P9-BVM-313

YOUNG CHILDREN
An Introduction to Early Childhood Education

YOUNG CHILDREN
An Introduction to Early Childhood Education

Stephen B. Graves
The University of Memphis

Richard M. Gargiulo
The University of Alabama at Birmingham

Linda C. Sluder
Texas Woman's University

with Patricia Holmes

West Publishing Company
Minneapolis/St. Paul New York Los Angeles San Francisco

Production Credits

Copyediting: *Christianne Thillen*
Art: *Nancy McClure, Hand to Mouse Arts*
Interior Design: *Maureen McCutcheon*
Cover image: *Bill Heinsohn/Tony Stone Images*
Cover design: *Tracy Trost, Fishbone Design*
Index: *Terry Casey*
Composition: *American Composition & Graphics, Inc.*
Production, prepress, printing, and binding by West Publishing Company
Photo credits and text credits follow the index.

West's Commitment to the Environment

In 1906, West Publishing Company began recycling materials left over from the production of books. This began a tradition of efficient and responsible use of resources. Today, up to 95 percent of our legal books are printed on recycled, acid-free stock. West also recycles nearly 22 million pounds of scrap paper annually—the equivalent of 181,717 trees. Since the 1960s, West has devised ways to capture and recycle waste inks, solvents, oils, and vapors created in the printing process. We also recycle plastics of all kinds, wood, glass, corrugated cardboard, and batteries, and have eliminated the use of Styrofoam book packaging. We at West are proud of the longevity and the scope of our commitment to the environment.

British Library Cataloguing-in-Publication Data. A catalogue record for this book is available from the British Library.

Printed in the United States of America

03 02 01 00 99 98 97 96 8 7 6 5 4 3 2 1 0

Library of Congress Cataloging-in-Publication Data

Young children: an introduction to early childhood education /
Stephen B. Graves . . . [et. al.].
p. cm.
Includes bibliographical references and index.
ISBN 0-314-04466-3
1. Early childhood education. I. Graves, Stephen B.
LB1139.23.Y59 1996
372.21--dc20 94-38891
CIP

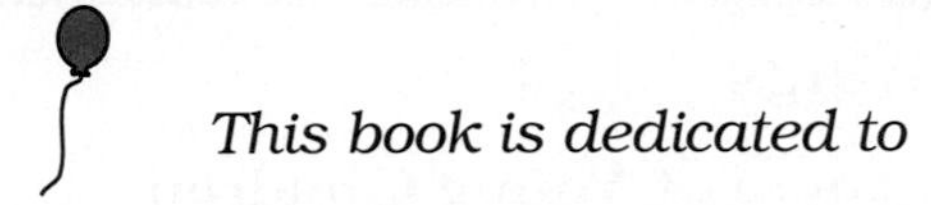

This book is dedicated to

My wife, Deborah, and to our children,
Molly, Jessica, Justin, and Laura
SBG

My daughters, Christina, Cara,
Victoria, and Elissa Marie
RMG

My family, Randy, Moleana,
Charles, and Cecile
LCS

BRIEF CONTENTS

APPENDIXES

CONTENTS

PREFACE

Welcome to the remarkable field of early childhood. You are beginning one of the most interesting, exciting, and important studies that can be imagined. Understanding and meeting the developmental needs of young children is both challenging and rewarding. Whether your goals are that of childcare provider, teacher, administrator, parent, or student, the authors of this textbook salute your decision.

The period from birth to eight years of age is identified as the early childhood years. It is considered by many to be the most significant developmental period of life. The mission of early childhood education is to nurture the intellectual, emotional, social, and physical growth of all children. Our responsibility, as parents and educators, community members and citizens, is to create developmentally appropriate educational environments that prepare all children for success in school and active participation in the civic, economic, and cultural lives of their communities.

These important years of change are served by a wide variety of early childhood programs, which guide children from periods of dependence to independence, or from infancy to the middle school years. The role of the early childhood professional is instrumental to a successful program. At the heart of their success as professionals is a well-defined training program for early childhood personnel. Effective programs guide individuals in their understanding of developmentally appropriate practices. Training programs must also include opportunities to know children through observations and interactions. In the real world of early childhood education, knowledge must be tempered by experiences.

This edition of *Young Children: An Introduction to Early Childhood Education* offers unique pedagogical features that bring students into the child care setting and offer views of parents and children as well as various child care professionals. The text includes discussions related to the development of early childhood as a profession, strategies for instruction, and topics related to individual differences as well as other issues in early childhood today.

GOALS AND OBJECTIVES

The primary goals in the development of this edition include the following:

- To present an introduction to the diversity of the early childhood profession.
- To integrate child development theory and practice into early childhood approaches.
- To report current perspectives of children from birth through age eight.
- To explore the applications of developmentally appropriate approaches to early childhood.
- To address the needs of all children including those who are culturally, linguistically, and developmentally different.

ORGANIZATION OF THE TEXT

Young Children: An Introduction to Early Childhood Education is divided into four main sections to explore the varied perspectives of early childhood education.

Part 1—Beginnings

In part 1, we examine the foundation of the early childhood profession. Chapter 1 explores the role of teachers in the lives of young children and introduces the reader to the diversity of the early childhood profession. Chapter 2 investigates the foundations of the field while drawing upon a long history and rich legacy. Many contemporary practices in education have their beginnings in the history of early childhood. The demand for early childhood programs and the evolution of child care as a profession are explored in the final chapter of part 1.

Part 2—Observing the Young Child

In part 2, we introduce techniques for observation and evaluation strategies. Chapter 4 provides the fundamentals of observing and assessing young children. The developmental phases of play as the work of the young child are presented from theory to practice in Chapter 5. Concepts of creativity in the young child are the focus of Chapter 6.

Part 3—Learning and the Young Child

We offer practical approaches to theory and curriculum in part 3. "Teaching and Learning Environments," Chapter 7, sets the stage for the development of appropriate classrooms and facilities. Chapter 8 presents a thoughtful plan for effectively meeting the physical and motor development of children. The significance of understanding the young child's initial efforts in literacy is presented in Chapter 9. The world of math and science is presented in a practical application approach through Chapter 10. Part 3 concludes with an investigation into the social and cultural foundations of young children in Chapter 11. Integrated curriculum approaches related to multicultural aspects, language, emotional, cognitive, and physical development are at the center of these discussions.

Part 4—Policies and Practices

In part 4, we direct the reader to focus on current issues in the profession. Chapter 12 presents a compelling introduction to the special needs of children with learning differences. This chapter addresses the diversity of young children with special needs, key legislation, and service delivery models. Chapter 13, "Administration and Supervision of Early Childhood Programs," emphasizes the role of administration in early education programs. The importance of meaningful parent and teacher partnerships is the focus of Chapter 14. An analysis of policies and practices would not be complete without an exploration of contemporary issues and trends. A thorough review of current literature and field experiences provides the backdrop for a careful investigation of these changing perspectives. Key issues encountered in Chapter 15 invite readers to consider their own professional opportunities.

LEARNING TOOLS

The text offers the following features to assist students in organizing chapter material:

- Each chapter begins with an **outline** and includes an introduction to **key terminology**.
- Chapter **summaries** are designed as review components.
- **Test Your Understanding** provides opportunities to explore the content of each chapter.
- Individual chapters provide **Learning Activities** designed to extend chapter topics through field experiences, discussion, and group and individual learning opportunities.
- Key terminology can be found in a comprehensive **glossary**.

- The book is distinguished as a **full-color** textbook featuring numerous photographs, tables, and descriptive charts.
- Supplementary supports include a comprehensive **Instructor's Manual** and **Test Bank**.
- Extensive **appendixes** provide a wealth of information for extending professional development.

PEDAGOGICAL FEATURES

The text provides pedagogical features drawn from practical experiences in early childhood education. Included are the following:

- *Spring Hill Child Development Center*, a fictitious center for young children, serves as a basis for discussion throughout the text. Readers are introduced to realistic situations and problems typically encountered by early childhood professionals, parents, and children. Each section opens with a scene from the Spring Hill Center. These scenarios establish themes for each of the four sections of the book.
- *Parents Speak Out*, *Teachers Speak Out*, and *Kids Speak Up* provide first-hand observations about chapter topics and offer personal, thought-provoking perspectives for the reader.
- *Anecdotes* based on the authors' professional experiences are presented in chapter introductions and provide advanced organization for the chapter content.

ACKNOWLEDGMENTS

Young Children: An Introduction to Early Childhood Education is possible only as the result of the combined efforts of our colleagues and associates. Their willingness to collaborate through authorship, discussions, interviews, and materials contributed to the overall development of this book. These include Donna Hester, University of Alabama at Birmingham; Peggy Goodman, Dallas Independent School District—Texas Woman's University; Laurie Dinnebeil, the University of Toledo; and Patricia Holmes, University of Central Florida.

In addition, we appreciate the assistance of the reviewers in the following list:

Nancy Bacot
Arkansas State University

Ramon Garcia-Barrios
Texas A & M University–Corpus Christi

Maryann Baumann
Community College of Denver

T. J. Betenbough
Western New Mexico University

Linda Brees
Greenville Technical College

Shelly Moss-Brooks
Oakland Community College

Margaret Budz
Triton College

Marlene A. Bumgarner
Gavilan College

Christine Catalani
San Antonio College

Laurie Dinnebeil
University of Toledo

Cyndra Fees
Bakersfield College

Audrey Flynn
Florida Community College

Janet Foster
Valdosta State University

Michael Henniger
Western Washington University

Jennifer Jackson
Iowa Western Community College

Kathy Kelley
Chabot College

Mona Lane
Oklahoma State University

Ann Marie Leonard
James Madison University

Marian McKinney
Owens Technical College

Glenn Olsen
University of North Dakota

Delia Richards
Prince Georges Community College

Robert Schirrmacher
San Jose City College

Carole Schwartz
University of South Florida

Janice Sherman
Winona State University–Rochester

Rosemarie Slavenas
Northern Illinois University

Carol Vukelich
University of Delaware

Kathleen Watkins
Community College of Philadelphia

Stephen White
University of Georgia–Athens

Karen Williams
University of Wyoming

Phil Wishon
University of Northern Colorado

The following child care centers participated in the creation of the Kids Speak Up, Parents Speak Out, and Teachers Speak Out features.

Medical Center Childcare

Daycare Services of Blair County, Inc.

State Employee Childcare Center

Roadrunner Parent Cooperative Preschool

Brookhaven College Parent-Child Study Center

World of Wonder Preschool

Sara Lawrence Early Child Care Center

Saint Joseph Child Care Center

Little Acorn Patch

Tennessee State Employee Child Care Center

The Stanford Hospital Children's Center

Towson State University Council Daycare Demonstration and Training Center

The Educational Research Center for Child Development

Greenville Technical College Child Development Center

Kansas State University Rosenwald Preschool Center

Zion Headstart

Oakton Community College Child Development Demonstration Center

Ruth Washburn Cooperative Nursery School

Vienna Baptist Children's Center

The Educational Research Center for Child Development

S.E.C.C.C.

UM CDC Community Children's Project

CCP Rainbow Preschool

Saint Andrew's Nursery School

Valley Community Services

East Millstone Country Daycare, Inc.

Norfolk Children's School

State Daycare Center

Medical Center Childcare

Daycare Services of Blair County

Cradle 'N' All Bureau Tots Daycare

Small World Learning Center and Academy

Martin Luther King Center

Eliza C. Frost Child Center

Texas Women's University Child Development Center

Briarlake Baptist Child Development Center

We also received information from Worthy Wage Coalition/The Child Care Employee Project

We also extend our sincere appreciation to the many early childhood professionals, administrators, parents, and children who shared their views for this publication. Their honest and open comments are deeply appreciated.

Finally, we acknowledge our colleagues at West Publishing. We extend our sincere gratitude to Joan Gill, our editor, who brought us together and directed this project. We also owe a great deal of thanks to our developmental editor, Becky Stovall, who provided support, guidance, and direction. Thanks also to Laura Evans, production editor, and our copy editor, Christianne Thillen, for their careful and thorough work.

YOUNG CHILDREN
An Introduction to Early Childhood Education

PART 1 Beginnings

SPRING HILL CHILD DEVELOPMENT CENTER

"Congratulations! You have just completed your required early childhood field experience." Several students smiled at each other as the professor complimented them on the quality of their work. It had been a long, difficult, and sometimes exhausting experience, yet surprisingly rewarding.

The professor had asked each team of students to include in their summary reports the following topics:

- Children served
- Professional staff responsibilities
- Curriculum
- Learning environment
- Physical facilities
- Support personnel
- Program philosophy
- Services for children with special needs
- Roles of parents
- Administration

Observation sites available to the students included a family day care center, a Head Start program, a parent cooperative preschool, a public school kindergarten, a campus laboratory school, an employer-sponsored child care center, a community child care center, the primary grades in a local elementary school, and both profit and nonprofit day care centers.

One team of four students chose to visit and report on a community child care center. Their report follows.

During the term, one student emerged as the team leader. Mildred, a former accountant and part-time student, was very interested in the families of the children. As leader, Mildred assigned each team member specific tasks: To Matt, a military veteran who is beginning his college career, she gave the task of describing the center.

She asked Stephanie, who has worked with young children since she was 12, to report on some of the children enrolled in the center. And she asked Lillian, whose youngest child is a senior at the same university, to report on the center's personnel.

The first speaker was Matt, who began by saying that his attitude toward young children has changed dramatically since he initially enrolled in the course (at first only because it fit his schedule). In describing the Spring Hill Child Development Center, Matt said it is located in the educational wing of a very large church, next to a neighborhood elementary school in a major metropolitan area of the Midwest. The center is licensed by the Department of Human Resources. Last year, after a great deal of work, Spring Hill was accredited by the National Association for the Education of Young Children. Parents are charged fees for their child's care. The center, which is eight years old, enjoys adequate supplies, materials, and space. Indoor and outdoor play environments are adequately equipped.

Matt said that Spring Hill has eight classrooms serving over 150 children:

Infant Room (ages 6 weeks–12 months)	8 children
Toddler Group (ages 12–18 months)	12 children
Preschool I (ages 18–36 months)	18 children
Preschool II (ages 36–48 months)	22 children
Preschool III (ages 48–60 months)	25 children
Kindergarten (5-year-olds)	18 children
After-School Care I (5- and 6-year-olds)	25 children
After-School Care II (7- and 8-year-olds)	25 children

In her report, Stephanie, who has always wanted to be a kindergarten teacher, shared the group's perceptions of some children who made impressions on the team members:

- *Infant Group.* Austin is a white male who can best be described as a difficult and demanding baby. The Infant

Specialist at Spring Hill believes that Austin might have a developmental problem.

- *Preschool I.* Carmelita, who was born in Mexico, recently immigrated to the United States with her parents. She is a very attractive and active young child, but somewhat shy and withdrawn around other children due to her difficulties with the English language.
- *Preschool II.* Howard can best be described as a mini-tornado. He is a black child from a large family. He craves attention and is very affectionate. Howard needs to have gentle reminders about his assertiveness several times each day.
- *Kindergarten.* Shelby is extremely popular with both the staff and children. She is a born leader with an outgoing personality. She has assumed the role of Carmelita's "big sister."
- *After-School Care.* Lee is an Asian-American child who spends most of his day in a special education classroom at the nearby elementary school. He is diagnosed as being mentally retarded and has a slight hearing loss. He is small for his age and is often picked on by other children in the after-school program.
- Staff members dread the days that Nathaniel attends the after-school program. He is verbally abusive and physically assaultive toward staff and classmates. His inability to follow directions and explosive anger lead to frequent telephone calls from the administrator to Nathaniel's dad.

Mildred, a single parent whose child is enrolled in the Spring Hill Center, started her speech by explaining that she is concerned with family issues and parent involvement with their child's education. Mildred said she was astonished to find such diversity among the families of children attending the center. Here are some of her observations:

- Austin is an only child of two blue-collar working parents.

- Carmelita is the youngest of two daughters. Her father is enrolled in graduate school, and her mother works on the weekends as a waitress in a restaurant.
- Howard is the youngest child in a single-parent home headed by his father, who works for a large investment firm.
- Shelby is being raised by her stepmother and her father. She has three stepsiblings, two older and one younger. Her biological mother has little contact with Shelby.
- Lee's parents are both professionals. Lee has a twin sister who is very proud of her brother. Lee's parents spend a great deal of time transporting Lee to his therapy sessions and doctor's appointments.
- Nathaniel lives in an exclusive neighborhood. His father is the president of a local bank, and his mother is actively engaged in volunteer work. Nathaniel's behavior at Spring Hill is beginning to cause some marital tension.

The final speaker was Lillian, an overachiever who has maintained the highest grades in the course. She enthusiastically reported on the Spring Hill Center professional staff:

- The Executive Director has a master's degree in Early Childhood Education with additional training in administration. The director is an African-American woman with 17 years of experience as a teacher and program administrator.
- The Infant Specialist is a middle-aged white female with over 25 years of experience in working with very young children. She is a high school graduate who recently received her Child Development Associate credential.

- The Preschool I teacher recently graduated from the local community college with an associate of arts degree in Child Development. She has been employed at Spring Hill for 6 months.
- The Preschool II teacher is a part-time student at the nearby state university. She is a senior majoring in early childhood education who hopes to be employed at Spring Hill upon her graduation.
- The Kindergarten teacher is a young Hispanic male who was previously employed as a social worker. Even though he has a bachelor's degree in Social Work, he is presently enrolled in a graduate teacher education program.
- Staff employed for the After-School Care II program are students from the local high school in addition to students from the state university who are fulfilling field experience requirements for various classes.

After the report, the professor asked each team member to lead small group discussions. The discussions were to focus on the early childhood profession, observing the young child, learning and the young child, and policies and practices affecting early childhood education.

The team decided to use their textbook to support their perspectives. Look for their viewpoints throughout this text . . . then, let's talk about it.

CHAPTER 1

Teachers of Young Children

CHAPTER OUTLINE

Young Children and You

- *Your Beliefs about Children*
- *Teacher Values and Philosophy*
- *A Philosophy of Teaching*
- *Teaching—Art or Science?*
- *Child Advocacy and Children's Rights*
- *Professionalism*
- *Ethical Behavior*

Characteristics of Early Childhood Teachers

- *Attributes of Effective Teachers*
- *Self-Awareness*
- *Bias and Prejudice*
- *What Makes a Good Teacher?*
- *Teacher Stress and Burnout*

Training of Early Childhood Personnel

- *Teacher Preparation*
- *Training Guidelines*
- *Child Development Associate*
- *Certification and Licensing*
- *Professional Growth and Development*

KEY TERMS

Values
Advocacy
Children's rights
Profession
Professional
Bias
Prejudice
Burnout
Child Development Associate

Tracy found a quiet area in the entrance hall of the main library to wait for the college orientation sessions to begin. As she thumbed through her campus catalog, the advice of friends and family mingled in her thoughts. It did not seem to matter to them that she had not identified a major area of interest. During her initial contact with a university advisor, she was assured that many students enter college as "undeclared majors." One thing was certain, she wanted to go to college.

As Tracy began to review the list of orientation majors one more time, a young child about 4 years old caught her attention. The child was industriously pulling at one sock that simply would not stay in place. The little girl's father was trying to complete an admission form while supervising the activities of his daughter.

"Here, Daddy," the little girl directed as she handed her father a treasure she had found under the bench where they were sitting. Tracy noticed that the man patiently took the object and attempted to redirect his daughter's interests.

Tracy silently marveled at the child's curiosity and enthusiasm. Soon the little girl noticed the silent observer and began to direct her attention to Tracy. As her dad continued completing the form, the child approached Tracy. "Hi," the little girl declared.

"Hi," Tracy responded.

"Want to see what I can do?" the child continued. Tracy nodded yes, and then watched as the child turned on one foot. "I can do this too . . . ," the child said, lifting her hands above her head and turning again.

For the next few minutes, the two chatted and laughed while the grateful father completed the back of his form. Tracy's own anxieties about the university orientation disappeared as she found herself fascinated by the questions and responses of the little girl. When their conversation was interrupted by an announcement directing new students to specific rooms for orientation sessions, Tracy listened for the room assignment for undeclared majors. Suddenly she heard "Early childhood majors, please meet in room 101."

"Early childhood," Tracy softly repeated under her breath. How had she missed it? The little girl and her dad regrouped and were preparing to find their meeting room when the father formally introduced himself and thanked Tracy for her help.

"Where are you going?" the little girl asked her newest friend.

Tracy smiled, "I'm on my way to room 101. I'm an early childhood major."

YOUNG CHILDREN AND YOU

Recent statistics indicate that approximately 6,660,000 young children are enrolled in preschool and kindergarten programs (National Center for Educational Statistics, 1991). This number has been

Early childhood teachers play an important role in the lives of young children.

steadily growing over the past few decades, and so has the demand for early childhood professionals. Each day more than 425,000 teachers of young children (U.S. Department of Labor, 1992) gaze into a vast sea of faces—most of them smiling, a few frowning, and some gazing back with wonder and amazement at their teacher.

You have *chosen* to become a teacher of young children. It is one of the most important commitments you will make. Occupational choice can profoundly affect your life. And your decision to teach affects not only your life, but the lives of many young children as well. Next to parents and siblings, teachers are probably the most significant individuals that children encounter. Your influence extends far beyond the classroom—and can last a lifetime.

The decision to become a teacher should not be made in haste or taken lightly. Teaching is something that not everyone can do. It is a profession that requires total dedication. Teaching young children is not an easy task. It is intellectually challenging as well as emotionally and physically exhausting. Yet, there is so much joy and satisfaction in working with young children. In most instances, experienced early childhood teachers report that the rewards far outweigh the difficulties.

It is perhaps wise to ask yourself, "How can I be certain that I am choosing the best career for me?" One obvious answer is gain as much direct experience with young children as possible. Your involvement should be in a wide variety of settings; for example, in kindergartens, day care centers, recreational programs, or Sunday school classes. Teachers of young children must be genuinely interested in them. You need to discover how you feel when a child disobeys you, has a temper tantrum, or hugs you and exclaims that they love you. Your answers to these questions (Seaver, Cartwright, Ward, & Heasley, 1979, p. 3) can also help in your decision to become an early childhood educator:

1. Why do I want to work with young children?
2. What personal qualities and abilities do I possess that will make me successful in working with young children?
3. What degree of involvement with children is best for me?

There are no absolute or correct responses. Answers reflect the uniqueness of each person. Because each teacher is different, responses will reflect your own personality, values, and attitudes. In fact, in the classroom, one of the most important contributions you can make is your uniqueness (Lindberg & Swedlow, 1985).

Your Beliefs about Children

Teaching, according to Maxim (1985), is something done *with* children rather than *to* them. Your ideas and attitudes about teaching and children significantly influence your interactions with your students. Personal views of children affect what and how early childhood educators teach (Morrison, 1993). If a teacher considers a group of youngsters to be "slow," she is likely to work with these children in a manner congruent with her beliefs. Likewise, if a teacher is challenged by an ambitious and eager learner, he typically provides experiences and opportunities to meet the unique needs of his pupil.

Child rearing and educational practices are frequently determined by adults' views of children and the value of childhood. Unfortunately, some people hold unfavorable beliefs. Different perspectives on childhood are the result of various political, social, and economic factors.

Maxim (1985) and Morrison (1993) describe historical and contemporary viewpoints about children. We briefly examine them in the following subsections. Which orientation do you subscribe to? What is your view of children?

Children as Miniature Adult. In some developing countries, and even in regions of the United States, preschool children are expected to be economically productive. In this regard, twentieth-century views parallel those of medieval Europe. Children are different from adults only in size and age. Although child labor laws protect some children from exploitation, modern media continually inform us about children involved in pornography, prostitution, drug abuse, and other adult activities. While we may dress our children in the latest designer outfits, treating them as tiny adults only leads to conflicts between expectations and capabilities. This is especially true when parents and teachers expect adult-like behavior that is incompatible with the youngster's developmental ability.

Sinful Children. With its foundation in religious doctrine, another viewpoint is that a child's inappropriate actions indicate inherent sin and are the work of the devil. Corporal punishment, therefore, is commonplace. This view was popular for over 400 years and lasted until the 1700s. In more modern times, this belief is evident in the insistence on unquestioning obedience and respect for adults. Rigid supervision of children is necessary. Schools are places where children are to be taught "correct" behavior by their teachers. The rise in the number of church-supported and private schools gives testimony to the popularity of this viewpoint.

Blank Tablets. Children are seen as blank tablets or slates (*tabula rasa*). Individual differences do not matter. The environment is important. The quality and nature of a child's experiences determine what happens to her. Children exposed to similar influences should behave the same. The role of the educator is to present material without considering the pupil's interest, needs, or readiness for instruction. It only matters that children learn what is taught. This viewpoint has its roots in the writings of the English philosopher, John Locke.

Growing Plants. Children are sometimes compared to flowers or blooming plants. They grow and develop, or unfold, according to a natural pattern within a nurturing environment. Maturation, therefore, is important. Proponents of this view believe there are opportune times for acquiring specific skills. Parents and teachers should not force learning on the child before he is ready. The concept of *readiness* evolves from this view of children.

PARENTS SPEAK OUT

Young children need positive, nurturing environments. They need a place where they feel accepted, a place with age-appropriate expectations and activities. Children are little people with their own feelings and ideas. They deserve to be treated with respect and love.

State Employee Child Care Center

Property. One belief with a long history is that children are the property of their parents. As their creators and primary caregivers, parents have broad authority and jurisdiction over their offspring. Few legal statutes interfere with the parents' right to exercise control over their children. Within limits, many parents believe that they may do whatever they wish with their children. Discipline techniques, religious training, educational experiences, and social customs are but a few examples of the areas in which parents exhibit their influence. Parents who see children as their personal property typically function as decision makers for them.

Investment in the Future. Another long-standing view of children is that they are vehicles for social reform and representatives of future productivity and wealth. Children are considered a valuable national resource. Many educational and social policies are based on the view that children are sound investments for the future. Several government programs have been developed around the assumption that prevention of problems in childhood often results in more productive adults. Prevention is also less costly and more effective than remediation. Head Start and Follow-Through are two programs that see children as human capital and profitable investments. Investing in the education of children is but one way of guaranteeing the future economic strength of our nation. Of course, relying on our country's youth as human capital perpetuates a utilitarian use of children and fails to consider their intrinsic human worth. "Trying to make a nation stronger through its children tends to emphasize national priorities over individuals" (Morrison, 1993, p. 8).

Children as Saviors of the World. Our final perspective on children is a somewhat controversial view. According to this viewpoint, children are valuable and worthy of protection, investment, and education because of their potential for saving the world from its problems. The future of our planet thus becomes the responsibility of the children. As you can well imagine, not everyone believes this a suitable role for children. World leaders should focus on resolving current problems instead of making this a duty of future generations. Children are not equipped to assume such a responsibility, nor is it an appropriate function of childhood.

Teacher Values and Philosophy

We all have values. Values are very important; among other things, they influence what you do to and say to young children. Simply stated, **values** are those things you believe in, that you consider important and meaningful in your life. "Values are concepts of the desirable" (Hildebrand, 1990, p. 358). Equality, freedom, individuality, and honesty are but a few examples of typical American values.

Where do our values come from? How are they developed? The answer is not simple. Values are developed through life experiences and typically begin when the child is young. Many individuals and institutions contribute to the development of values. Children develop their values through family and friends, from schools and religion, and from the society they live in. Once established, values are difficult to change, although they can be modified with concerted effort. As an adult, you will probably agree that the "oughts" and "shoulds" guiding your daily behavior can frequently be traced to values instilled in you as a young child (Hildebrand, 1990).

Hildebrand (1990), who believes in the importance of values for young children, has identified ten characteristics of values (p. 368):

1. Values are defined as concepts of the desirable.
2. Values are learned throughout life through study, instruction, and example.
3. Values can be either conscious or unconscious.
4. Values can be brought to the level of awareness.
5. Values guide actions and decisions of individuals.
6. Values have been enshrined in the Constitution, laws, and regulations.
7. Values are rarely identical for two individuals.
8. Values are reflected in an early childhood program.
9. Values are the basis for regulations and standards in early childhood programs.
10. Values can be changed through conscious effort of individuals.

Since young children are so impressionable, the values exhibited by an early childhood educator are very important. As a teacher, the values you subscribe to will significantly affect what happens in your classroom. It is crucial that the behavior and actions of the teacher are congruent with their values. The quality and kind of learning experiences you provide your students are greatly influenced by your personal value system and the philosophy of the program. Table 1.1 presents essential values of a "good" early childhood professional.

Professional values are different from personal values. Professional values are acquired through education, training, and experience. Conflicts about educational policies and practices are often due to differences in the value systems of the professional, for example, the relative merits of emphasizing structured activities versus free choice and spontaneity. When differences occur, they should be admitted and a solution developed. Perhaps there is room for compromise. This will require honest discussion and mutual respect for the beliefs of the other individual(s). Conflicting messages will be sent to colleagues, parents, and children if resolution is not possible.

Disagreements can also occur between teachers and parents over differences in values. Early childhood professionals need to listen carefully to the parent's concerns and assess the merits of their request. Most parents want what is best for their children, and this concern frequently causes them to confront the teacher about certain issues. For instance, "Why do the children spend so much time playing rather than learning how to read?" We believe it is important for early childhood educators to have a clear rationale for their ac-

TABLE 1.1 Core Values in Early Childhood Education

For Children and Adults

- To respect and recognize each individual as a unique human being
- To support children and adults in realizing their full potential
- To promote environments that foster well-being and positive self-esteem in children, staff, and families
- To foster autonomy and self-reliance in children, staff, and families

For Children

- To appreciate the special vulnerability of children and their need for safe and healthy environments
- To recognize that each child is an individual with unique needs and abilities
- To help children develop socially, emotionally, intellectually, and physically
- To help children learn in ways that are appropriate to their stage of development
- To appreciate childhood as a unique and valuable stage in the life cycle
- To base practice on the best current knowledge of child growth and development

For Families

- To recognize and support the interconnectedness of the child and family
- To support families in their task of nurturing children

For the Profession

- To protect children and advocate for their rights

Source: Reprinted with the permission of Macmillan College Publishing Company from *Who Am I in the Lives of Children?*, 3rd edition by Stephanie Feeney, Doris Christensen, and Eva Moravcik. Copyright © 1987 by Macmillan College Publishing Company, Inc.

tions and explain it to the parents. While due consideration of the parents' views is important, you should not compromise your beliefs about what you think is best for the child.

At times, circumstances can be such that compromise with fellow teachers, program administrators, and parents is not possible. The conflicts cannot be resolved. For example, you are opposed to the practice of corporal punishment, yet its use is fully supported by the administrator and the majority of the parents. In this situation, you should give careful consideration to resigning. While not an easy decision, it might be the most appropriate solution. Teachers should not abandon their beliefs. As Hildebrand (1990) states, "Teachers must live with themselves" (p. 366). Working daily in an environment that continually ignores your personal value system can be psychologically harmful. It is not healthy for you or the children.

A Philosophy of Teaching

Closely related to the issue of values is the concept of a personal philosophy of teaching. Like values, your beliefs about education are unique to you. A philosophy of education can be described as a statement of beliefs regarding how children learn, what they should be taught, and the most appropriate means of instruction. Your individual beliefs about education and teaching are derived from your value system, your experience with children, and your professional training and preparation. Your philosophy can serve as a guide for classroom practice. Unfortunately, a great deal of instruction is frequently accomplished without the benefit of a guiding philosophy, and some early childhood programs operate without a written statement of beliefs.

How do you develop a philosophy? We provide the following topics suggested by Morrison (1991, p. 484) as a useful starting point. You may find it helpful to complete the following open-ended sentences:

1. I believe the purposes of education are . . .
2. I believe that children learn best when they are taught under certain conditions and in certain ways. Some of these are . . .
3. The curriculum of any classroom should include certain "basics" that contribute to children's social, emotional, intellectual, and physical development. These basics are . . .
4. Children learn best in an environment that promotes learning. Some of the features of a good learning environment are . . .
5. All children have certain needs that must be met if they are to grow and learn at their best. Some of these basic needs are . . . I would meet these needs these ways . . .
6. The teacher should have certain qualities and behave in certain ways. Qualities I think important for teaching are . . .

TEACHERS SPEAK OUT

The real reward is not the pay but the smiles and hugs and rainbow pictures that are drawn for you again and again.

Morrison (1991, p. 484) also suggests that you evaluate your statements with the following six questions:

1. Does it accurately reflect my beliefs about teaching?
2. Have I been honest with myself?
3. Is it understandable to me and others?
4. Does it provide practical guidance for teaching?
5. Are my ideas consistent with each other?
6. Does what I believe make good sense?

Your philosophy about teaching young children will not be static; instead, it will slowly evolve and change as you gain additional knowledge and experience. Of course, having a philosophy of teaching does not guarantee that you will be a good early childhood teacher. But it does establish a basis to further develop your ideas about the process of teaching and learning.

Teaching—Art or Science?

Is teaching young children an art, or is it a science? Unfortunately, there is no universal agreement on the best answer to this question. Some believe that teaching is more an art than a science. While early childhood educators are generally credited with being creative, spontaneous, and intuitive in their interactions with children, Hildebrand (1990) argues for considering the contributions of science to the education of young children. She believes that teachers need a strong foundation in child development, curriculum matters, and guidance techniques in addition to an awareness of their own experiences and knowledge about the individual needs of children. This basis, coupled with the teacher's creativity and other attributes, allows the educator to satisfactorily meet the needs of young children.

Teaching is considered one of the "helping" professions, similar to social work, counseling, and nursing. As such, it shares some qualities with these other professions. Specifically, educating young children involves the *what* of teaching (science) in conjunction with the *how* of teaching (art) (Gargiulo, 1985). The science of teaching is based on theories of child development, principles of learning, skills training, and curriculum development, among other aspects. The art of teach-

The real art of teaching often occurs on the classroom floor.

ing speaks to the teacher as a person, to his or her affective qualities, and to how she or he interacts with children in the classroom.

In teaching, art and science go hand in hand. Teaching cannot be distinguished as an art or science; rather, it is correctly viewed as a marriage of both. While it is true that the real art of teaching often occurs with the children in a circle on the floor, effective teaching requires a joining of theory and professional skills with the individual's values, attitudes, and traits. The theories, principles, and techniques of teaching are typically presented in a college classroom—a place where teachers can be trained. But the necessary personal characteristics, values, and beliefs of a teacher are developed through life experiences. These are what the person brings with them to the college classroom. It is exceedingly difficult, if not impossible, to teach someone how to be caring, warm, genuine, friendly, and sincerely interested in young children and their welfare.

In conclusion, we believe that teaching is much more than using specific techniques or following a teacher's manual; it also requires the full utilization of yourself as a person.

Child Advocacy and Children's Rights

An important responsibility of early childhood educators is being an advocate for children and their families. **Advocacy**, according to Caldwell (1987), is simply trying to influence the political process. Concerned individuals realize that the needs of children must be promoted. This requires active involvement in the political process (Goffin, 1988). Early childhood teachers should not limit their concerns for young children to what happens only in their classrooms. As professionals, early childhood teachers are in a prime position to assume "a leadership role in promoting advocacy on behalf of the children, their families, and the early childhood profession" (Katz & Goffin, 1990, p. 204).

Being an advocate is an important role for the early childhood teacher. In recent years, early childhood professionals have increased their political activity in an effort to influence public policy as it pertains to young children and their families (Graves, 1990). Simply stated, public policies, in our field, are proposals designed to affect the lives of children and their families. These policies are frequently implemented through legislation or via official statements and position papers from groups such as the Children's Defense Fund and the National Association for the Education of Young Children (NAEYC), two organizations in the forefront of lobbying for children. Examples of recent advocacy efforts include supporting family leave legislation and taking positions on issues such as assessment of preschool children, kindergartens for 4-year-olds, early education for young children with special needs, and developmentally appropriate practices. Each of these topics affects a large number of children, their families, and the early childhood professional.

Early childhood professionals are capable of influencing the political process.

Traditionally, early childhood professionals have advocated for change by reacting to proposals and strategies offered by individuals working within the political structure. Frequently, these policymakers are not fully informed about the particular issue. Lombardi (1986) believes, therefore, that individuals working in the field of early childhood education need to use their skills and expertise in identifying problems and suggesting solutions. This will require working in partnership with politicians. It is regrettable, however, that early childhood professionals, teachers in particular, have been slow to recognize the benefits of advocacy (Caldwell, 1987; Graves, 1990). What causes this lack of involvement? Several reasons are typically given (Caldwell, 1987; Lombardi, 1986):

- Advocacy is beneath their dignity as a professional.
- They believe that they are powerless to change anything.
- Teachers are fearful of the political process.
- They lack confidence in their expertise.
- They lack the time to be advocates.

Today, there is an increasing awareness of the importance and benefit of advocacy efforts. Advocacy is being recommended as part of early childhood teacher training. Both Almy (1985) and Lombardi (1986) believe that a background in advocacy training should form an integral component of professional preparation. Educators anticipate that by developing advocacy skills, early childhood teachers will be motivated and better equipped to function as advocates for young children, their families, and the field of early childhood education. A further outcome of this training is that early childhood educators can take a proactive stance on important issues and move them forward in the political process (Ott, Zeichner, & Price, 1990).

According to Bettye Caldwell (1987), former president of NAEYC, professionals in early childhood should be committed to three types of advocacy: personal, professional, and informational. Basically, *personal advocacy* is one-on-one advocacy, in which you try to influence the beliefs of an individual. *Professional advocacy* efforts are frequently known as lobbying; yet the aim is still the same—working to benefit children and those who serve them. Wilkens and Blank (1986) suggest that "while lobbying may sound intimidating, it is nothing more than getting the right information to the right people at the right time" (p. 71). Caldwell's final advocacy activity is one of *informational advocacy*. A combination of the preceding two types, informational advocacy "refers to attempts to raise the general consciousness of the public both about the importance of events that occur during the early childhood period and about the capacity of quality programs to foster growth and development and to strengthen families" (p. 31). What role will you play?

Early childhood teachers need to become advocates for children. Advocacy requires that you stay current on issues affecting the lives of young children and their families in addition to learning how to utilize yourself as an instrument for change. As an individual, you can influence the political process in several ways, according to Seefeldt and Barbour (1990):

1. *Keep informed.* Stay abreast of legislative issues and proposals that can affect you as well as the children and families you serve. Express your opinion about the issues. Professional journals such as *Young Children* and *Dimensions* publish, in each issue, policy reports on national legislation and suggest what type of action is appropriate. The Children's Defense Fund is another source of information. They prepare an annual report of the status of children in America. Valuable information is available in this document.

TEACHERS SPEAK OUT

I enjoy working in the field of education. Preschool years are critical and provide the foundation for a child's future success. I get very excited about playing a role in these critical years of development.

2. *Contact your elected representatives.* With the information and knowledge you now possess, urge your elected officials to react to legislation in ways you believe will improve the quality of life for children. Personal contact is best. Form letters and telegrams are not as effective as sincerely written correspondence. Most legislators want to know how their constituency feels about issues. Do not be afraid to express your viewpoint.

3. *Vote.* Express your opinion in the ballot box. Follow the voting record of your legislators, at all levels of government, and support those persons who vote in ways that you favor.

4. *Inform others.* In many instances, friends, neighbors, and citizens without direct contact with children are unaware of issues affecting children. Thus, you need to become a spokesperson and inform them about the importance of supporting (or opposing) specific legislation. Seek the involvement of civic groups and community organizations. You may also want to invite elected officials to visit your early childhood program. Have these individuals meet the youngsters and their parents. Explain the needs of children and how what you do benefits children and families. Ask for their support with legislation that positively contributes to lives of children.

5. *Join organizations.* There is considerable truth to the belief of strength in numbers. By joining professional organizations such as NAEYC, Association for Childhood Education International (ACEI), Southern Early Childhood Association (SECA), and other groups, you add your voice to those who are concerned about children, families, and the profession. Collectively, you can make a difference in the lives of children. As a professional, you are responsible for ensuring that the best interests of children are always considered. For further discussion of the role of advocacy in early childhood education, see Chapter 15.

Another important function of professionals is to help to secure **children's rights**. Children are individuals with rights of their own. Increasingly, advocacy groups, professional organizations, and the judicial system are championing the rights of children.

This issue, however, is not without controversy. One point of view suggests that society tends to be indifferent to the issue of children's rights. Some believe that children are discriminated against and their rights continually trampled upon (Farson, 1978). On the other hand, many people believe that the rights of parents are ignored, and in some cases, may be secondary to the rights of children. It appears that, as a society, we need to strike a balance between the rights of the caregivers and the rights of the child.

Those who work in the field of early childhood education tend to be strong supporters of children's rights. In a 1984 survey examining the protection and rights of children, Kerckhoff and McPhee made some startling discoveries. These investigators examined the views of Indiana lawyers and members of the Indiana Association for the Education of Young Children (IAEYC). The responses of IAEYC members were statistically significantly different from those of attorneys. Unlike their legal counterparts, almost three out of four early childhood professionals (78 percent) were in favor of laws giving children greater protection; 67 percent favored giving children more rights; 72 percent were in favor of providing an advocate for children; and a majority of IAEYC members (51 percent) supported a proposal making it illegal to sell war toys to children. The survey also revealed that early childhood educators (41 percent) believe that children should be provided with an attorney when parents divorce. An approximately equal number (42 percent) also favored legislation making it illegal for parents to ridicule their children. But less than 10 percent of the early childhood respondents supported laws prohibiting parents from spanking their children. (Such a law exists in Sweden.) Kerckhoff and McPhee noted that those who work most closely with children were their strongest supporters, while those who most closely resemble the composition of lawmakers were least accepting of legislation extending children's rights.

FIGURE 1.1

National Education Association. Reprinted by permission.

Bill of Rights for Children

National Education Association Representative Assembly
July 4, 1991

We, the people of the United States, in order to achieve a more perfect society, fulfill our moral obligations, further our founding ideals and preserve the continued blessings of liberty, do hereby proclaim this Bill of Rights for Children.

I. No child in a land of abundance shall be wanting for plentiful and nutritional food.

II. A society as advanced in medical knowledge and abilities as ours shall not deny medical attention to any child in need.

III. Whereas security is an essential requirement for a child's healthy development, the basic security of a place to live shall be guaranteed to every child.

IV. To ensure the potential of the individual and the nation, every child at school shall have the right to a quality education.

V. The government, whose primary role is to protect and defend at all levels, shall assure that children are safeguarded from abuse, violence and discrimination.

National Education Association

It is anticipated that the trend toward gaining increased rights for children will continue. The National Education Association recently adopted a "Bill of Rights for Children" (see Figure 1.1). From a more global perspective, in 1979 the General Assembly of the United Nations sponsored the International Year of the Child, which focused attention on the rights of children worldwide. Part of this activity was a reaffirmation of the U.N.'s Declaration of the Rights of the Child (1959). This proclamation (U.N. Resolution No. 1386) addresses the following basic rights:

- The right to affection, love, and understanding
- The right to adequate nutrition and medical care
- The right to free education
- The right to full opportunity for play and recreation
- The right to a name and nationality
- The right to special care, if handicapped
- The right to be among the first to receive relief in times of disaster
- The right to learn to be a useful member of society and to develop individual abilities
- The right to be brought up in a spirit of peace and universal brotherhood
- The right to enjoy these rights regardless of race, color, sex, religion, national, or social origin

Professionalism

At the beginning of this chapter, we noted that you have chosen to become a teacher of young children. This decision also means that you will become a professional. What does this mean? The answer may be found in several concepts usually associated with being identified as a professional. But first we need to understand our terms. A **profession** can be defined simply as an occupation that results from a prolonged education and specialized training. A **professional** is viewed as a person who uses his or her skills and abilities to assist other people in improving the quality of their lives.

We now turn our attention to the field of early childhood education and look at it from several different aspects. Here are some of the components that make early childhood education a profession:

1. *A specialized body of knowledge.* Early childhood teachers have a command of a body of knowledge, a range of specialized skills, and a technical vocabulary (Katz, 1988; Lindberg & Swedlow, 1985; Maxim, 1985).

2. *Entry requirements and prolonged training.* Early childhood educators must meet the entrance requirements stipulated by the particular preparation program; not everyone can enter the field; training is specialized and the knowledge base is acquired through prolonged and difficult study and practice of the craft (Katz, 1988; Lindberg & Swedlow, 1985).

3. *A code of ethics.* Being a member of a profession typically requires allegiance to a code of conduct that governs a person's behavior and the delivery of their services.

4. *Standards of practice.* In a profession, there are norms of acceptable practice for ensuring that members perform their duties using generally accepted standards of professional judgment.

5. *Autonomy.* A profession regulates itself and retains internal control over quality; early childhood educators are assisted in this task by licensing requirements, guidelines from our professional organizations, and standards established by state education and human service departments.

6. *Altruism.* Katz (1988) believes that early childhood teachers are very altruistic: They give of themselves and use their knowledge and skills to improve the quality of life of young children and their families.

7. *Ongoing learning.* Professionals continually seek to upgrade their skills and acquire new knowledge; learning is an ongoing process; effective early childhood teachers are constantly looking for new ways to improve the quality of their instruction.

A close examination of our field clearly reveals that in certain respects we truly are a profession; in other areas, however, we need to work collectively to meet the challenges and opportunities presented to us as we move toward obtaining this status.

KIDS SPEAK UP

I like to play school when I can be the teacher.

Boy, 5 years old

Spodek, Saracho, and Peters (1988), as well as Lawton (1988), suggest that at present it might be best to consider early childhood education as a semiprofession. Teachers traditionally have not been viewed as full-fledged professionals. Howsam, Corrigan, Denemark, and Nash (1976) offer several reasons for this perception. In comparison to "learned professions" such as medicine or law, teachers have a shorter training period, a less developed body of knowledge, and a weaker theoretical foundation. Teachers also have less autonomy in professional decision making. Finally, teachers have lower occupational status and generally do not enjoy societal acceptance.

The preceding arguments notwithstanding, we agree with Lindberg and Swedlow (1985) that teaching *is* a profession due to the immense responsibilities involved in caring for and educating young children in addition to the knowledge and skills required to effectively meet their needs. We view early childhood education as a legitimate profession. Teaching young children is not just a job; it is a profession. It demands dedication, your full commitment to children, and a strong belief that you can make a difference in their lives. There is pride in teaching!

Ethical Behavior

A cornerstone of being a professional is ethical behavior. A professional person is an ethical person. As professionals, teachers are expected to adhere to a code of ethics and exhibit high standards of behavior. A code of ethics guides decision making. Teachers without a code of conduct are often aimless in their purpose and actions.

According to Graves (1987), a code of ethics is one way a profession acknowledges its responsibility to society. It involves establishing standards for the profession, developing guidelines to assist in decision making, and recognizing commitments to ourselves, the profession, and the individuals served. Maxim (1985) echoes this thought and focuses on the field of early childhood education. He identifies professional ethics as "personal responsibilities" that describe an individual's role in the field, and he clarifies the teacher's relationship with the children, their parents, and the community served.

A code of ethics includes statements about appropriate ways professionals should act as they go about implementing their programs (Graves, 1987). Early childhood teacher educator Stephanie Feeney and philosopher Kenneth Kipnis believe that professional ethics is a process whereby professionals critically examine their moral obligations. Ethical standards assist the early childhood educator in deciding what a responsible teacher should do as well as what she or he should refuse to do (Feeney & Kipnis, 1985). Ethical guidelines help teachers to act in ways they perceive to be right instead of doing what is expedient or easy (Graves, 1987). Katz and Ward (1978), two early thinkers in this area, summarize a code of ethics as statements that assist early childhood educators in dealing with complex situations inherent in our profession. A code of ethical behavior gives professionals a set of collectively agreed upon standards against which they can assess their own performance and actions with children, caregivers, administrators, and fellow workers.

Why should early childhood teachers need a code of professional conduct? First, early childhood educators should make choices and base their decisions on the values, judgments, and opinions shared by their colleagues rather than on their personal beliefs and values. Second, a code is necessary to ensure that young children are dealt with in just and responsible ways. As a profession, we need to assure parents and the public alike that our behavior is based on sound thinking and accepted practices that have the best interest of the child at heart (Katz & Ward, 1978).

Early childhood teachers continually confront ethical dilemmas in their daily work. A nationwide survey conducted by Feeney and Sysko (1986, p. 16) identified five areas of concern to early childhood educators:

- Discussing a child or family in a nonprofessional setting,
- Implementing policies you feel are not good for children because the program requires them,
- Letting children do an activity that may not be worthwhile or appropriate,
- Knowing that a program is in violation of state regulations, and
- Dealing with conflicting requests from divorced/separated parents.

In analyzing their data, Feeney and Sysko noted that each of the preceding concerns either directly or indirectly involved the well-being of children.

Their information revealed several other areas of ethical concern. Examples of troublesome situations include the unprofessional behavior of co-workers, managing confidential information, and reporting suspicion of child abuse or neglect. The area of greatest ethical concern for early childhood teachers was their relationships with parents. This finding is not too surprising. Katz and Ward (1978) also believe that "the most persistent ethical problems faced by early childhood practitioners are those encountered in their relations with parents" (p. 8). We suspect that this type of ethical issue will only increase as parents seek greater involvement and participation in their child's education.

You will most likely confront your own ethical problems, and frequently there will not be an easy solution. Regardless of the particular circumstances, we suggest that when in doubt, you always place the welfare of the child first.

In 1989, NAEYC adopted a Code of Ethical Conduct which, according to Feeney and Kipnis (1989), "offers guidelines for responsible behavior and sets forth a common basis for resolving the principal ethical dilemmas encountered in early childhood education" (p. 25). The code can be found in Appendix A.

According to this code, ethical behavior in early childhood education is based on a personal commitment to certain core values that have their roots in the history of our field. As early childhood teachers, we subscribe to the following six beliefs as stated by Feeney and Kipnis (1989, p. 25):

- Appreciating childhood as a unique and valuable stage of the human life cycle
- Basing our work with young children on the knowledge of child development
- Appreciating and supporting the close ties between the child and family

- Recognizing that children are best understood in the context of family, culture, and society
- Respecting the dignity, worth, and uniqueness of each individual (child, family member, and colleague)
- Helping children and adults achieve their full potential in the context of relationships that are based on trust, respect, and positive regard

A Statement of Commitment also accompanies the NAEYC guidelines. This document describes the personal commitment individuals must make to their profession (Feeney & Kipnis, 1989, p. 29):

> As an individual who works with young children, I commit myself to furthering the values of early childhood education as they are reflected in the NAEYC Code of Ethical Conduct.
>
> To the best of my ability, I will:
>
> - Ensure that programs for young children are based on current knowledge of child development and early childhood education.
> - Respect and support families in their task of nurturing children.
> - Respect colleagues in early childhood education and support them in maintaining the NAEYC Code of Ethical Conduct.
> - Serve as an advocate for children, their families, and their teachers in community and society.
> - Maintain high standards of professional conduct.
> - Recognize how personal values, opinions, and biases can affect professional judgment.
> - Be open to new ideas and be willing to learn from the suggestions of others.
> - Continue to learn, grow, and contribute as a professional.
> - Honor the ideas and principles of the NAEYC Code of Ethical Conduct.

This code and the accompanying principles and statements individually benefits us as early childhood teachers, and it helps our profession grow and mature. But perhaps the greatest gain is the guidance we get as we work with young children and their families.

CHARACTERISTICS OF EARLY CHILDHOOD TEACHERS

One of the most important components of a quality early childhood program is a good teacher. Teachers significantly affect what happens in the classroom. Their influence is far reaching. Early childhood educators have a lasting impact on young children and their families. Few individuals are as important in the lives of young children as their first teachers.

One determinant of effective early childhood programs is the personal characteristics of the teacher. The personal characteristics of teachers significantly affect how they behave in the classroom in addition to the kinds of relationships they have with children and other adults. The personality, behavior, and attitude of early childhood teachers determine the tone of the learning environment (Maxim, 1985). Spodek, Saracho, and Davis (1991) note that teachers who possess favorable attitudes about themselves are successful in fostering a positive and supportive learning atmosphere for children.

PARENTS SPEAK OUT

It's important to me, as a parent, to have a teacher for my child who is approachable and easy to talk with. When a teacher takes the time to tell me what my child did during the day—knowing details about what he did in the backyard or something funny he said or did—it makes it easier to be separated from him all day.

Attributes of Effective Teachers

What type of person makes a good early childhood teacher? Just as we find diversity among the children we work with, we also see great variation among early childhood teachers. There is no one best kind of early childhood educator. Many different types of people are successful in working with young children. What seems to be important is *who* you are as a person. Your personal characteristics—what you bring into the classroom—are vital in determining your effectiveness as a teacher. This is the art component of the teaching equation.

While there is no universal and complete list of desirable attributes of early childhood teachers, some characteristics are recognized as being essential. It must be remembered that these qualities are typically developed through personal experiences. A person is able to trust others, for example, if someone first trusted her. Likewise, an individual is able to demonstrate respect if he has experienced respect from others. The personal characteristics listed in Table 1.2 are presented for your consideration. Generally speaking, no one factor is considered more important than another. The perceived absence of a particular quality does not mean that you should not work with young children.

The characteristics identified in Table 1.2 are reflected in a list developed by Wittmer and Myrick (1974), who investigated the qualities of effective and ineffective educators. They found that "turn on" teachers were consistently described as good listeners, empathic, caring, concerned, genuine, warm, interested, knowledgeable, trusting, friendly, dynamic, possessing a sense of humor, and able to communicate. "Turn off" teachers were portrayed by students as insensitive, cold, disinterested, authoritarian, ridiculing, arbitrary, sarcastic, demanding, and punitive (p. 39).

TABLE 1.2
Desirable Characteristics of Early Childhood Teachers

Successful teachers of young children demonstrate:	
Flexibility	Friendliness
Sensitivity	Humor
Maturity	Honesty
Empathy	Open-mindness
Affection	Resourcefulness
Enthusiasm	Energy
Warmth	Trustworthiness
Respect	Patience
Understanding	Self-confidence
Compassion	Responsibility
Impartiality	Caring
Kindness	Intelligence

Are there other essential qualities of effective early childhood teachers? What do you think they are?

You may wish to privately and honestly evaluate yourself. How do *you* measure up to the list of desirable characteristics? Do you have the necessary qualities to be a successful early childhood teacher?

Self-Awareness

An honest appraisal of your personal qualities leads to heightened self-awareness. Understanding and accepting yourself is an important first step in becoming an effective teacher. Self-knowledge is the foundation for personal growth. A word of caution, however: Do not look at your individual characteristics as being good or bad, but rather as components that make you a unique person. What is crucial is that you become mindful of them and recognize that these qualities affect your daily interactions with students, parents, and colleagues.

A realistic evaluation takes courage and the willingness to take a risk. Yet, it may assist you in answering these vital questions posed by Feeney, Christensen, and Moravcik (1991): "Who am I?" and "What kind of teacher do I want to be?" (p. 11). Your answers to these questions may suggest certain changes, which in turn can increase your effectiveness and sensitivity as a teacher of young children. Being a good teacher also requires you to be a genuine or authentic person. Like other professionals in helping fields, a teacher cannot be afraid of being him or herself. Teachers must not be phony. Even young children quickly discover when a teacher's behavior is inconsistent with his or her innermost feelings. There must be harmony between your beliefs and your actions (Gargiulo, 1985). Good teachers have learned to accept themselves. Accepting yourself is the starting point for accepting children.

Bias and prejudice can affect teachers' interactions with children.

Bias and Prejudice

One beneficial outcome of an honest appraisal is recognition of your biases and prejudices. Do not be alarmed; these are traits everyone possesses in varying degrees. Biases and prejudice are products of your personality and your life experiences.

A **bias** may be defined as a tendency to accept or reject certain people or things. Exceptionally strong feelings result in **prejudice**, or preconceived opinions and attitudes typically formed without regard to facts or adequate knowledge. Prejudice can also refer to an intolerance of others. While prejudice may be favorable, it usually represents an unfavorable judgment. We typically find prejudice when we talk about views regarding race, culture, religion, socioeconomic status, disabilities, and even gender, to name but a few areas.

Teachers are frequently unaware that they harbor such beliefs. Confronting this reality can be very difficult. Yet, this self-awareness is extremely necessary due to the potential for harm to young children. Your true feelings will show in your dealings with your students. Children are astute observers of teacher behavior. There is also the risk that children will reflect your biases in their interactions with their classmates. Feeney et al. (1991, pp.13–14) suggest that you learn something about yourself by truthfully answering these questions:

- How do I respond to children who are dirty, ragged, smelly, or unattractive?

- How do I feel when children do not conform to my expectations about good or acceptable behavior?
- Are there children I immediately like or dislike or with whom I feel comfortable or uncomfortable? What are the characteristics of these children?
- Do I have strong feelings about children who are loud, verbal, and aggressive? What about children who are quiet, passive, shy, clingy, or whiny?
- Do I generally tend to prefer children of one sex?
- Do I have strong reactions to children from certain economic backgrounds, races, or culture?
- Do I have negative feelings about working with children who are precocious, developmentally delayed, or have handicapping conditions?
- What are my reactions to families who have lifestyles that are very different from my own, and do these influence my feelings about their children?

KIDS SPEAK UP

Why do I have to wash my hands, all I did was sneeze?

Boy, 4 years old

If you discover that you have a bias, and you most likely will, sometimes simple awareness of this fact is all that is needed to bring about a change. For some early childhood educators, however, intense reflection and critical examination may be necessary as they attempt to sort out deeply rooted views. In certain situations, your feelings may be so strong that it would be wise not to attempt to work with certain types of groups of children (for example, youngsters with special needs or children from different ethnic backgrounds). In a few extreme instances, it may be appropriate to ask yourself, "Should I become an early childhood teacher?"

Finally, the recognition of the role that bias and prejudice can play in our interactions with children has resulted in the popular and contemporary strategy known as the "anti-bias approach" to teaching young children (Derman-Sparks, 1989). Developed at Pacific Oaks College, this model stresses that all children, despite diversity, are deserving of respect and recognition as unique individuals. Differences are to be acknowledged and valued. Teachers, therefore, must be cognizant of their beliefs and behaviors that might deny any child their individual dignity. This approach has major implications for how teachers construct the classroom environment, develop curriculum and learning activities, and relate to their students and co-workers.

What Makes a Good Teacher?

As we conclude this discussion of the qualities of early childhood teachers, it might be interesting to look at what other individuals think makes a good teacher. There are several sources of information. The assessments of children, parents, and co-workers can be particularly valuable. According to Hess and Croft (1981, pp. 407–412) a good teacher has these characteristics:

Children say a good teacher

Holds you and reads to you
Sings songs to you
Doesn't slap you
Pushes you high on a swing
Goes to meetings
Puts a band-aid on a hurt finger right away
Smiles at you
Doesn't make you sit still or be quiet
Wears pretty beads
Lets you play with her hair
Fixes bikes
Doesn't get mad
Works hard
Builds with us
Makes you laugh

Mothers say a good teacher

Attends to the needs of the children
Is firm without being mean
Doesn't hold a grudge or play favorites
Gives him or her self to every child equally
Is able to handle unexpected situations smoothly and doesn't get excited in emergencies
Makes learning situations out of every "problem"
Watches and listens and concentrates on the children
Gives me specific information about my child and helps me learn how to teach what he or she wants my child to know
Reinforces what I think is important for my child to know
Is warm and friendly and smiles sincerely

Fathers say a good teacher is

[Someone] who is not afraid to get dirty
Someone who is patient and has a lot of self-confidence
Someone physically affectionate
[Someone] who is not afraid to be firm and discipline the child
[Someone] with a sense of humor
Someone who can create a special bond with each child

Someone with varied interests and an eager, joyful outlook on life
Someone who isn't all hung up with a sexist role

Teachers say a good teacher is

A teacher who is willing to do more than his or her share
A person who is cheerful
Someone who doesn't let his or her personal life interfere with classroom work
A person who is a good sport and knows how to work on a team
Someone who sees a need and fills it
A person who reinforces the consistency of the classroom goals
A teacher who does not contradict other members of the teaching team
A person who is emotionally healthy and is able to talk through the problems all teachers face
Someone with a sense of humor

Teacher Stress and Burnout

Teachers must be alert to the possibility of job stress and burnout. People employed in helping professions are especially vulnerable to burnout. Stress may well be an occupational hazard and an unavoidable consequence of the teaching profession (Beck & Gargiulo, 1983). It can affect both the novice and experienced educator.

When anxiety, tension, and frustration persist or increase, stress develops into a syndrome called **burnout** (Freudenberger, 1975). The burnout syndrome is characterized by physical and emotional exhaustion, which results from ongoing demands on personal energy,

Without proper precautions, the daily routine of being an early childhood teacher can lead to stress and eventual burnout.

strength, and resources (Freudenberger, 1977). Mattingly (1977) describes burnout "as a painful and personally destructive response to excessive stress" (p. 127).

What causes early childhood teachers to experience stress and, without intervention, eventual burnout? Several factors are involved. Hess and Croft (1981, p. 420) state that burnout in child care workers and teachers of young children is a reaction to three things:

1. Staff members who have unrealistic expectations and goals for the changes they want to bring about in the people with whom they work;
2. A job that has relatively constant demands for emotional interactions with others; and
3. Long-term goals that are difficult to achieve or do not provide day-to-day signs of progress.

Partin and Gargiulo (1980) found that there are a number of common classroom events and situations that can produce stress for teachers. Some of these factors are involuntary transfers, disruptive youngsters, unsatisfactory job performance, lack of adequate teaching materials and supplies, large class size, reorganization of classes, and denial of promotion. Failure of administrators to demonstrate support and concern for their teachers may also contribute to burnout.

A more recent reason for burnout among teachers of young children is suggested by Dresden and Myers (1989). They write that "burnout does not result from what we do or when we do it so much as it comes from a sense of not being able to make a visible impact with individual children and their parents, teachers, or caretakers . . ." (p. 65). Finally, teachers who do not take care of their own health and well-being are prime candidates for burnout.

It must be remembered that stress is not solely dependent on specific environmental factors, but on the reaction of the person to those stressors. Consequently, while teachers encounter a wide variety of stressful situations, "these sources cannot be viewed in isolation but only in relation to the teacher's capabilities, personality, and perceptions" (Beck & Gargiulo, 1983, p. 172).

Symptoms of stress vary with the individual teacher. The first step in burnout prevention is recognizing the early warning signs. Stress can be managed more constructively if it is recognized in the formative stages rather than in crisis. These signs may be both physiological and behavioral. Common bodily reactions include a change in eating habits (too little or too much), insomnia, elevated blood pressure, fatigue, ulcers, and frequent headaches, to name but a few of the physical ailments (Beck & Gargiulo, 1983). Behavioral reactions include heightened irritability (with staff and children), increased absenteeism, "clock watching," deteriorating relationships with colleagues, and a decreased willingness to be a "team player" (Hess & Croft, 1981).

What makes burnout so harmful is that it affects the teacher's attitude and often leads to low morale. Burnout also influences the teacher's performance in the classroom and their relationship with the children. When early childhood professionals are suffering from burnout, the quality of the children's experiences are also harmed. Teachers who suffer from burnout typically exhibit a loss of positive feelings toward their students. They are more concerned with survival than instructional responsibilities. Early childhood educators who are burned out contribute little to the quality of the students' daily experiences in the classroom. The children, in fact, may suffer from lower self-esteem as result of their teacher's uninvolved and uncaring behavior. Teaching young children is no longer rewarding or brings joy; instead, it is viewed as a boring and thankless routine (Beck & Gargiulo, 1983; Partin & Gargiulo, 1980). Quality early childhood programs need teachers who are fully committed to their duties.

Fancy toys and the latest equipment look good when you're touring through, but they don't really tell you how well the school will teach your child. Instead, the *consistency* of the staff—both in terms of quality and tenure— is a much better yardstick for evaluating the school.

Wise teachers do not let stress take control of their lives. They develop plans of action for alleviating stress before it becomes a problem. Some strategies that have proven useful for reducing stress and avoiding burnout are exercise and recreational activities, developing a hobby, and meditation (Beck & Gargiulo, 1983). Another helpful technique is effective utilization of time. Careful planning and prioritizing of what you hope to accomplish in the classroom is a great stress reducer. Many of the stresses identified by teachers result from a perception of trying to do "too much in too little time" (Partin & Gargiulo, 1980). Maxim (1985) offers the following ideas for "recharging" a teaching career and thus reducing the possibility of burnout:

- Change established routines; work with a new group of children; accept new challenges or assignments.
- Introduce yourself to innovative ideas by attending professional meetings, conferences, and workshops.
- Extend your circle of friends; socialize with people who work outside the profession.
- Give praise and recognition to fellow teachers; positive feedback is a powerful antidote to burnout.

- Plan for time away from your professional responsibilities; use vacation wisely—it is a time to renew energies and seek refreshment of the spirit.

Probably the most frequently mentioned method for reducing stress is the development of peer support groups. The value of teachers regularly meeting to reflect on professional concerns and encourage each other is well documented (Beck & Gargiulo, 1983). The stimulation, nurturance, and collegial support teachers can receive from each other is a powerful tool in combating burnout.

TRAINING OF EARLY CHILDHOOD PERSONNEL

Earlier, you read that teachers of young children need to be outstanding people. In fact, Maxim (1985) believes that they should be among the finest individuals imaginable. Good teachers, however, must also have a substantial educational background. Teaching young children demands more than just liking them; it requires knowledge and skill that are usually gained through a teacher training program (Spodek & Saracho, 1988). Good programs for young children rely on competent teachers. Essential to becoming a competent educator are preparation programs that provide specialized training (Perry, 1990). Teachers with preparation specific to the field of early childhood education provide a solid foundation for quality early childhood programs.

Teacher Preparation

Training early childhood teachers is a difficult task. Part of this difficulty arises from the wide variety of programs, that serve young children. Teachers work in kindergartens, preschools, day care centers, and Head Start programs, to name only a few settings that require competent professionals. Each of these programs differs in their purpose, sponsorship, and the children they serve. Distinctions can also be found in the qualifications and training background of the teachers. In some cases, those who work with young children only need to have a high school diploma and experience with young children. Other situations require a two-year college degree. Increasingly, however, a baccalaureate degree in Early Childhood Education is required to teach young children in public and nonpublic school settings. It is interesting to note that this diversity in qualifications is seen as a major obstacle to early childhood education becoming a *true* profession (Lawton, 1988).

One question that is not easily answered is, "What constitutes adequate preparation of early childhood teachers?" One characteristic of the field of early childhood education is the absence of a single model appropriate to the training of all early childhood teachers. This is a unique feature. Many realize that the training of early childhood personnel is the key to quality programs, but a common set of expectations does not exist either at the local, state, or national level (Maxim, 1985). Therefore, the professional qualifications of those who with young children greatly vary. It is not clear, according to Katz (1988), what kind of training nor how much of it is necessary to produce high quality teachers. Spodek et al., (1988) suggest that "no one model can serve to define standards for performance for all early childhood education practitioners" (p. 8). The level of preparation for practitioners is typically determined by the employer and the licensing/accrediting agency—either the state department of education or a department of human services.

While the research evidence suggests that the practitioner's level of professional preparation is related to improved outcomes in young children (Lawton, 1988; Powell & Dunn, 1990), teachers are essentially prepared according to a two-track system. We train individuals who work in public schools differently from those employed in nonpublic school settings such as private kindergartens, day care centers, and Head Start programs. Those who work in public schools must be certified (licensed) teachers. This requires at least a bachelor's degree from a college or university. Practitioners employed in the private sector or the federally funded Head Start program are usually trained at community colleges, which award an associate (two year) degree or in vocational home economics programs offered through high schools, vocational schools, and at the community college level. Persons with associate degrees assume an important leadership role in early childhood classrooms. They can serve, in the private sector, as teachers, assistant teachers, or even directors of early childhood programs. Vocational programs provide training for entry-level positions such as child care assistants or aides who function under the supervision of staff with greater training and experience (Powell & Dunn, 1990). An additional avenue of preparation is the **Child Development Associate** (CDA) credential. Originally developed in 1972 to meet the need for trained personnel in Head Start programs, this training opportunity is based on demonstrated competency in working with young children and provides an alternative to college-based preparation. This credential is also presently being used to certify child care practitioners. Unfortunately, specialized training is frequently not required for teachers in the private sector. Standards are often minimal and requirements typically less stringent. It is equally regrettable that these two main preparation tracks operate in relative isolation from each other (Spodek & Saracho, 1990).

Level of training leads to different roles and responsibilities. Adults other than teachers are important partners in delivery services to young children. Many early childhood programs recognize

TABLE 1.3 Preparation and Responsibilities of Early Childhood Practitioners

Level	Preparation	Professional Responsibility
I. **Early Childhood Teacher Assistant**	High school diploma or equivalent; no specialized training in early childhood; will participate in professional development program	Entry-level or pre-professional position, implements program activities under direct supervision of professional staff
II. **Early Childhood Associate Teacher**	CDA (Child Development Associate) credential or associate degree in early childhood education or child development	Professionals who independently implement program activities; may be responsible for the care and education of a group of children
III. **Early Childhood Teacher**	Bachelor's degree in early childhood education or child development; possesses greater theoretical knowledge and depth of practical skills	Professionals responsible for the care and education of a group of children
IV. **Early Childhood Specialist**	Advanced degree in early childhood education or child development or bachelor's degree plus 3 years full-time teaching experience with young children	Professionals who supervise and train staff, design curriculum, and/or administer programs

Source: National Association for the Education of Young Children. NAEYC Position Statement on Nomenclature, Salaries, Benefits, and the Status of the Early Childhood Profession, *Young Children, 40* (November 1984), pp. 52–55. © 1984 by NAEYC. Adapted with permission.

this and routinely follow the tradition of a teaching team. NAEYC has acknowledged that individuals with different levels of preparation are essential to early childhood programs. In a 1984 position statement on nomenclature, NAEYC outlined four levels of early childhood practice, each with different levels of responsibility and varying amounts of training. This hierarchical model is illustrated in Table 1.3.

Training Guidelines

As we noted earlier, the preparation of teachers is critical to the quality of early childhood programs. To ensure that young children are taught by highly qualified teachers, the two premier early childhood organizations, ACEI and NAEYC, published guidelines and recommendations that established a standard of excellence for baccalaureate teacher education programs (ACEI, 1983: NAEYC, 1982). These guidelines address broad areas of knowledge considered important for developing a teacher of high quality, rather than merely providing a list of specific courses. The preparation experiences should be sequentially organized and include the following.

- A broad liberal arts education
- Foundations of early childhood education
- Understanding of child growth and development (birth to age 8)
- Knowledge of early childhood curriculum
- Understanding of the principles and methods of teaching and learning
- Ongoing supervised field experiences with young children and their families
- Study of human relations, ethical issues, and cultural diversity

The preceding guidelines parallel the recommendations of Spodek and Saracho (1990), who view general education, foundations, instructional knowledge, and practice as essential components of a four-year teacher education program. More recently, the Association of Teacher Educators (ATE) and NAEYC joined forces and identified five characteristics essential for any early childhood teacher preparation program (Early Childhood Teacher Certification, 1991, p. 18):

1. Teachers must be educated in the liberal arts and knowledgeable about a variety of disciplines in order to recognize the learning embedded in children's activity. Early childhood teachers must be knowledgeable in various subject matter pedagogies to be skillful in interactive teaching strategies that advance children's developing understandings.
2. Early childhood teachers must be well informed about developmental theories and their implications for practice.
3. Early childhood teachers must understand the significance of play to children's educational development and develop skills in facilitating enriching play in early childhood classrooms.
4. Early childhood teachers must understand families as the primary context for children's learning and development, respect diversity in family structure and values, and develop skills in interacting with parents in ways that enhance children's educational success.
5. Early childhood teachers need to acquire the ability to supervise and coordinate their teaching with other adults. With the expansion of shared decision making in these settings, early childhood teachers also should be able to reflect on their own professional development.

These guidelines and preparation recommendations should provide the early childhood teacher with the competencies and skills needed to fulfill their roles. Early childhood teachers function, according to Saracho (1984), as diagnosticians, curriculum designers, organizers of instruction, managers of learning, counselors/advisors, and decision makers.

NAEYC has also addressed the issue of personnel preparation at associate degree granting institutions. Teachers prepared via two-year training programs have an avenue for immediate entry for working with young children (see Table 1.3). The guidelines, prepared in 1985, call for a minimum of 50 percent of the student's work to be in a professional studies component. In addition, prospective early childhood educators should have a strong foundation in liberal arts. The professional studies curriculum (NAEYC, 1985) provides for both practical skills and theory, distributed over the following nine areas:

- Introduction to early childhood education
- Typical and atypical child growth and development
- Curriculum planning
- Providing, implementing, and evaluating developmentally appropriate activities
- Child guidance and group management
- Child health, safety, and nutrition
- Young children with special needs
- Observing and recording children's behavior
- Family and community relations

Important elements of this model are field experiences with young children in a wide variety of environments and supervised practicum work totaling at least 300 hours.

Child Development Associate

A national credentialing program was inaugurated in 1972 to meet the growing need for quality child care. The goal of the Child Development Associate (CDA) program was to raise the skill level of child care workers and provide a ladder for career advancement. The CDA program was designed as an entry-level program for individuals with little or no training and/or experience with preschool children. Perry (1990) writes that the

> basic purpose was to design and promote a system of training and credentialing individuals based on their demonstrated competency with children rather than coursework taken at a university. A CDA was defined as a person who will be able to assume full responsibility for the daily activities of a group of young children in day-care centers, Head Start programs, private nursery schools, and other preschool programs. (p. 186)

Originally the credential was awarded only to persons working in center-based programs serving children between ages 3 and 5. In the mid-1980s, the credential was modified to include several settings:

A CDA credential requires that child care workers participate in formal training experiences.

preschool center-based, infant/toddler center-based, home visitor, and family day-care providers working with 3- to 5-year-olds. An option exists for bilingual (Spanish) specialization (Benson & Peters, 1988).

In 1972, the Child Development Associate Consortium was established with representatives from 39 professional organizations. This consortium managed the program until 1979, at which time it was administered by the Bank Street College of Education. Since 1985 the CDA has operated under the auspices of NAEYC through its Council for Early Childhood Professional Recognition (Powell & Dunn, 1990).

Individuals seeking a CDA certificate must demonstrate competency in six domains related to thirteen functional areas. The standards and functional areas, which use a "whole child" approach, are outlined in Table 1.4. The competency goals are the same for each of the settings. Yet, the functional areas vary according to the child care setting and ages of the child (Council for Early Childhood Professional Recognition, 1992).

Since June 1992, candidates are required to have completed, within five years, 120 clock hours of formal child care education. No less than ten hours of instruction must be taken in each of the following eight subject areas:

- Planning a safe, healthy learning environment
- Steps to advance children's physical and intellectual development

TABLE 1.4 Child Development Associate Competency Goals and Functional Areas

Competency Goals	Functional Areas
1. To establish and maintain a safe, healthy learning environment	1. Safe 2. Healthy 3. Learning Environment
2. To advance physical and intellectual competence	4. Physical 5. Cognitive 6. Communication 7. Creative
3. To support social and emotional development and provide positive guidance and discipline	8. Self 9. Social 10. Guidance and Discipline
4. To establish positive and productive relationships with families	11. Families
5. To ensure a well-run, purposeful program responsive to participant	12. Program Management
6. To maintain a commitment to professionalism	13. Professionalism

Source: CDA National Credentialing Program, *Assessment System and Competency Standards for Preschool Caregivers.* (Washington, DC: Council for Early Childhood Professional Recognition, 1992).

- Positive ways to support children's social and emotional development
- Strategies to establish productive relationships with families
- Strategies to manage an effective program operation
- Maintaining a commitment to professionalism
- Observing and recording children's behavior
- Principles of child growth and development

The formal training experiences must be under the auspices of an agency or organization with expertise in early childhood teacher preparation. Examples of these organizations include community or junior colleges, four-year colleges and universities, vocational schools, Head Start programs, and local school districts. The educational requirements can also be met via participation in training experiences typically available in the field, such as in-service opportunities, workshops, and seminars sponsored by recognized training providers (Council for Early Childhood Professional Recognition, 1992). The educational requirements are the same for all settings, with the exception of the home visitor credential. Regardless of the means, individuals seeking CDA endorsement must demonstrate their competency via their work with young children.

The backbone of the CDA program is the assessment process. From the beginning, CDA was conceived as a self-assessment procedure. The candidate (child care worker) is believed to be capable of evaluating her own competence as well as working toward strengthening those areas perceived to be weak (Benson & Peters, 1988). To seek the endorsement, the candidate must be at least 18 years old, possess a high school diploma or equivalent, be able to read, write, and speak well enough to fulfill the CDA standards, and sign a statement of ethical conduct. In addition, he must have access to a state-approved child care program where he can be observed working with children.

The CDA assessment system operates as follows:

1. The individual seeking a certificate applies to the CDA National Credentialing Program. The candidate verifies that he or she has completed at least 480 hours of direct work experience with young children in a group setting over a five-year period in addition to meeting the educational requirements.

2. The child care worker selects an early childhood professional to serve as an advisor and identifies parents who have children in the applicant's class.

3. The advisor gathers information about the candidate's work with young children and families. The applicant's performance is documented through formal observation(s) and is recorded on the CDA Observation Instrument. Parent perceptions of the candidate's abilities are a vital ingredient in the assessment process. Each parent with a child in the applicant's care is asked to complete a confidential Parent Opinion Questionnaire. It is expected that a minimum of 75 percent of the surveys will be completed.

4. The candidate also prepares a Professional Resource File containing a brief autobiographical sketch, a collection of specific resource materials, and written statements of competence describing her work in each of the six competency areas identified in Table 1.4.

5. After all the information is gathered, the candidate notifies the national office that he is ready to be assessed. The CDA program assigns an early childhood professional, trained in the credentialing process, to evaluate the performance of the child care worker. During a verification visit, the representative carefully evaluates all the materials and documents that have been completed. In addition, the representative administers a written exam, the Early Childhood Studies Review. The test is "designed to measure general knowledge of good practices in early childhood education programs serving children birth through age 5. The content of the Review is based on those current principles of developmentally appropriate practice widely accepted among early childhood professionals" (Council for Early Childhood Professional Recognition, 1992, p. 26). Upon conclusion of the examination, candidates participate in an oral interview. The interview consists of ten structured situations specific to the candidate's setting, age level endorsement, and specialization. The child care worker is shown photographs and given a written description of the situation depicted. Specific questions are asked and the candidate's responses recorded.

6. Upon conclusion of the verification visit, the evaluator gathers the appropriate documents and forwards them to the national office for review and evaluation by a committee. Based on the committee's assessment, the candidate may be awarded a credential, or suggestions for additional training will be made along with information on an appeals procedure (Council for Early Childhood Professional Recognition, 1992).

The candidate progresses through the assessment procedure at her own pace and is evaluated only when she is ready. The cost of the evaluation is primarily the responsibility of the candidate. The initial CDA credential is awarded for a three-year period and may be renewed for periods of five years. Requirements for receiving a credential are essentially similar for each of the settings.

The CDA program has been largely successful in accomplishing its main objective—improving the quality of child care for vast numbers of young children. The credential is a requirement for practitioners in the Head Start program. Military child care standards also require the CDA credential for lead teacher positions. Currently, all fifty states and the District of Columbia incorporate the CDA credential in their licensing requirements as a means of ensuring the competency of the staff. Powell and Dunn (1990) note that the six competency goals also function as guidelines in many two-year teacher training programs. Since the inception of CDA, over 50,000 credentials have been awarded.

Certification and Licensing

An issue important to the field of early childhood education is the certification and licensing of practitioners. All teachers in public schools must be certified. Increasingly, teachers in private and parochial schools are also certified educators. Teaching certificates are issued by state departments of education and are typically awarded on the basis of completing an approved program of study from an accredited institution of higher education. This usually requires four years of college preparation; however, in several states, an additional year or master's degree is necessary for receipt of a teaching credential. Standards for certification, and the specific requirements for receiving a teaching certificate, vary from state to state. A teaching certificate simply identifies those individuals who possess *minimum* competencies or a "safe level" of basic professional knowledge and skill needed to teach young children. (Spodek & Saracho, 1988).

TEACHERS SPEAK OUT

I had been employed as a crossing guard for the school district for a year and one half and at the same time became active as a parent volunteer at my son's preschool. I began taking child development classes at the community college and was hired as a preschool teaching assistant. I believe walking children safely across the street is important work. However, I was surprised that I was not paid more at my new position, which involves teaching and directing our children, the future of tomorrow.

State teacher certification agencies exert significant control over the preparation of early childhood teachers. Colleges and universities construct their teacher education programs around state certification standards. Professional organizations like NAEYC, ACEI, and the National Council for Accreditation of Teacher Education (NCATE) also influence the training and eventual certification of early childhood teachers via their guidelines and calls for professional standards. But due to the absence of standardized, nationwide credentialing requirements, each state establishes its own standards for early childhood teachers. This pattern results in a high degree of variability in the preparation, and thus the quality, of teachers of young children. In a 1988 survey, McCarthy found that almost half of the states offer neither certification nor an endorsement in early childhood education. Among the twenty-three states with specialized certification, only three incorporate NAEYC's definition of early childhood in their statutes. NAEYC reports that in 1993, thirty-five states offer credentialing in early childhood education.

NAEYC is very concerned about the inconsistencies in both the preparation and certification of teachers of young children. The goal of this organization is to achieve specialized early childhood certification in every state. NAEYC, in conjunction with ATE, is calling for a certificate exclusively for early childhood education. This credential should be distinct from, and independent of, existing elementary or secondary certifications (Early Childhood Teacher Certification, 1991). The position of these two associations is that such a certificate should be for children birth through age 8 and address the following certification standards:

- Growth, development, and learning
- Family and community relations
- Curriculum development, content, and implementation
- Health, safety, and nutrition
- Field experiences and professional internship
- Professionalism

As the need for qualified early childhood teachers increases, the joint NAEYC and NCATE goal is an important first step for ensuring that young children, regardless of where they live, are taught by teachers who demonstrate a high degree of professional competency.

As we noted earlier, teachers in nonpublic school programs such as day care centers and preschools are not required to have a teaching license. Qualifications for persons working in these types of early childhood programs are established by regulatory agencies other than departments of education. Standards are typically set by health or social service agencies. Perhaps more important than who is responsible for licensing is that this separation perpetuates the classic, yet highly artificial dichotomy between education and care. It appears that those who work in public schools are responsible only for education, while individuals in child care centers or preschools are solely responsible for care giving (Bredekamp, 1990). But when working with young children, it is vital for all concerned to recognize the inseparability of care and education.

Generally speaking, the standards for early childhood personnel working in nonpublic school settings are frequently minimal and lower than those for public school teachers. Like teacher certification requirements, state standards for personnel working in child care programs are diverse. Requirements usually address three areas: age, education, and work experience with young children. Because these are minimal qualifications, administrators are free to establish higher standards for their programs. The variation in employment requirements is great. In some states, only a high school diploma is necessary. Alabama's minimal regulatory standard requires that a person be at least 16 years old and be able to read and write. In California, the qualification for a "group leader" necessitates twelve hours of college coursework in early childhood or child development (Bredekamp, 1990). Bredekamp, Director of Professional Development for NAEYC, further notes that if NAEYC's accreditation criteria were met, persons responsible for the care and education of young children would possess at least a CDA credential or an associate degree in early childhood or child development. The reason why standards are so important is that the requirements for personnel tend to significantly influence the quality of programs offered to young children.

Professional Growth and Development

Teachers never stop learning. Beginning teachers quickly recognize that they have much to learn, despite having completed a rigorous preparation program. Experienced educators also appreciate the value of increasing their knowledge and improving their skills. Continually seeking to improve yourself is an important aspect of being a professional.

Your education does not cease upon obtaining a degree or securing a job; in fact, in many ways, it is only beginning. The educational needs of teachers change as they gain experience with young children. Katz (1972) recognized this fact several years ago and identified four stages of teacher development and the type of training activities appropriate for each state:

Stage 1. *Survival.* During the difficult first year, many teachers are concerned with survival. Questions abound. "Can I really do this on a daily basis?" "Can I make it until Christmas break?" "Am I doing a good job?" It is not unusual for beginning early childhood teachers to feel ill-prepared and inadequate. Support is typically necessary. Guidance and encouragement from experienced colleagues is beneficial. Specific suggestions and hints are also very helpful. Teachers are "learning the ropes."

Stage 2. *Consolidation.* After two to three years of experience, teachers have moved beyond survival and can begin to focus on individual students and specific areas of concern. Continued on-site support is helpful. Technical assistance and advice from consultants, colleagues, and supervisors is genuinely appreciated.

Stage 3. *Renewal.* A sense of boredom or dissatisfaction may develop after three to four years in the classroom. Teachers are tired of the routine in their jobs. They actively search for new activities for their pupils and investigate recent developments in the field. Teachers renew their enthusiasm by joining professional organizations, attending conferences, participating in workshops, and meeting other teachers.

Stage 4. *Maturity.* As a result of several years of teaching, the professional educator reaches a state of maturity wherein she comes to terms with herself as a teacher. Her years of experience allow her to become more introspective. A concern is expressed with the theories, issues, and beliefs that undergird the profession. Teachers begin to read widely, work on advanced degrees, and participate in professional meetings as a means of renewing their commitment to teaching.

Effective teachers are always looking for ways to improve themselves and consequently enhance the quality of the learning experience for young children. While program administrators and the schools bear some responsibility for staff development, it is the individual teacher who is ultimately accountable for his or her own professional growth and development. Several options are available to teachers who wish to engage in improvement activities. These experiences can be formal or informal and include the following:

- Participating in workshops and in-service activities
- Pursuing an advanced degree
- Joining a professional organization
- Reading the professional literature
- Visiting other classrooms and observing colleagues

- Organizing a teacher study group
- Serving as a mentor for a novice teacher
- Attending and participating in professional meetings
- Working on committees
- Writing an article for a professional journal or local newspaper.

Although teachers greatly benefit, both personally and professionally, from these activities, the true benefactors are the young children the teacher is responsible for.

SUMMARY

Choosing to become a teacher is one of the most important decisions you will ever make. You will be a significant influence in the lives of many young children. Your ideas and attitudes about teaching and children will greatly affect your interactions with them. Your personal values as well as your individual philosophy of teaching will also guide your actions in the classroom. As a teacher of young children, you have a responsibility of advocating for children and their families.

Being a teacher means that you are a professional. A professional person is an ethical person. You are expected to exhibit high standards of behavior and follow a code of conduct.

Of course, there is no one type of person who is ideally suited for working with young children. Early childhood teachers are diverse individuals. Yet, there are desirable characteristics associated with being an effective early childhood educator. The personal qualities of a teacher do influence the learning environment. Successful teachers are aware of their strengths and weaknesses. They also take steps to avoid burnout, a frequent occupational hazard.

There are many ways a person can become a teacher of young children. Some avenues are more formal and rigorous than others, but specialized training is essential. Qualified personnel are the key to quality early childhood programs.

The standards for personnel preparation, which vary greatly, are established by individual state departments of education or health and social service agencies. Unfortunately, these requirements specify only minimal competencies. Effective teachers, therefore, seek to continually improve themselves through professional growth and development activities.

TEST YOUR UNDERSTANDING

1. Identify three reasons why you want to be a teacher of young children.
2. Describe seven historical and contemporary viewpoints of children. Which perspective do you believe?
3. What values do you think are important for an early childhood teacher?

4. Why is it necessary to have a personal philosophy of teaching?
5. Do you think early childhood educators should be advocates for young children and their families? If so, why?
6. Is early childhood education a profession?
7. Why do early childhood teachers need a code of conduct?
8. List five personal characteristics you believe are essential for an early childhood teacher.
9. Why must teachers of young children be aware of bias and prejudice?
10. What is burnout? What can teachers do to prevent it?
11. Why is it important for early childhood personnel to have specialized training?
12. Describe three different types of early childhood teacher preparation programs.
13. What is the purpose of certification of early childhood practitioners?
14. Identify six activities appropriate to the professional growth and development of early childhood teachers.

LEARNING ACTIVITIES

1. Write your own philosophy of education.
2. "Anyone can be a teacher of young children." Do you agree or disagree with this statement? What is the thinking behind such a statement? How did this point of view emerge?
3. Read the NAEYC Code of Ethics located in Appendix A.
4. Describe the personal qualities of an ideal early childhood professional.
5. Interview several early childhood teachers. Find out what strategies they use to combat job stress and burnout.

CHAPTER 2

The Early Childhood Profession

CHAPTER OUTLINE

Definitions and Terminology

Typical Early Childhood Settings

- *Child Care Centers*
- *Preschools*
- *Federal Programs*
- *Kindergartens*
- *Primary Grades*

Need for Early Childhood Programs

- *Working Mothers*
- *Single-Parent Homes*
- *Child Care Availability*

Indicators of Program Quality

Benefits of Early Childhood Education

- *Perry Preschool Project*
- *Other Research Findings*

Cultural Diversity

KEY TERMS

Early childhood
Early childhood education
Child care center
Preschool
Parent cooperative preschool
Head Start
Project Follow-Through
Home Start
Chapter I
Even Start
Kindergarten
Prekindergarten
Primary grades

"Welcome Back," the sign above the teacher's door read. As Mrs. Johnson went through the door on her way home, she decided that for the most part, the first day back at school had gone as she expected. A few tears had fallen as moms and dads left their children to begin the routines of school that would become a familiar way of life for the next few months.

By 8:10 a.m., the children had learned their teacher's name. Around 9:00 a.m., they visited the class centers and ate their snacks. At 10:00 a.m., the librarian read a story and gave everyone a book marker. By about 10:15 a.m., two of the children chewed their name tags into pieces, and the teacher promptly found a place to put their tags until they dried. About 11:00 a.m., the little girl who had stood quietly and watched for most of the day sat close to another child while the teacher began a new song—and Brian began to put things into his backpack.

As Mrs. Johnson talked about what would be happening next, she noticed that Brian, now with a completely loaded backpack, was standing near the door. Approaching the little boy, she asked, "Brian, where are you going?"

He answered, "To my baby sitter's house."

Mrs. Johnson, suddenly aware of what he must be thinking, countered, "Not yet, Brian. You are in the first grade now. This year we stay at school all day. There are interesting things to do after lunch."

Brian frowned, slowly placed his pack on the floor, and responded with indignation, "I would just like to know who signed me up for this!"

Welcome! Welcome to the world of young children. As you enter the field of early childhood education, you will become part of a dynamic, vibrant, and growing profession. Early childhood education is a relatively young field, but one with a long and rich heritage. It is a legitimate profession filled with challenges and opportunities for the dedicated individual.

Many psychologists and educators believe that the early years of a child's life are one of the most important developmental periods. Much of what happens during this time can significantly affect later development. As an early childhood professional, you will play an important role in the lives of young children. While parents and siblings are often a youngster's first teacher, early childhood educators are also valuable contributors. In support of this belief, Graves commented recently that "studies on children's early years have shown that preschool experiences influence all areas of a child's development and later learning" (Graves, 1990a, p. 190).

It is not only professionals, but parents and the general public, who recognize the importance of early childhood education. Interest in the well-being of our youngest citizens has been increasing over the past few decades. Many caregivers are concerned with getting the child "off on the right foot." This emphasis is all around us. One of the authors, the father of a toddler, recalls attending hospital-sponsored courses for expectant parents, receiving promotional literature for stimulating and developmentally appropriate toys, getting complimentary copies of parenting magazines in addition to sample books designed to enhance prereading skills, and even receiving enrollment information about a class designed to assist parents in raising "bright" children. Although some parents have the desire and resources necessary to take advantage of these opportunities, there is a segment of our population whose children live in poverty, suffer from abuse and neglect, exhibit medical problems, or have learning difficulties. The early childhood professional serves the full continuum of our nation's young children. You will help shape the lives and minds of *all* youngsters. Our future lies with our children. They represent one of this country's greatest national resources.

DEFINITIONS AND TERMINOLOGY

Many different terms are used when talking about young children. It is important, therefore, that we have a common understanding of key terminology. Throughout this book, we use the term **early childhood** to refer to the time period between birth and 8 years of age. This description is fairly typical and is frequently used by professionals. It also reflects the thinking of the National Association for the Education of Young Children (NAEYC), the largest professional organization concerned with the well-being of young children. The term **early childhood education** is generally defined as the education and the delivery of services to youngsters from birth to age 8. It includes programs that serve children from infancy to the third grade in a wide variety of settings or environments. Thus it can be said that early childhood refers to the two main worlds of children—home and school. Current thinking suggests that early childhood education includes both the care and education of young children, including those with special needs.

As we just mentioned, early childhood education is provided in many different types of settings or locations. Examples of such places are child care centers, preschools, Head Start programs, kindergartens, or the primary grades of elementary schools. Some settings are more formal than others, such as schools that typically require full-day attendance. On the other hand, some services are delivered to young children on a flexible time schedule in less formal programs. We now turn our attention to some of the many different types of experiences available to young children.

TYPICAL EARLY CHILDHOOD SETTINGS

Programs for young children vary according to a number of factors (Table 2.1). Illustrations of these variables include the ages served, purpose of the program, public or private facility, profit or nonprofit organization, funding sources, type of children enrolled (typical, atypical, or both), and of course, as previously noted, the location and hours of service.

Child Care Centers

Child care or day care centers represent one type of program that is common for young children. These centers provide a service to parents who, for a variety of reasons, cannot stay at home with their children. **Child care centers** normally operate from approximately 6:00 a.m. until 6:00 p.m.; some provide extended hours until midnight. These programs typically serve children from infancy through age 5 or 6. Depending on the program, after-school care and services during school vacation periods may be available. Parents are charged fees by the centers for providing care. Federal income tax credits are available, however, to parents who pay for child care. A family is now allowed to deduct between 20 and 30 percent of their annual child care expenses from their tax bill. Up to $2,400 may be deducted for one child and $4,800 for two or more children.

Quality day care centers provide a safe environment under adult supervision. The physical, emotional, social, and intellectual well-being of the child is of primary importance. Contemporary thinking about child care focuses on the total needs of the youngster.

Child care centers may be located in the homes of friends or relatives, in the workplace as a convenience for parents, in local churches, and even in shopping malls and recreational centers such as health clubs. Some centers may be nationally franchised for-profit operations, while others are nonprofit and serve specific populations of children such as abused/neglected or homeless youngsters.

Child care centers may be licensed or unlicensed, depending on where the services are delivered (for example, in the home of a neighbor or at an industry-sponsored site). Although no national licensing standards nor any federal child care regulations exist, many local and state governments require the licensing of day care centers. But even at the state level, policies greatly vary and there is no one central licensing agency. The agencies responsible for licensing child care centers might be the local Department of Health, a state Department of Education, or the Department of Human Resources. Also of concern to both parents and early childhood professionals is the issue of quality of care and the training and experience of the child care worker.

TABLE 2.1 Types of Early Childhood Program Settings

Facility	Program Characteristics	Typical Ages Served
Preschool	Typically half-day program; usually privately operated in various locations; program emphasis varies (usually socialization skills and cognitive development)	2 to 4 years
Day Care/Child Care Centers	Usually designed as full-day experience for employed caregivers; variety of settings; physical care in addition to socialization and cognitive activities; both profit (e.g., Kinder Care) and nonprofit establishments (e.g., United Way agencies)	Infancy to school-age
Family Day Care	Small numbers of children cared for in private home; typically only custodial care; hours accommodate parent(s)	Variable
Parent-Child (Infant) Center	Provides health education, parenting information, and social services to parents in poverty; may include sensory and cognitive stimulation activities for at-risk and special needs youngsters	2 (3) months to 2 years
Head Start	Comprehensive health and social services for economically disadvantaged families; cognitive and social development of children in preparation for school entry; parental participation; federally supported program	2 to 5 years
Backyard Groups	Small groups of young children meet in the home of one of the youngsters; socialization and child care emphasis; supervision typically provided by one or more participating parents	Variable
Cooperative Preschool	Parent-operated program; provides cognitive and socialization activities; usually half-day; located in donated or rented space in churches or public buildings; nonprofit organization	2 to 5 years
Home Visitor Programs	Regularly scheduled home visits by professional or paraprofessional; direct instruction of child plus parent education; may be in conjunction with school program; typically used for infants and toddlers with special needs	Variable
Intergenerational Child Care	Program that integrates young children with nursing home residents; typically located in adult care facility; participation is voluntary;	Variable

(continued)

TABLE 2.1 Types of Early Childhood Program Settings *(continued)*

Facility	Program Characteristics	Typical Ages Served
	provides for mutually rewarding and beneficial experiences; some senior citizens function as "pseudo-grandparents"	
Nanny Program	Of recent popularity; usually used by upper-income families; well-trained individuals provide child care and many assume other household responsibilities; compensated position; lives with child's family	Variable
Ill Child Care	Popular service for single parents and two-income families; children with mild or noncontagious illnesses are cared for in separate facilities specifically designed for ill children, in special areas of child care centers, or in-home care may be provided	Variable
Employer Child Care	Child care facilities provided at or close to parent's workplace; employer-sponsored or provision for shared costs; physical care in addition to socialization and cognitive activities; provision for parent involvement if desired	Infancy to school age
School Age Child Care	Providing before- and/or after-school child care as a service to employed parents; located in local public schools and/or community agencies	6 to 12 years
Prekindergarten	Social and cognitive activities in preparation for school entry; public or private facilities	3 to 5 years
Kindergarten	Half-day or full-day programs; variable curricular emphasis; public or private organizations	4 to 5 years
Transitional Kindergarten	Opportunity for select children to extend kindergarten experience in preparation for entry into first grade; both public and private programs	6 to 7 years
Primary Grades	Public and private schools; academic skills associated with first, second, and third grades	6 to 8 years
Campus or Demonstration Schools	Research and teacher training opportunities; experimental and state-of-the-art practices; usually located on college or university campus; various funding sources	Infancy to adolescent years

Quality child care centers promote a safe environment under adult supervision.

Possibly the fastest growing segment of child care is the "cottage industry" of providing day care in private homes. This represents an alternative to center-based programs. This kind of caring for young children, while not highly visible, might well be the most common type of child care used by parents. Many of these sites are operated by women who accept a small number of children into their homes. These family day care homes may be licensed or unlicensed. The quality of care can range from minimal supervision to warm, stimulating, and nurturing environments.

Preschools

Another type of early childhood program is the **preschool** (or *nursery school*, as it is sometimes still called). These schools typically serve youngsters between the ages of 2 to 5 and are most often half-day programs (usually morning); thereby they provide a service to families who do not require full-day care. In some situations, full-day programs are available.

PARENTS SPEAK OUT

As a parent of preschoolers, finding a program that emphasizes social skills, encourages individuality, and enhances self-esteem is a priority.

Preschools traditionally focus on the social-emotional development of children in conjunction with enrichment activities. One basic purpose of a preschool is to provide a learning environment within a play setting. Play is at the heart of the preschool curriculum. This traditional function of a preschool is perhaps best recognized in the philosophy of Katherine Read, an early and influential advocate of nursery schools.

Read (1960, 1971) believes that a nursery school should be a place that nurtures young children and provides them with a secure, supportive environment for learning. A nursery school complements a youngster's home experience. It allows children an opportunity to develop socially, emotionally, physically, and intellectually. Teachers promote learning by creating a climate for discovery and exploration. Play and child-initiated activities are vital components of a quality nursery school program. Read also stresses the importance of the relationships children form with their classmates and teachers. These relationships help the child to develop self-confidence and a sense of adequacy and security, as well as a positive self-image.

Today, however, many preschools stress cognitive development. As a result, the focus has shifted from a child-centered program that emphasizes play to a teacher-centered program characterized by a downward extension of the kindergarten curriculum.

It is interesting to look at the public's changing attitude toward preschool experiences. According to the Gallup organization, a majority of Americans (55 percent) favor tax-supported preschools for 3- and 4-year-olds. This represents a considerable change in the public's opinion over the past fifteen years (Elam, Rose, & Gallup, 1991). A more recent survey reveals that a large majority (64 percent) of Gallup respondents favor federally subsidized child care for children from single-parent homes or from households where both parents are employed outside of the home. The cost of such a program should be shared—according to 85 percent of the respondents—between the federal government and the parents, based on their ability to pay (Elam, Rose, & Gallup, 1992).

Preschools may be publicly or privately sponsored. Examples of such sponsorship range from churches to colleges and universities that have laboratory schools or demonstration programs to a distinctively American concept, the **parent cooperative preschool**. In this model, parents are responsible for the operation and maintenance of the school. One parent might serve as an administrator while others assist on a regular basis, fulfilling a variety of roles.

Federal Programs

Another type of early childhood experience is the federally sponsored Head Start program. Head Start came into existence as a result of the 1964 Economic Opportunity Act. **Head Start** was part of a national agenda aimed at the War on Poverty. This compensatory program sought to overcome the effects of poverty in the lives of young children. With a focus on disadvantaged, low-income families with children between the ages of 2 and 5, Head Start sought to enhance the opportunities and increase the chances of school success for poor children. Head Start was unique in its emphasis on the total development of the youngster, on strengthening the family unit, and in its comprehensive nature of the services provided. The goals of the Head Start effort include increasing the child's physical, social, and emotional development; developing the youngster's intellectual skills and readiness for school; and improving the health of the child by providing medical, dental, social, and psychological services. Active parental participation and community involvement are also viewed as important components.

In 1990, Head Start celebrated its silver anniversary. In its 25-year existence, this program has provided services to more than 11 million children and their families (*Federal Register*, June 18, 1990). Unfortunately, because of government funding limitations, only a portion of the children eligible for services (approximately 20 percent) are able to receive them. It is also estimated that only 15 percent of Head Start centers operate on a full-day basis (Cohen, 1990). Adequate funding of Head Start is one of the goals President Clinton called for in his first State of the Union Address in February 1993. Many early childhood professionals are hopeful that full funding can

One aim of Head Start is to increase the chances of school success for poor children.

be obtained so that Head Start can improve and continue to effect meaningful change in the lives of young children.

Head Start provided the impetus for two other programs. In 1967, **Project Follow-Through** was initiated after some educational research data suggested that the positive impact of the Head Start experiment was not maintained once the children enrolled in elementary school. Follow-Through was introduced in an effort to continue the gains developed in Head Start. Using various models and educational approaches, students in kindergarten through the third grade continued to receive educational benefits in addition to health and social services.

In 1972 another program variation, **Home Start**, was created. Simply stated, this program took education into the child's home. The focus of Home Start was the parent and their preschool child. Efforts were aimed at developing and enhancing parenting skills through the use of home visitors.

TEACHERS SPEAK OUT

Head Start can make a difference and has made a difference.

More recent federal involvement in the lives of young children came about as a result of legislation. In 1988 Congress passed the Hawkins-Stafford Elementary and Secondary School Improvement Amendments, Public Law 100–297. One component of this enactment is known as **Chapter I** (originally called Title I, as part of the 1965 Elementary and Secondary Education Act; it was renamed in 1981). Chapter I provides substantial funds for the purpose of improving the academic achievement of disadvantaged and educationally at-risk students. Approximately 75 percent of all public elementary schools in the United States receive Chapter I support. Almost $4 billion was allocated for Chapter I in 1990 (Beatty, 1990). Realizing the value of early education, some school districts are being innovative and using Chapter I funds to serve young children and their families at the kindergarten and, in some instances, the prekindergarten level. This represents one attempt by educators to improve the chances for success in school of children from low-income families.

The 1988 Chapter I reauthorization legislation also gave birth to another early childhood program called **Even Start**. The focus of this parent-child education effort is threefold: (1) to provide early education experiences to young children from impoverished backgrounds, (2) to enhance the literacy of adult caregivers, and (3) to assist parents in becoming full partners in the education of their children.

The federal government continues to be concerned about the damaging consequences of poverty on young children and their families. Government officials and legislators have sponsored many other programs aimed at improving educational opportunity and the quality of life of our youngest citizens.

Kindergartens

Kindergartens represent one example of publicly sponsored early childhood programs. Most local schools offer kindergarten programs in their communities. In fact, kindergartens are viewed by many parents and professionals as part of elementary school. Eighty percent of Americans are in favor of making kindergarten a regular part of public education (Gallup, 1986). But it should be noted that kindergartens are not limited to our public schools. Private schools and church-based programs also offer kindergarten experiences.

Kindergartens are the most common form of early childhood education. Every state in our country provides for publicly supported kindergartens (Table 2.2). Approximately 2,604,000 5-year-old children are enrolled in public kindergartens, while another 411,000 youngsters can be found in private kindergarten programs (National Center for Education Statistics, 1991). About 93 percent of all 5-year-olds attend some form of kindergarten before entering the first grade (U.S. Bureau of the Census, 1992a).

Kindergartens primarily serve 5-year-old children, although public kindergartens for 4-year-old children are becoming increasingly common. These programs are usually identified as **prekindergarten** experiences. Kindergarten attendance for 5-year-olds is compulsory

Kindergartens are the most common form of early childhood education.

TABLE 2.2 Growth in Nursery School and Kindergarten Enrollment

	Nursery School			Kindergarten		
Year	**Public**	**Private**	**Total**	**Public**	**Private**	**Total**
1965	127,000	393,000	520,000	2,439,000	618,000	3,057,000
1970	333,000	763,000	1,096,000	2,647,000	536,000	3,183,000
1975	574,000	1,174,000	1,748,000	2,851,000	542,000	3,393,000
1980	633,000	1,354,000	1,987,000	2,690,000	486,000	3,176,000
1985	854,000	1,637,000	2,491,000	3,221,000	594,000	3,815,000
1990	1,212,000	2,188,000	3,401,000	3,332,000	567,000	3,899,000

Source: U.S. Department of Commerce, Bureau of the Census, *School Enrollment—Social and Economic Characteristics of Students: October 1990.* Current Population Reports, Series P–20, No. 460 (Washington, DC: U.S. Government Printing Office, April 1992), p. A–2.

in seven states; that is, parents are required, by law, to send their children to school at 5 years of age (Table 2.3). Compulsory kindergarten is favored by 71 percent of individuals surveyed in a Gallup poll (Gallup, 1986).

Primary Grades

The **primary grades** typically signify the upper limits of what is known as early childhood education. The first, second, and third grades are designated as the primary grades, serving children between the ages of 6 and 8. Public, private, and church-affiliated schools educate children in the primary grades. The curricula emphasis in many primary grades is on basic skills—reading, writing, and arithmetic. Although the curriculum is academically oriented, the social and emotional development of the young student is not completely forgotten nor neglected. A child's developing self-esteem and perceived competency as a learner are important to the primary-grade teacher.

Children receive instruction in other content areas besides the basics. Social studies, language arts, and science, for example, are also part of the school day. The primary grades provide creative experiences in art and music, and physical education is usually available. In contrast to other types of programs for young children, the learning environment in the primary grades is more structured and predominantly teacher-directed.

Currently, in many areas of the United States there seems to be a renewed interest in the "three Rs." Accompanying this movement is an emphasis on student performance and learner accountability. Assessment of student achievement in the early grades is becoming

TABLE 2.3 A Survey of State Kindergarten Policies

State	Compulsory School Attendance Age	Child Must Attend Kindergarten	Age 5 on or Before
Alabama	7	No	September 1
Alaska	7	No	August 15
Arizona	6*	No	September 1
Arkansas	5	Yes*	October 1
California	6	No	December 1
Colorado	7	No	Local option
Connecticut	7	No	January 1 of school year
Delaware	5	Yes	December 31
District of Columbia	5	Yes	December 31
Florida	6	Yes	September 1
Georgia	7	No	September 1
Hawaii	6	No	December 31
Idaho	6	No	August 15
Illinois	7	No	September 1
Indiana	7	No	June 1
Iowa	6	No	September 10–15
Kansas	7	No	September 1
Kentucky	6	No	October 1
Louisiana	7	No	Local option
Maine	7	No	October 15–16
Maryland	5	Yes	December 31
Massachusetts	6	No	Local option
Michigan	6	No	December 1
Minnesota	7	No	September 1
Mississippi	6	No	September 1
Missouri	7	No	July 1
Montana	7	No	September 10–15
Nebraska	7	No	October 15–16

(continued)

common. In some instances, promotion to the next grade depends upon passing tests of basic competency.

Since the mid 1980s, the primary grades have received increased attention from parents, state legislators, business people, and educators. We are now realizing the value of the first three grades. They provide the foundation for success in school and accomplishments in later life.

TABLE 2.3 A Survey of State Kindergarten Policies *(continued)*

State	Compulsory School Attendance Age	Child Must Attend Kindergarten	Age 5 on or Before
Nevada	7	No	September 30
New Hampshire	6 by 9/30	No	Local option
New Jersey	6	No	Local option
New Mexico	5	Yes	September 1
New York	6	No	December 1
North Carolina	7	No	October 15–16
North Dakota	7	No	August 31
Ohio	6	Yes	September 30
Oklahoma	5†	Yes	September 1
Oregon	7	No	September 1
Pennsylvania	8	No	Local option
Rhode Island	6	Yes	December 31
South Carolina	5	Yes*	November 1
South Dakota	6	No	September 1
Tennessee	7	Yes**	September 30
Texas	6	No	September 1
Utah	6	No	September 1
Vermont	7	No	Local option
Virginia	6	No	September 30
Washington	8	No	August 31
West Virginia	6	Yes	September 1
Wisconsin	6	No	September 1
Wyoming	7	No	September 10–15

**Waiver possible.*
***As of fall 1993.*
†Unless screened and deemed not ready.

Note: Data collected in the summer of 1992.

Source: Unpublished data from National Association for the Education of Young Children Division of Public Affairs, Washington, DC.

NEED FOR EARLY CHILDHOOD PROGRAMS

The need for quality early childhood programs is growing. An increasing number of families and individuals need child care for their children. Several factors have contributed to this phenomenon. The basic impetus is related to a variety of complex social issues and economic trends. Examples of these forces include an increasing number of women with young children in the labor force, a rise in the number of single parents, and a decline in the availability of traditional child care providers. According to Gullo (1992), these reasons, among others, have "contributed uniquely, as well as collectively, to contemporary early childhood education philosophy and practice" (p. 9). We now briefly examine some of the forces that are helping shape the field.

TEACHERS SPEAK OUT

If you promise not to believe everything your child says happened at the center, I promise not to believe everything your child says happened at home.

Working Mothers

A main contributor to the growth of early childhood programs is the number of mothers employed outside their home. While some women work by choice, most work out necessity. Life-styles are changing. Unlike mothers of the past, a large number of today's mothers need to return to the workforce as quickly as possible. They are no longer able to stay at home until their children enter school or are fully grown. A look at some statistics confirms this trend. Figure 2.1 dramatically depicts the increase in the percentage of children under age 6 with working mothers. Equally astonishing are data from the U.S. Bureau of the Census (1992b). According to that analysis, in 1977 13 percent of children younger than age 5, whose mothers were employed, were enrolled in early childhood programs. Eleven years later the percentage had doubled. A 1990 report from the Census Bureau estimated that over 9 million youngsters under the age of 5 were in day care (Hymes, 1991).

Changing attitudes and social policy are also related to the demand for early childhood programs. In 1971 then-President Nixon vetoed the Comprehensive Child Development Act. Despite the administration's presumed commitment to child care, this legislation was vetoed due to a belief that child care outside of the home was an attack on the very fabric of the American family. Former President Nixon is quoted in his veto message (regarded as a remarkable social policy statement) as saying that

> good public policy requires that we enhance rather than diminish both parental authority and parental involvement with children. . . .
>
> . . . for the Federal government to plunge head long financially into supporting child development would commit the vast moral authority of the National Government to the side of communal approaches to

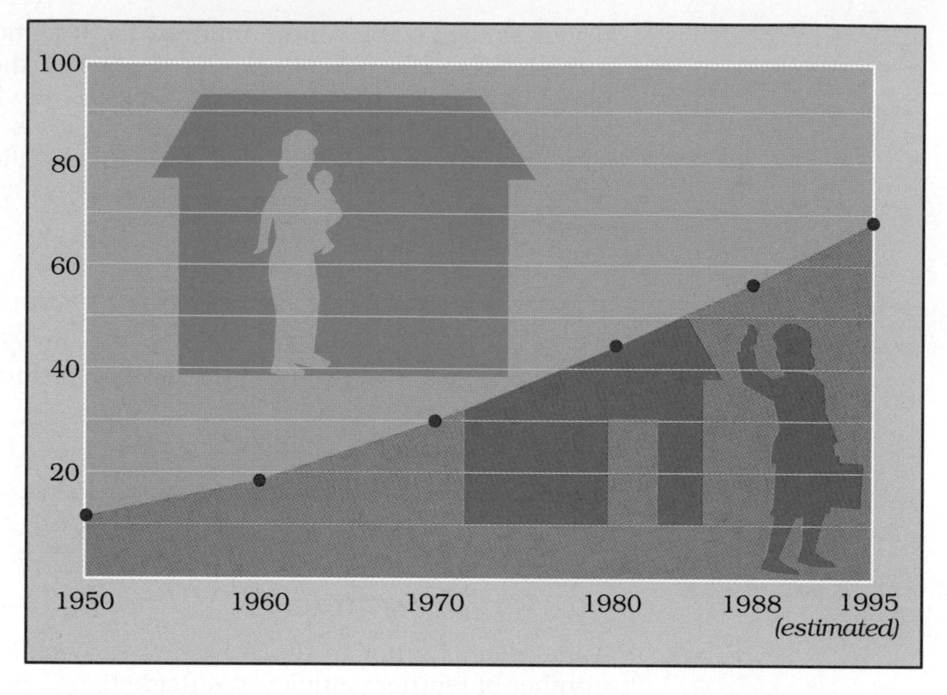

FIGURE 2.1
Percentage of Children under Age Six with Mothers in Workforce

Source: U.S. Department of Labor, *Handbook of Labor Statistics*, Bulletin No. 2070 (Washington, DC: U.S. Government Printing Office, December 1980); *The State of America's Children 1991*, Children's Defense Fund (Washington, DC, 1991).

> childrearing over against the family-centered approach. (Joffe, 1977, p. ix)

In light of this prevailing attitude, many early childhood professionals and parents were not too surprised when a 1970 White House Conference on Children and Youth suggested that "to maintain the relationship of infant and mother, children under three remain in their own homes unless there are pressing social or economic reasons for care away from the home" (Lawton, 1988, p. 45). Fortunately, this point of view is no longer popular. Presidential leadership is now calling for family leave legislation and full funding for Head Start. We suspect that a conference held today would reach a very different conclusion.

Single-Parent Homes

Another significant influence affecting the growth of early childhood programs is a rise in single-parent households. This increase is related to changing divorce statistics and greater numbers of children being born to persons who choose single parenthood. Government statistics indicate that in 1991, more than one out of four families

(26 percent) with children under the age of 18 were headed by a single parent (U.S. Bureau of the Census, 1992c). In 1980, approximately 23 percent of children in the United States lived in single-parent households. Great variation can be found depending on where the child resides. In North Dakota, for example, only 12.3 percent of youngsters are in single-parent families; in the District of Columbia, over 58 percent—almost five times as many children—live in single-parent homes (Children's Defense Fund, 1991). Graves (1990b) reports that 40 percent of American children will live in a single-parent home before reaching age 18. Almost half of all marriages end in divorce (U.S. Bureau of the Census, 1992c).

The following information reflects the trend in single-parent households. In 1950, approximately one out of twelve children under the age of 18 were living with a single parent; 25 years later this figure had doubled to one out of six children (Hess & Croft, 1981). In 1978 there were 50 percent more single-parent families than there were at the beginning of the decade. (Robinson, 1983). Projections suggest that more than 50 percent of all youngsters born today will spend part of their childhood in a single-parent home. The primary child care provider is typically the mother (Children's Defense Fund, 1991).

There is a disproportionate number of single-parent households in certain segments of our population. In 1988, 34 percent of Hispanic families were headed by a single parent; among African-American families, 59 percent were single-parent households (U.S. Bureau of the Census, 1989). All of these statistics, of course, affect not only the need for early childhood programs but also the role of the early childhood professional.

For many persons, being a single parent results in economic hardships. A large number of single parents need to work in order to support themselves and their children. Consequently, obtaining child care, and the ability to pay for it, are major concerns for many mothers and fathers (Table 2.4). Sadly, a large number of children are being raised in poverty. Information presented by Graves (1990b) reveals that 22 percent of the children in the United States, almost 5 million youngsters, live in poverty. Fourteen percent of children who live in poverty have a teenage mother. In 1990 terms, poverty is defined as a family income of under $12,700 for four persons. The latest figures indicate that approximately one out of ten white families were living below the government's poverty line; almost one out of three African-American families; and nearly one out of four Hispanic households.

Child Care Availability

Our last example of the forces that have aided the growth of early childhood programs is the reduced availability of typical child care providers. Changing demographics have caused this situation. As we

TABLE 2.4 Child Care Costs for Single Parent in Selected Cities

	Annual Cost		Percent of Salary*	
	1-Year-Old Child	4-Year-Old Child	1-Year-Old Child	4-Year-Old Child
Boulder, CO	$6,604	$4,472	77.7	52.6
Dallas, TX	$3,900	$3,380	45.9	39.8
Oakland, CA	$5,572	$4,836	67.9	56.9
Orlando, FL	$4,212	$3,120	49.6	36.7

*Working full time at minimum wage.

Note: Average fees in licensed child care centers, 1990.

Source: Adapted from *The State of America's Children 1991*, Children's Defense Fund (Washington, DC, 1991), p. 43.

just mentioned, more mothers are in the workforce; consequently, there are fewer traditional babysitters. For many families, customary providers such as grandparents or favorite aunts and uncles no longer live close to those who need daily child care (Spodek, Saracho, & Davis, 1991). In 1991 the Children's Defense Fund (1991) estimated that more than 6 million children, 2 million younger than age 3, spent all or part of their day being cared for by someone other than a parent or relative. If traditional providers are unavailable, who is watching the children? The United States government recently asked this same question. The answer reveals some interesting facts. Figure 2.2 portrays commonly used child care arrangements. These statistics provide for an interesting comparison with earlier data. You will notice a striking difference in the location of child care. The vast majority of working mothers (68 percent) with young children in 1975 typically had child care provided in their homes (U.S. Bureau of the Census, 1976). More recent surveys reveal that in 1988, less than 30 percent of young children were cared for in their own home, a reduction of almost 40% in this type of arrangement (see Figure 2.2). Out-of-home provisions accounted for only 32 percent of child care arrangements in 1975, but in 1988 this type of child care was used by approximately 63 percent of parents.

There is a great need for high-quality early childhood programs. "Support of the family," according to Robinson (1983), "is basic to our social structure" (p. 9). The more society and families change, the greater is our responsibility to children. Spodek and his colleagues (Spodek et al., 1991) note that early childhood education has always been responsive to social forces and the needs of young children. We must maintain this commitment. Failure to do so could very well result in the downfall of a future generation.

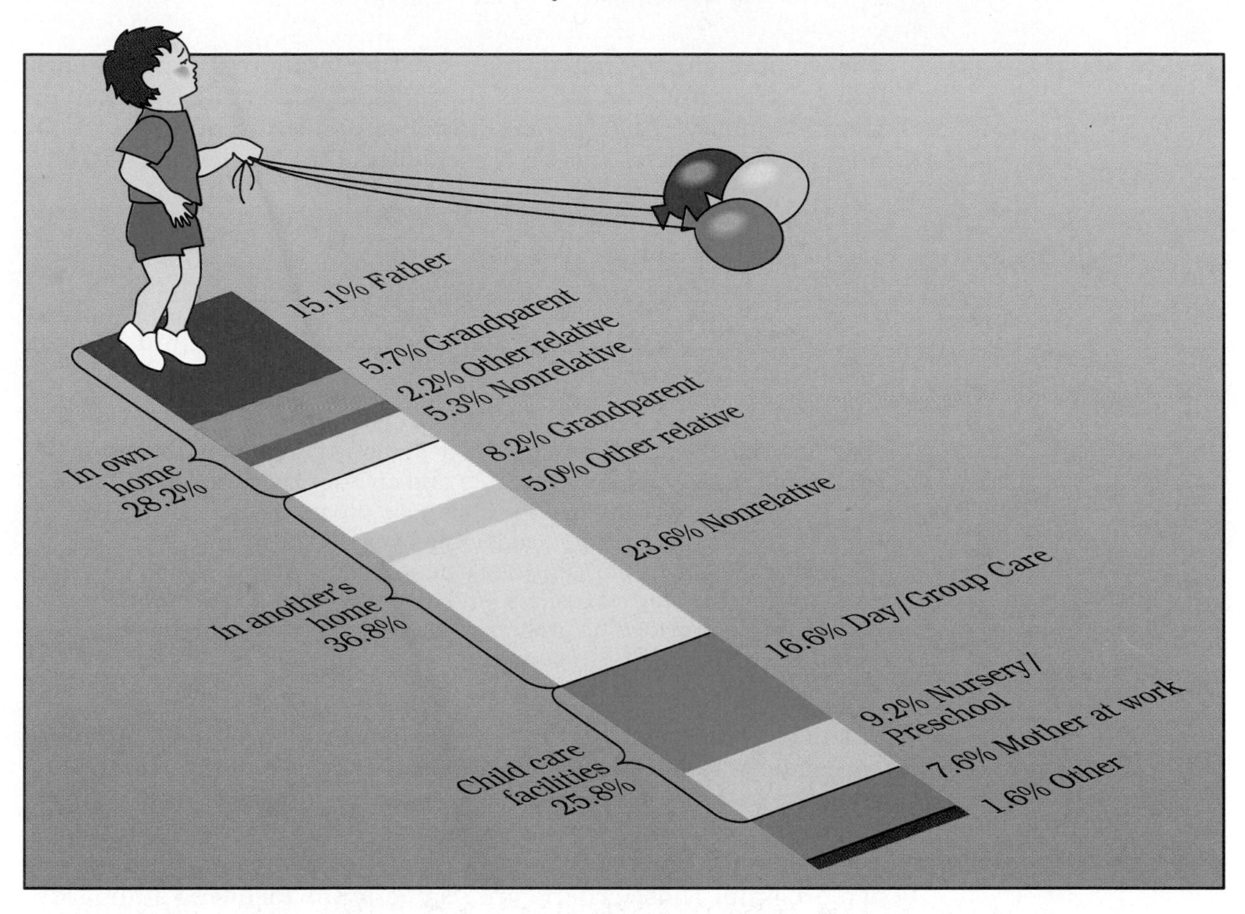

FIGURE 2.2 Primary Child Care Arrangements Used by Employed Mothers for Children under 5 Years of Age

Source: U.S. Department of Commerce, Bureau of the Census, Who's Minding the Kids? Child Care Arrangements, Fall 1988. Current Population Reports, Series P-70, No. 30 (Washington, DC: U.S. Government Printing Office, August, 1992), p. 4.

INDICATORS OF PROGRAM QUALITY

Parents not only want and need child care for their children, they also demand that the programs be of high quality. But how can you judge the quality of an early childhood program? Just because a facility has a license from a governmental agency, this does not indicate the quality of care provided. A license only signifies that the center has met minimum standards. The quality of care given to young children is an important issue. Studies have indicated that youngsters who have had quality child care exhibit fewer behavior problems and are more likely to develop appropriate social skills and good academic ability (Children's Defense Fund, 1991).

As we have already noted, there are many different types of early childhood programs; but most of them display the same essential indicators of quality. Three factors have been linked to quality care for infants and toddlers as well as preschoolers (Abt Associates, 1979):

- The teacher-to-child ratio
- Total size of the group (class)
- The experience and professional training of the staff

Schweinhart, Berrueta-Clement, Barnett, Epstein, and Weikart (1985) believe that

> quality is essential in early childhood programs if they are to have long-term benefits. We have developed a definition of quality in preschool programs that is based on research and on our experience in running such programs. Quality in early childhood programs calls for parent involvement, programmatic leadership by supervisors and directors, competent and genuinely enthusiastic teachers, an articulated curriculum of proven effectiveness, a sound inservice training program, and the feedback provided by program evaluation. If a program has these features, we believe it is a good one that will produce lasting effects. (p. 553)

Critical components of a high-quality early childhood program have also been developed by NAEYC (National Association for the Education of Young Children, 1984). Based on input from child care workers, early childhood professionals, and academic experts, NAEYC compiled a list of criteria that can be used to judge the quality of a program. These criteria are related to the following standards:

- Interactions among staff and children
- Developmentally appropriate activities
- Staff-parent communications and parent involvement
- Staff qualifications and training
- Staffing patterns
- Effective administrative procedures

PARENTS SPEAK OUT

During the past two years, our family had the opportunity to be involved in a parent cooperative preschool and school age child care center which is NAEYC accredited. I cannot begin to tell you all we learned as parents: speaking, listening, modeling for the children, and letting them work out their own disagreements. My son has really dedicated teachers who provide many learning experiences in a quality environment.

- Appropriate physical environments
- Provisions for health and safety
- Adequate nutrition and food services
- Evaluation of program effectiveness

These standards provide the foundation for a voluntary, national accreditation process through NAEYC's National Academy of Early Childhood Programs. Child care centers, preschools, and other types of early childhood programs are eligible for accreditation. Programs conduct a self-study and submit written documentation to the Academy. If the descriptions are judged to be complete and adequate, a trained early childhood specialist conducts a site visit to confirm the written information. On the basis of the evaluator's comments and the center's written materials, an accreditation certificate, valid for three years, may be issued. Although early childhood programs are not mandated to seek accreditation, a growing number are. The accreditation process serves as a vehicle for recognizing quality programs, and parents frequently ask if the program they are considering for their child is accredited.

KIDS SPEAK UP

My teacher is very, very neat. She can clap and whistle and drive a bus.

Girl, 6 years old

Parents, as well as early childhood professionals, recognize that the quality of an early childhood program is generally related to the training and experience of the staff. "The most important factor," according to Willer and Johnson (1989), "in determining the quality of an early childhood program is the quality of the staff. Children do best when a sufficient number of trained and experienced adults are consistently available" (n.p.). This thought was echoed in a survey of parents recently conducted by NAEYC in collaboration with two U.S. government departments. A majority of parents whose children were enrolled in either child care centers or family day care programs ranked the characteristics of the staff or provider as the number one factor they considered when selecting a program for their son or daughter (Willer, Hofferth, Kisker, Divine-Hawkins, Farquhar, & Glantz, 1991). This information seems to suggest that those individuals who provide care and education to young children are vital components of a quality program.

BENEFITS OF EARLY CHILDHOOD EDUCATION

Some may question the need for or the benefit of an early childhood education. "Does it make a difference?" "Is it necessary?" In many instances, the answer is a resounding yes. We will briefly examine some of the educational research on this issue. But first, it is important to remember that educational research is not an exact science. Professionals argue about the adequacy of the research design, the types of dependent measures used, the size of the sample investigated, and the conclusion or recommendations drawn from the study. Suffice to say that research with children in early childhood programs can be very difficult.

Perry Preschool Project

One of the best examples of the long-term educational benefit of early childhood experiences is the Perry Preschool Project. Begun in the 1960s, it was designed as a longitudinal investigation to measure the effects of a quality preschool education. Over 120 disadvantaged African-American children were followed from age 3 until late adolescence. The results of this project can be summarized as follows:

> Results to age 19 indicate long lasting beneficial effects of preschool education in improving cognitive performance during early childhood; in improving scholastic placement and achievement during the school years; in decreasing delinquency and crime, the use of welfare assistance, and the incidence of teenage pregnancy; and in increasing high school graduation rates and the frequency of enrollment in postsecondary programs and employment. (Berrueta-Clement, Schweinhart, Barnett, Epstein, & Weikart, 1984, p. 1)

Another advantage noted in the report on the Perry Preschool Program (*Changed Lives*) is an economic one. In social and financial benefits, an early childhood education is cost-effective; it more than pays for itself. Berrueta-Clement et al. (1984) estimated that value gained in terms of future dollars saved (e.g., in welfare and educational costs) versus the expense of the program for one year exceeds 7 to 1. A cost-benefit analysis demonstrated a net gain to society of almost $29,000 for a year of preschool. This is a truly remarkable return on an investment.

Other Research Findings

In a research effort sponsored by the United States government, Lazar and his colleagues (Lazar, Hubbell, Murray, Rosche, & Royce, 1977) documented the long-lasting benefit of early intervention.

These researchers examined the impact of fourteen infant and preschool projects in the lives of young children. In general, their report suggests that exposure to quality early childhood experiences results in a decrease in the number of children retained in a grade and fewer youngsters recommended for placement in special education programs. Academic achievement and IQ scores are also significantly affected when assessed in the early primary grades. The most important conclusion drawn from this body of data is that well-run early childhood programs improve, in some ways, the ability of young children to meet the requirements of their schools.

Hess and Croft (1981) summarized some of the research conducted in the 1970s on the influence of educationally based preschool programs. They discovered that in some instances, initial gains in IQ found among disadvantaged children enrolled in early intervention programs faded within twelve to twenty-four months after the participants left the programs and enrolled in public schools. There were, however, definite long-term positive effects on school performance. Compared to youngsters who did not participate in preschool experiences, children who did performed better on achievement tests and were more likely to be promoted, and fewer pupils were enrolled in special education. These findings parallel those reported by Lazar et al. (1977). The follow-up studies also revealed fewer disciplinary problems among the participants, a greater willingness to interact with classmates and adults, and overall, a better adaptation to school.

KIDS SPEAK UP

Teachers listen when you tell stories.

Boy, 4 years old

More recently, Schweinhart and Weikart (1985) analyzed the outcomes of seven preschool programs representing a cross-section of urban communities. Here is their conclusion, reported in the *Phi Delta Kappan*, a leading educational journal:

> The documented effects of early childhood education may be organized according to the major outcomes for participants at each period of their lives. These outcomes and the ages at which they occurred are: improved intellectual performance during early childhood; better scholastic placement and improved scholastic achievement during the elementary school years; and, during adolescence, a lower rate of delinquency and higher rates of both graduation from high school and employment at age 19. The best-documented preschool effect is an immediate improvement in intellectual performance as represented by intelligence test scores. (p. 547)

One of the most researched early childhood programs is Head Start. Two examples of this focus are the conclusions of Brown (1985) and Schweinhart and Weikart (1986) on the effectiveness of Head Start. Brown reported that children who participated in the Head Start program were less likely to be referred to special education, and that significant increases in IQ and school achievement could be attributed to high-quality early childhood programs. Equally positive conclusions were offered by Schweinhart and Weikart (p. 50):

1. Short-, mid-, and long-term positive effects are possible.
2. Adequately funded Head Start programs run by well-trained, competent teachers can achieve the level of quality operation that will lead to positive effects.
3. Equal educational opportunity for all people is a fundamental goal of the great American experiment and good Head Start programs can make a sound contribution to the achievement of this goal.

Despite the difficulties of the task, early childhood professionals needs to be consumers of research as well as producers. The growth of the field requires this commitment. The benefactors of these efforts are our country's young children.

CULTURAL DIVERSITY

The United States is an immensely diverse society. We live in a nation of many different people and cultures. The vast number of Americans are grandchildren of immigrants from other lands who entered through Ellis Island in the beginning decades of this century. Today, America is enriched by a new surge of immigration from Asia and the Middle East as well as Central and South America. A great strength of our country is its cultural diversity. We are rich in our diversity of national origins, languages, religious beliefs, and cultural backgrounds. As a nation we greatly benefit from this mix of people. Many citizens enjoy the food, music, sports, and games of different countries. While we celebrate and value these differences, all too often cultural distinctions generate prejudice, stereotypes, and misconceptions. The print and electronic media frequently send messages suggesting that certain groups of people or races are responsible for organized crime, rising welfare costs, and the decline in quality of American goods and products. Heward and Orlansky (1988) believe that for many Americans, being a member of a minority group often results in discrimination, misunderstanding, lower expectations, and lack of equal opportunity and access.

It is indeed unfortunate that the preceding statement characterizes, in many instances, the educational system in the United States. In the opinion of some educators, business leaders, and policymak-

Early childhood programs are serving a growing number of children from different cultures.

ers, the educational system confronting minority children is not only inadequate, but often damaging and openly hostile (Quality Education for Minorities Project, 1990). "In many public schools cultural differences are still translated as deviant, deficient, disabled, and/or disadvantaged" (Poplin & Wright, 1983, p. 368). But as teachers in a culturally diverse society, early childhood educators need to demonstrate respect for and sensitivity to the cultural and linguistic differences they will encounter in their classrooms.

There is no question that America's population is changing. Early childhood professionals are confronted with an increasingly diverse group of young children. The number of bilingual youngsters and children from different cultural backgrounds is expanding rapidly. The classrooms of the next century will be very different from today's. Teachers of young children will find it necessary to carefully evaluate curricula, teaching materials, and even their own attitudes and beliefs to guard against prejudice and stereotyping. Early childhood educators need to be sensitive to diversity and respect individuality. It is crucial that cultural awareness and sensitivity become a priority for early childhood teachers. This theme of cultural diversity and its implications for the early childhood educator is fully explored in a later chapter.

SUMMARY

Early childhood education is a rapidly expanding field. The demand for early childhood experiences is increasing due to the growing number of women with young children in the workforce and to the rise in the number of single parents, coupled with a decline in the availability of traditional child care providers. Some of the employment opportunities for early childhood professionals include child care centers, preschools, Head Start programs, and the primary grades of elementary schools, to name only a few of the sites that serve young children.

Today, there is an increasing demand by both parents and professionals for high-quality early childhood experiences. Quality is absolutely essential if programs are to benefit young children. Some indicators of quality include the use of developmentally appropriate practices, the experience and training of the staff, parent involvement, staffing ratios, and a concern for the safety and well-being of the children. The educational research evidence suggests that the lives of many young children can be positively affected by quality early childhood programs. Early childhood programs are now enrolling a growing number of young children from different lands. This diversity enriches our classrooms and ideally leads to greater understanding and respect for differences.

TEST YOUR UNDERSTANDING

1. What is meant by the terms *early childhood* and *early childhood education*?
2. Provide an example of one public and one private early childhood program.
3. What is the purpose of Head Start?
4. Do you think kindergarten attendance should be compulsory?
5. Identify two factors that have contributed to the increased demand for early childhood programs.
6. List five indicators of quality early childhood programs.
7. Provide examples of three benefits that quality early childhood programs produce.
8. What do you think early childhood teachers can do to meet the needs of culturally diverse children?

LEARNING ACTIVITIES

1. Using newspaper classified advertisements and personal visits to early childhood programs in your community, find out about job qualifications, duties and responsibilities, working conditions, salary ranges, and benefits.
2. Visit at least four different early childhood programs and note their differences. Suggested items for comparison include ages served,

number of children, staffing ratios, curricula, learning activities and materials, parent participation, degree of teacher direction/ involvement, tuition, and sponsorship.

3. Interview single parents of young children. According to these parents, what effect, if any, does being a single parent have on their children? What are the parents' concerns about child care for their children? What types of services do single parents of young children most desire?
4. Ask several parents what features they look for when choosing an early childhood program for their children. Compare their responses.
5. Develop a list of indicators of quality for early childhood programs. Compare your list with your classmates' lists.
6. Find out what the local and state licensing requirements are for various types of early childhood programs in your area. Do they meet NAEYC standards?
7. Visit an early childhood classroom. Notice if the bulletin boards and other illustrations represent culturally diverse groups in a positive fashion. Do the instructional materials reflect the cultural background of the children? Does the teacher respond in a notably different way to culturally different children?
8. Begin a picture file of magazine, newspaper, and other commercial images of diverse cultures depicted in a positive manner. What are some ways you might want to use your multicultural picture file with young children?

CHAPTER 3

Past and Present Dimensions of Early Childhood Education

CHAPTER OUTLINE

KEY TERMS

Gifts
Occupations
Progressives
Progressivism
Sensitive periods
Prepared environment
Schema
Assimilation
Accommodation
Equilibration
Adaptation
Works Progress Administration (WPA)
Lanham Act
DISTAR
Key experiences

> *"That little child of yours is a miracle, so child-like and unconscious, and yet so wise and able, attracting and ruling the children, who seem nothing short of enchanted." "No miracle, but only brought up in kindergarten," said Mrs. Schurz. "A kindergarten! What is that?" "A garden whose plants are human. Did you never hear of Froebel?" "No; who is he?" "A greater discoverer in education than Pestalozzi. He opened lectures to mothers, and instructed children's nurses and kindergartners by precept and exemplification."* (Peabody, 1882, p. 523)

Early childhood education has a long history rich with tradition. Investigating and appreciating the field's history is vital. Historical perspectives give us a sense of our professional roots as well as increasing our understanding of where we are today and our future direction (Graves, 1990). Maxim (1985) challenges the early childhood professional to "Investigate the past to explain what we are presently doing in early childhood education and examine the present in order to understand its historical significance for the future" (p. 29). It is interesting to observe that what we often consider as new or innovative in early childhood education has been written about and tried before. Earlier events and the efforts of past religious leaders, reformers, and philosophers have helped to shape contemporary early childhood programs and thinking. A sign in the National Archives perhaps says it best: "The past is prologue."

HISTORICAL PERSPECTIVES: PEOPLE AND EVENTS

The nineteenth century has traditionally been regarded as the birthdate of early childhood education. Before that time, the idea of childhood as a unique period was generally unaccepted. In fact, previous to the sixteenth and seventeenth century, childhood could perhaps best be described as a living nightmare for most young children. The child historian de Mause (1974) portrays childhood as a panorama of unbelievable cruelty and exploitation. As a result of common practices, Segal (1978) described young children as an endangered species. Several writers (de Mause, 1974; Gargiulo, 1990; Maxim, 1985) eloquently depict the typical treatment of children. It was commonplace in early history, for children to be sexually exploited, routinely beaten, starved, killed at birth (infanticide), or used as payment for debts or cheap labor, among other indignities. From medieval times until the 1800s, children were regarded as miniature adults and were given no special treatment or consideration (Graves, 1990).

Gradually, but dramatically, views of children and childhood have changed. Two factors are generally considered responsible for the changes—societal conditions and beliefs about the nature of childhood (Maxim, 1985). "The conditions of society," according to this early childhood educator, "often influence our views of childhood, and the ways we view children often determine how we interact with them, the expectancies we have, and the care we provide" (p. 29).

Roots of Modern Ideas of Childhood

We now examine some notable events and individuals that have influenced views of children, education in general, and what we now call early childhood education.

Martin Luther. Although Martin Luther (1483–1546) is mainly remembered as a religious reformer (the Father of the Reformation), he is also credited with proposing the concepts of literacy and universal, compulsory education. He was a strong advocate of preparing citizens for reading and interpreting the Bible themselves rather than relying on the interpretations of the Catholic church. This required that individuals read the Bible in their native language as opposed to Latin, the official language of the Catholic church. Thus, we have the beginnings of teaching and learning in people's native language.

Luther also believed in publicly supported schools for all children, including girls. The aim of schools was to develop the young child's intellectual, emotional, physical, and of course, religious growth. While religious instruction was the primary focus of most schools, Luther's insistence that music and physical education be part of the curriculum can still be found in many early childhood programs today. Equally modern was Martin Luther's idea that family involvement was an important part of a child's education. As a result of Luther's championing of education, citizens began to consider educational practices for young children.

John Comenius (1592–1670) believed that children should be actively involved in the learning process.

John Comenius. Another early proponent of educating young children was a Moravian (now part of the Czech Republic) bishop and educational theorist, John Comenius (1592–1670). Like the ancient Greeks, Comenius believed in the essential goodness and equality of all people. He also was an advocate of universal education, which he believed should begin in the early years of life due to the plasticity of the child. In his book, *The Great Didactic* (1657), he argues that early schooling should be at home, at the mother's knee ("School of the Mother's Knee"), and continue throughout the person's life. Education for Comenius, who was known as the "Teacher of Nations," would be natural and very much like play (Aires, 1962). This enlightened educator further believed that all children, including those with handicaps, should be educated (Gargiulo & Cerna, 1992).

Comenius was one of the first educational thinkers to realize the importance of readiness for an activity. Parents and teachers need to be aware of a child's development. Successful learning requires that activities and tasks not be presented before the youngster is ready.

This early concept can be found, centuries later, in the work of Maria Montessori and Jean Piaget—two major contributors to present-day thinking about children's learning and development.

Comenius also laid the foundation for the belief that children learn best by being actively involved in the learning process—learning by doing. Students learn to write, according to Comenius, by writing; to reason by being provided with opportunities to reason; and to speak by verbally interacting with others. Learning is to be a positive experience for children.

The use of concrete experiences and involving the senses (e.g., sight, touch, etc.) was another of Comenius' contributions to education. His book, *Orbis Sensualium Pictus* (1658), generally regarded as the first illustrated book for children, helped young children learn the names of concepts and objects (e.g., animals, plants, body parts) through words and pictures. Today, many early childhood programs and materials incorporate the ideas of sensory learning and concrete examples.

Jean-Jacques Rousseau. Rousseau (1712–1778) was not an educator, but a philosopher and social theorist who had a significant impact on education. He was a prolific writer who spoke out against corruption, injustice, and decadent life-styles. One of his most influential works was about a fictitious child, *Emile* (1762). In this novel, Rousseau describes his view on childrearing and education. Rousseau argued against the common theme that children are born with original sin. Instead, he saw youngsters as inherently good individuals who were subsequently corrupted by an evil society.

Jean-Jacques Rousseau (1712–1778) saw childhood as a distinct period wherein children develop according to their own innate time tables.

Rousseau also broke with tradition when he advocated that children were not miniature adults, and that childhood was a distinct and special period. During this stage, children developed or "flowered" according to their own innate timetables. Rousseau believed in the importance of early education, which was to begin in the home. Mothers especially were advised to allow their children to explore nature and provide opportunities for learning through discovery. He proposed a stage theory of child development. In the first stage, from birth to 5 years of age, children learn from physical activity; from age 5 until age 12, they learn best by exploration and direct experience with the environment. Rousseau firmly believed that education came about from three sources—nature, people, and things. He further insisted on using concrete teaching materials and reserving abstract and symbolic activities until the child was older. Schools, according to Rousseau, should be based on children's interest. He also was an opponent of strict discipline. He felt schools should be less restraining and designed to meet the needs of the students. In fact, Rousseau would rather send children to the country where nature would provide their education instead of sending them to school.

Some of Rousseau's ideas are commonplace in today's early childhood programs. Examples of his influence are the use of concrete rather than abstract materials and the idea of child-directed activities.

The Emergence of Early Childhood Education

Rousseau typically provides a dividing line between historical and modern periods of education. He was a strong influence on Pestalozzi, Montessori, and Froebel, three educational reformers and thinkers directly involved in the education of young children.

Johann Heinrich Pestalozzi. Strongly influenced by Rousseau, Johann Heinrich Pestalozzi (1746–1827), a Swiss educator, is credited with establishing early childhood education as a distinct discipline. He had a deep concern and love for the poor children and orphans from his rural area of Switzerland. Pestalozzi dedicated his life to education.

KIDS SPEAK UP

My grandma says she didn't go to kindergarten cause they didn't have them back then. I'm glad they have them now.

Boy, 5 years old

Fully convinced of the importance of education through nature, Pestalozzi purchased a farm he called *Neuhof*, or *New House*, and established a school where he could explore his educational theories. Although the school was a financial failure, his teaching methods and concepts significantly influenced the field of early childhood education. He believed that it was important to follow the youngster's natural development; school experiences were to be based on the child's interest. But he considered a child-centered approach to education insufficient. Learning cannot occur simply through a pupil's own initiative and exploratory behavior. He advocated, therefore, that teachers develop and direct "object" lessons to balance the student's experiences. His belief in the importance of sensory education and exploration lead to the use of manipulative activities such as touching, feeling, counting, and measuring concrete objects as ways for young children to learn important concepts (Lawton, 1988).

Pestalozzi was an early believer in the grouping of children for purposes of teaching. Older children could then assist the younger ones. He rejected corporal punishment and the use of rote learning as instructional strategies. The role of the educator, according to Pestalozzi, was to teach children, not subjects. He further stressed the education of the whole child. Teachers were to be concerned with the education of the head, the hand, and the heart of the child (Hewes, 1990).

Like Rousseau, Pestalozzi also realized the importance of the youngster's home and the vital role played by the mother in a child's education. Teachers, therefore, needed to plan activities aimed at integrating the student's home life in the educational process. The focus of these lessons was vocational education and reading and writing (Lawton, 1988). Because mothers are so influential, Pestalozzi wrote two books (*How Gertrude Teaches Her Children* and *Book for Mothers*) describing their responsibilities. He recognized the importance of parent involvement more than a century and a half before it became a popular part of many early childhood programs.

Jean Frederick Oberlin. The earliest known school for young children was established in the Alsace region of France in 1767 by Jean Frederick Oberlin (1740–1826). Oberlin's school taught handicrafts, language skills, and provided exercise and play activities to children as young as 2 or 3 years of age. Instruction was provided by Oberlin's spouse and two other women, Sarah Banzet and Louise Schepler. Schepler would talk to the young students as they gathered about her feet while she knitted. She would show the children pictures about nature and history and help them learn the names of the things portrayed in their local dialect as well as proper French (Graves, 1990).

Oberlin's "knitting school" was popular. Similar schools were established in five neighboring villages prior to his death. Further development and expansion were curtailed by the forthcoming French Revolution. Because Oberlin was a Protestant minister, there was some suspicion that instruction might be religious and antirevolutionary. Consequently, Oberlin's contribution to young children was limited to the region in which he lived.

Robert Owen. English social reformer and factory owner Robert Owen (1771–1858) is credited with establishing the Infant School in 1816. A firm believer in the principles espoused by Pestalozzi, Owen was genuinely concerned about the children and their families who worked in the textile mills during the Industrial Revolution. He wanted to reform the living and working conditions of citizens living in mill towns. These conditions were very much like those described by Charles Dickens (Spodek, Saracho, & Davis, 1991).

Owen managed a textile mill in New Lanark, Scotland, where he initiated his reform ideas. The minimum working age for children was raised from 6 to 10 years of age, and living conditions were improved. More important, however, Owen established a school (Institute for the Formation of Character) with a section for the youngest children (ages 3 through 10) known as the *Infant School*. He believed in starting education at an early age because it is the best time to shape character, and a child's behavior can be more easily influenced by the environment. Owen was convinced of the importance of the environment. Like other Utopians, he believed that by manipulating environmental conditions it was possible to modify and control a child's behavior. As a result a better, and perhaps more perfect society would emerge.

TEACHERS SPEAK OUT

Every day I learn something new about children. It makes me realize that there may be specialists in early childhood but I don't think anyone could be an "expert."

In Owen's Infant School, children received instruction in basic academic skills such as reading, history, and arithmetic; but they were also exposed to dance, music, and sewing activities. Field trips and other out-of-classroom activities in addition to visitors from the community were frequently used in the instructional process. Owen did not believe in forcing children to learn. He also was strongly opposed to punishment: Children would learn right from wrong by the natural consequences of their actions. Mutual respect and consideration between teacher and pupil were important components in the Infant School.

Owen's ideas, and his views about school, were spread by his books throughout Europe and even the United States. In fact, Owen established a community based on his visions in New Harmony, Indiana, in the early 1820s. Although this settlement lasted for only a few years, and his schools did not have lasting success in Great Britain, they did have an enduring impact on education. Many practices incorporated in today's early childhood programs have their roots in Owen's schools. Examples of his influence can be found in child-selected activities, play as a means for learning, and a nurturing classroom atmosphere under the direction of a nonpunitive teacher (Graves, 1990).

Friedrich Froebel (1782–1852) is generally considered to be the "Father of the Kindergarten."

Friedrich Wilhelm Froebel. The person who perhaps had the greatest impact on the field of early childhood education was Friedrich Wilhelm Froebel (1782–1852). A student of Pestalozzi and a teacher at one of his schools, Froebel was a strong believer in the education of young children. He translated his beliefs into a system for teaching young children in addition to developing a curriculum, complete with methodology. His efforts have earned him the well-deserved title, "Father of the Kindergarten."

Also influenced by the writings of Rousseau and Comenius, Froebel conceived an educational theory ("Law of Universal Unity") partly based on their thoughts as well as on his own personal experiences and religious views. His basic idea was essentially religious in nature and emphasized a unity of all living things, a oneness of humans, nature, and God. His notion of unity led Froebel to advocate that education should be based on cooperation rather than competition. Like Comenius and Pestalozzi, he also considered development as a process of unfolding. Children's learning should therefore follow this natural development. The role of the teacher (and parent) was to recognize this process and to provide activities to help the children learn whenever they were ready to learn (Graves, 1990).

Froebel used the garden to symbolize childhood education. Like a flower blooming from a bud, children would grow naturally according to their own laws of development. A kindergarten education, therefore, should follow the nature of the child. Play, a child's natural activity, was a basis for learning (Spodek et al., 1991).

Froebel established the first *kindergarten* (or "children's garden") in 1837 in an old powder mill near Blankenburg, Germany. This early program enrolled youngsters between the ages of 1 and 7. Structured play was an important component of the curriculum. Unlike many of his contemporaries, Froebel saw educational value and benefit in play. Play is the work of the child. Because he believed that education was knowledge being transmitted by symbols, Froebel devised a set of materials and activities to aid the children in their play activities as well as to teach the concept of unity among nature, God, and humankind. Education was to begin with the concrete and move to the abstract.

Froebel presented his students with "gifts" and "occupations" rich in symbolism. In his curriculum, **gifts** were manipulative activities to assist in learning color, shape, size, counting, and other educational tasks. Wooden blocks, cylinders, and cubes, balls of colored yarn, geometric shapes, and natural objects such as beans and pebbles are some examples of the learning tools used.

Occupations were arts and craft activities designed to develop eye-hand coordination and fine motor skills. Illustrations of these activities include stringing beads, embroidering, folding paper, cutting with scissors, and other psychomotor skills such as weaving. Froebel's curriculum also used games, songs, dance, rhymes, and finger play. Other components of his curriculum were nature study, language, and arithmetic work.

Teachers were to be designers of activities and experiences with children, using the child's natural curiosity. They are responsible for directing and guiding their students toward becoming contributing members of society (Graves, 1990).

Froebel also had several other "firsts" to his credit. He was the first person to advocate schooling for groups of young children outside of the home. This was in addition to the role played by mothers, who typically educated their children at home. He also called for the establishment of a training institute where young, unmarried women would learn to become kindergarten teachers. [See Hewes (1990) for an excellent historical discussion of Froebel's ideas.] Unfortunately, many of his beliefs and ideas were considered too revolutionary for the times (see Table 3.1). He was subject to a great deal of criticism. His kindergartens were even banned because he was wrongly accused of using them to promote socialism (Maxim, 1985). It was not until after his death that Froebel and his concepts received the recognition they richly deserved during his lifetime.

TABLE 3.1 Syllabus of Froebel's *Education of Man*

Education defined by the law of divine unity.
Free self-activity the essential method in education.
Unity, individuality, and diversity the phases of human development.
The several stages of childhood, boyhood, and manhood to be duly respected in their order.
The various powers of the human being to be developed by means of suitable external work.
Nature and value of the child's play.
The family is the type of true life and the source of active interest in all surroundings.
The games of boyhood educate for life by awakening and cultivating many civic and moral virtues.
The true remedy for any evil is to find the original good quality that has been repressed or misled, and then to foster and guide it aright.
The purpose of the school and its work is to give to the child the inner relations and meanings of what was before merely external and unrelated.
The essential work of the school is to associate facts into principles, not to teach isolated facts.
Mathematics should be treated physically, and mathematical forms and figures should be considered as the necessary outcome of an inner force acting from a center.
Writing and reading grow out of the self-active desire for expression and should be taught with special reference to this fact.
In the study of plants, animals, etc., the work proceeds from particulars to generals, and again from generals to particulars in varied succession.
From natural objects and the products of man's effort, the study should proceed to include the relations of mankind.
The prime purpose throughout is not to impart knowledge to the child, but to lead the child to observe and to think.
The general purpose of family and school instruction is to advance the all-sided development of the child and the complete unfolding of his nature.

Source: F. Froebel, *The Education of Man* (Clifton, NJ: Augustus M. Kelley, 1974), pp. 333–340. (Original English Publication, 1887)

Kindergarten in America

Froebel's kindergartens were very successful in his native Germany. With the wave of immigration from Europe in the 1800s, his program was exported to the United States. One believer in Froebel's philosophy was Margarethe Schurz (1832–1876), who is credited with establishing the first kindergarten in America. She began her German-speaking kindergarten in her home in Watertown, Wisconsin, in 1855. The first pupils were her own children and those of her German neighbors. While her efforts lasted for only a few years, she was successful in introducing to the United States the idea of schooling for young children.

The concept of early childhood education surged forward as a result of a chance meeting between Schurz and Elizabeth Peabody (1804–1894), an idealist and descendant of an original Puritan family. Mrs. Schurz explained the Froebelian system to Peabody, a sister-in-law of Horace Mann. Peabody was so impressed by what she heard that she and her sister, Mary Mann, opened the first private English-language kindergarten in Boston in 1860. Elizabeth Peabody also journeyed to Germany to study with Froebel's followers. With almost missionary fervor, Peabody traveled throughout the United States extolling the virtues of kindergarten programs. She co-authored a Kindergarten Guide (1864) and even convinced toy manufacturer Milton Bradley to produce and sell Froebel's gifts and occupations.

Peabody's promotion of kindergarten paid dividends. She was successful in winning public support for kindergarten programs. Evidence of this can be found in her ability to convince William Harris, superintendent of schools in St. Louis (and later U.S. Commissioner of Education), to establish a publicly supported kindergarten. Thus, the first public school kindergarten, under the direction of Susan Blow, opened in 1873.

Kindergartens proved to be very popular. In the early 1870s, there were approximately one dozen private kindergartens. In 1892 the number of programs had grown to almost 2,500 and involved over 33,000 young students. Many of these early kindergartens were located in the large urban areas of the East and Midwest (Maxim, 1985). Kindergartens were established by a variety of agencies in the nineteenth century. Churches, labor unions, factories, settlement houses, and the Women's Christian Temperance Union all sponsored programs. Kindergartens were seen as particularly important for poor children living in slums. By providing an early education, people thought that the ills of urban poverty could be eliminated (Spodek et al., 1991). Kindergartens were seen as an opportunity of increasing the chances of poor children for a better life.

By the end of the nineteenth century, kindergartens began to experience growing pains. Conflicting points of view began to emerge among leaders in the field. Some, such as Susan Blow, wished to adhere to Froebelian principles and practices; others, known as *progressives*, saw merit in focusing on child development, the interest of children, and the emerging philosophy of progressive education.

Reform in the Kindergarten

Around the beginning of the twentieth century, ideas about young children and kindergarten experiences began to change. Froebel's theories were under attack. Voices of dissent were being heard. A new breed of kindergarten teachers challenged the current thinking. These educators, called **progressives**, saw little value in adhering to Froebel's symbolism. "Kindergartens were paying too much attention to symbols and not enough to the child's life" (Spodek et al., 1991, p. 22).

Concurrent with this disenchantment with Froebel was a movement toward a more scientific basis for understanding young children. Formal observations were emphasized rather than speculation and philosophic idealism. The work of G. Stanley Hall, the father of the child study movement, was instrumental in guiding many kindergarten teachers away from a Froebelian perspective of children to one based on empirical study (Spodek, 1991). Observational data generated new ideas about what should be considered of educational value for children. Consequently, support for Froebelian kindergartens slowly began to erode.

The progressive kindergarten movement, with its emphasis on freedom and activity, also aided in the trend away from Froebelian practices. Kindergarten curriculum was reconstructed and included dramatic play, songs, and games as well as field trips and other innovations. The daily life experiences of the children became the focal point of kindergarten activities (Spodek et al., 1991). Progressive kindergartens based many of their ideas on the work of John Dewey.

John Dewey (1859–1952) is generally regarded as the founder of a school of thought known as progressivism.

John Dewey. Born in Burlington, Vermont, Dewey (1859–1952) was one of the first Americans to significantly influence education. He is generally regarded as the founder of a school of thought known as **progressivism**. This approach, with its emphasis on the child and his or her interests, was counter to the then-prevalent theme of teacher-directed, subject-oriented curriculum. Learning flowed from the interests of the child instead of activities chosen by the instructor. Dewey, who taught at both the University of Chicago and Teachers College, Columbia University, coined the phrases "child-centered curriculum" and "child-centered schools" (Graves, 1990). According to Dewey, the purpose of schools was to prepare the student for the realities of today's world, and not just for the future. In his famous work, *My Pedagogic Creed*, this philosopher emphasizes that learning occurs through real-life experiences, and describes education as a process for living. He also stresses the concept of social responsibility. Basic to his philosophy is the idea that children should be equipped to function effectively as citizens in a democratic society.

Traditionally, children learned predetermined subject matter via rote memory under the strict guidance of the teacher, who was in complete control of the learning environment. In Dewey's classroom, however, children were socially active, engaged in physical activities, and discovering how objects worked. They were to be continually afforded opportunities for inquiry, discovery, and experimentation. Daily living activities such as carpentry and cooking could also be found in a Dewey-designed classroom (Graves, 1990).

Dewey (1916) advocated the child's interaction with the total environment. He believed that intellectual skills emerged from children's own activity and play. He further rejected Froebel's approach to symbolic education. Spodek (1991) explains:

> Play, in Dewey's conception of education, was embedded in the child's natural impulses rather than in the need to manipulate materials in order to abstract the symbolic meanings in them. Children were given direct experiences with both physical and social phenomena. They were to reconstruct those experiences through play in the kindergarten. (p. 10)

Some have unfairly criticized Dewey as only responding to the whims of the child. This was a false accusation. Dewey did not abandon the teaching of subject matter or basic skills. He was opposed to imposing knowledge on children; instead, he favored using the student's interest as the origin of subject matter instruction. Dewey believed, according to Lawton (1988), "that teachers should look for opportunities during children's spontaneous, self-interest activities to include traditional subject matter" (p. 15). Teachers need to take advantage of these opportunities as they occur and build on the pupil's interest. Curriculum cannot be fixed or established in advance. Educators are to guide learning activities, observe and monitor, and offer encouragement and assistance as needed. They are not to control their students.

Some educators were critical of the progressive education movement. They believed that students were not learning basic skills. This mostly occurred because some of Dewey's followers were overly zealous, misinterpreted his beliefs, and consequently were unduly permissive.

Although Dewey's impact has diminished, his contributions to early childhood education in America, and other countries, is still evident (see Table 3.2). Many "traditional" early childhood programs today have their philosophical roots in Dewey's progressive education movement.

Patty Smith Hill. Hill (1868–1946) was an early innovator and one of the leaders of the progressive kindergarten movement. Although she was trained in Froebelian practices, Hill found that approach too rigid. After being introduced to the work of G. Stanley Hall and the philosophy of John Dewey, Hill also believed that the foundation for learning should be the child's life experiences, and

TABLE 3.2 What Dewey's Pedagogic Creed Means Today

Dewey Believed	In Today's Classroom
"I believe that only true education comes through the stimulation of the child's powers by the demands of the social situations in which he finds himself."	This tells us that children learn to manage themselves in groups, to make and share friendships, to solve problems, and to cooperate.
"The child's own instinct and powers furnish the materials and give the starting point for all education."	We need to create a place that is child-centered, a place that values the skills and interests of each child and each group.
"I believe that education, therefore, is a process of living and not a preparation for future living."	Prepare the child for what is to come by enriching and interpreting the present to him. Find educational implications in everyday experiences.
"I believe that . . . the school life should grow gradually out of the home life . . . it is the business of the school to deepen and extend . . . the child's sense of the values bound up in his home life."	This sets the rationale for a relationship between teachers and parents. Values established and created in the home should be enhanced by teaching in the schools.
"I believe, finally, that the teacher is engaged, not simply in the training of individuals, but in the formation of a proper social life. I believe that every teacher should realize the dignity of his calling."	This says that the work teachers do is important and valuable. They teach more than academic content; they teach how to live.

Source: Reproduced by permission from *Beginnings and Beyond*, 3rd ed. by Ann Gordon and Kathryn Williams Browne (Albany, NY: Delmar, 1993), p. 15. Adapted from *My Pedagogic Creed* by John Dewey (Washington, DC: The Progressive Education Association, 1897).

that the focus of the curriculum, derived from observation, should be based on the needs of the pupil.

Creative play was an important component in Hill's modernized kindergarten. Play, in a free and informal environment, was seen as a valuable learning experience for children. She is credited with introducing into the kindergarten classroom large blocks that children could use to construct play areas. Centers for water and sand play, and housekeeping activities, in addition to free expression in music and creative art, were also part of the redesigned kindergarten program. These child-oriented activities were viewed as a natural part of the child's life and in contrast to traditional teacher-directed tasks typically found in kindergartens. Hill also strongly advocated the importance of the youngster's home and the learning that took place there. The basic format of Hill's kindergarten remained popular until the late 1960s. Her model eventually became known as the traditional approach to early childhood programs (Maxim, 1985).

Hill made several other contributions to the field of early childhood education. She established a laboratory nursery school at Teachers College, Columbia University, in 1921. In 1925, she founded the National Association for Nursery Education, the forerunner of the National Association for the Education of Young Children. She and a sister introduced triangles and bells to kindergartners and wrote the song "Happy Birthday to You."

The Nursery School

Concern for poor, young children living in the slums of London lead Margaret McMillan (1860–1931), with help from her sister, Rachel, to establish the first nursery school in 1911. McMillan was a political and social activist who was born in the United States but moved to England with her family after her father's death. There, McMillan became an advocate for impoverished children. She advanced her beliefs through her election to the school board of Bradford, England, in 1894. She was convinced that the health and social problems of children from slum areas could be corrected or prevented by proper care before children entered school. Margaret and her sister championed nourishing meals, baths in school, and medical evaluations for youngsters (Graves, 1990). Her ideas were an early version of the Head Start program.

KIDS SPEAK UP

I like that my school has birds outside.

Boy, 3 years old

The McMillan sisters established an open-air nursery school as a preventative measure for children between the ages of 2 and 7. They believed that poor children should have the same advantages as youngsters growing up in London's more affluent neighborhoods. The school program sought to compensate for the conditions the children typically experienced in their homes. The sisters viewed the total development of the child as important. An educational program was combined with a concern for the child's health and overall well-being. They believed in a "whole child" approach to education and focused their attention on the physical, intellectual, and affective dimensions of each youngster. The underlying philosophy of the McMillan school was that of nurturance. Maxim (1985) explains, "Nurturance was viewed as the process of supporting the total development of the child, including the social, emotional, physical, and intellectual aspects of each child" (p. 42).

TEACHERS SPEAK OUT

The proposed new amendments to the Head Start Act will create programs that serve infants and toddlers from birth to age 3. My concern is that we must prepare people to meet this need.

In addition to valuing cleanliness and health issues, the first nursery school emphasized movement, play, creative experiences, and the development of the young child's imagination and self-expression through coloring, clay modeling, and block play. Teachers were expected to nurture the child and enhance their opportunities for play and creativity (Graves, 1990). Self-care skills, perceptual-motor development, gardening, and care for animals were also important aspects of their program. Students older than 5 were provided with formalized instruction in the basic skills of reading, writing, and arithmetic.

McMillan's untiring efforts aroused public concern and contributed significantly to the enactment of the Fisher Education Act of 1918, which provided tax money for the creation of nursery schools in the public school system. Unfortunately, adequate funding was never achieved, and financial difficulty stemming from World War I prohibited nursery schools from becoming universal in England (Maxim, 1985; Spodek et al., 1991).

Margaret McMillan also established a training program for "nurse-teachers," the McMillan Training College. Some of her graduates came to the United States in the early 1920s to demonstrate the British program. Abigail Eliott, a social worker who worked and studied with the McMillan sisters in the Deptford slums of London, is generally credited with popularizing the nursery school movement in the United States. Eliott served as the director of the Ruggles Street Nursery School and Training Center, which began operating in Boston in1922. But it was a nurse who established the first nursery school in America. In 1919, Harriet Johnson opened the City and Country School in New York City, which later became known as the Bank Street College of Education. Other nursery schools quickly followed, often privately funded or sponsored by colleges and universities. In the early 1930s, only about 200 such schools existed in the United States; by 1935, the number of nursery schools had increased about 850 percent—to approximately 1,900 (Maxim, 1985).

Contemporary Leaders

We now turn our attention to two individuals who have significantly influenced contemporary thinking about the learning and development of young children—Maria Montessori and Jean Piaget.

Maria Montessori. Montessori (1870–1952) was a major force in the field of early childhood education. A feminist, she became the first female to earn a medical degree in Italy. She began working as a physician in a psychiatric clinic at the University of Rome, caring for the insane. It was in this hospital setting that she came into frequent contact with "idiot children," or children with mental retardation. At the turn of the century, mental retardation was viewed as indistinguishable from insanity. A careful observation of these youngsters led Dr. Montessori to conclude that educational intervention rather than medical treatment would be a more effective strategy. She began to develop her theories for working with these children. Montessori was influenced by the writings of Pestalozzi, Rousseau, Froebel, and the work of Edouard Seguin, a French physician who pioneered an effective educational approach for children with mental retardation. She concluded that intelligence was not static or fixed, but could be influenced by the child's experiences. Montessori developed an innovative, activity-based sensory education model involving *didactic* (teaching) materials. She was eminently successful. Youngsters who were originally believed incapable of learning performed successfully on school achievement tests.

Montessori's unbelievable success, hailed by some admirers as a miracle, caught the attention of the director general of the Roman Association for Good Building, who in 1906 invited her to organize schools for the young children living in tenement houses. She accepted the offer, and in 1907 opened the *Casa dei Bambini* or "children's house" in the San Lorenzo slum district of Rome. It was there that she hoped to perfect her educational methods with typical preschoolers. Her first school served children between the ages of 30 months and 7 years. It operated from 8:00 a.m. until 6:00 p.m.

Montessori believed that children learn best by direct sensory experience. She was further convinced that children had a natural tendency to explore and understand their world (Graves, 1990). Like Froebel, she envisioned child development as a process of unfolding; however, environmental influences also had a critical role. Education in the early years is crucial to the child's later development. Montessori also thought children passed through *sensitive periods*, or stages of development early in life during which they are especially able, because of their curiosity, to easily learn particular skills or behaviors. This concept is very similar to the idea of a child's readiness for an activity.

To promote the children's learning, Montessori constructed an orderly or **prepared environment** with specially designed tasks and materials. Much like Froebel's gifts, these materials included items such as wooden rods, cylinders, and cubes of varying sizes, sets of sandpaper tablets arranged according to the degree of smoothness, and musical bells of different pitch (see Table 3.3). Dr. Montessori's program also emphasized three growth periods—practical life experiences, sensory education, and academic education. Each of these

TABLE 3.3 Examples of Montessori's Sensory Materials

Material	Purpose	How It Is Used By Children
Wooden cylinders	Visual discrimination (Size)	Ten wooden cylinders varying in diameter, height, or variations of both dimensions. Child removes cylinders from wooden holder, mixes them up, and replaces in correct location.
Pink tower	Visual discrimination (Dimension)	Ten wooden cubes painted pink. Child is required to build a tower. Each cube is succeedingly smaller, varying from ten to one centimeter. Repeats activity.
Green rods	Visual discrimination (Length)	Ten wooden pieces identical in size and color but varying in length. After scattering rods, youngster arranges them according to gradations in length—largest to smallest.
Material swatches	Sense of feel	Matches identical pieces of brightly colored fabric (e.g., fine vs. coarse linen, cottons, and woolens). Initially performs task without blindfold.
Sound cylinders	Auditory discrimination	Double set of cylinders containing natural materials such as pebbles or rice. Child shakes cylinder and matches first according to similarity of sound and then according to loudness.
Tonal bells	Auditory discrimination	Two sets of eight metal bells, alike in appearance but varying in tone. Youngster strikes the bells with a wooden hammer and matches the bells on the basis of their sound; first according to corresponding sounds and then according to the musical scale.

Source: M. Montessori, *Dr. Montessori's Own Handbook* (New York: Schocken Books, 1965).

components was considered important in developing the child's independence, responsibility, and productivity.

Practical life experiences focused on personal hygiene, self-care, muscular education, and responsibility for the environment. Examples of this last activity are tasks such as sweeping, dusting, and raking leaves, using child-size equipment. Sensory education was very important in Montessori's education scheme. She designed a wide variety of teaching materials aimed at developing the student's various senses. Her didactic materials are noteworthy for two reasons. They were self-correcting; that is, there was only one correct way to use them. Thus, the materials could be used independently by the children and help them become self-motivated students. The sensory training equipment was also graded in difficulty—from easiest to most difficult and from concrete to abstract. Her sensory train-

Maria Montessori (1870–1952) believed that children learn best by direct sensory experiences.

ing materials and procedures reflected her educational belief that cognitive ability results from sensory development. The final stage, academic instruction, introduced the child to reading, writing, and arithmetic in the sensitive period from ages 2 to 6. Various concrete and sensory teaching materials were used in the lessons of this last stage (Montessori, 1965).

Montessori's classrooms were distinguished by their attractive and child-sized materials and equipment. Furniture was moveable. The beautifully crafted materials were very attractive. They appealed to the child's senses. Teaching materials were displayed on low shelves in an organized manner to encourage the pupils' independent use. Children worked at their own pace. They were required, however, to complete one assignment before starting another.

Teachers in Montessori classrooms are facilitators and observers of children's activities. By using skillfully crafted lessons, teachers slowly and carefully demonstrate concepts to the children. Ideas are presented to the students in small, sequential steps and build on previous experiences that form the basis for the next level of skill development. Teachers foster the development of independence in their students. A Montessori-designed classroom is typically focused on individual student activities rather than group work.

Several distinct features of Montessori's work stand out:

- Children's freedom of choice in selecting activities and materials
- A practical, "real life" approach to curriculum

- Training of the senses
- Modifying the curriculum to meet the unique needs of the child

Her legacy also includes the materials she invented.

Montessori's ideas were extremely popular and successful. Her techniques and fame soon spread throughout Europe, the United States, and other countries as well. Her methods were exhibited at the 1915 World's Fair located in San Francisco. She lectured at Carnegie Hall in New York City as the guest of Thomas Edison. The Montessori Society was formed shortly afterward with Alexander Graham Bell as first president.

Popularity of the Montessori method was short-lived. Criticism began to be heard. Her approach to education, especially it emphasis on academics, was contrary to the popular child-centered philosophy of John Dewey. Discontent was also aimed at the absence of creative and expressive experiences like music and art, lack of language stimulation, peer interaction, and social development. In addition, because many of the Montessori programs in the United States were private, the 1929 stock market crash and the accompanying Depression led to the demise of the Montessori movement, at least in the United States (Spodek et al., 1991).

The late 1950s and 1960s saw a revival or rediscovery of Montessori's ideas. Today, Montessori schools can be found in many communities. Although most schools are private, and somewhat expensive, a few public school systems are offering Montessori programs and attracting a broader segment of America's children. Two professional associations currently support Montessori education in the United States. The American Montessori Society represents an Americanized version of the Montessori movement, and the Association Montessori Internationale adheres to the original thinking of Dr. Montessori.

Jean Piaget. Piaget (1896–1980) is one of the major contributors to our understanding of how children think. He is considered by many to be the premiere expert on the development of knowledge in children and young adults. Born in Switzerland, he was trained as a biologist. This preparation was influential in the development of his theories about cognitive development.

Piaget studied in Paris. There he had the opportunity to work with Theodore Simon, who in conjunction with Alfred Binet was constructing the first test for assessing children's intelligence. While standardizing the children's responses to test questions, Piaget became extremely interested in the incorrect answers given by the youngsters. His careful observations led him to notice that they gave similar wrong answers. He also discovered that the children made different types of errors at different ages. This paved the way for Piaget to investigate the thinking process that led to incorrect responses.

According to Piaget's point of view, children's thinking is profoundly and fundamentally different from that of adults. He also believed that children's thought processes are modified as they grow and mature. With the assistance of his wife, he began to formulate his theories, which were initially based on observations of his own three children. Piaget's ideas about intellectual development are complex, and a full discussion of his theory is beyond the scope of this chapter. Therefore, only his basic concepts are presented here.

First, it is important to understand Piaget's view of intelligence. As an epistemologist, he was concerned with *how* knowledge is acquired. Piaget avoids stating a precise definition of intelligence; instead, he attempts to describe it in general terms. Piaget speaks of intelligence as an instance of biological adaptation. He also looks at intelligence as a balance or equilibrium between an individual's cognitive structures and the environment. His focus is on what a person *does* as they interact with their environment. Knowledge of reality must be discovered and constructed. It results from a child's actions with their world. It is also important to note that Piaget is not concerned with individual differences in intelligence (Ginsburg & Opper, 1969).

Piaget's theory rests on the contributions of maturational and environmental influences. Maturation establishes a sequence of cognitive stages controlled by heredity. The environment contributes to the child's experiences, which dictate how he or she develops. Thinking is a process of interaction between the child and the environment. Graves (1990) describes children as "active agents who interact with the social and physical world" (p. 198). Youngsters are self-motivated in the construction of their own knowledge, which occurs through activity.

PARENTS SPEAK OUT

I've always enjoyed hearing anecdotes about my children's day at school. Just something they did or said. It makes me feel more a part of their school day. I also try to tell their teachers about things they do or say at home, especially if it involves school, teachers, or classmates.

One consequence of interaction with the environment is that the person soon develops organizing structures or **schemas**. These schemas, or mental concepts, become a basis from which later cognitive structures are established. Piaget developed three concepts that he believes individuals use to organize their personal experiences into a blueprint for thinking. He called these adaptive processes assimilation, accommodation, and equilibration. **Assimilation** occurs when the child is able to integrate new experiences and information into existing schemes (i.e., what the child already knows). Children view new situations in light of previous experiences in their world. As an illustration, when a toddler encounters a pony, she will most likely call it a dog, something she is already familiar with.

Accommodation is Piaget's second process. It involves modifying existing cognitive structures so that new data can be effectively used. Current thought patterns and behavior are changed to fit new situations. Accommodation involves a change in understanding. For example, 2-year-old Victoria visits Santa Claus at the mall. Later that day, she is shopping with her mother and sees an elderly gentleman with a long white beard. She calls him Santa Claus. Victoria's mother corrects her daughter's mistake. When she next meets a man with a white beard, she asks, "Are you Santa Claus, or are you just old?" Victoria has demonstrated accommodation; she has changed her knowledge base.

Assimilation and accommodation are involved in the final process of **equilibration**. Here an attempt is made to achieve a balance or equilibrium between assimilation and accommodation. Piaget believes that all activity involves both processes. The interaction between assimilation and accommodation leads to **adaptation**, a process of adjusting to new situations. Equilibration is the tendency to control the balance, and that accounts for the formation of knowledge. Intellectual growth, according to Piaget, is achieved through the interplay of these three processes.

Four stages of cognitive development were identified by Piaget. Children pass through these stages in an orderly, sequential fashion. Each stage is a prerequisite for the next one. The ages identified in Table 3.4 are only rough estimates of when a youngster enters each stage. Children progress at their own rate, which is influenced by their experiences and existing cognitive structures in addition to maturation.

Piaget also described several types of knowledge. Children come to know things in three ways; via physical knowledge, logico-mathematical knowledge, and social knowledge. Briefly, *physical knowledge* is gained by exploration of the physical world and sensory experiences. Hot vs. cold, flat vs. round are discovered by interaction with the objects. Discrimination is the primary cognitive process used in the development of physical knowledge. The second stage, *logico-mathematical knowledge*, evolves from various cognitive activities performed on physical items. This type of knowledge is not synonymous with formal mathematics; rather it refers, for example, to the ability of the individual to see spatial relationships, classify objects, and the Piagetian concepts of conservation and numeration, among others. Each person must formulate his or her own knowledge base; it cannot be directly transferred from one individual to another. The final stage of knowledge, *social knowledge*, is derived from a variety of sources—through social interactions, by being told

TABLE 3.4
Piaget's Stages of Cognitive Development

Approximate Age	Stage	Distinguishing Characteristics
Birth to 1-½ or 2 years	Sensorimotor	Knowledge constructed through sensory perception and motor activity. Thought limited to action schemes.
2 to 7 years	Preoperational	Emergence of symbolic thinking. Intuitive rather than logical schemes. Egocentric in thought and action.
7 to 11 years	Concrete operations	Beginning of logical, systematic thinking; limited, however, to concrete objects. Decreased egocentrism.
12 to 15 years	Formal	Abstract and logical thought present. Capable of solving hypothetical problems. Deductive thinking and scientific reasoning are possible.

or taught things, and by learning "the rules of the game." Culturally appropriate social customs, religious concepts, and moral codes are all illustrations of this kind of knowledge. Acquired through life experiences, social knowledge is frequently arbitrary (Piaget & Inhelder, 1969).

Piaget's work was known in Europe several decades before his ideas affected American education. Only in the past thirty years have his contributions been fully appreciated. Morrison (1991, p. 65) identified some of Piaget's concepts that have influenced early childhood education:

- Children play an active role in their own cognitive development
- Mental and physical activity are important for children's cognitive development
- Experiences constitute the raw materials children use to develop mental structures
- Children develop cognitively through interaction with and adaptation to the environment
- Development is a continuous process
- Development results from maturation and the *transactions* or interactions between children and the physical and social environments

Table 3.5 presents a brief sketch of some historical milestones that have contributed to the development of education and the field of early childhood education.

TABLE 3.5 Key Dates in the History of Early Childhood Education

Year	Event
1524	Martin Luther advocates for public support of education.
1657	John Amos Comenius authors *The Great Didactic*; urges early schooling, which should begin at home.
1658	Comenius publishes *Orbis Sensualium Pictus*, generally considered the first children's book with pictures.
1762	French philosopher Jean Jacques Rousseau writes *Emile*, espousing a child's innate goodness and the value of early education.
1801	*How Gertrude Teaches Her Children*, a classic in education, is published by Johann Pestalozzi; in this book, he argues for home education and schooling based on children's interest.
1816	The "*Infant School*," established by Robert Owen, begins serving young children whose parents worked in his cotton mill.
1822	First day care center is established by Robert Owen at his cooperative community in New Harmony, Indiana.
1826	Froebel describes a "children's garden" in his book, *The Education of Man*.
1837	First kindergarten, began by Froebel, opens in Blankenburg, Germany.
1856	The first American kindergarten, operated by Margarethe Schurz, begins serving German-speaking children in Watertown, Wisconsin.
1860	The first English-speaking kindergarten in the United States is established by Elizabeth Peabody in Boston.
1863	Elizabeth Peabody and her sister, Mary Mann, publish the first American textbook about kindergartens.
1868	First training school for kindergarten teachers in America opens in Boston.
1873	Susan Blow begins first public kindergarten program at the Des Peres School in St. Louis.
1896	John Dewey establishes a laboratory school at the University of Chicago.
1897	John Dewey publishes *My Pedagogic Creed*, describing his views on education.
1905	Alfred Binet and Theodore Simon publish the first intelligence test.
1907	*Casa dei Bambini* is opened by Maria Montessori in one of Rome's slum areas.
1911	Margaret McMillan establishes the first nursery school in London.
1916	First parent cooperative nursery school is opened at the University of Chicago.

(continued)

FEDERAL INVOLVEMENT IN EARLY CHILDHOOD EDUCATION

Who is responsible for the education of young children? This question is a major issue in the field and is typically surrounded by conflict and fundamental disagreement (Seefeldt, 1990). Traditionally, the needs of our youngest citizens were usually met by their families. In fact, it is generally assumed that families have the primary re-

TABLE 3.5 Key Dates in the History of Early Childhood Education *(continued)*

Year	Event
1919	A nursery school, first in America, is opened by Harriet Johnson in New York City.
1921	Patty Smith Hill establishes a laboratory nursery school at Teachers College, Columbia University.
1925	First public school nursery founded as part of the Chicago public school system.
1925	National Association for Nursery Education (NANE) founded by Patty Smith Hill.
1927	Dorothy Howard, an educator, establishes first black nursery school in Washington, D.C.
1929	First black laboratory nursery school established at Hampton Institute.
1933	Federal Emergency Relief Administration provides funds for Works Progress Administration (WPA) nursery schools.
1942	Lanham Act authorizes funds for nurseries so women could work in defense industries.
1943	Kaiser Child Care Service Centers, operated by a ship-building company in Portland, Oregon, provides 24-hour child care 364 days a year.
1962	Perry Preschool Project in Ypsilanti, Michigan, is opened.
1965	Project Head Start begins operations.
1967	Project Follow-Through is initiated, extending Head Start into primary grades.
1968	Handicapped Children's Early Education Program is established to fund model preschool programs for youngsters with special needs.
1970	Westinghouse Report investigates the effectiveness of Head Start.
1971	Stride-Rite shoe company initiates corporate-sponsored child care program.
1975	Public Law 94–142, Education for All Handicapped Children Act, is enacted, mandates services for exceptional children and their families.
1980	Separate Department of Education established; Department of Health, Education, and Welfare changes its name to Department of Health and Human Services.
1986	Public Law 99–457 is passed requiring early intervention services for young children, ages 3 to 5, with special needs; financial incentives available for serving exceptional infants and toddlers, birth through age 2.
1990	Public Law 101–508 is signed into law, a modified version of the Act for Better Child Care (ABC Bill).

sponsibility of providing for their children. Historically, however, religious groups, businesses, professional associations, and government (at all three levels), have at one time or another addressed the educational and other needs of young children.

Child and family policies initiated by government play a vital role in the lives of young children. Goffin (1990) recently explained the significance of public policy for the field of early childhood education:

> Public policies help define the social and economic context that describes the range of choices parents, early educators, and others can make for children. This critical understanding helps explain the significance of governments' role in early childhood care and education. Early childhood programs are part of children's child-rearing environments.

> Policies made by our governments about early childhood care and education can make it easier or harder to parent and for children to grow into competent, caring individuals. Public policies help make children's environments more or less supportive for their growth. (p. 10)

Goffin goes on to state that public policies "are more than just decisions in favor of particular programs or services for children. They are also reflections of the kinds of relationships policymakers believe should exist among families, various levels of government, and the needs of children" (p. 11). Yet, as we approach the twenty-first century, the United States does not have a national policy regarding programs for children. One public policy analyst (Steiner, 1976) describes the situation as follows:

> Child development policy is uncoordinated. Public involvement in the field is a federal-agency-by-federal-agency, congressional-committee-by-congressional-committee, state-by-state, or city-by-city assortment of unrelated decisions that are as likely to be contradictory as complementary. (p. vii)

Those who lament the absence of clear-cut and coherent family policies interpret this as a failure to recognize the importance of society's support for young children and their families (Goffin, 1990). This is in complete contrast to several European nations, which see value and importance in having well-defined government policies that support young children and their families. Typically, in Eastern European countries, young children are viewed as a valuable national resource and enjoy the benefits of government policy that acknowledge this role (Gargiulo & Graves, 1993; Graves & Gargiulo, 1994).

First Efforts

The earliest government efforts on behalf of children in the United States can be traced to the establishment of the Children's Bureau in 1912. This office was responsible for advancing the health, education, and welfare of young children. The primary mission of the bureau was to investigate and report child health and labor conditions. The 1920s saw little expansion and federal involvement in programs for young children.

The 1930s and 1940s

The onset of the Great Depression saw a resurgence of federal activity. The **Works Progress Administration** (WPA), under Franklin D. Roosevelt, established federally funded nursery schools. Two million dollars were allocated to provide jobs for unemployed teachers and relief work for other school personnel such as cooks and custodians. The WPA nurseries, in addition to being a source of employment for many Americans, also made it possible for mothers, who were typi-

WPA nurseries helped popularize the idea of out-of-home child care for young children.

cally at home, to go out and seek work. The WPA nurseries were comprehensive programs providing all-day services for children ages 2 through 6. These nurseries helped popularize the notion of out-of-home child care for young children and could be found in many communities across the United States. As of April 1934, WPA nursery programs were located in 31 states providing jobs for over 4,000 teachers and serving 61,000 youngsters (Osborn, 1980).

The New Deal nurseries had a long-lasting impact on the field of early childhood education. Besides the popularization of the concept of nursery schools, curricula were written, teacher training workshops were established, and services to young children were expanded. Unfortunately (or fortunately, depending on your perspective) when the Depression ended so did the WPA centers, and federal involvement with early education faded.

The government's absence from the field was brief. The Second World War brought with it a renewed interest in young children and their families. Unlike the previous decade in which there were not enough jobs, in the 1940s the problem was finding workers for all of the available positions. Women assumed new roles in jobs vacated by males who had entered the armed forces of the United States. Once again, child care became a problem as large numbers of women served in war-related industries. The federal government responded in 1942 via the Community Facilities Act, more commonly called the **Lanham Act**. This legislation established day-care centers in war-affected communities. Basic child care and education were provided in these centers on a daily basis. The war nurseries typically operated from 6 a.m. until 6 p.m., but some provided services 24 hours a day. At the height of their activity, almost 2,000 nurseries served 600,000 youngsters in 41 states (Osborn, 1980).

Perhaps the most famous war nursery was a model program operated by the Kaiser Shipbuilding Company in Portland, Oregon. This company-sponsored nursery was the largest of its kind in America. There were two Kaiser Child Care Centers (1943–1945), which operated 364 days a year providing around-the-clock services to just over 1,000 children. The Kaiser Centers were unique as well as exemplary in their design and services. (See Zinsser's description of the Kaiser program in the October 1984 issue of *Working Mother.*)

The Lanham Act called for the termination of government funding upon conclusion of the war. With the men returning from the war and reentering the job market, women, without a whisper, went back to their homes and children (Steiner, 1976). Peacetime brought a return to a traditional family situation. The prevailing viewpoint of the postwar era was that mothers belonged at home, taking personal care of their children. As a result, federal involvement in early childhood programs evaporated. In the period between 1946 and the early 1960s, there was little national attention and no government support for early childhood. The home was viewed as the ideal location for children to grow and flourish.

The 1960s and 1970s

The 1960s witnessed a rekindling of interest in early childhood. The needs of young children and their families were spurred on by several events. The successful Soviet launching of *Sputnik* in 1957 caused the American public to question the quality of education being provided in U.S. schools. The writings of several prominent educators and researchers such as Benjamin Bloom (*Stability and Change in Human Characteristics*) and J. McVicker Hunt (*Intelligence and Experience*) demonstrated how crucial the early years of a child's life were for intellectual development and later academic success. The discovery of Piaget's theorizing among U.S. educators added impetus to the importance of the preschool years.

The 1960s and the 1970s were a period of social unrest in this country. Issues of racial discrimination, inequality, and the devastating effects of poverty on children also helped to shape policy and social reform. It was believed that compensatory education could ameliorate the effects of environmental deprivation. The federal government thus began to focus its attention and resources on combating poverty. One outcome of this effort was the inauguration of Head Start as part of America's War on Poverty. It was the belief of President Lyndon Johnson "that education must begin with the very young, that the child of poverty is handicapped even before he begins school, is usually a year behind before he reaches the third grade, and three years behind before he reaches the eighth grade" (Steiner, 1976, p. 29). What was to begin as a federally funded eight-week summer program serving children from low-income families soon grew to become the largest federal commitment to young children. In that first summer program, almost 30 years ago, over a half million youngsters participated in Head Start. Federal involvement in the lives of young children increased with the establishment of Project Follow-Through in 1967 and Home Start in 1972.

TEACHERS SPEAK OUT

Perhaps the most significant influence of the past thirty years has been the rediscovery of early childhood education

The 1980s and 1990s

Dynamic changes in family structure and new roles for women in American society are two characteristics of the 1980s and 1990s. These social forces have contributed to increased demands for day care, preschool programs, and kindergartens (now available in all fifty states). Unfortunately, government involvement in the early 1980s was characterized by a reduction in federal participation. There was, however, an accompanying increase in state government responsibility and private sector involvement. During the last part of the 1980s and early 1990s, we have seen an increase in federal commitment. Illustrations of this revival include calls for increased funding and full availability of Head Start, reauthorization of Follow-Through, and passage of legislation supporting child care, Public Law 101–508. This law was first proposed in 1987 as the Act for Better Child Care (ABC Bill). Enacted in 1990, this latest federal attention to young children provides assistance with child care costs and improves the quality and availability of services.

It is safe to say that the involvement of the federal government in the lives of young children is well established. Most likely this commitment will increase in the future. Some (Seefeldt, 1990) would like to see the government play a larger role in the education of young children, just as it does with older children. Parents as well as early childhood professionals need to become strong advocates for young children and their families. Together we can successfully influence government policy so that services and programs improve and dollars are used effectively.

PARENTS SPEAK OUT

I thought I knew everything about being a parent. Until I became a parent.

PROGRAM MODELS

Historical events, influential individuals, and government involvement, among other factors, have contributed to the development of many contemporary early childhood programs. We will examine several well-known models, most of which have their origins in an experimental project called Planned Variation, which is closely linked with Project Follow-Through. This project was an attempt to continue into the primary grades the comprehensive efforts initiated in Head Start.

Teachers can select from a variety of approaches or program models when working with young children. These widely divergent models represent different philosophical positions and approaches to early childhood education. "The models differ," according to Klein (1973), a specialist on the Head Start program, "in basic philosophy, learning theory, goals, and steps to reach goals, classroom procedures, teacher training and curriculum materials" (p. 360).

There are several ways to distinguish between the models. One way is to arrange the programs according to theoretical perspectives. Klein (1973) provides one example (see Table 3.6). At one end of the spectrum are models based on a psychodynamic interpretation of development formulated around the work of Sigmund Freud. At the other end of the continuum are behavioral perspectives founded on the views of John Watson, B.F. Skinner, and other psychologists who believe that all behavior is learned.

Klein (1973) gives other examples on how to group program models. Her second classification scheme centers around the interactions between the teacher and the children. This strategy identifies three variations: (1) *preacademic programs* based on behavioral principles and advocating high teacher direction (for example, the Academic Preschool designed by Wesley Becker and Siegfried Englemann); (2) *discovery models*, which call for the early childhood teacher to act as a facilitator by establishing a stimulating learning environment and

TABLE 3.6
Curriculum Models Arranged According to Theoretical Perspectives

Curriculum Models
Open Education Model
Bank Street Approach
Parent Education Model
Tucson Early Education Model
Cognitively Oriented Model
Responsive Model
Institute for Developmental Studies Model
Responsive Environment Model
Learning Research and Development Center
Behavioral Analysis Model
Academic Preschool Model

Source: J. W. Klein, "Making or Breaking It: The Teacher's Role in Model (Curriculum) Implementation," *Young Children, 28*,6 (August 1973), p. 360. © 1973 by the National Association for the Education of Young Children. Used by permission.

guiding children in their interactions (Bank Street Approach); and (3) a *cognitive-discovery model* that lies somewhere between the first two approaches. In this third condition, teachers use "a specific sequentially defined curriculum as a broad framework" (p. 61), however, early childhood educators do not follow a set curriculum for each lesson or day (for example, the Cognitively Oriented Model developed by David Weikart in Michigan or the Tucson [Arizona] Early Education Model).

Other authorities in the field have constructed guides for examining program models. An example of this effort is Maxim's (1985, p. 65) configuration. He proposed three categories:

1. *Basic Skills Model.* These programs stressed the acquisition of reading, language, and number skills through programmed teaching with highly structured and sequenced learning activities. (A *product* approach)
2. *Cognitive/Conceptual Models.* These programs stressed the development of concepts and learning processes through activities such as problem-solving, observation, and manipulation. (A *process* approach)
3. *Affective/Development Models.* These programs try to strike an even balance among all areas involved in child growth and development: physical, intellectual, and social-emotional—but the primary emphasis is on the last.

Program variations can also be attributed to the roles assumed by the teacher and student. As in Klein's second classification scheme, Weikart (1971) also looks at who initiates the learning activities. When the curriculum is planned and directed by the teacher, program models are identified as *teacher-initiated.* This approach uses highly structured activities with predetermined goals and objectives. "Teacher-proof" materials are typically used in the areas of math and language arts. A good example of this strategy is the DISTAR model, initially developed by Carl Bereiter and Siegfried Englemann at the University of Illinois.

In some instances, children are the initiators and adults take their cues from the child's activities. The Bank Street College Model is one example of a *child-initiated* program. Similar to Klein's discovery model, in the Bank Street approach teachers are responsible for creating a rich and stimulating environment where children are safe to explore and initiate their own learning.

I never realized how many choices there are in early childhood care. My son's teacher is Montessori trained with a kindergarten endorsement who teaches in the Head Start Program.
My son just thinks she's a nice lady.

Weikart's third approach is based on a shared responsibility; both teacher and child initiate activities. A *teacher-child initiated* approach is an interactive process wherein both take cues from one another. On occasion, teachers may govern the learning experience typically by structuring the activity or establishing objectives; at other times, the child's needs and interests may direct the curriculum and what transpires in the classroom. Weikart's Cognitively Oriented Curriculum exemplifies this open approach.

Good teachers rarely accept a program model in its entirety. Approaches should act only as guidelines for planning and organizing experiences for young children. Teachers need to function as curriculum developers. The teacher is the crucial variable in the implementation of any curriculum. Early childhood educators usually select approaches compatible with their own preference in technique and teaching style (Klein, 1973). Teachers also incorporate their own experiences in the models they use. Thus, they are capable of customizing learning experiences for their students.

As you gain experience, you will most likely develop your own philosophy and ideas about what programs are best for young children. Your personal approach will frequently depend on how you respond to the following questions developed by Hess and Croft (1981):

1. Do I prepare a structured or unstructured curriculum?
2. Do I teach cognitive skills or affective skills?
3. Do I emphasize content or process?
4. Do I use planned instruction or self-discovery?
5. Do I use extrinsic or intrinsic motivation?

Of course, there is no right or wrong answer. Most teachers select positions between the extremes. As with any educational issue, it is important for teachers to keep an open mind and be receptive to alternative ideas and concepts.

We now turn our attention to three models typical of the various approaches used in teaching young children.

Academic Preschool

Perhaps the best-known direct instruction or behaviorist model is a program developed by Bereiter and Englemann in the 1960s. It was originally conceived as a compensatory education model designed to help economically disadvantaged preschoolers achieve academic success. Their work was controversial and received considerable attention. Unlike typical preschool programs, Bereiter and Englemann (1966) stressed a highly structured and formalized approach that emphasized academic objectives. One reason for this work-oriented philosophy was that Bereiter and Englemann believed that early childhood teachers have little time to help their students "catch up" before entering the primary grades. Therefore, the Bereiter and Englemann program, commercially marketed as DISTAR, focused on the systematic development of specific skills and abilities. Social and affective development are not integral parts of their model.

The foundation of the academic preschool approach is based on a behavioral perspective of learning. One component of this orientation is that children's performances or behaviors that are immediately followed by reinforcement or reward are likely to be repeated. This point of view requires that instruction be carefully sequenced and designed to provide maximum opportunity for reward. Creative experiences, free choice, and play, traditional components of many early childhood programs, are not part of the academic preschool. This is because Bereiter and Englemann do not believe that these activities adequately prepare students for academic tasks. The focus of the direct instruction approach is on academic goals in three areas: reading, language, and arithmetic. Very specific skills are presented in 20-minute lessons to small numbers of children grouped according to ability. Materials are methodically prepared and organized to motivate students. Repeated drill and demonstration distinguish this model. Information is presented to the children at a fast pace, and the workload is heavy. Off-task behavior or irrelevant activity is not tolerated. Verbal responses from the group are emphasized. Continual feedback is provided to the pupils.

A main characteristic of this model is the structuring of the teaching situation so that children give correct responses to questions. Appropriate behavior and correct answers are lavishly rewarded. Verbal praise is very frequent. It is commonly used in conjunction with other reinforcements such as cookies, special activities, and games. Incorrect responses are not rewarded. Instead, the teacher rephrases the question or restructures the learning activity until the correct answer is provided by the students.

Almost every minute of this half-day program is focused on academic skills; very little time is devoted to creative activities. The classroom is plain and uncluttered with few decorations. Bereiter and Englemann (1966) explain their objection to the overabundance of materials usually found in the many early childhood classrooms:

> an object-rich environment stimulates a culturally deprived child to attend to a glitter of superabundant stimuli. He darts from one object to the another, treating each only in terms of sensory gratification. When the toy no longer "feels good," another one is selected. By minimizing the inducement of noise in the environment, the preschool can be far more effective in directing the child not to the vehicle of the concept but to the concept itself. Sterilizing the environment is a firm requirement of the work-oriented preschool. Toys should be limited to form boards, jigsaw puzzles (which are usually favorites with the children), books, drawing and tracing materials, Cuisenaire rods (to be handled during free time under the direction of the teacher), and a miniature house, barn and set of farm animals. Paper, crayons, and chalk (but no paint) should be available for expressive play. Motor toys, such as tricycles and wagons, and climbing equipment are not necessary for the program. (p. 72)

Students are rewarded for being quiet and following strict rules of classroom behavior. Even during unstructured portions of the day, children are not allowed to be rambunctious. It is believed that such behavior makes it difficult for the youngster to get back on task. Spontaneous activity, typical of most preschoolers, is also discouraged.

Mounts and Roopnarine (1987, p. 132) outline three characteristics of behavioral teaching:

1. The teacher operates the class at various levels of response difficulty, ranging from merely pointing to the correct response to identifying a relationship in regard to given objects. Understandably, this allows the children the opportunity to become comfortable with new material before requiring them to respond verbally.
2. Teachers adhere to rigid, repetitive presentation patterns intended to give children a basic understanding of language. Language skills are further enhanced by requiring children to respond in unison and to speak in loud clear voices. The objective here is to enhance verbal facility and to help teachers identify children who are having difficulty with the material.
3. Teachers are permitted to generate many examples and questions, and to use repetition to increase children's mastery skills.

Bank Street Approach

The Bank Street Approach (BSA) has been described as a discovery-oriented model (Klein, 1973), a child-initiated program (Weikart, 1971), and a developmental interaction approach (Lawton, 1988).

While the labels may differ, the focus is the same. The Bank Street Approach has its roots in the writings of John Dewey and his theory of progressive education.

Educational goals, in this model, are constructed as developmental processes. The child's ability for organizing experiences through cognitive strategies are promoted in the Bank Street program. Learning, therefore, is seen as resulting from the child's active participation and involvement with his or her social and physical world. Play is an important aspect of BSA. It is the vehicle for the interactions between the child and various stimulus materials as well as the foundation for child-to-child and child-to-adult interactions. Play provides the opportunity for young children to experiment and explore their immediate environment (Lawton, 1988).

A BSA classroom is similar, in many respects, to other early childhood classrooms. It includes a wide variety of attractive materials designed to engage the young students' interests and allows them to be active learners. Typical equipment includes blocks, paints, dress-up clothes, plants, classroom pets, puzzles, games, books, and dolls. Many items are handmade and are typically organized around learning or interest centers to facilitate the students' interaction with them (Gilkeson & Bowman, 1976). In this model, the classroom is a rich and cognitively stimulating learning environment designed to promote learning (Zimiles, 1987).

The curriculum incorporated in the Bank Street model is sensitive not only to the interest of the children, but it also reflects an awareness of the pupils' conceptual development. The presentation

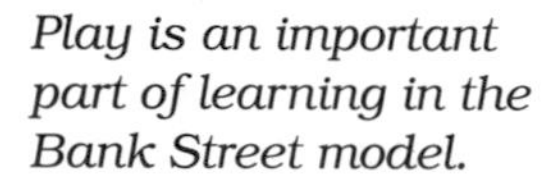
Play is an important part of learning in the Bank Street model.

of learning activities must be consistent with the individual's level of cognitive functioning (Zimiles, 1987). Lawton (1988) explains that the curriculum, which commonly uses a unit approach to instruction, focuses on the themes of "how," "what," and "why," as the children explore the physical and social world. Cognitive skills such as symbolic thinking, problem-solving, reasoning, and judgment are emphasized. By employing themes, teachers are able to include a wide range of activities and experiences linked to a particular task like baking cookies. The activity itself provides motivation; thus, intrinsic rather than extrinsic (external) rewards are used in a Bank Street classroom.

KIDS SPEAK UP

My favorite place at school is home living. It has some babies.

Girl, 4 years old

Classrooms allow the students freedom of choice. They might work independently or in small groups. Total class instruction is used by the teacher when appropriate. Teachers are flexible in using "teachable moments." Often, an unexpected event provides for a rich and valuable learning experience.

A final distinguishing characteristic of the developmental interaction approach is its emphasis on language. Both the spoken and written word are presented to the students as enjoyable and useful tools. Reading is taught as a communication skill (Zimiles, 1987). Teachers read to children daily, and children are encouraged to write their own stories based on their personal experiences. Teachers serve as recorders when necessary. The classroom also provides a functional reading environment through charts, labels, messages, class news, and other types of activity.

Cognitively Oriented Curriculum

The Cognitively Oriented Curriculum model is another example of a compensatory preschool program originally designed to benefit children of poverty. Its origins can be traced to the Perry Preschool Project in Ypsilanti, Michigan. The program is now known as *Young Children in Action.*

This curriculum model has its foundation in the work of Jean Piaget. It strongly emphasizes cognitive development. Children are active participants in the learning process. They learn best from activities that they plan and execute themselves. This strategy is in keeping with the Piagetian idea that development is a by-product of children's active manipulation, organization, and interpretation of events and objects in their environment.

The learning process in the Cognitively Oriented Curriculum matches the child's level of intellectual development to the curriculum. Children proceed at their own pace, and activities are selected according to the students' interests and competency. An emphasis is placed on developing the child's emerging intellectual abilities.

The important role played by teachers in guiding the learning of young children is stressed by Weikart and Schweinhart (1987), original framers of the Perry Preschool Project:

> . . . teachers must be fully committed to providing settings in which children learn actively and construct their own knowledge. The child's knowledge comes from personal interaction with the world, from direct experience with real objects, and from the application of logical thinking to this experience. The teacher's role is to supply these experiences and help the child to think about them logically. In a sense, children are expected to learn by the scientific method of observation and inference, at a level of sophistication consistent with their development. (p. 255)

Planning is an important part of the daily routine in classrooms using the Cognitively Oriented Curriculum. With the teacher's guidance, children are given the opportunity to decide what activities they wish to pursue within a consistent routine of daily events (see Table 3.7). Students are given a great deal of freedom to plan and carry out their intentions. Teachers continually support and encourage the children's involvement with their activities. Part of their daily routine is a Plan-Do-Review scheme. This element is an important part of the program. Children make their choices, engage in the activity, and then represent it in a variety of developmentally appropriate ways recalling how they carried out their plan (Weikart & Schweinhart, 1987).

Teachers are also responsible for planning part of the daily agenda. They plan certain **key experiences** which broaden and extend the pupil's self-designed activity. Hohmann, Banet, and Weikart (1979), authors of the *Young Children in Action* model, identify these eight experiences as:

- Active learning
- Using language
- Representing experiences and ideas
- Classification
- Seriation
- Number concepts
- Spatial relations
- Time

TABLE 3.7
Sample Daily Routines of the High/Scope Curriculum

Half-Day Program	
8:30–8:50 a.m.	Planning Time
8:50–9:45 a.m.	Work Time
9:45–10:00 a.m.	Clean-up Time
10:00–10:30 a.m.	Recall, Snack, and Small-Group Time
10:30–10:50 a.m.	Outside Time
10:50–11:10 a.m.	Circle Time
11:10–11:20 a.m.	Dismissal

Full-Day Program	
7:30–8:30 a.m.	As children arrive, adults plan with them and get them started on a short work time.
8:30–9:00 a.m.	Breakfast and brush teeth
9:00–9:20 a.m.	Planning Time
9:20–10:30 a.m.	Work Time and Clean-up
10:30–10:50 a.m.	Recall Time
10:50–11:20 a.m.	Outside Time
11:20–11:45 a.m.	Circle Time and preparation for lunch
11:45–12:30 p.m.	Lunch
12:30–1:30 p.m.	Nap Time. Children either sleep or lie quietly with a book.
1:30–2:15 p.m.	Small-Group and Snack Time
2:15–4:00 p.m.	Some children leave. Adults plan with the remaining children, who then work until they leave.

Source: M. Hohmann, B. Banet, and D. Weikart, *Young Children in Action: A Manual for Preschool Educators* (Ypsilanti, MI: High/Scope Press, 1979), p. 61.

Many of these components occur normally throughout the daily routine and are natural extensions of the children's interests and activities. It believed that these experiences, which are simple and pragmatic, promote intellectual development as well as providing a means for structuring the curriculum while still maintaining flexibility (Weikart & Schweinhart, 1987). Table 3.8 presents examples of the activities children encounter with the key experiences of active learning and number concepts. When planning key experiences, Lawton (1988) tells us that teachers are mindful that children's activities proceed from concrete to abstract, simple to complex, and from the "here and now" to the "there and then."

Classrooms that use the Cognitively Oriented Curriculum are arranged and equipped like many other preschool environments. The

TABLE 3.8
Key Experience Activities of the Cognitively Oriented Curriculum

Key Experience: Active Learning
• Exploring actively with all the senses • Discovering relations through direct experience • Manipulating, transforming, and combining materials • Choosing materials, activities, and purposes • Acquiring skills with tools and equipment • Using the large muscles • Taking care of one's own needs
Key Experience: Number Concepts
• Comparing number and amount: more/less, same amount, more/fewer, same number • Comparing the number of items in two sets by matching them up in one-to-one correspondence (example: Are there as many crackers as there are children?) • Counting objects and counting by rote

Source: D. Weikart and L. Schweinhart, "The High/Scope Cognitively Oriented Curriculum in Early Education." Reprinted with the permission of Macmillan College Publishing Company from *Approaches to Early Childhood Education* by Jaipaul L. Roopnarine and James E. Johnson. Copyright © 1987 by Macmillan College Publishing Company, Inc.

physical arrangement consists of a large, open area for group activities and games in addition to centers or work areas for specific activities (for example, quiet area, sand and water area, art area, block area). The work areas are located around the room. The equipment is also typical—trucks, dolls, wooden blocks, puzzles, stuffed animals, puppets, and a host of other items designed to engage the children in learning.

The teaching methods used in this curriculum model were summarized by Hohmann and her colleagues (1979, p. 291) in the following principles:

- Maintain a comfortable, secure environment.
- Support children's actions and language.
- Help children make choices and decisions.
- Help children solve their own problems and do things for themselves.

This early childhood curriculum model has been adapted for use with bilingual children and for young children with special needs. It has been introduced in the developing countries of South America. Weikart and Schweinhart (1987) report that the Cognitively Oriented Curriculum has also been extended into the elementary school years.

Research Findings

The question, of course, that comes to mind for many early childhood teachers is, "Which model is best for young children?" Unfortunately, there is no clear-cut answer. Research evidence has been inconclusive. No one model or program has proven to be superior to any other model or strategy.

Doing large-scale educational research of the type needed to answer this question is a formidable task. There are many variables and parameters to control. For example, different models have different goals; some stress academic objectives while others emphasize affective development. In addition, it is difficult to control for teacher effectiveness and student differences, and to find valid assessment instruments appropriate to the program's goals. These illustrations are just some of the factors that can influence the outcome of research efforts.

One attempt to look at the planned variations of Project Follow-Through was an evaluation study conducted by Abt Associates in 1977. This firm was commissioned to investigate the effectiveness of various program models. Basically, their findings were inconclusive. The effectiveness of the program varied from community to community, and no one approach was successful everywhere it was implemented. Results typically reflected the purpose of the model (Abt Associates, 1977).

Katz (1988) sounded an appropriate note for early childhood educators. She believes it is best to look at the long-term cumulative outcomes of programs as demonstrated by the student's interest in learning. Probably the only conclusion we can safely draw is that we have a great deal to discover about the learning of young children. Klein (1973) may offer the best summary about *all* curriculum approaches. She writes, "in the final analysis, it is the *teacher* who makes or breaks the model. Without the teacher, the curriculum is just a lifeless piece of paper" (p. 365).

SUMMARY

The field of early childhood education has a long history rich with tradition. Many contemporary practices and programs such as the value of play, parent involvement, and kindergartens have their roots in the work of earlier philosophers, reformers, and educational thinkers.

Despite the absence of a well-defined national policy, the federal government, for over sixty years, has played a vital and significant role in the lives of countless young children. This involvement has often been in response to the collective needs of our society. Many of the advantages that youngsters enjoy today are the result of government working cooperatively with early childhood professionals, parents, advocates, and policymakers.

Early childhood professionals need to function as curriculum decision makers. Many program models and approaches are available; but which one is best? Teachers need to choose wisely. Their decisions are based on several factors—the experiential background of the teacher, the needs of the children, views on learning and development, and thoughts about the role of education are but a few of the factors that frequently guide personal philosophy. As we noted earlier, it is the teacher, working with young children, who brings life to the curriculum.

TEST YOUR UNDERSTANDING

1. Describe the typical treatment of children prior to the 1800s.
2. What was the contribution of religion to the development of education?
3. Identify the roles philosophers and social/educational reformers played in shaping early education.
4. Why was symbolism important to Froebel?
5. Describe the "gifts" and "occupations" of Froebel's children's garden.
6. Explain Dewey's ideas about educating young children.
7. Identify the main features of *Casa dei Bambini.*
8. What is a prepared environment?
9. How does Piaget believe intelligence develops?
10. Provide examples of the concepts of assimilation and accommodation.
11. How does Piaget describe the stages of cognitive development?
12. Trace the role of government in the field of early childhood education since the 1930s up to the present.
13. List five significant events that have helped to influence federal involvement in the lives of young children.
14. Explain the differences between behavioral, discovery, and cognitive models of early childhood programs.

LEARNING ACTIVITIES

1. Read books and articles written by influential people in the field of early childhood education (e.g., Dewey, Piaget, Froebel, Montessori). How have their ideas been incorporated into present-day early childhood programs?
2. Interview the coordinator of kindergarten programs in your local school district(s). Find out how kindergartens developed in your area.
3. Argue for or against the following statement: "Government should play a larger role in the education of all children younger than age 6."
4. Interview early childhood educators working in different types of programs. Discuss with these teachers their program philosophy and goals, teaching strategies, training requirements, and other issues. What are the similarities and differences among the programs?

LET'S TALK ABOUT IT

As Mildred reviewed her notes in preparation for leading the discussion on the early childhood profession, she realized that the four team members had radically different experiences despite the fact that they had all observed the same children, staff, and program. She began to wonder if they had all been at the same place! She decided to present their observations.

Why is the Preschool I teacher spending so much time with Carmelita?

How could the teacher meet Carmelita's needs without ignoring the needs of the other children?

If you were Matt, what would you do?

What caused the behavior change in this award-winning teacher?

If you were this teacher's colleague, what would you do to help?

What do you think is the philosophy of each teacher?

Mildred was very impressed with the Preschool I teacher, who was especially effective in working with Carmelita. She noticed this teacher usually gave Carmelita individualized attention. Her patience and understanding allowed Carmelita to gain in self-confidence. Other team members reported that most of the teachers really seemed to genuinely care for their children. Matt, however, questioned the wisdom of devoting so much time to one child while the other eleven children were encouraged to be more independent.

Matt shared a concern with Mildred that his observations of the kindergarten teacher were limited. After he had been at Spring Hill for only two weeks, the kindergarten teacher would leave the classroom, thus placing Matt in charge of the children. Because Matt had very limited experience with young children, he wondered what he should do.

One teacher in particular stood out in the minds of each of the group members. This teacher continually sat and read a newspaper while children played independently in the learning centers. She repeatedly ignored the childrens' requests for assistance, continually complained, and often talked of changing professions. Stephanie and other team members were really surprised by this teacher's actions, since she had recently been named the outstanding early childhood teacher by the state association.

Mildred concluded her presentation to her classmates by describing some of the programs at the Spring Hill Center. In one classroom the children were actively engaged in a variety of learning experiences. The teacher guided the children's learning. Many of the activities in this classroom were small group and child-initiated. Lillian noted that in her classroom, the children spent a great deal of time on teacher-directed tasks, while Lillian spent much of her time at the copy machine. She was also surprised at the limited responses of the children to the teacher's questions.

PART 2

Observing the Young Child

SPRING HILL CHILD DEVELOPMENT CENTER

During the class break, team members Lillian, Matt, Stephanie and Mildred were reflecting on some of their observations at Spring Hill Child Development Center. Lillian was comparing Austin's behavior with the behavior of her children when they were babies. She was baffled by how demanding Austin was. He seemed to require so much of the teacher's time. Lillian said, "I've raised three kids of my own and none of them were like Austin. Although each of my three were different, none of them, as I recall, exhibited the kinds of problems and behaviors that Austin exhibits every day. I am physically exhausted at the end of the day from dealing with Austin. I realize times are different, but when I was raising my children, I made sure that I stayed home and was always there when my kids needed me. You know, if his mother stayed home with him, he would be different."

"Austin is nothing compared to Nathaniel," Matt replied. "The other day when he was in the block center, he intentionally hurt another child who accidentally knocked his tower over. This is not the first time that his teacher and I have witnessed this kind of behavior. His dad spends more time in the center than the teacher I observed. I think it is interesting that neither of us have ever met his mother."

Stephanie added, "As long as we're talking about those kids, the only way I could get Howard to do anything was to sit with him."

"Let's remember that not all children are like these kids," Mildred cautioned, "Although these kids seem to stand out more, there are a far greater number of kids like Shelby. Don't you wish that all children were like Shelby?"

The professor joined the group, commenting on how well the class discussions were going. She asked, "Have you noticed that even though you visited the same program, you all came away with different experiences? That's the value of working with a team and learning from each other. Of course, how you see things is a reflection of your individual background and experiences. It's also related to your views of children, your philosophy of teaching, and your value system."

Matt responds, "You know, before I took this class, I didn't realize that kids are more alike than they are different. As future teachers, I think it's important for us to focus on similarities and strengths rather than differences and weaknesses."

The professor then reminds the group that it is time to return to class and continue the discussions. "I'm very pleased with the quality of the presentations so far. You can tell your classmates are genuinely interested by the number of questions they are asking."

The team members decided that the topics for the remainder of the morning's discussion should include the different ways of assessing young children. At Spring Hill, they decided, there was no one best way to assess what a child knows and has learned. They agreed that observation, anecdotal records, and portfolios are three effective ways of assessing children's progress.

"Hey, we can't forget about play," Matt reminded the team. "Play is the work of the young child. I learned a great deal about children by watching them play.

Mildred added, "I never realized how creative young kids are. Given the opportunity, they truly are imaginative. Too bad that adults often stifle it."

CHAPTER 4

Observation and Assessment

CHAPTER OUTLINE

KEY TERMS

Assessment
Systematic observations
Anecdotal records
Work samples
Checklists
Rating scales
Developmental scales
Interviews

"I don't know," Jason signed as he carefully considered two drawings he had recently completed. Tony propped his cheek on his hand and watched his friend as they contemplated the two pictures. The children in Ms. Garcia's kindergarten enjoyed selecting work to be placed in their scrapbooks. The books served as a collection or portfolio of each child's efforts. Today the two boys were dealing with the dilemma of selecting a picture of their families for the collection.

As the two boys considered the drawings, the teacher noticed that Jason had illustrated his family members using circles with extended lines for arms and legs. She noted that the illustrations supported her observations of Jason's development. Ms. Garcia was intrigued by the intensity of the boys and moved closer to listen. From the teacher's perspective, the illustrations were very similar. But she recognized the importance of Jason choosing the picture he would place in the collection.

After selecting one picture, Jason began to identify the members of the family while the teacher recorded the names under each illustration. Tony watched carefully as his friend pointed to a circle with lines and said, "That's my mother."

As the teacher printed the name, Tony pointed to one of the four circles and asked Jason, "Is that your brother John?"

"Uh-huh," Jason replied. Ms. Garcia studied the two boys for a moment and then carefully printed the name of John under the circle. While she was printing, Jason asked Tony, "How did you know that was my brother?"

Tony confidently replied, "Cause it looks just like him."

Ms. Garcia noted the discussion for future reference. She thought about the development of the children and was reminded how important it is to observe and listen to children.

A central part of teaching young children is gathering information about each child to make informed decisions about the child's learning and development. Teachers make many daily decisions about children that should be professional judgments based on accurate information. The subject of how curriculum and assessment are linked in programs for young children has received increasing attention during the 1980s and 1990s. Much of the discussion has focused on the inappropriateness of standardized testing for young children. Some of the discussion has failed to recognize the importance of the knowledge we have about children's natural development. The question of how achievement and performance of children should be measured or judged has just recently received appropriate attention.

DEFINITIONS

Curriculum is an organized framework that includes the content children are to learn, the processes children engage in to reach teacher's goals, and the context in which teaching and learning take place. The early childhood education profession defines curriculum in a way that includes theories, approaches, and models. Assessment includes observing, recording, and documenting the work and play children engage in. This process, which should be continuous, focuses on what children do and how they do it. The information guides the teacher's planning, assists in the communication process with parents, and informs the teacher of the children's developmental levels and needs (National Association for the Education of Young Children, 1991).

TEACHERS SPEAK OUT

Evaluation completes the cycle of good planning.

PURPOSES OF ASSESSMENT

Assessment, curriculum, and teaching must be united in effective early childhood education programs. **Assessment** provides information necessary to assist the teacher in making very important decisions which influence the child. Among the many questions assessment can answer are the following:

- What are the child's strengths, needs, and styles of learning?
- How is the child doing in comparison to the teacher and parent expectations?
- How will this child's instruction be planned?
- How can this child's needs be best met?
- Is the program meeting its goals and objectives?

THE NEED FOR CHANGE

In the 1980s and 1990s, we have witnessed numerous calls for educational reform. Many of the reform plans have included significant changes in curriculum, teacher education programs, school structure, governance, and accountability issues such as assessment. Many national organizations representing subject/content disciplines and administrators have issued calls for change. These include the National Council of Teachers of Mathematics, the American Association of the Advancement of Science, the International Reading Association, the National Council of Teachers of English, the National Commission for the Social Studies, the National Association of Elementary School Principals, the National Association of State Boards of Education, and the Association for Supervision and Curriculum Development, among others.

PARENTS SPEAK OUT

I wish the schools would use portfolio assessment all the way through the system. For the first time, I understand my child's strengths.

Several professional organizations in early childhood education, such as the Association for Childhood Education International, the National Association for the Education of Young Children, and the Southern Early Childhood Association (formerly called the Southern Association on Children Under Six) have published position statements, monographs, and other materials addressing the inappropriateness of standardized testing. Some extend the issue by describing the appropriateness of multiple types of assessment for young children (see Appendix B).

These reports reflect a position that rejects many traditional teacher-directed, drill and skill activities that focus on isolated academic skills. These approaches fail to consider current knowledge of children's learning and fail to produce students who possess the problem-solving and critical thinking skills that will be required in the next century. Many organizations are calling for more performance-based assessments that match current views of curriculum and children's growth, development, and learning.

We believe it is important for teachers to know the differences between assessment, evaluation, and testing. Many teachers erroneously use these terms interchangeably. The focus in this chapter is to describe types of assessment that assist teachers in providing a developmentally appropriate program for young children (see Table 4.1).

The following are other purposes for individual assessment (Brown, 1988):

- Determine progress toward goal.
- Obtain samples of experiential background.

TABLE 4.1 Assessment Serves a Variety of Purposes

Term	Definition	Purpose
Assessment	The process of observing and recording the work that children do and how they do it	To keep current on children's progress in order to make informed educational decisions in planning (See other purposes in section below.)
Evaluation	The systematic collection and analysis of program-related data	To understand how a program delivers services or what the consequences of its services are for the participants (Northwest Regional Educational Laboratory, 1991); to determine program effectiveness
Standardized Test	An instrument composed of empirically selected items that have definite instructions for use, adequately determined norms, and data of reliability and validity (NAEYC, 1991)	To yield a score that is often used to make decisions regarding labeling grouping or placement (This is not considered an appropriate form of assessment for young children.)
Achievement Test	A standardized instrument	To measure the extent to which a person has mastery over a certain body of information or possesses a certain skill after instruction has taken place (NAEYC, 1991) (This is not considered an appropriate form of assessment for young children.)
Intelligence Test	A standardized instrument	To yield a score indicative of cognitive functioning (This is not considered an appropriate form of assessment for young children.)
Screening Test	A procedure used to gain information about a child	To identify strengths and to determine if special services are needed
Criterion-referenced Test	A standardized test	To measure specific objectives to determine what a person can and cannot do

- Determine ability to complete tasks.
- Ascertain physical attributes.
- Monitor processing skills.
- Measure communication skills.
- Sample social skills.
- Identify special needs and strengths.
- Formulate reports to parents.
- Provide information for planning curriculum.

ESTABLISHED CRITERIA FOR APPROPRIATE ASSESSMENT

Established criteria for the appropriate assessment of young children should include the following components (Southern Association on Children Under Six, 1990):

- Assessment must be valid. It must provide information related to the goals and objectives of a program.
- Assessment should not include standardized tests, which are multiple choice, group administered, and claim to measure achievement.
- Assessment must encompass the whole child. Programs must have goals and assessment procedures which relate to children's physical, social, emotional, and mental development.
- Assessment must involve repeated observations. Many observations help teachers find patterns of behavior and avoid quick decisions which may be based on isolated behavior by children.
- Assessment must be continuous over time. Each child should be compared to his or her own individual course of development over time rather than to an average for the group.
- Assessment must use a variety of methods. Gathering a wide variety of materials and information from different sources permits informed and professional decisions.

ASSESSMENT PROCEDURES FOR YOUNG CHILDREN

One of the newest types of assessment for young children is the use of the portfolio. The portfolio can provide the teacher with an excellent way to assess children as they learn and grow. It gives the teacher a record of the child's progress over time. Like an artist's portfolio, it can show the child's best work in a variety of areas. It may contain documentation of how the child thinks and creates, as well as how the processes of learning occur.

According to Meisels and Steele (1991), portfolios serve a variety of purposes, including:

- Helping to integrate instruction and assessment.
- Providing students, teachers, parents, administrators, and other decision-makers with essential information about children's progress and various classroom activities.
- Enabling children to participate in assessing their own work.
- Keeping track of individual children's progress.
- Forming the basis for evaluating the quality of children's overall performance.

Other tools used to assess young children are often components of the portfolio. These include systematic observations, anecdotal records, work samples, checklists, rating scales, developmental scales, and interviews. The use of these types of procedures demonstrates an understanding of children's learning and a recognition that learning is a continuous process. It also represents an awareness that children learn at different rates and in a variety of styles (Grace & Shores, 1991).

Systematic Observations

One of the most commonly used and most important techniques in assessing young children's progress is the **systematic observation**. Teachers watch children as they work and play to determine their developmental level, skill levels, interests, and needs. To use this approach effectively, teachers must be deliberate, thoughtful, and reflective as they watch children. They must also have a keen understanding of children's growth, development, and learning, as well as specific goals for the individual child being observed.

Children should be observed when they are playing and working alone, in small groups, large groups, at various times of the day, and in a variety of situations and contexts. Effective observation must be objective, unobtrusive, and carefully and accurately recorded. You will find the following guidelines from Cook, Tessier, and Armbruster (1987) helpful in using systematic observations:

- Note the date, time, setting, and record exactly what the child says and does. Note gestures, reactions, what prompted behaviors, what followed behaviors, and other factual information.
- Record observation as things occur. Important documentation can be lost if one tries to recapture it much later than it occurred. It takes practice and skill to facilitate classroom activities while simultaneously observing and documenting behaviors and children's progress. It is important to plan classroom observations as unobtrusively and efficiently as possible.

Small group reading activities led by a parent allow the teacher time for observation.

- Observe children at different times of the day and in different settings. Changes in time and context may yield information about a child's style, mood, interests, and patterns of behavior.
- Focus on one child at a time. The process of watching individual children combined with other assessment techniques assists teachers in developing observational skills.
- Protect confidentiality. Make certain that notes are not left in a place where they can be read by other teachers or parents of other children. A system of coding names and other information may be helpful in protecting the identity of the children.
- Choose a practical, workable system. Teachers should refer to individual children's goals as well as classroom or program goals and objectives. Some teachers have been successful using clip boards, post-it notes, file cards, notebooks, three-ring binders, and other tools and materials. Find a system that works well.

Anecdotal Records

Anecdotal records are factual, nonjudgmental observations of activity. These are most useful for recording events, activities, and behaviors that are unanticipated. Descriptions of children's gestures, expressions, and direct quotes are most helpful in this approach. Anecdotal records are usually brief and describe one incident at a time (see Table 4.2). But they can provide a complete account of a child's progress when examined in a cumulative manner. Often, teachers record notes about the documented events that may provide insight and perspective. In Appendix C, we provide an anecdotal record form.

TABLE 4.2
Sample Anecdotal Record

Name of child:	Molly	**Date:**	October 5
Observer:	B. Hammond	**Time:**	9:15
Setting:	Language Arts Center		
Incident:	Molly wrote a three-page story about Lad, her dog. The writing was very descriptive with well-developed, complete sentences.		

Beaty (1990) reminds teachers that it is important to separate observations from the intention of recording the observation. Guidelines to help teachers develop good anecdotal records are as follows:

1. *Determine what you will observe.* Choose behaviors that will inform you about the child. Record the behaviors as they relate to both program and individual goals.

2. *Keep the anecdote in context.* Note the date, time, setting, situation, etc. Recording a specific action or behavior in isolation does not yield instructive information.

3. *Use specific information in the anecdote.* The analysis is easier if your notes are precise, simple, and specific.

4. *Keep the anecdotal information objective.* Use facts. If you need to write notes about the observation, use parentheses and separate these comments from the anecdotes.

5. *Keep the recording process simple.* The notes should not be too wordy, rambling, or take too much time away from your teaching.

Reflecting on a variety of children's work over time helps the teacher assess and plan appropriately.

Work Samples

Work samples are an important part of the assessment procedure and package. Samples included may be of the child's informal and formal work, academic and nonacademic, samples of writing (drafts; revised and edited works), processes and results of investigations, experiments, photographs, products, art work, audiotapes, videotapes, interviews, lists of books read, etc. As with the use of artist's portfolios, these materials should represent the best work of the child. They should show the variety and depth of work the child is able to do over time.

Checklists

The **checklist** is an easy and popular tool used by teachers for recording children's progress. Any checklist should be based on instructional objectives. By checking off skills or abilities, the teacher can verify the child's progress. Checklists are often divided into areas on development such as social, emotional, physical, and intellectual. Some contain a section on perceptual growth, some include language, and some contain a self-help section (see Table 4.3).

In general, observations should be noted casually, not on specially planned or artificial activities. Sometimes, though, it is necessary for the teacher to "set up" a situation to assist in the assessment.

See Appendix F for a complete sample checklist.

Rating Scales

Rating scales are appropriately used when behaviors observed have different elements or components. Typically, each behavior is rated on a continuum that goes from the highest level to the lowest level, with the points between marked off at regular intervals. The teacher/observer must decide where on the scale the child's behavior or progress lies. Some rating scales are numerical and have numbered items,

TABLE 4.3
Sample Checklist

Student: Shelby Stone	**Age:** 5 years, 5 months		
Skill	**Month**		
	1	4	8
Responds to rights and teachings of others		X	
Asks questions for information and meaning		X	
Enjoys looking at books	X	X	
Exhibits understanding of one-to-one correspondence			
Understands *before* and *after*			

such as 1 = needs more time or experience; 2 = satisfactory; and 3 = excellent. Others may be graphic with choices to be circled, such as daily; several times a week; once a month; once a week; and never.

Scales may look like one of the following examples.

Rating scale with continuum of choices

Cognitive skills	1	2	3
Is able to recognize his or her name	X		

1 = needs more time or experience
2 = satisfactory
3 = excellent

Rating scale with choices to be circled

Remains involved until a task is completed

daily (several times a week) once a month never

Developmental Scales

Developmental scales and screening tests are sometimes used to identify children's strengths and weaknesses and to assist the teacher in planning. The assessment information revealed by many of these instruments is not appropriately used for grading, labeling, grouping, or retaining children. In choosing one of these instruments, teachers should carefully consider the purpose for using such a test as well as the program goals and individual children's needs.

Interviews

One of the easiest and most effective methods of obtaining information is to ask the child direct questions. This technique can also be used with parents and other significant people in the child's life. Many teachers ask parents to answer specific questions about the child's experiences before enrolling in the classroom or school. This can give the teacher a wealth of background information about the child. Parent **interviews** can also reveal information about patterns of behavior and activities in the home. Teachers should remember that a relationship must be created, nurtured, and maintained with parents if they expect to receive honest, helpful information. See Table 4.4 for a summary of assessment procedures.

WHO IS INVOLVED IN ASSESSMENT?

The stakeholders in the assessment process in early childhood education are the children, the teachers and administrators, and the parents. All assessment results should lead to benefits for the child.

TABLE 4.4 Summary of Assessment Procedures

Type	Advantages	Disadvantages
Systematic Observation	Informs the teacher about the child's growth, development, and learning. Gives information in all areas of development and subject/content areas.	It takes time, practice, skill, and a workable system.
Anecdotal Records	Informs the teacher about the child's growth, development, and learning. Documents important incidents in the classroom.	It takes time, practice, skill, and a workable system.
Work Samples	Demonstrates growth and learning over time. Documents success and progress. Valuable resource. Supports teacher's judgements about children's development.	It takes space, time, and keen organizational abilities.
Checklists	Good tool for recording progress and assisting with planning.	It takes time and keen observational skills.
Rating Scales	Informative and instructive in illustrating patterns of behavior.	It requires that teachers know individual children extremely well and are able to accurately interpret behaviors.
Developmental Scales	Good tool for recording progress and assisting with planning. May identify strengths or special needs.	It takes time and may not yield much information.
Interviews	Easy and effective way of gathering information. Can yield information from contexts other than school.	It takes time.

The teacher is best positioned to assess the needs of each child with the program goals and objectives. The teacher should keep parents informed about the assessment information. Parents need specific information about their child. Administrators, school boards, policy committees, and others have needs for assessment information related to programs and large groups of children. In most cases, their needs should not include specific information on individual children. All adults involved in the assessment process have responsibilities.

Role of Children

Hills (1992) states that children can have four roles in assessment:

- As the subjects of assessment
- As sources of assessment information

The importance of thorough planning by teachers cannot be overemphasized.

- As observers and critics of their own thinking processes and progress
- As beneficiaries of the ways information is used

In attempting to engage in any of the assessment procedures discussed in this chapter, the teacher must carefully consider traits and characteristics of young children. Because young children are continually changing at a rapid pace during the early years, they must be assessed frequently. They experience significant changes in their physical development, in language abilities, in social and emotional growth, and in other areas. They are also very sensitive to their environment. This may contribute to certain reactions that could skew their behavior or the assessment item. In general, many children do not have much interest in being assessed. If the assessment procedures interfere with the children's agenda, they may approach the task with a lack of enthusiasm. All of these factors may lead to difficulties on an assessment procedure.

KIDS SPEAK UP

Once, when I was little, I drew pictures that were really funny . . . Now I draw good.

Boy, 4 years old

Role of Teachers

Teachers need information about each child in their classroom. Before making important decisions about how, what, and when to teach certain things, teachers must discover how the children are progressing, how they are thinking and solving problems, and how they are approaching and thinking about their own learning. It is important for the teacher to examine how the child is thinking, learning, constructing ideas, interacting, and responding. Teachers need to continually examine these issues and reflect about how to best meet the children's needs.

The teacher's responsibilities for assessment include

- Integrating instruction and assessment in the planning and implementation of the program
- Using knowledge about young children's growth, development, and learning to assist in making decisions about planning, implementation, and the evaluation of instructional practices
- Exchanging information with parents and involving them as partners in the child's development and education

Role of Parents

Parents are the primary receivers of assessment information. They have a need to know that their children are developing and learning. They have knowledge about their children that can be very helpful to the teacher. Building a good relationship with parents is critical for the teacher of young children. See Chapter 14 for additional information about the parent-teacher partnership.

Role of Administrators

As we said earlier, administrators do not generally need information about individual children. It has become increasingly important for program administrators to give special attention to program evaluation. They need to know how groups of children are doing in relation to a standard of expectation. Administrators should be well informed about the types of assessment being used, and they should be the teacher's advocate for appropriate assessment. See Chapter 13 for more detail on the role of the administrator.

PRINCIPLES FOR GUIDING THE ASSESSMENT PROCESS

If teachers of young children succeed at providing curriculum and instruction that is both age-appropriate and individually appropriate, an assessment plan is essential. Many teachers use an initial assessment that informs them about the child's likes, dislikes, and favorite activities. This helps the teachers get to know the child and assists them in making curriculum decisions. The beginning teacher needs to find out what the child already knows and is able to do. To then provide an accurate look at the child's capabilities, the teacher must carefully observe the child and gather information from a variety of sources and contexts. If the teacher ignores assessment data as it relates to planning, then the process of collecting the date is futile. The data should guide the planning process and the adjustment of plans to better meet the individual needs of the children. It should not be used to make decisions on labels, grouping, or retention.

TEACHERS SPEAK OUT

A key to portfolio assessment is organization. You do not keep everything a child does. It is best to have a plan and stick to it.

The following principles (National Association for the Education of Young Children, 1991, pp. 32–33) should assist the teacher in the assessment process:

- Curriculum and assessment are interrelated and integrated throughout the program.
- Assessment data should be used to assist the teacher in providing more individualized instruction and curricular improvements.
- Children's growth, development, and learning in all areas of development should be continually assessed by the early childhood teacher.
- Assessment data should be used to support children's learning and development and to communicate with parents.
- Assessment involves periodic and continuous observation in a variety of situations that are representative of children's progress and behavior over time.
- Assessment depends on the documentation of typical daily activities rather than contrived artificial situations which may disrupt the natural learning practices of young children.
- Assessment relies on a variety of sources of information. Among other data sources, these may include observations, work samples, checklists, developmental scales, interviews, audiotapes, and videotapes.
- Assessment takes into account that children learn at different rates and utilize diverse styles.
- Assessment supports children's learning and parents' relationships with their children.
- Assessment illustrates children's strengths and progress.
- Assessment is a collaborative process involving all stakeholders in the child's development and education.

SUMMARY

In this chapter, we examined the variety of assessment procedures that teachers of young children can use. The definition, use of multiple sources, and purpose for observing and assessing children's behavior and progress has changed over the last two decades. Assessment is much more integrated and interrelated with curriculum issues in programs today. A large number of professional organizations in education in general, and in early childhood in particular, have published papers regarding appropriate assessment practices. Some of these have grown out of reactions against standardized testing, and some have grown from educational reform efforts. Teachers should view assessment as an essential component of programs, curriculum, and planning. We also addressed the roles of children, teachers, parents, and administrators in the assessment process, and provided guiding principles for the teacher. For more information on assessment, see Chapter13.

TEST YOUR UNDERSTANDING

1. Define and explain the differences between curriculum and assessment. How are they related?
2. Discuss the purposes of assessment and the questions that are answered through the assessment process.
3. Discuss the issues and influences that have caused so many professional organizations to publish statements concerning testing. Name several of these organizations.
4. Name and discuss the established criteria for appropriate assessment for young children.
5. Discuss several ways to monitor and assess children's progress and development.
6. Discuss guidelines for developing good anecdotal records.
7. What are the four roles that children play in the assessment process?
8. Discuss the roles and responsibilities related to the assessment process.
9. Describe the differences between screening, assessment, and evaluation.

LEARNING ACTIVITIES

1. Interview the director of an early childhood program serving children from birth through age 4 and a kindergarten, first grade, second grade, or third grade teacher. Find out what types of assessment are used with the children in each program. Ask how assessment data is communicated with the parents and how it is used by the teacher in planning curricular activities.
2. Interview the parents of a child in an early childhood education program. Ask the parents about the assessment practices that are

implemented in the child's classroom or program. Ask if the parents believe they receive adequate information about their child's progress. Ask questions to determine if the parents agree with and support the program's methods of assessment.

3. Interview three children, ages 3, 5, and 8. Ask them how their teacher decides if they are learning what they are supposed to learn. Ask the children if they know other ways to discover this information.

CHAPTER 5

Play

CHAPTER OUTLINE

Definitions and Characteristics
Theories of Play
- *Surplus Energy*
- *Recreation*
- *Recapitulation*
- *Pre-exercise*
- *Other Theories*

Changes in Play Development
Assisting Children's Play
Benefits of Play
- *Development of Intelligence*
- *Development of Personality*
- *Development of Competencies*

Adult Roles in Children's Play
Types of Play
- *Functional Play*
- *Construction Play*
- *Symbolic Play*
- *Sociodramatic Play*

Facilitating Play
- *Preparing for Play*
- *Time*
- *Space*
- *Materials*

Playgrounds

KEY TERMS

Surplus energy theory
Recreation theory
Recapitulation theory
Pre-exercise theory
Unoccupied play
Solitary play
Onlooker play
Parallel play
Associative play
Cooperative play

The field trip to the county fair had been quite enjoyable, but the children were becoming quite restless as they waited for the school bus. They waited and waited, and still no bus arrived. Suddenly, one young boy said, "Look! Look! I found a ticket to the pony ride!" The other children, hearing the comment, grew excited and began to collect debris from the bus area. To discourage littering the sidewalk again, the teacher calmly asked the group to put the items into her shopping bag, thinking she would throw them away later. That afternoon, the children were preparing to make a collage by retelling the story of their trip. When one child recalled finding the treasured items at the bus stop, the findings became materials for the project. The collage materials became a creative outcome of the field trip, adding closure to an exciting activity.

The subject of children's play has been the focus of many articles and research studies over the past twenty-five years. Educators and researchers have been concerned that the value and legitimacy of play is not recognized. The emphasis on developmentally appropriate practice for young children has caused a renewed commitment toward a play-centered curriculum.

I thought I sent my child to school to learn how to read and write. I realize now that playing gives her something to read and write about. Play is a part of learning.

Play-oriented programs in early childhood education are certainly not new. We can look to Froebel's kindergarten as well as to the work of Maria Montessori to see the importance of activity and play in children's growth, development, and learning. Play began to be accepted as a legitimate educational activity at the time of the nursery school movement in England and the reform kindergarten movement in the United States. These educators observed children and recognized that play provides multiple opportunities for learning. Children use play to construct knowledge, test ideas, and integrate what they are learning. Play fosters all aspects of the child's learning: intellectual, social, emotional, physical, and linguistic.

Play supports children's growth, development, and learning in building competencies such as self-direction, industry, decision-making, problem-solving, cooperation, and initiative (Van Hoorn, Nourot, Scales, & Alward, 1993). When addressing issues about play in this chapter, we take a whole-child approach and recognize that all areas of development are related and intertwined. Play is the foundation for growth, development, and learning because of its role in fostering and enhancing all these areas.

We begin the chapter with definitions and characteristics of play as well as theories about the value and function of play. We address types of play and discuss the relationship of play to the development of intelligence, personality, and competencies. A discussion of how play changes over the early childhood years follows. We also examine ways of assisting and enhancing children's play, the benefits of play, and the time, space, and materials related to play. We conclude the chapter with a brief discussion of playgrounds.

DEFINITIONS AND CHARACTERISTICS

Play has received much attention from educators, researchers, psychologists, and parents for many decades. Many attempts have been made to define it, explain it, understand it, and discover its relationship to many other activities children engage in (Spodek, Saracho, & Davis, 1991). Schwartzman (1978) defined play in terms of what it is not:

> Play is not work; play is not real; play is not serious; play is not productive; and so forth . . .
>
> (Yet) work can be playful while sometimes play can be experienced as work; and likewise, players create worlds that are often more real, serious and productive than so-called real life. (p. 4–5)

This definition, like many others, reflects a difficulty in separating work from play. Neumann (1971) suggests that an activity can be determined to be play according to three criteria, placed on a continuum from work to play. Her work indicates that many activities fall somewhere in this continuum. The three criteria she has identified are as follows:

1. *Control.* There is a difference between internal control and external control of activities. To the extent that control is internal, an activity is play. To the extent that it is external, it is work. In most cases, the control is neither totally internal or external. The only time people can totally control their own play activities is when they are playing alone. As soon as more than one player is involved, control is shared, and this involves a move from internal to external control for each individual.

2. *Reality.* There is a differentiation between internal reality and external reality. One criterion of play is the ability of the player to suspend reality, to act "as if," to pretend, to make believe, to suppress the impact of external reality, to let the internal reality take over. To the extent that an activity is tied to the real world, it stops being play. To the extent that you can act in an as-if way, you are acting in a playful manner. Most play, however, maintains some tie with external reality.

3. *Motivation.* To the extent that an activity is internally motivated, it is play. As soon as the motivation is external, it stops being play. Seldom is the motivation entirely internal or external.

Rubin, Fein, and Vandenberg (1983) suggest that most definitions identify play by the state of mind of those who are playing. Motivation is also important in their definition. They have identified the following criteria:

1. Play is personally motivated by the satisfaction embedded in the activity and not governed either by basic needs and drives or by social demands.
2. Players are concerned with activities more than with goals. Goals are self-imposed and the behavior of the players is spontaneous.
3. Play occurs with familiar objects, or following the exploration of unfamiliar objects. Children supply their own meanings to play activities and control the activity themselves.
4. Play activities can be nonliteral.
5. Play is free from rules imposed from the outside, and the rules that do exist can be modified by the players.
6. Play requires the active engagement of the players.

THEORIES OF PLAY

The work of Neumann (1971), Schwartzman (1978), Rubin et al. (1983), and other researchers provides useful information in defining play more clearly and communicating about play more accurately. But we still need to understand why people (and especially children) play. Gilmore (1971) identified the various theories dealing with the reasons why people play. The classical theories date back to before World War I and are not based on any research. These include the surplus energy theory, the recreation theory, the pre-exercise theory, and the recapitulation theory (see Table 5.1). Although educators continue to use these theories in their discussions about why children play, none of these theories adequately explains the causes of play in all situations (Frost, 1992).

TABLE 5.1 Classical Theories of Play

Theory	Originator	Major Purpose of Play
Surplus energy	Schiller and Spencer	Eliminate surplus energy
Recreation	Lazarus	Regenerate energy expended in work
Recapitulation	Hall	Eliminate ancient instincts
Pre-exercise	Groos	Perfect instincts needed for adult life

Surplus Energy

The **surplus energy theory** suggests that we, as organisms, are continually generating energy. Most of that energy is used up by working or taking care of our basic needs. When we have energy that is left over, we expend that energy by playing. This theory could be used to explain why children still have so much energy at the end of the school day and are able to play into the evening before bedtime.

Recreation

The **recreation theory** focuses on energy in a different way. In this theory, play serves to restore the energy we expend during work or meeting our basic needs. After a period of sustained work, we need a period of play in which we can relax. This theory reinforces the notion that children need an active experience if they have been asked to sit quietly for awhile. It also explains the need for adults to engage in a an active experience like jogging or racquetball after a sedentary day at the office.

Recapitulation

The **recapitulation theory** suggests that we all go through stages in our personal development that we have gone through in the development of the human race. Play is an instinctive way of ridding ourselves of primitive skills and drives that have been carried through the ages of civilization. In this theory, play prepares the child for activities of modern life. Therefore, the play of children more closely resembles the activities of primitive people than those of modern adults. You might say this theory implies that the need to play baseball could be traced back to the primitive behavior of a hunter-gatherer.

Pre-exercise

The **pre-exercise theory** (sometimes called the practice theory) suggests that play is instinctive behavior and prepares children for their adult life. Play is viewed as preparation for future work. An example is the child taking on adult roles in the housekeeping center of the kindergarten.

Other Theories

Two contemporary theories that view play in a more dynamic way are the psychodynamic and the constructivist theories. According to Sigmund Freud and Erik Erikson, the proponents of psychodynamic theory, play allows children to express ideas, feelings, fears, and anxieties. In this view, play is seen as a cathartic activity. It enables children to express feelings they cannot handle rationally.

Constructivist theory is rooted in the work of Jean Piaget. He viewed the development of knowledge in children as being created or constructed by two related processes, called assimilation and accommodation. In the process of assimilation, the child takes in information and experiences and fits these structures into the already existing structural framework for understanding. Sometimes new information cannot fit into the existing framework. As a result, a change or modification must occur. Changing the sense of what a child knows in relation to new information is called accommodation.

TEACHERS SPEAK OUT

There is so much to be learned from play. Children discover things we could never teach them as they interact with each other and the materials around them.

Play, according to Piaget (1962), is a way of abstracting elements from the outside world and changing them so that they fit the person's existing framework. As such, play serves a vital role in the developing intellect of children. Piaget defined three distinct stages in the development of play. The first is the sensorimotor stage, which has practice play as its dominant type. This is based on reflexive physical behaviors. The second is a level of symbolic play, demonstrated by the preschooler through pretend play. In the third stage, children's play involves games with rules. This play is typical of the child in the primary grades.

Other theories have been recognized as contributing to the explanation of why children play and what function play serves. Vygotsky (1967) found that play assists with the development of language and thought. He sees play as an aspect of the young child's experience that enables the child to advance beyond the ordinary accomplishments of the age period. As Vygotsky states, the young child is "always above his average age, above his daily behavior." Accordingly, "play creates the zone of proximal development of the child" (p. 16).

Ellis (1973) suggests that people are normally mentally active. He seeks to understand play as information processing. According to Ellis, people are continually attempting to make sense out of the information that is being processed. The young child often uses play as a way of creating information internally through fantasy play. White's (1959) theory of competence motivation suggests that children gain satisfaction from being competent in play situations. Play helps children develop competency because it allows them to act on their environment and experience some control over objects, ideas, and situations.

CHANGES IN PLAY DEVELOPMENT

Another issue adding to the complexity of the study of play is that it changes as children grow and develop. Changes have been noted in social and intellectual aspects by several child development specialists. Mildred Parten (1932) identified social play of young children as either **unoccupied play** (not playing), **solitary play** (playing alone), or **onlooker play** (watching others play). Parten also states that children engage in **parallel play** (playing side by side), **associative play** (shifting between parallel play and cooperative), and **cooperative play** (engaging in play with other children). Parten's work continues to be used in discussions about children's play, although more recent studies have raised doubts about when children engage in these types of play.

Parten viewed parallel play as a bridge between solitary play and cooperative play or group play. A number of studies suggest that children sometimes move directly from solitary play to social play, with parallel play serving as the transitional type. In a replication of Parten's study, Barnes (1971) found children to be less social than those in Parten's sample of 3-, 4-, and 5-year-olds continuing to engage in solitary play. Researchers and educators tend to view these activities as types of play rather than stages of play (Eddowes, 1991).

This child constructs knowledge about structures and space as she exhibits solitary play.

Among other skills, these boys learn science and math concepts as they explore with materials in the water table.

Jean Piaget (1962) outlined early stages in play development as practice play, symbolic play, and games with rules. These stages correspond with Piaget's stages of cognitive development (discussed earlier in the text) called *sensorimotor*, *preoperational*, and *concrete operations*. Smilansky (1968) used Piaget's stages for her study of young children. She defines functional play as simple motor activity or routine use of play materials. She views constructive play as purposeful, sequential, and resulting in a finished product. She defines dramatic play as role play that involves transforming situations or objects.

Teachers continue to use the work of Parten, Piaget, and Smilansky to determine the level at which children are playing in their classrooms. Rubin, Maioni, and Hornung (1976) have used this information in researching the impact of interventions on the play behavior of young children. Teachers can observe their children's play and modify the setting by asking questions, replacing materials, and assisting children in directing their play. Knowing the types of play would help prevent teachers from distorting the play situation and help prevent children from becoming so reality oriented or sensitive to adult authority (Spodek, Saracho, & Davis, 1991).

ASSISTING CHILDREN'S PLAY

There is no doubt that play is a critical activity in the lives of young children. Play serves as a way for children to develop understanding about their world and their experiences (Swick, Brown, & Graves, 1984). It gives children an opportunity to express ideas and feelings. By nurturing and facilitating children's play, teachers become supportive rather than directive in their teaching (Spodek & Saracho, 1988). Teachers who understand the value of play are more likely to develop strong, positive attitudes toward it and provide many opportunities for children to engage in play experiences (Dimidjian, 1991).

Most programs for young children provide a large part of the day for play activities. These activities are often initiated simply by making materials available to children. It is important for teachers to carefully plan these experiences. Planning should include considerations of space, materials, time, and expectations. Spodek, Saracho, and Davis (1991) suggest that teachers should be active in initiating and extending children's play. Spodek and Saracho (1988) recommend that to maximize the effectiveness of children's play, teachers must

(*a*) Offer a supportive environment with sufficient play areas, materials, and equipment;

(*b*) Foster positive social interactions; and

(*c*) Extend (i.e. make home productive) children's play.

A short meeting between the teacher and children to plan for the play activities can be very valuable. In this meeting, the teacher can introduce new materials, discuss expectations and limits about the materials, and review any time or space issues. These discussions can stimulate children's interests, thinking, and planning. A new medium, material, or activity should pique children's imaginations.

Teachers can facilitate children's play by adding or taking away materials from the play environment. If an activity is totally new in the children's experience, they may need a lot of guidance and assistance in the process. If the children have experience with the activity, they may require less guidance and facilitation. The teachers may need to make signs, assign roles, and provide resources. Teachers must be careful to monitor materials, information, and structure.

BENEFITS OF PLAY

Although researchers have distinguished various forms of play (functional play, rough-and-tumble play, constructive play, pretend play, and games), in this section we address the functions and benefits of

Much intellectual and social learning occurs as these children work cooperatively on putting puzzles together.

play for young children (Pellegrini, 1988; Rubin et al., 1983). We focus here on how play assists the child in developing intelligence, personality, and competencies. In Chapters 6 through 8, we will examine the benefits of play in greater detail.

Development of Intelligence

Natural activities that young children engage in are almost exclusively in play situations. The character and context of nonplay activity demand a way of guiding your own activity that young children are incapable of in the early childhood years. During these early years, the child's intelligence is marked by a lack of equilibrium between the two functions of intelligence—assimilation and accommodation. The child's understanding of the world is full of contradictions because of the inability to use logic. Until this equilibrium is achieved, the child is bound in intellectual ability by this inability to form a stable, logical, objective view of the world (Van Hoorn et al., 1993).

Development of Personality

The entire range of children's needs, emotions, and ideas are expressed in play. Their play themes deal with fear, power, acceptance, rejection, and many other feelings. Emotions and social interactions are practiced and connected to children's real needs, but are also imagined in play situations. These experiences help shape children's personalities. Piaget discussed a process called *reflective abstraction*, which is necessary and inevitable in the case of intelligence, but not inevitable in the case of personality. He created this concept to describe the way intelligence works its way up the developmental ladder. In reflective abstraction, the child, through representation, brings into recognized forms the unrealized or unrecognized relationships that already exist in the child's practice or practical behaviors. This is a natural, regulative process that advances intelligence through the activity of bringing unrealized ideas into representational focus (Piaget, 1977).

In the case of intelligence, this process is inevitable because the child attempts to formulate goals and direct actions to reach those goals. Reflective abstraction causes the child to represent goals, represent links between goals and actions, and to realize goals. For example, in trying to put a necklace of beads in a cup, a toddler might imagine (represent) what would happen if the beads fell over the side, knocking the cup and beads over onto the floor. In bunching the beads into a ball and dropping it into the cup, the child represents the goal (getting the necklace into the cup), the obstacle (the necklace knocking the cup over), and the solution (bunching the necklace into the ball).

In the case of personality, the child's psychological and emotional self can remain relatively unconscious and focused on actions that can remain unreflected throughout life. As an illustration, consider a child who develops a certain coping mechanism that becomes a large part of her behavior and personality. The origin of this behavior may be unknown and not available to the child for reflection. For the personality to continue the process of development, it requires constant reflective activity. Play serves an important role in this endeavor.

Development of Competencies

During the early childhood years, children develop a large number and variety of competencies in all areas of their development. Before entering a 5-year-old kindergarten class, many children have developed most of their language system, can dress themselves, can initiate social interactions, can express their needs and feelings, and have good motor coordination. Play provides the context as well as the practice for these competencies and others to develop and increase.

ADULT ROLES IN CHILDREN'S PLAY

Wood, McMahon, and Cranstoun (1980) discovered that teachers become involved in children's play in four different ways, which have different effects on children (see Table 5.2). Through their study of teacher-child interactions in British preschools, they labeled the kinds of involvement as:

(*a*) Parallel playing
(*b*) Co-playing
(*c*) Play tutoring
(*d*) Being a spokesperson for reality

Parallel playing is demonstrated when the adult is close to the child and plays with the same materials. The adult does not attempt to take over the play, however. You can usually see this type of play during functional play or constructive play. For example, if a child is sitting on the floor playing with Lincoln Logs, the adult sits near the child and builds with some of the materials. The adult may talk about the structures being built, but does not attempt to engage the child in conversation about the structures. The adult's presence in this context can comfort the child and validate that the activity is valuable. Children are likely to persist longer when an adult is close. Another benefit is that the children may learn some new possibilities for creating structures by observing the adult. In this scenario, however, it is important or appropriate for the adult to attempt to guide the child's play.

TEACHERS SPEAK OUT

One of the hardest aspects of teaching is learning to let go; learning to follow the child, not forcing the child to follow you.

Co-playing occurs when an adult joins in a play episode in progress, but allows the child to control the play episode. The adult may respond to the child's comments and possibly ask questions that could extend the play. Co-playing offers the same type of approval and encourages persistence in the same way as parallel playing. But adults extend these benefits building rapport and influencing the play. This type of play provides an opportunity for the adult to model appropriate social behaviors and language. It does not involve tutoring or teaching the children any new behaviors. Co-playing is most often noted in sociodramatic play or constructive play.

Play tutoring differs from co-playing in three important ways. In play tutoring, the adult often initiates a new play episode, where the adult co-player always joins in a play episode in progress. Another difference is that in play tutoring, the adult takes a more dominant role in the play. The third distinction in this type is that the adult teaches the children new play behaviors. Play tutoring is typically used to teach children how to engage in sociodramatic play. According to Smilansky (1968), sociodramatic play contains the following five elements:

1. *Role playing.* The child adopts a make-believe role, such as doctor or teacher, and communicates this transformation verbally and with role-appropriate behavior.

2. *Make-believe transformations.* Objects, actions, and words are used to substitute other objects, actions, or situations. For example, a child may use a block to represent a microphone and deliver the evening news to the other children.

3. *Social interaction.* At least two players must interact with each other in the play episode.

4. *Verbal communication.* The children engage in verbal exchanges related to the play episode. These exchanges are usually classified as metacommunications or pretend communications. In metacommunications, the children comment about the play (i.e., "You be the doctor and I'll be the patient"). Pretend communications describes the children's comments that are appropriate for the role that they are enacting (for example, "Now I need to examine your eyes and ears, Mrs. Jones").

5. *Persistence.* The children engage in sustained play episodes. Most young children can sustain at least a ten-minute episode.

If the teacher or other supervising adult learns through observation that children are missing some of these elements in their play, play tutoring may be advised. Smilansky (1968) identified two types of play tutoring in her play-training study: outside intervention and inside intervention. In outside intervention, the adult remains on the outside of the play episode. From this vantage point, the adult suggests ways to encourage sociodramatic play behaviors. Inside intervention occurs when the adult takes on a role in the play episode and directs the course of the play by actions and comments.

TABLE 5.2
Adult Roles in Children's Play

Type	Adult Roles
Parallel playing	Plays with the child and materials but does not take charge.
Co-playing	Joins a child in a play episode but allows the child to control the play. Modeling social behaviors and language is appropriate. No tutoring or teaching.
Play tutoring	Initiates new play episodes. Takes a more dominant role. Teaches new play behaviors.
Spokesperson for reality	Remains outside the play but encourages children to connect play with the real world. Interjects reality into the play episode.

The fourth type of adult involvement in play, according to Wood et al., is being a spokesperson for reality. This usually occurs when play is used as a medium for academic instruction. The adult remains outside the play but encourages children to make connections between their play and the real world. Instead of encouraging make-believe, the adult in this type interjects reality into the play episode. This form of involvement is particularly effective with older children.

TYPES OF PLAY

Children engage in and illustrate various types of play during the early childhood years (see Table 5.3). We discussed the social play of young children in an earlier section of this chapter. Parten (1932) identified those social types of play as unoccupied, solitary, onlooker, parallel, associative, and cooperative. In this section, we address the following types of play:

- Functional
- Construction
- Symbolic
- Sociodramatic

Functional Play

Functional play is described by some as the child's first type of play. It consists of simple, repetitive actions. This type usually occurs in the infancy stage and is sometimes called *exercise play*. This stage soon evolves into a time when the baby discovers that if she hits the mobile, she can make it sway back and forth. Play begins when the child engages in this type of activity for functional pleasure (Buhler, 1935), often smiling and laughing at her actions. Functional play may also include humming, babbling, and other vocalizations.

The young child learns very quickly about physical capabilities and cause-and-effect relationships by acting on objects in the environment. For example, a baby learns that if she strikes the square on the busy box, it makes a certain sound. She also learns that if she strikes the circle, it makes a different sound. Functional play is usually thought of as occurring in the first two years of life, but it can continue through the childhood years whenever the child learns a new skill.

Construction Play

Construction play is not viewed by Piaget as a distinct stage of play like functional play, symbolic play, and games with rules. This is in contrast to Buhler and Smilansky. Piaget maintained that construction play occupies a position between play and work. While the three stages of play (practice, symbolic, and games with rules) correspond to the three forms of intelligence (sensorimotor, representational, and reflective), construction games are not perceived as a distinct stage. Piaget described them as occupying "at the second and particularly at the third level, a position half-way between work or between play and imitation" (1962, p. 113).

KIDS SPEAK UP

I like to play house in the sand.

Girl, 4 years old

Smilansky viewed construction play as a distinct stage that typically emerges around the age of 22–24 months. This is when the toddler plays with a purpose. For example, the child who makes a mountain out of his mashed potatoes and says proudly, "It's like our vacation mountain," has made his creation with a goal in mind. Preschoolers become more purposeful in their play through language, movement, manipulating objects and ideas, imitation, and dramatics. Providing the child with a wealth of materials contributes to this type of purposeful play and learning.

Symbolic Play

Symbolic play, frequently called *dramatic play*, involves representation of an absent object. The child who puts the empty cup to her mouth and drinks all the iced tea is engaging in symbolic play. In this way, young children create their own reality. Frost (1992) uses an example of a 2-year-old child whose mother refuses his request for a cookie because it's almost time for supper. The child then brings his hands to his mouth and smacks his lips as if he were enjoying a cookie. Through this type of symbolic play, the child learns to resolve a conflict.

Sociodramatic Play

Sociodramatic play is the most highly developed form of symbolic play. It occurs when the child is pretending to take on the role and responsibilities of someone else. Often in this situation, the child takes on the actions, speech, and gestures of someone she has en-

TABLE 5.3
Types of Play

Type	Description
Functional	Child's first play. Exploratory, simple, repetitive actions. Usually thought of as occurring in infancy.
Construction	Plays with a purpose. Usually emerges about 22–24 months.
Symbolic	Represents absent objects. Assists in learning to resolve conflicts.
Sociodramatic	Child pretends to take on roles and responsibilities of someone else. Assists in learning control, flexibility, and responsibility.

countered. This type of play contains two elements, the imitative one and the reality element. Pretending aids in imitation and gives children pleasure when they "try on" adult roles. Sociodramatic play enables the child to learn responsibility, control, and flexibility.

FACILITATING PLAY

It is very important for teachers to use the information about play that we present in this chapter. With this information, teachers can assist and facilitate children's play processes and experiences. Teachers should always consider the developmental levels of children, the benefits of play, the competencies that are developed, and the roles adults play in children's playful experiences.

Preparing for Play

Among the most important considerations for the teacher in preparing for children's play are time, space, and materials. If the play is unstructured, not teacher-directed, these considerations help teachers decide the range and quality of play. Many decisions focusing on these issues must be made. Questions about time should include the following:

- How much free play time should I allow?
- Will there be enough time to complete child-initiated projects?
- How long will children remain engaged in play?
- How should I balance indoor play time and outdoor play time?

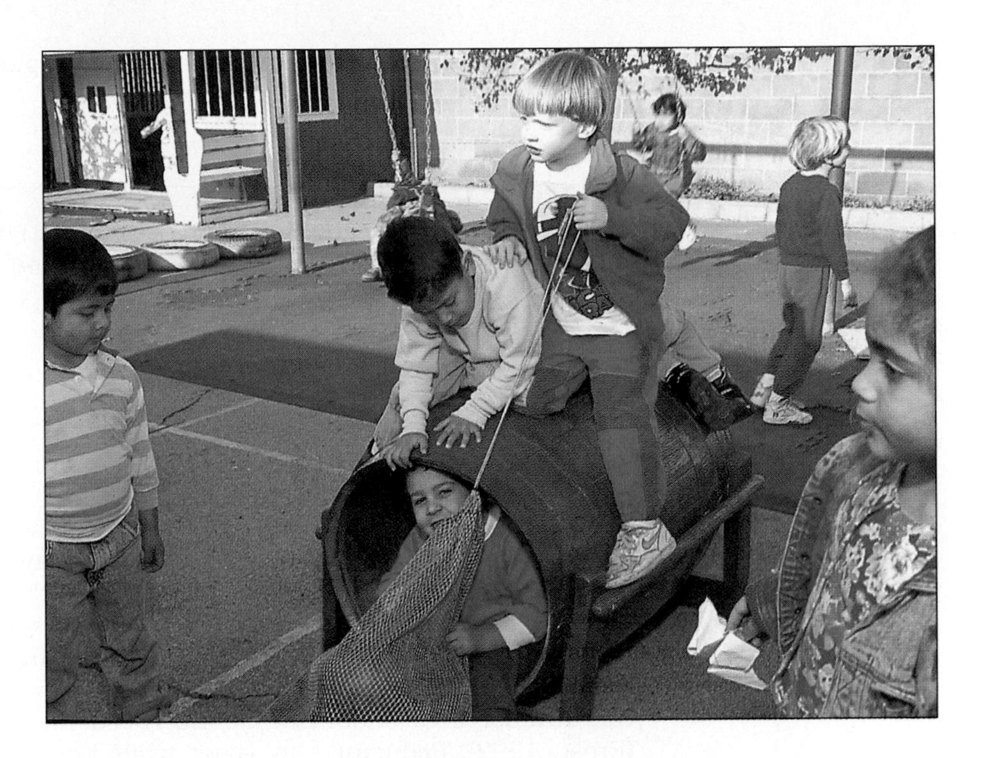

Ample time, space, and materials on the playground provide opportunities for children to engage in learning.

Time

If children are provided an ample amount of appropriate materials and are relatively free (with limits) from adult intrusion, their imaginative play tends to increase in time and intensity (Frost, 1992). For example, several preschoolers initiate astronaut play in a learning center. It takes them only a short time before they begin assigning roles to the players: "You watch the controls while we get ready for liftoff." As blastoff time nears, the astronauts perform many jobs to assist with the preparation.

As other children join in, more time and materials are needed. Play roles of children are enhanced by time for developing the play situation. Careful planning, readily available materials, and defining the play space are important in facilitating play.

Since all children are different, it is difficult to determine the amount of time needed for this scenario. If children are really engaged, this scenario may extend for 20 minutes. Many programs for 4- and 5-year-old children provide 30- to 50-minute periods for free play (Johnson, Christie, & Yawkey, 1987). In full-day kindergarten programs, an hour may be needed (Peters, Neisworth, & Yawkey, 1985). It is much better to provide large blocks of time for preschoolers and primary-aged children because play themes require time to develop and should take place in a relaxed, undirected setting. Many programs provide more time than we mentioned above. Some teachers are inclined to be very rigid about ending free-play times. This behavior risks a separation from the flow of play and learning and sometimes from meaning and memory.

> **TEACHERS SPEAK OUT**
>
> All the wonderful equipment cannot replace a teacher who is committed to and understands Early Childhood.

Space

Play spaces may be as varied as a throw rug, a table, a housekeeping center, or an outdoor superstructure. The player usually selects the space, and the boundaries are determined by the themes that emerge. In this sense, the child's energy, imagination, age and developmental levels of the players, materials and equipment, and time determine the space. The indoor space should be about 50 square feet per child; the outdoor area should be about 100 square feet per active child (Frost, 1992). Reducing play space while holding the number of children constant has been found to increase physical contact (McGrew, 1972), increase onlooker behavior (Peck & Goldman, 1978), decrease participation (Phyfe-Perkins, 1980), and increase aggression and decrease group play (Smith & Connolly, 1980).

Questions about space should include the following:

- Have I defined the play spaces to allow for freedom, but not to encourage chaos?
- Should I limit the number of children in different spaces?
- Have I separated noisy spaces from quiet ones? Private spaces from more public ones? Wet or messy spaces from dry spaces?
- Can I monitor all the spaces I have provided?
- When should I change the size of spaces?
- Are the spaces set up in such a way that running is not encouraged?
- Are the spaces safe and healthy?

Materials

Setting up the environment for play determines for the children what should happen in the area. If an area in the classroom is set up with a sand and water play table and props, the children know precisely what is expected to go on in that area. But this type of table may be filled with sand, water, packing pellets, rice, beans, or other materials. Children should also be provided with measuring and pouring containers, scales, paper for recording, and other props.

KIDS SPEAK UP

You be the mommy—and I'll be the daddy—and you be coming home from work—and I'll be looking for a pan to cook—and you be telling me about the dog and. . . .

Girl, 6 years old

The best type of indoor or outdoor area is one that changes and evolves over time. If the area is designed for imaginative or dramatic play, then appropriate props should be provided. In addition to dress-up clothes, numerous household items should also be found in this area. This area may be a launching pad one week and a veterinary office or a post office the next week. Appropriate items should be provided to enhance the play of the children. Items such as juice cans, pipe cleaners, and paper towel rolls may be helpful to supply, but do not encourage as much imagination. Pretend roles are encouraged more with items like cardboard boxes or large, hollow blocks. Manipulation and construction are aided by materials like large cylinders, large pieces of foam, and unit blocks (Dodge & Frost, 1986).

Questions about materials should include the following:

- Are there ample appropriate materials in all play spaces?
- Are there enough materials to provide multiple uses and a variety of play themes?
- Are there enough materials that are more than one-dimensional (boxes, blocks)?
- Am I recycling materials and props enough so that children are not growing tired of the same materials in the same spaces?

Teachers of young children should regularly ask themselves these and other questions. More information on these issues can be found in Chapter 7, "Teaching and Learning Environments."

PLAYGROUNDS

Playgrounds for young children differ as much as young children in classrooms. Some are ample in space, rich with equipment, and abundant with levels, platforms, safe surfaces, and climbing appara-

Wide slides and multi-level platforms allow for planning, interaction, and reflection.

tus. Some are barren, uninteresting, uninviting, and unchallenging. The values and benefits of play are widely documented by researchers. Play is fun, spontaneous, and can enhance learning and development. Playgrounds, like large boxes, should offer open-ended types of play and play themes. Outdoor play can assist the child in developing responsibility, problem-solving abilities, cooperation, spatial abilities, and a variety of other skills and abilities.

The playground should offer a variety of forms, textures, colors levels, and challenges (Frost, 1992). It should challenge the child in all areas of development, yet be comfortable and inviting (Guddemi & Jambor, 1993). It should also support the basic developmental needs of the child. A good playground allows and encourages interaction with children, materials, themes, and adults.

Many playgrounds of today are built around a superstructure. This focal piece of equipment is a fixed structure that usually offers several platforms linked with steps, clatter bridges, cargo nets, ropes, fireman's poles, climbers, slides, swings, etc. Many of these commercially made superstructures are designed so that other structures can be added. All climbing and moving equipment should be installed over a safe surface. Surfaces, especially in "fall zones," have received much attention in the last decade because of injuries. Surface materials under equipment vary, but are usually sand, pea gravel, bark mulch, or shredded tires. Many of these superstructures are designed, built, and treated not to seep, splinter, or crack. Designers are much more aware of the necessity of covering bolts or screws for safety.

Most playgrounds have a sand area enhanced by props such as buckets, shovels, strainers, and other accessories. Some underside areas of superstructures provide a sand play space as well as a storage space. Storage is an important consideration for support materials, wheel toys, building materials, outdoor art supplies, balls, sand and water play materials, and other materials. Natural features add to the quality of playgrounds. Nature areas, grassy areas, sand areas, mounds and hills, animal habitats, and gardens all contribute to the playground. For more information on playgrounds, see Chapter 8 and Appendixes G through I.

SUMMARY

Programs that are play-oriented have a rich history in the field of early childhood education. Play experiences support children's growth, development, and learning in a variety of ways. Play activities enable children to test ideas, construct knowledge, and integrate what they are learning.

In this chapter, we focused on the types and theories of play as well as on changes in play development. We addressed the functions of play and the relationships of play to the development of intelligence, personality, and competencies. We also discussed the roles adults assume in children's play. Teachers should be constantly aware of the importance of play in young children's growth, development, and learning. We considered the ways of facilitating play related to time, space, and materials; and ended the chapter with a brief examination of playgrounds.

TEST YOUR UNDERSTANDING

1. Where are the roots of play-oriented programs in early childhood education?
2. Describe the benefits of play.
3. Discuss the definition of play.
4. Discuss the pros and cons of the four historical theories discussed in this chapter.
5. Compare the relationship of Piaget's views on play and his stages of cognitive development.
6. Identify classroom situations or scenarios that illustrate Parten's types of social play.
7. Discuss how play contributes to the development of intelligence, personality, and competencies.
8. Describe appropriate adult roles in young children's play.
9. Identify differences between functional play, construction play, symbolic play, and sociodramatic play.
10. Explain how the issues of time, space, and materials can influence children's play.

LEARNING ACTIVITIES

1. Observe three children—ages 2, 4, and 7—engaged in play. Note similarities and differences in the children regarding type of play, type of materials used, type of language accompanying the play, type of social interactions, and other behaviors.
2. Interview a day-care teacher and a second-grade teacher about the play opportunities available in the classroom. Find out how much time is allocated for "free play," what materials are available, what types of instruction the children receive before free play, what limits are placed on the children, how much time the children are allowed to play in each area, and other related questions.
3. Observe the play of an early childhood classroom to determine if the children exhibit all the five elements of Smilansky's sociodramatic play.
4. Observe a group of young children at play on a playground, and complete the Infant-Toddler Playground Maintenance Checklist (Appendix I).

CHAPTER 6

Creativity

CHAPTER OUTLINE

What Is Creativity?

Creativity and the Early Years

- *Stimulating Creativity*
- *Significance of Creativity*

Identifying Creativity in Children

- *Creativity and Intelligence*
- *Creativity and Giftedness*

Origins of Creativity

- *Hemispheric Functions*
- *Creative Concepts*

Fostering a Creative Environment

- *Benefits to Children*
- *Benefits to Teachers*
- *Parents and Creativity*
- *Schools: Creativity vs. Conformity*
- *Motivating Creativity*

Self-Expressive Activities for Creativity

- *Two-Dimensional Self-Expressive Activities*
- *Three-Dimensional Self-Expressive Activities*
- *Creative Dramatics*
- *Music and Rhythm*
- *Literature*

KEY TERMS

Creativity
Creative impulses
Right cerebral hemisphere
Left cerebral hemisphere
Self-expressive activities
Convergent thinking
Divergent thinking

The children in the early childhood center each selected a story or poem and decided to illustrate their favorite parts of the literature. Austin chose the "Owl and the Pussycat" and used water colors to paint an illustration. As the teacher watched him complete the project, it became apparent that his design was a carefully detailed ship with no owl or pussycat.

When Austin sought approval of the work, the teacher assumed he had neglected to include the animals due to an oversight, or perhaps the characters were too difficult to paint. Of course, the beautiful "pea green boat" could have interested Austin more than other aspects of the story. As the teacher interacted with him, she commented, "Your painting is interesting. Tell me about the picture."

When Austin began to discuss the painting, the reason for the absence of the characters became clear. "You see," he explained, "the Owl and the Pussycat went out in this boat so they could go swimming under the water. So, I painted them under the water."

The teacher responded enthusiastically, "That is a very creative idea. Let's hang your painting up so others can see it."

The teacher's acknowledgement of Austin's thought as creative suggests appreciation and approval of the effort. The painting is a concrete representation of a child's creative thought. This interaction between Austin and his teacher will surely foster feelings of success and encourage him in continuing to explore other creative interpretations.

Both casual and planned opportunities for creative experiences abound within the early childhood setting. Issues such as problem solving, investigating, discovering, understanding, learning, and inventing may be perceived as creative. But do teachers recognize the value of these experiences in terms of their creative potential? What does the word *creative* mean in the development of a young child? What approaches do teachers use to encourage creativity? Throughout this chapter, we consider these questions as well as some issues of the origins of creativity, approaches to defining the term, and the influences parents, teachers, and schools have on creative development.

Creativity involves a flexibility of thought that appears to be a natural process in human beings. In its simplest form, creativity involves initiating approaches to accomplish a simple goal (such as getting out of a jacket when the zipper is jammed). In its most complex form, it is the unification of psychology, biology, sociology, culture, education, intellect, physiology, and experiences that prompt a new and original concept or product. This collaboration is critical to the processes of discovery, formulating new hypotheses, implementing innovations, and conducting experimental research (Chukowsky, 1968). The relationship between creativity and imagination appears to be significant in problem solving and essential to survival.

KIDS SPEAK UP

Sometimes when we play with the music instruments, I use a bowl and spoon to make a drum. I can do that at school . . . not at home, ok?

Boy, 5 years old

The importance of nurturing creative development is enhanced by our need to invent, discover, and resolve the continuing issues of society. Certainly, few questions and issues have easy answers. Consequently, our ability to look beyond expected approaches and investigate with confidence is essential. This ability to move beyond the expected or known is by its nature creative.

WHAT IS CREATIVITY?

Although there are many approaches to defining creativity as a process, product, innate ability, or fostered skill, no single definition appears to be universally accepted. But some terms seem to unify discussions on creativity. *Creativity* is most often identified as the ability to approach something in a novel or unusual manner. As a process of thought, creativity suggests a unique solution to a problem, product, or an effort (Baer, 1993).

In some interpretations, creativity is explained as the ability to generate an original idea or to adapt the ideas of others. Gardner (1989) further suggests that creativity is the capacity to regularly solve problems or produce work in a manner that is not only novel, but is also ultimately accepted by society.

For purposes of this discussion, we choose to define the term based on the approaches children use to resolve problems. As children confront the challenges of each day, they initiate creative approaches to construct the answers they need. Therefore, creativity in young children is defined as "an approach to thinking, acting, or making something that is original to the child and may be appreciated by the child and others." With this definition, we recognize the process of creativity as an individual effort. We do not necessarily suggest that the idea has never been considered by anyone before the child generates the thought, demonstrates the style, or initiates the act. Creativity is, by this interpretation, a very personal process. If the innovation is new to the child, valued by the individual, and appreciated by others, it is creative.

Each developmental milestone can offer a new way for children to explore, discover, and create ideas.

CREATIVITY AND THE EARLY YEARS

We all use innovative approaches to investigate the world from birth and throughout life. A progressive unfolding of developmental skills enables children to continually explore the world creatively. As a new skill develops, such as speech, children explore the possibilities that new skill offers. Each developmental milestone presents opportunities for imagination to flourish (Fein, 1986). These imaginative efforts may be encouraged through adult-to-child, child-to-material, and child-to-child experiences (Jalongo, 1990). Table 6.1 summarizes some developmental characteristics of imagination and suggests ways of stimulating creativity in very young children.

Stimulating Creativity

As children invest ways to respond to a situation, they use techniques described as **creative impulses** (Maxim, 1989). This term means that before children have determined the correct or acceptable answer to a situation, they initiate systems that satisfy their own needs and interests. This independence of investigation does not depend on the behaviors expected by parents, teachers, or society.

TABLE 6.1 Age-Related Developmental Characteristics of Imagination

Age	Nature of Development Related to Imagination	Stimulation
Birth to 2 yrs.	Speech begins. Explores through touch, taste, sight, hearing, smell. Imagination begins to develop.	• Large blocks, dolls, sensory materials. • Encourage verbal play. • Accept the verbal tags children use. • Listen. • Introduce songs including the child's words.
2 to 4 yrs.	Learns from direct experiences. Develops ways to discover. Short attention span. Independent and curious. Asks questions.	• Representational toys for many things. • Offer environmental experiences such as flowers, pets, etc. • Needs freedom to explore new experiences.
4 to 6 yrs.	Developing planning skills. Work and play evident. Pretend play. Experiences many roles.	• Blocks, paint, manipulatives. • Modeling objects. • Integrate ideas. • Provide opportunities to create.

Considering the nature of the creative impulse, which appears to be the resolving of a situation, even a very young child uses problem-solving strategies. Imagination and opportunity combine with prior experiences to prompt a new approach. Individuals who work with young children will discover a myriad of creative impulses as children seek to fulfill their needs in unexpected ways. Often, the most common examples of creative impulses include the misuse of materials. A toothbrush becomes a hair brush. A shoe may be utilized as an impromptu container. A wagon may be used to reach objects out of the child's reach, or a tablecloth may become a cape.

PARENTS SPEAK OUT

The most creative thing our son has done recently was carefully wrap an entire role of bathroom tissue around his foot so he could have a cast like his teacher who broke her leg.

E. Paul Torrance (1962), a recognized authority on creativity, emphasizes the sensitivity of creative imagination during the early childhood years as a peak time for development. He suggests that children reach the height of creativity between 4 and 4½ years of age, followed by a decline in creativity at about 5 years. This decline correlates with the time most children enter school. The drop in creativity has been regarded by some as a developmentally inevitable phenomenon of maturation. But recent indicators demonstrate that the decline in creativity is not an issue of maturation. The limiting of creativity is best characterized as an environmental effect, and not the product of nature. Current research (New, 1993; Bredekamp, 1987) suggests that children in stimulating and nurturing environments continue to demonstrate creative development. This finding is supported by recent attention to the instructional approaches used in Reggio Emilia, a regional community school system in Italy, which has generated an enthusiasm for the creative potentials for school curricula (Gandini, 1993; Bredekamp, 1993).

The products of young children observed in Reggio Emilia, Italy, suggest that such approaches enhance the development and continuance of creative processes in young children. Through a multistimulus environment, the children of Reggio Emilia are encouraged to use all of their senses and communicative abilities to express their interpretations and understanding in very creative forms. For example, following a visit to a poppy field, children plan and create a wide range of personal interpretations of the experience. These interpretations are left to the creative responses of the children. Teachers serve as guides to the experiences but do not intervene with directives. The resulting efforts of the students are child centered and considered highly creative in comparison to children of the same age who attend other schools.

Katz (1990) observes that the children in these Italian schools are basically no different from children of the same age in any school in the world. The primary difference appears to be the philosophy of the Italian schools to empower children to explore the world through innovative approaches. The remarkable artwork of the school children suggests a discrepancy in the belief that creativity naturally declines during early childhood (New, 1990; Katz, 1990).

Significance of Creativity

The significance of fostering creativity during the early years is its lifelong influence. It has been suggested that although creativity seems less apparent during the middle childhood years, adults who demonstrate creative early childhood initiatives return to them in later life. "Imagination developed during early childhood serves as a foundation for adult creativity" (Gardner, 1993, p. 115).

Preschoolers are openly creative. They are willing to try a variety of ways to use materials. These children are risk takers in exploring ideas that are new to them. But this natural tendency toward creativity may be changed by others. It has been suggested that three points relating to the analysis of creativity can influence an individual's willingness to continue to respond creatively (Csikszentmihalyi, 1988):

- The child's personal attitudes toward the activity
- The work itself in relation to a field of work (For instance, how does a painting compare to other styles of painting?)
- The influence of teachers or adults (Is the child's creativity supported?)

In many instances, a child's success is directly related to his or her ability to conform to adult expectations and follow the rules. In other words, success is often based on meeting the needs of the teacher, parent, or community.

IDENTIFYING CREATIVITY IN CHILDREN

Clearly, "all" children are creative in their approaches to discovering how the world works. But some children appear to be more creative than others. Some children demonstrate creativity in a particular area. Such people are often characterized as being "so creative."

Perkins (1984) identifies six characteristics common to highly creative individuals. The elements contributing to creativity are reflected by the six points of a snowflake model, with each point representing a specific characteristic. The more indicators the child demonstrates, the more creative that person is considered to be by personal and societal standards (Santrock & Yussen, 1992).

According to this model, creative children seek beauty. They consider aesthetics to be practical and necessary. Creative children excel in identifying problems. Such children resolve problems with flexibility and enjoy the challenges of open-ended activities.

Creative thinkers are objective. They not only analyze their work, but also seek the criticism of others. A creative characteristic is the child's willingness to take risks. They are intrinsically motivated and are prompted to be creative in order to satisfy their personal needs. Figure 6.1 illustrates Perkin's approach to creativity.

Often subtle signs of creativity can be noted in children if we take the time to listen and observe. One of the best opportunities for identifying creativity is to consider children during free or independent play. Watch the child who spends a long time with materials. Creative children typically explore many possibilities for using a material before moving to another item.

A creative child often uses resources in unusual or surprising ways. A cardboard box may be far more satisfying to a creative child than the most elaborate toys and materials available. Adults should ask questions and *listen* to the ideas and opinions of the children. Creative children often have variations of events and episodes. Elaborate and detailed stories may demonstrate imagination. Adults

FIGURE 6.1
Snowflake Model of Creativity

Source: Adapted from D. Perkins, Creativity by design. *Educational Leadership* (September 1984), pp. 18–24. Reprinted with permission of the Association for Supervision and Curriculum Development.

should be aware that creative children may exhibit behaviors that are sometimes challenging. Table 6.2 offers an overview of behavioral indicators as well as some remarks that may be signals of a creative child.

Creativity and Intelligence

In addressing the creative development of young children, some foundation information is important. Creativity is sometimes combined with discussions of intelligence and giftedness. It is important to differentiate the terms *creativity*, *intelligence*, and *gifted* (Elkind, 1994).

Just how strongly is creativity related to intelligence? If we accept that creativity is a cognitive and thoughtful process, it must follow that higher levels of creativity are related to higher levels of intelligence. Although a certain level of intelligence is required for an indi-

TABLE 6.2 Signals of Creativity

- *Intense absorption in listening, observing, or doing:* "But I didn't hear you call me for dinner."
- *Intense animation and physical involvement:* "But I can't sit still, I'm thinking."
- *Use of analogies in speech:* "I feel like a caterpillar waiting to become a butterfly."
- *Tendency to challenge ideas of authorities:* "Why do I have to go to school?"
- *Habit of checking many sources:* "Mom, I looked at all the books and watched a TV special and asked my teacher and still can't find where God lives."
- *Taking a close look at things:* "Hey, this centipede only has 99 legs."
- *Eagerness to tell others about discoveries:* "Guess What, Guess What, Guess What...."
- *Continuing in activities after the scheduled time for quitting:* "I did my artwork right through recess today."
- *Showing relationships among apparently unrelated ideas:* "You know what? Your new hat looks just like a butterfly."
- *Following through on ideas set in motion:* "Tomorrow, I'm going to dig for gold in our back yard."
- *Various manifestations of curiosity and wanting to know:* "I just wanted to see what the yard looked like from the top of the roof."
- *Spontaneous use of discovery or experimental approach:* "I thought flour and water would make bread, but all I got was white goo."
- *Excitement in voice about discoveries:* "Flour and water make paste!"
- *Habit of guessing and testing outcomes:* "I put detergent in the birdbath but no birds came to clean up. Can I try some bubble bath today?"
- *Honesty and intense search for truth:* "Mom, I hope this doesn't upset you, but I've come to the conclusion that there is no tooth fairy."
- *Independent action:* "There are not any good books on racing cars. I'm going to write my own."
- *Boldness of ideas:* "But, I think that children should be allowed to vote."
- *Low distractibility:* "I can't come out to play. I'm waiting for my chemicals to dissolve."
- *Manipulation of ideas and objects to obtain combinations:* "I'm going to take this string and this pencil and make a compass."
- *Penetrating observations and questions:* "When snow melts, where does the white go?"
- *Tendency to seek alternatives and explore new possibilities:* "This old shoe would make a great flower pot."
- *Self-initiated learning:* "Yesterday, I went to the library and checked out all the books on dinosaurs."
- *Willingness to consider or toy with strange ideas:* "What if dogs were masters and people were pets?"

Source: Adapted from E. P. Torrance, *Creativity.* (Sioux Falls, SD: Adapt Press, 1969).

vidual to be creative in most fields, many highly intelligent individuals, as measured by standardized tests, are not necessarily creative (Wakefield, 1991).

Experts in creative research believe that intelligence and creativity are not the same thing (Winner, 1989; Gardner, 1993). Everyone has some degree of creativity. Educators should realize that creativity is as natural to the average person as it is to a genius (Torrance,

1962). Four possible relationships between intelligence and creativity are explored in the following discussion (Wallach and Kogan, 1965):

- **Children with low IQs may demonstrate highly creative characteristics**. They are typically frustrated with traditional school settings. These children may appear cautious and lack self-confidence. They become disruptive in situations which do not allow creative outlets.
- **Children with low IQs may demonstrate low creativity characteristics**. Such children do not appear to understand the purpose for school. When interacting with others they may demonstrate characteristics which are intensely physical, passive, or they may retreat from a challenging situation.
- **Children with high IQs may demonstrate highly creative characteristics**. Individuals who excel in both areas appear to be flexible to changes. They adapt easily to different learning environments. These children are able to balance personal behaviors to meet serious situations when necessary or be relaxed and playful when appropriate. They appear to be very self-confident and may at times engage in attention-getting and disruptive behaviors. Typically, children with high IQs and high levels of creativity attend to school tasks and enjoy their own successes. They are self-motivating.
- **Children with high IQs may demonstrate low creativity characteristics**. Such children are devoted to school achievement. They typically exhibit high attention spans and self-confidence. These children conform to rules and characteristically respond well to positive reinforcement.

TEACHERS SPEAK OUT

Children are born with a talent and flair for creativity which we, as early childhood educators, must nurture. All our art should be process-oriented, investigative, imaginative, hands-on, and open-ended. Preschool is the last time that children will be allowed to explore the various media and to expand their creativity. Once they enter elementary school, it will be drummed out of them by the "necessity" to cut along lines, color within lines, glue pre-cut shapes onto pre-ordained spaces, keep everything neat and tidy, etc., etc., etc.

Getzel and Jackson (1962) found teachers preferred students with high IQs who demonstrate less creativity, because they also display characteristics that suggest greater conformity to rules and expectations. Children who are creative at both high and low IQ standards exhibit styles of learning that require more opportunities to explore and are seldom concerned with the boundaries of an assignment.

Creativity and Giftedness

The terms *gifted, talented,* and *creative* are often associated, although there are distinctions. Giftedness is the ability to excel in a given area. A person may be musically gifted but not creative. The talent or gift may be the ability to perform, which does not necessarily include the ability to create a new song. The creative songwriter may not possess the talent or gift to perform the creation.

In some school systems, children who are identified as gifted have above-average intelligence (an IQ of generally 130 or higher), a superior talent for something, or both high IQs and exceptional talent. Many school systems emphasize intellectual superiority and academic aptitude when selecting children for gifted programs (Sisk, 1987). Creativity in this context extends beyond the individual's process and creation of a new and unique form. It is the extension of both the highly creative characteristics and intelligence.

In summary, research suggests that intelligence, creativity, and giftedness can indeed be distinguished as separate (Moran, Milgram, Sawyers, & Fu, 1983). Creativity may be a characteristic of giftedness. But individuals may be gifted and not creative. Creativity may also be a characteristic of intelligence; but likewise, individuals who are intelligent may not be creative (Sisk, 1987).

ORIGINS OF CREATIVITY

It has been suggested that current studies in brain functioning may provide some insight into the origins of creativity (Maxim, 1989; Hendricks, 1994). Ornstein (1977; 1978), Restak (1988), and Galin (1976) are among the early researchers to identify the nature of two interactive thinking systems within the brain. The term "brain lateralization" refers to the specialized functions and control of each hemisphere of the brain (Schiamberg, 1989).

Hemispheric Functions

Studies in brain lateralization provide some insights as to how a creative thought may be formed and refined. The cerebrum (the highest brain center) is composed of two halves, which are identified as brain hemispheres and are united by a thick band of connective fibers called the *corpus callosum* (Heller, 1990). Although each hemisphere of the brain looks similar, each performs different functions (Grady & Luecke, 1978; Hellige, 1990). The **right cerebral hemisphere** con-

The left and right hemispheres are responsible for different functions.

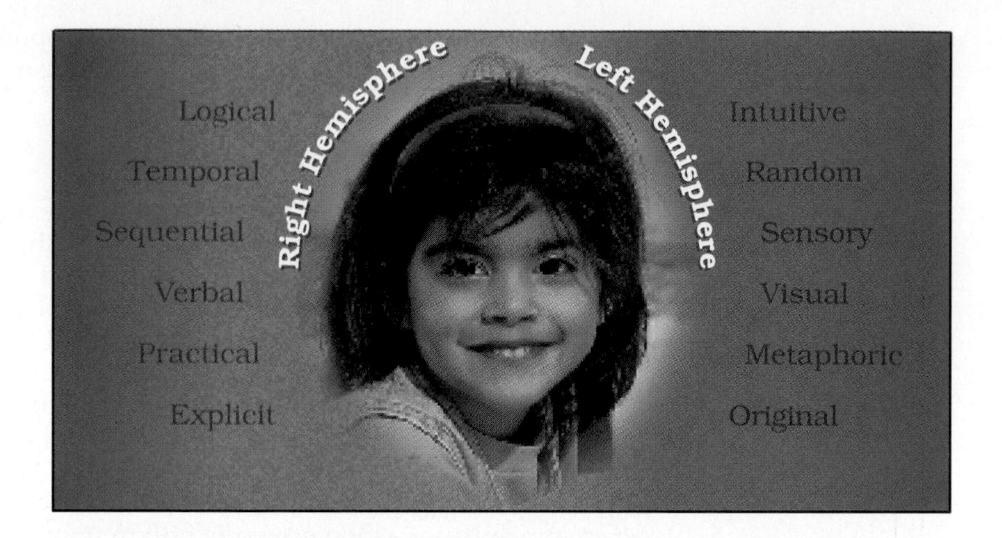

trols the left side of the body, and the **left cerebral hemisphere** controls the right side of the body. The left cerebral hemisphere, which is often referred to as the logical brain, has centers that control such functions as hearing, speech, and processing of verbal information (recognizing groups of letters as words, groups of words as sentences, and motor movements).

Many traditional school tasks that require specific answers or actions are handled through activity originating in the left hemisphere. The right brain interprets information through patterns, images, and emotions. The right brain is frequently viewed as approaching problems in a wholistic manner. It has been suggested that the right hemisphere focuses on the total image, while the left hemisphere focuses on the parts that ultimately make a whole. Lateralization of brain function does not mean that the hemispheres operate independently of each other. The two hemispheres communicate across the corpus callosum to integrate the functions of each hemisphere (Siegler, 1991). Table 6.3 provides an introduction of the hemispheric functions of the brain. As can be surmised, the characteristics of the right hemisphere seem to be more creative, although creativity does not specifically appear in either the right or left hemisphere.

Cherry, Godwin, and Staples (1989) suggest that the production of a creative act is a complex integration of communications between the right and left cerebral hemispheres. An idea originating in the right hemisphere is of limited value unless it is refined and organized for action by the left hemisphere. The two brain hemispheres operating together produce the elements that are referred to as creative.

An issue is the educational or instructional approaches that challenge only one hemispheric domain. Young children have developed skills using the right brain to interact with the environment. School systems often emphasize specific task activities that use basically left hemisphere orientations. As a result, the potential for later-

TABLE 6.3 Asymmetry in Hemispheric Functions

Left Hemisphere	Right Hemisphere
• Analytic Analyzes the data • Logical • Uses logic in handling information • Temporal Is aware of time: past, present, and future • Sequential Deals with information in a variety of systematic ways • Linear • Reduces whole to parts and reassembles parts to the whole • Verbal • Processes language into meaningful communication: receptive and expressive • Compositional Writes music scientifically • Computational Uses mathematical and computations • Practical Concerned with cause and effect • Abstract • Has abstract-oriented cognitive functions • Factual • Uses facts • Concrete Explicit, precise	• Intuitive Responds to data intuitively • Spontaneous • Handles information spontaneously • Atemporal • Processes information without consideration of time • Random • Deals with information according to the need of the moment • Wholistic • Sees the gestalt (wholeness) of information and objects • Nonverbal • Responds to tones, body language, and touch • Responsive • Responds to tones and sounds • Visual-spatial perceives shapes and intuitively estimates • Originative • Concerned with ideas and theories • Sensory • Has sensory-oriented cognitive functions • Visual • Uses imagery • Metaphoric • Symbolic, representational

Source: C. Cherry, D. Godwin, and J. Staples, *Is the left brain always right? A guide to whole child development.* (Belmont, California: David S. Lake Publishers, 1989), p. 13.

alization may be limited. Clearly, the biological maturation of the child, experiences, and individual differences offer an added dimension to the creative process. Effective programs for children must stimulate the whole brain through a wide range of experiences.

Creative Concepts

One common distinction between intelligence and creativity involves the process of thinking. **Convergent thinking** produces one correct answer and is characteristic of the kind of thinking required on standardized intelligence tests, whereas **divergent thinking** produces many possible answers to the same question and is more characteristic of creativity (Guilford, 1967; Runco, 1991). For example, the following intellectual problem-solving tasks characterize an intelligence test that has one answer. How many pennies are equal to a nickel?

Convergent activities elicit one correct answer (Baer, 1993), but divergent activities stimulate a multitude of responses. Divergent activities therefore encourage creativity. A balance of convergent and divergent experiences is the challenge of knowledgeable teachers.

It is essential that teachers be able to recognize and distinguish activities that promote creative experiences and those that inhibit creativity. The simplicity of the definition is misleading when faced with the perspective of making careful choices. For example, most educators would agree that simply asking a child how many pennies equal the value of a nickel is a one-answer question, and therefore convergent. But the same teacher may find it difficult to accept that game boards, picture puzzles, and coloring sheets are convergent. All of these activities result in limited correct responses. Traditional activities that require cutting out patterns and putting them together to look like the teacher's model are convergent. Questioning strategies that prompt a specific answer are also convergent.

KIDS SPEAK UP

My picture was going to be of a blue flower but now I think it's the sky or maybe a lake!

Boy, 5 years old

Divergent activities provide an opportunity for many answers. Benjamin Bloom (1956; 1964) and Baron and Sternberg (1987) suggest that divergent approaches produce higher levels of thought, which include evaluation and creation. Questioning strategies that provide opportunities to extend ideas include "What do you think; what could we do; how could we make it better?" Consider the following list of materials or activities that are classified as convergent or divergent processes:

Material	**Process**
Picture puzzles	Convergent
Blocks	Divergent
Dolls	Divergent
Water paints	Divergent
Collage	Divergent

Patterns	Convergent
Crayons	Divergent
Coloring sheets	Convergent
Worksheets	Convergent

Real objects and events may promote many creative experiences. Before children are able to understand the meaning of symbols such as letters and numbers, enthusiasm for discovery emerges as young children explore materials and interact with people. Throughout early childhood, concepts evolve to enable children to understand more symbolic and abstract information (Williams & Kamii, 1987). Pictures and stories should be used frequently to enhance children's experiences. Workbooks, worksheets, coloring books, and adult-made models are not appropriate for young children, especially children under age 6 (Bredekamp, 1987). The nature of such approaches is convergent. These activities do not promote creativity or curiosity. The controversy related to coloring sheets is not new (Moyer, 1990). But their continued use prevails in many early childhood programs. Lowenfeld (1954) responds to the issue of coloring books in Table 6.4.

TABLE 6.4 Using Coloring Books, Workbooks, and Worksheets

What about coloring books?

From *Your Child and His Art*

by Victor Lowenfeld

I have heard many teachers or parents say, "but my children love coloring books." This is quite true. Children in general, however, do not discriminate between things good for them or things detrimental. That they love things is not always an indication that they are good for them. Most children prefer sweets to vegetables and without doubt would always prefer them. This, however, does not mean that we should adjust their diet to sweets.

A child, once conditioned to coloring books, will have difficulties in enjoying the freedom of creating. The dependency which the coloring book creates is devastating. It has been revealed by experimentation and research that more than half of all children, once exposed to coloring books, lose their creativeness and their independence of expression, and become rigid and dependent.

Some teachers may still tell you that with the coloring book the child learns the discipline of staying within the lines of a given picture (area). It has also been proven by experiment that this is not true at all. More children color beyond the given boundaries in coloring books than in objects they draw themselves. If Johnny draws his dog, he has much more incentive to remain within his boundaries than if he colors a dog in a coloring book to which he has no relationship.

Coloring books, as well as ditto sheets, workbooks, cutouts, patterns, and clay models are of little value in teaching preschool children.

They learn better from real hands-on experiences such as field trips, cooking and science activities, manipulative materials, and opportunities for dramatic play and creative expression.

Source: V. Lowenfeld, *Your child and his art: A guide for parents.* (NY: Macmillan, 1954), pp. 12–14.

Does developmentally appropriate mean convergent activities should never be used? It is important to respect, reinforce, and uphold the expectations of society, traditions, and your culture without sacrificing individuality in the process. "Children need both divergent and convergent thinking" (Tegano, Moran, & Sawyers, 1991, p. 28).

Although specific information is typically viewed as convergent, information in action stimulates creativity. Playing store, for example, extends a child's understanding of the value of coins. It is important not to confuse memorization with knowledge. Knowledge is creative, applicable, and transferable.

FOSTERING A CREATIVE ENVIRONMENT

If, as we have suggested, creativity is a natural process of human beings, a question arises as to the ability to teach creativity. Torrance (1969) and others have conducted research efforts in the pedagogy of creativity, resulting in some important thoughts for teachers of young children.

Benefits to Children

Currently, no hard data exist to suggest that we can increase the natural creative potential of an individual. Perhaps the secrets of individual creativity are locked in genetic coding. But we can prompt more creative approaches to problem solving through opportunities to think divergently (Getzel & Csikszentmihalyi, 1976). Here are some benefits of such activities for children:

- Children learn to seek many answers to a problem and select the most effective answer based on the resources available.
- Children extend their potential for thinking through several levels of complexity, which moves them from the known to the new.
- Children develop higher levels of self-concept and an appreciation for their own individuality.
- Children are stimulated to explore new skills without fearing risk of failure.
- Children demonstrate an acceptance for the ideas of others.

Benefits to Teachers

The benefits of a creative environment influence not only the children but also the teacher. It is suggested that teachers who provide environments for creative thinking and experiences have greater variety in their programs. Often, children are less dependent on the teacher, allowing more time for the teacher to observe and interact with individuals. In addition, teachers who encourage creative experiences for children appear to have fewer behavioral problems (MacKinnon, 1962).

The role of the teacher in developing the potential for creativity is significant. The following are some suggestions that invite creativity:

- Allow and encourage children to ask questions.
- Grant responsibilities and provide opportunities for independence.
- Present situations that are open-ended.
- Emphasize self-initiated explorations that incorporate observations, inquiries, feelings, classifying, recording, translations, inferences, communications, and problem solving.
- Provide multicultural experiences.
- Provide social and cooperative experiences.

Parents and Creativity

A survey of creative adults indicated that their childhood home environments were reinforced by parents who respected the creative efforts of children. Such parents were confident in their child's abilities and granted freedom and opportunities for the child to explore and make decisions. Discipline was always consistent and predictable. The family values appeared to stress integrity, quality, intellectual, and cultural efforts. Success and ambition were considered secondary to respect for the child's own initiative (Helson, 1993).

Creativity has a different meaning for me now that I am a mother. My six-month-old amazes me every day with the new ways she is discovering how things work. Today she learned about gravity and I spent most of the day picking up the things she tossed across the room. Creativity and discovery seem to go hand in hand.

Obstacles to creativity have also been found as a result of family interactions. It has been noted that creativity is inhibited by specific family expectations. Creative children do not conform easily to rules and standards of behavior (Draper, Larsen, Haupt, Robinson, & Hart, 1993). They question authority and do not act or behave in an expected manner. Such actions may be perceived as misbehavior. Responses that do not meet the normal expectations of the family may be viewed as inappropriate. Because creative actions may be viewed as odd, immature, or abnormal, parents need more information about the nature of creativity (Clemens, 1991). Communications between teachers and parents are critical to the facilitation of a child's creative potential. Torrance (1969) suggests the following ideas for parents to use in fostering the creativity of young children at home:

- Provide materials that develop imagination.
- Offer materials that enrich imagery.
- Permit time for thinking and daydreaming.
- Encourage children to record their ideas.
- Accept and use the tendency to take a different look.
- Prize rather than punish true individuality.
- Be cautious in editing children's products.
- Encourage children to play with words.

Schools: Creativity vs. Conformity

For most children, entry into the school setting represents a shift from an independent and creative life-style to a structured, shared environment. By their nature, schools may encourage conformity to the standards and expectations of others (Eisner, 1992). In recent years, much emphasis has been placed on the academic demands of education as the indicator of success (Hanna, 1992).

TEACHERS SPEAK OUT

Give children the least amount of assistance to be successful. This will foster independence which will be a lifelong skill.

It should be noted that there is no research to substantiate that structured academic programs in early childhood promote long-term (beyond age 9) academic gains that are superior to divergent, focused early childhood experiences (Weikart, 1990). Short-term academic results that diminish around age 9 cannot justify the sacrifice of the long-term benefits of creative development.

Children whose experiences include creative development demonstrate 50 to 75 percent higher scores on class performance measures over the long term (Parnes, 1967). Such measures consider vocabulary, attention span, and the child's interests in school topics.

The school curriculum may be perceived as potentially detrimental to the development of creativity as a result of some noteworthy examples. The following list represents observations of noncreative influences:

- Most assignments are narrow. Children have few opportunities to generate innovative answers, or even select from among possible answers.
- Aesthetics or the appreciation of beauty is rarely discussed outside of fine arts classes.
- Risk taking is not encouraged and is often perceived as negative.
- Classrooms and activities are often structured to encourage children to be dependent on the teacher or care provider.

Amabile & Hennessey (1988) suggest that individuals from birth through adulthood are more actively creative under circumstances that foster self-reliance and intrinsic motivations. Situations that promote dependence on external motivation and rewards stimulate less creativity. In the schools, activities that contribute to dependent behaviors include grades and performance evaluations.

Competition for prizes has been found to inhibit creativity as children seek to perform at a level they anticipate will be sufficient to achieve a reward. Finally, supervision and close monitoring by teachers and caregivers are other activities that were found to undermine creativity in the classroom (Amabile & Hennessey, 1988).

Motivating Creativity

An environment that fosters creativity is well within the reach of teachers and caregivers. It begins with an analysis of the nature of activities and materials. Clark (1986; 1988) recommends the following points for establishing a creatively motivating environment:

- The environment should be rich and varied in stimulation.
- Use materials and methods that are age and developmentally appropriate.
- Keep in mind the aims of a creative program and avoid activities for the sake of adults.
- Make sure that the environment and materials are friendly and nonthreatening.
- Allow disagreement without hostility so children can engage freely in behaviors that support creativity.
- Reduce the level of anxiety in the classroom, especially anxiety created by the teacher.
- Search for integrative elements. Consider how things work together.
- Consider all elements of a child's development as materials are selected. This concern should include cognitive, affective, and physical development.

- Treat children with respect and allow them freedom to explore their universe.
- Create an atmosphere with variety in books, music, and pictures.
- Treat ideas and questions with respect.
- Respect the child's privacy.
- Value the unusual.
- Help the child learn by mistakes and support when needed.
- Interfere as little as possible.
- Choose self-expressive activities.
- Emphasize process—not product.
- Remember that providing appropriate materials is a beginning. Encouraging the creative use of the materials is equally important.

SELF-EXPRESSIVE ACTIVITIES FOR CREATIVITY

Self-expressive activities are optimum for divergence of thought. These activities may be defined as open-ended and nonrestrictive with regard to a product. They stimulate imagination and do not necessarily result in a product. When effectively introduced, these activities let children express themselves without conforming their

Through the scribble stage, a child's drawings progress from random marks on a page to repeated and controlled efforts.

The basic form stage is characterized by the more controlled use of triangles, circles, and connected lines.

answers to any closed standards. The concept of self-expressive activities is by no means new. But the pedagogical concepts of their use have warranted careful appraisal regarding the developmental appropriateness of their implementation (Bredekamp & Rosegrant, 1992). The term *developmentally appropriate* refers to issues including age appropriateness and individual appropriateness. An example of the need to understand these two aspects of the philosophy may be noted in simple drawing activities.

Simple drawings may represent self-expressive experiences and serve as an effective activity for creativity. The drawings of very young children may seem to be more creative than older children. In judging creativity, it is important to be aware of the corresponding stages of development that we might expect in children.

Lowenfeld and Brittain (1987), in their classic study of children's drawings, describe six stages of artistic development. The stages appear to progress in much the same way that cognitive development occurs. Table 6.5 provides an overview of the six stages of simple drawing through early childhood.

Self-expressive activities involve a variety of mediums and approaches. Such experiences may include two-dimensional arts or crafts, creative dramatics, music, and literature.

Although the following discussion is by no means a comprehensive review of self-expressive activities, we present it to introduce you

TABLE 6.5 Characteristics of the Development of Drawings

Scribble Stage
(Ages one and a half to three years)

Early Scribble Stage: Disordered scribbling

- Child does not have control over movements and marks on a page.
- Marks go in many directions.

Later Scribble Stage: Controlled scribbling

- Child has found it is possible to control marks.
- Able to make marks go in a desired direction.
- Child tries new motions; zig-zags or circles appear.
- Repeats motions to gain control.
- Becomes very involved with the process.

Basic Form Stage of Early Drawings
(Ages three to four years)

Early Basic Form: Circle and oval phase

- First form is usually oval or circle which develops from scribbles.
- Curved lines or arcs are evident.
- Arcs become less curved and develop into horizontal and vertical lines.

Basic forms with straight lines.

- Squares and rectangles are noted.
- Much repetition of the same form appears.
- Rough and unclear forms appear in the early stage.

Later Basic Forms: Rectangles and square phase

- More clear repetitions of patterns.
- Rectangles and squares appear when child can draw separate lines of any length desired.
- Child joins the lines to form the rectangle, etc.
- Forms will be clearly drawn.

First Drawings
(Ages four to five years)

Early First Drawings: Perfects symbols

- Repeats the same symbols over and over.
- Pictures are completed quickly.
- Symbols may change constantly while the child is seeking new ideas.
- A man may be drawn differently in every picture.

Later First Drawings: Schema

- Draws more exactly and easily.
- Begins to organize for neatness and order.
- Complexity of pictures increases to include more complexity of symbols.
- Four- and five-year-olds are able to use their drawings to tell a story or describe an event.

Source: Adapted by permission from Mary Mayesky, *Creative activities for young children*, fourth edition (NY: Delmar, 1990), p. 140.

to basic approaches. The creative potentials of these and similar activities depend on the teacher. The role of the teacher is that of a facilitator. Each of the following discussions offers suggestions for materials and variations of the basic approaches (Edwards & Springate, 1993).

Two-Dimensional Self-Expressive Activities

Two-dimensional arts and crafts describe experiences that have one working surface. The term is used to describe any artwork that is flat. Drawings, finger painting, easel painting, and collage are examples of two-dimensional art (Clemens, 1991).

During early first drawing, children perfect symbols to illustrate what they know about their subjects. This four-year-old often draws people with exaggerated knees.

Drawing. As we described earlier, creativity can be enhanced as children explore the natural stages of artistic development through simple drawings. Experiences for simple drawing can be provided in all areas of the classroom. Materials should be readily available and easily accessible to invite the child's participation. Teachers should support and encourage the efforts of children without patronizing their products.

Basic drawing materials. Nontoxic crayons, nontoxic markers, pencils, and chalks represent possible tools for simple drawing. A surplus of paper—new and recycled including various sizes, shapes, colors, and textures—should be readily available.

Variations for simple drawing activities. As children discuss their drawings, record the child's thoughts. A tape recorder can be used to capture the child's terms and phrases. Teachers will find the recordings to be effective resources for dictation and later references. Often, children provide insights to their creative initiatives as they share and compare their projects with one another.

Finger painting. Finger painting is a process-oriented activity. This experience provides opportunities for creativity, sensory percep-

In the first drawing stage, children illustrate boundaries including horizons and baselines.

tions, motor development, spatial relationships, color awareness, and reversibility.

Basic finger painting materials. Basic materials include nontoxic water-based paints (such as tempera or commercial finger paints), aprons or smocks, painting surfaces such as paper, laminated table tops, meat packing trays, and additional materials.

Variations for finger painting activities. Introduce soft background music. Add texture to the paints with sand or use a textured surface for the paint base. Provide tools such as spoons, plastic utensils, or other materials that will extend exploration.

Easel painting. Easel painting is an enjoyable, creative activity for children. This activity is a tradition in most early childhood classrooms. The creative value of the experience depends on the child's opportunity to plan and initiate the project. Children who have become dependent on adults may ask what they should paint. Adults can prompt the child's interest and imagination without assigning a theme or project. Large motor skills, eye and hand coordination, and balance are some skill benefits of this creative activity.

Basic easel painting materials. Sturdy easels and paint brushes of varied width and size are essential to the painting process using this approach. Tempera or other water-based paints are economical media for the process.

Variations for easel painting. Add a small amount of liquid starch to the paints to make the consistency thicker. Display illustrations of famous artists near the art center. Exhibit the children's work. Plan a painting environment in which drips or spills do not distract from the child's creation.

Collage. The term *collage* refers to the process of gluing small pieces of paper or materials to a surface. You can prompt creativity by allowing children to freely interact with collections of potential collage items. Allowed to investigate the materials, children may develop representations of the world as they see it.

Basic collage materials. Quality white glue and base surfaces such as cardboard, scraps of poster board, wood, and boxes serve as the foundation for collage activities. An abundance of possible collage materials should be available. Collage materials are limitless. They may include cloth, paper, natural resources, packing materials, or similar items. Parents are excellent sources for collage materials and often enjoy contributing to the supplies with things that might otherwise be discarded (Clemens, 1991).

Variations for collage activities. Children may collect materials during field experiences. Recycling may become more understandable to young children as they gather materials for collage.

Three-Dimensional Self-Expressive Activities

Three-dimensional arts and crafts are representative of freestanding forms such as sculptures or mobiles. Puppets, costumes, and staging are three dimensional. Such materials provide creative experiences for concept development related to depth and space.

Clay and playdoughs. Clays and playdoughs are soft media for creativity. These materials typically hold a shape for the time that children choose. After the product has satisfied a child's creative spirit, children may change or redesign the materials. Physical, cognitive, emotional, language, and social opportunities are increased as children manipulate the materials.

Basic clay and playdough materials. Soft clays and commercial or homemade playdoughs are the foundation for the development of many activities. Extension devices such as cookie cutters, rolling pins, toothpicks, or pipe cleaners may prompt the elaboration of play.

Cookie cutters, rolling pins, and toothpicks are materials that can be used to prompt elaboration of activities with clay and playdoughs.

Variations for clay and playdough activities. Scents may be added to playdoughs. Photographs may be used to record the children's models. Store the materials in the refrigerator to provide a different type of stimulus.

Creative Dramatics

Creative dramatics, role playing, and puppetry allow children to explore the world from the perspective of others. Working with situations and not scripts enhances the children's understanding as they resolve problems from a different view.

Basic creative dramatics materials. Props may include a wide range of clothing and staging materials. Puppets, dolls, and stuffed animals extend the potential for creative dramatics.

Variations for creative dramatics activities. Make props readily available in all centers. Use story starters, children's literature, and familiar and new situations to encourage open explorations. Change props frequently to extend the experiences.

Music and Rhythm

Creative experiences with music stimulate an understanding of tempo (fast/slow), pitch (high/low), dynamics (loud/soft), and articulation (smooth/rough). The freedom to exercise musical explorations extends thinking, language, physical, emotional, and social development (Warner, 1990).

Basic music and rhythm materials. The tools for making sound form the fundamentals for music discovery. Such tools may include rhythm band instruments, tapes, and records of varied sounds and music. Authentic instruments may also be used as basic tools.

Variations for music and rhythm activities. Encourage the use of rhythms and sounds that children discover. Allow new words to be used in familiar tunes. Make music a part of the total learning environment, not relegated to a given time and place. Take field trips to places where music is created, practiced, or used. Invite musicians to your classroom.

Literature

The generous use of stories, poetry, and books invites the creative potential of children. Literature in all forms should be a nurturing part of the early childhood environment.

Basic literature materials. Exposure to stories, books, poetry, and print provides the foundations for literary innovations. Chapter 9 offers a variety of literary ideas to invite creative endeavors in literature.

The self-expressive activities suggested in this section offer only the potential for creativity. Activities do not, in and of themselves, foster creativity without the thoughtful use of teachers and caregivers. Teachers do not need to be creative in a given area in order to promote the creativity of others. The teacher who proudly displays the tissue models of Thanksgiving turkeys and discusses the creativity of the students has forsaken process for product. The discovery of how a real turkey looks, sounds, smells, and feels cannot be replaced by assembly line models or coloring sheets.

SUMMARY

Creativity has been defined in many ways, but the common elements of each interpretation suggest that creativity is novel and new to the individual. An indication of highly creative individuals is that they exhibit several characteristics of creativity. These indicators include such things as an appreciation for beauty, flexibility in thought, elaboration of ideas, and consistency in their ability to produce new or novel ideas and products.

Although the origins of creativity have not been definitively identified, one concept is that creativity originates as a result of the interaction between right and left cerebral hemispheres. Such interactions may be stimulated by divergent activities that offer the potential for many answers.

The belief that creativity reaches a peak and then diminishes as children attain school age has been challenged by the results of children who are encouraged by parents, teachers, and schools. Fostering creativity in young children benefits society as a result of their creative contributions.

Teachers, parents, and schools play a vital role in the creative development of children. The ability to provide and nurture creativity results from an awareness of the nature of creative individuals. The inclusion of self-expressive activities promotes divergent experiences. Adults do not need to be creative themselves to appreciate and encourage creativity in children.

TEST YOUR UNDERSTANDING

1. List two common terms found in definitions of creativity.
2. Why are the early childhood years important to the development of creativity?
3. Define convergent and divergent concepts. List three activities in each category.
4. Discuss how schools and teachers may inhibit creativity. What are some recommendations for teachers to encourage creativity in their classrooms?
5. Define self-expressive activities. How do they foster creativity?
6. List five self-expressive activities. Describe how teachers might use the activities to promote creativity.
7. Discuss the role of the parent in nurturing creativity.
8. For each of the following combinations, what types of behaviors might you expect?
   Highly creative-low intelligence
   Highly intelligent-low creativity
   Highly creative-highly intelligent

LEARNING ACTIVITIES

1. Think of an individual whom you consider creative. List the traits you used to categorize that person as creative. Compare your list to Perkin's model for creativity. Which of his indicators does the person you chose demonstrate?
2. Visit an early childhood classroom. List the creative influences you observed during your visit.
3. Review the goals for an early childhood program in your area. Identify how creativity may be encouraged while meeting the goals of the system.
4. Develop a collection of children's artwork that represents at least one example for each of the developmental categories presented in the stages of simple drawings.

LET'S TALK ABOUT IT

Stephanie was the first team member to begin sharing her observations with her classmates. She told them that the one thing she learned is that there are many ways of looking at kids. "I didn't know there were so many ways to gather information about one area. I mean, like, she used six ways to assess the child's language."

Matt's group was considering the importance of play. He reported that a teacher can learn a great deal about how kids are doing by watching their play. "The problem my teacher had was convincing the parents of the importance of play."

After Lillian finished her report, one of her group members told about a classroom she had observed. She was very impressed with how neat, attractive, and orderly the classroom was. In every corner of the room, the teacher had large, colorful, teacher-made and commercially prepared materials. The student said, "I bet she spends a fortune on decorating her classroom."

Mildred began her discussion by relating an incident she had observed at the recent Open House at Spring Hill Center. One child was proudly showing his parent his painting. Tears formed in the child's eyes after the parent said, "Don't you know that grass isn't purple?"

What is the value of having many ways of assessing children's progress?

How do teachers convince parents that their child is learning through play and that play has value?

Considering the observation from Lillian's classmate about the organization of one teacher's room, what can you infer about this teacher's philosophy?

How do you feel about the parent's reaction to the child's painting?

PART 3

Learning and the Young Child

SPRING HILL CHILD DEVELOPMENT CENTER

The question-and-answer section of the team's report on Spring Hill Child Development Center generated more questions than answers. Many of the concerns expressed by their classmates focused on questions like these:

- How do you teach young children?
- What is important for young children to learn?
- When do they learn certain things?
- What is appropriate for a young child to know?
- How do you get it all in?

Unfortunately, the team members couldn't provide all the answers from their field experiences alone. But theirs was just one of six group presentations.

The professor said, "I believe the more questions you have, the better you understand. I am finding some very interesting comparisons and contrasts emerging. Those students who observed a Head Start program had a totally different experience from yours. And your classmates who spent time in a second-grade class reported an even greater variety of observations. This is why I asked the class to share their experiences with each other."

The team members felt that many of the things they had read about in their textbook were observed in action at the Spring Hill Center. Not everything they saw was good; not everything was bad; but there was something to learn from each experience. They agreed that sometimes you can learn more from a bad experience than from an ideal situation. They decided to finish their report by describing some teaching strategies for working with young children.

Stephanie discovered that a well-planned learning center requires careful preparation and serves as an important instructional tool. "I saw many different kinds of learning experiences occurring as the children explored the various centers," she said, "And I was sur-

prised by how much a child's motor ability influenced their success and interest in the different materials found in the learning centers."

Lillian was impressed by the amount of print material that she observed in her classroom. "The environment was rich with print and books," she said, "But I never saw the teacher formally teach reading skills." Lillian said the children seemed to be interested in writing, "but I was frustrated by their frequent misspelling."

Matt, who had always found math and science to be challenging, said he was impressed by the knowledge the children were discovering through their own explorations. "I could hardly believe how much they enjoyed math and science," he said, "And I wish the same level of enthusiasm could be maintained throughout elementary school."

Mildred said, "I was amazed by how much the teaching of social studies has changed in twenty-five years." She was struck by the variety of topics included in the social studies curriculum. "Today, social studies seems to cover just about everything," she reported. But perhaps more important, Mildred said she was astonished by how much the children knew about the various topics. "Times certainly have changed!"

CHAPTER 7 Teaching and Learning Environments

CHAPTER OUTLINE

Environments for Young Children

Philosophies and Goals

Direct Instruction Program Environments

Academic Preschool Environment

Traditional Primary Environment Model

Behavioral Environment

Developmental and Maturational Program Environments

Prepared Environment

Cognitively Oriented Environment

Activity or Learning Center Environment

Environmental Ownership

Physical Space

Planning Physical Space

A Space of Their Own

Responding to Environmental Conditions

Sound

Light

Color

Temperature, Humidity, and Success

Organizing for Early Childhood

Learning Centers

Art Center

Block Center

Communications Center (Library, Listening, Writing)

Home and Dramatic Play Center

Math and Manipulatives Center

Music and Sound Center

Science Center

Sand and Water Centers

Woodworking Construction Center

Room Arrangements, Schedules, and Monitoring

Room Arrangement

Schedules

Grouping Children for Experiences

Monitoring

Parents as a Resource

KEY TERMS

Prepared environment

Environmental ownership

Play spaces

Empty spaces

Learning center

Manipulatives

Room arrangement

Rachel, who was beginning her first day in the class, was a little reluctant to select an activity when Elizabeth, another child, confidently volunteered, "Hi, let me show you our room." The teacher was sure that the child would be an excellent guide for the new student. Elizabeth continued, "Over here we build stuff with the blocks. We can write stories or draw pictures about our blocks."

As the two girls toured the room, it became clear that the children in this class were comfortable and very knowledgeable about what was expected of them and how to use their classroom. While the children continued their tour, the teacher was involved with an equally important job—explaining the program to Rachel's parents.

Teachers are often asked to explain the approach they use in arranging and selecting materials for their early childhood centers. In their response, teachers and child care providers attempt to integrate their use of child development, individual differences, opportunities for experiences, and developmentally appropriate strategies and practices. Before an educator can confidently weave theory and practice into a personal philosophy and instructional goals, he or she must form a careful plan of action. Few teachers will disagree that once the excitement of getting a new job has diminished, additional concerns arise regarding their preparation for children.

In this chapter, we consider the issues for establishing and maintaining an appropriate learning environment for young children. These topics include philosophy, room arrangement, space, colors, climate, materials, supplies, grouping, and scheduling.

ENVIRONMENTS FOR YOUNG CHILDREN

Certainly, the term *environment* refers to many aspects of the world that influence children. Home environments, neighborhoods, and schools each provide the conditions and surroundings that comprise a type of developmental ecology. It is through this ecology that children are nurtured. As providers of care and education, teachers of young children are also a part of this ecosystem. The classrooms, strategies, techniques and climate that teachers design for children provide environments for learning (Burton, 1991; Day, 1992).

The classroom arrangement, color, texture, temperature, and schedule influence those who work, grow, and learn within the walls of the classroom and on the playground. Teachers direct the environment through which children may flourish in their development of skills (Ard & Pitts, 1990). Every aspect of sensory, emotional, social, cognitive, and linguistic growth is affected by a well-organized, attractive, and participatory environment. In *School zone: Learning environments for children*, Taylor and Vlustos (1983) note that the school environment contributes to both student behavior and learning.

Successful early childhood centers provide a variety of materials for children to openly explore.

PHILOSOPHIES AND GOALS

The selection of materials and the arrangement of a classroom to create a learning environment reflect the philosophies and goals of a program. Experienced observers suggest that even an empty classroom communicates the philosophy of the teacher and the goals of an early childhood program. In the following sections, we address the environmental approaches that characterize different philosophies and goals.

DIRECT INSTRUCTION PROGRAM ENVIRONMENTS

Programs that are teacher-oriented follow a direct instruction model. We will now focus on classrooms where students are presented information by an adult and children are guided to specific experiences.

Academic Preschool Environment

A preschool environment that emphasizes an academic or instructional focus may appear to have few distractions. Visuals and manipulatives are at a minimum. Bereiter and Englemann (1966) suggest that distractions should be limited in order to meet the requirements of an academic preschool curriculum. A visitor in such a classroom may be aware of limited toys and stimuli. Children are dependent on the teacher to direct the learning (Cryan & Surbeck, 1979). Bulletin boards and displays could be considered distracting.

Traditional Primary Environment Model

Although at first glance the academic preschool may seem more in keeping with the traditional primary approach to early education classrooms, there are differences. In a traditional primary classroom, the setting may appear somewhat restrictive when judged by developmentally appropriate standards. Desks are usually placed in rows or patterns, and individual seats are the central focus of the classroom. A table may be located in the back of the room so that the teacher can work with small groups while maintaining a view of the other children. A traditional classroom, unlike the academic preschools, often features bright commercial or teacher-made displays. The observer may note that the traditional environmental setting exhibits student-made artwork that suggests the use of a pattern or design.

Behavioral Environment

Behavioral-oriented environments display management systems, such as charts with stars to recognize student's accomplishments. Teachers using this philosophy typically create environments that require the child to respond to a prescribed system of rules. Appropriate responses result in the distribution of rewards. Classroom designs promoting this philosophy encourage the child's dependence on the teacher. Play materials, used as rewards, are usually stored in cabinets or storage shelves away from the regular classroom activities.

DEVELOPMENTAL AND MATURATIONAL PROGRAM ENVIRONMENTS

In contrast to programs that focus on a direct instructional approach, the visitor to a classroom whose teacher's philosophy is developmental or maturational discovers a very different environment. These rooms appear to be organized to meet the needs of a child's development (Day, 1992).

Prepared Environment

The teaching and learning approaches of the Montessori method, an example of the prepared environment, are highly individualized. The materials for the classroom may be divided into four types (Almy, 1985):

- Materials that target motor activity, such as grooming, sweeping, and cleaning
- Materials that encourage sensory discrimination skills to enhance logic and language through visual, tactile, auditory, and olfactory experiences
- Materials that focus specifically on language training activities through naming, recognizing, and pronunciation
- Materials that prompt cultural and artistic stimulation

While visiting this classroom, you will discover an environment that reflects a program philosophy designed to encourage autonomy. Materials are self-teaching, self-checking, and one of a kind. The items are organized and coordinated. The environment is scaled to physically and conceptually meet the needs of children.

Cognitively Oriented Environment

The influence of Piagetian concepts can be observed in many environments where children are provided materials to investigate through active involvement and hands-on experiences. Materials found in a cognitively oriented environment give children opportunities for classifying items on the basis of relationships (Hohmann, Banet, & Weikart, 1979). Objects may also be included to stimulate arrangement by size, quality, or quantity. Spatial relations materials, such as puzzles, should be available to encourage concepts of proportion and placement.

Temporal activities enable children to deal with time in terms of periods having a beginning and an end. The daily schedule is characterized by a teacher-pupil session in which children formulate a plan and determine activities. The room includes areas for exploration such as a block center, home center, or an art center. The room organization also features a large gathering space where groups can discuss the outcomes of their plan.

Activity or Learning Center Environment

When visiting a classroom that focuses on activity centers, you will find the class space organized into related sections. The room arrangement suggests that wet or messy activities are located in areas where easy cleanup is possible. You may observe a home-like atmosphere stocked with everything from a mock refrigerator to a typewriter or a computer. Blocks and tools, pencils and paper, tape recorders and books, playdough and plastic utensils have unity and cohesiveness in this setting. Art displays and photographs are at the children's eye level. Closer evaluation suggests that this classroom is actually an environment under the direction of a teacher who is guiding a developmental approach to learning.

ENVIRONMENTAL OWNERSHIP

The philosophy and program goals initiated by adults make a difference in a child's attitude toward school. Gehrke (1979) and Dodge, Goldhammer, and Colker (1988) found that children in traditional or restrictive environments were less likely to exhibit ownership behaviors related to the classroom. This failure to relate or "own" the environment may result in negative actions. In restrictive environments, the teacher appears to control any movement. "Children quickly learn to ritualize being in one's seat and can be depended upon to tattle and make judgment of others on the basis of who gets into or out of, or stays put in, seats" (Gehrke, 1979, p. 107).

Although young children may consent to and adjust to rigid classroom requirements, research suggests that the environment is not optimal for the child's development of ownership of their class. (Lewis, 1979). Children must have some autonomy to adjust successfully to the early childhood environment.

Day (1983) suggests that conditions of establishing a secure environment are related to space. Activities, which are by their nature noisy, should not be located in an area that disturbs children working in a naturally quiet domain such as the library center. Children need both collaborative and private moments.

PHYSICAL SPACE

As teachers begin to develop the physical space for their programs, they encounter and must consider immediate limitations. Few teachers have the opportunity to design the classroom structure. But knowing about the effects of physical space helps them make choices that positively influence the environment (Kennedy, 1991).

PARENTS SPEAK OUT

It is important for a teacher to make a room comfortable and inviting. The materials in a classroom say a lot about the kind of experiences my children will have.

Planning Physical Space

The National Association for the Education of Young Children recommends allotting 35 square feet of indoor play space per child and 75 square feet of outdoor play space per child (Bredekamp & Rosegrant, 1992). Appropriate use of physical space is significant to overall program success as well as to the accomplishments of children in early childhood programs (Zimring, 1981). Stress factors related to inadequate or poorly managed space can influence the users of an environment. Children need personal space, shared space, and private space in order to be successful.

As teachers develop their classrooms, they will find it valuable to consider room arrangements that serve multiple purposes and extend space. For example, a library center may also serve as a quiet center and a listening station. By including a small table with chairs in the library center, the teacher can extend the space to accommodate a small-group activity base for children who are working with projects or themes.

Teachers should determine the permanent features of the environment, including electrical outlets, water resources, and paths for entrances and exits. These items are permanent elements of the classroom that may determine the best location for centers and instructional uses of the environment. The following list suggests some possible permanent features that should be considered in planning the use of physical space:

- Light sources
- Ceiling height
- Quiet areas
- Noisy areas
- Carpet
- Flooring
- Acoustics

It may be effective to develop a map of the class to gauge the initial room arrangement and the anticipated traffic flow. Figure 7.1 illustrates a simple floor sketch of an area designated for an early childhood classroom. Note that the room has been divided into four zones, based on permanent features as a starting point. To this sketch, the teacher would record the additional fixed features of the classroom (such as electrical outlets) that may restrict or extend the potential for specific use.

It is important to recognize how children respond to physical space. Kritchevsky, Prescott, and Walling (1977) studied the approaches that children take in using space. This classic study determined that classroom spaces can be identified as either play space or empty space. **Play spaces** are specifically identified with materials and designated to serve a particular purpose. **Empty spaces** are

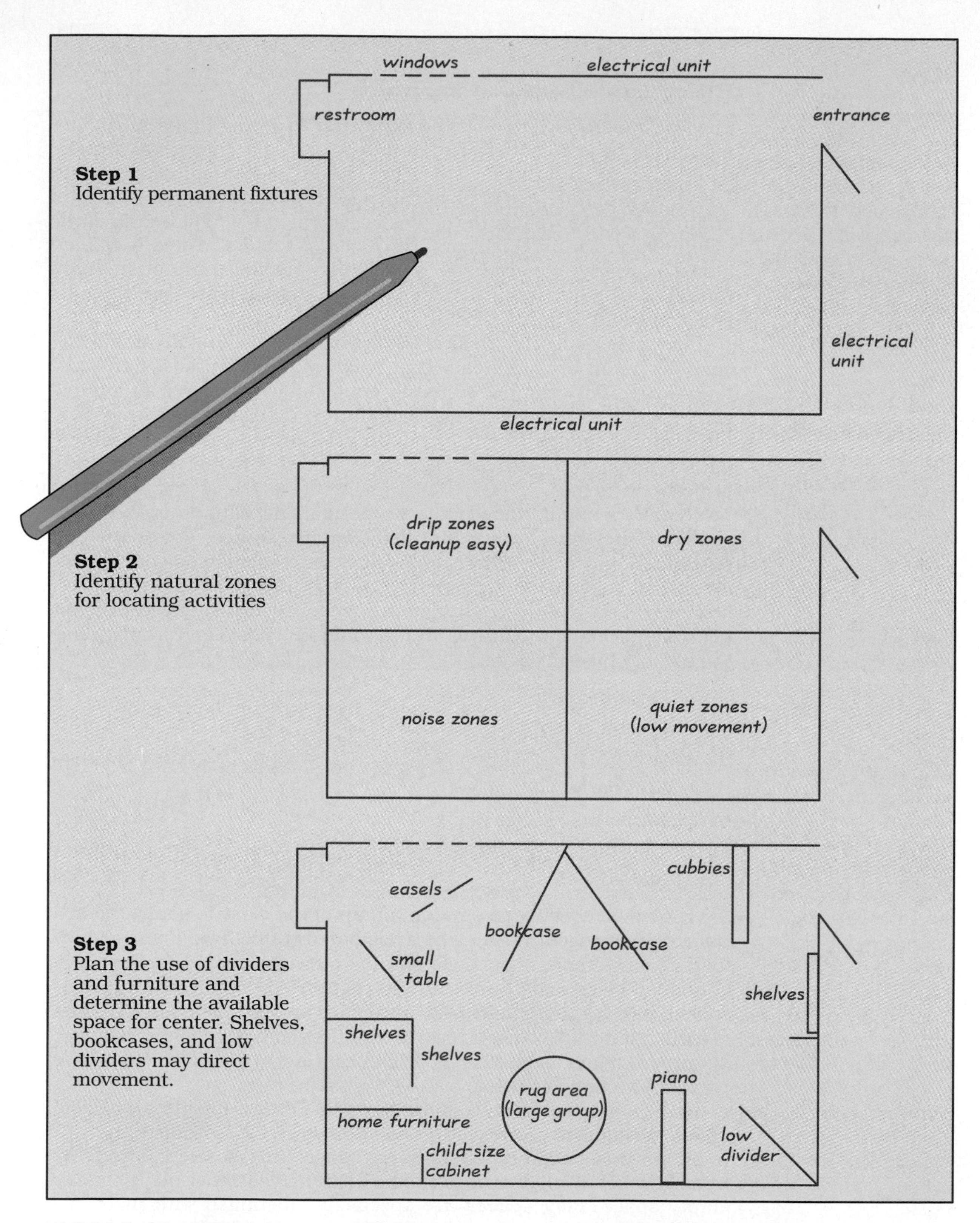

FIGURE 7.1 Steps in Designing Physical Space for an Early Childhood Classroom

paths, dividers, or undesignated areas. Undesignated areas can be used for activities that occur throughout the year (for example, an occasional display or a table for a meeting). A well-designed environment includes both play spaces and empty spaces.

A Space of Their Own

Children need a space to call their own (Meltz, 1990). The term *cubbies* is derived from the word *cubicle*, which refers to a small space allotted for children to place the things they bring from home. Children also use cubbies for storing activities and projects they will take home with them at the end of the day. Clearly identified spaces give children a feeling of proprietorship. Such spaces may include commercially divided lockers or mailbox systems. These "territories" are essential to classroom management and organization as well as psychologically beneficial to the child. If commercial space is not available, alternatives may include using boxes or cartons to individualize a space (Readdick, 1993). The containers should be located near the entrance of the center in order to catch items as children arrive and offer easy access to belongings as children leave for the day.

Individual spaces should be clearly identified with each child's name. Attaching a sealed photograph of the child to the corner of the cubbie helps children and adults make sure that materials go in the right place. Teachers should resist the urge to rearrange names and spaces during the year.

Restrooms represent another space-related issue for young children. Restrooms should be easily accessible and always available to the young child (Zeegers, 1991). Regulatory agencies monitor the basic needs for restrooms with regard to number, size, and accessibility (Willis & Lindberg, 1967). Teachers should remember that using a public restroom is foreign and intimidating for the very young child (Foster & Rogers, 1970). Considerations should be made for making the environment attractive and pleasant. Certainly, the restroom should be one of the first stops on a tour of the new classroom.

RESPONDING TO ENVIRONMENTAL CONDITIONS

Each classroom offers unique conditions that make up the learning environments of young children. Teachers who are alert to the influences of such things as sound, light, color, temperature, and humidity discover they can influence the classroom settings. Various strategies exist for responding to the environmental conditions that teachers may encounter.

Sound

The effects of sound on individuals has been well documented (Malecki, 1990). Children in an early childhood environment may respond in several ways. Some children will openly voice their concern that "it's noisy" and ask the teacher to make other children be quiet. Children who may be less aware of what is troubling them, or less anxious to call attention to themselves, may seek seclusion under tables or in corners away from others. Some children will escape the stress of sound by spending more time in the restroom. Teachers should try to resolve inappropriate noise conditions before class begins and respond to any symptoms of a noise-stressed environment as they occur. The dimensions of noise can influence the behavior of students and may hinder success (Leeper, Witherspoon, & Day, 1984).

A noisy environment perpetuates itself and presents concerns for specific planning considerations. Both large and small classrooms may present acoustical problems as active learners participate in the construction of knowledge. Structural dynamics of the room may offer immediate clues to the potential for undesirable noise levels. Although a rectangular classroom may present more opportunities for the creative use of physical space, teachers will discover that square rooms are less noisy (Jefferson, 1968).

Schools are traditionally *hard surface* environments. Tables, desks, and ceiling height contribute to the resonating of sound. By *softening* the environment, teachers can not only decrease environmental noise but also provide a more visually and texturally inviting classroom.

Materials including soft furniture, rugs, plants, pillows, and pets absorb sound waves and minimize noise. Table 7.1 provides a list of suggestions for creating a room in which children can talk and play without becoming distracted by sound.

Light

In assessing an early childhood environment, teachers should carefully consider appropriate lighting with regard to the scope of visual activity and the emotional well-being of children. Recent studies suggest the significance of exposure to appropriate amounts of lighting (Decker & Decker, 1988). The mood and nature of children's reactions may be influenced by light.

According to Stein (1975), regulatory agencies frequently recommend a prescribed range of lighting for early childhood settings. Typically, fifty to sixty footcandles of glare-free illumination is suggested. But the most effective lighting environments are designed to meet the children's needs with relation to the activity. Art activities are significantly more successful where natural lighting is available. In contrast, natural lighting may be too intense for reading print on a

TABLE 7.1 Solutions for Classroom Noise Pollution

Ten Steps to a Quieter Environment

1. *Use carpet, throw rugs, or carpet squares.* Absorb sounds and can be used to suggest a special place, such as the library or home center.

2. *Hang curtains or cloth drapes on the windows, or children's artwork on the windows or blinds.* Influence the lighting and the sound of a room.

3. *Lower high ceilings by using permanent mobiles, dropping signs from the ceiling to announce the names of learning centers, or hanging children's artwork from the strings.* Visually attractive, communicate where things are to visitors, and help with echoes.

4. *Arrange plants throughout the classroom.* Absorb sound, filter the air, provide opportunities for children to care and learn about plants.

5. *Include pets.* Pets soften the environment on several levels. Children often lower their voices to nurture pets.

6. *Scatter pillows around the room.* Bean bags, throw pillows, and stuffed animals absorb vibrations and offer a cozy warmth for independent and shared experiences.

7. *Use the teacher's influence.* Soften voice, plan activities, and establish a predictable place.

8. *Provide books, magazines, and paper.* Materials may influence every area of the room. These tools promote literacy and absorb the sounds of activity.

9. *Use baskets.* Using baskets for containers and transports for tools provides an attractive and soundproofing alternative to other containers.

10. *Add bulletin boards.* Cloth-covered bulletin boards absorb sound. If the room has limited display space, provide portable boards or make space by securing cloth to the walls.

white page and may be avoided as an area for some activities. Therefore, intense lighting suggests the need for one approach in room arrangement while the lack of light presents other concerns. Teachers should determine their lighting needs and access the class resources as they develop their environmental strategy (Sampson, 1970).

If additional lighting is necessary, teachers may increase the quantity of reflective light by adding lamps. Carefully placed lighting may imply a special area such as the library center. Lights secured on the tops of cabinets may offer peripheral light to suggest that the room is large. Florescent lighting provides a nonglare light that works well for young children.

If a classroom appears dark, teachers can redirect the available light by using reflective surfaces such as light colors of enamel paints, formica table coverings, or carefully placed mirrors. Lighted fish aquariums and plants with plant lights also help to extend the illumination. If the classroom is too bright, teachers should redirect the light from overhead by using carefully placed mobiles and lower-wattage bulbs. Colored blinds with nonreflective textures and shades will provide a cozy effect. The display of children's artwork and the use of flat or matted paint may assist in controlling the reflective light.

Color

The color climate of the classroom should be stimulating and not agitating. Color and balance within patterns and design should lead to the success of the child and not constitute a distraction.

The behavior of children typically indicates ineffective environmental conditions including color (Irlen, 1991). Studies in the selection of color suggest that coordinated color schemes are the most conducive for success. Young children respond favorably to bright colors (Irlen, 1991), but too many bright colors may prompt excessive movement. Studies reviewing environmental criteria imply that the color red is successful in areas of physical activity, gross motor skills, and concept formation (Irlen, 1991). Children respond positively to art and music in areas where the color scheme is yellow, while shades of green, blue, and purple appear to be effective for reading and language learning areas.

Softer colors are often considered by adults to be restful and soothing. This point may be in contrast to the child's perspective that these colors are less interesting (Irlen, 1991).

Color and lighting are related to the needs of the children and the environment. Soft colors that absorb light may be effective if the class windows are located on the southern or western wall. But if light is at a minimum, reflective shades of yellow or white may be the best selection for a center that draws its natural lighting from the north (Headley, 1966).

An essential element in selecting color for the class setting is that it be aesthetically pleasing (Leeper et al., 1984). Many children spend more time in this setting than in their homes. The child's environment should be safe, secure, constructive, and attractive.

Temperature, Humidity, and Success

Comfortable temperature and humidity influence the cooperative and intellectual success of children. Willis and Lindberg (1967) recommend a room temperature of between 68 and 72 degrees Fahrenheit (20 to 22 degrees Celsius). An efficient measure of the temperature is to record the thermometer readings at the eye level of the children.

A humidity level of 50 to 65 percent increases the productivity and comfort of children (Willis & Lindberg, 1967). Teachers may find that practical alternatives to a humidifier could include a carefully placed vaporizer secured out of the traffic flow and reach of children.

An open aquarium, plants, and a water table may offer additional humidity.

ORGANIZING FOR EARLY CHILDHOOD

Once the school philosophy, space, and design have been evaluated, teachers continue the planning phase through an analysis of who will actually use the classroom. The diversity of skills in early childhood classes can be challenging (Kostelnik, 1992; Elkind, 1994).

The terms *multiage grouping, multi-skilled, inclusion,* and *diversity* all present issues related to how teachers will organize for optimal experiences. For example, with a multiage grouping of 3- through 6-year-old children, the discrepancies in abilities and skills are clear. But are they as clear as you might first expect? In classroom settings where children begin school at a common age, there is a marked diversity in developmental differences.

Some public school systems address the entry level by regulating a specific entry schedule based on the calendar year. For instance, if a child is 5 years of age on or before September 1 of the current school year, the child may be allowed admission to public school. Therefore, a child whose fifth birthday is August 31 is eligible to enter school at the same time as a child who will be 6 on September 2. From a developmental perspective, the day a child begins school is arbitrary—provided that the focus is on the individual child and not the chronological age.

LEARNING CENTERS

A **learning center** approach to early education enables teachers to individualize experiences and optimize their opportunities to engage children in meaningful activities. Centers that are designed to provide developmentally appropriate challenges support the needs of the child, not necessarily the age of the child.

The concept of learning centers to individual instruction is not new. Froebel and Pestalozzi provided glimpses of how individualized and small group activities may have provided for the needs of children during their times (Osborn, 1991).

While there have been some discussions as to the names used to represent the approach—learning centers, activity centers, or interest centers—the basic principles remain the same. Areas designated as learning centers have an element of independence that is common in their relationship to the goals and themes of the program. Learning center spaces may be framed with dividers, bookcases, displays, or tables. The intended effect is that children enter clearly defined spaces with well-established goals. Specialities are

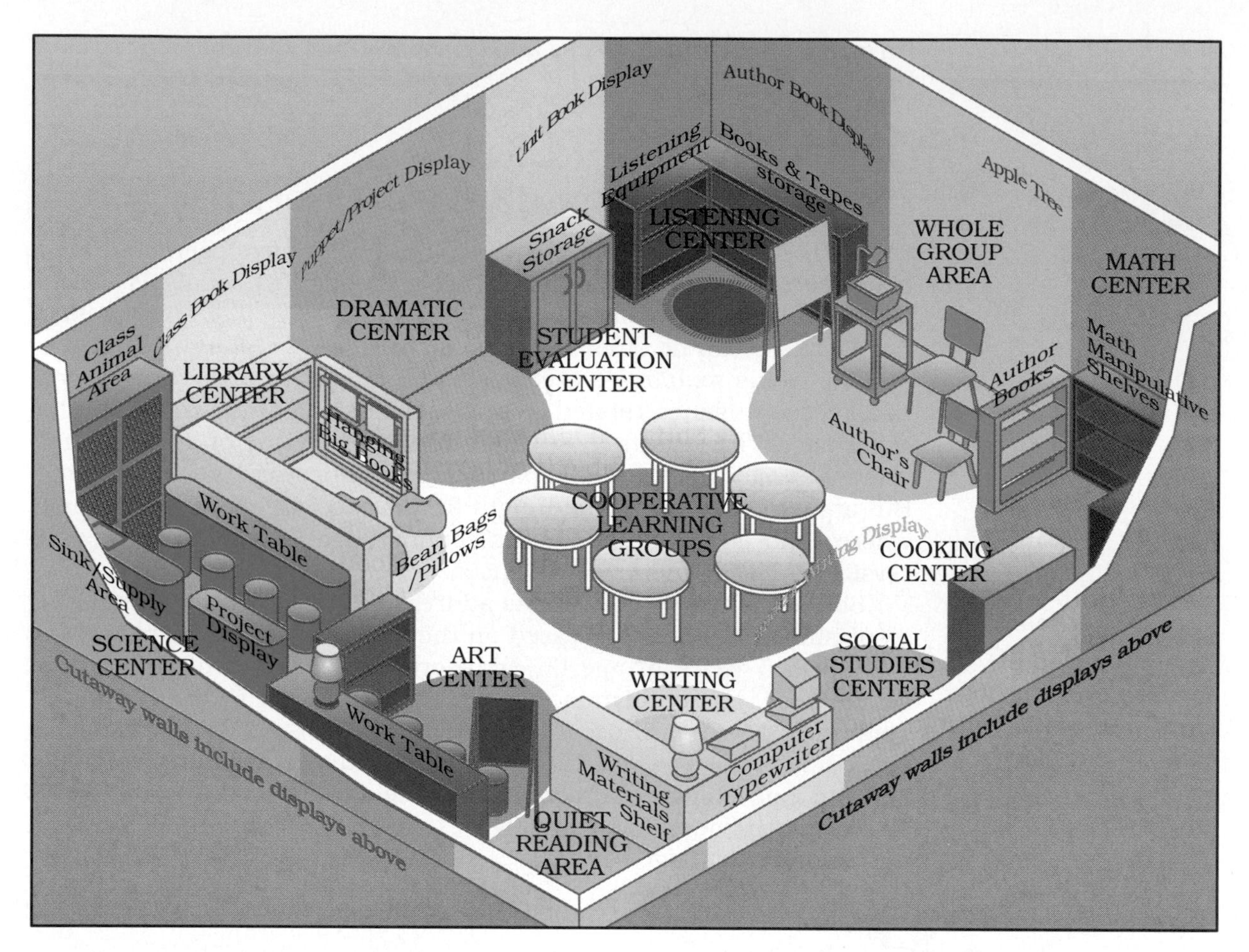

FIGURE 7.2

Learning Center Classroom Design

Source: S. L. Snider, *Integrating developmentally appropriate curriculum and learning style preferences.* (Unpublished master's thesis, Texas Woman's University, Denton, TX, 1994), p. 97.

available in each center. Figure 7.2 illustrates a classroom design for a first-grade setting.

The numbers of learning centers and options in each area are guided by several factors (Pattillo & Vaughn, 1992). Certainly, the needs of children are foremost in the selection of centers and materials, but other considerations must include space as well as the availability of materials and resources. Safety and the health of children cannot be overemphasized in the selection and organization of centers and materials for early childhood programs.

You can see the following types of learning centers in many early childhood programs, but you should consider each discussion as suggestions only. Because the materials for the centers should reflect the development of the children in each setting, no list can comprehensively satisfy all individual requirements or surpass the imagination and ingenuity of motivated teachers.

Art Center

The art center provides opportunities for creative expression while encouraging artistic appreciation (Nunnelley, 1990). It is best suited for a wet area location where children need not be concerned about drips or spills. A source of natural light facilitates the success and creativity of children in this center. The center should provide children with the challenges of working with a wide variety of mediums. Material selections should be varied in sizes, shapes, and textures.

The manipulation of assorted media promotes discovery. Children may be encouraged to express their emotions through painting, working with clay, and construction resources.

Art activities foster the refinement of motor skill development, including eye-hand coordination, ambidexterity, and fine motor functions. Psychomotor functions are encouraged as children cut, paste, and arrange materials. The implementation of a child-generated plan promotes problem-solving strategies as well as creative techniques (Waldrop & Scarborough, 1990).

Respect for oneself and others is promoted as children share their activities and projects. Collaboration and skills in sharing are often observed as children explore the art center. Visual arts become a means of expression and communication through which children are introduced to the art of others, including well-known works. Table 7.2 offers some suggestions for materials that could be collected for the art center.

Block Center

The use of blocks for young children has been well documented throughout much of the history of early childhood education. Osborn (1991) reported that Froebel included blocks in his teaching materials. Although pedagogical philosophies may differ, the developmental value of experiences with blocks remains unchallenged. As early as 1933, Johnson identified characteristics of block play (Johnson, 1933; Apelman, 1984).

The stages are typically observed between 2 and 6 years of age. They reflect physical, cognitive, social, emotional, and language development (Apelman, 1984). Here are some characteristics of each stage of development through block play:

- *Stage one* occurs as the child focuses on carrying a single block. During this stage, the independent block is not used for construction.
- *Stage two* is identifiable by the use of repetitive patterns. Blocks are placed in rows either side by side or end to end.

TABLE 7.2
Developing Materials for an Art Center

- Aprons (old shirts or smocks)
- Art prints and art objects
- Art tissue
- Bags (varied sizes)
- Books of crafts, artists, prints
- Brads
- Buttons, shaped macaroni, bottle caps
- Cafeteria trays for painting
- Cake tins for separating materials
- Chalk and pastels
- Cloth scraps
- Construction paper
- Corn starch, laundry starch
- Corrugated cardboard
- Crayons
- Display area
- Drip cloths, old rugs, shower curtain
- Drying rack
- Easels
- Finger paint
- Food coloring
- Formica-top tables or plastic tablecloth
- Flour, salt (for texture and playdough)
- Glue (white, water based)
- Glue sticks
- Looms
- Magazines and catalogs
- Magic markers
- Materials for weaving and sewing
- Modeling clay and playdough
- Orange juice cans (keep the lids)
- Paper (different sizes and colors)
- Paper scraps
- Paint (water based)
- Paintbrushes (varied sizes)
- Pencils and colored pencils
- Plastic containers with lids
- Paper clips
- Pins
- Pipe cleaners
- Rulers
- Scissors
- Socks
- Stapler and staples
- Tape (varied)
- Toothpicks
- Wallpaper samples
- Water colors
- Yarn

- *Stage three* is evidenced by the development of overlays of blocks. Children leave space between blocks while connecting them with a second layer. The effect is something like a bridge.
- *Stage four* suggests closure of formations. The structures begin to assume rectangular or square formations.
- *Stage five* serves as a transitional phase during which the builder forms symmetrical and decorative patterns. The structures provide repetitive formations but are still unnamed.
- *Stage six* is representational of a form or structure. Children name their structures and incorporate dramatic play elements in their activities with blocks.
- *Stage seven* is illustrated by the specific representation of buildings and structures that are familiar to the child. The

Block play provides opportunities for cooperation and collaboration.

child assumes roles and relationships relevant to the block design.

As children organize and design block structures, they are engaged in a wide range of concept development. These concepts include fundamentals of space and physical orientation. Balance and design are explored through problem-solving approaches to construction. Elements influencing mathematical foundations including more than, less than, seriation, classification, and categorization are enhanced by hands-on opportunities with blocks (Cartwright, 1990).

Social and language concepts are extended through the group dynamics of play. Children's block play begins with solitary interactions and extends to structures that include games and rules with other children. Children interpret their world through structures, creativity, and methods of exploration. The following block sets are typical of materials that may be found in an early childhood setting:

Unit blocks

- Set of solid wooden blocks including ramps, curves, elliptical, circular, Y shapes, triangles, cylinders, squares, single units, double units, quadruple units, pillars, half pillars, switches, arches, half arches, Gothic doors, curves, and buttresses.
- Sets contain 750 blocks; accommodate 18 to 20 children.

Hollow blocks

- Large hardwood blocks used to extend unit blocks.
- Sets include square (5½" × 11" × 11"), double square, half square, ramp, short board (⅝" × 3¾" × 22"), and long board (¾" × 5½").
- Classroom set contains 60 to 80 hollow blocks.

Table blocks

- One-inch solid wood cubes.
- Collection of 50 to 100 blocks.

Foam blocks

- Large blocks (8" × 8" sizes to 11" × 11½") of lightweight, dense foam.
- Light weight has appeal for the needs of 2- and 3-year-olds.

Waffle blocks

- Lightweight, sturdy plastic pieces.
- Large pieces about 14".
- Set contains 50 blocks.

Interlocking blocks

- Lego and Duplo blocks.
- Interlocking pieces standard and large blocks.

Magnet blocks

- Plastic blocks with internal magnets.
- Set contains varied shapes and colors.

Because playing with blocks is noisy, the center should be located in an area where other centers will not be disturbed. Low, open shelves provide easy access to the blocks and serve as a divider between other centers. Housing for the blocks should appear inviting and offer a simple organizational plan for storage (Hirsch, 1984). Teachers may use symbols for children to identify the best location for materials during cleanup. A low pile carpet will insulate sound and provide a suitable base for building. Block centers should be placed in a low traffic area. Corner locations or dividers can be used to limit movement to a single entrance. Since block projects may be extended over several days, a single-entrance system is a wise choice to prevent structures from being tumbled.

Early childhood teachers will find that the cost of a set of blocks is well worth the investment. Supplementary materials may be provided to extend the center's potential and enrich the environment for social dramatic play through props (Myhre, 1993). Supplements to the block center for extending its potential are listed in Table 7.3.

KIDS SPEAK UP

I can build tall buildings with my blocks.

Boy, 4 years old

Communications Center (Library, Listening, Writing)

The communications center, often identified as the library center, should be designed to promote literacy through explorations in language. Organize the center so that all strands of communications are present. These strands include listening opportunities, oral language experiences, and writing opportunities, as well as an environment rich with books and prints. A center-based approach to language promotes the natural evolution of a child's emerging language interests, skills, and abilities.

Library Component. Although a goal of all learning centers should be to promote literacy, a thoughtfully arranged and supplied library serves as an essential resource in the classroom. It is through

TABLE 7.3
Props for Block Center

- Wheel toys (tractor and trailer, derrick truck)
- Small vehicles (airplane; helicopter; dump truck; open-ended, simple toys that allow for imagination)
- Toy zoo and farm animals
- People models (health care professional, farmer, firefighter)
- Traffic signs
- Steering wheel
- Ropes
- Homemade blocks
- Tinker toys
- Lincoln logs
- Sheets for tents and imagination
- Balance beam
- Boxes
- Puppets
- Hard hats
- Architect designs
- Graph paper
- Camera with film to record structures
- Paper and pencils to illustrate plans and label structures

this center that children are stimulated to develop an understanding of the relationship between oral language and symbols of print. Success and satisfaction for beginning readers is promoted as children make choices and refine interests and preferences in literature. Resources in this center encourage developmental understandings of such things as how books "work." Book knowledge, including front, back, pages, and left-to-right progression of print are significantly more meaningful to the child as a result of selective encounters with books.

Children are invited to read for pleasure, achievement, and information (Kostelnik, Soderman, & Whiren, 1993). Language is extended through concepts of story telling and enhancing the concepts of sequence and comprehension. This center encourages the transfer of ideas and skills to cross content areas through the selections available (Danielson, 1990).

The library center should be located in a quiet part of the room. Since this area is a low-mobility center, it should have a single entrance and exit. Provide a large rug or carpeted area as the base for an inviting center. Pillows, carpet squares, or floor cushions help children to identify personal space. Rocking chairs, couches, or bean bags are appropriate for children in this center. Open shelving, tables, and chairs are also important for an effective library center.

Teachers may gather an assortment of books as resources. Some teachers will place books related to a project or unit theme in the center, in addition to a wide range of books to meet several diverse interests. Selections should be evaluated for their structural quality and developmental appropriateness. Magazines, catalogs, and encyclopedias are an asset to promote and extend the interests of children.

Including Authorship. Child-made books and equipment to extend writing are essential to this center. Such tools range from the obvious, such as paper and pencils, to less traditional items such as colored pens, markers, typewriters, or computers. Dictionaries and children's pictionaries should be available. Leftover stationery, cards, and envelopes promote the transitions to print as a natural flow in communications.

Literacy and Technology. Microcomputers and typewriters may be effectively located in the library center (Burns, Goin, & Donlin, 1990). Children who are invited to use equipment in the process of development are risk takers and openly construct understanding as they explore (Swick, 1989; Hyson & Eyman, 1986). Select software that meets the developmental needs of children who will use the center. Today's state-of-the-art software offers a variety of experiences for children (Haugland & Shade, 1990). Teachers must become the careful consumers of such materials (Anselmo & Zinck, 1987). Swick (1989) suggests that the inclusion of computers in a naturally

An environment that offers easy access to literacy tools promotes enthusiasm for communication.

approachable forum introduces children to more than technology; it also promotes social exchanges, invention, and an effective way of encouraging children to think.

Listening Concerns. Listening stations, filmstrip stations, and flannel-board equipment are prompts for language extension. Simple directions provide children the autonomy to create, imagine, and appreciate communications.

Teachers will find that an overnight checkout system encourages children to select a favorite book from their time in the center and extend that enthusiasm to the home. The responsibility of returning the book the next day for others who will visit the center may be set early in the year. Teachers will discover a wide range of materials and techniques for extending and modifying this center to promote the development of the children they serve.

Home and Dramatic Play Center

One of the most popular and developmentally significant learning centers is the home center or dramatic play center. This center serves as the location for child-size home equipment including cabinets, refrigerators, stoves, sinks, tables, and chairs. Telephones,

Simple props may be provided to encourage sociodramatic play.

mirrors, dolls, and stuffed toys are among the materials located in the center to stimulate nurturance and empathy.

The home and dramatic play center requires space. A corner location provides a natural barrier, communicating a more homelike atmosphere and resolving some issues of movement. The materials provided within the center offer children experiences such as social, culture, language, mathematical, and scientific concepts. Physical and emotional skills are among the many possible targeted areas for children's use of the center. Teachers should rotate the materials in the center to promote continued interest. We suggest the following items as possible materials to be included in the home and dramatic play center:

Puppets
Brooms, mop, dustpan
Brushes
Dishpan
Small table, chairs
Small rug
Dolls
Doll bed
Sponges, cloths
Dishes, silverware
Rocking chair
Puppet stages, boxes, or a television case
Clothes rack
Child-size sink, stove, refrigerator, cupboard
Open shelves
Doll clothing
Cooking utensils
Doll carriage
Full-length safety mirror
Curtains for window area

- Artificial foods
- Ironing board, iron
- Jewelry, shoes, handbags, hats, coats, dresses, wigs, pants, ties
- Clotheslines
- Clock
- Stuffed animals
- Telephone and book
- Pails
- Newspaper, grocery list pads
- Seasonal household items, wrapping paper, cards
- Sheets, pillows, blankets
- Dried beans and peas

Prop collections are sources of materials related to a specific theme. Collections are designed to promote sociodramatic play. Themes are limited only by the careful decisions of teachers. General topics may include occupation or community helpers. A prop collection contains the tools of the trade.

Math and Manipulatives Center

The term **manipulatives** refers to development of skills through the movement of materials. These materials are referred to as concrete in that they visually and physically occupy space. They serve as the tangible representations of a child's understanding. Piagetian theory suggests that young children are not abstract thinkers. Consequently, assigning concepts such as name, number, volume, or quantity is a complex skill for young thinkers. Meaning and value are reinforced as the child touches and moves concrete materials.

Typically, manipulatives include items that engage the child in motor and concept development. These materials might include beads (for stringing), puzzles, construction sets, and board games. Other materials may include clocks, measuring spoons, and cups. Teacher-made games, unit rods, number lines, balances, play money, pegs and pegboards, geometric shapes, dominoes, and things to measure may be accumulated to promote and direct concepts of math.

Teachers might include items for counting such as blocks, beads, sticks, straws, buttons, clothespins, or bottle caps. Scales and objects for weighing, rulers, yardsticks, meter sticks, tape measures, paper clips, straws, or other objects used to measure might also be included in the center.

The use of small manipulatives has been related to reading readiness, fine motor skills, social studies, and math. Increased attention span, auditory discrimination, visual discrimination, language skills, and concept formation are included as benefits for the successful use of manipulatives (Seefeldt & Barbour, 1990).

As children interact with manipulatives, the potential for organization, classification, and categorization abound. Focusing on math as a component of this center, children explore and experiment with the underlying principles of problem solving. Measurement and sequencing are actively investigated. Explorations of geometric and nontraditional shapes are also possible.

Center materials may be stored on open shelves in small baskets. Teachers may find that this center is an effective starting point for children as the day begins. The location should be away from the entrance, and enough materials should be included to allow for choices and involvement of every child. See Chapter 10 for further discussion of math and science themes and concepts.

Music and Sound Center

In many centers, the once-traditional piano has given up its space for a keyboard, record player, or tape recorder. Whatever the central source for the music and sound center, teachers should recognize the value of this center (Hitz, 1987). Teachers promote these objectives through the use of music and sound as a learning center:

- To encourage understanding of the basic elements of music: melody, harmony, rhythm, tempo, dynamics of tone, mood and texture (through singing, playing instruments, and movement).
- To listen and react through self-expression and placing a value on music, thus encouraging appreciation for all types of music.
- To use music as a vehicle for creativity, to develop individual self-confidence, and to build self-esteem in the student.
- To develop skills in identifying environmental, animal, and human sounds.
- To encourage language development through the use of songs, chants, and fingerplays.
- To develop motor control by stimulating the use of musical instruments.
- To foster a love for music.
- To appreciate and respect historical, cultural, and social diversity of music.

Equipment for this center should include commercial or teacher-made rhythm instruments. Materials children can use to make instruments include sturdy paper plates, boxes, dowel rods, bottle caps, pebbles, stones, beans, marbles, and cans. Tape recorders, varied tapes, and earphones extend music experiences. Sound relationships may also be explored through materials including glasses of water and spoons, as well as authentic musical instruments.

Posters of musicians, music, and musical instruments lend themselves to establishing the center. This center should be located in an area where acoustics may compensate for a noisy environment. A carpeted area with low mobility is best for a music center.

Science Center

The science center is designed to encourage the development of concepts through exploration and experimentation as a result of both incidental and contrived situations. Children are natural scientists and enthusiastically explore the boundaries of this center. One result is that they discover ways to use the scientific method of problem solving in observing and identifying problems. They are encouraged to perform research in order to test their predictions and generalize their findings. Through these efforts, they are encouraged to discuss their discoveries with others (Malecki, 1990).

TEACHERS SPEAK OUT

I believe in the developmental approach to many activities. In setting up an art table for the children, I've found it very enjoyable for them when they've had a variety of tools (scissors, tape, glue, paper, one-hole punch, stapler, markers, etc.) from which to choose. From these materials the children have created books, spaceships, costumes, and anything their hearts desire.

Children learn to care and have respect for plants and animals. They are exposed to a classification of systems. As an outcome of working in the science center, children develop a positive attitude toward living things and the environment.

Science centers should be exciting. They should be located near a source of light where drips and spills will not hinder investigations. Displays and equipment should be inviting. The teacher should provide resources to promote the enthusiastic exploration of ideas. The center might include donated lab coats and photo name tags to identify the children in this center as scientists.

Equipment for the center might include magnifying glasses (individual and tripod), insect cages, pets, different kinds of soil, magnets, prisms, seeds, watering cans, objects that float and sink, terrariums, thermometers, and objects that can be assembled and disassembled. Theme materials such as simple machines, pulleys, levers, and inclined planes promote understanding.

Sand and Water Centers

Sand and water centers are viewed by many as a complex medium. Children work creatively in a social setting. Large and small muscle skills are challenged as children dig, move, and build with sand. The open-ended materials allow children to build and mold formations.

Both sand and water tables extend the concept of exploration through quantity, measurement, and volume. Water tables further incorporate concepts of sinking or floating as items of classification.

Social, language, emotional, and group collaborative skills are extended.

These centers should be located in zones where cleanup is easy. It is beneficial to be near a source of water. Teachers have found that the traditional water table may be replaced by filling a sink or a plastic dishpan with water. Indoor sand tables may be filled with rice, beans, uncooked oatmeal, birdseed, or packing foam. If carpeting is a concern, teachers may secure a plastic table cloth or shower curtain to the floor.

Toy cars, trucks, and people may be used to extend play. Pots, pans, dishes, and silverware added to the center will foster extended activities. Parents may be encouraged to share clean milk cartons, food containers, and towel rolls for the center. Squeeze bottles, shovels, scoops, sifters, strainers, and funnels may also serve as extension resources for the center.

Woodworking Construction Center

The enthusiasm with which children meet the tasks of woodworking and construction is a springboard to a full range of skill potentials. As children plan and implement strategies of building, they express themselves creatively. The organization of resources, balance of materials, and use of equipment must operate together to secure the child's goal.

Children use many skills as they participate in woodworking activities.

Through the enterprise, children discover the relationships of equality, inequality, and proportionate comparisons while building and constructing with wood and other materials. They communicate with one another while solving common problems.

Woodworking also provides a positive release for emotions through nonverbal expressions. The reward of woodworking is the continuing process of discovery through investigation.

Children develop eye-hand coordination by manipulating tools. Muscle coordination is enhanced as children hammer, saw, lift, and carry. Teachers may find that a woodworking center located inside is not practical for all projects. But manipulation of some woodworking activities that do not require hammering may find a place indoors. This center should be handled as a construction site. Children should be encouraged to follow specific safety precautions. Goggles and hardhats should be regular equipment in the building zone, just as they are at any building site. This center does require the supervision of an adult. Often, parent and community volunteers may be solicited to participate in construction activities.

It is important that children have real tools for their projects. Toys or poor-quality equipment are as frustrating for a child as they would be to an adult craftsman. A well-supplied wood and construction center might include these materials:

Sturdy workbench
Storage shelves
4" C-clamps
Pliers
Vise for workbench
Miter box
Plane
Nails (variety)
Paint (water based)
Wood scraps
Scissors
Sawhorse, hand saw
Hand drill with several bits
Hammers (7 to 10 oz. claw)
Screwdrivers (Phillips and standard)
Brushes (varied)
Broom, dustpan
Hooks and screws
Rulers, yardstick
Rags
Glue (white, water based)

Old carpet may be used to cover the workbench and reduce hammering sounds. In addition, supplies for the center could include blueprints, illustrative sketches, and photographs of the children's work. Extensive woodworking or construction centers can be effectively implemented outdoors to increase collaborative planning and encourage ongoing activity. It is essential that the center, whether indoors or out, be carefully monitored to ensure that tools are in good operating condition and that safety is a priority. The developmental value of this center is well worth the considerations necessary for its operation.

ROOM ARRANGEMENTS, SCHEDULES, AND MONITORING

Learning centers accommodate materials for children to discover such concepts as classification, seriation, and temporal influences. The dynamics of the experience are gently guided by the teacher, whose skills in grouping students, organizing materials, selecting materials, and scheduling are critical. The process is not an art or a coincidence. The learning that occurs as the result is not incidental.

Research suggests that the successful use of learning centers should not be regarded as child's play (Cummings, 1989; Day, 1988). Psychological, sociological, physiological, linguistic, and cognitive structures are being formed as children interact within this environment.

Room Arrangement

Carefully selected materials, attractively displayed and arranged, are the beginning of an effective learning environment. Loughlin and Martin (1987) suggest that knowledge of the "arranged environment" is necessary to successfully meet the needs of children (p. 6). Every aspect of the early childhood environment offers the potential for a learning experience. The placement of centers and materials, according to Loughlin (1977), is an instructional device that reinforces and inspires learning.

Children are not concerned with the same use of space as adults. The arrangement of a center should focus on the environment from an approximate level of three feet to the floor. This space is the actual operational space of children in the classroom. As teachers establish room design, they should take a child's view by sitting down to consider a child's perspective.

Shapiro (1975) suggests that dividing the room into L- and U-shaped formations increases the opportunities for successful arrangements of centers. An L shape is obtained with the use of corners. The U form provides single entrances and exits. Figure 7.3 illustrates how furniture, shelves, bookcases, and low dividers can be used to form traffic flow patterns and determine the possible number of learning centers.

A teacher may develop a profile for appropriate arrangements of centers, combining the conditional needs of each center with regard to low traffic, light, noise, water, and space. Early review of available space, combined with an understanding of the needs of each center, gives the teacher a framework for decision making. Consider Table 7.4, which is an inventory of two learning centers.

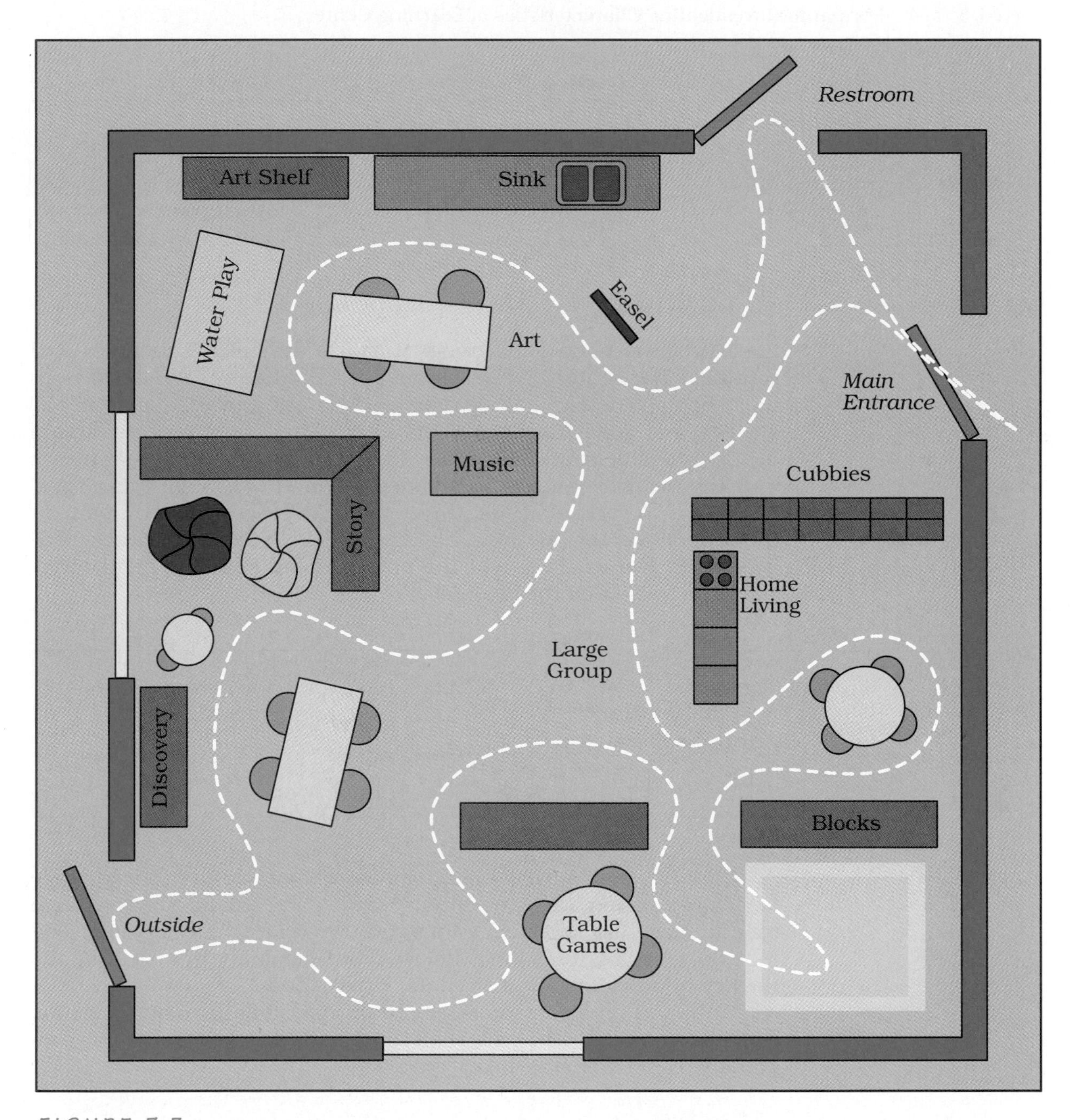

FIGURE 7.3
Determining Potentials for Room Arrangement

Source: L. Ard and M. Pitts (Eds.), *Room to grow: How to create quality early childhood environments.* (Austin, TX: Texas Association for the Education of Young Children 1990), p. 20.

TABLE 7.4 Format for Investigating Characteristics of Learning Centers

	Space	Light	Traffic	Noise	Water	Additional
Art	Open	Natural	Low	No	Yes	Need place to dry, display art.
Blocks	Single entrance	No	High movement	High	No	Possible to leave structures?

Schedules

Each program philosophy brings with it a system of schedules and routines. The center-based approach is no different. Several factors must be considered, including arrival, planning, transitions, meals, snacks, and quiet times (Crosser, 1992). The use of centers should be a predictable part of each day. Children respond to daily routines and the security and certainty that such rituals can bring (Bredekamp & Rosegrant, 1992; Crosser, 1992). If the teacher organizes the room in center rotations, children quickly recognize their schedules. They will easily accept the predictability of which center they will be in today and the next day.

KIDS SPEAK UP

The dress up center is on Monday. Blocks are tomorrow and the next day we paint. This week I am going to make a house when I get to the block center.

Girl, 5 years old

Christie and Wardle (1992) indicate that children need large blocks of time to engage in center activities. Each child needs enough time to close the activities initiated during play. Teachers may find that 30 to 45 minutes are sufficient, but flexibility in scheduling is the key to providing effective center explorations.

Table 7.5 provides some scheduling possibilities using learning centers in daily plans for half and full day programs of pre-kindergarten through primary grades.

Grouping Children for Experiences

Piaget (1952), Vygotsky (1978), and Erikson (1963) are among the theorists whose work emphasizes the importance of social interactions in the developmental process. Knowledge is constructed as a result of dynamic and reciprocal exchanges between the child and the physical and social settings (Bredekamp & Rosengrant, 1992).

TABLE 7.5 Planning for Integrating Learning Centers

Half-Day Schedules		Full-Day Schedules	
Programs for Four-Year-Olds		***Programs for Five-Year-Olds***	
8:00 a.m.	Focused Opening Activity. Children have an activity that brings them together as they begin the day. Examples include small manipulatives box, puzzles, or an art activity. Circle Activity. Teacher and children discuss the day and plan their activities. Transitions may include music, stories, or fingerplays.	8:00 a.m.	Opening, Sharing, Planning, Discussion
		8:30 a.m.	Learning Center Activities
		9:30 a.m.	Outdoor Play
		10:00 a.m.	Story Time
		10:30 a.m.	Whole Group Activities
		11:00 a.m.	Lunch
		11:30 a.m.	Quiet Time
		12:00 noon	Small Group Activities
		12:30 p.m.	Learning Center Activities
8:30 a.m.	Learning Center Time. Examples include dividing children into small groups to work in individual centers. Teacher observes and directs.	1:30 p.m.	Library, Music, Art, or Physical Activity
		2:00 p.m.	Story Time
		2:30 p.m.	Sharing Events, Evaluation of Day
9:30 a.m.	Outdoor Play	3:00 p.m.	Dismissal
10:00 a.m.	Snack Time	***Programs for Primary Grades***	
10:30 a.m.	Story Time	8:00 a.m.	Opening, Planning for the Day, and Discussion
10:45 a.m.	Preparing to Go Home		
11:00 a.m.	Dismissal	8:30 a.m.	Learning Center Time, Teacher conferences with children
Programs for Five-Year-Olds			
8:00 a.m.	Opening, Planning, Sharing	10:30 a.m.	Outdoor Play
8:30 a.m.	Learning Center Time	11:00 a.m.	Whole Group Activity
9:30 a.m.	Whole Group Activities	11:30 a.m.	Lunch
10:00 a.m.	Outdoor Play	12:00 noon	Story Time
10:30 a.m.	Story Time, Evaluation of Day, Preparing to Go Home	12:30 p.m.	Small Group Activities
		1:00 p.m.	Learning Center
11:00 a.m.	Dismissal	2:00 p.m.	Library, Music, Art, or Physical Activity
		2:30 p.m.	Closure, Review of the day
		3:00 p.m.	Dismissal

These constructs of knowledge appear to be fundamental to all areas of development (DeVries & Kohlberg, 1990; Ferreiro & Teberosky, 1982; Teale & Sulzby, 1986).

Considerations for children should include careful observations related to the individual needs of children. Often this process of grouping is an opportunity for children with compatible needs to work together in small social settings to the mutual benefit of each child. Although it is not possible to assume what the personal chemistry of a group will be without being in the classroom, teachers can make certain predictions based on common sense. For example, the combination of several aggressive children in a single group may encourage a negative situation. A center grouping that includes only quiet children may not stimulate the group members to initiate invention and exploration. Teachers will find that using flexibility in groupings gives them opportunities to observe and balance the placement of children. Determination of groupings should not be perceived as permanent. In Chapter 5, we emphasized the benefits of play and socialization that are related to group dynamics.

TEACHERS SPEAK OUT

I enjoy working with young children because you can see the joy they get out of discovering new things and mastering them. There is always something new to learn, and children will challenge you in a way that keeps you motivated.

The grouping and rotations of children within the centers is clearly significant to the development of children. Two approaches are typically used in the process. The first and most common is the external regimenting of group and center assignments. This approach is a teacher-directed strategy used to manage the centers in a prescriptive technique. Children are grouped for reasons such as mixed abilities, developmental and age grouping, gender, and culture. Groups are routed through areas of the room, often using management techniques such as color codes rather than student selection. For instance, group 1 could be in the green center on Monday, and group 2 could be in the blue center. While most teachers suggest this scheme is a successful management philosophy, it is not the most appropriate developmental approach to center scheduling (Hohmann et al., 1979). The rotation system does not meet the interests or unique skills and talents of the individual child.

A second approach to grouping is student decision. Teachers can initiate a system that lets the children select the center they work in during the day. Educators will find it important to limit the numbers of children in each center. A master chart can be used to follow the children's work selections for the week. Such charts help the teacher in gathering information about student preferences as well as in determining center changes.

Monitoring

Fundamental to the operation of learning centers in the early childhood setting is the teacher's ability to intelligently observe and make decisions. In Chapter 4, we presented a broad scope for observation and assessment strategies that are applicable to monitoring and assessing individual development in learning centers.

Children can be included in the monitoring process. Teachers can use rebus checklists to determine student satisfaction with a particular center or a child's self-evaluation of performance. Children mark the face that best expresses how they feel about their work in the center. They may circle the centers they enjoy the most, or indicate the centers they did not enjoy. Teacher-child conferences are effective systems of evaluation as well.

PARENTS SPEAK OUT

The entire family participates in gathering things for the preschool. This month we are saving tissue rolls.

Teachers should maintain records of each child's activities and modify, replenish, and implement regrouping strategies based on these observations. The effective teacher soon discovers that the center schedule is one of the most productive and busiest for the child and the professional.

Staff members contribute significantly to the success of children in the class environment. They become much more than observers of behavior; they can greatly influence the success of children through their own behaviors (Bredekamp & Rosegrant, 1992):

- Staff members are available to children.
- Adults are responsive to children.
- Staff members are courteous, friendly, and inviting.
- Staff members use positive guidance and redirection when needed.
- Staff members help children to deal with problems such as anger, disappointment, frustration, or sadness.
- Staff members encourage and model positive social behavior.

PARENTS AS A RESOURCE

Parents are genuinely interested in the philosophies and strategies implemented in early childhood. The use of learning centers and their effectiveness are common concerns. Teachers can encourage a supportive base for developmentally appropriate practices by communicating the purposes of learning centers to parents. Involving parents in the development and implementation of materials extends the potential for a child's success. Parents who are aware that the world their children live in is an extended center for learning become enthusiastic about the approach.

Parents and families are an excellent source of materials for extending the learning centers. Adults working together form a coalition of well-informed early education supporters. Communications frame understanding and cooperation. In Chapter 14, "Parent-Teacher Partnerships," we extend the discussion of family and school communications.

SUMMARY

Visitors to an early childhood classroom will discover physical indicators of the program and a teacher's philosophy. These cues inside room arrangement, environmental design, and materials. Academic preschools, traditional primary programs, and behavioral approaches address direct-instruction programming.

Developmentally motivated programs include activity center environments, cognitively oriented approaches, and prepared environments or maturational strategies. Environmental designs suggest the role of the child and the teacher in the educational approaches taken. Children need a feeling of ownership in reference to their school, room, and teacher.

Sound, light, color, temperature, humidity, and space contribute to a climate of success for young children. Concerns for developing space must include issues of private and public areas.

Learning centers refers to specific areas where materials have been gathered as a topic or theme. The use of learning centers is an efficient way of meeting the needs of the multifaceted developmental levels in an early childhood class.

The selection of centers depends on resources, space, and the needs of individual children. Center selection may include, but should not be limited to art, blocks, communications, home and dramatic play, math and manipulatives, music and sound, sand and water, science, and woodworking.

Room arrangement plays an important part in the movement and use of an early childhood center. Coupled with the selection of materials, teachers can gently guide the direction of learning. The choice of materials should emphasize the safety and health of children while meeting developmental concerns.

Two thoughts on grouping emphasize the difference between teacher-controlled and teacher-directed use of the centers. As children interact with materials and people, the potential for learning is enhanced. A well-documented system of observations and monitoring generates modifications and an extension of developmental opportunities for children.

TEST YOUR UNDERSTANDING

1. What is meant by the phrase "environment of a classroom"?
2. What is a classroom learning center?
3. List some environmental characteristics of each of the following programs:
   a. Academic preschools environment
   b. Traditional primary environment
   c. Activity centers environment
   d. Prepared environment
4. List the permanent features teachers must work with in designing an early childhood classroom.
5. Identify five environmental conditions that must be considered in preparing an early childhood classroom.
6. Discuss a child's environmental ownership as it relates to the classroom.
7. You have just observed two children playing in the block center. One is holding a block and watching others play. The second child has arranged the blocks end to end. Discuss the stage of development each child is demonstrating.
8. How can the use of learning centers help teachers individualize their approaches to teaching?
9. What are the values of using learning centers?
10. Discuss three strategies for involving parents in the development of classrooms that may help them understand a learning center philosophy.

LEARNING ACTIVITIES

1. Design a floor plan for an imaginary early childhood classroom.
2. Select three learning centers and develop a wish list of materials you would place in the center.
3. Write a paragraph for an elementary school newsletter about the value of dress-up materials in the home center.
4. Develop a list of indoor plants that would be appropriate for an early childhood classroom.
5. Design a communications center for a kindergarten. What materials would you include?

8. Brainstorm a list of resources in your community for free or inexpensive materials that might be used in developing learning centers.
9. Visit an early childhood classroom in your area. Describe how the teacher uses learning centers.

CHAPTER 8 Motor Development and Movement

CHAPTER OUTLINE

Motor Development
- *Principles of Development*
- *Physical Growth and Development*

Educational Movement Programs
- *Movement Program Goals*
- *Developmental Characteristics*
- *Phases of Motor Skill Development*
- *Developmentally Appropriate Movement Activities, Teaching Strategies, and Equipment*

Characteristics of a Good Playground
- *Using the Playspace*
- *Installing and Maintaining the Playspace for Safety*

KEY TERMS

Motor development
Cephalocaudal
Proximodistal
Maturation
Physical growth
Learning to move
Learning through movement
Perceptual motor development
Foundational movement
Fundamental motor skills

The teacher for the after-school program had been watching the children on the playground. That day, the usual reenactments of television heros were forgotten as one boy worked on teaching another how to skip. Jamie, a boy of about 8, had spent most of the afternoon trying to teach a younger friend how to maneuver his feet in a skipping pattern. When he decided a break was necessary, Jamie sat down beside the teacher and announced, "I've been trying to teach Turner how to skip, but he just can't get it." The teacher listened as Jamie continued, "He does this goofy hopping thing. When I tell him he's not skipping, he gets real mad and yells, 'I *am* skipping,' and then he takes off doing that hopping thing again."

The teacher looked thoughtful for a moment before suggesting, "You know, Turner is 5 years old."

Without thinking, Jamie responded, "He just doesn't pay attention, and I'm getting mad!"

"Jamie, do you remember when your little sister was starting to walk?" the teacher asked. Jamie nodded yes, remembering the tiny steps. "Do you remember how she climbed stairs?" she continued. Jamie nodded again, thinking of how she scooted from one step to the next. "Skipping is like that for Turner," she explained.

"But Turner can walk and climb stairs," Jamie protested.

"Yes, and before long he'll be skipping, too," she concluded.

"Oh, I get it—when he grows up like me." Jamie stretched the words to indicate he understood.

"In the meantime, maybe you can help Turner by just letting him hop while you skip," the teacher suggested.

"You're a neat teacher," Jamie observed. "How do you know so much about skipping?"

"Oh, I read it in a book or studied it in class," she replied. Noticing that the boy did not look satisfied with her answer, she added, "Or maybe I learned it from watching you and Turner."

Jamie giggled, and as he skipped backwards to Turner, he wondered what his teacher might know about whistling.

The importance of movement is evident early in life. Movement is the basis for all learning and serves as the foundation for psychomotor, cognitive, and affective development. It is through movement that infants discover and gain control over their environment. Movement serves as a vehicle for nonverbal communication, expression, and learning (American Alliance for Health, Physical Education, Recreation, and Dance, 1986). Therefore, quality, daily movement programs should be an integral part of early childhood programs and should be available to all children.

The Council on Physical Education for Children (COPEC), a subgroup of the American Alliance for Health, Physical Education, Recreation, and Dance (AAHPERD), has developed a position statement, *Developmentally Appropriate Practice in Movement Programs for Young Children* (in press). This document, modeled after the developmentally appropriate practices published by the National Association for Education of Young Children (NAEYC), identifies appropriate and inappropriate practices (i.e., do's and don'ts) for early childhood movement programs. The following premises provide the basis for quality early childhood movement programs:

- "Young children learn through interaction with their environment" (p. 3). Children must be active participants, not passive or inactive observers.
- "Teachers of young children are guides or facilitators" (p. 4). Teachers design activities with specific goals in mind, but allow children to make choices and explore.
- "Young children do not learn or develop according to narrowly defined subject areas" (p. 4). All domains of learning (psychomotor, cognitive, and affective) are related. Movement program activities should draw upon the natural connections among these domains.
- "Movement programs and play are different" (p. 4). Play is essential and results in learning. But play should not be viewed as a substitute for planned movement experiences, nor should planned movement experiences be viewed as a substitute for play.

In this chapter, we describe the elements of developmentally appropriate movement programs for young children and the basis upon which such programs are developed. This basis includes the nature and principles of motor development. Educators of young children should have a strong knowledge base of child development, including motor development. In the following section, we introduce you to basic motor development.

MOTOR DEVELOPMENT

Motor development is the study of changes in performance of motor skills throughout the lifespan and the factors that influence these changes. Two factors are the principles of development and the nature of physical growth. Such factors are interactive in nature and help explain the way motor skills develop (see Figure 8.1). Familiarity with the developmental principles and physical growth trends helps teachers

- Understand how young children acquire motor skills
- Identify children whose development may be delayed
- Design appropriate movement programs based upon the abilities of the children

FIGURE 8.1
Interactive Factors Affecting Motor Skill Development

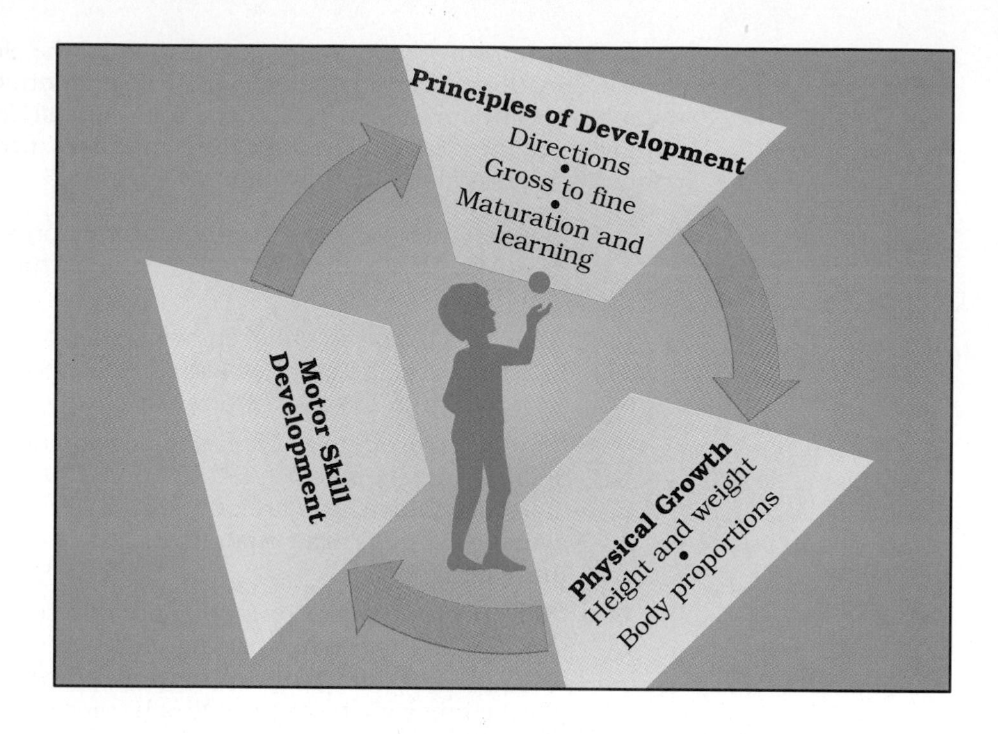

Principles of Development

Principles that apply to many aspects of development include the directions of development, gross to fine muscle development, and the roles of maturation and environment. We provide here a brief overview of each principle.

Developmental Directions. Cephalocaudal and proximodistal describe the orderly and progressive directions in which growth and the development of motor skills occur. **Cephalocaudal**, literally interpreted, means "head to tail." Physical growth patterns and the nature of motor control illustrate this direction of development. The relative sizes of the body segments at birth show that the head and trunk have undergone the most growth up to this point. At birth, the head constitutes two-fifths of total body length. By maturity, the head has increased only twice its birth size, while the legs have grown five times their birth length.

PARENTS SPEAK OUT

The physical development of our child has been one of the most exciting aspects of parenthood.

Motor control is gained in a cephalocaudal direction. The infant first develops control of the head, followed by the neck, trunk, and finally the legs. The order in which the major motor milestones emerge also illustrates this point (i.e., lifting the head, turning over, sitting, crawling, creeping, independent standing, and walking).

Proximodistal, meaning "from the center or midline to the periphery," is also illustrated by growth patterns and motor control. Development during the prenatal period occurs from the midline of the body around the spinal column outward to the extremities. The attainment of the skill of grasping clarifies the proximodistal direction of motor control. Initially, infants move the arm and hand as a unit when grasping an object. With maturity, differentiated movements of the arm and hand are evident as infants grasp an object with the fingers and thumb.

This direction of development is also clear when considering the developmental progression of the skill of catching. That is, at first children use their arms and body to maintain possession of the tossed object in a "scooping" motion before using the hands and fingers in a cuplike fashion. Thus, it is inappropriate to expect a child who uses the scooping motion to catch a small object such as a tennis ball. In the activities and equipment section of this chapter, we address this concept further.

Gross to Fine Muscle Development. Children first establish control over the large (gross) muscles of the body, followed by control over the smaller (fine) muscles. Traditionally, motor skills have been categorized as either gross or fine motor. A more contemporary view is that few movements are totally of one type of another (Payne & Isaacs, 1991). Instead, they are the combined movements of the large and small muscles. For example, the skill of throwing involves using the large muscles of the arm and shoulder as well as the small muscles in the hand and fingers. The large muscles are essential in producing the force of the throw, while the small muscles are important for controlling the accuracy of the throw. Knowing that gross muscle control develops before fine muscle control, it is important for teachers and parents to stress force production with young children before emphasizing accuracy.

Roles of Maturation and Environment. The third principle of development relates to the combined influence of maturation and environment upon motor development. **Maturation** is the qualitative changes occurring with age that cause an individual to progress to a higher functioning level. Maturation is a fixed order of progression that is primarily innate and genetically determined. Individuals follow a predictive, progressive sequence of development; but the rate of development varies among individuals.

The experiences children have within their environment may speed up or slow down their maturation rate. But until a child is physically *and* cognitively mature enough to learn a skill, he or she does not benefit from instruction and practice of the skill (Gabbard, LeBlanc, & Lowy, 1987). Because not all children of the same chronological age are at the same point in the sequence of development, they are not all necessarily ready for the same experiences.

Physical Growth and Development

Physical growth refers to the quantitative, structural changes that occur with age, that is, increases in the size and number of cells in the body. Physical growth affects the development of motor skills. Growth within the skeletal and muscular systems that results in changes in height, weight, and body proportions are most relevant to this discussion. A brief overview of the trends in physical growth and their relationship to motor skill development follows.

Height and Weight. The most rapid growth period in life occurs from the prenatal period through the first year. At birth, the average length (height) is about 20 inches for males and 19.75 inches for females. From birth to age 1, there is a 50 percent increase in length; by age 2, children reach one-half their adult stature. After age 2, there is a slow but steady increase in height (about 2 inches per year). Some children experience a mid-growth spurt between 5-½ and 7 years of age (Gabbard, 1992).

At birth, the average weight is 7.5 lbs. for males and 7 lbs. for females. As expected, the average weight among infants is more variable and is more readily influenced by environment than is height (length). Weight generally doubles by 3 to 4 months of age, triples by the end of the first year, and quadruples by the end of the second year. Weight gain slows down following the second year and remains steady for the next three years, with a gain of about 4.5 lbs. per year (Lowrey, 1986).

The effect of children's height and weight upon their attainment of motor skills during infancy and the toddler years is inconclusive. Studies of the relationship between weight and height and the onset of independent walking (Jaffe & Kosakov, 1982) show that while longer, lighter infants tend to walk earlier, most of the shorter, heavier infants catch up within one year (Payne & Isaacs, 1991). Later in childhood and on into adolescence and adulthood, the excess weight for height does influence various movement abilities, such as those that require moving the body through space (e.g., jumping).

Body Proportions. As we stated earlier, while each child follows the same sequence of development, they do not do so at the same rate. This pattern is also true of the growth of various body segments (see Figure 8.2). That is, from birth to the completion of growth, the head doubles in size while the trunk triples, the arms

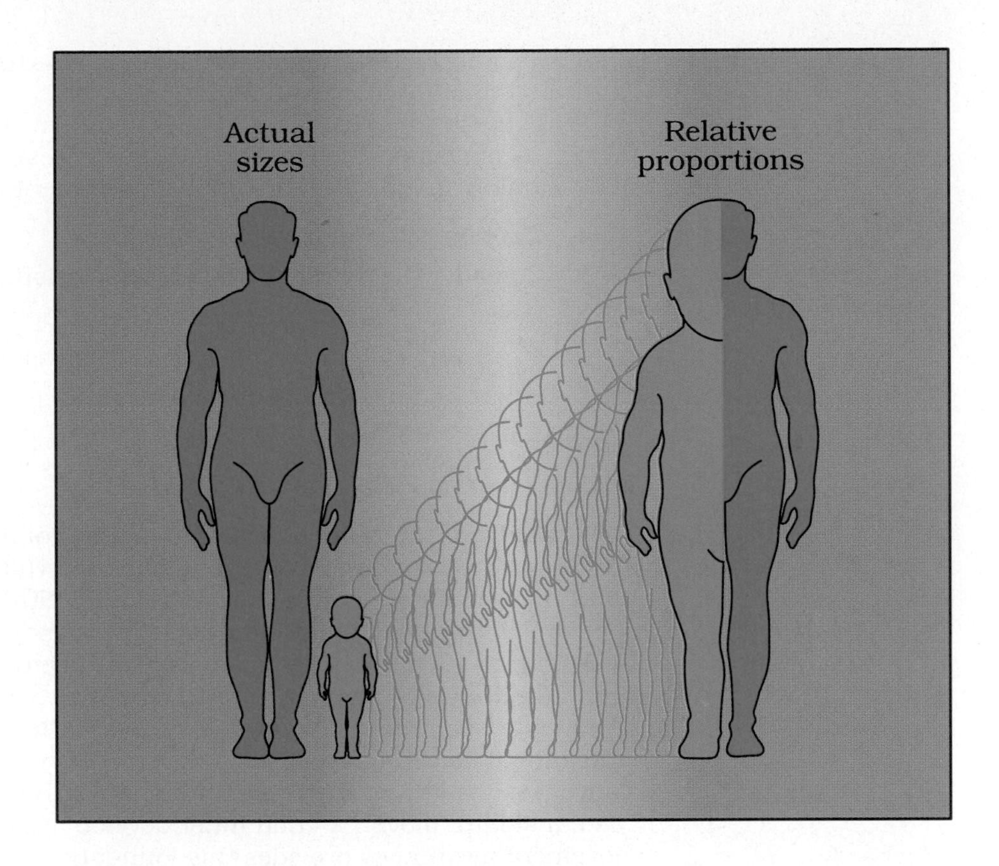

FIGURE 8.2
Variable Growth of Body Segments

quadruple, and the legs grow five times their original length (Martin & Vincent, 1960).

Because of this disproportionate growth, the body's center of gravity varies considerably during childhood. Young children carry most of their weight in their upper bodies and are therefore top heavy. This high center of gravity, along with a small base of support (i.e., small feet), typically results in poor balance. Because balance is an underlying influence of motor skill development, teachers must have realistic expectations for young children in learning motor skills that rely on balance (e.g., running and kicking).

EDUCATIONAL MOVEMENT PROGRAMS

To develop effective curricula for an educational movement program, a sequential and progressive design should be followed. Too often educators begin to select content without considering the underlying factors that may determine the success or failure of a performance. The first consideration when developing the educational movement curriculum is the principles of motor development and physical growth factors. For example, in the previous discussion of these principles and factors, we clearly established the impact of strength development and balance on motor behavior.

With the principles of motor development and physical growth factors as our foundation, we next discuss these steps in the process of developing an effective educational movement curriculum:

1. Develop goals, general and specific.
2. Consider the developmental characteristics.
3. Review the phases of motor skill development.
4. Use a variety of teaching styles or methodologies.
5. Select and design the movement tasks.

Movement Program Goals

The initial consideration for program development is the general goal(s) for the program. We support the idea that the goal of educational movement programs is to develop skillful and fit movers. To accomplish this goal, children must learn to move and move to learn. **Learning to move** focuses on movement awareness, skills acquisition, and fitness enhancement. Movement awareness, an awareness of how the body moves through space, is an integral element of any educational movement program. Movement awareness includes body awareness, space awareness, and relationship awareness. To become a skillful mover, a child must develop a movement foundation; movement awareness provides this foundation.

Skills acquisition, the second component, does not automatically occur because of maturation. Most fundamental movement skills must be taught if the mature level of ability is to be achieved. For example, unless taught, a child does not learn the correct movement patterns needed for throwing (e.g., stepping on the foot opposite the throwing hand). The learning environment could range from a formal setting with a trained movement specialist to a less formal setting where the "teacher" is a parent, a peer, or a sibling. Regardless of the teacher, the learning environment should reflect the developmental characteristics of the age if skill acquisition is to occur. For example, 5-year-old children should not be involved in competitive activities if the goal is motor skills acquisition. Children exposed to a developmentally appropriate movement program can become skillful, knowledgeable, and expressive movers.

TEACHERS SPEAK OUT

Motor skills enhance whole development.

Another component of the learning to move approach recognizes the importance of physical fitness. Early childhood educators should not accept the premise that all children are physically fit and physically active. Research suggests that the sedentary life-style patterns of many children should be of major concern to parents and educators (Ross & Pate, 1987). Movement programs should include moderately vigorous, large muscle activities that are fun. Fun associated with movement lays the foundation for developing positive attitudes related to fitness and an active life-style.

Learning through movement recognizes the positive relationship between educational movement and development in the cognitive and affective domains. The relationship between educational movement, perceptual motor development, and learning cognitive concepts has long been recognized by early childhood educators. Developmentally appropriate movement programs focusing on self-discovery and problem solving enhance critical thinking skills. The social-emotional aspects of development are also a primary focal point of educational movement programs. Affectively, a developmentally appropriate movement program enhances a child's cooperative skills, self-esteem, and socialization skills. Additionally, attitudes related to the importance of an active life-style can originate during early childhood. An active child usually becomes an active adult.

Specific goals are best categorized according to the three domains of learning:

1. *Psychomotor domain.* Psychomotor outcomes include movement awareness, skills acquisition, and enhanced physical fitness.
2. *Cognitive domain.* Cognitive outcomes emphasize the relationship between movement and critical thinking skills.
3. *Affective domain.* Affective outcomes include enhanced self-esteem, socialization skills, and positive attitudes related to movement.

The National Association for Sport and Physical Education (NASPE) defines the physically educated person as one who:

- Has learned the skills necessary to perform a variety of physical activities
- Does participate regularly in physical activity
- Is physically fit
- Knows the implications of and the benefits from involvement in physical activities
- Values physical activity and its contributions to a healthful life-style

A developmentally appropriate movement program is an important first step in ensuring that children become physically educated people. Movement programs should be an integrated part of the total curriculum. Movement experiences provide the medium for learning concepts related to cognitive and affective skills.

Indications are that life-style patterns related to physical activity develop during childhood (McGinnis, 1987). Therefore, children need the opportunity to experience a wide range of activities and develop a variety of physical skills. Children choose to participate in activities in which they feel competent and confident. Because life-style once established is difficult to change, early positive movement experiences are essential. Children who experience success in a movement environment are more likely to develop positive attitudes toward movement that in turn may influence future movement behaviors. Children who feel inferior about their skill level will generally avoid opportunities to participate in activities. This lack of participation prevents improvement in skill and may result in the development of a negative self-concept and negative attitudes toward movement.

In summary, the goal of early childhood movement programs is to develop skillful and fit movers. To achieve this goal, a child must learn to move and move to learn. An educational movement program must be designed that is basic to sound developmental practices if general and specific goals are to be attained.

After determining the long-term and specific goals, the next consideration is the developmental characteristics of the age group that will participate in the program. A program dominated by large muscle group activities and lacking a developmental framework is not appropriate.

Developmental Characteristics

Several developmental characteristics are of particular concern when designing and implementing a movement program. We present these characteristics here, and discuss the programmatic implications for each.

Egocentric. Young children are egocentric and self-centered. Games and activities that require children to function as a team in which the performance of one child affects the success of another child, as in a kickball game, are inappropriate.

Physically Active. Because young children want to move and be physically active, activities should be selected and designed to ensure maximum participation. According to the developmentally appropriate practices published by AAHPERD (in press), educators should avoid the following kinds of activities:

1. Games and activities requiring children to stand and wait for a turn (such as relays)

Educators should avoid games that require children to stand and wait.

2. Games where teams are chosen (Choosing teams takes away activity time and always results in some children being chosen last.)
3. Sedentary games such as "Duck, Duck, Goose"
4. Elimination games and activities that result in children waiting for periods longer than 30 seconds (such as musical chairs and dodge ball)

Short Attention Span. Another characteristic of young children is their short attention span. A variety of movement opportunities using developmentally appropriate equipment should be available. Activities that recognize the uniqueness of children are recommended, instead of activities requiring them all to perform in the same way, at the same rate, for the same amount of time. Children typically move in short bursts of energy, rarely staying with any task for very long. When tired or bored with an activity, their attention shifts to another more intriguing activity. For example, 5-year-olds should not be expected to run a mile. While they are physically capable, their emotional immaturity usually keeps them from completing the task.

Large Muscle Development. Since the large muscle groups are more developed than the smaller muscle groups, locomotor, stability, and manipulative skills are dominant in a movement program. But fine motor skills develop at a consistent rate during early childhood, so educators should provide ample opportunities to enhance the development of smaller muscle groups. Examples include large-piece puzzles, shape tracing, and pegboard games.

Improved Balance. The preschool child's center of gravity is continuing to stabilize. At birth, the center of gravity is in the approximate area of the sternum. As the child gets taller, the center of gravity continues to shift downward until it stabilizes in the area of the iliac crest (just below the waist). As a result, static and dynamic balance continue to improve throughout early and middle childhood.

These movements are observed as children refine perceptual motor development. This development refers to how a child brings together new experiences, past experiences, and movement as a response to something.

Movement tasks should be designed to enhance both static and dynamic balance. Dynamic balance movement tasks involve low balance beams, incline ladders, and stair climbing. Balance boards, balance blocks, and balancing on selected body parts are ways of improving static balance. Safety is a primary concern when designing balance movement tasks. Use developmentally appropriate equipment that is low to the floor, and carefully supervise all activities.

Vision and Coordination. Binocular vision, eye-hand coordination, eye-foot coordination, and eye-hand-foot coordination continue to improve throughout childhood. Many children do not show effective tracking skills until middle or late childhood. Various movement tasks involving object manipulation are included in the movement program, such as catching large, slow-moving objects. Activities such as catching and striking, perceptual motor tasks, and climbing tasks are an integral part of the movement program.

Hand, Foot, and Eye Dominance. Young children often do not have a demonstrated dominant or preferred hand, foot, or eye when performing movement tasks. Therefore, it is important to provide experiences using both sides of the body. For example, the child who does not display a preferred leg should be encouraged to kick with the right foot and left foot. Movement tasks should not force the use of a specific limb.

Phases of Motor Skill Development

Figure 8.3 illustrates the progressive and sequential nature of motor skill development. Movement programs that reflect the developmental nature of this ladder of motor skill development are an integral

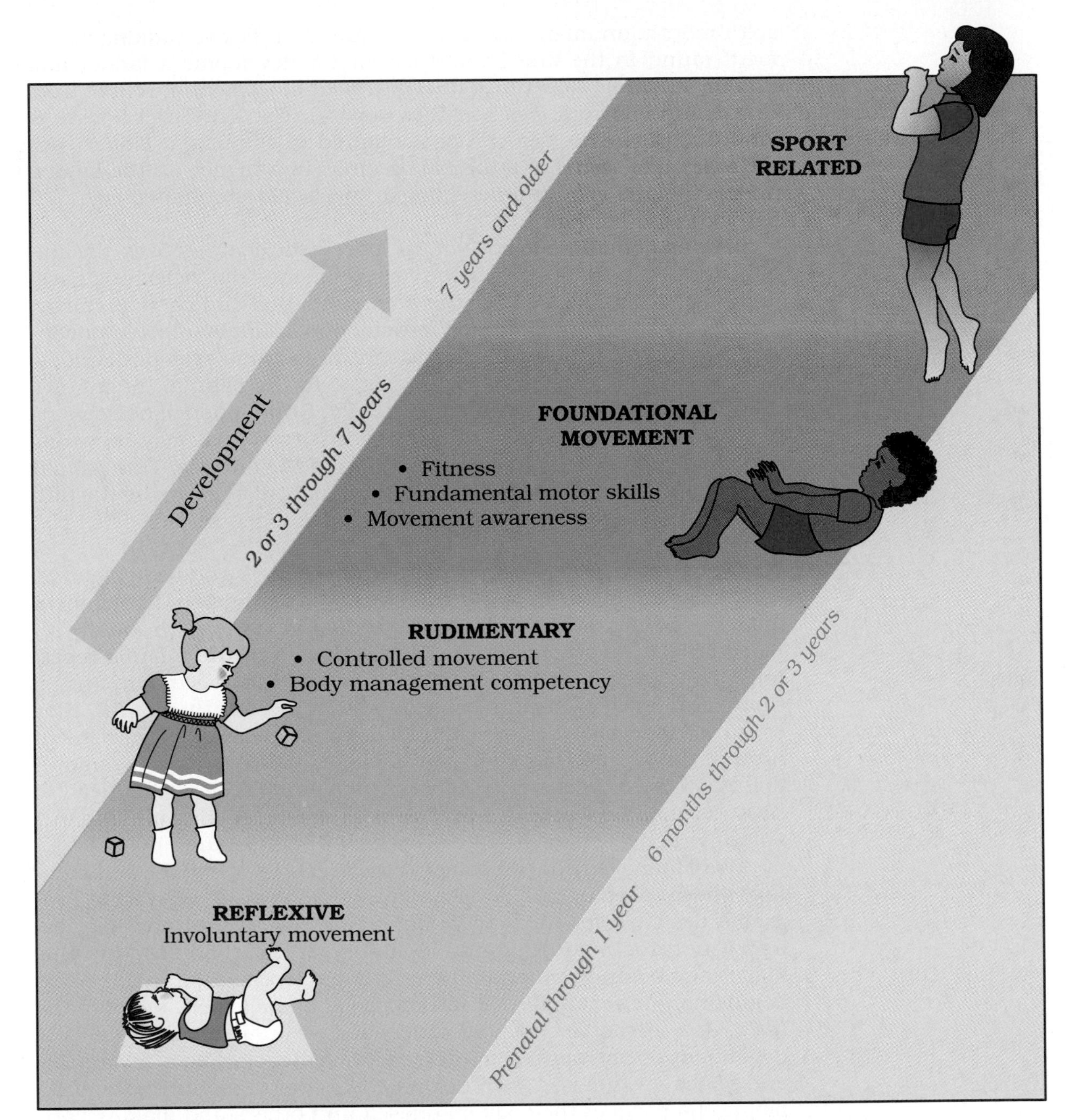

FIGURE 8.3
Ladder of Motor Development

part of any educational program designed for children. At each level, the new skills build upon the skills learned at the previous level. Although one level provides the foundation for the next level, these phases interrelate; therefore, a child does not necessarily complete one level before entering the next. For instance, during the fifth or sixth month, an infant may demonstrate the reflexive walking movement found in the first level of the motor development ladder and may also be able to perform the controlled movement of rolling from a supine to a prone position that occurs in second level (Payne & Isaacs, 1991). This idea can be compared to climbing a ladder with the feet on one rung and the hands on a rung higher up the ladder. That is, a child may be functioning at two levels simultaneously.

Reflexive Phase. *Involuntary movement* characterizes the initial rung of the ladder of motor development—the reflexive phase. This phase is evident during the prenatal period and persists during the first year of life. Controlled movements gradually replace uncontrolled reflexive movements as the central nervous system develops. As an example, when an object is placed in the palm of the infant's hand, the fingers close or grasp the object. Stimulation of both palms at the same time results in an involuntary grasp that may be strong enough to allow the infant to be lifted from the surface. This palmar grasp reflex, one of the first to appear, usually disappears by the fifth month as voluntary, *controlled* grasping action begins.

Rudimentary Phase. *Controlled movement* and *body management competency* form the second rung of the motor development ladder—the rudimentary phase. Controlled movements gradually replace reflexive movements. During the first year, the infant's repertoire of movement includes both reflexive and controlled movements. Controlled movements first appear about the fourth month. They continue to evolve and become the primary source of movement around the seventh month (Payne & Isaacs, 1991). Controlled movements progress from simple actions such as holding up the head to basic locomotion (crawling and creeping), basic stability (pulling to a stand), and basic manipulation (reaching and grasping).

Body management competency, the second stage of the rudimentary phase of motor skill development, is the focus of movement programs designed for the very young child. The level of physiological and conceptual maturity of the 2- to 3-year-old child suggests this stage may be an appropriate time to begin working on motor skills acquisition in a more formal setting. Body management refers to the ability to control the body in a variety of environments. This ability is dependent on the movement awareness elements of body awareness and space awareness. *Body awareness* refers to identifying and labeling the parts of the body on oneself and others and making various shapes with the body. *Space awareness*, an extension of body awareness, includes the spatial dimensions of self space, general space, levels, and directions. Basic control, not proficient control, is the anticipated outcome of this stage. Body management continues to develop throughout the foundational movement phase.

The movement environment should provide opportunities for children to experiment and explore with a variety of body positions—

stationary and moving, upright and inverted, on the ground and on various pieces of developmentally appropriate apparatus. The movement environment should include apparatus to practice the following skills:

- Climbing (both level and inclined structures designed to climb over, under, up and on)
- Hanging and swinging (from hanging and inverted positions)
- Bilateral alternating movements (ascending and descending ladders and incline boards)
- Balancing (floor balance beams)
- Jumping (boxes of various heights for jumping down and obstacles for jumping over)

In addition, a variety of balls, puzzles, rings, and striking implements in a variety of sizes, shapes and textures should be provided. Remember, the movement program at this stage should focus on experimentation and exploration.

Foundational Movement Phase. The foundational movement phase, the third rung of the motor development ladder, provides the building blocks needed for participation in a lifetime of activity. A solid foundation at this phase ensures success with sport-related skills. As we stated earlier, attainment and improvement of motor skills are not automatic. How far a person goes up the movement development ladder depends on the combined influence of innate ability (heredity) and opportunity (environment). Through success-oriented, developmentally appropriate movement experiences, all children can develop skills at each level of the progression.

The **foundational movement** phase includes three movement categories: movement awareness, fundamental motor skills, and fitness (see Table 8.1). Basic performance ability within each category of movement is necessary if a solid movement foundation is to be achieved. In the following section, we describe the movement categories. Later in this chapter, we discuss activities appropriate for each category.

Movement awareness. As stated by Gabbard (1992), the movement awareness category refers to elements of the perceptual-motor system that are necessary for movement efficiency and motor skill performance. These elements include the aspects of kinesthetic, visual, temporal, and auditory perception that contribute to skill development and are necessary for development of body management competency. Various authors classify the perceptual-motor components in different ways. In this chapter, we use the terms *perception* and *awareness* interchangeably.

TABLE 8.1 Foundational Movement Phase

Movement Awareness	Fundamental Motor Skills	Physical Fitness
Kinesthetic Awareness • Body awareness • Space awareness –self-space –general space • Directional awareness –laterality –directionality • Vestibular awareness –balance—postural, static, and dynamic –temporal awareness	***Stability Skills*** • Axial movement –twist/turn –bend/stretch • Support movements –balance—postural, static, and dynamic	***Health-Related*** • Cardiorespiratory efficiency • Musculoskeletal functioning –muscular strength –muscular endurance –flexibility • Body weight fitness
Visual Awareness • Figure ground discrimination • Perceptual constancy • Depth perception • Perception of movement • Visual motor integration	***Locomotor Skills*** • Run • Jump • Leap • Hop • Gallop • Skip • Slide	***Skill-Related*** • Speed • Agility • Power • Coordination • Reaction time
Auditory Awareness • Sound localization • Figure ground discrimination • Temporal auditory perception	***Manipulative Skills*** • Throw • Catch • Strike –kick –volley –dribble	

1. *Kinesthetic awareness* refers to the body's sensations relative to bodily movements and positions. The muscles, tendons, joints and vestibular system supply the sensory input. Kinesthetic perception, the "feel of the movement," includes the aspects of body awareness, space awareness, directional awareness, and vestibular awareness (Gabbard, 1992). The previously discussed components of body awareness and space awareness are expanded during the foundational movement phase.

a. Knowledge of *body awareness* extends to include not only an understanding of the names and locations of the body parts, but also their relationship to each other, and their abilities and limitations.

b. *Space awareness*, an extension of body awareness, refers to your perception of your body in space. Concepts related to space awareness include the following progressive abilities to:

- Perceive the space occupied by the body
- Locate objects in relation to your body
- Make spatial judgments using something other than your body as a point of reference (This concept includes the child's ability to judge the location of objects in relation to his or her body.)

Children need to experience movements requiring spatial judgment relative to the body's location and the amount of space it occupies (Gabbard, 1992; Gallahue, 1993). In addition, activities focusing on moving in self-space and general space should be provided. *Self-space* is that area immediately around the body, and *general space* is the available activity space within the boundaries of the room or playground established by the teacher.

TEACHERS SPEAK OUT

Toddlers are movers and runabouts.

c. *Directional awareness*, an extension of body awareness and space awareness, includes laterality and directionality. *Laterality* is an awareness of the two sides of the body, and that each side can move independently or in coordination with the other side (Haywood, 1986). *Directionality* is the "motoric expression of laterality" (Gabbard, 1992, p. 171) such as moving up/down, forward/backward, and left/right. Developmentally appropriate activities involve identifying these spatial dimensions and moving the body within these dimensions in self-space and general space.

d. *Vestibular awareness* refers to the body's ability to maintain balance or equilibrium. *Balance* requires the integration of information from the kinesthetic, visual, and vestibular systems and is subdivided into three types: postural balance, static balance, and dynamic balance. *Postural balance*, the unconscious leveling of the body, involves involuntary movements that attempt to keep the head upright and level. *Static* and *dynamic balance* refer to maintaining equilibrium while stationary and moving, respectively. A developmentally appropriate movement program includes a variety of activities to improve static (stationary) balance and dynamic (moving) balance. Balance is recognized as an underlying ability that transcends most fundamental movement skills.

e. *Temporal awareness* relates to the "timing" mechanisms in the body (Gallahue, 1993). This sensation includes the ability to:

- Move the body parts together smoothly (synchrony)
- Move body parts together smoothly to an imposed tempo (rhythm)
- Put actions of a skill in the proper order (sequence)
- Predict when an object will reach a specific point (coincidence-anticipation)

Synchrony, rhythm, and sequence are important elements when performing such synchronized tasks as skipping and jumping rope. The successful performance of many manipulative tasks (striking and catching) requires coincidence-anticipation timing. When striking a tossed ball, the child's ability to predict when the ball will arrive is built into the success of the task. Judgments related to the speed, trajectory, and weight of the ball must be made. The child's ability to process and appropriately respond to this incoming information determines whether he or she successfully executes the skill. The child must coordinate bodily movements with the arrival of the ball (Payne & Isaacs, 1991).

2. *Visual awareness* plays a dominant role in the development of most skills. Visual awareness includes figure ground discrimination, perceptual constancy, depth perception, perception of movement, and visual motor integration.

a. *Figure ground discrimination* refers to the ability to locate and visually distinguish an object from its background. To stop a rolling ball, a child must focus on the figure (ball) against the background (floor).

b. An aspect of *perceptual constancy*, size constancy, is the ability to judge the sizes of different objects that are varying distances from the observer. The object maintains a constant size regardless of its proximity to the observer's body. For example, although a bird "looks smaller" in the air, it is the same size that it is when sitting on the ground. Another aspect of perceptual constancy, form constancy, includes recognition of various shapes and sizes of objects. A triangle keeps its triangular shape regardless of its color, position, or size.

c. *Depth perception* allows children to judge the distance from their body to an object or surface, as when walking up or down stairs. This aspect of visual perception is particularly important for motor skills acquisition. The ability to recognize the three-dimensional nature of objects continues to improve throughout childhood and is shown by the increase in successful judgments of space.

d. *Perception of movement* "is the ability to detect and track moving objects with the eyes" (Haywood, 1986, p. 177). Often called *dynamic depth perception*, this ability is obviously critical to motor performance. Since tracking skills may not be proficient before age 10, a developmentally appropriate movement environment should provide a variety of activities to enhance these skills.

e. The final visual perception category, *visual motor integration*, refers to a combining of the "timing" mechanisms of temporal awareness; synchrony, rhythm, and sequencing. Eye-hand coordination, eye-foot coordination, and eye-hand-foot coordination all require visual motor integration.

3. *Auditory awareness.* Though not as directly related to motor behavior as kinesthetic perception and visual perception, auditory awareness plays an important role in the execution of many movement tasks. Auditory perception includes sound localization, figure ground discrimination, and temporal auditory perception. *Sound localization*, judging the location of sounds, is fairly well developed by age 3. Limited information is available about *figure ground discrimination*—the ability to attend to relevant sounds while ignoring others. *Temporal auditory perception* involves the ability to perceive and discriminate variations of sounds presented in time (Gabbard, 1992). This aspect of auditory perception, combined with temporal awareness, allows an individual to move rhythmically to auditory stimuli.

The perceptual motor development checklist found in Figure 8.4 can be used to screen various movement awareness abilities. We describe how to use this checklist in the Learning Activities at the end of this chapter.

Fundamental motor skills. As shown in Table 8.1, the **fundamental motor skills** include three categories: stability, locomotor, and manipulative. These skills are the building blocks for future sport skill development. Fundamental motor skills, especially those in the locomotor and manipulative categories, develop in a predictable, sequential fashion. This sequential progression is evident in three ways:

Observer: ______________________ Date: ______________________

Child's Name: ______________________ Sex: ______________ Age: ________

Characteristic	*Procedure*		*Score*	
Body Awareness				
Identification of body parts	Ask the child to touch each of the following body parts:	Eyes	Y	N
		Nose	Y	N
		Feet	Y	N
		Stomach	Y	N
		Chin	Y	N
		Elbows	Y	N
Comments:				
Lateral Preference		**Trial**	**Preferred**	**Side**
Hand dominance	Place a basket of five 3-to-4-in. yarn balls in front of the child at the midline. Ask the child to pick up and throw the balls one at a time. Note the hand used to perform each throw.	1	R	L
		2	R	L
		3	R	L
		4	R	L
		5	R	L
Foot dominance	Place a 7-to-9-in. ball on the floor in front of the child at the midline. Ask the child to kick the ball. Observe which foot is used to perform each kick.	1	R	L
		2	R	L
		3	R	L
		4	R	L
		5	R	L

FIGURE 8.4 Perceptual Motor Development Checklist *(continued)*

1. *Among the stability, locomotor, and manipulative categories.* Full development of many locomotor and manipulative skills requires an appropriate base of support (e.g., hopping requires stability on one foot). In addition, successful completion of many complex manipulative tasks requires development of locomotor skills (e.g., dribbling a soccer ball requires controlled kicking while running).

2. *Among the skills within each category.* Within the locomotor skills category, the skill of running precedes hopping, which precedes skipping.

3. *Within each skill.* Within each locomotor and manipulative skill, a child progresses through four distinct yet related phases: initial, elementary, intermediate, and mature. For ex-

Comments:	
Vestibular Awareness	
Static balance	Ask the child to balance on one foot. Record the number of seconds balance was maintained. Score _______
Comments:	
Dynamic balance	Ask the child to walk the length of a floor balance beam (4–6 in. wide by 8 feet long). Record the number of steps the child can take without stepping off the beam.
Comments:	
Perceptual Constancy	
Size constancy child——ball—ball—ball 15" 1 3' 2 3' 3	Arrange three balls that are the same size (7 to 9 in.) but different colors according to the diagram. Ask the child each question and record the correctness of each response (Y—correct, N—incorrect). 1. Which ball is the largest? Y N 2. Which ball is the smallest? Y N 3. Which ball is closest to you? Y N
Form constancy	Have a variety of sizes and textures of triangles, squares, and circles (at least five of each). Ask the child to group the like shapes together. Give the child 2 minutes to complete the task. Record as a pass/fail.
Comments:	

FIGURE 8.4 Perceptual Motor Development Checklist *(continued)*

ample, when a child is learning to throw, the following progression is generally evident:

a. *Initial phase.* The trunk is parallel to the target; only the hand and arm are involved in the action, with limited (if any) follow-through.

b. *Elementary phase.* A step with the foot on the dominant-hand (i.e., throwing) side of the body initiates the throw; the throwing hand finishes next to the hip on the dominant-hand side of the body.

c. *Intermediate phase.* The child stands with the nondominant side to the target; a step with the foot on the nondominant-hand side of the body initiates the throw; the follow-through of the throwing hand finishes across the body.

We were interested in a well balanced early child care program that included motor development.

d. *Mature phase.* The child steps in opposition to the throwing arm; the body rotates backward with the shoulders turning first, followed by the hips; the forward motion is characterized by hips leading, followed by the shoulders; the follow-through of the throwing hand goes beyond the point where the ball is released and finishes diagonally across the body.

The process of learning all of the manipulative and locomotor skills can be broken into these four developmental phases. Vast amounts of information are available about how a child progresses from using the initial form to the mature form of the movement (Gabbard, 1992; Gallahue, 1993; Payne & Isaacs, 1991).

Developmentally appropriate movement programs for young children focus on the process of learning motor skills, not on the product of the motor performance. Activity selection and design should focus on teaching a child how to throw (process), not throwing accuracy (product).

1. *Stability skills* are an underlying component in the execution of most fundamental skills. The ability to maintain balance and control in a variety of situations and body positions indicates a child's stability. Stability skills are subdivided into axial movements and support movements, upright and inverted.

Axial movements are those in which the axis of the body moves around a fixed point. These include bending, stretching, twisting, and turning. *Support movements*, upright and inverted, include the previously discussed movement behaviors of static and dynamic balance.

2. *Locomotor skills* involve movements that transport the body from one location in space to another and include single skills and integrated skills. Single skills (walking, running, jumping, leaping, and hopping) develop before the integrated locomotor skills (galloping, skipping, and sliding). As we said earlier, children learn upright locomotion in a rather distinctive and sequential order. With physiological and conceptual maturity, a child increases the factors needed to execute many locomotor skills. For example, a 2-year-old does not have the leg strength or balance to hop, nor the conceptual processing abilities to execute a skip.

Locomotor skills are an integral part of any developmentally appropriate movement program. Remember that most skills must be taught—they do not naturally evolve with age. The developmentally appropriate movement program incorporates activities to work on the skills appropriate for the age level. The following locomotor skills are defined in the order they usually develop. Activities should be designed for the age levels accompanying the definitions to ensure skill acquisition.

a. *Run (ages 1–7).* To move rapidly so that for a brief moment, both feet are off the ground. Leg strength and balance determine when a child will start to run.

b. *Jump (ages 2–7).* To take off on one or both feet and land on both feet. This includes jumping down, jumping across, and jumping up.

c. *Leap (ages 3–7).* An elongated step designed to cover distance or go over a low obstacle. Running usually precedes a leap.

d. *Hop (ages 4–7).* The body is moved up by one foot and lands on the same foot. Because hopping requires more strength and balance than running, jumping, and leaping, mastery of this skill occurs later.

e. *Gallop (ages 4–7).* One foot leads with the other foot brought to it, similar to a slide but executed in a forward direction.

f. *Skip (ages 4–7).* A combination of steps and hops with alternate feet. Hopping is a prerequisite skill for skipping.

g. *Slide (ages 5–7).* A gallop to the side; one of the last locomotor skills learned because of the sideways movement.

3. *Manipulative skills* involve projecting and receiving objects with the hands, feet, or an implement such as a bat or paddle. They occur in a fairly predictable sequence depending on the physiological and conceptual maturity level of the child. Initial attempts at throwing are evident during the first year of life, but throwing with a purpose is not observable until later. Developmentally appropriate movements programs provide extensive opportunities to develop the manipulative skills of throwing, catching, and striking. The use of developmentally appropriate equipment (discussed later in this chapter) is vital to the success of learning the skills.

Activities should be designed for the age levels accompanying the definitions to ensure skill acquisition.

a. *Throw (ages 2–7).* To project an object into space using one or both hands; force production is very important.

b. *Catch (ages 3–7).* To control or stop an aerial or rolling objective by using the hands and arms or the feet (trapping).

Catching is more difficult than throwing and requires force absorption and visual tracking skills.

c. *Strike (ages 3–7).* To project an object by contacting it with a body part (kicking, volleying, or dribbling) or implement (batting or striking with short- and long-handled implements). Striking, like throwing, requires force production.

KIDS SPEAK UP

I can climb higher than anybody.

Boy, 5 years old

Physical fitness. Fitness is divided into health-related components and skill-related components. Health-related components are basic to functional health and quality of life (e.g., cardiorespiratory efficiency; musculoskeletal function including muscular strength, muscular endurance, and flexibility; and body weight fitness.) Skill-related components include the elements needed to be a skillful mover (e.g., speed, agility, power, coordination, and reaction time). An appropriate movement program incorporates activities to develop both types of fitness.

The major fitness emphasis for young children is to develop positive attitudes toward movement and thus encourage an active life-style. The focus should be on positive health behaviors rather than extensive fitness testing or training. Children should be provided age-appropriate activities designed to help them understand and appreciate the basic concepts related to fitness.

Research shows that children are not active enough to produce the desired health-related benefits. The belief that children "play, therefore, they are physically fit" has been questioned within the last two decades (Kuntzleman & Reiff, 1992). A review of the literature in this area suggests that educators working with young children should evaluate current practices and focus more attention on developmentally appropriate movement experiences that will have a positive effect on the long-term physical fitness of children.

The fitness segment of the movement program involves more than moderately vigorous physical activity. Age-appropriate movement experiences focus on the concepts related to physical fitness and the importance of a physically active life-style. Since young children cannot do most calisthenic exercises correctly, such exercises are inappropriate. The development of fitness is enhanced through innovative and fun activities.

Developmentally Appropriate Movement Activities, Teaching Strategies, and Equipment

The relationship of the cognitive, affective, and psychomotor domains must be recognized and included in the movement experiences selected and designed for young children. Movement experiences should

- Meet long-term and specific goals
- Address the developmental characteristics of the age group
- Incorporate a variety of teaching strategies
- Reflect the progressive and sequential development of motor behavior

A quality educational movement program incorporates teaching strategies that reflect the previously mentioned developmental characteristics. A teacher-centered, command approach is not appropriate. Guided discovery and problem-solving strategies encourage children to explore the movement environment actively and to make decisions in response to movement challenges. The teacher's role is to facilitate and design a stimulating movement environment consisting of challenging and motivating movement tasks. Tasks are designed based on their ability to contribute to the program goals.

Group size is a primary consideration when planning movement experiences for young children. The developmental characteristics of the age group determine the appropriate size of the group. For example, an educator has more success teaching a group of ten 5-year-olds than teaching a group of twenty-five 5-year-olds. Larger than appropriate groups result in managing rather than teaching. Therefore, in the following discussion of developmentally appropriate activities, we consider appropriate group size and appropriate expectations based on the previously discussed developmental characteristics.

A developmentally appropriate movement program features a broad range of movement experiences designed to enhance motor skill performance, physical fitness, positive self-concept, socialization skills, and creativity. Movement experiences focus on improvement of the skills included in the foundational movement phase of development (see Table 8.1).

Developmentally appropriate equipment and apparatus are essential for a successful movement program for young children. A piece of equipment or apparatus is developmentally appropriate if it matches the characteristics, needs, and abilities of the children using it. Siedentop, Herkowitz, and Rink (1984) offer various strategies in the selection and construction of equipment.

The first strategy is to provide children with several pieces of equipment that are of the same shape but of different size. For example, several sizes of balls should be available for children whose catching abilities range from unskilled to skilled. Vertical and horizontal ladders with rungs different distances apart accommodate children of various heights, muscular strength, and endurance levels.

The second strategy is to provide equipment that children can adjust to match their developmental levels. Here are some examples of this technique:

- Jumping standards that allow each child to raise or lower the crossbar to match his or her jumping ability
- A batting tee with an adjustable-length tube that the user raises or lowers to change the height of the supported ball
- A ball attached to a length of rope that is adjusted to the child's waist level by an adjustable knot

Another strategy promotes force production in skills such as striking, kicking, and throwing by using large targets. Large targets lessen the need for highly accurate performance and encourage a child to throw, kick, or strike as hard as possible. This strategy in turn promotes the use of a more mature movement pattern.

In recent years, equipment companies have begun offering more items that are appropriate for young children. But it is important to supplement this inventory with homemade equipment for two reasons: Many of the items available for purchase can be made less expensively, and much of the equipment is not developmentally appropriate for young children. As an example, a traditional commercially made target is a clown's face painted on a 2-by-3-foot board with holes cut to represent the clown's eyes, nose, and mouth. A target of this nature encourages a child to toss underhand or use a "dart-throwing" motion rather than the full overarm throw with force. A more appropriate target (shown in Figure 8.5) is one with a picture of a familiar character sewn or drawn onto a 4-by-8-foot piece of material (such as a bed sheet). A teacher can find many opportunities to use images related to a unit topic. A winter theme might have a snowball toss. A spring theme could include a baseball activity.

By using developmentally appropriate equipment and apparatus, teachers can design activities to allow children of all skill levels to participate successfully. In the following discussion, we focus on activities and equipment appropriate for each skill category. General considerations are followed by three or four specific activities. Appendix J contains descriptions on constructing equipment marked with an asterisk (*).

Movement Awareness. Movement awareness activities are designed to enhance the various sensory systems of the body (e.g., kinesthetic, visual, and auditory). Just as these systems work in an integrated fashion, many of the following activities require the use of

FIGURE 8.5
Large Targets Encourage Forceful Overhand Throw

more than one sensory system. Many movement awareness activities can be done individually, with a partner, or in small groups.

Part-to-part (body awareness). Begin by having children use a locomotor skill (walk, jump, or run) to move about the general space.

Children respond enthusiastically to small group movement awareness activities.

As you call out a body part, have them stop and touch that body part. The next time, have each child touch the called body part on another child.

Body part puzzles (body awareness). Begin with the puzzle put together and have the child identify various body parts on both his body and on the puzzle. For example, "show me your nose; now show me the nose on the clown." Or ask the child to identify the body parts as he puts the puzzle together. Puzzles may be constructed of plywood or poster board.

FIGURE 8.6
Body Part Puzzles

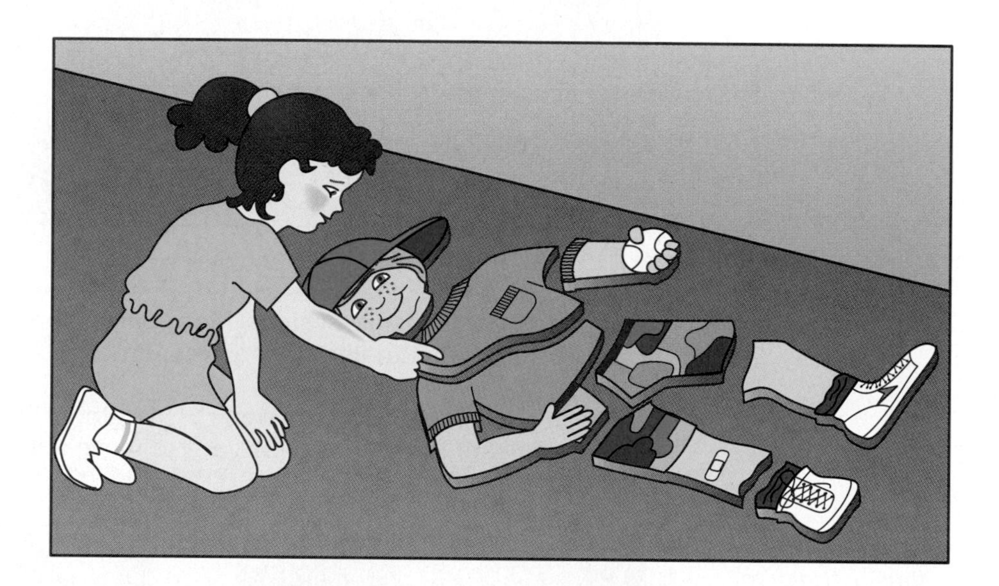

****Lummi sticks (body awareness, auditory awareness, vestibular awareness).*** Have the child hold one stick in each hand and tap the sticks together, on called body parts, or on the floor (you can begin with the child using only one stick). When put to music, this activity enhances all aspects of auditory awareness.

Ropes (vestibular awareness, perceptual constancy). Have the child make various shapes, letters, or numbers with the rope. After identifying the formation of the rope, have the child walk on the rope in different directions or use the locomotor skills to move around and over the rope. Cloth ropes of any length can be used for this activity.

Fundamental Motor Skills. Two goals of early childhood programs are the refinement of stability and locomotor skills. Teachers may direct activities that target the development in these areas.

Stability. Stability activities enhance static and dynamic balance. As with climbing, arrange balance beams, walking boards, ladders, etc. in a motivating and challenging pattern. When the children readily negotiate the configuration, for an additional challenge have them balance a beanbag on specific body parts while moving through the area.

Locomotor skills. The nature of the locomotor skill influences activity selection and design. A continuous movement approach (e.g., miniature track or obstacle course) is the best way to practice running, leaping, galloping, skipping, and sliding. Jumping and hopping should first be practiced in a more controlled environment, such as on the rebounder and jump-the-stream (described later). Since jumping and hopping require more leg strength and control, these activities use the skills individually. When the child is jumping, the emphasis is on taking off and landing on two feet. When first attempting to hop, a child may need your help because of a low level of leg strength.

1. *Miniature track.* Use large cones and flags to lay out a miniature track. Have the children move around the track using various locomotor skills (e.g., run, gallop, skip, and slide). Begin the activity by "clapping" the **starter* and turning the **birdseed timer.* Remember to vary the locomotor skills to sustain interest and motivation.

FIGURE 8.7
Miniature Track

2. **Jumping mat.* This horizontal jumping activity provides a visual cue regarding the distance jumped. Encourage the children to jump as far as they can, to promote a strong push off with the legs and full use of the arm swing. The colored lines on the mat provide feedback to the children on their performance. Emphasis is not on the distance covered but on a strong jump forward using both feet.

3. *Jump-the-stream.* This challenge is also a horizontal jumping or hopping activity. Have the children jump or hop over the various animals and objects found in the "stream" (e.g., fish, frogs, lily pads). Skipping and galloping around the stream are good variations of this activity.

FIGURE 8.8
Jump-the-Stream

4. **Jumping standards.* The multicolored standards provide visual feedback regarding the height jumped. The crossbar height adjusts to the skill level of the child. Have the child stand behind the crossbar and jump over it in the direction that will allow the crossbar to fall freely from its support if hit by the child's feet. The standards can also be used for leaping. In this case, have the child stand several feet away, then run and leap over the crossbar.

5. *Rebounder.* During this activity, the child jumps from the rebounder onto a specified number, letter, shape, or colored card

FIGURE 8.9
Rebounder

placed on the floor around the rebounder. Challenges are individualized to the child's level of ability. For example, have the children jump to the first letter of their name, or have them jump to the number that equals two plus two.

Manipulative skills. Developmentally appropriate activities can be categorized as "closed" or "open" movement tasks. Closed tasks remove as many factors as possible that could jeopardize the successful execution of the skill. In contrast, open tasks tend to make execution more difficult. For instance, a closed kicking task uses a stationary ball, while an open kicking task requires the child to kick a moving ball. When designing movement tasks to teach manipulative skills, it is important that you follow the progression from closed to open tasks.

1. *Throwing.* Use large targets to stress forcefulness and improve technique when teaching throwing. Small targets are not appropriate. Accuracy is not stressed until the throwing pattern is functioning at an intermediate level. **Neat feet* provide a visual cue for stepping with opposition and using body rotation. You determine when the child is ready to use the opposition neat feet (i.e., when hand dominance is obvious) and when to progress to the body rotation neat feet (i.e., when the child steps with opposition without using the opposition neat feet). As throwing technique improves, increase the distance from the target.

- *a.* **Large stationary targets*: Large targets made from cloth or wood (4 feet by 8 feet) are used when teaching young children to throw. Targets depicting animals, clowns, etc. are motivating and fun. Remember, the key word is *large.* Have the children throw as hard as they can to encourage force production. This action, in turn, increases the probability of the child using the full overarm throwing pattern. Suggesting that the children hit the clown's mouth promotes the use of an underhand toss or dart-throwing motion. This type of activity ensures failure and development of poor technique.
- *b.* **Pendulum target*: When the child no longer needs to use the neat feet for opposition, he or she is ready to throw at the pendulum target. This activity is a closed activity if the pendulum is a stationary, and it is an open activity if the pendulum is swinging. Due to the smaller size of the target, more accuracy is required to be successful, making this activity more difficult.
- *c.* *Moving hoop*: This activity is more advanced and is appropriate for the child who uses opposition consistently without a visual or verbal prompt and who can hit the pendulum target with some degree of accuracy. It is an

open activity designed to work on the temporal aspect of the throw, that is, hitting a moving target. Use a shower curtain hook to attach a large hula hoop to an inclined cable. As the hoop slides down the cable, have the child throw various objects (e.g., **yarnballs*, beanbags, foam balls) through the hoop.

FIGURE 8.10
Moving Hoop

2. *Catching*: Use large (7 to 9 inches), soft-textured balls when teaching a child to catch. Remember the previously discussed developmental characteristics that influence a child's ability to learn to catch (e.g., developing binocular vision, proximodistal direction of development). After the child learns the catching technique and is comfortable with the activity, begin using smaller balls of various textures.

a. Suspended ball for catching. This activity is designed to improve tracking skills and lessen the tendency of the child to turn his or her head in fear of the ball. Suspend several sizes of foam balls (for example, 9, 7, and 4 inches) from a horizontal rope by means of a shower curtain hook and tape. Use an adjustable knot to allow the height of the ball to be moved to waist level for each child. Use the larger ball for the less skillful child and progress to the small ball as skill improves. Begin by "sending" or "pushing" the ball to the child. As skill improves, let the child "send" or "catch" the ball independently. Later, two children can successfully participate in this activity by cooperatively sending and catching the same ball to each other.

FIGURE 8.11
Suspended Ball for Catching

b. *Catching ramp.* The purpose of this activity is to improve tracking skills. Toss a ball onto the ramp and have each child catch the ball as it descends the ramp. Begin by having the child stand close to the ramp, eliminating approach steps. As skill improves, the children can take a running approach to the ramp when catching. Later, have the children toss the ball onto the ramp for themselves or for another child.

c. *Roll/toss/bounce and catch.* You can design a variety of movement challenges to accommodate a variety of skill

FIGURE 8.12
Catching Ramp

levels with this activity. It is easily individualized by using the progression of large, soft balls to smaller balls. For example, roll a large foam ball to a less skillful child and bounce a tennis ball to a child who is more skillful.

d. **Scoops.* This activity is designed for the more skillful catcher to improve eye-hand coordination by using a piece of equipment (the scoop) rather than the hands. Have the children hold the scoop in their nondominant hand and catch balls or beanbags they or the teacher have tossed at different levels (i.e., low, medium, and high). Partner activities are introduced as skill improves (i.e., when each child can throw to a partner with a fairly high degree of accuracy).

3. *Striking.* The activity progression for teaching striking proceeds from closed activities involving a stationary ball to open activities involving a moving ball. When teaching striking, you should design activities to progress from using the hand to using a short-handled implement such as a table tennis paddle to using a long-handled implement such as a light weight tennis racket or bat. This progression reflects the processes that occur as eye-hand coordination develops.

a. **Suspended ball.* This procedure is a closed activity designed to improve eye-hand coordination. Have each child stand on the neat feet and face the suspended ball. They can use their hand or an appropriate implement to strike the ball. Remember to encourage force production ("hit the ball hard"). The neat feet provide visual cues to assist

FIGURE 8.13
Suspended Ball for Striking

in learning the proper stepping technique. The ball is suspended from a horizontal rope using the tape and adjustable knot previously described.

b. *Tee batting.* Place balls of various sizes, progressing from 7 to 4 inches, on a **batting tee* with the ball height adjusted to the child's waist level. Using the neat feet, if necessary, have the child strike the ball from the tee with the appropriately sized implement. When the child has learned the stepping pattern, the neat feet are no longer needed.

c. **Nylon paddles/balloons.* The purpose of this activity is to improve eye-hand coordination and tracking skills. The slow-moving balloon allows the child to track a moving object and contact it with an implement. Initially, have the children practice hitting the balloon with their hand, then progress to using the nylon paddle. Depending upon skill level, two children can work together on this activity.

4. *Kicking.* The activity progression for kicking proceeds from closed activities using large, stationary balls to open activities using smaller, moving balls. Activities progress in the following way:

- Stationary ball with no approach or a one-step approach
- Stationary ball with a walking approach
- Moving ball with a limited approach
- Moving ball with a running approach

a. *Kicking chimes.* This activity is designed to give auditory feedback upon success. Working with the progression listed above, have the child kick a ball from a **rope coil* into the chimes. For the more mature kicker, stopping the ball between kicks may not be necessary.

b. *Kicking ramp.* This activity is designed to provide visual feedback upon success. The procedures described for the chimes are appropriate for the kicking ramp. A large target or a parachute suspended in the corner of a room are useful as kicking ramps.

c. Bumper ball. This activity is designed to improve eye-foot coordination and introduce the technique of punting. Tie a string or piece of elastic onto the valve of a small beach ball. Have the child hold the string and kick the ball, releasing the string on contact. At first, you can hold the ball for the child.

FIGURE 8.14
Kicking Ramp

Physical Fitness. Fitness is stressed within many activities. Because upper-body strength is recognized as an area of weakness among children, numerous activities are designed to enhance this area. Recognizing the importance of cardiorespiratory efficiency, developmentally appropriate activities are selected to improve this component of fitness as well. In many cases, activities enhance motor skill acquisition as well as fitness.

Moving gymnastics. These activities are designed to improve upper-body strength by having the children partially support their body weight on their hands and arms while moving. Moving gymnastics include crabwalk, seal drag, lame dog walk, and other activities that require a portion of the body to be supported by the shoulder girdle area. Children enjoy obstacle courses that include moving gymnastics and locomotor movements.

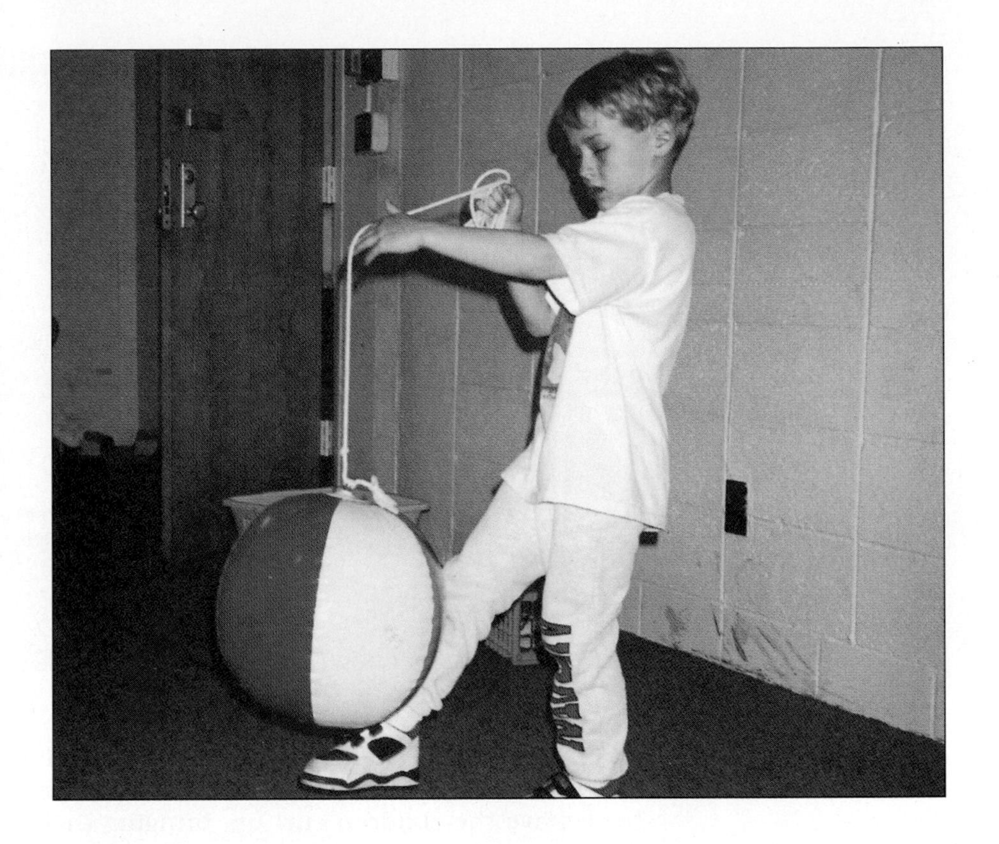

FIGURE 8.15
Bumper Ball

Climbing. Climbing activities provide an excellent way to enhance fitness. Arrange a variety of apparatus in motivating and challenging configurations to facilitate bilateral, unilateral, and contralateral movements. Such apparatus include ladders, cargo nets, climbing frames, jumping boxes, slides, bolsters, and wedge mats.

Miniature track. With modification, this activity (previously described as an activity to enhance locomotor skills) becomes a fitness activity. To improve fitness, the distance covered or the time spent doing the activity should be sufficient to elevate the heart rate. It is a good idea to change the locomotor skill every 20–30 seconds to sustain interest.

Parachutes. The parachute is useful in developing all aspects of fitness. Cooperation is a key factor when children are working with the parachute. Therefore, these activities are best suited for children ages 5 to 8. Arm and shoulder strength, abdominal strength, cardiorespiratory efficiency, and leg strength can be improved by the following activities. In addition, we present one age-appropriate game.

1. *Arm and shoulder strength.* With children sitting around the parachute, have them lift the chute and look at the person across from them. Have them repeat this process while lying on their backs.

FIGURE 8.16
Climbing

2. *Abdominal strength.* Have the children lie on their backs and stretch the chute taut. With their feet flat on the floor and knees bent, have the children curl up, bringing their palms to their knees (keeping the arms straight). A variation requires the children to lie flat on their backs, raising only the head to look across the taut chute and wave with one hand at the person directly across the chute.

3. *Leg strength.* Standing and holding the chute taunt, have the children do various locomotor movements. For example, tell the children to hold the chute with their right hand and gallop.

4. *Cardiorespiratory efficiency.* Do the previously described activity for leg strength for a longer period of time. Use a variety of locomotor skills, changing directions often.

5. *Pop-up.* Place several 4-inch yarnballs on the parachute, which is stretched out on the floor. On the signal, have the children stand and shake the chute until all the balls have been bounced off.

CHARACTERISTICS OF A GOOD PLAYGROUND

The characteristics of a good playground revolve around three important elements: using the playspace, designing and equipping the playspace, and installing and maintaining the playspace for safety.

Volumes have been written on the subject of playground design and safety. In the following section, we give an overview of what to look for in a quality playspace and how it can be used and maintained for safety. The terms playground and playspace are used interchangeably in this discussion.

Using the Playspace

Using in this section refers to how the playspace fits into the educational program or perhaps the purpose of the playspace rather than specific playspace activities. Obtaining full benefit from the time spent on a playground is a two-fold challenge. According to Esbensen (1990), early childhood education programs must allow a sufficient amount of time for outdoor play and ensure that a high-quality outdoor play environment is available. Esbensen promotes the concept of the playspace as an outdoor classroom designed to meet curriculum objectives. This concept opposes the traditional view of time spent on the playground as a way for children to get rid of their excess energy or to provide the teacher with a break. While children do in fact need time away from adult direction, the playspace should not be used solely for this purpose.

Designing and Equipping the Playspace. Just as all activities should be developmentally appropriate, so should the playspace. The sizes and types of equipment, toys, and structures should match the developmental characteristics of the children using them. A playspace designed for an elementary school is not appropriate or safe for a group of preschoolers, nor is one designed for a preschool appropriate or safe for infants and toddlers. A developmentally appropriate playspace is one that gives children opportunities to engage in activities that suit their needs and abilities.

KIDS SPEAK UP

Playing on the monkey bars is fun.

Girl, 5 years old

According to Wortham and Frost (1990), "the best early childhood playground is not just a play area equipped with play structures" (p. 1). A quality outdoor playspace stimulates children to engage in physical, social, fantasy, and creative play and thus develop skills in all domains of learning (i.e., physical, affective, and cognitive). To promote all types of play, designers of playgrounds propose a design framework based on zones (Esbensen, 1990; Frost, 1992). Each zone, by nature of its layout and the equipment, toys, and structures available, encourages a specific type of play. For example, the physical zone includes an open space for running as well as structures for balancing and climbing. "Zoning the play area serves to facilitate the organization of the space in such a way as to incorporate the developmental needs of young children, safety considerations such as size and surfacing of areas, and the learning opportunities available" (Esbensen, 1990, p. 62).

Frost (1992) suggests the following factors when zoning and equipping a play space:

1. Complex structures that serve multiple functions are more useful than simple, single-function structures.
2. Provide a broad range of equipment to accommodate every form of play naturally engaged in by the children.
3. Arrange structures and equipment for integration of play between structures.
4. Define play zones by boundaries that set them apart functionally and visually and integrate them spatially with adjacent zones.
5. Arrange space to invite movement within zones, between zones, and between points of entry and exit.

Installing and Maintaining the Playspace for Safety

The most important characteristic of a good playspace is its safety. A severe injury to a child quickly negates the perceived good provided in a play setting (Thompson, Bruya, & Crawford, 1990). Safety begins with the design of the playspace and includes the selection and installation of quality equipment, toys, and structures. Once the playspace is built, safety continues through supervised play and regular inspection, maintenance, and repair.

Supervision may be the most important element of playground safety. More than "watching children play," supervision includes establishing rules for safe play as well as teaching children how to play safely. According to Warrell (1988), it is best to involve the children when making the rules. In addition, if a specific curriculum is used with the play environment, children will be more likely to use the equipment safely (Sommerfield & Dunn, 1988).

Inspection of the playspace is an ongoing, systematic process. The use of a safety checklist helps to ensure the inspection of all items and verifies that the inspection has in fact taken place. Checklists of this nature can be found in the references cited at the end of

TABLE 8.2 Playground Safety Considerations

Surfacing

Use force-absorbing material under all structures where falls are most likely to occur. Apply a minimum of 10 inches of loose sand or mulch to cushion falls of several feet (the depth of the material must be proportional to the height of the structure). The most effective materials include chopped tires, sand, and granulated pine bark. Each materials has its advantages and disadvantages. For example, while an appropriate depth of pea gravel is also effective, it is not appropriate for infants and toddlers because it is easy to place in the nose, ears, and mouth.

Enclosures

Surround the playspace by a barrier, such as a 4-foot fence, that prevents children from entering or leaving the area without adult supervision. The fence should be free of sharp edges and protrusions.

Accessibility

Position equipment to be easily and readily accessible. Equipment should be designed to accommodate more than one child at a time. Children should not have to wait in line to use equipment such as slides, ramps, and climbing nets. Impatience often results in injury.

Size and Spacing of Equipment

Place equipment for infants and toddlers in a separate area. An individual piece of equipment should be at least 10 feet from any other structure including trees, fences, or other pieces of equipment. In addition, appropriate "fall zones" are needed around each structure to prevent children from falling onto other pieces of equipment.

Visual Barriers

Ensure that partially enclosed equipment, which encourages dramatic and quiet play, is large enough to allow adults to supervise visually and large enough for the passage and movement of both children and adults.

Entrapment and Protrusions

Check that open spaces on equipment (e.g., ladder rungs) is large enough to avoid entrapment of body parts. Nuts and bolts should be countersunk. Protrusions result in skin lacerations and torn clothing.

this chapter. For example, Wortham and Frost (1990) include a detailed series of checklists developed by the American Association for Leisure and Recreation (AALR) Committee on Play, while Jambor and Palmer (1991) provide a more condensed version. Table 8.2 summarizes the various safety elements to be considered.

Constant use of a playspace naturally results in necessary maintenance and repairs. Maintenance of a playspace is an ongoing process that should be scheduled regularly. Routine maintenance includes replacing scattered ground cover under structures as well as tightening loose bolts, etc. Repair or replacement of worn or broken parts should take place immediately with the equipment or structure remaining off limits until reinspection has taken place.

A good playground allows children to have fun safely. It gives children the opportunity to make choices and explore. In addition, a well designed playground is developed with a purpose in mind and is an integral part of the early childhood program's curriculum.

SUMMARY

Educational movement programs designed for young children must be based on the developmental characteristics and developmental principles that affect the motor development of the young child. Effective programs select and design developmentally appropriate activities and equipment and use a variety of developmentally appropriate teaching methodologies and strategies. The goal of movement programs designed for young children is to develop skillful and fit movers.

The ladder of motor development illustrates the progressive and sequential nature of motor skill development. Progression through the phases of the ladder is dependent on heredity and environment. Heredity sets the potential for achievement; opportunity (environment) determines the amount of that potential achieved. The foundational movement phase should be the focus of movement programs for young children and include activities that improve movement awareness, fundamental motor skills, and physical fitness.

A safe playground that is used to meet curriculum objectives is an important element of a quality educational program for young children. The playground should encourage all types of play that helps the children develop physically, socially, and cognitively.

TEST YOUR UNDERSTANDING

1. Discuss the Developmentally Appropriate Practices as suggested by COPEC and the NAEYC.
2. Identify several developmental characteristics that impact the motor skill development of the young child.
3. Explain how the concepts of "learning to move" and "learning through movement" are different but related.
4. Identify and define the components of perceptual motor development. Provide one developmentally appropriate activity for each.
5. Describe the relationship between the following principles of development and motor development: developmental directions, gross and fine motor development, maturation, and environment.
6. Identify at least one characteristic of each phase of motor skill development: reflexive phase, rudimentary phase, foundational movement phase, and sport-related phase.
7. Discuss the three movement categories of the foundational movement phase.
8. Describe fundamental motor skills, identifying the skill category classifications and the specific skills included in each.
9. Distinguish between health-related and skill-related fitness.
10. Identify several aspects that should be considered regarding developmentally appropriate equipment.
11. Discuss one aspect to consider when designing activities to teach each of the following: striking, catching, kicking, and throwing.

12. Discuss the three elements that should be considered when investigating the characteristics of a good playground.

LEARNING ACTIVITIES

1. Arrange to visit a preschool or kindergarten. Observe one child while he or she is engaged in various forms of physical activity (i.e., free play or organized activity). Note the socialization characteristics displayed (e.g., egocentric/self-centered; short attention span; solitary, parallel, or group play) and write a summary of your observation.

2. Develop a checklist of developmentally appropriate activities and practices. Arrange to visit a preschool or kindergarten during their educational movement lessons. Complete your checklist regarding the appropriateness of the activities/practices you observed. In addition to your complete checklist, prepare a summary of your impression of the class.

3. You are responsible for the educational movement program at the preschool where you work. Design a developmentally appropriate activity to teach each of the following skills: body awareness, space awareness, dynamic balance, jumping, throwing, and striking.

4. Select a 3- to 5-year-old child. Complete the perceptual motor development checklist in Figure 8.4. Write a summary of the child's perceptual motor maturity.

CHAPTER 9

Literacy

CHAPTER OUTLINE

How Language Proceeds

- *Setting Up a Literate Environment*
- *Planning Literacy Events*
- *Providing Literate Environments in Early Childhood Settings*
- *Providing Literate Environments: Primary and Elementary*
- *Characteristics of Literacy-Rich Classrooms*
- *Literacy Development Factors in the Home*
- *Views on Language Development*

Approaches to Literacy Instruction

- *Basal Approach*
- *Whole Language Methods*
- *Reading as a Vehicle for Developing Literacy*
- *Literature-Based Programs*

Appropriate Literacy Practice

KEY TERMS

Nativist theory
Behaviorist theory
Cognitive developmental theory
Vygotskian theory
Zone of proximal development

The two 5-year-old girls noticed each other as they explored in the reading-writing-listening center of the kindergarten classroom. One said to the other, "This is where we can write stories, read books, and listen to all sorts of exciting tales!" She added, "Don't you think you will like playing here?" The other girl answered by saying, "Read books." As the two girls continued their conversation, the teacher, who was observing, noted that young children have very different language abilities depending on their experiences.

During the last few years, research on language arts and literacy development has increased tremendously. This research has brought new knowledge into the areas of language, reading, and writing. It has also raised questions about some common practices in literacy instruction of children. In this chapter, we draw on current research and examine various theories and successful practice. We believe that language arts programs for developing children's literacy must be based on the following rationale (International Reading Association, 1985):

1. Literacy learning begins in infancy.
2. Parents need to provide a rich literacy environment to help children acquire literacy skills.
3. School personnel must be aware that children come to school with prior knowledge of oral and written language.
4. Early reading and writing experiences at school should build upon that existing knowledge.
5. Learning requires a supportive environment that builds positive feelings about self as well as about literacy activities.
6. Adults must serve as models for literacy behavior, by demonstrating an interest in books and print.
7. During their literacy experiences children must interact within a social context so that they can share information and learn from each other.
8. Early literacy experiences should be meaningful and concrete, and should actively involve the child.
9. A literacy development program should focus on a whole language approach, utilizing functional experiences that include the use of oral language, listening, writing, and reading.
10. Differences in cultural and language background must be acknowledged and addressed.

In this chapter, we build on the work of learning theorists, psychologists, psycholinguists, educators, and researchers who have described how children learn. Our emphasis here is on the development of literacy through the teaching and learning processes of language, listening, reading, and writing. Table 9.1 lists the milestones in children's language development at various times during the early childhood years.

TABLE 9.1
Overview of Language Development: Birth to 5 Years

Age	Appearances
Birth–1 year	Responds to sudden noises. Recognizes familiar voices.
1–2 years	Recognizes some words. Performs for family. Imitates sounds. Obeys some directives. Recognizes own name. Enjoys songs and rhyming poems. Engages in familiar routines (bye-bye, pat-a-cake). Begins to use words and sounds to show needs.
2–3 years	Points to and names objects. Begins to use pronouns (*mine, me, you*) and two-word utterances. Uses own name. Asks questions. Enjoys simple stories and rhyming games. Talks while playing.
3–5 years	Listens to learn. Shows longer memory. Begins to understand terms like *on, over, in.* Uses words to express ideas. Uses speech that can generally be understood. Enjoys books and being read to. Uses articulation to show feelings (anger, pleasure, fear).

HOW LANGUAGE PROCEEDS

The first word spoken by a young child is greeted by the parents as one of the most significant events in the child's life. It represents a milestone equal in importance to the first step or the first tooth. Ask the parent of an infant or a preschool teacher how a child's language is acquired, and the answer probably will contain some personal stories combined with theories about the way children gain mastery over language. When the same question is asked of linguists or others who have studied language acquisition, the answer probably will reflect some of the major research studies that have been done in the last hundred years (Smith, Aldridge, & Graves, in press).

The linguist Michael Halliday (1975) carefully observed his young son when his vocalizations were clearly exhibiting an intention to communicate. He noted that his son's vocalizations were assuming consistent phonological form. Halliday was able to distinguish seven different functions, or uses, of his son's speech (see Table 9.2). He believed these functions or uses of speech to be models of the child's conception of what speech is for.

The first function to emerge is that of speech as instrumental, a means of satisfying needs. The second function, regulatory, is when children discover that others seek to control them by talking, and that they can also control the behavior of others. Children also recognize the interactional function of speech. This is when children sense that they can establish and maintain contact with others by talking. Next, language has a personal function. This is demonstrated as children express their individuality through talking, as they make choices and take some responsibility. The heuristic or learning function of speech is demonstrated in the questions "Why?" and "What's this?": Children use talk to learn about and describe their world. Language serves the imaginative function of pretending, which may overlap with an aesthetic function. This occurs as children discover the ability to create images through language. Finally, the representational function is using language to inform. As adults, we view language as a means of expressing or conveying information (Halliday, 1975).

In addition to these functions, Griffiths (1979) found that children between 1.0 and 1.6 years of age made references as they solicited adult's attention. One study of the meaning of words by Clark (1979) suggests that such words are overextended. For example, one child's "mooi," originally used to refer to *moon*, was also used to refer to a cake, round shapes in books, and marks on a frozen window (Clark, 1973). Because a young child has only a few words but many experiences, the few words are used for many things. The words also illustrate how infants focus on certain attributes and use one term to

TABLE 9.2
Halliday's Functions of Language

Function	Interpretation
1. Instrumental	Child uses language as a means of satisfying needs.
2. Regulatory	Child discovers others seek to exert control through speech. Child also discovers the ability to control others through speech.
3. Interactional	Child discovers ability to establish and maintain contact with others by talking.
4. Personal	Child demonstrates personal function through making choices and expressing individuality in speech.
5. Heuristic	Child demonstrates through (learning function) questions "Why?" and "What's this?" Child uses talk to learn about and describe the world.
6. Imaginative	Child discovers the ability to create images through language (pretending).
7. Representational	Child uses language to inform: expressing or conveying information.

Source: M. Halliday, *Learning how to mean.* (New York: Elsevier).

express like concepts. For example, "big" might be used to describe something adults would refer to as "tall" or "wide."

Children's word comprehension at this stage is much greater than is demonstrated by the number of words uttered. Not only are children overextending meaning, but they are also underextending meaning. For example, a child may use "cat" to describe cats like her pet, rather than all cats. The process of acquiring the specific terms for relational concepts takes many years (Donaldson & Balfour, 1968).

Golinkoff (1983) proposed that infants acquire new words through a negotiation process with parents when communication fails. The infant with a high degree of motivation attempts to communicate a strong need that the adult does not understand. As the adult names objects in an attempt to understand, the child's interest in heightened toward new structuring. Through this negotiation process, the children restructure their prelinguistic communication into linguistic communication. Therefore, when parents carry out negotiations with young children who have developed the faculties for learning new words, new words are acquired. Support for this idea is found in Nelson's (1973) study of first word acquisition. She found that children with mothers who were aware, receptive, and responsive to their child's language made greater language progress. She described this type of responsive relationship between mother and child as being "in tune" with each other. These mothers consistently provided names of objects and linking or function words when children needed them. This is often described as expanding or extending language (Smith et al., in press).

Setting Up a Literate Environment

Teachers of young children generally want their classrooms to be attractive, cheerful, and inviting; but making a classroom a literate environment takes more than classroom decorations. Holdaway (1979) recommends making the classroom a "total environment alive with print, displaying all its functions, from things as simple as signs and labels right through to literature" (p. 71). A classroom alive with print contains many signs, lists, labels, and charts. The children easily recognize these types of classroom environmental print. Along with these items and books, the environment should include magazines, brochures, and pamphlets for browsing, investigating, and eventually reading. An essential component is a library with many types of books within easy reach. There should be chairs, rockers, pillows, rugs, or even bathtubs for comfortable "reading." Even if it is just a book corner or nook, the library should be attractive and inviting. Favorite books, books written by children in the classroom, books written by the teacher, and classics in children's literature should be included. Catalogs, telephone books, recipe books, poetry books, and "big books" can all be a part of the library (Smith et al., in press).

Children love writing and illustrating their own stories and books.

Planning Literacy Events

Three key behaviors—integration, exploitation, and demonstration—can strengthen the literacy environment for beginning readers and writers. *Integration* refers to the organizational structure teachers use in tying the curriculum together, with the mastery of reading and writing skills as a unifying thread. Planned literacy activities flow easily from an integrated curriculum in which purposeful goals are set for mastery of content information. For example, when children write or dictate stories about their experiences, an opportunity exists for them to gain knowledge in science, social studies, math, and creative art.

Exploitation refers to the teacher's ability to seize opportunities for children to use their own skills and knowledge, to use reading and writing, and to talk about literacy. Many teachers believe they miss some of these "teachable moments" because of time constraints and the pressures of having large classes (Salinger, 1988).

Demonstrations are experiences and activities that illustrate the way reading, writing, print, and other literacy components function. Children who are developing literacy skills must have opportunities to practice, experiment, test, and refine skills. Activities such as copying, matching, coloring, or circling words do not allow these important and necessary skills to be tested and refined. Such activities can be confusing, boring, and hold very little learning value.

Providing Literate Environments in Early Childhood Settings

A teacher who understands and facilitates children's natural acquisition of literacy skills is critical in providing an appropriate environment for beginning readers and writers. A classroom rich with print that offers opportunities to act on and react to environmental print is also critical. The teacher must possess skills in planning and organizing the environment as well as in evaluating children's literacy progress. To maximize the acquisition of literacy skills, the teacher must provide a positive, supportive setting that allows children to progress at their own rate. Salinger (1988) suggests the following tips for teachers who work in early childhood classrooms.

Arrival. When children arrive, allow them to sign in as a record of their attendance. This may involve a check on a chart or enlarged attendance book. Depending on the child's level of ability, it may involve an initial or a first name. Children's belongings should be placed in a cubbyhole marked prominently with their own names. Before children are able to recognize their names, the cubbyholes may have a special picture displayed on them. The picture can later be replaced by an initial, an initial and a picture, or a first name. Upon arrival, children may be invited to select a familiar book for browsing before circle time.

Circle Time. A whole group time usually occurs after all children have arrived. This is when the teacher discusses opportunities for the day, by introducing charts, special events, news items, and other enlarged texts for visual learning. Other communications may be written on charts for visual reinforcement and to convey the idea of having a visual equivalent to what is said. The teacher of preschool and kindergarten realizes that the children cannot read these texts in a formal way, but seeks to make the children familiar with print directionality and sight words.

Center Time. Learning centers in the classroom are clearly labeled with pictures, signs, rules, and the number of children able to occupy the center. Visual cues are found in all the centers to enable children to complete the tasks and activities provided. Children in the art center are encouraged to write their name (or make a symbol) on their work. Captions for pictures may be dictated to the teacher or to other children. The housekeeping center contains many writing materials for taking telephone messages, paying bills, writing letters or notes, and making shopping lists. Snack time is ideal for following a recipe written on chart paper with pictures or words (or both) for ingredients and measurements. Through this process, children are "reading" the recipe. Other learning centers contain visual cues that

Children's learning thrives with hands-on materials and clear instructions.

communicate to the children directions and information that help them to successfully complete tasks and activities.

Free Time. Any scheduled free time should allow children ample opportunities to browse through books of all types, including telephone books, catalogs, letters, menus, etc. Children may use typewriters, computers with word processing programs, or crayons, pencils, and paper to write stories. The teacher may transcribe or take dictation of stories related to play and work in the learning centers. These processes allow the children to see their actions and thoughts in print and provide a feeling of ownership of their work.

Story Time. During a scheduled story time or the daily news, children have opportunities to "read along" with a familiar story by inserting words or specific parts of the texts. The teacher points to words on a chart or an enlarged book, which helps the children recognize the words.

Letters Home. Communications about field trips or classroom activities are often sent to parents from preschoolers and kindergartners. Teachers often allow time for children to add their own letters to the teacher-written notes. This provides a time for parents and children to read the teacher-written and child-written notes at home. All of these reading and writing experiences are building literacy skills as children see the purpose and function of print.

Providing Literate Environments: Primary and Elementary

The teacher in a primary or elementary classroom must also understand and encourage children's natural acquisition of literacy skills. These classrooms must be rich with print and must support a variety of reading, writing, speaking, and listening activities. They should also have a library, media center, and literacy center. The library would contain a wide variety of books including those written or reviewed by the children and teacher. Opportunities for journal writing, story writing, report writing, record keeping, and note taking are always possible. Charts and folders for writing, story starters, grammar rules, and other literacy information are displayed. Much of the work in the classroom related to all subjects is accompanied by stories and reports that children have written. Literacy events are an important and vital part of the daily routines of the classroom. Salinger (1988) suggests the following specific ways to enhance the literacy learning of school-age children.

Arrival. The children enter the room and take their places at the desks and begin with a reading or writing activity (or both). The teacher can initiate the activity with the use of a story starter on the board. During this activity, the teacher reinforces the children's enthusiasm for independent reading and writing. As with similar activities for younger children, the emphasis should be placed on the process rather than the product. As the teacher completes clerical tasks such as collecting lunch or book club money and checking attendance, she involves the children in the reading and writing activities associated with the tasks.

Reading Instruction and Independent Work. Whatever the teacher's approach is for reading, it regularly contains time for independent reading and writing, browsing through books, drawing, illustrating, and editing stories. The students and teacher ask questions about the reading that focuses on main ideas, story structure, and details. The children read or hear the questions, suggest answers, and with teacher guidance, check for evidence to support their opinions and answers in the reading material. The emphasis is on reading for enjoyment as well as reading for meaning.

Composition. Teachers who are successful in providing literate environments for their children find opportunities for writing about different subjects in the curriculum. Children can compose stories on science and math subjects that report measuring, observing, and recording information. They can also write reports on current events, community activities, and community places and personalities that are a part of the social studies curriculum. Teachers can write music on charts for the primary and elementary child to learn. Emerging writers and readers can create reports about the song's historical origins. Subject related to geography, cooking, history, language arts, and other content naturally lend themselves to writing. Personal stories about new baby brothers and sisters, family outings, and significant events are easy and fun for children to write about.

Reading Time. A special time each day should be set aside for reading. This time might include a story or a portion of a book read by the teacher. It might be a time for the children and the teacher to engage in silent reading. Programs called DEAR (Drop Everything And Read) and SSR (Sustained Silent Reading) are in place in many schools throughout the country. In many of these schools where the programs are used, everyone in the school engages in self-selected reading. This includes the principal, custodians, cooks, secretaries, and other school personnel.

Throughout the day, children in environments rich in print are motivated to experiment with literacy and are encouraged to build literacy skills. Children perceive and understand reading and writing as ways to communicate that are different from oral language. They understand the natural development and playfulness of language. Children must see adults read and write, be read to, and be allowed to use their whole set of language skills to explore and make discoveries about literacy. This foundation will only enhance the future learning of skills and refining of skills throughout the school experience (Smith et al., in press).

Characteristics of Literacy-Rich Classrooms

One way that has been used to learn more about how to support children's literacy learning in schools is to examine the homes of children who have learned to read and write "on their own" or who have become successful readers and writers in school. Home environments that are described as literacy-rich have characteristics that apply directly to literacy-rich classrooms. Identifying home-related factors should enable teachers to provide classroom environments that support literacy learning. Children in literacy-rich homes own an average of 80 books (Morrow, 1983). Many of these children also have library cards and visit libraries frequently; they have access to many other books. Their homes are filled with a variety of reading materials such as magazines, catalogs, junk mail, cookbooks, reference books, and many other publications (Teale, 1978). Materials for reading and writing are readily available and are often in plain sight in a variety of rooms where children spend time (Taylor, 1983). McGee and Richgels (1990, pp. 79–82) concluded that literacy-rich classrooms should have:

1. A variety and quantity of reading and writing materials appropriate to the age and interests of the children. These materials should be

These girls could spend hours reading in their literacy-rich classrooms.

available and accessible to children. Searfoss and Readence (1985) call such a classroom a "print lab."

2. A physical setting supportive of literacy activities, including comfortable reading and writing centers and attractive displays of literacy products and activities. Literacy-rich classrooms should have a comfortable reading center where children can browse through books. There should be a writing center that is large enough for children to talk and write together.
3. Teachers who read and write and who plan activities involving children reading and writing for everyday purposes and not just for the purpose of learning reading and writing. Teachers in literacy-rich classrooms should be aware that reading and writing are learned for a purpose. They should recognize the value of play in supporting children's literacy learning. Reading and writing should be integrated into content study, literature study, and daily classroom routines.
4. Daily literacy "routines." Teachers in literacy-rich classrooms should read aloud to children daily. They should write with children for routine reasons such as making a list of activities accomplished at the end of the school day. Children should be given time each day for free choice reading and writing activities.
5. Children and teachers who interact as they read and write. Teachers in literacy-rich classrooms should know that children need to interact with other children and with their teacher as they read and write. They should know that the questions children ask and the comments children and teachers make during reading and writing activities are important avenues of literacy learning.

6. Teachers who feel responsible for helping children learn about reading and writing and who believe that their children are readers and writers. They should believe that their students can learn about reading and writing, and indeed, that they are readers and writers.
7. Teachers who are knowledgeable about the individual and unique needs of their children and who are willing to accept children's nonconventional reading and writing efforts. Teachers in literacy-rich classrooms should expect children's literacy efforts to be childlike and not adultlike. They should be aware of each student's level of knowledge and respond in appropriate ways to individual children's different approaches to literacy learning.

Literacy Development Factors in the Home

Leichter (1984) suggests that families influence literacy development in three ways: (1) interpersonal interaction, (2) physical environment, and (3) emotional and motivational climate. Interpersonal interaction consists of the experiences related to literacy shared with a child by parents, siblings, and other individuals in the home. The physical environment consists of the literacy materials available in the home. The emotional and motivational climate consists of the relationships among those in the home and their attitudes toward literacy.

Many research studies have been completed in homes where children have read early without direct instruction. Results in these studies have consistently established that certain characteristics are common to these children and their homes (Morrow, 1989):

1. The I.Q. scores of early readers range from low average to above average.
2. Early readers are interested in paper-and-pencil tasks, letters and words.
3. Their parents read to them, readily help them with writing and reading activities, and are readers themselves.
4. The parents read a great variety of materials, including novels, magazines, newspapers, and work-related materials.
5. They own and borrow books both for themselves and for their children.
6. Reading material can be found throughout the homes, in living rooms, bedrooms, family rooms, playrooms, kitchens, and bathrooms.
7. Parents often take their children to libraries and bookstores.
8. Reading is valued as an important activity.
9. Books are associated with pleasure and literary activities are rewarded.

Many researchers have described home environments in which children's ability and desire to read develop quite naturally (Durkin, 1966; Holdaway, 1979; Taylor, 1983; Teale, 1984). These homes provide rich reading environments and social contexts that encourage and enhance literacy activities. Hansen (1969) argued that a literacy-rich environment was more of a determinant in reading than parents' education, occupation, or socioeconomic level. Children who show an early interest in reading tend to spend time writing and drawing with paper and crayons and looking at books. They are rated by their teachers as higher than average in social and emotional maturity, work habits, and general school achievement (Morrow, 1983). The children also spend less time watching television than other children who do not show an early interest in reading.

KIDS SPEAK UP

I can write my name . . . Want to see?

Girl, 3 years old

In the past, teachers and parents believed that the way to help children learn to read and write was to drill them on the letters of the alphabet and help them with the sounds of letters. The new research on early literacy suggests a different approach. When parents provide a rich literacy environment at home, helping children to read and write becomes much easier for both the teacher and the child at school. It is a more natural support system provided in the home environment (Smith et al., in press).

Views on Language Development

There are various theories and views on how children develop their language. Like other types of learning, language learning is developmental in nature. Despite individual differences among children, there are predictable patterns in children's language development. The differences among the major views relate to the environment, the role of parents and teachers, and the cognitive processes that accompany language learning. In this section, we discuss the main premise of each theory. Table 9.3 summarizes the basic beliefs of each theory.

Nativist Theory. Linguist Noam Chomsky advanced the view that language is creative and develops innately. This position was developed further by Lenneburg (1967) and McNeil (1970) and became known as the **nativist theory** in 1965. According to this theory, children figure out how language works by internalizing the rules of grammar. This process is accomplished without the assistance, reinforcement, or modeling of an adult.

TABLE 9.3
Theories of Language Development

Theory	Theorist	Basic Belief
Nativist	Noam Chomsky	Language is creative and develops innately.
Behaviorist	B. F. Skinner	Language is learned through imitation and reinforcement.
Cognitive Developmental	Jean Piaget	Children construct knowledge through their actions and sensory experiences.
Vygotskian	Lev Vygotsky	Children learn through maturation and the stimulation of social interactions.

Behaviorist Theory. Behaviorists have influenced our thinking by stressing the importance of imitation and reinforcement. Although it is evident that children imitate adult models and can be positively reinforced to use language, behaviorism does not explain the total picture. Through imitation, children often demonstrate erroneous comprehension or none at all. For example, the child reciting the "A-B-C's" may say "L-M-N-O-P" as one letter. Often when children encounter unfamiliar words in context, they substitute similar-sounding words from their own experiences. Morrow described a child singing "torn between two lovers" as "torn between two mothers." The verse obviously had meaning for this 4-year-old.

Cognitive Developmental Theory. Jean Piaget's theory of **cognitive development** is built upon the principle that children construct knowledge through their actions and sensory experiences in the environment. According to this theory, children's first words are egocentric, or centered in their own actions. Their early language relates to actions, objects, and events they have experienced through their senses (Piaget & Inhelder, 1969). By the end of the sensorimotor stage (about 18 months), children reach an important milestone. They begin to think of themselves as separate objects in a world of permanent objects.

Several important changes occur in the preoperational stage (about 18 months to 7 years). Children are able to use symbols in play and thinking, they learn that objects have permanence, and they also begin to make drawings that help to organize their thinking. Finally, children develop the ability to form mental images of objects not present (like a unicorn). Once these images are formed and are named, children discuss and describe absent objects and past evens (Piaget & Inhelder, 1969).

This teacher records the child's story as he tells it. This process helps children understand that writing is made up of spoken words that have been written down.

Vygotskian Theory. A Russian cognitive psychologist named Lev Vygotsky had a different view about the role of thought in children's language. According to Vygotsky, children learn through maturation and the stimulation of social interactions. He viewed the language acquisition process as follows: Adults provide names for objects, give directions and suggestions, and gradually reducc thc level of their language assistance as children gain more competence and confidence with language. He described a **zone of proximal development** (1978) to operationalize the role of the teacher. The zone is "the distance between the actual developmental level as determined by independent problem solving and the level of potential development as determined through problem solving, through adult guidance, or in collaboration with more capable peers" (Vygotsky, 1978, p. 86). Therefore, instruction should take place between the child's independent level and the level at which the child can operate without adult help.

APPROACHES TO LITERACY INSTRUCTION

In this section, we discuss four approaches to literacy instruction currently being used in early childhood programs and the primary grades: the basal approach, whole language, reading as a vehicle for developing literacy, and literature-based programs. The two main philosophies being reflected in literacy approaches today are skills-based and whole language.

Basal Approach

The basal approach reflects a skills-based orientation founded on the belief that literacy is learned when the skills of literacy are identified, learned, and taught in a systematic way. The main source for teaching this approach is the basal series. Many of these basal approaches draw from the behaviorist view of stimulus-response. According to this theory, teaching involves demonstrating a behavior and supplying learners with immediate feedback on how well they performed the behavior. Many reading programs have been organized around four or more major skill areas: word identification (decoding), vocabulary, comprehension, and study skills. Because the behaviorist orientation required that skills be simple and easily demonstrated, the skill areas were broken into smaller components. Word identification skills encompass a large number of skills for decoding words (phonics). Another set of word identification skills involves recognizing and using prefixes and suffixes (structural analysis). Another set of skills involves being able to use context or the surrounding words in a text (contextual analysis). Vocabulary skills include the ability to read a large number of words without having to "sound them out" (sight vocabulary).

Many basal approaches have adopted much of the skills orientation. These programs usually have lists of skills (sometimes called a *scope and sequence chart*) and often use criterion-referenced or competency-based tests. Teachers should exercise much caution in considering the use of basal approaches. Literacy involves much more than the sum of several separate parts. Readers know many things related to reading that cannot be restricted to skills and that cannot be taught by the stimulus-response approach. Chomsky (1968) has demonstrated that language is not a behavior, and that behaviorist theory is woefully inadequate for describing how children learn language.

Whole Language Methods

One of the most important influences on instruction today is an integrated language arts process called *whole language*. The implementation of whole language teaching methods in American schools is a recent phenomenon, although this method of instruction has been an integral part of reading programs in Australia, New Zealand, and Canada for many years.

Whole language is more often described as a set of beliefs or a perspective than a practice. In comparison to other views of literacy learning, it is neither a whole-word approach, in which the goal for the learner is to simply "get the words," nor is it just another term for language experience. Since definitions and descriptions of whole language vary greatly, we will discuss some interpretations of this method. The main purpose of this section is to examine the origins and basic tenets of the movement and to discuss the principles of instruction, the implementation of the whole language curriculum, future trends in classroom applications and research designs, and the evaluation process.

KIDS SPEAK UP

I know everything about dinosaurs. I got a book about them.

Boy, 5 years old

A Historical Perspective. Whole language has been described as a grassroots movement. The movement includes teachers, administrators, researchers, and teacher educators. These committed professionals are participating in study, discussion, and support groups, raising questions, engaging in research, and writing articles.

Kenneth Goodman (1986) proposed that the use of the term *whole language* came from teachers' awareness of the knowledge explosion surrounding real and written language development and the processes of reading and writing. With this new knowledge, teachers were developing insights about language learning as they observed their students using language to solve meaningful and significant problems in their daily lives (Goodman, Smith, Meredith, & Goodman, 1987). Through this process, teachers began to realize the necessity of changing their views about how language was learned and taught. Teachers, administrators, and teacher educators first used the term casually in discussions about classroom practices. This informal use of the term came before its use in curriculum guides, newsletters, professional articles, and books.

Many people's names are associated with the whole language movement. In describing how teachers developed a theoretical view of the reading process, Jerome Harste and Carolyn Burke (1977) used a paradigm called *a whole language view of reading.* In 1978 Dorothy Watson of the University of Missouri and others from Columbia, Missouri, formed the first teacher support group to meet under the organizational name Teachers Applying Whole Language (TAWL). Two of the most familiar proponents of the movement are Kenneth and Yetta Goodman of the University of Arizona, who wrote an occasional paper in 1981 titled "A Whole Language Comprehension-Centered View of Reading Development."

Orin Cochran, Ethel Buchanan, and a teacher support group in Winnipeg, Canada—called Child-centered Experience-based Learning (CEL)—began to present workshops about whole language teaching and learning in 1980. Most believe that the early users of the term were not consciously naming a new movement or a belief system, but were instead talking about some new ideas about language and language learning. More important than who used the term is how the movement has influenced teaching, research, and teacher education programs (Smith et al., in press).

Bases for Whole Language. The base for the whole language movement has come primarily from the knowledge explosion in the fields of reading and writing. Research in these areas over the past twenty years has caused educators and teacher educators to rethink teaching and learning practices about beginning reading and writing. Many educators who believe in an integrated approach to language learning have reexamined the works of John Dewey, Jean Piaget, Lev Vygotsky, M. K. Halliday, and others. Influences from the field of reading have come primarily from Ken and Yetta Goodman, Gary and Maryann Manning, Frank Smith, Don Holdaway, Marie Clay, Jeanette Veatch, and others. Among the major influences from the field of writing are Don Graves and Lucy Calkins.

Pedagogical Influences on Whole Language. John Dewey's work provides a theoretical rationale for the integration of language with all other studies, the learner being at the center of the active learning process, and the power of reflective teaching. He envisioned classrooms as laboratories with "the materials, the tools with which the child may construct, create, and actively inquire" (Dewey, 1943, p. 32). One of the tools he spoke of was language:

> The child who has a variety of materials and facts wants to talk about them, and his language becomes more refined and full, because it is controlled and informed by realities. Reading and writing, as well as the oral use of language, may be taught on this basis. It can be done in a related way, as the outgrowth of the child's social desire to recount his experiences and get in return the experiences of others. (1943, p. 56)

Dewey (1938) was concerned that students of all ages participate in their own learning by solving real problems of concern.

The work of Jean Piaget has also influenced the whole language movement. One of the questions he explored throughout his life was how people come to know concepts, ideas, and moralities. Piaget and his colleagues have shown how children are actively involved in understanding and constructing knowledge about their world. They discovered that children do not wait for someone to transmit knowledge to them but rather learn through their own experiences with external objects and their own conceptualizations. Piagetians have taught us that children think differently from adults and have different views of the world than adults (Duckworth, 1987). Children play an active role in learning and learn oral and written language in similar ways (Ferreiro & Teberosky, 1982).

TEACHERS SPEAK OUT

The fundamentals of literacy including talking, listening, reading, and writing unite every activity that we do in school.

Lev Vygotsky, a Russian psychologist, contributed to understandings of whole language learning through his examination of the relationship between individualized student learning and the influences of the social context. His zone of proximal development emphasizes the important role teachers play in students' learning. The student does not learn in isolation, but is supported (or discouraged) in language and thinking development by others in the school environment. Vygotsky also explored the important social aspects of the role of peers and the relationship of play and intellectual development:

> Play creates a zone of proximal development of the child. In play, a child behaves beyond his average age, above his daily behavior; it is as though he were a head taller than himself. As in the focus of the magnifying glass, play contains all the developmental tendencies in a condensed form and is itself a major source of development. (1978, p. 102)

M. K. Halliday, a systemic linguist, has provided understanding about the power of language for whole language advocates. Halliday explored questions about what constitutes functional and natural language use (discussed earlier in the chapter). Halliday (1975) contents that while learners are using language, they are also learning through and about their language. This notion has made an impact on the integration of language arts and other subjects in the development of whole language curriculum (Pinnell & Haussler, 1988).

Terms and Definitions Describing Whole Language. Like any educational movement, whole language has been defined and described in a variety of ways. It has also been mislabeled and misinterpreted. One of the most reliable sources of information about whole language is Ken Goodman of the University of Arizona.

In *What's whole in whole language?*, Kenneth Goodman (1986, p. 40) defines whole language in this manner:

- Whole language learning builds around whole learners learning whole language in whole situations.
- Whole language learning assumes respect for language, for the learner, and for the teacher.

- The focus is on the meaning and not on the language itself, in authentic speech and literacy events.
- Learners are encouraged to take risks and invited to use language, in all its varieties, for their own purposes.
- In a whole language classroom, all the varied functions of oral and written language are used and encouraged.

Whole language teachers collect, proudly share, and enthusiastically talk about students' work that demonstrates their excitement about reading and writing. Preservice teachers in college and university courses study the research and theory of whole language and look forward to finding practical classroom applications when they begin teaching. Parents are reading and hearing more about literacy programs using the writing process, author's chairs, invented spelling, and literature-based approaches. Administrators are increasingly listening to, and supporting teachers understand and can articulate, the principles and practices of whole language. Researchers and teachers around the globe are working together to describe the new curriculum and classrooms in which it takes place (Smith et al., in press).

Manning, Manning, Long, and Wolfson (1987) remind readers that whole language is not simply a set of blueprints to follow. They clearly make the point that teachers create the curriculum based on personal goals, values, and understanding of theory and research coupled with their understanding of how children construct knowledge. Teachers who successfully implement whole language programs are those who agree with and consistently demonstrate the following beliefs (Manning et al., 1987):

- Reading and writing should be a natural outgrowth of oral language development.
- Children construct their own knowledge from within.
- Reading is comprehension, that is, creating meaning from text.
- Communication is the main aim of writing.
- Learning to read and write is a social process.
- Risk taking and making mistakes are critical to reading and writing.

According to Watson (1989), whole language is difficult to define for a least three reasons. First, most whole language advocates reject a simple definition that can be looked up and memorized. Teachers have come to use whole language approaches from many different paths. Because of this, their definitions may vary greatly depending on their own developmental level, personal growth, and professional development. To even arrive at a definition requires great honesty in evaluating your own personal and professional beliefs. It also requires time, patience, and reflection. This process may result in significant differences, but also yield many similarities (Watson, 1989). Second, whole language is difficult to define because of the passion teachers feel about it. Sometimes the emotionalism expressed on either side prevents critical examination. Third, the teachers who are informed and confident about the definition have not often been asked. Knowledgeable teachers who are experts sometimes remain silent. This seems to be changing, however, with the advent of support groups such as Teachers Applying Whole Language (TAWL).

A sampling of definitions. Even though it is difficult to define, whole language has different definitions. It is safe to assume from the following list that the authors did not intend to present an all-inclusive definition:

- "Whole language is clearly a lot of things to a lot of people; it's not a dogma to be narrowly practiced. It's a way of bringing together a view of language, a view of learning, and a view of people: kids and teachers." (Goodman, 1986, p. 5)
- "Those who advocate a whole language approach emphasize the importance of approaching reading and writing by building upon the language and experiences of the child." (Weaver, 1988, p. 44)
- "Whole Language: Written and oral language in connected discourse in a meaningful contextual setting." (Anderson, 1984, p. 616)

PARENTS SPEAK OUT

Before the baby was born, I found myself in the children's book section of the shops looking for the stories of my childhood. I hope my child loves hearing these classic stories as much as I did.

- "It is built on practical experience and the research of educators, linguists, and psychologists. Whole language utilizes all the child's previous knowledge and his/her growing awareness of the aspects of language." Southside Teachers Support Group, 1985, p. 1)
- "Whole language is a shorthand way of referring to a set of beliefs about curriculum and not just language arts curriculum, but about everything that goes on in classrooms . . . Whole language is a philosophical stance; it's a description of how some teachers and researchers have been exploring the practical applications of recent theoretical arguments which have arisen from research in linguistics, psycholinguistics, sociology, anthropology, philosophy, child development, curriculum, composition, literary theory, semiotics, and other fields of study." (Newman, 1985, p. 1)

- "Whole language is a way of thinking, a way of living and learning with children in classrooms." (Bird, 1987, p. 4)
- "Whole language is a perspective on education that is supported by beliefs about learners and learning, teachers and teaching, language, and curriculum." (Watson, 1989, p. 133)

These definitions address many different aspects of whole language. They are as diverse as children in a classroom because of different personal and professional histories of the authors. Many of the definitions focus on the wholeness of language. Language is whole and intact in natural settings, but in some instructional approaches language is broken into small segments or fragments. The belief supporting breaking language into small parts is that learners can manage small pieces easier, and teachers can monitor learning easier. Whole language takes the position that language is integrative, not broken into small pieces. It follows, then, that language is learned and should be taught with all its systems intact. All systems must be maintained and supported if language is to be learned in a natural process (Smith et al., in press).

Frank Smith recommended that teachers find out what kids are trying to do and help them do it. He felt that through this process students would be helped to become proficient language users (Smith, 1973). Yetta Goodman (1985) added the term "kidwatching" to describe this observational process. This term grew out of her belief in the importance of observing children's beginning reading and writing. For teachers to be the "kidwatchers" Goodman described, they must know language development, realize that errors are a part of the learning process, watch children in a variety of interactive settings, collect samples of their work, and keep records of the observations. Harste, Woodward, & Burke (1984) described children in whole language classrooms as "curriculum informants." Based on what teachers learn about their students and what they know about content, whole language teachers develop curriculum with their students. They are advocates for their curriculum as well as for themselves and their students.

Basic tenets of whole language. As advocates would agree, a whole language classroom is not automatically achieved simply because the teacher hears about the concept and decides to use it. A balanced and coherent language arts program based on whole language principles evolves gradually over time. Fountas and Hannigan (1989) believe these basic tenets of whole language will enable teachers to reach their goal of a holistic approach to language learning:

1. *Children are empowered as language learners.* Young learners must be actively engaged in their language learning. They must use language for real, meaningful, and functional purposes. They must learn the power of language. Students are encouraged in a positive way to try things out, predict, hypothesize, explain things, and reflect. Their active involvement encourages self-regulation and responsibility.

2. *Oral language assumes greater prominence.* Whole language advocates emphasize the use of oral language in all its varieties in communication and enjoyment. Readings of stories, songs, chants, and poems assist children in internalizing rhythm and intonation. Whole language also helps in word recognition, vocabulary, and fluency. Children are exposed to rich vocabulary and sentence structure through the teachers' reading-aloud sessions.

3. *Reading is considered a thinking process.* Reading is viewed as an active, constructive process. When the text does not make sense, the reader reviews and adjusts to discover meaning. Community reading in a supportive environment helps beginning readers build their skills and love for reading.

4. *The use of whole text is emphasized.* Only a total text can convey its full meaning and intent. Using a whole text, song, chant, poem, or story assists the beginning reader with an understanding of structural patterns in print.

5. *Classic literature experiences a revival.* The renewed emphasis on using literature allows the beginning reader to be introduced to a rich variety of rhythms, rhymes, dialects, registers, and genres. This richness in literature helps the child discover that reading is enjoyable. Using a variety of literature allows teachers to open up a new world of cultures, peoples, and places.

As a result of her experiences to date, my daughter is entering first grade with a tremendous sight vocabulary, a sense of herself as a reader and writer, a sense of sound/letter connections—all of which I perceive to be a solid basis for her continued success as a reader, writer, talker, listener.

6. *Writing is taught as a process.* Writing, like reading, is also viewed as an active, constructive process. Creating meaning and taking risks are important parts of the writing process. Empowering emerging writers is encouraged through drawing and approximating the spelling of unknown words by writing the sounds heard. In this process, the fluency of the writing is not interrupted. Whole language advocates realize that writers do not separate and isolate skills from context. After a draft is prepared, the writer re-reads the text, possibly refocuses, then revises. In the early stages of writing, the beginning writer focuses on the content of what is written, rather than the specific mechanics of the text.

7. *Skills are taught in the context of reading and writing.* The goal in whole language teaching as it relates to skill development is to provide opportunities for the student to see and understand skills and strategies within contexts that make sense. Whole language teachers do teach skills—in contexts that are child-centered and meaning-centered.

8. *Connections between reading and writing are fostered.* At very early levels of learning, children are given opportunities to dictate stories as a way to express their ideas and see them in print. At the same time, they are drawing, scribbling, and using other techniques to communicate their ideas. With a variety of rich language experiences like these, students are gradually moved toward more conventional writing. As they read good writing, they become more aware of the qualities of good writing. In a language-rich classroom, writing encourages reading and reading encourages writing.

9. *Curriculum becomes integrated.* In whole language classrooms, children experience a curriculum that flows naturally from childrens' interests and teachers' knowledge of childrens' growth, development, and learning. The curriculum is not fragmented. Units of study engage children in active involvement, exploration, discussions, and sharing ideas about content. Reading and writing experiences are woven into learning activities that focus on science, math, social studies, health, art, drama, music, and other subjects. Children learn to read through reading and learn to write through writing.

10. *The teacher's role is of great importance.* The key ingredient in any classroom is the quality of the teacher. Whole language teachers know themselves, know child development, and are able to effectively plan learning opportunities that match the childrens' developmental levels and interests. Teachers also model literate behavior as they look at errors and risk taking as important parts of the learning process for emerging writers and readers.

Role of the Teacher. To effectively implement a whole language program, the teacher must firmly believe in certain principles of teaching and learning. Because of the creative nature of teachers and classrooms, teachers who use the whole language approach may have classrooms that look and function differently to observers. Learning needs of children, school environment, and types of relationships dictate a variety of approaches.

Effective whole language teachers place the children and their needs at the center of all instructional strategies. The teachers must be flexible in their approach, but grounded enough to defend their lack of rigidity. Whole language teachers also recognize that accountability is important and can demonstrate that children in a whole language program compare favorably to those in a traditional basal reading setting. As noted earlier, whole language views the curriculum in an integrated way. Using predictable books is one strategy that teachers adopt in guiding children's reading and writing development. These stories and books have a logical sequence of plot and allow the reader to predict the outcome of the story. Allowances should be made for "wrong guesses" and disagreements over the predicted ending. Predictions can be discussed in pairs, small groups, a large group, or written in a creative, supportive environment. Some teachers also audiotape predictions of story endings.

Literature Sources. Whole language teachers use a wide variety of literature sources in their classrooms. Trade books, Big Books, magazines, newspapers, cookbooks, lists, telephone books, plays, poetry books, and other types of literature are available to the students. With a rich variety of materials, children are encouraged to read for many purposes. Content area materials such as those found in science, social studies, and health provide the basis for many writing and reading activities.

Activities. Integrated language activities are constructed to assist learners in becoming fluent with language. All lessons, activities, and experiences in language arts recognize how children learn and use language. This recognition also has implications for how curriculum is developed, implemented, and evaluated.

Peer writing workshops are sometimes used in the whole language classroom. This approach involves a team of learners who write short stories or poems, analyze the writings, and make suggestions for improvement. Journal writing or use of writer's notebooks are also used. Illustrations and invented spelling are encouraged and accepted. This nonthreatening acceptance of creative ideas allows the learner to develop a love for language that is sometimes not as encouraged in traditional classrooms.

Independent reading is also used as part of the whole language program. Many teachers incorporate fifteen to thirty minutes each day to allow reading for enjoyment. This can be done with children of varying ages, whether the child is identifying pictures or reading at a third-grade level. Children select their own reading materials at this time, and they read for sheer enjoyment. In some classrooms, students keep records of their independent reading by logging in the number of pages read and the source. Teachers also keep records of students' books and documentation of the readers' strengths. Reading aloud by the teacher and students is an excellent opportunity to share favorite books. Don Holdaway's (1982) shared book experiences have been proven to increase literacy competence among beginning readers (Brown, Cromer, & Weinberg, 1986).

Reading conferences are also used by the whole language teacher. During a reading conference, a teacher can have a child read aloud, tell a story, respond to questions, or just discuss a reading selection. Through the process, the teacher can assess how much meaning the child is getting from the text (Manning et al., 1987).

The classroom environment. As we stated earlier, teachers who use the whole language approach may have classrooms that look and function differently. It would be very difficult to give a recipe for the whole language classroom. But some elements are found in all whole language classrooms where teachers are consistently showing their students that literacy is attainable, enjoyable, and useful. In addition to some of the techniques mentioned above, whole language teachers also use demonstrations in their teaching. Demonstrations are provided not only by teachers, but by children, products, acts, and artifacts (Smith, 1984). A teacher who demonstrates a love of writing and reading teaches that writing and reading are precious gifts.

KIDS SPEAK UP

It's a good thing to take care of books.

Girl, 4 years old

Teachers who abide by and demonstrate a commitment to the basic tenets described earlier will have children who are successful language learners. Important elements for success are a clear understanding of children's growth, development, and learning; knowledge of how children learn to read, write, and acquire language; an ability to engage children in learning; a genuine respect for the learner; and a passion for learning.

Evaluating Whole Language Approaches. A critical issue in every area of the curriculum is evaluation. Many criticisms have been made recently against procedures used to evaluate and assess students' progress in reading and the language arts. Most of these criticisms center around the fact that assessment procedures are too narrow and do not adequately measure the students' abilities or level of functioning. We discuss here the importance of observing, using a variety of assessment tools, and emphasizing continuous informal procedures.

Observation. One way to assess the progress of children's reading is to observe how they are processing print as they read. The teacher asks the child to read a text and then asks him or her to retell the story. The retelling is then followed by questions about what the reader has already related about the story. If the child is able to retell the story with most of its meaning, then the child is successfully reading.

Miscue analysis. Miscue analysis is another assessment that is helpful to whole language teachers. When assessing readers with difficulties, teachers are encouraged to use the complete procedures outlined in Reading Miscue Inventory (Goodman, Watson, & Burke, 1987). The cloze procedure is also helpful in determining whether children are comprehending what they are reading. In this procedure, individual words are deleted from meaningful texts, and the children are asked to supply the missing words. The emphasis in this approach is to get the children to select words that make sense to them and are consistent with the author's intent. This approach is often used with children in pairs or small groups (Rye, 1982).

Continuous assessment. The emphasis of any assessment is on continuous, informal procedures that are related to specific language use such as oral language experiences, book handling, print awareness, reading, and writing experiences. The evaluation criteria used for evaluating whole language are increasingly more process focused. Whole language teachers are much more concerned with aspects such as children's interests, levels of functioning and understanding, and stage of literacy development. These aspects take a more prominent role in importance than traditional criteria, such as instructional reading levels and grades. In addition to the assessment procedures mentioned, teachers should consider children's willingness to read, ability to select books independently, self-concept about reading, demonstration of basic comprehension skills, and ability to read independently for information and pleasure (Cushenberry, 1989).

Future Trends in Classroom Applications and Research Design. A major factor in determining the future use of whole language techniques in classrooms will most likely be teachers' beliefs about literacy learning. Another factor is the teachers' willingness and ability to use whole language teaching. As teachers gain knowledge about literacy learning and expand their own experience across age and grade levels, they seem to grow more open to whole language approaches. Social and political factors obviously will also influence the widespread implementation of whole language teaching. As the use of standardized tests measuring mastery of isolated skills decreases, the door may swing open wider for the acceptance of whole language approaches.

KIDS SPEAK UP

Why didn't you read the book with the same words momma uses?

Boy, 3 years old

The future of whole language also depends on quantitative and qualitative research on whole language teaching. Pickering (1989) has predicted that the following approaches will be used in the future:

1. Teachers will increase their use of literature in the curriculum, not just in language arts, but in other content areas, as well.
2. Students from kindergarten through high school will write more in all subject areas.
3. Teachers will use a variety of materials for language arts curriculum (newspapers and other periodicals, anthologies of student writings, almanacs and other informational publications), rather than a small number of major texts.
4. Reading and writing tests will address the major components of literacy, reading and writing, in contrast to tests now in use which place more emphasis on discrete skills than on overall literacy competence.
5. Literacy curricula will stress communication of significant ideas first, with form viewed as a vehicle for effective communication rather than an end product of curriculum.

The topic of literacy for children and adults has been of critical importance during the last twenty years. The next few decades promise to be an exciting time for educators committed to improving literacy for all learners. Whole language continues to positively influence the development of improved techniques and theories of literacy instruction.

Reading as a Vehicle for Developing Literacy

Attitudes and ideas about early childhood instructional strategies and literacy development have been changed by recent research in cognitive development, language acquisition, and early learning about books, print, and writing. Until recently, reading, writing, listening, and speaking were thought of as separate skills taught independently of one another. Courses in colleges and universities tended to separate those in reading from those in language arts. We now realize that literacy involves all of the related communication skills, and that each skill enhances the other as they are learned concurrently (Morrow, 1989).

New concepts are replacing older ideas about reading readiness. The term **emergent literacy**, first used by Marie Clay (1966), has captured the attention of educators and parents interested in children's language, reading, and writing. Emergent literacy assumes the child has acquired some knowledge in these areas before beginning school. Literacy development begins very early in life and is part of a continuous process. Development occurs through interactions with print and materials and through interactions in social contexts. Emergent literacy acknowledges children's attempts at telling stories while looking at a book. Similarly, recognizing differences between written words and illustrations in a book is acknowledged as legitimate literacy behavior. Even though these activities traditionally have not been described as reading or writing, they are accepted as essential components of the reading and writing learning processes (Smith et al., in press).

Reading Is Acquired through Social Interactions. Literacy is viewed by Teale (1982) as the result of children's involvement in reading activities and their interactions with literate significant others. Through interactive literacy events, children learn the conventions of reading, while gaining an appreciation for and a continuing interest in literacy activities. Teale's emphasis on the social aspects of reading development relate to Vygotsky's (1981) ideas on intellectual development. Vygotsky believed firmly that all higher mental functions are internalized social relationships.

Holdaway's (1979) theory of literacy development is consistent with Teale's:

> The way in which supportive adults are induced by affection and common sense to intervene in the development of their children proves upon close examination to embody the most sound principles of teaching. Rather than provide verbal instructions about how a skill should be carried out, the parent sets up an emulative model of the skill in operation and induces activity in the child which approximates towards the use of the skill. The first attempts of the child are to do something that is like the skill he wishes to emulate. This activity is then "shaped" or refined by immediate rewards . . . From this point of view, so called "natural" learning is in fact supported by higher quality teaching intervention than is normally the case in the school setting. (p. 22)

Holdaway believes that this type of developmental teaching is appropriate for literacy instruction in school. His model is characterized by self-regulated, individual activities, peer interaction, and an environment rich with printed materials. He derived this model from observations of home environments where children learned to read without direct instruction. Features of these home environments were discussed earlier in this chapter.

Holdaway (1986) states that four important processes enable children to acquire reading abilities: observation, collaboration, practice, and performance. Observation includes being read to and watching adults reading. Collaboration is when a responsive individual is interacting, encouraging, and helping the reader. Practice is when the reader tries out what has been learned through role playing, experiments, or other reading activities. This process gives the reader an opportunity to evaluate, make corrections, and increase skills. The fourth process, performance, allows the reader to share what has been learned and seek approval from those who are helping. These ideas by Holdaway (1986) are also articulated by Calkins (1986), Clark (1976), Read (1975), and Smith (1983).

Reading Is Acquired as a Result of Life Experiences. Children's strength in literacy varies within individuals and certainly is influenced by the home environment and experiences. Most children, before entering first grade, have a general command of their language, a sizable vocabulary, and some internalized rules of language. Some children are already reading before any formal reading instruction occurs. Many young children begin their first-grade experience with a wealth of information about environmental print. Research during the last twenty to thirty years has reinforced our awareness of early childhood competencies and skills in literacy. Children as young as three are able to read such common words in their environment as Burger King, McDonald's, Exxon, and Sugar Pops (Goodman & Altwerger, 1981). This awareness of print, letters, and words coupled with an ability to identify familiar symbols constitutes the beginning of reading.

PARENTS SPEAK OUT

The Sunday funny paper is an afternoon ritual at our house. The little ones "read" the pictures first then we "read" the words.

According to Goodman (1980), the "roots of literacy" are established in the early childhood years in most literate societies. Environmental print helps readers to discover how print is organized as well as different ways it is used. Children in their early years also demonstrate knowledge of books and book handling, including where to begin reading, the differences between pictures and print, awareness of the left-to-right progression of print, the difference between the beginning and the end of the book, and how to turn pages (Wiseman & Robeck, 1983).

Efforts to expand children's reading abilities into fluent reading need to build on their strengths, prior knowledge, and prior experiences. This is the basis of the psycholinguistic definition of reading. Reading is an active process in which children are anticipating what the message is likely to state as they are reading. Readers are continually searching for cues based on the knowledge they already have. The meaning comes from what they already know in language and from their experiences. The most meaningful cues are those in whole pieces of print, rather than in isolated words.

Readers Acquire Skills When They See a Purpose and Need for the Process. Children are more likely to engage themselves in reading activities if they have seen and have begun to appreciate reading, writing, and speaking as useful, functional, and purposeful (Morrow, 1989). Studies by Taylor (1983), Goodman (1980), and Heath (1980) have clearly concluded that children acquire their first information about reading and writing through their functional uses. Children come into contact with functional literacy information daily: recipes, telephone numbers, grocery lists, directions on toys and games, menus, mail, magazines, storybooks, newspapers, and many more. Children are familiar with these items, interact with them, and understand their purposes.

Readers Acquire Skills When They Are Read To. Research clearly indicates that reading to a child benefits the child's acquisition of reading ability. Chomsky (1971) and other researchers have found that reading to a child aids in the development of literacy skills, increases interest in books and reading, enhances background information and sense of story structure, and familiarizes children with the language of books. A well-structured story has a setting (a beginning, time, place, and introduction of characters), a theme (the main character's problem or goal), plot episodes (a series of events in which the main character tries to solve the problem or achieve the goal), and a resolution (the accomplishment of the goal or solving of the problem and an ending). Through the process of hearing many well-structured stories, children begin to predict what will happen in the story based on their awareness of the story's structural elements (Morrow, 1985).

Literature-Based Programs

The primary goal in using literature as a reading approach is to promote an appreciation and enjoyment of reading. Developing an awareness, appreciation, and love for print is an integral part of the instructional process. Children who have opportunities for positive, pleasant interactions with literature are more likely to believe that reading can and should be its own reward.

Several years ago, a national commission regarding reading instruction (Commission on Reading, 1984) made several recommendations relating to the importance of literature-based reading instruction, including the following:

1. Children should spend more time in independent reading by reading a minimum of two hours per week at the third- or fourth-grade level. The books should include classics and modern works of fiction and nonfiction.
2. Schools should maintain well-stocked and managed libraries in order to assure a constant access for children to read a large number of interesting and informative books. A professional librarian is also important for encouraging young readers to read widely in books that match the interest and ability levels of the learners.

Providing a variety of worthwhile reading materials to children in all grade levels is an essential component of any reading curriculum. Teachers must also allow time for children to read and talk about what is read. The richness in variety of reading materials allows for a diverse group to find materials that are of interest to all individuals. A good rule of thumb is that each classroom should contain at least four books per child. When purchasing these books, teachers should consider the interests of the learners, the age groups, and the readability level of the books (Cushenberry, 1989).

TEACHERS SPEAK OUT

Preschool parents, take a minute to write a short note to your child—place it in their lunch box. This helps motivate your child's curiosity to want to read and print words; plus it feels good to both of you.

A learning environment in which children can select books, discuss books, and build new reading interests is desirable. Teachers who learn as much as possible about their children's interests and attitudes are better able to make informed decisions about arranging furniture, ordering reading materials, and planning activities in reading, writing, speaking, and listening.

A generous amount of time should be allocated for the children to read in any classroom. In many traditional reading programs, the time allowed for reading is planned primarily for teaching a variety of isolated reading skills. There is a tremendous increase in the number of classroom teachers who allow more time for recreational reading designed to match the learner's interests and abilities. Teachers who use this approach also recognize that reading should be pleasurable. One program related to this technique is Sustained Silent Reading (SSR), which is usually twenty or thirty minutes each day. Another program is called Drop Everything and Read (DEAR). Often accompanying these programs are individual reading conferences in which the teacher asks the reader specific questions about their reading interests and the content of what is being read. Provisions must be made for readers to talk to each other about their reading. This type of sharing can be with pairs, in small groups, or in large groups. Extension activities such as dramatizing a story, making a videotape of a story, or illustrating stories may be added.

Research Findings. Those who use literature-based reading instruction have boasted of high success rates with many different types of readers. The whole language movement, which gained much momentum during the 1980s, has given renewed attention to redefining and refining the processes involved in using literature to develop literacy (Tunnell & Jacobs, 1989).

A number of studies have compared literature-based reading with more traditional reading approaches. Some others have examined children's literacy growth in whole language classrooms using literature-based reading programs. A study by Cohen (1968) used a control group of 130 second graders who were taught with basal readers and compared them to 155 children in an experimental group that was using a literature component along with regular instruction. The experimental treatment consisted mainly of reading aloud to children from fifty carefully selected children's trade picture books, followed by meaning-related activities. The books had no fixed vocabulary or sentence length. The children in the study were encouraged to read the books any time.

The experimental group showed significant increases over the control group in word knowledge, reading comprehension, and quality of vocabulary. Instruments used were the Metropolitan Achievement Test and a Free Association Vocabulary Test administered in October and June. When the six lowest classes were compared, the experimental group showed an even more significant increase over the control group. Cohen's study was replicated a few years later by Cullinan, Jagger, and Strickland (1974) and yielded basically the same results.

A study by Eldredge and Butterfield (1986) compared a traditional basal approach with five experimental methods, two of which were literature-based programs. Using the Gates-MacGinitie Reading Test and a Pictorial Self-Concept Scale, the researchers found that 14 of 20 significant differences among the instructional methods favored the literature approach coupled with a series of decoding lessons. The other literature group also placed highly. The researchers concluded that "the use of children's literature to teach children to read had a positive effect upon students' achievement and attitudes toward reading—much greater than the traditional methods used" (Eldredge & Butterfield, 1986, pp. 37).

In New Zealand, a literature-based program called the Shared Book Experience has been adopted throughout the country, which is currently the most literate country in the world. That program has also influenced many practices in the United States and elsewhere. A study by Holdaway (1982) found that an experimental group using this approach proved equal or superior to other experimental or control groups on a variety of measures, including Marie Clay's *Diagnostic Survey*. In this approach, all word-solving skills are taught in context during real reading. The Ohio Reading Recovery Program, an American version of New Zealand's Reading Recovery Program, is targeted at beginning readers who are likely to fail at reading. Results of studies using this approach have been impressive. In one study, 90 percent of the children whose pretest scores were in the lowest 20 percent of their class caught up to the average of their class or above and never needed remediation again (Boehnlein, 1987).

A literature-based reading program in New York City (called the Open Sesame program) involved children who were at high risk of failure. Of these 225 kindergarten children, 92 percent came from non-English speaking homes, 96 percent lived below the poverty level, and 80 percent spoke no English when entering school. The Open Sesame program gave these children the opportunity to read in a pleasurable, unpressured setting that used neither basals nor workbooks (Larrick, 1987). The major goals were immersion in children's literature and rich language experiences. As the school year ended, all children were able to read their dictated stories and many of the picture books in the classroom. Some were even reading at second-grade level. School officials were so impressed with the results, they decided to extend the program gradually through sixth grade. The following year, all 350 first graders were reading.

These approaches create a nonthreatening, success-oriented, pleasurable atmosphere in which children are invited and encouraged to discover the joy and wonder of reading. By falling in love with books and stories, children invest themselves in the process, and consequently reap greater benefits.

Basic Elements of Literature-Based Programs. Though each study mentioned employed its own type of literature-based reading program, several common aspects are found in the different approaches. In all of the programs, Tunnell and Jacobs (1989) have found the following elements either clearly demonstrated or implied.

Premises learned from "natural readers." Advocates of whole language and literature-based reading programs generally believe that reading skills are acquired much the same ways that language is acquired (Holdaway, 1979). In a study involving readers in fifteen countries (Thorndike, 1973), researchers discovered two attributes of strong readers. All the strong readers had been read to from an early age and had come from homes that truly respected education. Immersion in natural texts at a young age has the same effects on reading as immersion in aural and spoken language has on speech. Hoskisson (1979) agreed that natural readers learn to read as they construct their knowledge of written language. This natural process begins as parents read to children, allow children to handle books, and then integrate books into a variety of content in the school setting.

PARENTS SPEAK OUT

"Read it again, Daddy" is one of my best memories of our kids. Some of those books I can recite with my eyes closed even today.

Use of natural text. In each study mentioned, the researchers strongly believed in using children's literature written in natural, uncontrolled language. Kenneth Goodman (1988) has been one of the most vocal supporters of whole language approaches and literature-based reading programs. One of Goodman's main criticisms of basals is that they tend to isolate sounds, letters, and words from the total system. This isolation deemphasizes the meaning of the text. He believes that basals "often produce distorted abstractions, loss of contextual meanings, and loss of grammatical function due to letter-sound relationships taught in isolation or words used out of context" (Tunnell & Jacobs, 1989, p. 474).

Neurological impress methods. In the studies involving beginning readers, a variation of this method was generally used. In the study by Eldridge and Butterfield (1986), children were grouped into reading pairs (dyads) or groups of three (triads) in which poor readers were mixed with average readers. They sat together and read aloud from the same book. The faster reader touched the words as they were read, and the slower reader repeated them. Even the use of "Big Books," as suggested by Holdaway and others, allows for a type of neurological impress. Big Books are usually trade books reproduced in a large enough format to be seen from 20 feet away. Using Big Books allows the reader to follow their fluent reading.

Reading aloud. All literature-based programs have teachers who read aloud to their children. Daily reading aloud from children's trade books provides the stimulus for many children to fall in love with books and stories. While reading aloud, teachers can model their own love for books and reading.

Sustained silent reading. A time of uninterrupted silent reading of self-selected materials is a part of every literature-based reading program. This time is sometimes called SSR or DEAR. Giving children time to read for pleasure and to reread favorite books and stories is one of the best ways teachers can encourage reading.

Teacher modeling. Another element not frequently discussed is modeling. One of Holdaway's three requirements of the Shared Book Experience (1982) is that teachers should present new books with wholehearted enjoyment. This modeling takes place during the SSR time and at other times. Part of the message this modeling communicates is that the teacher knows books, loves books, and values reading.

Emphasis on changing attitudes. A recurring element in literature-based programs is an affective approach to reading instruction. Studies by Tunnell (1989) and others have shown marked improvement in student attitudes.

Self-selection of reading materials. Allowing children to select their own materials has been correlated with a positive attitude about reading. Each study had a specified time when children at all levels could find and read books of their own choosing. Successful silent reading approaches allow children to choose their own books.

Meaning oriented with skills often taught in meaningful context. Most studies cited suggest teaching reading skills as they directly relate to the books, stories, and writings of the children (Holdaway, 1982: Larrick, 1987; Boehnlein, 1987).

Process writing and other output activities. In every instance of the studies, some sort of follow-up activity accompanies the reading experience.

Patterns of Literature-Based Instruction. Hiebert and Colt (1989) have identified three distinct patterns of literature-based reading instruction. The differences are found in the instructional format and the literature selection process. These researchers recommend that all patterns can be combined to form a total reading program. The descriptions of each pattern illustrate their functions.

Pattern 1: Teacher-selected literature in teacher-led groups. In the first pattern, the teacher shares the content of the literature with the beginning readers. This includes the text structures and the author's strategies. This approach is not simply a didactic technique with the teacher making all the decisions. It involves modeling, demonstrating, and coaching. The teacher uses information received from the children's interests and inquiries. When teachers want to influence children's thinking about specific authors, themes, or topics, they select passages for students to read or guide students to a particular book or resource. In this approach, a careful balance must be found between teacher guidance and independent reading.

TEACHERS SPEAK OUT

Did you know that show and tell is a child's first formal experience with public speaking?

Pattern 2: Teacher- and student-selected literature in teacher- and student-led small groups. Small groups provide an opportunity for satisfying self-selection needs in literature-based classrooms. In smaller groups, teachers are better able to focus on individual children's needs and interests. Children are freer to share their ideas and interpretations of favorite books and authors. Responsibility for learning can also be fostered in small groups.

Small groups in literature-based programs serve a very different function than the traditional ability groups that were the central focus for reading instruction in decades past. The basis for membership in literature groups is much more flexible than the ability groups. These groups may be formed by interests, by specific needs, or for other reasons. The composition and purpose of the groups may also change frequently during the school year. Children who are beginning readers need time in independent and group settings to develop their reading abilities. One strength of this approach is that the responsibility of learning begins to shift from the teacher to the children.

Pattern 3: Student-selected literature read independently. Independent and lifelong reading depends on numerous classroom opportunities for children to read in authentic reading situations. Far too often, reading instruction has emphasized the practice of reading skills for unclear purposes. To become a better bicycle rider, a child does not need to know all there is to know about each part and function of the bicycle. What a child needs is to ride the bicycle and gain more skill in competence as a rider. Through the process of riding, the child naturally gets better. The same can be said about reading: The child who wants to become a better reader needs to read. When students practice skills, the tasks often become tedious and are isolated from any logical meaning for the children. Independent reading is very important but lacks the critical opportunity for readers to discuss, share ideas, and ask questions about texts. These activities allow children to gain the essential reading strategies they need to become proficient readers.

Visitors to classrooms where teachers are using literature-based reading programs may see all three of these patterns being used each day. Some teachers may use the patterns at different times during the school year. A total reading program should contain a variety of combinations of teacher and student interactions and selection of literature (Hiebert & Colt, 1989).

APPROPRIATE LITERACY PRACTICE

Many organizations (International Reading Association, National Association for the Education of Young Children, Southern Association on Children Under Six, and others) involved with young children and committed to appropriate teaching strategies have issued statements of concern about current practices in pre-first-grade reading instruction. At the beginning of this chapter, we included a set of principles about children's developing literacy skills. That rationale for programs assisting children's developing literacy was developed and published by the International Reading Association (1985). The statement describing recommendations for improving literacy instruction and kindergarten is presented in Appendix K.

The National Association for the Education of Young Children describes appropriate and inappropriate practice in language and literacy programs for the primary grades (Bredekamp, 1987, p. 70). This statement is presented in Appendix L and includes appropriate literacy experiences for children in first through third grades.

SUMMARY

We open this chapter with an introduction to literacy and to the work of learning theorists, psychologists, psycholinguists, educators, and researchers who have described how children learn. We emphasize that the development of literacy is a natural learning process in which language, listening, speaking, reading, and writing skills emerge without direct, formal instruction by parents, caregivers, and teachers. A brief review of the research related to language acquisition follows. In that section, we include the "nativist" view held by Chomsky, Lenneberg, and McNeil that language is creative and develops innately. According to this theory, children figure out how language works by internalizing the rules of grammar. We briefly discuss the behaviorists' view of language learning primarily through imitation and reinforcement.

Next, we review Piagetian approach describing language learning, which emphasizes the developmental stages children move through as they construct answers to language problems. We briefly discuss the development of language as related to the development of thought. Lev Vygotsky's work stresses that writing and reading are intentionally communicative through maturation and the stimulation of social interactions.

We explain how language develops with Halliday's seven functions, or uses, of talk. Literacy development factors in the home are discussed, including specific characteristics of children who have read early without direct instruction. New concepts like "emergent literacy," first used by Marie Clay, have begun to replace older ideas about reading readiness.

In the next section of the chapter, we address how teachers can adequately and appropriately provide literate environments and literacy events for their children. We also examine literacy development factors in the home.

Following that section is a discussion of the whole language movement. Beginning with the history of the movement, we include an overview of the whole language approach. We introduce various professionals participating in the movement and examine factors contributing to the acceptance of whole language in the classroom. After defining various whole language terms, we consider the major tenets of the approach. Following that, we focus on the whole language curriculum, including practice, techniques, and instruction methods. We conclude the section on whole language by describing future trends in classroom application of the approach.

We conclude the chapter by discussing the ways reading is acquired: through social interactions, as a result of life experiences, when readers see a purpose and need for the process, and when readers are read to. Statements of concern about literacy learning and teaching approaches by professional organizations are included. The beginning teacher will find the discussion on appropriate literacy practice helpful in planning print-rich environments for beginning readers and writers.

TEST YOUR UNDERSTANDING

1. Discuss what types of literacy events take place in infancy.
2. Describe the types of literacy activities that can be provided when children arrive at school.
3. List several of the beliefs shared by teachers who use whole language methods.
4. Name several indicators of a literacy-rich classroom.
5. What are some of the elements found in most whole language classrooms?
6. Discuss the process by which young children acquire reading skills as a result of life experiences.
7. List the pros and cons of using literature as a reading approach.

LEARNING ACTIVITIES

1. Write a one-paragraph summary of each theory of language development discussed in the chapter.
2. Observe a preschooler and a primary-grade child using Halliday's Functions of Language. Note any specific language used by each child that illustrates the functions.
3. Interview a teacher who uses DEAR (Drop Everything and Read) or SSR (Sustained Silent Reading), and survey the teacher (and/or the children) to see what types of materials are read. As a follow-up activity, you could interview another teacher and compare the reading materials.
4. Interview a teacher who uses a whole language approach. Ask the teacher these questions: What is your definition of whole language? What types of learning activities are provided in your classroom? What is the source of your ideas for reading and writing activities? Whom do you communicate with about literacy? Ask any other questions you think are pertinent.
5. Collect language samples of children ages 2, 5, and 8. If possible, include children from different cultures.

CHAPTER 10 Discovering Math and Science

CHAPTER OUTLINE

KEY TERMS

Constructivist
Discovery learning
Inquiry method
Problem solving
Classification
Comparing
Class inclusion
Attribute
Seriation
Operations
Spatial relations
Kinesthetic
Graphing
Ordering
Temporal
Neonate

The autumn air was crisp as the elderly couple sat quietly enjoying the serenity of nature while seated on the park bench. Their quiet moment was interrupted by children's voices.

"Miss Kelley, Miss Kelley, look at this big old tree!" shouted Chad.

"I see," replied the teacher as she placed a picnic basket on a nearby bench. The group of children had been following the activity of a squirrel when Chad made the discovery.

"Good grief!" said Mindy, "What a tree." The other children, excited about the "find," began hugging the tree, feeling the bark, and softly kicking the exposed roots. As the group stood in awe, Mindy offered an idea. "I know. I've got a long scarf we can tie around the tree to show we discovered it."

The children moved toward Mindy to help her in positioning the brightly colored scarf. "No," said one boy, "It's bigger than a scarf."

Another boy, who had been quietly observing until then, said, "I know what to do! I know!"

"What?" asked Miss Kelley.

"We can make a circle around the tree! We can see how many kids big it is."

"Okay!" said several children at once. As the children encircled the tree, arms outstretched and hands linked together, they concluded that twelve children were too many. As they eliminated one child and then others, they came to a conclusion. "Miss Kelley, look! One, two, three, four! The tree is four kids big."

"Wow," said Miss Kelley, "What a big tree!"

The idea caught on quickly as the children measured tree after tree. Finally tiring of the experience, one, two, and finally all of the children began rolling in a bed of leaves.

When the teacher asked, "Hey kids, are you about ready for lunch?" The children's enthusiastic cry of "Okay!" told her the decision was unanimous. As the teacher, picnic basket in hand and followed by twelve lively children, marched up the hill to the picnic area, the elderly couple looked on.

"Hilda," said the old man, "Were our kids like that?"

"Oh my, yes," replied the old woman, "Our children were always just as curious as could be, and they got into things too—just like kids do now!"

APPROACHES TO MATH AND SCIENCE

As instructional techniques have been explored, a number of approaches to math and science have been tried. These curriculum methods include concrete and abstract models. Methods that have demonstrated particular success with young children include constructivist influences, discovery, inquiry, and problem-solving strategies.

Science and math are areas that naturally appeal to the inquisitive nature of young children as they discover their world. It is quite common for the parents of a young child to comment that their child "asks so many questions." Many parents have scratched their heads at questions such as, "Why is the sky blue? Why can't we see the wind?" or "How can a one and a zero make ten?" Though explanations of such questions would necessitate a discussion far above the child's comprehension, we must recognize the importance of children's efforts to make sense of their world. This building of a child's knowledge begins at birth and develops throughout the years of early childhood. Theorists have considered how this construction occurs as young children explore math and science. Three areas we address in this chapter include **constructivist** influences (Piaget, 1954), discovering learning (Dewey, 1910), and the inquiry method.

Constructivist Influences

Piaget explains that knowledge builds with experience, continues to expand on prior knowledge, and is continually revised and affirmed through the processes of assimilation and accommodation. The action results in a balance of old and new knowledge. Thus, children actively expand the potentials of mathematical and scientific understanding.

Piaget firmly believed that "all knowledge, including the ability to reason logically, is constructed by the individual as he acts on objects and people and tries to make sense out of his experience . . . that knowledge is acquired by construction from within" (Kamii & DeVries, 1978, p. 16). Children enhance their perspectives of the world through active experiences that allow them to discover information for themselves.

KIDS SPEAK UP

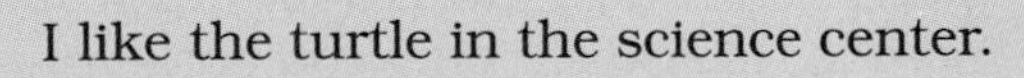

I like the turtle in the science center.

Boy, 4 years old

Three fundamentally distinct types of knowledge were identified by Piaget: physical knowledge, logico-mathematical knowledge, and social-conventional knowledge (Kamii, 1982). While physical knowledge and social-conventional knowledge are directed by society and have limited need for the child's modification, logico-mathematical knowledge is more complex. It is dependent on the ability of children to internalize and apply concepts. The act of this modification must be achieved within each child. External influences such as the teacher or parent may serve only as a guide for providing challenges. It is the child who accomplishes understanding. No one can think for the child. Educators may assist in the development of logico-mathematical knowledge by providing challenges that encourage active learning and discovery experiences. Many contributing factors promote the development of logico-mathematical knowledge. These factors include maturation, experience, and intelligence. The skills of math and science are formulated through the integration of physical knowledge and social knowledge, and organized within the structures of logico-mathematical concepts.

Discovery, Inquiry, and Problem Solving

One approach used to describe the acquisition of new information is the **discovery learning** method (Bredderman, 1982; Klein, 1991; Shymansky, Kyle, & Alport, 1982). It is through this series of strategies that children determine questions, form a methodology for discovery, develop a hypothesis, implement procedures, and summarize their findings.

The discovery method is guided by the teacher who provides the stimulus for **inquiry** and allows children to learn through actions. Dewey (1910) viewed the method as a **problem-solving** approach that requires children to be actively involved in the learning process. Children question, manipulate, and register their discoveries. The process fosters a child's acquisition of scientific and mathematic competencies.

CONCEPTS OF MATH AND SCIENCE

Both math and science require the acquisition and refinement of specific skills. Ard and Pitts (1990) suggest that these unified domains include classification, comparison, seriating, measuring, graphing, counting, numbers, operations, spatial relations, time, and sets.

Classification

The child's ability to observe the attributes of objects, and focus on similar characteristics, is essential to the process referred to as **classification**. This activity requires that the child be able to recognize how elements are alike or different. The classification of simple shapes may initially prompt the child to put all things that are square into one simple classification. Later, the system may take on multiple classification components through which the child will focus on additional similarities or differences. This approach may result in the child placing small squares into one category and large

Children are actively interested in the environment. Field trips provide a multitude of opportunities.

squares into a second category. It is suggested that the capacity to classify develops progressively in children (Hohmann, Banet, & Weikart, 1979). Babies appear to resolve approaches to different materials with different behaviors. For example, they shake some things while they quickly put others in their mouths, suggesting that even very young babies have formed a system of classification.

As children acquire and refine language, the organization of various attributes influence what children do with objects. The use of multiple classifications becomes evident as children demonstrate logical organization of **class inclusion**. Table 10.1 summarizes the development of a child's capacity to classify using Piaget's four stages of development.

The term **attribute** refers to the identifiable features of an object, situation, person, or event. The foundations of mathematical and scientific understanding are closely linked to the child's expanding abilities to classify information.

Comparison

Comparisons represent a process which allows children to consider the physical characteristics of their world. The ability to distinguish how things are alike and different is a prerequisite of increasingly

TABLE 10.1 Development of Classification Capabilities

The child	Sensorimotor Stage (0–2½ yrs.)	Preoperational Stage (2½–7 yrs.)	Concrete Operational (7–11 yrs.)	Formal Operational (12+ yrs.)
Makes different responses to different objects	x	x	x	x
Explores attributes	x	x	x	x
Makes graphic collection	x	x	x	
Sorts by identity	x	x	x	
Sorts into two groups		x	x	x
Uses multiple class relationships			x	
Uses class inclusion			x	
Controls variables				x
Generates hypothetical classes				x

Source: Adapted from Mary Hohmann, Bernard Banet, & David P. Weikart, *Young children in action.* (Ypsilanti, MI: High/Scope Press, 1979), p. 194.

more sophisticated skills such as seriation, measurement, and other concepts. The ability to conceptualize comparisons appears to follow developmental patterns. The rate of this development is dependent upon the unique dynamics of each child. The child's initial point of reference for comparison is focused on only limited aspects. Maturation, experience, and the child's developmental predisposition contribute to the rate of comparisons as an applied skill.

A very young child may identify a collection of objects as red while ignoring the size, shape, or dimension of the objects. An older child will extend the comparisons to include more observation cues that will allow greater potential for success.

Seriation

Seriation is the concept through which children sequence objects in accordance to a ranked order. Aspects of seriation include rankings such as weight, length, height, value, or age. From birth to approximately 2½ years, children characterize seriation through the systems of actions such as fitting nesting blocks together or building towers. During the period from 2½ to 7 years of age, children become more capable of comparing differences and ordering structures based on experimentation. In addition, the child demonstrates a seriation of elements focusing on one attribute such as length. By age 11, children are constructing systematic seriations and are capable of considering more than one dimension of the objects. As children refine their development of seriation, typically around age 12, seriation has reached an abstract and hypothetical level enabling the child to predict and theorize the serial relationships of abstract entities.

Measuring

Measurement may be defined as the comparison of objects and the discovery that objects can be compared in known or accepted units of measurement. From infancy to age 3, children are involved in a growing awareness of objects and size discrimination. At age 3 or 4, children begin to understand and verbalize concepts such as "taking a long walk" or "going faster in a swing." At 5 years, children may polish discrimination skills by applying concepts such as full and empty, heavy and light, more and less, high and low, short and tall, or most and least. Children 5 and 6 years old have attained skills to measure using nonstandard units such as paper clips, footsteps, pencils, or tongue depressors. According to Piaget (1965), development of measurement concepts using standard units occurs at about age 8 and is dependent on grasping the concept of conversation.

Counting

Counting involves the ability to use cardinal and ordinal numbers in the context of concrete objects. At age 3 to preschool age, children develop a fascination of rote counting. The memorization of counting the numbers one to ten, by 4- to 5-year-olds, is important in familiarizing young children with number name and numerical order, though children of this age may not understand that the number represents a specific number of objects. Meaningful counting occurs at about 5 or 6, when a child has developed the ability to confirm the number property of a group of objects by counting sequentially while touching objects in the set (one-to-one correspondence).

The concept of ordinal counting, using a number to describe a position in a sequence, perhaps has its inception when the child of 3 or 4 realizes the advantages of position and wants to be first. Ordinal counting of objects up to ten develops around age 5 or 6. The understanding of position evolves to a correlation of cardinal and ordinal numbers; for example, the number four position is fourth, when the child is about 7 or 8 years of age.

Numbers

Concepts of number and numeration include recognition of numeral names and various ways that numbers are used. Awareness of the various ways that adults and children use numbers begins at about

A child's ability to internalize the concept of number is influenced by development, maturity, and experiences.

age 4 and, like other areas of concept formation, is dependent on the child's environment, experience, and maturity. At about 5, children are capable of beginning to recognize numerals that are introduced in relevant situations. Five-year-olds will usually become aware of numerals through functional activities before reading them and read numerals before attempting to write them. The acquisition of reading and writing numerals for 5-year-olds may vary according to individual development of the child.

Operations

Operations involves the understanding that sets of objects may be placed together to produce another number. Preparatory skills for operations begins in early childhood as children manipulate objects, put them together, and take them apart. At about 7 years, the child grows in abilities to use and understand concepts that advance competence in operations: reversibility, order, classification, temporal-spatial relations, and seriation. Foundations for the operations of addition, subtraction, multiplication, and division are laid at this time. These become basic skills for future learning in areas of math and science.

Spatial Relations

Spatial relations include awareness of space in relation to one's body, relationship of objects, and shapes of the objects. Experience with the external world allows the child to construct knowledge of spatial relations, with the child's body serving as the reference point. A baby recognizes its mother's face in any position. The concepts of nearness, separateness, order, and enclosure develop as the child, starting as early as 6 months, moves to more organized thought and controlled motor behavior such as crawling, standing, sitting, and picking up objects.

By age 2 to 3, children are aware of space in relation to themselves through ordinary experiences at home or play. Children of this age develop awareness of their own shape because they have seen their shadow or viewed themselves in a mirror. Concepts of smaller or larger develop as children compare their size to adults, other children, or pets. Investigation into a variety of spaces (from crawling into kitchen cabinets to trying on mother's shoes) promotes additional understanding of space concepts. When young children are aware that the size of an object changes according to position, perception of spatial relations is beginning to develop.

By 5 or 6 years of age, manipulation and observation are used by young children to perceive and identify squares, triangles, and circles in an intuitive way. Some children of this age lack the visual perception to identify two- and three-sided figures, skills that can be improved through further manipulative experiences.

Time

Time is a measuring system that represents the present and refers to the past and the future. Young children are confined to limited concepts of time, because the abstract concept is dependent on understanding ordering and a change of perspective. At 3 years, young children view time in relation to themselves and their daily routine: time for snacks or time to take a nap. Three-year-olds generally know how to respond when asked their age, though the word *year* is a vague concept to them. At 4 years, children generally understand the meanings of words such as *morning, afternoon, night, now,* and *tomorrow.* The concept of time, for this age group, is usually related to events of daily living and may be occasionally confused when applied to other contexts. Five-year-olds use "time words" in conversation and are aware of the sequence of events within a day. Remembering events that happened last year is difficult for children of this age, as is understanding lengths of time before an anticipated happening. Children of this age become impatient for a new baby to arrive when they are told several months prior to the event. Six- or seven-year-olds appear interested in time, may "tell" time without thoroughly understanding it, and may become aware of the length of time for specific activities. When children understand the passing of time as the clock moves in a sequential progression, they have a true understanding of time that may be applied to experience.

Sets

A *set* is a collection of anything that has common characteristics. The number of a given set remains constant, though the members may be arranged differently by space, position, or pattern. Collections acquired during play encourage the development of sets concepts. Sorting of objects with common properties, joining sets of objects, removing subsets, counting objects within a set, and determining which sets have more or less are common activities for the preschool child. Children below the age of 6 depend primarily on visual perception to determine whether sets change as the number of objects is rearranged. Piaget discovered that children usually conserve number by the age of 7 years; they recognize that five objects will not become another number regardless of arrangement (Scott & Gardner, 1978). The various concepts of conservation occur at different intervals in the development of children's thinking: first with number, followed by quantity, weight, and finally volume at around 10 to 11 years of age (Copeland, 1970).

STRATEGIES, TECHNIQUES, AND TOOLS

The concepts of mathematics and science can be introduced to young children through a variety of life experiences. Teachers of young children will find the following tools, strategies, and techniques especially practical in organizing a curriculum for children.

Mathematics

The National Council of Teachers of Mathematics, in order to suggest uniform standards, has set goals for mathematical literacy (see Table 10.2).

Providing a Math-Rich Environment. Children come to school with knowledge of various mathematical concepts that were discovered in an environment rich in mathematics. Simply by living in the world, children are exposed to a number of mathematical survival concepts as part of their existence. Language of early childhood reflects these skills: "He has more," "This is bigger," or "Is this enough?" Children's day-to-day behavior requires engaging in a multitude of mathematical skills: matching (finding the other shoe), sorting (putting toys away), measuring (pouring half a cup of juice), counting (determining the number of days until a special event), one-

TABLE 10.2 Goals for Mathematical Literacy

General Goals for All Students:	Mathematics Content:
1. Learn to value mathematics.	1. Number sense and numeration.
2. Become confident in their ability to do mathematics.	2. Estimation.
3. Become mathematical problem solvers.	3. Concepts of whole number operations.
4. Learn to communicate mathematically.	4. Whole number computation.
5. Learn to reason mathematically.	5. Fractions and decimals.
Goals for Mathematical Thinking (Kindergarten–Fourth Grade):	6. Geometry and spatial sense.
1. Mathematics as problem solving.	7. Measurement.
2. Mathematics as reasoning.	8. Graphing and probability.
3. Mathematics as communication.	
4. Mathematical connections.	

Source: Adapted from *Curriculum and evaluation standards for school mathematics.* (Reston, Virginia: The National Council of Teachers of Mathematics, 1989).

to-one correspondence (a cookie for each hand), size (dressing dolls), sequencing (placing blocks in order from smallest to largest), pairing (putting gloves together), and producing patterns (developing repeating patterns with canned goods as children are helping to put away groceries). Parents often unconsciously immerse young children into a mathematics-rich vocabulary: "It's nine o'clock—bedtime," "I have two toys, one for you and one for your sister," "Your glass is the smallest one," or "Your birthday is four days away."

While we cannot expect a child to fully appreciate a math-rich environment at an adult level, exposure to the language of math promotes awareness, an important prerequisite to more structured learning. Because much of children's early learning is incidental, their casual introduction to the language of math offers a link to growing skills. By becoming aware that children's learning is integrated with play activities and social experience, adults may informally provide mathematical opportunities for the child or seize opportunities that occur spontaneously. Relevant and stimulating questions by adults, at appropriate times, will encourage the child's curiosity.

Practical Experiences with Math. Though adults may view the world of mathematics in a formal way, children see it as "a way of viewing the world and their experiences in it" (Brewer, 1992, p. 284). Parents and teachers may provide mathematical experiences for children with naturally occurring events of everyday life. The suggestions given here should serve as ideas that can be revised and tailored to suit the child's interest, needs, or life-style. Adults should be limited only by their imagination and the child's developmental level.

One-to-one correspondence activities. The child's experience with *one-to-one correspondence* may occur as part of a daily routine. A good introduction to this skill involves adults asking children to get one item (glasses, cookies, or crackers) for each member of a group. Once the task is accomplished, the child may be asked to distribute snack food evenly among the number of guests to be served. Allowing the child to serve with a partner is helpful as the dialogue between the pair encourages thinking, counting, decision making, and problem solving. Discussion between the pair and those being served provides immediate feedback on the equality of the activity.

Classification activities. To encourage *classification* skills, adults should permit young children to sort various household items: stockings, mittens, buttons, or money; to arrange rocks by texture or color; or to sort game pieces according to function. A particularly good activity involves sorting plastic dinnerware, which is arranged by types. Adults should prepare for the activity by gluing a knife, fork, or spoon in the bottom of separate containers, to show an

Cooking activities introduce children to real life experiences in mathematics.

example of each type of dinnerware. By using **kinesthetic** and visual awareness, the child may learn to sort and later use the information in a practical way at home or during group activities at school.

Measuring activities. Opportunities for *measuring* are plentiful in the child's home and school environment. Through cooking activities, children can measure a variety of materials while participating in a naturally appealing way. Another area that appears fascinating to young children is measuring growth. At home or school, adults may place paper over a wall section and designate the area for comparing the child's individual growth. The height of the family could be charted in a similar fashion to encourage comparisons between the height of parents, siblings, and the child. A good classroom variation of this activity allows the children to work in pairs as they draw the shape of their bodies. The teacher should cut out the various shapes and allow the children to create a wall display. The children's silhouettes can be ordered from shortest to tallest, or from tallest to shortest. **Graphing** skills are therefore implemented in a meaningful context.

Counting activities. Opportunities for young children to experience *counting* skills are numerous and easily motivated. Adults may encourage the practice of these skills by asking the child to count various objects: number of chairs at the table, number of an ingredient needed for a cooking experience, number of cold drinks, or other familiar items that children can count while helping. Adult play with the child may include suggesting variations that enhance mathematical skills. Bouncing a ball with a partner can become a good counting activity. The child should bounce a ball while the partner listens. The listener tells the bouncer how many times the ball bounced. Then the roles are reversed. A variation of the activity involves allowing the listener to turn around and count the bounces by sound. Counting should be done with objects or manipulatives, related to the child's experience, tied to interests, recognized as part of functioning as a helpful family or class member, or integrated into play situations.

TEACHERS SPEAK OUT

My class thinks the best math manipulatives are in the "junk box." Members of the class have contributed everything from buttons to bottle caps. We use it for counting, classification, ordering, etc.

Ordering activities. The **ordering**, or seriation, of numbers can be practiced by young children through the use of household objects. Adults may allow children to perform tasks such as picking up shoes and placing them in size from largest to smallest. Laundry sorting presents the opportunity to place items in varied sizes. Simple activities such as putting crayons away into separate containers according to various lengths will promote development of ordering skills.

Number recognition activities. While engaging in routine activities, children may gain experience in *number recognition.* Many young children enjoy telephone conversations with their grandparents, a favorite friend, or another relative. Adults may assist the child by saying the numbers in sequence as the child identifies the numeral by dialing (or pushing the touch tone) to complete the call. Another home activity that requires number recognition is changing the television channel, a task many children enjoy. Children may be motivated as they need to know numerals such as the number of their address, or perhaps their room number at school.

Geometry activities. To involve children in *geometry*, adults may call attention to shapes by purposely asking the child to bring objects of various shapes such as the round ball, the triangular puzzle piece, or the square pillow. While riding in the car or traveling, children may be motivated in a game to identify various shapes (circles on a traffic light or a triangular yield sign). Walks through the school or home neighborhood can provide a similar experience in exploration of geometry.

Spatial relations activities. Adult or peer interaction is often beneficial in encouraging the child's exploration of *spatial relations.* Directions that include words such as *over, under, above, below, beside,* or *on top of* can aid in the child's understanding of these concepts. A parent may provide practice in spatial relations by asking the child to look under the table for a missing item. The teacher of young children should be alert for the numerous possibilities of developing spatial relationships concepts through similar activities or games.

Time activities. **Temporal** understanding, the concept of time, should not include the actual telling of time in preschool or kindergarten. Day-to-day activities that are predictable within the daily classroom schedule give the child a sense of time. References to morning, afternoon, night, yesterday, today, or tomorrow, part of normal adult vocabulary, should encourage children's use and internalization of the concepts. Children will soon familiarize themselves with events and the time of day repeated events occur. They will recall when it is time for something pleasant—perhaps an afternoon class party. The structure of routinely reoccurring events allows children to frame a concept of time.

Sets activities. Children may become acquainted with the concept of *sets* by collecting things, putting like things together, or participating in center activities at school. Simply by interacting with toys that have various pieces, such as blocks or dominoes, children determine that blocks go with other blocks and dominoes should be placed with the rest of the dominoes. Most children have collections of some type, though the objects may not be referred to as collections: cars, trucks, rocks, airplanes, dolls, dollhouse furniture, or cards. By encouraging the child to place like objects together while maintaining an orderly room, adults are advancing the discovery of sets. "Clean up time," when center materials are returned to their place, promotes experience with sets.

Materials for Mathematics and Science. The child's environment provides a variety of resources for mathematical and scientific exploration. Use of familiar objects serves as an interesting transition to discovery. In the following list, we offer some easily accessible math and science resources that will challenge inquisitive minds and invite exploration:

- *Classification.* A class junk box may serve as a source for wonder and classification. Children may be invited to contribute to the classification treasury. Bottle caps, small toys, leftover socks or mittens, etc. will provide a foundation for matching, pairing, and the development of more sophisticated classifications of attributes.
- *Comparison.* Material samples, rug scraps, pieces of net, paper scraps, hard things, soft things, and smooth or bumpy things are a starting point for enticing children to compare the nature of properties.
- *Measurement.* Measuring cups, measuring spoons, different lengths of yarn, ribbon, scales, paper clips linked in chains, tape measures, and yardsticks are but a few of the limitless items that can be used to provide children opportunities for measuring.

PARENTS SPEAK OUT

Each week the teacher sends home a class letter of things we can do as parents. We read them with the kids and then try to put them into action. We had no idea so many household chores are a foundation for math principles.

- *Counting.* Play money, tongue depressors, blocks, plastic spoons, and other items of quantity should be accessible for young children as they gain enthusiasm for counting.

- *Fractions.* Old pizza boxes, unit blocks, and real objects such as cookies, oranges, and apples are ideal for problem-solving investigations in fractions.
- *Pattern reproduction.* Beads and string, dominoes, checkers, geoboards, and colored blocks allow children to follow patterns and create their own sequential designs.

Teachers should investigate the additional commercially produced materials and resources for mathematics and science that are presently available. Trips to teacher's stores, toy shops, and garage sales may prove fruitful in finding classroom materials.

Science

Science offers excitement to children as they investigate the environment by observing, hearing, tasting, smelling, touching, manipulating, and exploring. Through a kaleidoscope of experiences, children are true scientists. Motivated by their natural curiosity, children question, experiment, and discover just as scientists do, though the inquiry varies according to the developmental level of the child.

Developing through Discovery. Piaget's stages of child development chronicle the construction of concepts that are achieved through discovery and experience. The skills acquired during each stage are cumulative, making the foundation of one stage the commencement of the next.

Sensorimotor stage. Piaget gives *sensorimotor stage* (birth to 2 years) particular attention, detailing important achievements according to phases within the stage. Exploration begins in infancy (*modification of reflexes phase*—birth to 1 month) as the **neonate** (newborn) gradually modifies reflexive behavior to meet various situations. In a basic sense, the baby begins to discriminate between objects; for instance, though babies suck on a variety of objects, a hungry baby will not confuse a pacifier for a nipple. The infant continues to suck, watch, feel, and interact within a limited environment to explore the world. At 1 to 4 months (*primary circular reactions phase*), the infant repeats behavior (thus, the term *circular*) involving primary responses centering around the infant's body, rather than objects from the environment. The infant experiments by repeating such activities as thumb sucking, visual investigating, and vocalizations in the form of cooing sounds.

By approximately 4 to 8 months (*secondary circular reactions phase*), the infant "branches out" by exploring the external world. At this stage, the baby likes toys that can be manipulated to make sounds, because the child enjoys producing the effect. The child's coordination of visual and grasping skills to interact with objects, a "meshing together" of schemes, is a skill basic to discovery. During the *coordination of secondary schemes phase* (about 8 to 12 months), infants can apply their experience to new situations. By combining skills, they can reach and explore new territory, anticipate events, and use objects to obtain what they want.

During the *tertiary circular reactions phase* (approximately 12 to 18 months), the child becomes an active experimenter, a miniature scientist. Toddlers enjoy repeating actions in a trial-and-error fashion. They may throw an object repeatedly to determine where it lands. At this age, throwing bits of food from a high chair is typical behavior. Hallmarks of development from 18 to 24 months (*invention of new means through mental combinations phase*) include the child's ability to react spontaneously to solve problems, use mental imagery to represent objects and events, and recall a previous event.

Developmental changes occurring during the sensorimotor stage are impressive, as the child discovers and learns primarily through the senses and manipulation. One of the great achievements of this stage is the acquisition of *object permanence*, the gradual knowledge that objects exist even though they are out of hearing distance, touching range, or sight. Piaget outlines sensorimotor intelligence as a motion picture in which the action is delayed so that "all the pictures are seen in succession but without fusion, and so without the continuous vision necessary for understanding the whole" (Piaget, 1950, p. 121).

Preoperational stage. The preoperational stage (approximately 2 to 7 years) is characterized by representational thought, marked by the child's use of words, symbols, and signs. Piagetian theory supports the premise that cognition is not dependent on language, but the availability of increasing language assists the developing child.

Two phases make up the ***preoperational stage***: the *preoperational phase* (2 to 4 years) and the *intuitive phase* (4 to 7 years). *Egocentrism*, the inclination to perceive, comprehend, and interpret the world from one's own visual and social perspective, is characteristic of 2- to 4-year-olds. Preoperational children cannot imagine that a person looking at an object from an opposite viewpoint can see anything other than the what the child perceives. Egocentric speech occurs often during group play activities, when several children are talking, yet their comments are unrelated to each other. *Centration* is a form of rigidity of thought that permits the child to believe a tall, thin glass holds more liquid than a short, wide glass, when actually an equal amount of water has been poured into each container. The child considers only the water level when determining which container holds the greater amount. The child's *lack of flexibility* permits him or her to think about the beginning and end of the process, yet disregard the liquid as it is being poured. The child's *lack of reversibility* prohibits mental reversal of a series of events, transformations, or steps in reasoning. Mentally returning the poured liquid to its original container is not within the child's capabilities. During the preoperational period, *semilogical reasoning* is demonstrated by attempts to reason by explaining natural or scientific events in terms of human behavior. Children may talk about the sun "going to sleep at night." They believe anything that functions or moves is alive.

During the ***intuitive phase*** (4 to 7 years), children intuitively make classifications, though they do not understand the underlying concepts. At this age, ideas of number and relationships are developing, and children are beginning to see that water may appear differently in various-sized containers. Through ages 6 or 7, children believe that all objects have a force. To these children, the sun comes out when it wants to, or so small children can play outside.

Concrete operational stage. The ***concrete operational stage*** (Approximately 7 to 11 years) is marked by the child's involvement in mental operations that are integrated through the use of concrete objects. During this stage, the child grows in abilities to use and understand concepts that advance mathematical and scientific understanding: reversibility, order, classification, temporal-spatial relations, and seriation. Foundations for the basic mathematical operations of addition, subtraction, multiplication, and division are built during this period. Children of this age are capable of class inclusion—dealing with more than one attribute at one time—to solve problems. Operations, at this age, include *relations*; for example, if Jake lives farther than Donald and Donald lives farther than Scott, then Jake must live farther than Scott.

Formal operational stage. As children enter the ***formal operational stage*** (approximately 11 to 15 years), they become capable of abstract, coherent, and flexible thought. During this period, children become proficient at thinking scientifically, developing and testing their hypotheses.

Preparation for scientific learning and mathematical concepts that complement that learning are present throughout early childhood. Teachers should be aware of strengths and limitations of each stage in order to create a developmentally appropriate environment for young children. Promoting scientific and mathematical learning requires, first, knowing the child.

The Natural Scientist. The process of science is one that is familiar to young children. A young child may pick up a board in the garden and find a bug crawling in the dark, moist earth. As the child picks up the insect, rolls it into a ball, and puts it down to see if it rolls into a ball on its own, the child is experimenting with science. The child is forming conclusions (this is a bug), forming predictions (the bug will roll up when I put it down), and arriving at conclusions about insect life (no, it only rolls up when I touch it). Science is all around us as a natural part of the world that children explore through active experimentation and sharing with peers and adults. It also provides numerous avenues for exciting learning (Krough, 1990). This learning is particularly important during the early years, because the foundation for scientific thinking is developed before children enter the primary grades (Iatridis, 1986; Seefeldt & Barbour, 1990).

Going on field trips with my kids has reminded me of many of the things I had forgotten. My kids know all sorts of stuff about machines, animals, and the weather. I find *myself* getting excited when the teacher introduces a new unit.

Children should be active doers as they explore their environment. "Science is thinking and doing and making the two come together" (Holt, 1977, p. 2). Adults working with children should view their role as providers of a science-rich environment and language to describe and label the child's experience. Piaget's research (Schickendanz, York, Stewart, & White, 1990, p. 234) suggests some indicators for use in teaching science: 1) Science and thinking possibilities are present in every classroom; 2) in seeking to understand classification, causality, and relationships in first-hand experiences, children are developing meaningful, abstract concepts; 3) all children cannot be expected to learn science concepts or develop science skills at the same time; and 4) if a child cannot learn a particular concept, perhaps the objective, inferring, classifying, and communicating should be encouraged as children experience the world of science. (Seefeldt & Barbour, 1990).

Numerous experiences, inside and outside the classroom, can be used to promote scientific awareness. Because learning that results from these experiences becomes a foundation for future knowledge, it is rational to begin exposure to scientific experiences with the child as a unique individual and the child's knowledge of self.

The Child's World of Wonder. Children take note of everything around them, indoors or outside. "Impelled by wonder, children are constantly exploring and investigating things all around them" (Maxim, 1989, p. 465). Science experiences provide a world of amazement for the young child. The following plan for young children includes only basic suggestions. Adults working with young children should expect many innovative ideas to appear as a result of children's questioning and imaginative thinking. The ideas should guide the teacher in tailoring the curriculum to fit the children's needs.

Introduction. The distinctive features of individual children can be a starting point for scientific thinking. As the child focuses attention on personal attributes and observes the features of others, an awareness of likeness and differences will occur. The following activities provide opportunities for the development of self-identity.

1. *I am special.* The children may explore unique features of each class member. Children, assisted by the teacher, could identify something "special" about each classmate—the child with the brownest eyes or the longest ponytail.

2. A "VIP" book, including photographs of individual children, would create additional interest, along with print awareness when each child's name is recorded underneath the photograph.

The human body. Children are naturally curious about the human body. Their awareness and interest sets the stage for motivating learning in this area.

1. *My body.* The children should explore topics related to the child's body: its parts, care, health, nutrition, growth, exercise, and safety. Body awareness would include activities of comparing heights, size of feet, or size of hands through math (measurement) and art activities. An interesting way to motivate discussion of growth is to have each child bring a baby picture to be displayed.

2. *My senses.* The children should explore and experiment with activities in hearing, tasting, touching, smelling, and observing. Encourage use of the senses as part of the scientific process. Have a special day for each sense. For example, on "Smell Day," the children could bring perfume, room spray, an onion, an orange, a cedar branch, or a garlic clove. Blindfold individual children and allow them to identify smells and classify them into "good" smells and "bad" smells.

Life science. Exploring life science provides a variety of ways for children to investigate, compare, categorize, classify, experiment, and form new ideas about their environment. The following activities offer a broad perspective of experiences for young children.

1. *Living and nonliving things.* The child should explore and discuss living things and nonliving things, the variety of living things, categories of living things, contributions of living things to human beings, and the interrelatedness of life. A simple way to begin exploring the topics is to bring pictures and allow children to classify them into the categories of living and nonliving for a display.

2. *My classroom world of plants.* Provide a classroom rich in botanical resources for the children to explore. Encourage and assist the children in using observational experiences, experiments, and hypotheses to discover kinds of seeds, growth from seeds to plants, variety of plants, parts of plants, and plant needs. Allow beans to sprout on a wet paper towel. Sprout carrot tops or sweet potatoes. Assist the children in creating a classroom terrarium. Collect and ex-

Children learn about the world through exploration and discovery.

periment with seeds from home, such as peach, avocado, or lemon. Allow children to investigate sizes, textures, and colors of seeds. Measure the growth of plants and make a pictorial growth chart.

3. *The outside world of plants.* Encourage the children to explore grass, wildflowers, and trees in areas rich in these resources during "nature walks." Encourage children to feel the texture of tree bark. Allow the children to experiment by planting a garden or flower area on the school campus. Discuss plants we eat, plants that are harmful, and ways plants are useful to humans. Classify pictures of plants in those categories. Allow children to collect and compare leaves and make leaf rubbings. Extend learning with resources from the surrounding area and community.

4. *My classroom world of animals.* Provide experience in zoology with animals that are appropriate for classrooms: turtles, rabbits, gerbils, hamsters, or mice. Encourage children to use observational skills while caring for and interacting with the animals. Make a pictorial chart showing feeding times per day for each animal. Invite parents to bring pets for a classroom pet show. Hatch some chicks with an incubator, place the eggs over an overhead projector so the children can see the development, and send out birth announcements to parents.

5. *The outside world of animals.* Bring pictures of various animals from elephants to baby chicks. Discuss whether they should be outside or inside. Hypothesize what would happen if a hippopotamus came to school, and allow the children to dictate and illustrate a story about it. Provide a number of books, films, and film strips that enhance the children's knowledge of animals. Visit the zoo or take the class to a circus.

Physical science. The context of the world in which the child lives is the foundation for physical science. Children are innately challenged by such things as space, weather, change, and movement as well as the influences of the five senses. The following are suggestions for encouraging exploration of the physical sciences.

1. *Space.* Provide pictures of the sun, moon, stars, and space as a discussion point for astronomy. Ask children to observe the moon: whether it is full, a half-moon, or a crescent. Record the observations for a month. Allow children to draw night and day pictures of the same scene. Encourage children to observe the colors in the sky at sunset, describe their observations, and compare them to others. Expose the children to knowledge about space travel by reading about the first landing on the moon. As a group, watch a space lift-off on television and update the children, by summarizing news briefs, on what the astronauts are doing each day.

2. *Weather.* Make a pictorial calendar to record the daily weather each month to create awareness of weather conditions. Allow the children to determine whether the month had more of one condition, such as cold, warm, hot, rain, snow, clouds, or sunshine. Provide cut-out pictures or allow children to illustrate individual pictures for weather booklets; for example, things to do on a snowy day, clothing for a snowy day, or scenes from a snowy day. Fly a kite on a windy day. Take the children outside and observe pictures they see in clouds.

3. *Exploring change.* Allow children to observe things that freeze by putting fruit juice in small cups, placing a stick in the middle, and freezing them to make popsicles. On a hot day, allow children to place items in the sun to determine whether they will melt: use ice, ice cream, small candles, or crayons. On cold days, allow children to place various liquids such as liquid hand soap, water, or milk outside to determine which ones will freeze. Make pictorial charts depicting the experiments. Provide various items such as salt, pepper, cinnamon, or sugar and allow children to determine which items dissolve in water, cheese soup, bullion, or cooking oil. On a very hot day, record the changing temperature throughout the day, or bring an electric skillet to demonstrate that heat makes various changes. Provide additional cooking experiences for children to observe changes such as melting, solidifying, expanding, growing smaller, color differences, or texture variation. Allow children to experiment with blowing bubbles to observe the change in liquid soap.

4. *Movement.* Encourage children to experiment with toys with and without wheels. Allow children to make paper airplanes to determine which one moves in the air most efficiently. Ask them to predict what will happen and draw conclusions about their experience. Experiment with various objects to determine how they move in water, or whether they sink or float. Encourage children to modify their creations to produce varying results. Allow children to move objects across water by blowing on them to have races (Kamii and DeVries, 1978).

5. *Sound.* Encourage children to explore things that vibrate. Stretch a rubber band to various lengths, and let the children listen to the variation in sound and the vibration. Allow the children to bring small combs from home and experiment with vibrations by placing wax paper over the teeth of the comb and humming.

Earth science. The children of today will be the guardians of our planet. Experiences that allow them to develop respect for the environment can encourage a sense of lifelong responsibility for the world in which they live. The discussions to follow are designed to foster an awareness of earth science. Teachers will discover many exercises to promote such experiences.

Respect for the environment begins with first-hand experiences.

1. *Seasons.* Bring seasonal pictures and discuss typical weather, clothing, and activities of each season. Prepare a chart depicting fall, winter, spring, and summer and allow children to classify pictures and place them in the appropriate place on the chart. Make flannel-board figures with clothing for each season. Allow children to dress the figures for the appropriate season. As you read books to the children, ask them to identify the season of the year.

2. *Protecting our world.* Discuss with children the topics of respecting animals, plants, air, and water. Initiate a "Keep it Clean" project involving waste management around the campus. Encourage children to collect cans, plastic containers, and paper to be recycled. Discuss ways to conserve water at home.

INTEGRATING MATH AND SCIENCE: AN INTERDISCIPLINARY APPROACH

Science and math are considered simply as "the sciences" by many early childhood educators because of their similarities. In both areas, children manipulate and explore to solve problems, whether the questions involved are mathematical or scientific. The skills of classification, comparing, ordering, measuring, counting, numbers, time, and spatial relations are commonly used in mathematics and science experiences. Though the skills of mathematics and science are naturally integrated, opportunities in these areas can be further enriched by an interdisciplinary approach. In a developmentally appropriate classroom, there is much overlap in learning providing natural opportunities for the teacher to integrate experiences.

Thematic Unit: Dental Health

Using a thematic unit, such as this one on dental health, may allow teachers to develop topics of interest to enrich and reinforce the learning of young children.

Language, Literature, and Communications. The thematic unit may promote the child's awareness of dental health and increase oral language and vocabulary relative to the topic. Encourage children to dictate original stories about dental health after some exposure to the topic. Investigate appropriate literature, provide books related to dental health, and allow the children to retell the story (practice in sequencing and comprehension).

To incorporate mathematics skills into the theme, children may begin a "Missing Tooth Club" to record a major event in early childhood—losing a tooth. Create a display of tooth-shaped paper forms, one labeled for each child. The children can place a silver star for each tooth and a red star for each missing tooth. As a tooth is lost, a silver star may be replaced by a red star. The children will enjoy recording their missing teeth and counting the missing teeth of classmates.

Music. Create songs by writing original words to familiar tunes. For example, the lyrics to "Here We Go Round the Mulberry Bush" can be adapted to a dental health theme by using the following words: "This is the way we brush our teeth, brush our teeth, brush our teeth. This is the way we brush our teeth so early in the morning." Additional verses could include, "This is the way we floss our teeth," or "This is the way we rinse our teeth," and other ideas.

This activity can be extended to creating original verses about dental health to songs such as, "This Old Man," a song that includes number words to ten.

Art. Children may use pink clay and manicotti pasta or large macaroni to make dentures. The children should be encouraged to look at the inside of their mouth through a mirror to view the shape, and then make two clay palates (one for the top and one for the bottom). They should use their math skills to count their teeth (top and bottom) to determine how many pasta pieces to place on the clay before the two pieces are joined. This activity may also be done with red poster board, with the children gluing pasta to each end and folding the poster board in the middle. When the project is completed, children may brush the teeth and use an ice cream stick and clay to "fill" the teeth while playing dentist.

TEACHERS SPEAK OUT

When I'm working with the children in my group with problem solving, it is exciting to hear the exchange of ideas as children invent the best answers. True problem solving can be a noisy process but well worth it.

Drama. The teacher should provide two white smocks, a nurse's hat (paper will do), male dress-up clothing, and female dress-up outfits so the children may act out a visit to the dentist. Encourage male and female children to enact various roles. Math skills can be incorporated into dramatic play by encouraging children to determine the order of patients: first, second, or last. Provide play money so the characters can "pay" the dentist, creating an awareness of money exchange. Puppets may also be used to portray various characters. Encourage children to engage in dramatic play by determining the characters, providing the story line, and improvising the dialogue.

Health and Safety. Address the topic of keeping the child's teeth healthy by having a dental hygienist visit. Ask the hygienist to show pictures or models of both children's and adult mouths. Children can compare the numbers of teeth to create a mathematics awareness experience. Often, the local dental association provides a similar service, including a demonstration of good brushing habits and suggestions for proper care and health foods. In some locales, toothbrushes are provided at a minimal cost. The hygienist can also address safety precautions related to preserving teeth.

Kinesiology. Have the children interpret movements for brushing their teeth by improvising dance steps to music. They can also use background recordings to recreate "a visit to the dentist," in

TABLE 10.3
Resources for Expanding the Classroom

Topic or Subject	Resource
Mathematics	The local bank
Body awareness	Pediatrician (health and care) Doctor (health and care) School nurse (health and care) Hair stylist (hair care) Cafeteria manager (nutrition) Aerobics instructor (exercise) Law enforcement officer (safety) School crossing guard (safety)
Plants	Local park City garden Parent's flower garden Parent's vegetable garden Fruit/vegetable market Plant nursery Florist shop State park or national forest County agricultural agent Farmer Horticulturist Garden club member
Animals	Zoo or petting zoo Pet shop Farm Stable Dairy farm Chicken farm
Space	Planetarium
Movement	Airport Train station School bus
Sound	Guitarist Piano tuner Symphony concert

mime. Integrate mathematics by having the children count measures of the music while feeling the pulse of the music, listening, or dancing, for example, 1---, 2---, 3---.

Social Studies. Combine learning about community helpers with dental health by having the children visit a pedodontist (a specialist in children's and differently-abled people's dentistry) or a general dentist. The health professional could acquaint the children with visiting the dentist in a natural way, which could affect attitudes about future dental checkups. While at the dentist's office, ask the receptionist or office manager to tell the children how numbers are used in his or her job to increase awareness of how adults use numbers.

COMMUNITY RESOURCES

Resources from the community provide excellent ways to extend learning and to diversify experiences of young children. New emphasis on the partnerships of home/school and community/school has created a receptive community awareness in many places. Adults working with children should create a list of available persons to contact for classroom visits and people who will grant permission for children to visit. The resource contacts may include parents, associates, friends, community people, and company representatives (see Table 10.3).

SUMMARY

The discovery of mathematics and science is a vital, yet natural, part of young children's cognitive development. Adults working with young children can encourage development by creating an environment full of opportunities that encourage children to investigate through inviting experiences. To create a developmentally appropriate environment, teachers need a basic knowledge of child development that enables them to appreciate children's strengths, limitations, and interests. These interests should be related to, and considered in, the selection of various activities and materials. Use your awareness of how young children learn as a guide in selecting developmentally appropriate materials that enable children to engage in active participation, diverse experience, and use of manipulatives.

Use the children's natural curiosity to develop characteristics of investigation that are guided through questioning techniques to encourage more complex thinking and problem solving. The questions should "pull learning from the experience." Also encourage the children to record results of mathematical and science experiences on simple graphs and charts.

Promote peer interaction as children discover new knowledge to be shared with others. Other sources for learning can include films, filmstrips, videos, books, community persons, and community resources. The greatest source of learning is the children themselves; and the most significant learning will be the outcome of the children's own activity as they construct their world of mathematical and scientific knowledge.

TEST YOUR UNDERSTANDING

1. How do young children "discover" mathematics and science?
2. Discuss the resources available to teachers for teaching math and science to young children.
3. Explain some of the limitations of young children during the preoperational stage.
4. Define and elaborate on the types of knowledge according to Piaget.
5. Describe a math-rich environment.
6. List science items you would find in an ideal classroom environment for 5-year-olds.
7. Determine what math concepts may be discovered by children using the following materials:

straws	balls of cotton
playing cards	rocks
paper clips	grocery store tape
dominoes	pizza boxes
rug scraps	checkers

LEARNING ACTIVITIES

1. Make a list of manipulatives to be used in an early childhood classroom. Correlate the items to a multicultural theme. For instance, chopsticks can be used in counting for a thematic unit on China.
2. Design a science-rich environment for children ages 2 to 4.
3. You are speaking to teachers of early childhood in a large urban school district. This group neglects science activities due to the principal's insistence on standardized testing. Compose a speech to support the value of science activities for young children.
4. Make a list of do's and don'ts about having animals in the classroom. Consider selection, diseases and parasites of the animals, and health considerations of the children.
5. Make a list of experiences and places to visit that would encourage a broader understanding of how adults use math and science.
6. The principal has given you $200 to purchase math materials for starting your kindergarten class. Using a materials catalog, select developmentally appropriate items that assist children in learning basic concepts.
7. Develop a list of children's songs that can be used to teach mathematical and science concepts.

8. Write an original children's book that could be used to teach science concepts for young children. Illustrate it with original artwork, cut-out pictures, or photographs.
9. Compile a file box of recipes that can be used for math and science experiences. Include an original drawing of the finished recipe, or have a child you know complete the artwork.

CHAPTER 11

Social Studies: A Changing Perspective

CHAPTER OUTLINE

KEY TERMS

Physical knowledge
Logico-mathematical knowledge
Socio-conventional knowledge
Adaptation
Preconventional reasoning
Conventional reasoning
Postconventional reasoning
Self-concept
Socialization
Trust vs. mistrust
Multisensory approach
Visual discrimination
Auditory discrimination
Tactile discrimination
Olfactory discrimination
Project approach

A small group of people stands anxiously waiting at the window of the delivery room while a nurse prominently exhibits a newborn baby girl. For each member of the baby's first audience, the world has just changed significantly. David, age 3 and a nursery schooler, has just begun a very different journey in his life. He is no longer the only child and only grandchild. He has become a brother, another grandchild, and somehow older as he assumes the responsibilities of a big brother. His world now includes a form of sharing foreign to him. The impact of this birth for the moment means only that "he" has a baby.

For David's parents, grandparents, aunts, and uncles, this gathering to meet the newest member of the family carries with it the realization of both the old and the new. This birth represents the continuation of family, the sharing of tradition, culture, and the future.

Later, David goes to day care, carrying with him photographs of his new sister for "show and tell." The pictures are displayed on the "Me" bulletin board beside his name and other mementoes.

His aunt leaves the hospital to seek an appropriately colored traveling dress (according to family tradition) for the new baby, while both sets of grandparents linger to discuss the baby's new name, "Rachel," as a continuation of the two families. Exhausted, David's and Rachel's parents are still charged with the emotions of the last few hours.

For baby Rachel, her social studies are just beginning. The future will hold many lessons as she matures and gets to know these people and her world. The family will use her to look forward to the future and remember the past.

A child's developing awareness and understanding of the environment is a foundation of social studies. In the educational setting, the term *social studies* is assigned to a curriculum that embraces the social sciences. The content is limitless. The significance is profound. Its themes have the potential to afford interventions into the lifelong attitudes of an individual. The issues emphasized and integrated through the social studies are the responsibilities of well-informed teachers, administrators, and communities. Traditional approaches to the study must be modified and tempered by the trends of a changing world in which the child will soon become an active and successful participant.

The school by no means represents a solitary influence for a child's experiences in society. The evolution of the family, technology, media, and cultural sensitivity, as well as economic entities, are only a few of the social influences on childhood. Such compounding issues prompt careful considerations regarding the approaches teachers use in their instructional applications.

DEFINING SOCIAL STUDIES

Defining social studies is no small assignment for most educators. Since its first appearance in the American educational vernacular in 1916, the term has been used to encompass all aspects of the social sciences (Clemens, Fielder, & Tabachnick, 1966). John Dewey (1944) considered that education when viewed "in the broadest sense, is the means of the social continuity of life" (Seefeldt, 1989, p. 5). This principle of education is summarized by Seefeldt (1989) as the preservation of a culture, which extends "knowledge, skills, attitudes, and values required to perpetuate society" (p. 5). If this interpretation is accepted, a synthesis of the term *social studies* produces some common expectations that include the preparation of a child to accept his or her role in the community. Educators traditionally consider history, geography, economics, psychology, sociology, environmental education, drug education, antibias, multicultural issues, values, and moral development to be concerns for the expanded social studies.

Considering the potential of the social studies curriculum, it is surprising that the subject receives only limited emphasis with regard to daily schedules. Social activities that occur throughout the day are seldom recognized as curriculum. "Social studies" may, therefore, best be considered a subject representative of a necessarily inclusive approach. The focus of this approach may not be con-

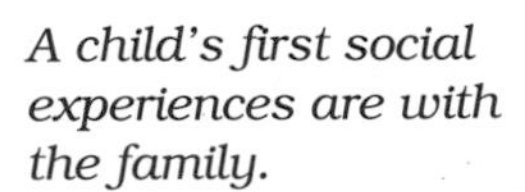

A child's first social experiences are with the family.

strained by a time period or schedule. It should be explored throughout each day and within the lives of our children. As such, it is a natural and approachable theme. It represents both complex and simple issues. "Social studies" is the curriculum of life.

History of Social Studies

The inclusion of social studies as a content area does not appear in the United States pedagogy before 1916. But suggestions for the improvement of the human condition through education are historically evident in philosophical discussions dating from Socrates, Plato, and Aristotle.

Issues of political and social reform have inevitably focused on children. As captives of a structured educational system, children are subject to the influences of their instructional settings. With attention to the past, present, and future, social studies programs are responsive to the trends and issues of the times (see Table 11.1). National, cultural, and social motivators direct the focus through which educators incorporate particular topics, themes, and ideals.

TABLE 11.1 The History of Social Studies Education In The United States

Before 1893

Analysis of educational history suggests that early efforts in the social studies movement were limited to the preservation of history. Before 1893, the emerging social studies curriculum included elements that supported this approach. These influences incorporated geography and civil government. Reading and Bible study were routinely emphasized. The term *social studies* did not exist, but the social studies curriculum was served through formal instruction in good behavior, manners, and morals as school subjects. This early social studies approach is evident in Frederick Froebel's *Education of Man* (1887). This review of the "father of kindergarten's" curriculum for children between the ages of 3 and 6 years emphasizes social issues. The early childhood program was "designed to train children in habits of cleanliness and neatness, courtesy, punctuality, and deference of others" (Osborn 1975, p. 20). The early Froebelian kindergarten movement in the United States combined the elements of social studies into the curriculum. Margarethe Schurz, a former student of Froebel's, established the first successful American kindergarten in 1856 (Snyder, 1972).

1893 to 1916

The inclusion of United States history was first involved in the social studies curriculum during this period. Under the leadership of important national committees (the National Association of Teachers and the National Council for the Social Studies), greater emphasis was placed on the geography of the immediate region. Limited amounts of economics and sociology were introduced. The desired outcome of the "history-geography" centered curriculum was loyal American citizens. Some emphasis was placed on the history of the world and geographical wonders abroad.

1916 to 1936

Genuine "social studies" came into educational terminology. The traditional role of history was challenged with the inclusion of political science, economics,

(continued)

Foundations for the Social Sciences

The implications for social studies in the early years are profound. A significant base of research emphasizes that fundamental social perspectives are formed during the preoperative and concrete operational periods of development, which include ages 2 through 8 (Block, 1986; Morrissett, 1983; Atwood, 1986).

Human beings are social by their nature. But for children to successfully interact with others, their basic personal needs must be satisfied. Maslow's "hierarchy of motives" (1954; 1971) suggests that individuals have five needs that must be sequentially satisfied in the order of physical needs, safety, love and belonging, self-esteem, and modest pride in one's own abilities—or self-actualization (see Figure 11.1). Issues relevant to the traditional concerns of the social sciences (including psychology, geography, ecology, economics, sociology, political science, and anthropology) cannot be embraced by a child who is hungry, frightened, or insecure. The core of a child's respect for society is therefore assumed to depend on the satisfaction of his basic needs as motivators.

TABLE 11.1 The History of Social Studies Education In The United States *(continued)*

human geography, and sociology as vital phases of the social studies. John Dewey and others, through movements such as progressive education, suggested the role of social interaction and play education of young children.

1936 to 1955

From approximately 1936 to 1955, there occurred a period of reaction domestically and internationally to economic and political upheavals. The results were critical attacks on social studies programs that had not met the challenge. The system was criticized as unorganized and lenient. The public demand was for locally determined curricula, stressing such contemporary themes as societal needs, citizenship, and individual adjustments for student needs.

1955 to 1967

From 1955 to 1967, there was a return to many of the earlier approaches which coupled with greater attention to structure of the social studies disciplines. The transition year between complacency and action in social studies education would appear to be 1963. During this period, educators took advantage of technological growth and attempted to unite student, society, and the social studies. The goal was to produce individuals who, knowing the working methods of social studies, would apply inquiry to new problems.

1970s

Beginning in 1970, educators continued the tradition of history, geography, and economics as the backbone to the social studies curriculum. The emerging concerns for students of this period were culture, drug education, career education, and economics.

1980s

The decade of the 1980s hailed an awakening of social awareness. Included in curriculum were social and self themes. Gender, cultural, and linguistic differences became issues of an expanding social studies agenda. These issues extend into the 1990s with the expansion of international and global issues, as well as domestic issues including violence.

FIGURE 11.1
Human Perspective of Interdisciplinary Social Studies

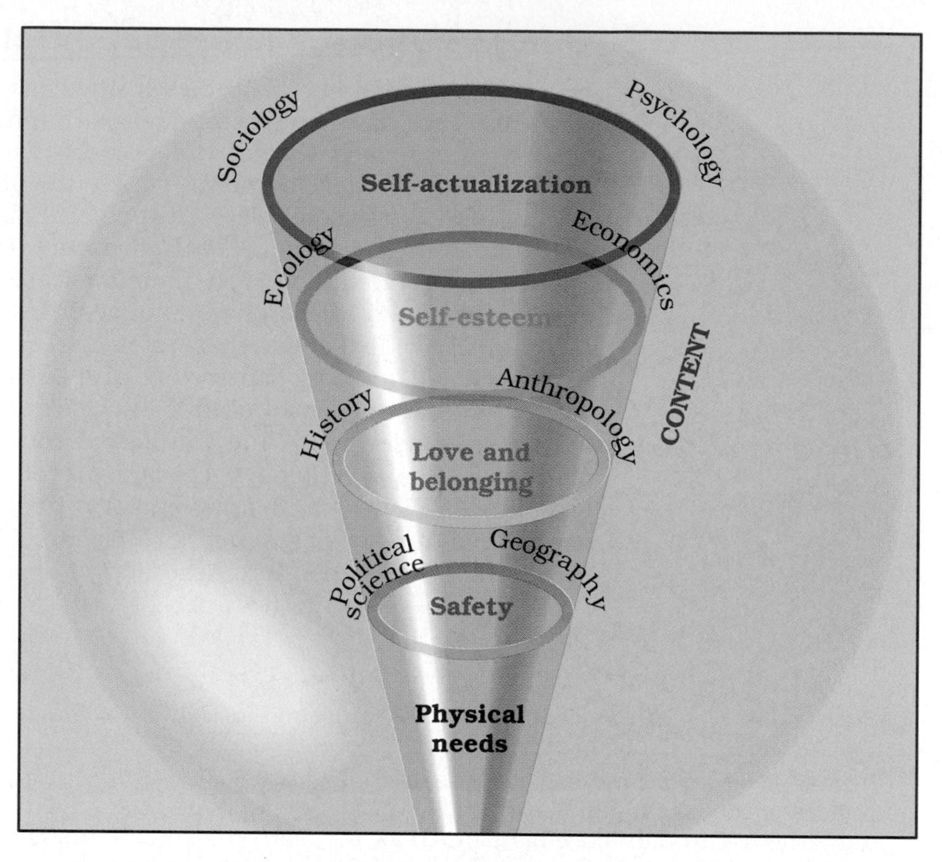

Source: Adapted from A. H. Maslow, *The farther reaches of human nature* (New York: Viking Penguin Inc., 1971). Also adapted in part from A. H. Maslow, ***Motivation and personality***, 3d ed. Revised by Robert Frager, James Fadiman, Cynthia McReynolds, and Ruth Cox. Copyright 1954, © 1987 by Harper & Row, Publishers, Inc. Copyright © 1970 by Abraham H. Maslow. Reprinted by permission of HarperCollins Publishers, Inc.

GOALS FOR EARLY CHILDHOOD SOCIAL STUDIES

The focus of a quality early childhood program may be lost in a proliferation of thematic considerations. A holiday curriculum, tourist curriculum, or mandated units should not overpower the central issue, which is a child's success in the environment. The term *holiday curriculum* refers to the initiation of activities and skills that are introduced under a regional or seasonal topic. An example of a holiday curriculum might be a Halloween study or a rodeo theme. The term *tourist curriculum* is used to describe an instructional approach that provides information about a country or a group of people in an introductory format. An example of tourist approaches to the curriculum could include a brief study on Mexico or a unit on Indians. These approaches may be misleading and inaccurate.

The third approach introduced is a mandated unit theme. These types of units may be organized so that a guide for social studies may be followed on a weekly basis. An example of this approach could be a September unit, Week One, "Let's Go to School." The goals for an effective early childhood social studies program should reflect the following ambitions:

- Investigate the concepts of socialization.
- Apply information to problems that are real to the child.
- Obtain physical information from the environment.
- Discover concepts of social science appropriate to the development of the child (geography, history, anthropology, and political science).
- Explore an abundance of authentic materials.
- Teach children about school skills. Included in this theme are rules, roles, tools, and other people.
- Teach children how to work with others.
- Help children to discover the community in which they live.
- Help children to become aware of their own cultural traditions and learn respect for the cultural traditions of others.

A DEVELOPMENTAL PERSPECTIVE OF SOCIAL STUDIES

From birth and throughout life, human development influences the perceptions and manner in which an individual meets the challenges of a society. In this discussion, we recognize that individuals will respond to a situation based on their stage of development, intelligence, and experience. Our focus in the following discussion is on the developmental milestones of cognitive development, intellectual processes, moral development, and social-emotional development. We also address the influences of specific antibias approaches—including culture, gender, and social bias.

The ability to accept and to manipulate the dynamics of a society depends on a series of events occurring simultaneously and at an appropriate point in a child's development. Havighurst (1953) suggests that when a child is both physically and intellectually prepared to address a learning experience, the experience will be successful. The developmental task theory suggests that when an infant is physically capable of walking and mentally desirous of walking, the activity will be best accomplished. The process should not be forced.

The same result may be true of any age group and carries some special considerations for developmentally appropriate activities with young social scientists. For example, a group of children may be asked to listen to a story, look at pictures, and then draw and label a mural representative of their understandings. The success of the activity clearly relies on each child's ability to operate cognitively, physically, emotionally, linguistically, and with a sense of social responsibility. The dynamics of the tasks we require of children are essential to the choices we make in the social studies curriculum. Before addressing the content and instructional issues for early childhood, it is important to consider child development.

Intellectual Processes and Social Studies

Early care and education providers interact with a unique range of intellectual and cognitive skills in children from birth through age 8. While many approaches have been taken to explain these processes of development (Piaget, 1970; Gardner, 1983; Elkind, 1993), the work of Jean Piaget remains at the pinnacle in understanding the stages of cognitive and intellectual development.

In the following discussion of intellectual processes, we consider the relationship of a child's development to the internalization of social studies concepts. We address the two early childhood stages of birth through approximately age 7 (note that these stages are represented by approximate age ranges that sometimes overlap).

PARENTS SPEAK OUT

One of the best child care centers I know puts all of the babies in play pens together (about four in a group). They add to this mixture toys and time. An adult is always nearby to lend a hand when necessary but most of the time the kids are great. I much prefer this to programs where children are left alone in their cribs. Somewhere in the ear twisting, slurping, and crawling over one another, they are having a giggling good time.

Sensorimotor Thought (birth to age 2). Piagetian scholars have provided much information about the characteristics of the young child. From birth to approximately 2 years of age, children expand and refine the skills of the sensorimotor stage. A brief review of this stage suggests that the six substages are the foundation for cognitive development, which later influences the child's ability to understand and associate social perspectives. The six substages (or phases) include simple reflexes; repeated movements; secondary reactions and the coordination of reactions; tertiary circular reactions; novelty or curiosity, and the internalizations of concepts. Although these initial phases of development have been somewhat neglected for their intellectual significance, recent perspectives suggest that an infant's ability to differentiate and perceive the world is much more sophisticated than previously believed. In addition, researchers have found that memory and other forms of symbolic activity occur by at least the second half of the first year of a child's life. The implications for social understanding and the framework of early experiences are more significant than earlier believed. Developmentally appropriate social experiences for the very young child include multisensory approaches and interactions with new and different situations. Attention to the infant's schedule, including sleeping and eating, provides more positive opportunities for social experiences. Opportunities such as playing with other babies and older children, as well as carefully structured outings, provide valuable social experiences.

Preoperational Thought (2 to age 7, approximately). The cognitive developmental characteristics for preoperational children are well documented. The observable features of this age group are particularly significant to those individuals who are developing approaches to meet the goals of the social studies. Hallmarks of this stage include

- Egocentrism (the inability to work with concepts contrary to their frame of reference)
- Fantasy-reality issues (If you can see something, it is real. Santa Claus is real because you can see him)
- Lack of conversation skills (This deficit suggests that the child has difficulty transferring information to new situations. Piaget considered this deficiency a classic flaw in children's thinking.)
- Acceptance of inanimate objects as life forms (Children may understand that the puppet is operated by a person and at the same time spank their shoes for causing them to fall down.)
- A propensity toward magical thinking (A preoperational child may attend to only the end product and is willing to accept the result with little or no concern for the cause of an event.)

Another feature of Piagetian theory suggests that there are three categories of knowledge. These categories are identified as physical knowledge, social-conventional knowledge, and logico-mathematical knowledge. According to Piaget, all knowledge may be classified into these three types of knowledge, which are reorganized by individuals as they mature intellectually. A brief review of each of the types of knowledge offers some insights as to the potential for concept development and the expectations we may realistically have for the development of a successful social studies curriculum.

- **Physical knowledge** is descriptive of the properties of an object, place, or thing. Color, weight, texture, and shape give the

Children acquire knowledge about a society through contacts with others. Holidays, customs, traditions, and expectations of a culture are socio-conventional knowledge.

thinker a blueprint of information. The primary method of stimulating a child's success with physical knowledge is hands-on interactions with the environment. Real objects, field experiences, observations, and guests will contribute to the expansion of physical knowledge. The child who has been exposed to what cows are like from pictures, films, and discussion cannot conceptualize the size, sound, smell, and differences in the animals without firsthand experiences.

- **Social-conventional knowledge** allows the learner to discriminate between the taboos, rituals, and representative assignments of information about the environment. In the United States, the "Fourth of July" represents a holiday, a green street light means "go," and moving your head up and down means "yes." Children acquire this knowledge through direct information from others.
- **Logico-mathematical knowledge** requires the internalization of information. Through this process, children arrange, organize, and assign value to their world. The abilities to classify, categorize, and seriate represent an individual's expanding understanding of the world. The ability to address relationships develops as we are encouraged to explore information. Pictures, objects, maps, literature, and social experiences

offer the context for logico-mathematical knowledge (Spodek, Saracho, & Davis, 1987).

The characteristics of preoperational thinkers suggest that there are limitations to the approaches children use in constructing information. Artifacts relevant to a topic may be explored with regard to a material's physical knowledge. But the social meaning of the material as it relates to a culture may be beyond the conceptual development of the child's self-centered (egocentric) nature. While logico-mathematical concepts such as time and historical understanding are notably beyond the child's abilities to process on a mature level, information and understanding can be nurtured on another level. A young child's interpretation of the pilgrim's story may best explain a preoperative's perceptions:

> A long, long time ago when momma was little, the pilgrims didn't have any good clothes, so they made stuff. But, they were really glad they could make stuff, so then, they went to the store and bought stuff and had the Indians come to Thanksgiving to say "thank you."

The concrete images and manipulatives used to present the historical study best formulate the child's ability to understand. The information is processed by the child and assimilated to a level of relationships at which the child is confident of an understanding and interpretation of the information. Only as children begin to struggle with new concepts and ideas to make sense of the information will they construct a more precise interpretation. Piaget offers that the constructivist approach to the development of knowledge is a series of activities that all humans are continuously involved with from birth throughout life. The process, referred to as **adaptation**, begins with the assimilation of information to fit a former understanding or old knowledge. The new information may force the child to accommodate another category of understanding if the new idea does not fit into an old frame of understanding. Table 11.2 provides an example of how social interactions with other children contribute to a child's construction of new information.

The adaptation model is used to build new information dependent on the individual's age and stage of development. A 3-month-old assimilates that all things go into the mouth, while a 5-month-old explores gravity by throwing the same objects. A 5-year-old, on the other hand, can demonstrate how to use a new tool, exhibiting a more sophisticated collection of experiences. Each child is actually responding to the material in a manner characteristic of a level of knowledge that is much different from the way an adult would use the tool. According to Piaget, using the adaptation model is a continuing process of life through which we formulate individual knowledge.

TABLE 11.2
Adaptation of Social Studies Information

Zoo Animals

Presented with a collection of toy animals, a group of children are classifying animal families. Tom places the camel and the horses together. Jeff argues that the camel does not belong in the group. Although Tom may give in to Jeff's conclusions that the camel belongs in another setting, he has not abandoned his internal model. Tom's ownership of the knowledge that animals are different requires that this schema must be modified through the adaptation model:

Assimilation + Disequilibrium + Accommodation = Equilibration

Assimilation

The camel has many physical characteristics like a horse. These properties of physical knowledge are satisfying to Tom and serve as the base of reference to place the animal in the category.

Disequilibrium

In this scenario, a peer (Jeff) contributes to Tom's awareness that the classification is not correct. Initially, confusion and a sense of being off balance replace the security of "knowing." They prompt the need to expand and discover more about the differences.

Accommodation

As Tom formulates an understanding of the issue, a new category is formed. This new knowledge is the property of Tom.

Equilibration

The security and control that Tom has over personal knowledge allows him to operate successfully. That is, of course, until something does not fit into his resources of the known, at which time the process begins again.

Issues of Moral and Social Development through Social Studies

A major objective of early childhood should be to provide socialization opportunities to help children bridge their home life with the shared experiences in the early childhood environment. The transition from an individual perspective to a social perspective is not automatic. Compounding this transition are issues of child experiences and child development.

It is suggested that values are formed through an individual's association with members of a society. The fundamental acquisition of values is inferred by adult models (Walker, 1993). A powerful secondary influence is that of peers (Walker & Taylor, 1991; Wall, 1993).

Damon (1988) proposes that the decision to include value education is a delicate issue for early childhood professionals; it requires knowledge of the community as well as child development. The relationship between intellectual or cognitive development and moral development are central to understanding the motives and responses of young children.

PARENTS SPEAK OUT

I feel that in preschool my children are learning lessons they will use for the rest of their lives. They are learning to share, take turns, respect others of different backgrounds, and enjoy learning. This will help them not only in school but in relationships, work, and play.

Kohlberg (1978), Piaget (1932), and Turiel (1966) suggest that a child's sense of right and wrong ascends a hierarchy of moral stages. These stages form a child's ideas regarding justice and social responsibility. A young, inexperienced child does not focus on the motivation of an action, but on the outcome of an event. "He hit me," requires reciprocity according to the child's system of moral justice. The fact that another child bumped him by accident does not satisfy the immediacy of his understanding. Kohlberg's (1978) theory of moral development provides some insights into the nature of the child's behavior. The three major stages of the Kohlberg model have two substages, which offer specific indicators of an individual's moral attainment. Consider the social implications of the following discussion of Kohlberg's stages of moral development.

Preconventional Reasoning of Moral Issues. Stage I is identified by Kohlberg as the **preconventional reasoning** of moral issues. The first indicator of this stage, or substage 1, is a time *punishment and obedience orientation.* The moral concerns are confined to obedience to a more powerful authority based on fear of punishment. Decisions related to actions are valued in terms of physical consequences. A child who is operating from this stage of moral development might reason that "if you break the rule, you will be in trouble." The goal of this level of moral understanding is simply to avoid punishment.

A second level of this stage is that of *individualism and purpose.* At this substage, a child does not consider the other person's needs unless it benefits the child. The underlying philosophy appears to be "I'll do this, if you do that." The moral goal is the gratification of a reward.

Conventional Reasoning of Moral Issues. The second stage of moral development identified by Kohlberg is **conventional reasoning** of moral issues. It is also identified by two substages.

They begin with *interpersonal norms*. Through this level of moral development, the child's goal is directed to being one of the crowd. A common objection for the child whose moral development is at this stage is "but everybody else . . ." This child avoids the disapproval of the group by performing roles that maintain the expectations of the group. Desired affection of others plays a strong role at this level of moral development.

A second phase of this stage is that of *social system morality*. The goal of this phase is to do what society expects. Children determine that "if something was wrong yesterday, it is wrong today."

Postconventional Reasoning Moral Issues. The highest level of moral reasoning is the **postconventional reasoning** of moral issues, which begins with a phase of *community rights versus individual rights*. The goal of this moral level is that principles accepted by the community be applied to all situations. The individual believes that some values, such as liberty, are more important than law.

The *universal ethical principle* is the highest level of moral development. The goal of this moral level is to do the right thing. At this level, the individual may respond, "I cannot live with a decision that I do not believe is right."

Both Piaget and Kohlberg "believed that peer relations are a critical part of the social stimulation that challenge children to advance their moral reasoning. The mutual give and take of peer relations provide children with role-taking opportunities that give children a sense that rules are generated democratically" (Santrock & Yussen, 1992, p. 590).

KIDS SPEAK UP

I like my friends at school, and doing art, and being a leader.

Girl, 4 years old

Group decision making, drama, puppets, play, and props for social drama provide opportunities for the child to explore moral reasoning. It is during early childhood that Damon (1988) found children become more alert to the uniqueness of other perspectives. These perceptions include that others may have a different point of view. A growing awareness of human reactions may account for a child's attempts at appropriate responses to another person's distress. Although it is typically not until middle childhood (around age 8) that children are capable of genuine empathy to the plights of those in less fortunate situations such as the homeless, the targets of cultural bias, or the physically compromised. Young children may follow the expectations of others with regard to such concerns, but a true empathetic response to socially complex issues may not be fully developed until later.

Self-Concept and Social Studies

According to Carl Rogers (1961), a child's **self-concept** is central to social success. Children who think positively of themselves respond positively toward others. Although there is discussion between genetic behaviorist and social learning theorists as the proportions of influence from nature and nurture in the child's sociability, it is generally conceded that the environment is very significant. Central to the child's success in the basic tenets of social studies is the child's ability to feel personally successful.

Erikson (1950) provided a psycho-social paradigm that offers the potential for positive social development resulting from appropriate social interactions as well as the potential for negative traits. The influence of others on the successful development of self is central to the theory. According to the theory, human development encounters critical periods for **socialization**, which begins at birth. The following stages demonstrate the significance of parents, caregivers, teachers, and peers in social development:

1. *Basic Trust vs. Mistrust (birth to 1 year of age)*
   a. Period of infancy
   b. As infants develop trust for others, a lifelong sense of well-being is established.
2. *Autonomy vs. Shame and Doubt (1 to 3 years of age)*
   a. Period of infancy to toddler
   b. The positive exploration of independence sets the tone for later life.
3. *Initiative vs. Guilt (3 to 5 years of age)*
   a. Period of preschool
   b. While children openly explore new skills, the support and encouragement of others is essential.
4. *Industry vs. Inferiority (6 to 10 years to age)*
   a. Period of middle to late childhood
   b. The mastery of skills is foremost. The positive support of adults and peers becomes more significant to the child's success.
5. *Identity vs. Role Confusion (10 to 20 years of age)*
   a. Period of early to later adolescence
   b. The discovery of role is critical. Peers take on a more influential aspect in the child's development.
6. *Intimacy vs. Isolation (20 to 30 years of age)*
   a. Period of early adulthood
   b. The formations of personal relationships are critical.

7. *Generativity vs. Stagnation (40 to 50 years of age)*
   a. Period of middle adulthood
   b. Adults in this period seek fulfillment by assisting younger generations to be successful.
8. *Ego Integrity vs. Despair (60s to later age)*
   a. Period of late adulthood
   b. Adults in this period view their life accomplishments as positive or negative.

School classrooms are as much social places as are families and communities. It is from these resources that children refine images of self-esteem: From external reinforcement, children internalize values of themselves as "good" or "not good" at a given task.

If socialization is to occur successfully, children must be given opportunities to interact. According to John Goodlad, it may be observed "that youngsters in our nation's classrooms usually work alone" (Bricker, 1989, p. 43). The social and emotional development of the young child can be viewed from many perspectives. Clearly, environmental influences on the way children view themselves are important to understanding how children interact with others. Diversity, gender roles, and cultural awareness channel emotional and social issues that are components of the social studies curriculum (Clark, DeWolf, & Clark, 1992).

Learning to work with others is an important part of a child's social learning.

CONFRONTING BIAS THROUGH SOCIAL STUDIES

The term *antibias* is used to describe the strategies and techniques implemented by adults to encourage the development of constructive human images. The premise of an antibias curriculum is that exposure to positive images of individuals who are in some way different will provide a framework for appreciation and acceptance of differences (Jones & Derman-Sparks, 1992; Gough, 1993).

It is suggested that the first step in promoting antibias is to determine what restrictions racism, prejudice, and sexism place on the development of a child's personal expectations for life (Kohn, 1992). Table 11.3 provides a rating system for teachers to use in analyzing their environments for bias.

Gender Role Identity and Social Studies

Essential to becoming a successful contributor to a group is the identification of the self and the expectation of that identity. Erikson (1968) suggested that self-identity is fundamental to the determination of personal goals and the prediction of a person's future. Gender carries with it the social dimensions of being male or female, which appear to influence the reactions and expectations of a culture or society.

By age 3, most children have determined their gender as male or female. But it is important to note that the determination of gender identity at an early age is often based on social cues. Such cues as hair length have been noted as indicators of the sex of another child. The interpretation may be that boys have short hair and girls have long hair.

It has been suggested that preoperational children (3 to 7 years of age) believe gender may be changed as easily as changing clothes or getting a hair cut. By the time a child reaches concrete operations (7 to 10 years of age), gender consistency has occurred and the child's affiliation with gender identification becomes a life-forming process.

Although research is inconclusive as to the significance of gender-linked behavior as inherent or culturally influenced (Tavris & Wade, 1984), concern for a child's positive self-concept is significant. It appears that environmental influences as to "what boys are like" and "what girls are like" begin at birth.

During the past decade, as a dynamic of changing vocational interests and family responsibilities, gender differences are more closely observed as gender similarities (Archer, 1991). The traditional roles of gender are presumed to be less sexist than in previous years. Research indicates that females maintain stronger emotional bonds

TABLE 11.3
Checklist for Antibias Environment

Am I Creating An Antibias Environment?

To gain a sense of whether you're creating an antibias environment in your program, score yourself on this checklist. Rather than relying on memory, have this checklist with you in the classroom. If your answer to an item is "a lot," give yourself 2 points; if your answer is "a little," give yourself 1 point; and if your answer is "no," give yourself 0.

Do I use materials/do activities that teach about . . .

- All the children, families, and staff in my program?
- Contemporary children and adults from the major racial/ethnic groups in my community, my state, and American society in their families, at work, and at play?
- Diversity within each racial/ethnic group?
- Women and men of various ethnic backgrounds doing "jobs in the home"?
- Women and men of various ethnic backgrounds doing "jobs outside the home" including blue collar work, pink collar work, white collar work, and artistic work?
- Elderly people of various backgrounds doing a variety of activities?
- Differently abled people of various backgrounds working, being with their families, and playing?
- Diversity in family lifestyles, including single mom or dad; mom works, dad's at home; dad works, mom's at home; mom and dad work; two moms or two dads; extended families; interracial and multiethnic families; foster families; families by adoption; families with differently abled members; low-income families, middle-class families?
- Individuals of many different backgrounds who contribute to our lives, including participants in movements for justice?

Now total your points and examine the results ________________

–If your score is between 16 and 18, you are using an antibias approach.

–If your score is between 11 and 15, you are moving away from a tourist approach in some areas.

–If your score is between 5 and 10, you are using a tourist approach.

–If your score is 4 or below, you are using a dominant Euro-American culture-centered approach.

Source: From "Meeting the Challenge of Diversity" by E. Jones and L. Derman-Sparks, 1992, *Young Children 47*(2), p. 16. Copyright © 1992 by the National Association for the Education of Young Children. Reprinted by permission.

and relationships than males. In addition, female identity development is more complex than male identity (Archer, 1989; Gilligan, 1990; Marcia, 1990).

The parents of preschool children provide gender models for social situations and expectations. Studies indicate that these family relations are the most significant influences in the development of gender role identity (Hendrick, 1990). But parents represent only one of many sources from which children acquire gender identity. Culture, peers, the media, schools, and extended family members influence the child's gender identity and self expectations that may relate to such identifications.

Observations in early childhood settings suggest that males are reinforced for more independent academic behaviors. Females receive more emotional support from adults. Often, teachers perpetuate stereotypical expectations by responding to the needs of boys and girls with different approaches. A review of the gender-related research in Table 11.4 illustrates the subtle influence adults use toward the reinforcement of gender bias.

Appreciating Diversity

Remarkable cultural diversity exists in a world whose technological boundaries are diminishing daily. At the touch of a single key on a computer, we can communicate with peoples anywhere in the world.

TABLE 11.4 The Role of Adults in Gender Bias

Adult Behavior	Related to Girls	Related to Boys
Interrupts while the child is speaking	Grief, 1979	
Encourages stereotypical play activities		Lewis, 1987
Provides more attention for inappropriate behavior		Maccoby, 1989
Provides rewards for gender-appropriate behaviors		Eccles, 1993
Provides a greater amount of support when they ask for assistance		Serbin, O'Leary, Kent, & Tonick, 1973
Reinforces math skills		Eccles, MacIver, & Lange, 1986 Eccles & Midgley, 1990
Reinforces the use of three-dimensional materials such as blocks and manipulatives		Serbin, 1980
Expects to excel in reading language arts	Sluder, 1987	

Children in America can share information with a classroom in Australia in a matter of minutes. With the increased potentials for communication, a continuing responsibility for social studies must be to reflect approaches of multicultural understanding and diversity, and to foster attitudes. The emphasis on human similarities will serve to bond relationships among people and encourage respect and appreciation for others.

The United States has enjoyed a unique period of influence in economic, political, military, and cultural awareness (Anderson, 1990). As the world becomes smaller with the increasing international ability to communicate, the need to appreciate diversity of society, cultural values, and cooperation becomes ever more important:

> A child who associates with children who speak other languages, who worship in other ways, who eat other foods, whose skin color differs from one's own, and whose behavior suggests different upbringing, learns about the basic similarities of all people everywhere and can understand and appreciate their fascinating differences. Such children have many points of reference when they meet people with other values and when they encounter new situations. (McCracken, 1990, p. vii)

Extensive research exists to support the influence of positive social experiences through early childhood educational programs. These studies suggest that children who experience positive multicultural interactions during the impressionable early years are far more likely to become productive, responsible adults than children who are not influenced by positive preschool settings. (Lazar & Darlington, 1982; Lally, Mangione, Honig, & Wittmer, 1988; Weikart, 1989; Weikart, 1993).

In this age of social awareness, many of the things we have discovered about traditional approaches to social studies do not satisfy our personal and professional goals for children. The celebration of our differences may become superficial rhetoric with only vague introductions to cultural traditions without thoughtful preparation and planning.

Perhaps central to this issue is that early childhood care providers must forgo the appeal of teaching to a world that no longer exists and accept the challenges that today's children face as pedagogical implications for curricula. As a global society, shared responsibilities are an increasingly important issue. Traditionally, people are separated by more than language. They are also separated by the interpretations of cultural and social perspectives.

Americans may offer the world a most unusual feature of a global society. By its very nature, the United States of America is composed of many and various people of the world. And through this unique cultural diversity, a unified and yet stratified identity exists. The citizens of the United States may serve as translators of the goals and needs of individual countries and their counterparts (Cawelti, 1993). Figure 11.2 illustrates the global diversity of the world's population.

FIGURE 11.2
An Analysis of the World's Population

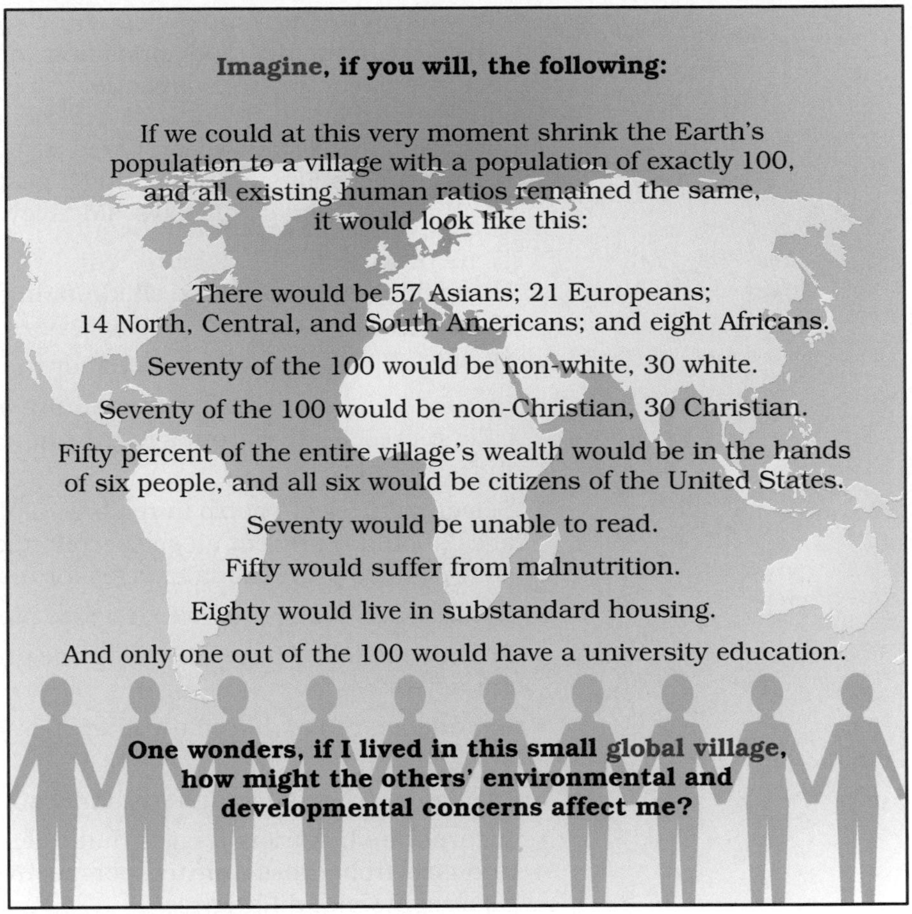

Imagine, if you will, the following:

If we could at this very moment shrink the Earth's population to a village with a population of exactly 100, and all existing human ratios remained the same, it would look like this:

There would be 57 Asians; 21 Europeans; 14 North, Central, and South Americans; and eight Africans.

Seventy of the 100 would be non-white, 30 white.

Seventy of the 100 would be non-Christian, 30 Christian.

Fifty percent of the entire village's wealth would be in the hands of six people, and all six would be citizens of the United States.

Seventy would be unable to read.

Fifty would suffer from malnutrition.

Eighty would live in substandard housing.

And only one out of the 100 would have a university education.

One wonders, if I lived in this small global village, how might the others' environmental and developmental concerns affect me?

Source: C. Hanson. Imagine, if you will, the following. (New York: U.N. Demographic Data Division, United Nations Children's Fund, 1993).

Multicultural Awareness

The dynamics of childhood in American are changing. The adoption of multicultural philosophy must be more than a superficial approach to curriculum. Effective multicultural curricula are threefold (Phillips, 1992). They include these elements (Derman-Sparks, 1993):

1. Fostering development within the child's home culture
2. Bringing diversity into the classroom
3. Counteracting bias and stereotypes

Children may be exposed to the influences of cultural and personal diversity in many ways. The most productive social influences appear to be those we do not "teach." These encounters are the experiences to which we contribute by carefully selecting materials, organizing the environment, and providing opportunities for social exchanges. Constructive use of the learning centers contributes to the positive assimilation of cultural experiences when coupled with the understandings of a well-prepared teacher. The following approaches are suggestions for promoting a positive multicultural environment through visual displays (McAvoy-Baptiste, Baptiste, & Hughes, 1993):

- Use photographs of all the children, families, faculty, and staff.
- Display photographs at eye level for the child.
- Present images of children and adults from racially and ethnically representative groups in the immediate community and in the country.
- Select pictures of people in realistic daily activities. These images should represent all socioeconomic professions and present positive professional images for males and females.
- Avoid stereotyping and overt reverse stereotyping.
- Provide realistic images of varied age groups involved in different activities.
- Include images of differently abled persons involved in work and play.
- Display a variety of images of family styles.
- Incorporate historical images that reflect men, women, boys, and girls from cross-cultural perspectives. Emphasize accomplishments, not differences.
- Maintain artwork and illustrations from a variety of artists whose contributions to the world of art have enriched humanity.

Multicultural education can be incorporated effectively into the core of the education of young children. The fundamentals of self-concept and cooperation should be embraced by the early childhood educator. Criticisms of multicultural education include separatism and disunification, lowered standards of expectations, and fragmentation of curriculum (Ornstein & Levine, 1990). These issues may actually be reduced through positive and consistent approaches in early childhood.

The role of the adult is central to a child's acceptance of appropriate behaviors related to cultural appreciations. Caregivers and teachers should be aware that young children need simple feedback to their questions and concerns. Table 11.5 emphasizes the role of positive adult models in promoting cultural awareness.

TABLE 11.5
Models for Cultural Awareness: Adults as Models

1. Use accurate and appropriate terms.
2. Listen to children.
3. Respond to curiosity.
4. Respect the ideas of children.
5. Express positive images.
6. Accept differences.
7. Allow children to express themselves constructively.
8. Create a safe and independent setting.
9. Recognize self weaknesses.
10. Provide opportunities for cooperation.

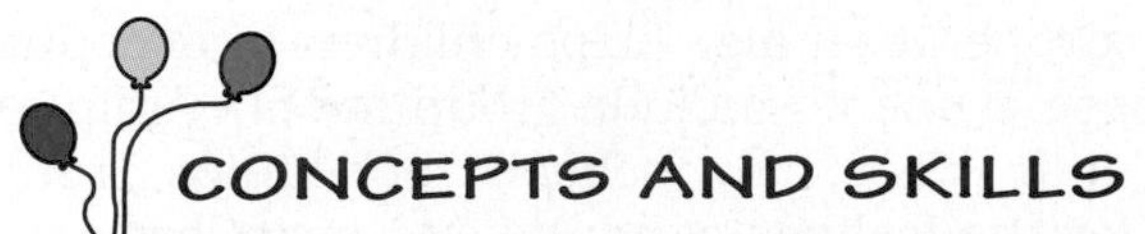

CONCEPTS AND SKILLS

The refinement of concepts and skills through social studies must be considered in relationship to many concerns. Seefeldt (1989) offers that these processes include the acceptance of individual learning needs, the hierarchy of skills from simple to complex, the accumulation of concepts, and the adult's acceptance that the interpretations offered by children are "often inaccurate" (p. 131).

Cooperative Skills

The term *cooperative learning* is applied to activities that involve two or more children planning and following through an activity. While cooperative experiences clearly provide a stage for children to solve a problem, the value of such experiences is far more significant as a process than a product.

Children working together learn to negotiate, mediate, understand, and create. Intellectual skills are stimulated as the members of the cooperative group modify and apply their contributions.

TEACHERS SPEAK OUT

When working with parents, an accepting, non-judgmental attitude helps in establishing and maintaining a positive relationship. A director shows acceptance by behaving in a way that exhibits respect and concern. When you are compassionate, gentle, and sympathetic, a parent feels the freedom to express herself or himself. Do not be concerned with blame or praise—only with understanding and cooperation.

Teachers provide opportunities for children to exercise all modalities for channeling knowledge through interactions between children. Cooperative interactions among peers stimulate heightened successes as children extend their knowledge. Peers encourage the growth of understanding. Cooperative experiences help the child to accept that there are many ways of working through a problem. Each child in the collaboration demonstrates a special perspective on the world that encourages other children to consider alternative approaches.

Peers provide experiences for developing and maintaining friendships. These relationships include skills in conflict resolution and in sharing. Successful cooperative experiences provide mutually satisfying conclusions to problem solving. Children learn to stand up for themselves and assert themselves when they are right. Peer relations also provide children with skills in avoiding conflicts, in resolving issues without violence, and in accepting others.

Peer cooperation also helps children in accepting the school culture. These elements include group membership as a sense of community (our class, my school). Schedules, routines, rules, and respect for the feelings of adults and peers are aspects of the school culture.

Interdisciplinary Awareness

The early childhood environment provides a setting for the elaboration of social studies objectives. As children explore the content of social studies, the potentials for cross-disciplines are reinforced through an effective use of content and centers.

Art

- Develop self-respect through personal achievement
- Work with others to complete group projects
- Solve problems through trial and error
- Explore diversity of color
- Express feeling through art
- Discover cultural artistic characteristics
- Complete tasks

Blocks and Manipulatives

- Role play with animals, people and or puppets
- Improve skills for sharing and working with others
- Use materials to present the world
- Express emotions in acceptable verbal and nonverbal manners

Dramatic Play

- Explore feelings

- Explore the emotions of others
- Role play issues and circumstances related to social contexts

Library and Language Arts

- Provide exposure to themes of social studies
- Provide accurate information without stereotyping
- Expose children to different languages, sign, and Braille
- Provide books for cultures
- Extend vocabulary

Music

- Provide experiences in cultural backgrounds
- Provide instruments, songs, and vocabulary

House and Family Living

- Explore family roles
- Explore social and community expectations
- Provide role settings

Woodworking

- Provide cooperative experiences
- Develop skills in sharing

Play in Social Studies

Play serves as a forum through which children investigate social roles. Sociodramatic play allows children to think and act on their interpretation of the social world. Piaget (1970) believed that such play provides concept testing for egocentric children. When children agree on the elements of their play, they are jointly assimilating experiences. In contrast, disagreements in the play sequence means that accommodation is necessary because old ideas have been challenged.

Children who are exposed to sociodramatic play episodes are more likely to modify their perspectives. Since play continues to be a major activity of childhood, the realization that social attitudes may be influenced has educational possibilities.

Changes in children's attitudes as a result of play episodes have been documented through research (Burns & Brainerd, 1979; Matthews, Beebe, & Bopp, 1980; Rosen, 1974; Smith & Sydall, 1978). Additional studies regarding the influence of sociodramatic play include the following:

- Cooperation with peers and groups appear to be enhanced as a result of play (Rosen, 1974; Smith & Sydall, 1978).
- Social interactions appear to be more cooperative (Smith, Daglish, & Herzmark, 1981).

As children interact with one another, their shared understandings of the world enrich the potential for learning

- Impulsive behaviors are less evident and self-control efforts are more often observed in studies of children exposed to play episodes (Saltz, Dixon, & Johnson, 1977).

APPROACHES TO INSTRUCTION

Although techniques and strategies for social studies are often dependent on many factors, the central issue is the child. Topics or themes may be determined by school systems, grade-level decisions, individual teachers, or as a result of student discussion.

Multisensory Approach to Social Studies

Montessori (1912) and others have emphasized the sensory learning channels of children as essential to the successful acquisition of information and the refinement of knowledge. Approaching social studies through multisensory concepts is an observably successful process of learning. These target skills are fundamentally the five senses.

Proponents of the **multisensory approach** consider that visual discrimination, auditory discrimination, tactile information, taste, and olfactory discrimination serve as channels through which physical information is accumulated. The acquisition of such information provides greater contexts for social and cultural knowledge, and is the catalyst for children to compare, contrast, categorize, and initially access information.

KIDS SPEAK UP

My mommy works in a big city. My daddy works in his truck.

Boy, 4 years old

Multisensory approaches to classifying, categorizing, or grouping are necessary for the young child to expand reasoning skills. The ability to understand objects and terms that are related becomes meaningful for context clues in comprehension and exploration of the natural world.

The following list of objectives demonstrates concepts and skills enhanced through a multisensory approach.

Visual Discrimination (sight)

- Identify and discriminate between colors
- Identify and discriminate between shapes
- Discriminate and reproduce patterns and designs
- Learn to use left-to-right progression
- Discriminate and identify letter and number form

Auditory Discrimination (sound)

- Identify human, animal, musical, and environmental sounds
- Discriminate likenesses and differences of sound
- Discriminate initial sounds
- Develop auditory decoding and oral language skills

Tactile Discrimination (touch)

- Identify an object held in the hand using descriptive terms
- Discriminate between various temperatures by touch
- Elaborate on the nature of materials based on their tactile qualities

Taste and Olfactory Discrimination (taste and smell)

- Explore new tastes and smells
- Develop descriptive language
- Assimilate relationships

Project Approach to Social Studies

Katz and Chard (1992) have provided educators with a paradigm for unifying the themes or topics that address the interests and needs of children. The **project approach** to engaging the minds of children involves the learner in the development of units or themes.

The teacher may begin with a reoccurring topic or question from a social studies issue. Initially, the topic is explored through a concept web as the children relate their ideas and understandings (see Figure 11.3).

Once the possibilities have been explored, other elements of the study can be developed. These additional elements include the vocabulary, related themes, and activities. Support activities should be classified by their nature as independent of the teacher and group or dependent on the teacher or group. This approach facilitates the delivery system. Activities can be used in centers for individuals or with small groups of children. A balance of developmental issues must be considered.

The emphasis of the project approach is on the firsthand experiences of children through social interactions. The projects cross disciplines as children measure, create, and investigate the components

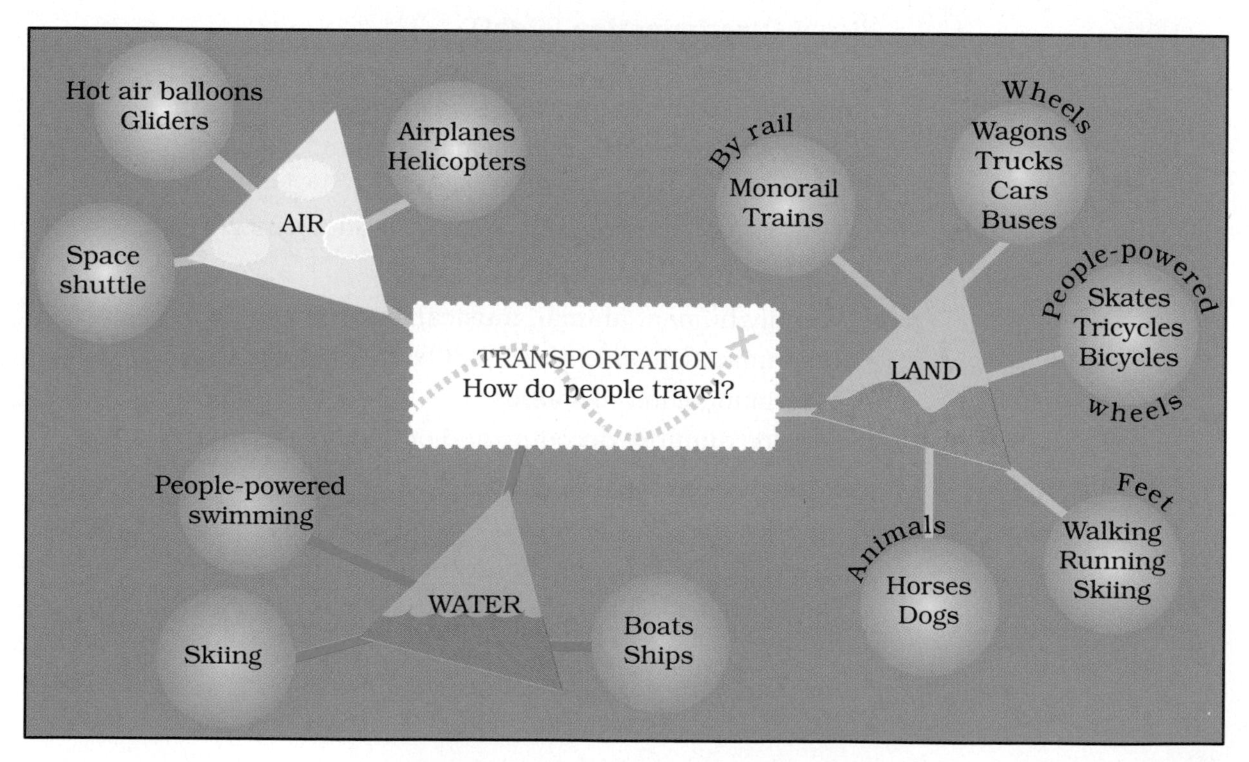

FIGURE 11.3
Concept Web for Transportation

of the theme. Table 11.6 demonstrates the responses of a group of 4-year-olds to questions about the four seasons. The responses of the children are dependent on experience, intelligence, and maturation. As children present their ideas, the teacher records the discussion on chart paper. The list is then displayed, and the children develop a plan for further investigations.

TABLE 11.6 Project Approach Responses to Questions for Seasons Theme

What clothes would you wear?	What food do you eat?	What are winter sports?
Summer	***Summer***	***Summer***
Swimsuits	Ice cream	Swimming
Shorts	Melons	Baseball
Fall	***Fall***	***Fall***
Jackets	Pumpkin	Football
Sweaters	Turkey	
Winter	***Winter***	***Winter***
Coats	Hot chocolate	Snow skiing
Mittens	Apple cider	Ice skating
Boots		
Spring	***Spring***	***Spring***
Short sleeves	Strawberries	Basketball
Sweaters	Peaches	Golf
		Track

What is the weather like?	What do animals do?	What are things you do?
Summer	***Summer***	***Summer***
Hot	Eat	Go to grandparents
Rain	Play	Play
Fall	***Fall***	***Fall***
Cool	Build houses	Go to school
Rain	Eat	
Winter	***Winter***	***Winter***
Cold	Sleep	Play in snow
Snow		
Spring	***Spring***	***Spring***
Cool	Baby animals	Fly kites
Rain		Plant flowers
Fog		

The possibilities for such elaborations are limited only by the imagination of the children and teachers. As children become active participants in the planning process, the sophistication of their understanding is enhanced through a developmentally appropriate approach to an integrated curriculum.

SUMMARY

Social studies is the curriculum of life. Its foundations as a content area include traditional social science curricula such as history, geography, sociology, ecology, and psychology. Trends in society greatly affect the responsibilities of the social studies.

A child's ability to succeed in the social studies depends on the teacher's understanding of child development. Cognitive, moral, and social development influence the child's acceptance of the view of others. If a child's basic human needs and self-concept needs are met, the potential for the acceptance of others is greater.

Multicultural, gender, and diversity influences affect self-esteem and perspective. Play is a modality through which children explore their role and the roles of others in context formation. Instructional approaches to social studies should reflect the nature of the learner. Multisensory approaches and concrete experiences through learning centers are effective approaches. The multidisciplinary approach to social studies through projects provides the child with the potential to participate in the development of concepts and skills.

TEST YOUR UNDERSTANDING

1. What are the curriculum content areas associated with social studies?
2. Historically the subject of social studies or social science has reflected the trends of the times. How is this trend true today?
3. Discuss the problems you see suggested in the following activities:
    - A one-week unit on the American Indians.
    - Asking the girls to prepare the cooking activity.
    - Assigning the boys to play in the block center.
4. What are the stages of moral development according to Kohlberg?
5. Define the term *diversity*.
6. What are the functions of play as they relate to social studies?
7. What are the concepts and skills you might weave into a social studies curriculum?

LEARNING ACTIVITIES

1. Visit an early childhood center. List ways that the child care providers and teachers you observed promote self-concept.
2. Discuss three social studies topics that reflect the community in which you live. Develop a concept web for one.
3. Review several current magazines and journals, and collect illustrations that suggest positive models of cultural and gender diversity.
4. Using the multisensory approach discussed in this chapter, develop two activities for a social studies topic.
5. While observing an early childhood setting, list the ways that the teacher incorporates concepts of physical knowledge, social-conventional knowledge, and logico-mathematical knowledge.

LET'S TALK ABOUT IT

As the professor walked around the room listening to the discussions, some students had genuine concerns about how to plan learning activities for young children. Many of the students were apprehensive about being able to meet the individual needs of all their children and doing a good job at teaching. The professor made a mental note to review some of the earlier lecture material with the class. The professor then approached each of the team members and asked them to share specific examples of teaching strategies used by their cooperating teachers.

How does the teacher decide what materials to use in the learning centers?

What is the role of the teacher in using learning centers?

In Lillian's review of how the learning centers were set up for different classrooms, she expressed some confusion about how to use them. As she explained, "One teacher used learning centers early in the morning, while completing clerical responsibilities and the lunch count, but I also saw another teacher who used the centers to engage the children in meaningful activities."

Mildred was enthusiastic about the project approach used by one teacher. The children were involved in selecting the themes as well the activities. She had discovered that all curricula were being developed under a single topic. "I couldn't believe how much time the teacher spent in planning and organizing without the aid of a teacher's manual," she concluded.

How important is a teacher's manual?

Stephanie said, "I have always thought that planning is the key to success in teaching young children. The teacher should always stick to the schedule." Her cooperating teacher, however, believed that children should determine when you change from one activity to another. "As a result," Stephanie said, "I was very frustrated with my field placement experience."

Is it important for the teacher to stay on schedule?

Should teachers allow children to determine what they are taught?

Every team member who visited the kindergarten classroom remembered Shelby. The teacher used her as a teacher's helper, despite the fact that Shelby often didn't complete her own activities. This little girl took her responsibilities to the teacher very seriously. Matt said, "I'm concerned that Shelby doesn't interact with her classmates or exhibit age-appropriate behavior."

What kind of planning do you think is necessary for Shelby?

PART 4

Policies and Practices Affecting Early Childhood Education

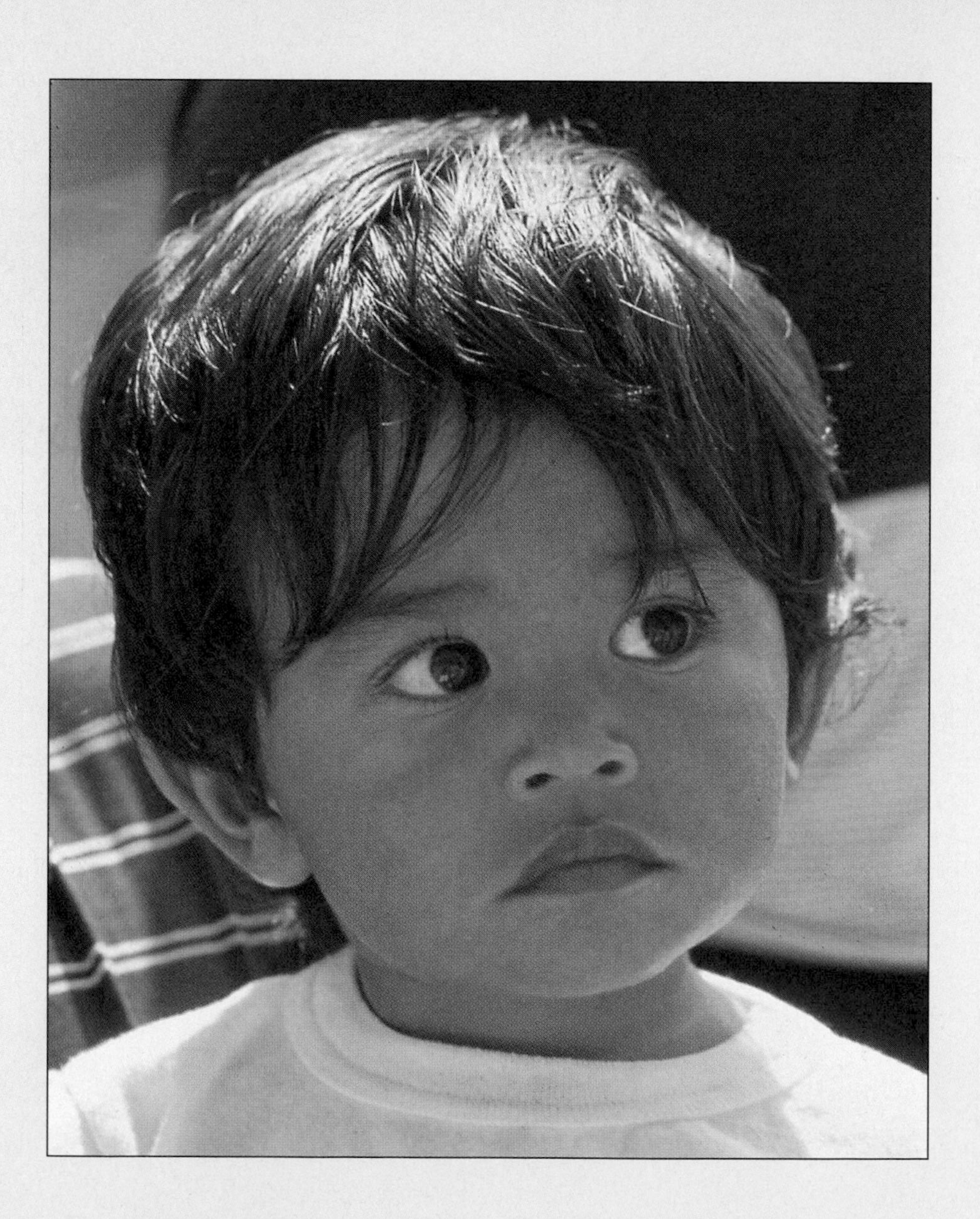

SPRING HILL CHILD DEVELOPMENT CENTER

The professor told the class that it was almost time to end the discussion session. "Team leaders, you have about 30 minutes left. Please don't forget to share your observations about young children with special needs, your impressions of the program administrator, and ways parents were involved."

The students exclaimed, "But there is so much more to talk about." They quickly regrouped to include some of their experiences that highlighted topics the professor suggested.

Lee was the focus of Mildred's observations of a child with special needs. Diagnosed as being mildly mentally retarded, Lee spends the majority of his day in a special education classroom. He is integrated, however, for the rest of the day with nonretarded children. "I was particularly interested in how Lee's typical peers relate to him," Mildred said, "But I'm not convinced that mainstreaming is an especially good idea for all children with special needs."

Lillian said, "I can't understand why public schools would want to serve very young children with disabilities. I think it's a waste of good tax money." Youngsters below the age of 2 (like Austin) should not be served, according to Lillian.

Matt reported that at the Spring Hill Center, teachers, parents, and the administrator all work together to build a quality program. "Each person plays a very important role in constructing developmentally appropriate experiences for young children," he said, "And the relationship between the child's home and Spring Hill is vitally important to the child's success." Matt concluded by saying that the Spring Hill staff members work very hard at maintaining effective communication with parents.

Stephanie said, "I want to share my concerns about the issue of kindergarten readiness. I feel that kindergarten has become too much like the first grade." At Spring Hill, however, Stephanie observed children experiencing success while working at their individual developmental level.

As a group, each one of the students saw the value of being an advocate for young children and their families. Issues like homelessness, violence, changing family structures, and economic insecurity demand concerned and well-informed voices speaking on behalf of young children.

Lillian said, “I regret that today many children don’t have the type of childhood my children experienced.”

“I agree with Lillian,” said Mildred, “And I believe that advocacy is an ethical responsibility for all early childhood teachers.”

CHAPTER 12

Young Children with Special Needs

CHAPTER OUTLINE

Definitions and Terminology
- *Exceptional Children*
- *Disability and Handicap*
- *Developmental Delay and At-Risk*
- *Least Restrictive Environment*
- *Mainstreaming*
- *Inclusion*
- *Normalization*

Rationale for Early Childhood Intervention
- *Reasons for Early Intervention*
- *Early Intervention Programs*
- *Research Evidence*

Key Federal Legislation
- *Public Law 94–142*
- *Public Law 99–457*

Young Children with Special Needs

Identifying and Assessing Young Children with Special Needs
- *Key Terms*
- *An Evaluation Model*
- *Considerations in Testing Young Children with Special Needs*

Service Delivery Models
- *Center-Based Services*
- *Home-Based Services*
- *Combination Programs*
- *School-Age Children*

Curriculum Considerations for Young Children with Special Needs
- *Individualized Educational Program (IEP)*
- *Curriculum Domains*

Partnerships with Parents
- *Parental Reactions to Exceptionality*
- *Parent Involvement*
- *Parent-Professional Relationships*

KEY TERMS

Exceptional children
Disability
Handicap
Developmental delay
At-risk
Least restrictive environment (LRE)
Mainstreaming
Inclusion
Regular education initiative (REI)
Normalization
Individualized educational program (IEP)
Individualized family service plan (IFSP)
Center-based services
Home-based services
Curriculum domains
Enabling
Empowering

"Do you have a moment to join me, Jean?" the director asked the second-grade teacher. "I think Karen said "good morning' to me today," he continued.

Jean smiled and responded. "I know. She has accomplished a great deal since the beginning of the school year." Karen was the first profoundly disabled child to be included in a regular class setting at the school. For Jean, it had been very special to have Karen in her second-grade class.

The year before, Karen had attended a regular class for the first time. She began with virtually no language, limited movement in her hands, no prior social experiences, and possibly serious mental limitations. Karen's seizures and tantrums compounded the problems faced by the school as it attempted to plan for her. The possible ramifications had been felt by every child, parent, and member of the educational community. Today, only the people who had played an immediate role in the transition could appreciate just what a success it had been.

The director handed a delicate white card to the teacher, saying, "This note is to all of us, from Karen's mother." Jean read this message:

> Dear Teachers, Staff, Administrators, Parents, and Children,
>
> Today is the second anniversary of our daughter beginning school on your campus, and we just want to say "thank you." Before you took on the task of bringing Karen into your school, we felt lost and isolated. We were not a part of the usual parent activities. We could not take Karen out in public. Somewhere deep inside, we believed there must be more for her than what private institutions and self-contained programs were able to offer. You met the challenge. We know that it has not always been pleasant, but you have always been professional and understanding. Karen's participation in a regular class has been an open door for her desire to learn. It has been a team process, and we want to thank every one of you: To the parents who understood and supported a child with differences being a part of your child's class. To the children who treat Karen like another kid who simply needs to learn in a different way. To the teachers who modify and accommodate to allow learning to occur. To the administrators, counselors, therapists, and specialists who keep us on task and focused. We thank you all.
>
> Sincerely yours,
> Jana Baker
> (Karen's Mom)

Jean was silent for a few minutes, and then commented, "Sometimes it takes many to do the best for one. But that one could be a Karen."

We live in a society that cherishes achievements, accomplishments, and being number one. Many individuals are taught, from childhood onward, that being the best and obtaining perfection is vitally important. As adults we witness the attention and praise given to those who excel and succeed athletically, scholastically, financially, and in their personal lives. Indeed, some parents believe that their children must also be perfect. Unfortunately, this does not always happen. Gargiulo (1985) eloquently describes the myth of the perfect child and the emotional consequences that often occur when dreams are destroyed and children fail to live up to the cultural stereotypes of beauty, popularity, and academic success.

According to one mother, "there is something very magnificent and very wonderful about having a child, unless that child is handicapped. Parents of handicapped children face something that is not wonderful, not magnificent" (Michaelis, 1980, p. 61). Being the parent of a child with a disability is not a role that mothers or fathers anticipate or prepare for. Consequently, many parents will turn to professionals for assistance and guidance. Frequently this task is fulfilled by the classroom teacher. The purpose of this chapter, therefore, is to provide the early childhood educator with a basic understanding of policies, programs, and procedures for serving preschool and young children with special needs.

DEFINITIONS AND TERMINOLOGY

A prerequisite to understanding young children with special needs and the educational services rendered on their behalf is knowing the definitions and terminology used by professionals. What do the terms *handicap* and *disability* mean? Who are exceptional children? What is mainstreaming? Clear-cut answers to these questions are sometimes difficult to obtain. Confusion and misinterpretation are common, even among professionals. The following definitions, developed by special educators, are an attempt to clarify terminology appropriate to this chapter.

Exceptional Children

Exceptional children, according to Heward and Orlansky (1988), are children who differ from the norm—they may be above or below and therefore require an individualized program of special education to meet their unique needs. Peterson (1987) believes that this expression is an encompassing term and refers to those individuals whom society views as differing from "normal." Such persons may be above our understanding of normalcy (intellectually gifted and talented youngsters), or they may be below (a child who is identified as mentally retarded). Meyen (1990) simply states that an exceptional child is one who differs from the norm. He reminds us that some exceptionalities are obvious, while others are hidden. Furthermore, exceptional individuals are different in ways that are either helpful or a hindrance in their daily lives.

Disability and Handicap

In everyday speech, the terms **disability** and **handicap** are frequently used as synonyms. But they do have separate and distinct meanings. When professionals talk about a preschooler with a disability, they are referring to an inability to do something, an incapacity or a reduced function (Heward & Orlansky, 1988; Hallahan & Kauffman, 1991). Sometimes the terms *impairment* and *disability* are used interchangeably. A young girl, for example, who is missing a leg might experience difficulty in walking up a flight of stairs. On the other hand, a handicap refers to the problem(s) confronting the child with the disability as she attempts to function and interact in the environment. A disability may or may not be a handicap, depending upon the circumstances. What might be a hardship in one situation might not be a difficulty in another. A child labeled mentally retarded will most likely encounter difficulty in the classroom when competing academically with classmates, but shouldn't experience problems when playing football on the playground at recess. Use of the term *handicap* should be restricted to explaining the consequences or impact imposed on the child by the impairment. Hallahan and Kauffman (1991) observe that as we work with pupils who have a disability, it is important that we strive to separate the disability from the handicap.

As a matter of convenience and for ease of communication, where appropriate, we will use the term *children with special needs* to describe children with disabilities or impairments.

It is vital to remember that youngsters with special needs are first and foremost children who are more like their typical classmate than they are different. Furthermore, we must focus on the individual, not the impairment; look for similarities, not differences; and finally, try to see the student's abilities and strengths, not their disabilities.

Developmental Delay and At-Risk

Young children with special needs are sometimes identified as exhibiting a **developmental delay** or being **at-risk** for future problems. Public Law 99–457 (to be discussed later) incorporates both of these terms. But, because legislators realized that these concepts would be difficult to define, they left the responsibility for developing satisfactory definitions to the individual states. Pennsylvania, for example, proposes to define developmental delay as occurring when scores on developmental assessments, which yield a score in months, indicate that a child is delayed by at least 25 percent of his or her chronological age in one or more developmental areas such as cognitive, lan-

A youngster with a disability is first and foremost a child who is more like his typical classmates than he is different.

guage/speech, physical, social/emotional, and self-help; or when scores on standardized assessments yield a score that is 1.5 standard deviations below the mean. New Hampshire constructed a definition that suggests a "developmentally delayed child" is

> a preschool child between 3 and 5 years of age, who, because of impairments in development needs special education or special education and educationally related services, may be identified as being developmentally delayed provided that such a child must first be determined to have an educationally disabling condition.

Finally, the Arizona Education Code uses the following description for children who may be moderately or severely developmentally delayed:

> "Moderately developmentally delayed" means a child who is at least three years of age but who has not reached the required age for kindergarten and whose performance on a standardized test measures at least one and one-half, but not more than three, standard deviations below the mean for children of the same chronological age or whose performance on a criterion referenced test that has been approved by the department of education measures at least twenty-five percent but not more than fifty percent below the mean for children of the same chronological age in two or more of the following areas:
>
> *a.* Cognitive ability.
>
> *b.* Motor ability.
>
> *c.* Sensory ability.
>
> *d.* Language skills.

e. Psychosocial skills.

f. Adaptive behavior.

"Severely developmentally delayed" means a child who is at least three years of age but who has not reached the required age for kindergarten and whose performance on standardized tests measures more than three standard deviations below the mean for children of the same chronological age or whose performance on a criterion referenced test that has been approved by the department of education measures more than fifty percent below the mean for children of the same chronological age in one or more of the following areas:

a. Cognitive ability.

b. Motor ability.

c. Sensory ability.

d. Language skills.

e. Psychosocial skills.

f. Adaptive behavior.

Obviously, there are many different ways to define this concept. No one definition is going to be completely satisfactory or meet with the approval of all professionals.

In developing an understanding of *at-risk*, however, educators have met with some success. Peterson (1987) defines at-risk children as individuals who

> have been subjected to certain adverse genetic, prenatal, perinatal (at birth), postnatal, or environmental conditions that are known to cause defects or are highly correlated with the appearance of later abnormalities. (p. 138)

As Peterson notes, at-risk factors suggest that the potential or probability for developing future difficulties and delays is present, but problems are not necessarily inevitable consequences.

Understanding of this concept has been greatly helped by Tjossem's (1976) description of three at-risk categories. Since its introduction, many professionals have accepted his classification scheme.

1. *Established risk.* Children with a diagnosed medical disorder of known etiology (cause) and a predictable prognosis or outcome are considered to manifest an established risk. An illustration of such a condition would be a child born with cerebral palsy or Down syndrome.

2. *Biological risk.* Included in this category are youngsters with a history of pre-, peri-, and postnatal conditions and developmental events that heighten the potential for later atypical or aberrant development. Examples of such conditions or complications include premature births, infants with low birth weights, rubella (German measles), or bacterial infections like meningitis.

3. *Environmental risk.* Environmentally at-risk children are biologically typical, but their early life experiences and/or environmental conditions are so limiting or threatening that the likelihood of delayed development exists. Severe poverty, abuse, and absence of adequate shelter and medical care, as well as limited opportunities for nurturance and social stimulation, are all examples of potential environmental risk factors.

The preceding categories are not mutually exclusive. They often overlap or occur in combination, for example, having a hearing-impaired child (established risk) living in extremely impoverished surroundings (environmental risk). As a result, the potential for future delays and learning difficulties increases.

Early childhood educators frequently encounter several other key terms, especially when discussing educational environments for young students with special needs. Next we examine four related terms and supporting concepts—least restrictive environment (LRE), mainstreaming, inclusion, and normalization.

Least Restrictive Environment

Today, in many schools across the United States, it is not unusual to find both typical and atypical children in the same classroom. In fact, many parents as well as some professionals believe that such arrangements always existed. But this now-common situation is a direct result of Public Law 94–142, the Education for All Handicapped Children Act, which was enacted in 1975 (to be discussed later). A major component of this legislation is a provision stipulating that "to the maximum extent appropriate, handicapped children, . . . are educated with children who are not handicapped . . . " [Section 612 (5) (B)]. This feature, known as the principle of **least restrictive environment (LRE)**, has generated significant controversy and debate. What does it mean? What is appropriate? Are all children to be taught and grouped together? Many of these questions revolve around the meaning of the word *appropriate*, which must be individually defined for each pupil. There is no one "best" placement. What is an appropriate learning environment for one child might be an inappropriate placement for another student. The attempt of the LRE principle is to prevent the unwarranted segregation of exceptional learners from their typical peers (Turnbull & Turnbull, 1990). It is perhaps best to think of the LRE concept as a continuum of placement opportunities that can meet the unique needs of the individual child (see Figure 12.1).

Public Law 94–142 does *not* require that all pupils with special needs be placed in regular education classrooms. There are levels of restrictiveness, according to Meyen (1990), which depend on the type and degree of the child's disability. Only being with special needs children is considered restrictive, while placement with nondisabled youngsters is viewed as least restrictive. The meaning of *restrictiveness* refers to the degree of integration between typical and atypical

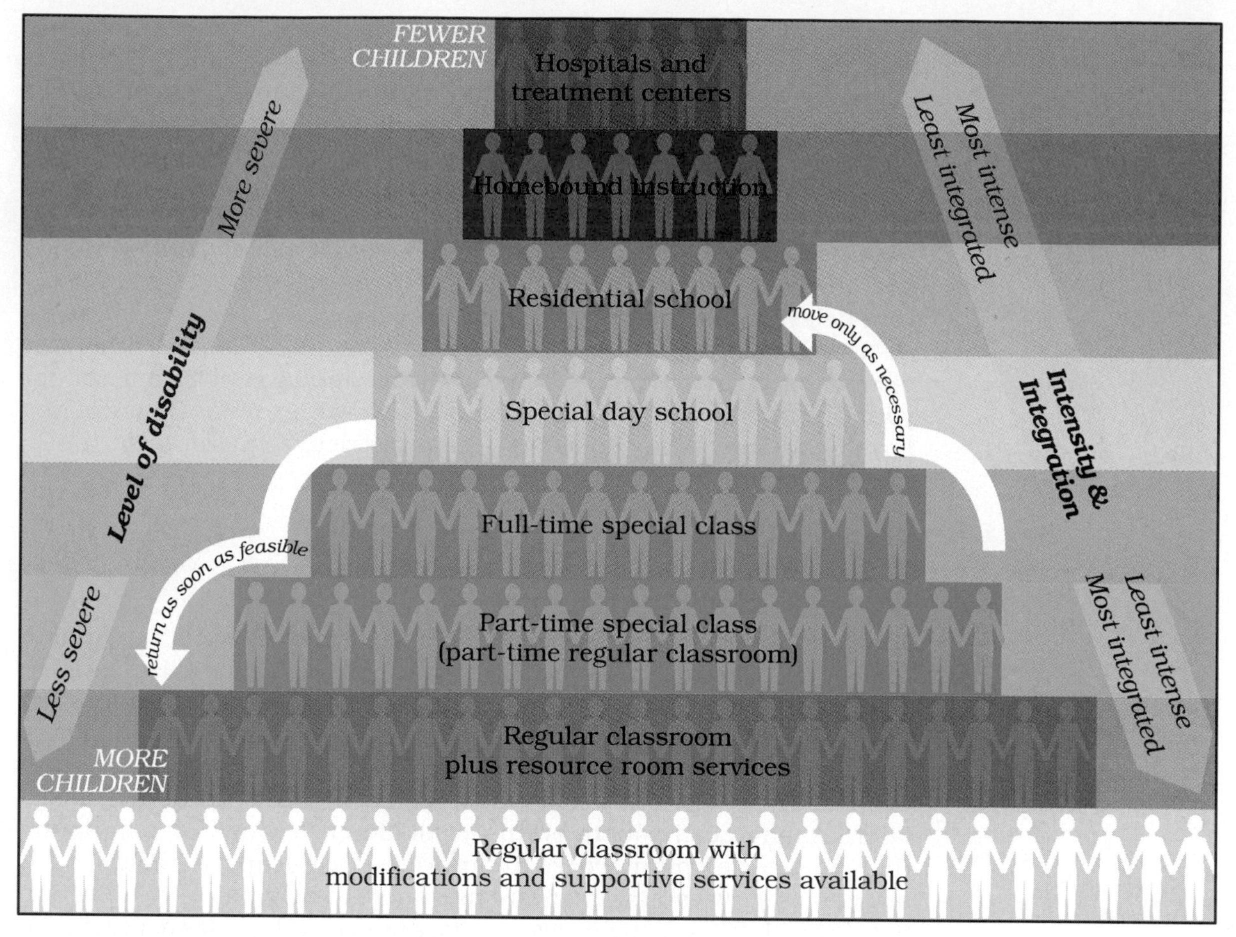

FIGURE 12.1
Hierarchy of Services for Special Education Programs

students. It is important to remember that the LRE is not always the most appropriate environment. Each situation must be carefully considered on a case-by-case basis.

Mainstreaming

A term often used in conjunction with the LRE is **mainstreaming**. Although linked together, LRE and mainstreaming are not synonymous. In fact, mainstreaming is not even referred to in the Education for All Handicapped Children Act, although the philosophy grew out of Public Law 94–142. These terms are frequently used interchangeably, but they are seldom well defined (Cook, Tessier, & Klein, 1992). An early attempt to define mainstreaming is still appropriate today. Kaufman, Gottlieb, Agard, and Kukic (1975) believe that

> mainstreaming refers to the temporal, instructional, and social integration of . . . exceptional children with normal peers based on an ongoing, individually determined, educational planning and programming process. (pp. 40–41)

Two recent authors offer simpler explanations. Heward and Orlansky (1988) propose that mainstreaming describes the process of integrating children with exceptionalities into regular classes and schools. Hallahan and Kauffman (1991) parallel this belief by stating that mainstreaming is "the integration of exceptional students into classes with their nonexceptional peers" (p. 75). *Mainstreaming* and *integration* are often used synonymously and interchangeably (Allen, 1992; Hanson & Lynch, 1989).

We agree with this approach, but other writers disagree with this viewpoint and distinguish between mainstreaming and integration. Odom and Speltz (1983), for example, consider mainstreaming environments as programs primarily developed for typical youngsters with exceptional learners placed in them. But the child with special needs constitutes less than half of the student population. In contrast, integrated early childhood programs are principally designed for atypical pupils who make up more than 50 percent of the enrollment.

Effective teachers of young children with special needs focus on the students' abilities rather than their disabilities.

More recently, Streifel, Killoran, and Quintero (1991) emphasized instructional programming. These authors believe mainstreaming refers to grouping of children, including those with and without disabilities, in the same classroom without the benefit of planned involvement in common instructional and social activities. On the other hand, when planning and structured involvement exists, integration is the appropriate term. Thus, mainstreaming refers to the physical placement, while integration focuses on active participation in common social and instructional matters. As Kaufman and his colleagues (Kaufman et al., 1975) remind us, mainstreaming is much more than just placing a youngster with special needs in a regular classroom rather than in one for exceptional learners. Placement conducted in isolation from planning and instructional programming does not result in effective mainstreaming.

Inclusion

A recent concept that has generated significant debate and controversy among professionals and parents alike is a full inclusion model of educating all students with disabilities. Full **inclusion** is an extension of a trend initiated in the late 1980s, whereby special and regular educators would work cooperatively in delivering services within the regular classroom. This shared responsibility for educating exceptional pupils is known as the **regular education initiative** or, more commonly, REI (Will, 1986).

Advocates of full inclusion believe that the present system of serving students with special needs is ineffective. These youngsters are labeled and stigmatized, their programming is fragmented, and regular educators assume little or no ownership for special education students. Placement in a regular classroom, with a true partnership between special education teachers and regular education teachers, would result in a better education for special needs students; and it would occur within the least restrictive environment. Opponents of this movement argue that regular educators are not trained to assist students with special needs, the classrooms are already overcrowded, and funding as well as support services are inadequate to meet present needs. Special educators, on the other hand, obviously have the necessary training; and a special education environment is the more appropriate location for delivering interventions, specialized instruction, and preparing students for their return to the regular classroom when appropriate (Hardman, Drew, Egan, & Wolf, 1993).

As currently being used, the term *inclusion* has come to mean the education of *all* exceptional students in the regular education classroom, particularly in the preschool and elementary years (Sailor, Gerry, & Wilson, 1991). In one proposal, full inclusion is advocated for day care, preschool-age youngsters, and kindergartners regardless of the type or severity of the child's disability (Sailor, Anderson, Halvorsen, Doering, Filler, & Goetz, 1989).

Six principles are found in most full inclusion models (Sailor et al., 1991):

1. *"Home school" attendance.* Defined as the local school the child would attend if nondisabled.

2. *Natural proportion at the school site.* The percentage of special needs children enrolled in a particular school is in proportion to the percentage of exceptional pupils in the entire school district; in regular education classes, this would mean approximately two or three students with disabilities.

3. *Zero rejection.* All students are accepted, at the local school, including those with severe impairments; pupils are not screened out or grouped separately because of their disability.

4. *Age/grade-appropriate placement.* A full inclusion model calls for serving special needs children in regular classrooms according to their chronological age rather than basing services according to the child's academic ability or mental age.

5. *Site-based management or coordination.* Recent trends in school organizational reform suggest a movement away from central office administration for special education programs to one in which the building principal (or other administrator) plays a large role in planning and administering programs for all children in the school.

6. *Use of cooperative learning and peer instructional models.* Instructional practices that involve children learning in a cooperative manner rather than in a competitive fashion and using students to assist in the instruction of classmates with disabilities can be effective strategies for integrating exceptional learners in the regular classroom.

One perplexing issue, however, needs to be resolved. If full inclusion indeed means educating all children with special needs in a regular classroom, then it represents a radical departure from the idea of a continuum of services (see Figure 12.1) and may well be a violation of current federal law.

Normalization

One final term related to our discussion is the principle of normalization. **Normalization** is a Scandinavian concept advanced in the United States by Wolfensberger (1972). Simply stated, it is a philosophy that every individual with a disability should have the opportunity for as normal or typical a life as possible. The term commonly includes education, living arrangements, vocational opportunities, and recreational activities. Regardless of the degree or type of impairment, every person should be integrated in all aspects of society to the greatest extent possible.

Young children with special needs should have every opportunity for as typical a life as possible.

RATIONALE FOR EARLY CHILDHOOD INTERVENTION

What are the benefits of early intervention? Why bother; does it really make a difference? The answer to both of these questions is a resounding yes. There is a wealth of information attesting to the advantages of intervening in the lives of young children with special needs. But first we must establish an understanding of what intervention is. According to Fallen and Umansky (1985), intervention refers to the process of intruding upon the lives of youngsters and their families for the purpose of altering the direction and consequences of a disability or delayed development. These writers state that "the action required is individual, but it encompasses any modification or addition of services, strategies, techniques, or materials required to maximize the child's potential" (p. 160). Likewise, Peterson (1987, pp. 72–73) echoes these thoughts when she states that the purpose of intervention for young children with special needs is to:

1. Minimize the effects of a handicapping condition upon a child's growth and development and maximize opportunities to engage in the normal activities of early childhood;

2. Prevent, if possible, at-risk conditions or early developmental irregularities from developing into more serious problems that become deviant to the extent that they are labeled as handicapping;
3. Prevent the development of secondary handicaps as a result of interference from a primary disability. . . .

Reasons for Early Intervention

Several authors (Hanson & Lynch, 1989; Meyen, 1990; Peterson, 1987; Striefel et al., 1991) have identified a variety of reasons why early childhood education is important for youngsters with disabilities and at-risk children. Many of these reasons are derived from research evidence, theoretical arguments, and societal values. Here are some frequently listed themes:

- A belief that early environmental stimulation can positively influence subsequent learning and development.
- A critical periods hypothesis, which suggests that intervening during key periods in a youngster's life is vital if the child is to acquire more complex skills and competencies later on. This notion, however, has been questioned by some professionals (Clarke & Clarke, 1976).
- An assumption that early intervention can minimize the impact of a particular disabling condition such as the effect of a severe hearing loss on speech and language development or the cognitive development of a child born with Down syndrome.
- The proposition that intervention programs can ameliorate learning deficits and problems frequently attributed to certain at-risk factors such as cultural and environmental conditions.
- The benefits that accrue to parents of youngsters with special needs and at-risk children. These children usually present many new challenges and additional responsibilities for caregivers and can potentially affect the entire family. Early childhood programs can assist parents in developing effective parenting skills, as well as provide emotional support, factual information, and specific training in addition to meeting other requests for assistance.
- Benefits that extend beyond the child and his or her family to society at large. Early intervention is cost effective. Effectiveness has been documented in terms of dollars saved and the need for special educational services.

In summary, early childhood programs for children with special needs have advantages for society, the family, and, of course, the child. Early childhood special education can make a significant difference in the lives of young children.

Early Intervention Programs

The preceding reasons are part of the philosophical underpinnings of several well-known early childhood and compensatory education programs. For example, Project Head Start (see Chapter 2), the first nationwide compensatory education program, was conceived in 1965 as an early intervention effort aimed at reducing the potential for school failure in disadvantaged young children from low socioeconomic, impoverished communities. This first volley on the War on Poverty, while not specifically directed at special needs children, represented a coordinated federal effort at comprehensive intervention in the lives of young children (Zigler & Valentine, 1979). Head Start was unique not only in its intent—to bring about change for the child, the child's family, and the community, but also for its use of a multidisciplinary intervention model wherein the importance of seeing the whole child was recognized (Brain, 1979). Head Start set the stage for later efforts directly aimed at young children with special needs. In fact, in 1972 a governmental requirement called for the project to reserve no less than 10 percent of its pupil population for children with disabilities.

TEACHERS SPEAK OUT

The one truth I have found in working with children of diverse abilities is that children are more alike than they are different.

A companion program, Project Follow-Through, was developed in 1967 in response to the controversy surrounding the effectiveness of the Head Start efforts. Professionals quickly realized that short-term intervention programs were ineffective in overcoming the effects of poverty. Therefore, a new model was created that extended the Head Start concept to include kindergarten through the third grade while maintaining its ecological emphasis of change in the home and community. Unfortunately, a funding crisis precipitated a retooling of the project's goals and objectives. According to Peterson's (1987) review, the emphasis shifted from a service operation like Head Start to an experimental R&D (research and development) program dedicated to assessing various approaches aimed at increasing the educational attainments of young disadvantaged and at-risk students. Rather than offering a single model of early childhood education for low-income pupils, Project Follow-Through studied a variety of approaches and strategies, realizing that a singular model would not meet the needs of all children. Public schools were free to adopt the model they believed best met the unique needs of their community.

Other representative projects and experiments of this era include the Milwaukee Early Intervention Project (Garber & Heber, 1977; Heber & Garber, 1975). Hailed as the "Miracle in Milwaukee," the Milwaukee Project demonstrated the benefits of early intervention and maternal education in reducing the incidence of mental retardation in young children considered at-risk due to sociocultural and economic conditions.

Like the efforts in Milwaukee, the Carolina Abecedarian Project also attempted to modify environmental forces impinging upon the intellectual development of children living in poverty. During the project, which was designed in 1972 as a longitudinal experiment, Craig Ramey and his colleagues (Ramey & Campbell, 1977, 1984; Ramey & Smith, 1977) found that young students exposed to early learning experiences achieved higher IQs when compared to matched age-mates who did not participate in the project. Both the Milwaukee Project and the Carolina program demonstrate the plasticity of intelligence and the positive effects of early environmental intervention.

Research Evidence

Over the past thirty years, numerous investigators have attempted to document the effectiveness of early intervention with atypical and disadvantaged preschoolers. Many reviews of these research efforts have been published; as expected, the findings were frequently contradictory. Heward and Orlansky (1988) expertly summarized some of the empirical evidence and interpretations. They noted that according to one analysis conducted by White, Bush, and Casto (1986), almost all of 52 previous reviewers found distinct advantages for at-risk, disadvantaged, and special needs youngsters who participated in early intervention programs. Benefits observed include (among others) improved cognitive, language, social-emotional, and motor performance. Lazar and Darlington (1979, 1982) issued two major documents reporting on results from twelve follow-up studies of children enrolled in cognitively oriented preschool programs. None of the projects focused specifically on children with special needs, although several selected participants on the basis of low IQ (range 50–85). Socioeconomically disadvantaged enrollees achieved better in school when compared to nonparticipants. The analysis also revealed that fewer of the early intervention children were receiving special education services (14 percent vs. 29 percent) and fewer repeated a grade level (26 percent vs. 37 percent).

While the long-term effects of early intervention are generally positive, several investigators comment on the difficulty of conducting methodologically sound experiments (Dunst, 1986; Strain & Smith, 1986). Potential problems lie in choosing assessment instruments, selecting participants with similar characteristics, and handling ethical issues, as well as in accommodating variations in curriculum emphasis.

Casto and Mastropieri (1986) conducted an analysis of over seventy early intervention efforts specifically involving preschoolers with disabilities. As in previous analyses, these researchers found not only positive effects but also that early intervention programs of longer duration and greater intensity usually demonstrate greater effectiveness. Two intriguing findings emerged, however, both of them contrary to conventional wisdom. First, Casto and Mastropieri found no support for the belief that the earlier intervention commences, the greater its effectiveness. Second, they disagreed with previous reviewers who asserted that greater parental participation leads to enhanced program effectiveness.

As expected, the findings of Casto and Mastropieri were subject to criticism. Critics (Dunst & Snyder, 1986; Strain & Smith, 1986) assailed the conclusions, claiming that the analysis was methodologically and conceptually flawed. But today many professionals and researchers agree that the earlier intervention is begun, the better.

KEY FEDERAL LEGISLATION

At one time, education of exceptional pupils was a privilege; today it is their right. Thanks are in large part due to litigation brought on behalf of children with special needs and legislative enactments mandating or requiring that such children are entitled to an education.

Over the past thirty years, a variety of federal laws have in many ways affected the education of typical and atypical young children. Of particular importance to students with special needs are two landmark pieces of legislation: Public Law (PL) 94–142, the Education for All Handicapped Children Act,[1] and PL 99–457, the Education of the Handicapped Act Amendments of 1986.

Public Law 94—142

Viewed as a "Bill of Rights" for exceptional children, PL 94–142 is considered by many individuals as one of the most important pieces of legislation enacted on behalf of children with special needs, if not the most important. Some advocacy groups consider this enactment a vital first step in securing the constitutional rights of citizens with disabilities (Allen, 1992).

Many professionals wrongly consider PL 94–142 an independent enactment, when in fact it is an amendment to earlier legislation (PL

1. PL 94–142 is now known as the Individuals with Disabilities Education Act (IDEA). Change came about with the enactment of PL 101–476 (the Education for the Handicapped Act Amendments of 1990) on October 30, 1990.

Exceptional children are to be educated, to the maximum extent possible, with their typical peers.

93–380) that initially established a federal commitment to the education of special needs children.

The purpose of this bill is

> to insure that all handicapped children have available to them . . . a free, appropriate public education which includes special education and related services designed to meet their unique needs, to insure that the rights of handicapped children and their parents or guardians are protected, to assist States and localities to provide for the education of all handicapped children and to assess and insure the effectiveness of efforts to educate handicapped children. [Section 601 (c)]

In addition to these four purposes, six major components are incorporated in this legislation:

1. *The right to a free appropriate public education. All* children must be provided an education appropriate to their unique needs at no cost to the parent(s) or guardian(s). Included in this feature is the concept of related services, which requires that children receive, as necessary, occupational, physical, and speech therapy among other services.

2. *The principle of least restrictive environment (LRE).* Exceptional children are to be educated, to the maximum extent possible, with typical students. Placement must be consistent with the pupil's educational needs.

3. *An individualized educational program (IEP).* This document, developed in conjunction with the parent(s) or guardian(s), is an individually tailored statement describing an educational plan for each exceptional learner. The IEP is required to address (a) present level of academic functioning; (b) annual goals and accompanying instructional objectives; (c) educational services to be provided; (d) the degree to which the pupil will be able to participate in regular education programs; (e) plans for initiating services and length of service delivery; and (f) an annual evaluation procedure specifying objective criteria to determine if instructional objectives are being met.

4. *Procedural due process.* The act afford parents or guardians several safeguards as it pertains to their child's education. Briefly, parents or guardians have the right to examine all records; obtain an independent evaluation; receive written notification (in parent's native language) of proposed changes to their child's educational classification or placement; and a right to an impartial hearing whenever disagreements occur regarding educational plans for their son or daughter.

5. *Nondiscriminatory assessment.* Before placement, a child must be evaluated in all areas of suspected disability by tests that are neither culturally nor linguistically biased. Students are to receive several types of assessments; a single evaluation procedure is not permitted.

6. *Parental participation.* PL 94–142 mandates parental involvement. Sometimes referred to as the "Parent's Law," this legislation requires that parents participate in the decision-making process that affects their child's education.

Congress mandated by 1 September 1980 a free appropriate public education for all eligible children ages 3 through 21. But the law did *not* require services to preschool children with disabilities. An exception was contained in the legislative language:

> except that, with respect to handicapped children aged three to five and eighteen to twenty-one, inclusive, the requirements . . . shall not be applied . . . if such requirements would be inconsistent with state law or practice, or the order of any court, respecting public education within such age groups within the state. [Section 612 (2) (B)]

Thus, since many states were not providing preschool services to typical children, an education for young children with special needs, in most instances, was not mandated. Although this legislation fails to require an education for our younger students, it clearly focused attention on the preschool population and recognized the value of early education.

PL 94–142 did, however, contain benefits for children under school age. The enactment offered small financial grants to the individual states as an incentive to serve young children with special needs. It also moved from a census count to a child count, or the actual number of children served. The intent of this feature was to encourage the states to locate and serve children with disabilities. In its

Fourteenth Annual Report to Congress, the U.S. Department of Education (1992) reported a significant increase in the number of 3- to 5-year-old youngsters served. In the 1978–1979 reporting year 214,885 preschoolers were receiving services; however, 368,869 children were counted in 1990–1991 (a 71.5 percent increase).

Public Law 99–457

In October 1986, Congress passed one of the most comprehensive pieces of legislation affecting young children with special needs and their families—PL 99–457. This law not only changed the scope and intent of services provided to preschoolers with special needs but also formulated a national policy for at-risk and special needs infants, toddlers, and young children with disabilities.

PL 99–457, the Education of the Handicapped Act Amendments of 1986, contains several parts, or in legislative terms, Titles. Our attention focuses on Title II (Part B), the preschool provision. We also briefly examine Title I (Part H), a new section allowing for services to be provided to infants and toddlers with special needs.

As noted earlier, PL 94–142 contains language that gave states the opportunity, via financial incentives, to provide an education and related services to preschool children with disabilities. This was a permissive or voluntary element of the act, not a mandated requirement. Trohanis (1989) reported Congressional data revealing that less than 80 percent—or 260,000 of the estimated 330,000 exceptional youngsters ages 3 to 5—were being served. An estimated 70,000 preschoolers were therefore unserved. Koppelman (1986) found that thirty-one states and territories did not require special education services for special needs preschoolers. PL 99–457 was enacted to remedy this situation.

Simply stated, Title II is a downward extension of PL 94–142, including all rights and protections. It requires that as of the 1991–1992 school year, *all* preschoolers with special needs, ages 3 to 5 inclusive, are to receive a free and appropriate public education. This element of the law is a mandated requirement. States will lose significant amounts of federal funding if they fail to comply. Other provisions of the earlier legislation also apply, such as an education in the least restrictive environment, IEPs, due process safeguards, and confidentiality of records. Family services are also recognized as being vitally important; thus, family counseling and training are allowable as a related service. Depending on the needs of the child, service delivery models can either be home-based or center-based, full-time or part-time. It is also interesting that each state is not required to report to the U.S. Department of Education the number of children served according to a disability category. This means that preschoolers do not have to be labeled with a specific disability (e.g., mental retardation).

All states were required to modify their state plans and policies to ensure compliance with the law. Funding for serving these children has also been dramatically increased.

Title I of PL 99–457 created the Handicapped Infants and Toddlers Program (Part H), a new provision aimed at at-risk and special needs children from birth to 3 years of age. This component of the legislation is discretionary; states are not compelled to comply.

In its findings, Congress asserted that "there is an urgent and substantial need"

1. To enhance the development of handicapped infants and toddlers and to minimize their potential for developmental delay,
2. To reduce the educational cost to our society . . . ,
3. To minimize the likelihood of institutionalization of handicapped individuals and maximize the potential for their independent living in society, and
4. To enhance the capacity of families to meet the special needs of their infants and toddlers with handicaps. [Section 671 (a)]

Several definitions and features of this law are worthy of examination. Under this act, infants and toddlers are eligible for services if:

- They are experiencing developmental delays in one or more of the following areas: cognitive, physical, language and speech, psychosocial or self-help skills.[2]
- They have a physical or mental condition that has a high probability of resulting in a delay (e.g., cerebral palsy, Down syndrome).
- At the state's discretion, youngsters are medically or environmentally at-risk for substantial delay if early intervention is not provided.

Eligible children and their families must receive a multidisciplinary assessment conducted by qualified professionals and a written individualized family service plan (IFSP). Like the IEP, the IFSP is designed as a guide to the delivery of services to infants and toddlers. The IFSP, which is developed by a multidisciplinary team, must contain:

- A statement of the infant's or toddler's present levels of physical development, cognitive development, language and speech development, psychosocial development, and self-help skills . . .
- A statement of the family's strengths and needs . . .

2. Terminology changed due to the enactment of PL 102–119, the Individuals with Disabilities Education Act Amendments of 1991 (October 7, 1991). Congress indicated that "language and speech" should be referred to as *communication development*; "psychosocial" should be referred to as *social or emotional development*; and "self-help" should be referred to as *adaptive development*.

Individualized family service plans (IFSPs) are developed by professionals in collaboration with the child's parent(s).

- A statement of major outcomes expected to be achieved for the infant and toddler and the family . . .
- A statement of specific early intervention services necessary to meet the unique needs of the infant or toddler and the family . . .
- The projected dates for initiation of services and the anticipated duration of such services,
- The name of the case manager . . .
- The steps . . . supporting the transition of the handicapped toddler to services provided under Part B [preschool]. . . . [Section 677 (d)]

The focus of the IFSP is on the family rather than the individual child, resulting—according to Widerstrom, Mowder, and Sandall (1991)—in a comprehensive and multidisciplinary plan. Parents are viewed as full-fledged partners with professionals. Their participation ensures that services occur within the context of the family unit.

The final noteworthy aspect of PL 99–457 to be discussed is the concept of case management.[3] A case manager is a professional selected from the discipline closest to the child's primary problem (e.g., a speech and language pathologist for toddlers with delayed language, or a physical therapist for a youngster with cerebral palsy).

3. Terminology changed due to the enactment of the PL 102–119, the Individuals with Disabilities Education Act Amendments of 1991 (October 7, 1991). Congress indicated that "case management" should be referred to as service coordination services and "manager" should be referred to as service coordinator.

The case manager's role is to function as an advocate for the family, to ensure the coordination of early intervention services, and to monitor the implementation of the IFSP.

PL 99–457 is the culmination of many years of dedicated effort by both parents and professionals. It represents an opportunity to intervene and effect meaningful change in the lives of the nation's youngest and most vulnerable children.

YOUNG CHILDREN WITH SPECIAL NEEDS

At the conclusion of 1990, the U.S. Department of Education (1992) reported that approximately 600,000 youngsters birth to age 5 were receiving some kind of special educational services. Preschoolers with disabilities, ages 3 to 5 inclusive, accounted for almost 67 percent of the number of children served. Since the enactment of PL 99–457 (Part B) in 1986, there has been a significant increase in the number of young students with special needs. Table 12.1 reflects this growth pattern.

As mentioned previously, due to the legislative requirements contained in the 1986 amendments, child counts are no longer reported by specific disabilities. Thus, the figures in Table 12.1 cannot be partitioned into specific conditions. But that provision refers only to the preschool population. School-age children with special needs are described by disability category. The U.S. Department of Education (1992) reported that as of 1 October 1991, over one million children in the primary grades manifested some type of exceptionality (see Table 12.2).

Early childhood educators working in preschools, kindergartens, and the primary grades will teach children with special needs. But

TABLE 12.1 Increase in Number of Preschoolers Served under the Individuals with Disabilities Education Act (Part B)

	Year					Change 1986-90	
Ages	**1986-87**	**1987-88**	**1988-89**	**1989-90**	**1990-91**	**Numbers**	**%**
3-year-olds	31,162	36,501	47,860	53,944	59,095	27,933	89.63
4-year-olds	62,327	71,819	89,379	104,245	111,787	47,550	74.02
5-year-olds	170,415	179,874	184,121	194,338	197,807	27,392	16.07
TOTAL	265,814	288,293	321,360	352,527	368,689	102,875	38.70

Source: From U.S. Department of Education, 1991, *Thirteenth Annual Report to Congress on the Implementation of the Individuals with Disabilities Education Act* (Washington, DC: U.S. Government Printing Office); and U.S. Department of Education, 1992, *Fourteenth Annual Report to Congress on the Implementation of the Individuals with Disabilities Education Act* (Washington, DC: U.S. Government Printing Office).

TABLE 12.2 Number of Children Served under the Individuals with Disabilities Education Act (Part B)

Disability	Ages			Total
	6 Years Old	7 Years Old	8 Years Old	
Mental retardation	18,337	25,178	33,065	77,121
Speech or language impairments	196,236	202,053	179,903	577,382
Visual impairments	1,194	1,378	1,596	4,168
Serious emotional disturbance	7,416	13,386	20,283	41,085
Orthopedic impairments	4,139	4,250	4,068	12,457
Other health impairments	3,552	4,368	4,790	12,710
Specific learning disabilities	31,935	81,049	145,897	258,881
Deaf-Blindness	47	72	79	198
Multiple disabilities	6,892	6,911	7,511	21,314
Hearing impairments	3,104	3,414	3,824	10,342
All disabilities	272,852	342,600	400,206	1,015,658

Note: Data reported for school year 1990–1991.

Source: From U.S. Department of Education, 1992, *Fourteenth Annual Report to Congress on the Implementation of the Individuals with Disabilities Education Act* (Washington, DC: U.S. Government Printing Office).

who are young children with special needs? The federal government, through PL 94–142, defines a child with a disability to mean:

> those children evaluated as being mentally retarded, hard-of-hearing, deaf, speech impaired, visually handicapped, seriously emotionally disturbed, orthopedically impaired, other health impaired, deaf-blind, multi-handicapped or having specific learning disabilities, who because of these impairments need special education and related services. (Federal Register, 1977, p. 12478)

These conditions are defined via regulations accompanying PL 94–142. The definitions, which can be found in Appendix O, provide the foundation from which the various states develop their own policies and standards as to who is eligible to receive special education. But note that gifted and talented children are excluded from the federal definitions. Other national legislation provides us with a definition of gifted and talented children. According to Public Law 97–35, gifted and talented children

> give evidence of high performance capabilities in such areas as intellectual, creative, artistic, leadership capacity, or specific academic fields, and who require services or activities not ordinarily provided by the school in order to fully develop such capabilities. (Section 582)

Because such children are viewed as exceptional rather than disabled, federal law does not mandate or require public schools to provide services to these children. Each state, therefore, is free to decide how it will service the unique needs of gifted and talented youngsters.

IDENTIFYING AND ASSESSING YOUNG CHILDREN WITH SPECIAL NEEDS

Before providing services to the young child with special needs, the early childhood professional must first recognize and identify who needs early intervention or special education. We begin our examination of identifying and evaluating special needs and at-risk children by reviewing appropriate terminology.

Key Terms

It is unfortunate that many terms and concepts used frequently by professionals are not standardized. This is a source of repeated confusion and misunderstanding, especially when discussing the process of assessing and evaluating children with exceptionalities. A clear understanding of the following four terms is critical to our discussion. Expert opinion is used to define the terminology.

Screening. Screening, according to Dumars, Duran-Flores, Foster, and Stills (1987), "is the application of a simple accurate method for determining which children in the population are likely to be in need of special services in order to develop optimally" (p. 111). Put another way, screening is a mechanism for quickly surveying the child population to identify those youngsters who may require special services (Lerner, Mardell-Czudnowski, & Goldenberg, 1987).

Diagnosing. Janet Lerner and her colleagues (Lerner et al., 1987) consider a diagnosis as one step in an ongoing process in which an in-depth evaluation is conducted on children identified through screening. Cross (1977), who parallels this view, writes that a diagnosis is "a process designed: (1) to confirm or disconfirm the existence of a problem, serious enough to require remediation, in those children identified in a screening effort and (2) to clarify the nature of the problem (is it organic, environmental, or both?)" (p. 25).

Assessment. Simply defined, assessment refers to "either a test or an observation that determines a child's strengths or weaknesses in a particular area of development" (Cook et al., 1992, p. 474).

Evaluation. "Evaluating refers to the ways of determining a child's progress within a program" (Lerner et al., 1987, p. 71). Salvia and Ysseldyke (1978) offer a second purpose, stating that "evaluation differs from other purposes of testing in the sense that the educational program rather than the student is being evaluated" (p. 16).

We now explore and expand the role of the preceding concepts in the following evaluation model.

An Evaluation Model

Determining who is eligible to receive special education services involves separate but related components of an evaluative process. Several early childhood theorists and practitioners have developed models designed to illustrate the procedures involved (Cook et al., 1992; Fallen & Umansky, 1985; Lerner et al., 1987; Peterson, 1987; Widerstrom et al., 1991). Although the elements vary slightly and the terminology may differ, the outcomes are essentially the same—delivering quality services to young at-risk or special needs children and their families.

Placing our special needs child in a regular kindergarten program would have been much more difficult had she not attended a wonderful day care program that let her just be a child. She feels good about herself and is ready and willing to try anything.

Borrowing from these professionals, we have constructed the following five-step model.

Step 1—Locating. Locating or case finding is the first step. It refers to the process of finding young children who might be eligible for early intervention. In communities this requires both concerted and systematic efforts at building awareness and informing the public, social service agencies and clinics, child care facilities, and professionals of available services. A primary goal of these activities is to elicit referrals of potential candidates for screening.

For a young child enrolled in a public school, the process is generally the task of the child's teacher, who makes a referral to the appropriate source depending on local school policies and procedures.

Step 2—Screening. The intent of this step is to identify those youngsters who may have a problem or a potential problem that warrants further investigation. Children with obvious or severe disabilities are generally not subjected to screening procedures. These children are identified through step 1 and typically proceed to a diagnosis phase.

Screening is a limited procedure with the goal of identifying suspected problems as early as possible. Professionals generally agree that early identification allows for more effective intervention and treatment. Screening does not indicate the nature and extent of the problem, nor does it offer explanations for its occurrence. The results of a screening procedure should not be used to label a child. Allen (1992) further cautions early childhood professionals that the "results from screening tests do not constitute a diagnosis; never should they be used as a basis for planning an intervention program" (p. 73).

Step 3—Diagnosis. The third element in this model is an in-depth, multidisciplinary assessment of a youngster detected through step 2. While the intent of the screening procedure is to sort out youngsters who may have a potential problem, the aim of a diagnostic evaluation according to Peterson (1987, p. 295) is to answer the question, "What exactly is the problem, and how severe is it?"

The term *diagnosis* as used by educators differs in meaning from its use by health care professionals. Traditionally, *diagnosis* describes a condition such as cerebral palsy or the etiology of a disorder. But educators use the term when talking about the nature and extent of a disabling condition. In many instances, the cause of the child's problem has little educational relevance and is frequently unknown or difficult to determine.

An in-depth, multidisciplinary evaluation of the child should assist in the decision-making process about (1) the severity of the youngster's problem, (2) possible causes, (3) type of treatment or intervention required, and (4) the most appropriate means for delivering the needed services (Lerner et al., 1987). The goal of the diagnostic process is to determine the type of intervention appropriate for the child. A diagnosis does not suggest what the student should be taught, nor does it recommend instructional strategies.

Information about the child is gathered from a variety of sources, both formal and informal. Data can be obtained from standardized tests, observations, parent and caregiver interviews, and case histories as well as specific diagnostic tests. This information must then be synthesized, evaluated, and interpreted so that a complete picture of the child's strengths and weaknesses develops. This task is frequently the responsibility of the teacher, who plays a critical role as part of a multidisciplinary team. Under the teacher's leadership, placement options are considered and the child's needs are evaluated in regards to necessary services.

Step 4—Assessment. Determining a child's strengths and weaknesses and developing individualized educational prescriptions is the basis of step 4. Current levels of performance are assessed, and areas of development to be mastered are noted. Assessment establishes a starting point or baseline from which instruction can be planned. Peterson (1987) observes that instructional objectives are generated from assessment data whereby the youngster's developmental level and learning needs are matched. Educational assessments are completed at the conclusion of step 3 but before constructing the student's IEP. IEPs are developed on the basis of assessment information.

Assessment data can be gathered from a variety of sources. Early childhood educators have an assortment of data-gathering tools at their disposal. Useful information can be gleaned from observations, criterion-referenced tests where a child's performance is compared to a specific standard, and standardized testing (norm-referenced tests), in addition to checklists and instruments designed to evaluate specific areas of development.

Assessment is an ongoing rather than a static process. As instructional objectives and goals are accomplished, the IEP needs to be modified and new instructional targets established.

Step 5—Evaluation. The final component of our evaluation model is an evaluative phase during which both student achievement and program effectiveness are scrutinized. The ongoing, systematic monitoring of student progress (or lack of it) assists (or impedes) educators in determining the effectiveness of instructional programming. It also provides useful information that may suggest

Assessment data provide the foundation for developing instructional objectives.

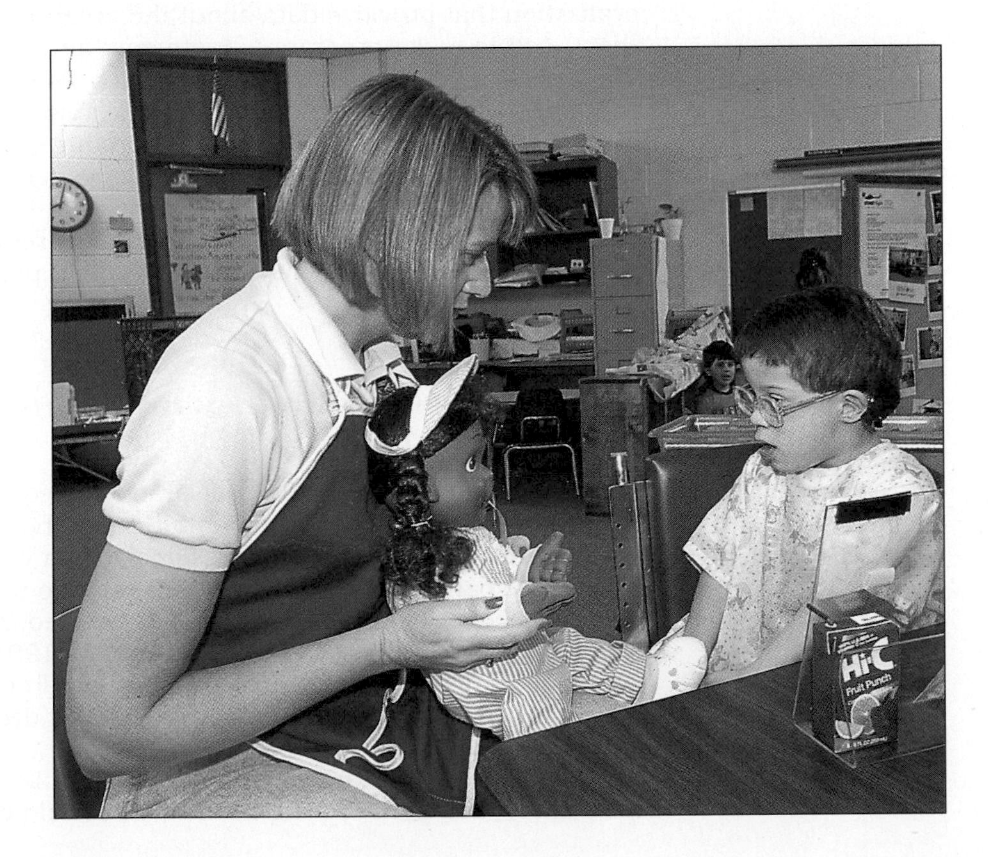

alteration of specific instructional objectives. Peterson notes that evaluation is designed to assess what happens once instruction is initiated. Peterson (1987, p. 307) suggests that educators ask the following three questions.

1. Is each child making continuous progress in specific skill areas as a result of the learning activities?
2. Is each child reaching the goals defined in his or her IEP?
3. Are the teaching techniques selected for each child working?

It should be obvious that tracking a student's performance is an individualized activity. Each pupil's progress is evaluated differently, depending on his or her IEP.

Educators are frequently asked to document the impact or effectiveness of the early childhood special education program. Administrators, consumer groups, funding agencies, and other decision makers are often concerned with the issue of accountability: Is the program doing what it said it would do, in an effective and efficient fashion? Program evaluation provides an opportunity to determine if changes need to be made.

Program evaluation must be an organized, coordinated, and well-planned activity in order for useful information to emerge. Program evaluation typically includes two types of evaluation: (1) formative evaluation that provides data about the program's progress, which is then used to make program adjustments and modifications if needed; and (2) summative evaluation, which assesses final results or overall outcomes and program success. Typically, the professional staff members closest to the program produce formative evaluations (internal reviews), and outside evaluators generate objective and unbiased summative reports (external reviews).

Each of the five components of this model represents a crucial element in an overall effort at ensuring quality programming for eligible children.

Considerations in Testing Young Children with Special Needs

Legislative requirements and best practices require that the assessment process be conducted by a multidisciplinary team. The composition of the team includes professionals from various disciplines as well as the parent(s). As a group, decisions are made as to what is to be evaluated and how the data will be obtained. According to Widerstrom and her colleagues (Widerstrom et al., 1991), obtaining an accurate picture of a child's strengths and weaknesses necessitates a collaborative relationship from which joint decision making and shared planning emerges.

The assessment process is useful only if it leads to the delivery of needed services to the young child with special needs. Obtaining this goal requires that examiners adhere to the following practices identified by Fewell (1991). First, evaluators should be cognizant of the reason(s) for the child's assessment. Evaluation tools appropriate for assessing a youngster's eligibility for services will most likely be invalid for developing instructional objectives and strategies. Selected instruments should be appropriate to the purpose of the evaluation and the desired outcomes. Second, Fewell reminds professionals that test selection must be appropriate for the child and consider his or her disabilities. PL 94–142 and PL 99–457 both mandate that testing be appropriate and not penalize children for their disability. As an example, tests must be administered in the child's native language or other modes of communication appropriate for the student. There also must be a match between test requirements and the child's capabilities, such as the ability to verbally respond to a question or point to a test item. Finally, tests must be administered by qualified individuals in a fashion consistent with test requirements. The issue of adapting or modifying standardized instruments in order to accommodate the individual needs of the student has generated controversy among professionals. Questions about test validity and appropriate interpretation of results are frequent concerns.

KIDS SPEAK UP

Jason is neat. He has a red wheelchair.

Boy, 5 years old

Peterson (1987) developed a list of six factors that may influence the performance of children with special needs in standardized testing situations. Early childhood professionals need to be aware of fatigue and short attention span, high distractibility, absence of motivation, lack of attentiveness, noncompliant or uncooperative behavior, and finally, fearfulness of strangers and unfamiliar situations.

Fallen and Umansky (1985) also note that situational variables are capable of influencing test performance of young children with special needs. Such variables include the general condition of the child's overall health; the rapport between the evaluator and the child; time factors including the length of the testing sessions as well as when the evaluation is scheduled (first thing in the morning, after recess, before lunch). Other considerations mentioned are the color and size of the materials involved, and auditory or visual distractions surrounding the testing environment.

Skillful evaluation of young children with special needs requires that professionals fully appreciate the uniqueness of each child and the importance of variables that can influence the assessment process.

SERVICE DELIVERY MODELS

There are a variety of administrative options for delivering services to young children with special needs. These arrangements are typically referred to as service delivery approaches, that is, where intervention or education is provided. The location of services often depends on the age of the students to be served, geographical considerations, costs, child characteristics, and community resources in addition to child and family goals and objectives.

Early childhood special education programs are frequently identified as center-based, home-based, or combination programs. One early childhood authority (Peterson, 1987), however, views these traditional categorizations as too restrictive and advocates a process-oriented approach to the concept of service delivery.

Center-Based Services

As the name implies, **center-based services** are located away from the child's home. Settings may be in churches, day care centers, preschools, public schools, or other locations. Center-based models are usually group oriented and the most common setting for 3- and 4-year-old children with special needs (Bailey & Wolery, 1992; Hanson & Lynch, 1989). Children are transported to the site, where they receive services from professionals representing a variety of disciplines. This strategy is in concert with the current transdisciplinary model of working with special needs and at-risk youngsters. Professionals share their expertise and work cooperatively as a team in delivering individualized educational plans. Many programs like to involve parents as part of the team and consider their participation both valuable and beneficial. Parental involvement increases program effectiveness. Children typically attend for several hours each day, often on a daily basis.

Experts (Bailey & Wolery, 1992; Meyen, 1990; Peterson, 1987) consider center-based programs to have several advantages. Frequently mentioned aspects include

- Opportunities for social interactions between typical and atypical peers
- Access to specialists from many different professional fields
- Availability of specialized equipment and materials
- Greater efficiency of program staff
- Caregiver involvement and the chance to observe other parents and their children

The center-based model is not without its limitations and drawbacks. Disadvantages can include

- Expense of transportation to and from the site
- Cost and maintenance of the center itself
- In comparison to home-based models, less opportunity to establish effective working relationships with families

Center-based administrators are also confronted with the issue of providing services with the LRE as mandated by PL 99–457. Currently, too few local schools provide preschool programs for typical pupils; therefore, alternative models for serving preschoolers with disabilities will need to be explored.

Home-Based Services

For some young children, the most appropriate location for providing services is in their home. With **home-based services**, intervention can individually be provided by the primary caregiver in the youngster's most natural environment. The caregiver, typically a parent, is instructed by professionals on how to implement specific instructional objectives and strategies developed by a multidisciplinary team. Specialists make regular frequent visits to the home to work directly with the child, assist and instruct the service provider, and monitor the child's progress.

Delivering services in the child's home has multiple advantages. The primary advantage is that services are provided in a setting that the child is familiar with and by the youngster's first teacher—a parent. Disruptions in the child's and family's routines are also minimized. With home-based programs, costs are generally lower, transportation is not a concern, and services are responsive to family needs. This model is especially appropriate for rural or sparsely populated communities.

There are certain disadvantages to home-based models. A commonly noted drawback is the commitment required and responsibilities placed upon the caregiver. Not all parents are capable of providing effective intervention, nor is it a role they wish to fulfill. Furthermore, in some situations, the effectiveness of this model may be diminished due to family circumstances such as a single-parent home, conditions of poverty, or other at-risk factors. Opportunities for social interaction with other children are also absent in home-based models. Finally, a considerable amount of the professional's time is usually spent traveling from one home to another.

Combination Programs

Services to young children with special needs may require that program philosophies be merged in order to best serve the child and the family. Combination programs provide this flexibility and reflect the advantages of both settings. Heward and Orlansky (1988) believe that the most commonly used model is one that allows for center-based activities as well as home visitations. Typically, children less than 36 months of age are served via home-based programs, while older preschoolers receive instruction in centers. Parent involvement and participation is an important component of both delivery systems.

Research (Filler, 1983) fails to distinguish the superiority of one model over another. Many professionals agree that what is most important is matching the service delivery options to the needs of the child and the family. What is an appropriate program for one family may be inappropriate for another. "The optimal model for service delivery depends on family and child characteristics and needs, intensity of services, and geographic characteristics of the service area" (Meyen, 1990, p. 145).

School-Age Children

Special needs children in the primary grades will also encounter various service delivery options. Two typical placement alternatives in elementary schools are variations of regular class placement or assignment to a special class. Many children with mild disabilities are served in the regular or typical classroom, while young students with moderate or severe impairments are usually placed in a special class (See Figure 12.1). While placement decisions may be based partly on the degree of the disability, legislative requirements mandate that an appropriate education must be provided to these pupils in the LRE. In a recent report to Congress on the implementation of IDEA (U.S. Department of Education, 1991) the prevalence of these two placement options was noted. Because the report uses an age grouping of 6 to 11, only a general impression can be obtained for children in the first, second, or third grades (ages 6 to 8).

TEACHERS SPEAK OUT

The children in our school discover that there are many different kinds of people and that everyone deserves respect and care.

The regular classroom was the most common learning environment (over 40 percent). A resource classroom, where a student spends time in both the regular class and a special education classroom, accounted for 35 percent of the enrollment. Therefore, almost three out of four young children with special needs are served in some form of regular class placement. Only 20 percent of the students are enrolled in a special class. These enrollment patterns suggest that early childhood educators will have varying degrees of responsibility for educating pupils with special needs.

CURRICULUM CONSIDERATIONS FOR YOUNG CHILDREN WITH SPECIAL NEEDS

Once the issue of *where* the child will be served has been decided, the question of *what* the student will be taught needs to be addressed. In other words, what is the curriculum? Curriculum, according to Lerner (Lerner et al., 1987) means "the planned arrangement of experiences designed to bring about the desired changes in the child's behavior" (p. 134). A more elaborate interpretation is proposed by Hanson and Lynch (1989), who believe that

> a curriculum is an organized set of activities and experiences designed to achieve particular developmental or learning objectives. This organizational structure dictates both the content (what should be included) and the method (how the targets are to be taught) for intervention implementation. As such, it involves a carefully planned and arranged sequence of events. (p. 158)

Meaningful curriculum for young children with special needs calls for elements from both early childhood and special education models. Curricula from these two areas must be blended in order to construct educational interventions that will meet the unique needs of each child (Lerner et al., 1987; Peterson, 1987). Cook and her coworkers (Cook et al., 1992) remind early childhood educators that when choosing or developing a curriculum, they must keep in mind what their goals and the parent's educational goals are for the student. Equally important are the strengths and learning styles of the pupil, as well as the teacher's teaching style. Another expert (Peterson, 1987) suggests that curriculum planning for exceptional pupils requires (1) accommodation of the IEP objectives of each student; (2) activities appropriate to the developmental level of the children; and (3) consideration of the competencies of each pupil, such as their ability to follow directions or work in groups. Curriculum planning and development for special needs children is not an easy task, especially when professionals consider the high degree of individualization needed in early childhood special education programs.

Individualized Educational Program (IEP)

One of the cornerstones of building appropriate curricula for young children with special needs is the student's IEP. Based on a multidisciplinary evaluation of the pupil's strengths and weaknesses, an individualized plan of learning activities and objectives is prescribed. Curriculum decisions, therefore, flow from the educational assessment. Furthermore, in contrast to many early childhood programs, which traditionally incorporate a group-oriented approach to instruction, the benchmark of early childhood special education is individualization: Rather than the child fitting into the program (curriculum), a curriculum is developed for what is appropriate or fits the individual student. It is perhaps best to envision the IEP as a management tool or vehicle for ensuring that children with exceptionalities receive an individualized education appropriate to their needs. The IEP is the foundation of the entire process of teaching and assessment.

Polloway, Patton, Payne, and Payne (1989) identify three of the most prominent purposes of an IEP. First, IEPs furnish instructional direction, acting as a blueprint to providing integrated instruction. Next, an IEP can serve as a basis for evaluation. Goals can function as a measure of instructional effectiveness and student progress. Finally, well-written IEPs have the potential to improve communication among team members—educators, parents, and other professional staff.

IEPs are written by a team. Participants must include a representative from the school district; the child's teacher(s); one or both parents or guardians; when appropriate, the student; and other professionals whose expertise is desired at the discretion of the parent or school. In the IEP process, the regular and special education teachers are the main individuals, for they ultimately have the responsibility for implementing the IEP. Pavia (1992) believes that both the special educator and early childhood teacher should be viewed equally as the youngster's teacher and therefore play a supporting or complementary role in developing the IEP. Early childhood educators "could be primarily responsible for most aspects of the young handicapped child's educational experiences" (Pavia, 1992, p. 39). Unfortunately, Smith (1990) feels that the importance of the regular educator in the IEP process has yet to be realized. Failure of these two key professionals to collaborate often leads to ineffective implementation of the IEP.

As a review, the minimal components of an IEP include

- The child's present levels of educational performance
- Annual goals and short-term instructional objectives
- Specific educational services to be provided
- The extent to which the child will participate in the regular education program
- Projected date for initiation of services and expected duration of these services
- Objective criteria and evaluation procedures

Legislation does not require, however, any provision for family goals and services as found in PL 99–457. But there is no empirical or theoretical reason for excluding this component (Bailey & Wolery, 1992). We agree with this point of view. In fact, it could reasonably be argued that this element is as important for preschool and school-age exceptional children and their families as it is for infants and toddlers.

Finally, IEPs are not meant to be so detailed or complete that they function as the *total* instructional agenda. "They are designed to target remediation of particular developmental lags or to accelerate learning" (Cook et al., 1992, p. 160). Goals and objectives, listed by priority, form the foundation from which daily lesson plans are developed within the developmental domains that are the framework of curricular content in early childhood special education (Peterson, 1987). It is to these broad developmental domains that we now turn our attention.

Curriculum Domains

Several authors (Bailey & Wolery, 1992; Fallen & Umansky, 1985; Meyen, 1990; Peterson, 1987) have identified key domains of curricular emphasis for youngsters 36–60 months of age. The six typical elements of **curriculum domains** include

- Cognitive development—developing concepts, understanding relationships, attention and memory, problem-solving, preacademic skills
- Motor development—gross motor (walking, jumping, throwing, rolling) and fine motor skills (cutting, writing, painting, eye-hand coordination)
- Language development—includes verbal and nonverbal communication as well as expressive and receptive skills
- Social/emotional development—socially appropriate means of interacting with family, friends, other adults and children; self-concept; understanding the emotional needs of others
- Self-help skills—ability for managing activities of self-care, such as eating, dressing, personal hygiene, and toileting
- Play skills—toy play, peer interaction, games, fantasy roles

"These developmental domains are the primary objects of curricular, or instructional, emphases in early childhood special education" (Meyen, 1990, p. 152). Although the key areas are presented separately, in practice teachers frequently formulate goals and objectives that cut across content areas. As the pupil cognitively and physically matures, the interrelatedness of the domains increases. These areas form the foundations from which instructional objectives are tailored. Specific objectives and individually planned activities are based on student characteristics and needs as well as on the impact of the disability on learning and development (Meyen, 1990).

KIDS SPEAK UP

Michelle showed me how to say "I love you" with my fingers.

Girl, 4 years old

Two broad perspectives tend to characterize the curricular framework for young children with special needs—developmentally based and functional approaches. Briefly, a developmentalist orientation sees development as a product of maturation that proceeds in an orderly, sequential, and hierarchical fashion. As children grow and develop, they become increasingly capable of accomplishing more complex behaviors. Piaget's model of cognitive development and Gesell's work on identifying developmental milestones reflect this viewpoint.

A developmental approach may not be appropriate for all young children with special needs. A functional focus is common with severely impaired pupils. Teachers select skills that enable the young student to improve their interaction with the environment and increase their independent functioning.

Early childhood educators are not forced to choose between the two perspectives. Meyen (1990) remarks that these viewpoints are not in opposition to each other; effective early childhood teachers frequently teach developmentally appropriate skills within a functional framework. Heward and Orlansky (1988) agree:

> Many early intervention programs for handicapped children use a combination of two approaches, relying on a normal sequence of development as a general guide to the curriculum while using functional considerations in the selection of specific instructional targets for each child. (p. 538)

It is this blending of philosophies that has given rise to the current ecological relevancy factor in curriculum consideration. This "best practices" approach suggests that curricula goals must not only be functional and consider developmental stages but also be relevant to each student within the context of their caregiving environment, that is, school, home, and community (Bailey & Wolery, 1992; Cook et al., 1992). A related and equally important issue addressed by these authors is a transactional perspective. This viewpoint suggests that social interactions between children and adults are interdependent, and each person reciprocally influences the other in positive and negative ways.

Parental Reactions to Exceptionality

"No, it can't be true, there must be a mistake." "Why us?" "It's your fault!" "Don't worry, everything will be okay."

How parents will react to the news that their son or daughter has a disability is difficult, if not impossible, to predict. Each situation is unique. This is a highly emotional experience for many parents, one capable of affecting their psychological well-being. Being the parent of a child with special needs is not a role that any parent asks for, and very few are prepared for the responsibility that in some instances, may last a lifetime.

Experts generally agree that parents will exhibit a wide range of emotional responses (Cook et al., 1992; Gargiulo, 1985; and Peterson, 1987). These feelings are often characterized as a series of stages or phases that many, but not all, parents appear to experience. The wisdom of a stage approach in understanding parental reactions is sometimes questioned (Blacher, 1984; Turnbull & Turnbull, 1990). But with the proper cautions, this strategy provides a useful point of departure for examining parental reactions to exceptionality. Teachers should remember, for example, that parents do not pass through these stages in a sequential or rigid fashion; each parent individually responds in his or her own way, according to their own timetable. Some parents also recycle or revisit earlier reactions. Feelings are continually being dealt with. Adjustment and adaptation is an ongoing process.

Early childhood professionals rarely give meaningful considerations to how parents *feel* about being the mother or father of a youngster with a disability. But parental reaction to exceptionality can significantly affect the quality of the parent-professional partnership. Parents' conduct and behaviors often reflect their interpretation of what exceptionality means to them as well as their child (Gargiulo & Graves, 1991).

PARENTS SPEAK OUT

Parents need to feel respected and have an open and honest dialogue with teachers.

Although there are no universal reactions, frequently identified emotions such as shock, denial, anger and resentment, guilt, and depression—to name but a few—are very common and typical reactions for many parents. One authority (Gargiulo, 1985) strongly believes that these

> reactions are legitimate, automatic, understandable, and normal. They are also necessary. Parental responses to a handicapped son or daugh-

ter are generally not abnormal but represent common reactions of people to frustration and conflict. (p. 21)

Teachers who agree with this philosophy are in a strategic position to truly understand parents and effectively interact with them (Gargiulo & Graves, 1991).

The following suggestions, developed by Gargiulo and his colleague Graves, provide useful ideas for facilitating effective and meaningful partnerships with parents. These hints specifically evolve around consideration of the parents' emotional state (Gargiulo & Graves, 1991, pp. 177–178):

- Explain terminology. Many parents have no previous experience with exceptionality. This may be their first exposure to a disability label. The parents' conceptualization of cerebral palsy or mental retardation is most likely different from that of the professional.
- Parents will frequently exhibit negative feelings when confronted with the news that their son or daughter is handicapped. Workers need to send a message that it is okay to have these feelings. They need to be acknowledged and then understood.
- Teachers must listen! If one wishes to discover the parents' agenda and wishes concerning their child, active listing is of critical importance. Effective helpers want to know what the parent is thinking as well as feeling.
- Use a two-step process when initially informing parents that their child requires special education services. After sharing diagnostic information, it is strongly suggested that professionals allow parents time to comprehend and absorb what they have been told. The parents' affective concerns must be dealt with prior to proceeding with matters such as intervention recommendations, treatment regimens and strategies, or duration of services. These issues should be addressed in a follow-up interview as the parents' emotional state permits.
- Recognize that diverse family structures and parenting styles will influence parent participation. In some circumstances the responsible or concerned individual may not be the child's biological parent. Therefore, respect the parent's right to choose his or her level of involvement. Turnbull and Turnbull (1982) urge professionals to tolerate a range of parent participation matched to needs and interests.
- The needs of the parents reflect not only their ability to cope but also the developmental needs of the child (Schulz, 1987). Professionals must be cognizant of this and customize their interactions with parents to meet these changing needs.

These experts conclude by noting that early childhood teachers will frequently encounter parents who are carrying so much emotional and attitudinal baggage that truly effective working relationships are difficult to establish. Professionals, however, must find ways, rather than excuses, for involving parents.

Contemporary thinking sees the family as a system of interactive, reciprocal relationships.

Parent Involvement

It is obvious that teachers now recognize the importance of parent participation. But what does parent involvement mean? Morrison (1978) provides a useful interpretation. He defines the term as "a process of actualizing the potential of parents; of helping parents discover their strengths, potentialities, and talents, and using them for the benefit of themselves and their family" (p. 22). Although this is an early definition of parent involvement, it is very much in keeping with current thinking about **enabling** and **empowering** families (Dunst, Trivette, & Deal, 1988). Notice the similarities between the two concepts.

> Enabling families means creating opportunities for family members to become more competent and self-sustaining with respect to their abilities to mobilize their social networks to get needs met and obtain goals.
>
> Empowering families means carrying out interventions in a manner in which family members acquire a sense of control over their own developmental course as a result of their own efforts to meet needs. (Deal, Dunst, & Trivette, 1989, p. 33)

Currently, the concept of parent involvement is being looked at as family involvement. In fact, when teachers design activities, services, and programs for young exceptional children, they need to keep the entire family constellation in mind (Graves & Gargiulo, 1989). Swick (1987) believes that intervention efforts must support the parents as well as other family members. This emphasis represents a change for many early childhood special education professionals from child-focused to family-focused intervention. It emerges from Bronfenbrenner's (1979) persuasive arguments for acceptance of an ecological perspective, that suggests that a child's behavior cannot be understood without appreciating the influence of the family on the behavior of the youngster. Professionals must also recognize that a child is part of a larger social milieu—their family (Meyen, 1990). This interrelatedness also extends to other social systems such as the extended family and the community, which influence the functioning of the family.

Contemporary thinking about parent involvement now focuses on the family and emphasizes the family as a system of interactive, reciprocal relationships. Families consist of interlocking subsystems in which members do not function in isolation from each other (Cook et al., 1992). Events that affect one member, such as a child being labeled mentally retarded, are likely to influence the rest of the family. The Turnbull's (Turnbull & Turnbull, 1990) family systems approach is an example of one model that considers the interrelatedness of family functioning within the broader societal context. This model provides a framework for understanding and working with families. The Turnbulls identify four major components that should, according to Hanson and Lynch (1989), be considered when establishing parent-professional relationships. They propose that the effect of a child with a disability on the family (and vice versa) is influenced by the interactions between and within family characteristics, interaction, functions, and life cycle. Hanson and Lynch (1989) appropriately summarize the benefits of this approach by stating that "interventions planned from the perspective of a family as a system can be designed to better promote the needs and priorities of all family members rather than solely the needs of the member with the disability" (p. 244).

Parent-Professional Relationships

Meaningful parent-professional partnerships do not just happen; as with any relationship they must be created, cultivated, and nurtured (Graves & Gargiulo, 1989). Sefton and her colleagues (Sefton, Gargiulo, & Graves, 1991) believe that collaborative relationships should be built on mutual trust, respect, sensitivity, and cooperation. Mutual understanding is also important. Peterson (1987) supports this viewpoint. She reminds us that "parent-professional cooperation and teamwork involve a reciprocal relationship" (p. 439). As with teacher-student or parent-child interactions, in parent-professional relationships each party affects the other and influences the success or failure of the partnership. Each individual brings to the relationship his or her own set of baggage—strengths and weaknesses, skills and limitations, beliefs and attitudes.

PARENTS SPEAK OUT

Children are a product of their surroundings and experiences. A child who knows the love and affection of family can be happy and productive regardless of external limitations.

Sefton et al. (1991, p. 40) developed the following nonprioritized list of helpful suggestions aimed at constructing effective parent-professional relationships:

- DO examine your attitude toward handicapped children. Remember that the child with special needs is more like the typical preschooler than he or she is different.
- DON'T compare the typical and atypical youngster. Each child is an individual. DO recognize each child's uniqueness.
- DO focus on the youngster's strengths and abilities, not weaknesses.
- DON'T be critical of parents. Be sensitive to the unique demands encountered daily by parents of atypical children.
- DO remain open and accepting of parents' feelings and behavior. DON'T make judgments about the family situation or the parents' manner of dealing with their child.
- DO respect the parent's right to choose their level of involvement and participation.
- DO demonstrate respect, concern, and a sincere desire to work cooperatively with parents.
- DON'T threaten or manipulate parents into actions which may be uncomfortable for them.
- DO encourage parents to keep you informed of changes in the child's daily schedule or any situation that may affect the child, such as an illness or the birth of a sibling.
- DO share information with parents. Keep parents informed of progress, activities, or special events. Use a variety of techniques: telephone calls, personal notes, bulletin boards, or newsletters.
- When communicating with parents, DO listen with the "third ear." DON'T hear only what the parent is saying; DO listen for the underlying feelings.
- DO remember that nonverbal communication often can convey feelings more accurately than words. Verbal behavior must be consistent with your body language.
- DO be accountable. If you agree to assume responsibilities or gather information, be certain to follow through.
- DO communicate to parents in terms that are meaningful and understandable to them. DON'T use professional jargon.
- DO urge parents to discuss their concerns with you. Be available for the parents.
- DO solicit the parents' input. Seek suggestions from the parents about successful strategies for working with their son or daughter.

- DO express, in a nonthreatening manner, concerns and problems you have with the child. DON'T focus on the child, focus on the behavior.

Graves and Gargiulo (1989) encourage early childhood professionals to consider two other components. First, recommendations for tasks and activities should be individualized and family-focused. Second, teachers should be sensitive to how parents and caregivers cope with their role as a parent of an exceptional child. Parental reaction to exceptionality can significantly affect parent-professional interactions (Gargiulo, 1985).

Working effectively with parents should be a goal for all early childhood educators. Parental involvement is no longer a privilege but a right. IDEA and PL 99–457 both carry a ringing declaration for parent involvement and full participation. The aim of working together as a team is to provide children with disabilities the opportunity to achieve their maximum potential. The ultimate benefactor of collaborative efforts will be the young child with special needs.

SUMMARY

From its infancy twenty-five years ago, the field of early childhood special education has rapidly grown. Young children with special needs are now common in many early childhood programs and include youngsters with a wide range of exceptionalities. Empirical evidence strongly suggests that early childhood special education programs make a significant difference in the lives of young children and their families.

Federal legislation has played a major role in securing educational benefits for young children with special needs. Both IDEA and PL 99–457 mandate a variety of procedures and provisions ensuring that preschool and young school-age children with disabilities receive a full range of services appropriate to their unique and individual needs. Education for these children is now a right rather than a privilege.

To provide meaningful programming, it is important that early childhood educators first locate and identify who might need special services and then accurately diagnose the youngster's problem. An assessment of the child's strengths and weaknesses provides the foundation from which individualized instruction can be planned. Finally, early childhood teachers must evaluate the student's progress and effectiveness of their intervention.

Youngsters with special needs receive services in a variety of settings. These options range from center-based to home-based models and from preschool programs to the primary grades.

The curriculum for young children with special needs is individualized. It is based on the IEP goals and, for infants and toddlers, the tasks contained in the individualized family service plan. The curricular focus for preschoolers with exceptionalities is usually formulated around teaching developmentally appropriate skills within a functional framework.

Parents are important and active participants in the decision-making process affecting their child's education. They have a right to be involved.

Contemporary thinking suggests that parent involvement be expanded and become family-focused.

TEST YOUR UNDERSTANDING

1. What is the difference between a disability and a handicap?
2. Describe a least restrictive environment for a young child with special needs.
3. Identify at least four benefits of early intervention for youngsters with disabilities and at-risk children.
4. List the six major provisions contained in PL 94–142 (IDEA).
5. What is an individualized family service plan (IFSP)?
6. Discuss the differences among the following four terms: screening, diagnosis, assessment, and evaluation.
7. Identify three service delivery models for preschool children with special needs.
8. What is the function of an individualized educational program (IEP)?
9. Distinguish between developmentally based and functional approaches to curricula for young children with special needs.
10. Why should early childhood professionals establish meaningful partnerships with parents of young children with special needs?

LEARNING ACTIVITIES

1. Observe a young child with special needs who is being served in an integrated early childhood program. Observe a youngster with special needs in an early childhood program serving only children with special needs. How do the programs differ in meeting the children's needs? What are the strengths and weaknesses of each setting? Which program do you believe is better for young children with special needs?
2. Develop a comprehensive list of the services available in your community for children with special needs birth through age 5.
3. Interview the parent(s) of a young child with special needs. Ask the parent(s) about child care issues, access to medical care, educational opportunities, relationships with any siblings, financial considerations, discipline techniques, emotional reactions to being a parent of a young child with special needs, and any other issues affecting their lives and that of their child on a daily basis.

CHAPTER 13

Administration and Supervision of Early Childhood Programs

CHAPTER OUTLINE

The Demand for Child Care

Leadership: Control, Care, Collaborative, or Careless

- *The Leadership Factor*
- *Theories of Management*

Introduction to Administrative Planning

- *Purpose*
- *Goals*
- *Philosophy*
- *Policies and Procedures*
- *Budget Planning*
- *Annual Plan*

Administrative Procedures

- *Selecting Staff Members*
- *Staff Development*
- *Mentoring*
- *In-Service and Continuing Education*
- *Curriculum Development and In-Service*

Accreditation and Licensing

Parent and Community Relations

Budgets, Forms, and Records

The Evaluation Process

- *Environmental Evaluations*
- *Teacher Evaluation*
- *Evaluation of Children*
- *Administrator's Self-Evaluation*

KEY TERMS

Autocratic management

Democratic management

Laissez-faire management

Theory Z management

Mentoring

In-service

Accreditation

Licensing

National Academy of Early Childhood Programs

Department of Human Resources and Services

As the director interviewed Chris, the most recent applicant for the infant care position, it was clear that she was genuinely concerned about meeting the needs of young children. As they discussed the program, Chris frequently used the term *developmentally appropriate*.

"The term 'DAP' may mean different things to different people," the director commented. "What does it mean to you?"

Following a thoughtful pause, Chris responded, "It means understanding how children typically develop according to their age. So, in some ways, it is what we expect of children based on their ages—but it's really more than that. It also means knowing each child and taking care of individual and social needs as well." Chris was hired.

The foremost goal of quality child care and early education is to provide a total learning experience for children that fosters a young child's development. The frequent rationalization that "I want to own or direct an early childhood center because I love children" is admirable, but it is only a starting point in meeting the demands of an increasingly complex profession. From a management and business perspective, early childhood education has changed dramatically. Terms such as *effective schools, total quality management, site-based decision making*, and *outcome-based education* are finding a place at all levels of education and child care. The common threads of the new language are the essence of the administrators' and supervisors' task. A total quality management system incorporates an administrative plan that includes assessing the need for child care, staff, budget, communications, collaboration, evaluation, and in-service, as well as an ongoing study of child development, trends, and issues.

THE DEMAND FOR CHILD CARE

As a result of the compounding issues in America's dynamic society, the demands for child care have increased at exponential rates. The development of child care programs, as well as childhood education, appears to be influenced by the continuing trend of mothers entering the work force.

TEACHERS SPEAK OUT

I feel that the role of the director is most important in the success of a good day care center or an early childhood program. Just as a good principal can make or break a school, so can a director of an early childhood program. Find a good school and you have a great principal who knows his or her role, and how to carry out the duties; this applies also to a great director.

To meet the challenges of today's child care culture, an increased body of knowledge and research has given rise to programs for young children through churches and synagogues, in storefronts, in basements or city projects, in private homes, in elaborately built structures, in hospitals and factories, in public schools, and in state and federal [illegible] over the last twenty [illegible] day care, nursery, child [illegible] hild-hood, and many other child-[illegible] young children have been addresse[illegible] kindergartens, and primary programs fr[illegible] public sectors of society. The need for such [illegible] exceed current resources.

The Children's Defense Fund (1994) reports t[illegible] lion children under the age of 5 are cared for by so[illegible] a parent. Although society necessitates the demand [illegible] also suggests that child care professionals are "friend[illegible] family life" (Joffe, 1986, p. 1). The intrusion represents f[illegible] meeting the demographic needs of a community. It rep[illegible] the sensitivity of early childhood administrators to address fa[illegible]y and social challenges through the careful direction of programs [illegible]undy, 1991).

LEADERSHIP: CONTROL, CARE, COLLABORATIVE, OR CARELESS

Whether in private or public settings, early childhood programs must be effectively "managed and directed" to provide the best possible settings for young children. The importance of administration and supervision in early childhood programs is often overlooked.

The Leadership Factor

The positive results of effective administration and supervision cannot be denied. David Weikart (1979) presented a striking example of administrative supervisory significance in his review of three diverse preschool programs. In comparing a traditional school format for preschool to approaches such as the cognitively oriented curriculum, Schweinhart and Weikart (1986) found similar results in the academic aptitude and achievement of children. Weikart surmised that the common components of the observed settings were positive, active administrators and supervisors. It may be suggested that effective supervision contributed to the academic success of the children. It may be well to emphasize the close connection between the quality of administration and supervision and the effectiveness of the program. According to the National Academy of Early Childhood Programs, a division of the National Association for the Education of Young Children (NAEYC), effective leadership is a highly significant factor for the success of any early childhood program (Click & Click, 1990).

TEACHERS SPEAK OUT

As a director, it's my job to balance the day-to-day effectiveness of day care with the varied needs of parents, teachers, and children. On some days, this delicate balance tips in favor of one group or another. Then, the director steps back to assess the needs of all and prioritize them. She becomes the peacemaker, the soothsayer, and an advocate for all.

Several major reviews of preschool evaluation data identify the need for administrative and supervisory support as a key influence. The administrator's title may be that of instructional supervisor, director, supervisor, or principal. In the majority of schools for young children, the same person serves as the administrator, supervisor, and director. Titles may vary as well as the extent of responsibilities. For clarity, we use the term *administrator* in referring to this role in the following discussion.

The functions of an early childhood administrator are broad. Essentially, they are directed toward keeping the channels of communication open. Everyone in the organization is a part of a team, in which each person provides a unique and essential contribution (Bredekamp & Rosegrant, 1992).

Theories of Management

Theories of management would label the administrator we have been describing as a "democratic manager" or a "Theory Y manager." Management styles make a difference. Table 13.1 illustrates three administrative styles and perspectives of employee success. Theory X managers demonstrate the leadership style known as **autocratic management**. They are perceived as "controlling," while Theory Y approaches are more closely related to the **democratic management** style. Theory Y administrators are typically considered to be "caring" directors. A third style of leadership is **laissez-faire management**. The strategy for such an approach is "careless." The system is inconsistent and provides few reliable supports for employees, parents, or children. A final leadership style for purposes of this discussion is **Theory Z management**, in which the administrator integrates a democratic style when possible and an autocratic approach if immediate decisions are required. This management style is typically viewed as "collaborative."

Few successful administrators would disagree with the value of including staff members in the decision-making process. Staff inclu-

TABLE 13.1 Influences of Leadership Styles on Staff Performance

Laissez-Faire	Democratic	Autocratic
Productivity with administrator on site		
Limited productivity	Greater productivity	Short-term productivity
Productivity without administrator on site		
Limited productivity	Minimal decline of productivity	Disjointed productivity
Performance quality		
Lower quality than democratic style	Higher quality than other styles	Lower quality than other styles
Employee satisfaction		
Discontentment	Less discontentment	Direct and indirect discontentment
Interpersonal relationships		
Limited professional relationships	Greatest sense of community and professional relationships	Hostile, distant relationships
Absenteeism		
Less absenteeism than autocratic style	Less absenteeism than other styles	More absenteeism than other styles
Self-motivated independent behavior		
High levels of motivation and independent behavior	Less self-motivation and independent behavior than other styles	Dependent behavior

Source: Adapted and reprinted with the permission of Macmillan College Publishing Company from V. Hildebrand, *Management of child development centers*, 3rd ed. p. 114. Copyright © 1993 by Macmillan College Publishing Company, Inc.

sion in the decisions that govern the materials, policies, and procedures of a school allows all members to feel they are contributing to the success of the program. It is important to recognize the expertise of the early childhood teaching staff and effectively use their talents and knowledge to enhance the program for young children.

INTRODUCTION TO ADMINISTRATIVE PLANNING

Kaplan-Sanoff and Yablans-Magid (1981) view the early childhood administrator's role in three board areas. These areas are planning, operations, and evaluation. Under these titles, the major and minor responsibilities of the administrator's position can be categorized.

A closer look at the planning process offers a wide spectrum of duties. Management considers planning as the primary function of early childhood administration. Planning is required in each of the other areas. The philosophy of the program, short- and long-term goals, objectives, policy and procedure, and the utilization of staff and personnel are developed in the planning stage. Good early childhood programs do not just happen; they are developed by individuals who understand the physical, emotional, cognitive, and social needs of children.

Purpose

The planning process begins with an in-depth look at the purpose of the program and the need for early childhood in the community. Hewes and Hartmen (1972) observe the "purpose" for child care as the task professionals are motivated to achieve through careful planning. In other words, it is the reason for doing something. It is the "why" of the early childhood center. An assessment of the societal needs for the school will enable the administrator, staff, and planning committees to determine appropriate goals.

KIDS SPEAK UP

When you go to your office, are you in trouble?

Boy, 5 years old

Goals

Goals are defined as the long-term plan for a course of action with the hope that these directions will best meet the needs of the children. Information concerning the socioeconomic level of the area, local businesses, census reports, and local early childhood organizations suggest questions for planning (Almy, 1985).

Philosophy

The next step in the planning process concerns the administrator's personal philosophy of early childhood. The philosophy and commitment of the director is the framework of such a philosophy.

Kaplan-Sanoff and Yablans-Magid (1981) suggest that the purpose of the program can only be achieved through a well-defined plan of action. This approach does not mean the mechanizing of teaching activities. It does emphasize the need for a statement of goals and general objectives. The goals of early childhood programs will vary. But most educators would agree that the following developmentally appropriate elements should be considered in planning goals for child care:

1. To provide a wide range of experiences for the purposes of:
   a. Stimulating the child's interest in the world
   b. Motivating the child to desire and seek information and understanding
   c. Providing a basis for the development of concept
   d. Developing all the cognitive processes appropriate to the young child, including communication skills
2. To provide the child with a sense of self-worth and well-being
3. To accustom the child to a varied social environment
4. To establish rapport with parents

Policies and Procedures

The fourth step in the planning process is the development of written policies and procedures. Health and safety policies, admission policies, and personnel policies should be responsive to the situation.

Budget Planning

The final point to be considered in the planning process is the budget. It is the administrator's responsibility to maintain a sound understanding and ongoing control of the budget. A carefully planned system of collecting tuition, predicting major and minor purchases, and determining long-term capital outlay goals must be developed. We address the management of budgets in more detail in the discussion on administrative operations processes.

Annual Plan

Many hours and much confusion can be resolved before the school year begins through a clearly defined annual plan. In the *Nursery school and day care center management guide*, Cherry, Harkness, and Kuzma (1987) offer an overview of general planning concerns extending from general organizational points to specific elements of the children's programs. Table 13.2 suggests a checklist to assist in planning for a new year.

ADMINISTRATIVE PROCEDURES

The "operations process" involves the implementation of long-term plans. A saying among administrators is "plan the work and work the plan" (Carmichael, Clark, & Leonard, 1977, p. 123). An early childhood center requires literally hundreds of day-to-day activities.

TABLE 13.2 Checklist for Planning Early Childhood Programs

General Areas
- Planning the early calendar
- Planning and scheduling administrative responsibilities
- Determining class schedules
- Scheduling responsibilities of the teaching staff
- Scheduling the use of shared classroom space and equipment

Fiscal Areas
- Preparing the annual budget
- Purchasing equipment and supplies
- Organizing long-term needs

Spacing and Equipment
- Planning for equipping outdoor areas
- Ordering equipment for indoors
- Replacing equipment

Staffing
- Preparing job descriptions
- Recruiting applicants to fill staffing
- Preparing procedures that lead to wholesome interpersonal relationships
- Preparing the staff handbook for the new year

Enrollment
- Planning for the gradual orientation of newly enrolled children
- Being alert to enrollment needs

Parents
- Planning policies and procedures for parent orientation
- Preparing parents' library
- Planning and maintaining an active system of parent-school relationships

Health
- Determining systems for implementing health programs for the center or school
- Contacting recognized agencies able to help children with special problems

Safety
- Investigating safety aspects and determining programs for the school
- Keeping informed of the school's legal responsibilities and liabilities
- Planning for fire drills

Children's Program
- Organizing procedures for managing the children's program
- Planning field trips
- Planning the educational program for children with special needs
- Arranging for a sound nutritional program

Source: Adapted from C. Cherry, B. Harkness, and K. Kuzma, *Nursery school and day care management guide*, 2nd ed. (Belmont, California: David S. Lake Publishers, 1987).

Generally, the operating process includes overseeing the staff, in-service, curriculum development, forms, records and the law, parent and community relations, and budgets. Organization and self-analysis of time and resources are vital to the success of the administrator.

Selecting Staff Members

Perhaps the most important operational task of the administrator is that of staffing. Research indicates that the quality of each staff member is a critical issue in the development of programs for chil-

Interviews and a careful review of an applicant's credentials are essential in selecting qualified staff members.

dren (Decker & Decker, 1988). Because young children are learning from their environment and observations of adults, every member of the staff is a teacher despite role or title. For this reason, a major task of the administrator is to recruit and retain qualified staff members.

To employ a successful staff member, administrators must base their judgments on definite criteria. Some suggestions for selecting highly qualified staff members include observing whether the applicant has a professional philosophy that complements the goals of the center, the appropriate training and qualifications, and a pleasant, compatible personality.

Caruso and Faucett (1986) provide a comprehensive listing of possible professional positions related to child care personnel. An overview of the titles and descriptions found in Table 13.3 suggests the scope of staffing issues challenging an administrator.

Positions can be announced in several forms, including the newspaper, professional journals, and other media. Job descriptions should be brief but precise. The announcement should include required qualifications (experience, training, degrees), position duties, employment dates, and statements of salary or indication of competitive salary.

TABLE 13.3 Job Title of Personnel in Center-Based Early Childhood Programs

Supervisors		**Classroom Staff**		
Owner-Operator	Recreational Leader-Program Director-Supervisor-Head Teacher	***Teacher/Caregivers***	Unit Director	Program Aide
Director	Minister of Music and Church Growth	Teacher	Supervisor of Infant/Toddlers	Helper
Owner-Administrator	Director-Master Teacher	Lead Teacher	Manager	Classroom Assistant
Teacher-Administrator	Owner-Manager	Day Care Worker	Teacher/Director	Classroom Aide
Owner-Administrator-Teacher	Supervisor of Infant/Toddlers	Special Ed Teacher	Program Coordinator	Paraprofessional
Assistant Director of Education	Teacher/Director of Preschool	Group Teacher	Teacher/Director of Preschool	Teacher Aide
Lead Teacher	Teacher/Director	Group Leader	Assistant Director	Assistant Instructor
Administrator	Education Specialist	Foreign Language Teacher	Center Coordinator	Recreational Assistant
Administrator-Owner, Chair of the Board	Unit Director	Infant Caregivers	***Paraprofessionals***	Assistant Teacher
Lecturer-Head Teacher	Toddler Director	Potty Training Caregiver	Funding Aide	***Other***
President	Pre-primary Director	Co-teacher	Foster Grandparent	Assistant Professor
Executive Director	Assistant Administrator	Caregiver	Helping Teacher	RN Caregiver
Education Coordinator	Business Manager	Preschool Teacher	Teen Assistant	Nutritionist
Teacher		Head Teacher	Volunteer	Home Visitors
Pastor-Director		***Administrators***	Cook/Teacher Aide	Nurse
Child Care Coordinator		Pre-primary Director	Secretary/Aide	Education Specialist
Supervisor and Bookkeeper		Toddler Director	Floaters	Graduate Assistant
		Site Director		

(continued)

TABLE 13.3 Job Title of Personnel in Center-Based Early Childhood Programs *(continued)*

Non-classroom Staff		
Provide Support to Staff, Family, Children	Social Worker	Landscaper
Family Worker	Speech Therapists	Painter
Parent Advisory Committee President	Psychologists	***Clerical/Administrative Services***
Coordinator of Handicapped	***Security, Maintenance, Food, Transportation***	Secretary
Health Coordinator	Security Guard	File Clerk
Family Counselor	Custodian	Office Manager
Home-Based Visitor	Cook	Bookkeeper
Family Service Health Assistant	AM-PM Bus Monitor	Personnel Dept. Worker
Parent Volunteer Coordinator	Bus Driver	Office Assistant
Outreach Specialist	WEP Kitchen Aide	Assistant Bookkeeper
Fieldtrip Director	Food Service Manager	Purchaser
Community Developer	Maid	
Faculty Director	Housekeeper	
Faculty Advisor	Cleaner	
Helpers	Yard Supervision	
Volunteer		

Source: J. Caruso and T. Faucett, *Supervision of early childhood education: A developmental perspective* (New York: Teachers College, 1986), p. 34.

Using these basic criteria to eliminate applicants that obviously do not meet the standards of the recruiting statement, the next step in attaining a quality staff member is the interview process. Schedule the interview in advance, allowing enough time to evaluate the potential of each candidate. Although interview schedules are subject to individual expectation, twenty to thirty minutes is usually enough time to evaluate an applicant's abilities. Table 13.4 offers key issues for a quick check of an applicant's qualifications.

During the interview, it is essential to determine the applicants' personalities, knowledge of child development, and teaching styles. Questions should be open-ended to allow applicants an opportunity to express themselves. For example:

- Where do you look for ideas for activities for young children?
- When you have gathered a group together to sing as part of the planned sequence, but the children do not seem interested in singing, what do you do?
- What do you do when a mother complains that something must have happened at school because her child does not want to go to school anymore?
- When a child spends most of his time wandering around with his thumb in his mouth, not participating in the play activities, what do you do?
- What do you do when a 3-year-old refuses to do finger painting?

The interview should be followed with a careful review of the applicant's credentials and answers. The administrator may choose to invite the prospective staff member to visit the center when classes are being conducted. The visit may be followed by a second interview.

Staff Development

New employees need a period of orientation. During this time, the administrator must maintain close, continuous relationships that are both constructive and professional. If the new staff member is to

TABLE 13.4
Early Childhood Professional Application Quick Check

1. *Philosophy*. Does the candidate exhibit a philosophy similar to that of the program? Would this person be able to work within the framework of the program?
2. *Qualifications*. Is the candidate appropriately qualified for the position? (Consider the job description for the staff position.)
3. *Compatibility*. Would the personality of the candidate be compatible with the personalities and work habits of the staff members currently working in the center?

do the best possible job, orientation arrangements must convey the responsibilities and opportunities that the school offers (Bloom, 1988).

Mentoring

Mentoring refers to the process by which one experienced professional guides the development of a new professional. First-year teachers are often assigned to mentors for the duration of their initial year. Participants in such programs agree that the process is definitely beneficial. Through the critical first year, mentors provide insights and practical assistance in many first-time experiences. Although the potential for success in a positive mentoring environment is significant (Galvez-Hjornevick, 1986), the decision to implement a mentoring relationship cannot be made without considering essential issues. In the following sections, we discuss some key concerns regarding the process of mentoring and mentorships.

Identifying Mentors. An important administrative step is the identification of individuals who will serve as mentors for new employees. Daresh and Playko (1990) address this point by emphasizing that mentors should effectively and consistently demonstrate the highest professional standards. Successful mentors are selected from volunteers who are willing to share their expertise with others. They should be assigned to the same campus as the new employee and preferably work with the same age group of children (Playko, 1990).

Characteristics of potentially successful mentors include keen analytical abilities, good communication skills, and effective techniques for organization. A final concern must be the prospective mentor's ability to work well with others, including parents and colleagues. The mentor is a guide, not an evaluator or supervisor. Effective mentoring relationships often evolve into mutual respect and friendship.

Determining the Mentor's Tasks. A mentoring or "coaching" relationship allows the new staff member to interact with an experienced colleague. Such experiences promote a feeling of professional community and program continuity. To accomplish such outcomes, a mentor's tasks may include the following (DiGeronimo, 1993):

- Answer questions about the system, including routines, processes, and expectations.
- Offer advice about instruction and planning, including lesson development, strategies, and teaching approaches.
- Help with information about deadlines and records.

Early childhood mentors model effective teacher/child activities for new teachers.

- Share ideas for parent communications.
- Assist in establishing routines and transitions.
- Consult during school and after school, as needed.
- Address the perceived needs of colleagues.
- Maintain an encouraging and supportive posture.
- Serve as a professional confidant or sounding board.

Training Mentors. The selection of highly qualified mentors does not guarantee success. Training and administrative support are vital to the project. Mentor orientation includes the following points:

- Provide opportunities to develop mutual confidence and set the stage for the new staff member to build rapport with staff members.
- Interpret and clarify the school's purposes, goals, philosophy, and general operating principles of the program.
- Provide written information, oral explanations, and demonstrations of the job expectations.

Concrete information can dispel many teacher insecurities and reinforce that mentorships are a collaborative effort. Working with young children is both physically and emotionally demanding. Teachers must be able to control emotional expressions, including anxiety and anger as well as enthusiasm. Teachers need opportunities for the stimulation of adult intellectual exchanges so that their teaching styles do not stagnate. Mentorships provide not only support for the new staff member but also stimulation for the mentoring faculty.

In-Service and Continuing Education

Effective early childhood programs embrace new ideas, the development of professional skills, and continuous training. The terms *staff development, in-service,* and *continuing education* are used to describe professional growth experiences. A successful administrator gives staff members opportunities to exchange ideas and information. Many licensing agencies require that the administrator allot a prescribed number of training hours or days per year (Bloom, 1993).

Group Dynamics of Staff Development. **In-service** has been described as participatory supervision. Continuing training may take many forms. These experiences should be developed to meet the needs and interests of the various teachers. Administrators have found the following techniques to be effective in-service strategies for involving group dynamics:

- Staff meetings involving group discussion
- Presentations by staff members
- Presentations by guest specialists selected by the faculty
- Participation by staff members in the selection of topics
- Video tapes screened and selected by faculty members
- Demonstrations by the administrator

Individualizing Staff Development. Staff development can take the form of a one-to-one, in-service approach between the administrator and the early childhood teacher or care provider. After observing the classroom for a few days, the administrator briefly assumes the teacher's role to demonstrate specific teaching or management styles. This method, combined with frequent discussions with the teacher, constitutes positive in-service training.

Cooperative In-Service. Teachers can provide their own in-service in much the same way as individualized staff development. Early childhood teachers can be encouraged to exchange classrooms for a short time, work with each other's children, and develop a prescription for changing each other's environments. The teachers may contribute ideas for resolving class management concerns or the problems of individual students.

Administrators can provide additional in-service by creating a professional library that is easily accessible by the teachers. A pleasant setting, where teachers can escape the daily routine, could include journals and periodicals offering practical solutions to child care, development, and management. A bulletin board for articles, notes, and announcements establishes an open-ended forum for disseminating ideas.

Since staff meetings and in-services should have a purpose, prepare an agenda in advance. Teachers should not be expected to listen attentively for great lengths of time. To make the in-service more relevant, the administrator can involve the teachers in the selection of topics. A discussion list might include the topics listed in Table 13.5. General topics can be developed to address specific age groups from birth through childhood (ages 0–11 years).

Curriculum Development and In-Service

In-service offers a format for curriculum development as well as professional growth. The term *curriculum* has changed in meaning as it relates to early childhood. Originally, it referred to a course of academic study. During the 1960s, it assumed a much broader meaning, encompassing all classroom experiences. By the late 1970s, it again acquired a narrower definition, which limited its meaning to a set of activities prescribed for some clearly defined purpose. But gradual

TABLE 13.5 In-service Discussion Topics

Topic	Age Group
Health and safety of children	Birth through childhood
Personality of the child	Birth through childhood
Sensorimotor development	Birth through 2 years
Auditory and visual perception	Birth through 7 years
Cognitive development issues	Birth through childhood
New ways of using old materials	Birth through childhood
Improving the class environment	Birth through childhood
Improving parent-staff relationships	Birth through childhood
Continuing child evaluation	Birth through childhood
Emotional growth of the child	Birth through childhood
Visitors in the center or class	Birth through childhood
Spaces and places in the learning environment	Birth through childhood
Stereotyping of sex roles of young children	Birth through childhood
Animals in the center	Age 2 through childhood
Cooking as preparation for learning	Age 2 through childhood
Music centers in the center	Birth through childhood
Creative ideas for the classroom	Birth through childhood
Management of learning centers	Birth through childhood
Project approaches and unit themes	Age 3 through childhood

changes through the late 1980s and into the 1990s suggest that the term *curriculum* is currently used to refer to all activities engaged by the child. This approach addresses both prepared and incidental episodes. Such a definition of curriculum is more reflective of the developmentally appropriate philosophy of early childhood that identifies the child as an active participant of learning. Children are therefore perceived as the catalysts of curriculum and not necessarily as recipients of curriculum (Bredekamp, 1992).

The word *curriculum* is often replaced in educational jargon by the work *program*. Programs are conceived as planned experiences. This interpretation would suggest that teachers serve as guides who manipulate experiences through which children construct their own learning.

As the instructional and curriculum leader, the administrator is responsible for developing an appropriate curriculum philosophy. The curriculum must ultimately lead to the individual development of those who are directly or indirectly involved. In some aspects of instruction, the teacher needs only to ensure that the necessary props are available. In any case, planning is necessary to provide materials appropriate to children at their particular stage of development.

The implementation of an appropriate leadership style may well make the difference between successful and unsuccessful coordination of curriculum. First, the administrator must exhibit the ability to guide staff members in completing the fundamental steps of the curriculum development process. The administrator must understand and use both group and individual communication skills to motivate and involve the staff in the curriculum philosophy. The ability to apply the principles of planned change while working with teachers and staff members often requires diplomacy and compromise.

Our high-quality school is a place where our children are safe, nurtured, and stimulated. A valuable bonus to our family is that the teachers and director serve as an excellent resource and sounding board on parenting, child development, and family issues that do and don't relate directly to school life.

The utilization of informal and formal authority is essential to the success of curriculum changes. The inclusion of proper group process skills throughout the initial procedures for change contribute to a sense of community and mutual respect for differences of opinion and interpretation. The collaborative development of curriculum is often the key to change and innovation.

The administrator must be well versed in the wide range of programs available, curriculum designs, and scheduling. Expertise in these areas will assist in guiding the development of a curriculum in keeping with the philosophy of the school.

ACCREDITATION AND LICENSING

Another role of the administrator that cannot be neglected in this discussion regards the legal aspects of supervising and managing an early childhood center. The administrator has the responsibility for maintaining required licenses. If the center chooses to participate in a voluntary accreditation system, the administrator is ultimately accountable for maintaining the guidelines. Whether the center is accredited or licensed, agencies exist for the purpose of setting and enforcing the minimum operational requirements for the health, safety, and general welfare of children served by the facilities under their jurisdiction.

Although state-required licensing elements vary, some issues are common to all. Table 13.6 describes generalized licensing and registration requirements.

TABLE 13.6
Accreditation and Licensing Requirements

1. Regulations concerning space
   a. Zoning
   b. Building codes
   c. Fire
   d. Health
   e. General regulations concerning room size, toilets, sewage, ventilation, and number of children served
2. Using the space
   a. Parking
   b. Furnishings and equipment
3. Children
   a. Ages of children
   b. Number of children for the space
   c. Nondiscriminatory provisions
   d. Physician's verification of health
4. Staff
   a. Minimum age
   b. Educational requirements
   c. Physician's report of physical and mental health
5. Financing and management
   a. Record keeping
   b. Board of directors

Public schools are accredited by the state agency in which they operate and are regulated by the interpretations of the local school district. Early childhood programs in the public schools are therefore associated through the primary and middle elementary school settings. The administrator or building principal must therefore be effective in the full spectrum of childhood education and supervision. Standards for licensing and accreditation may also be directed by the National Academy of Early Childhood Programs (The Academy) or licensed state-associated systems such as the Department of Human Resources and Services (Decker & Decker, 1988). Because regulations vary from agency to agency, it is the direct responsibility of the administrator to understand and maintain the standards required by the agency that accredits the school. In this regard, the administrator's role cannot be ambivalent. To appreciate the administrator's role, we must first understand the administrator's position as a middle manager. Typically, the center is owned by its patrons. The patrons may be citizens of a state and community who are afforded ownership through tax revenues. This system is best represented through the public schools.

In private or proprietary programs, the patrons may be the owners by virtue of their functions as "customers" of the center. Their tuition and support provide a degree of direction for management by virtue of their customer status. The owners of the system collectively decide the direction of a center. As individuals, however, they can recommend—but not change—the goals and objectives of a system. The administrator has been charged by virtue of the objectives established for the program. The administrator has been placed in a role of leadership as a result of his or her training, experience, and credentials.

PARENT AND COMMUNITY RELATIONS

Schools represent a major community and family investment. They function not only as consumers but also as valuable resources. Opportunities abound for the community to become involved in the school. Effective administrators "read" their communities well, enabling them to determine the best solution to major issues. It is generally accepted that the public is sincerely concerned about "its most valuable resource—their children." Consequently, the administrator may frequently be called upon to interpret the early childhood program's philosophy, goals, and purposes to the public.

Many of the public's questions are predictable and may be answered in a brochure. The brochure should include:

- The school name, address, phone number, and contact person
- The hours and days in session

Administrators, faculty, and parents provide a well rounded decision making panel for early childhood programs.

- Ages of children served, and any restrictions
- Tuition and other fees
- Purpose, philosophy, and goals
- Professional affiliation, if relevant

To increase community support, the administrator can involve parents in a wide variety of ways. Parents can be invited to serve as classroom assistants or substitutes. A parents' bulletin board could be used for articles, ideas, and announcements. The administrator might arrange for parent conferences to tell the community about the services an early childhood center provides. Parent organizations can contribute significantly to the success of a program.

Often, parents are unable to attend parent meetings. Administrators of effective programs recognize that alternatives are necessary to maintain an open line of communications. Table 13.7 provides some suggestions for maintaining a parent and community exchange.

Parents who are treated as welcome friends will be among the school's best supporters. The administrator has the opportunity to communicate with parents in many positive ways. Unfortunately, many parents and administrators do not meet unless there is a problem.

TABLE 13.7 Positive Parent and Community Relations

1. Assure parents they are welcome.
2. Allow parents to use the facility on evenings and weekends for meetings, special occasions, organizational meetings, etc. Some rules must be followed.
3. Make a comment each day to every parent about their child: a special activity he enjoyed, his or her clothing, or an appreciated personality trait.
4. Provide a pad for parents to jot down special instructions for the day.
5. Offer coffee or tea to early morning visitors.
6. Sponsor a winter boot and snowsuit exchange.
7. Have a lost-and-found box for small items.
8. Consider adopting an attendance policy that requires the parents to sign the child in and out for the day. Parents must accompany the child into the room, providing a contact point between the staff and parents.
9. Collect fees in person, and use the opportunity to solicit comments on the services parents are receiving.
10. Provide regular newsletters. Include requests for special needs items, the words to new songs, fingerplays, and announcements.
11. Invite parents to arrange their lunch hours so they can be their child's guest for lunch.
12. Always respond to parents' suggestions and criticisms.

Source: Adapted from L. Curtis. "Twenty ideas to help parents enjoy your program," *Day Care and Early Education*, 6 (Fall 1978), p. 43.

The administrator who actively participates in the community demonstrates an enthusiasm for the city and its people. By remaining actively visible, the administrator keeps the lines of communication between the school and the community continuously open. Professional associations outside the field of education can considerably influence the long- and short-term success of the program.

BUDGETS, FORMS, AND RECORDS

The term *accountability* has been used repeatedly in recent years with regard to education. Financial accountability is a major concern in the administrator's operation of an early childhood center. Budgets should be carefully designed systems for managing the financial aspects of the school. Early childhood programs are expensive. In combination with the maintenance of records, forms, and files, budgets can be extremely time-consuming. The business aspects of early childhood administration are often the most demanding and least interesting (Boyer, Gerst, & Eastwood, 1990).

Approximately 85 percent of the money for private child care comes from tuition. For this reason, estimates of enrollment and tuition are vital in determining the type of program an administrator can plan. Specific systems of money collection and recording must be developed. A clearly identified procedure allows for time efficiency. To determine an effective budget for a tuition-based program, the administrator must first consider the previous two years of enrollment and funds collected. The second concern is that of required expenditures. Expense factors to be considered are found in Table 13.8.

The major funding of a school budget goes into providing high-quality standards of staffing that ensure maximum benefits to the children. Many administrators satisfy this problem by supplementing their teaching staff with volunteers, aides, or students from local universities. Where such programs are possible, older children (fifth or sixth grades, or junior high school age) can serve as student aides during the day.

Public schools do not handle the staffing dilemma in the same way. Depending on the state and personnel units granted to the schools, one staff member can be assigned large numbers of children.

In the tuition-based program, as much as 50 percent of the budget may be appropriated for the salaries of staff members. Many administrators find it necessary to supplement their programs with extra sources of money. Possible sources of income for the early childhood program include

- A nonrefundable registration fee
- Grants for research or special services
- Federal subsidies for children of working parents
- Direct tax support, such as public-funded programs
- Community groups
- Tuition payments (sometimes referred to as scholarships) for individual children, given by group or individual donors

TABLE 13.8
Budget Considerations

1. Salaries
- *a.* Director
- *b.* Teachers
- *c.* Nonteaching staff members
- *d.* Custodial staff
- *e.* Maintenance

2. Fixed expenditures
- *a.* Housing for school
- *b.* Insurance
- *c.* Seasonal and annual events

3. All other expenditures
- *a.* Food
- *b.* Equipment
- *c.* Supplies
- *d.* Utility
- *e.* Advertising
- *f.* Telephone
- *g.* Transportation

4. Petty Cash

5. Deductibles

6. Miscellaneous items

- Specific items donated by organizations of parents
- Fund-raising by the school
- Schools in private settings that may be subsidized through religious affiliations

The importance of careful planning and constant management cannot be overemphasized. In review, the operations process of early childhood programs includes a wide range of responsibilities. Additional concerns for early childhood administrators include nutritional responsibilities, equipment purchases, time management, daily routines, and substitute staff. Each of the previously mentioned areas requires considerable time and administrative consideration.

THE EVALUATION PROCESS

Evaluation is a critical function of the early childhood administrator. Not unlike the planning and operation processes, the evaluation process includes several areas. If an early childhood program is to continue to succeed, there must be a realistic means of providing in-

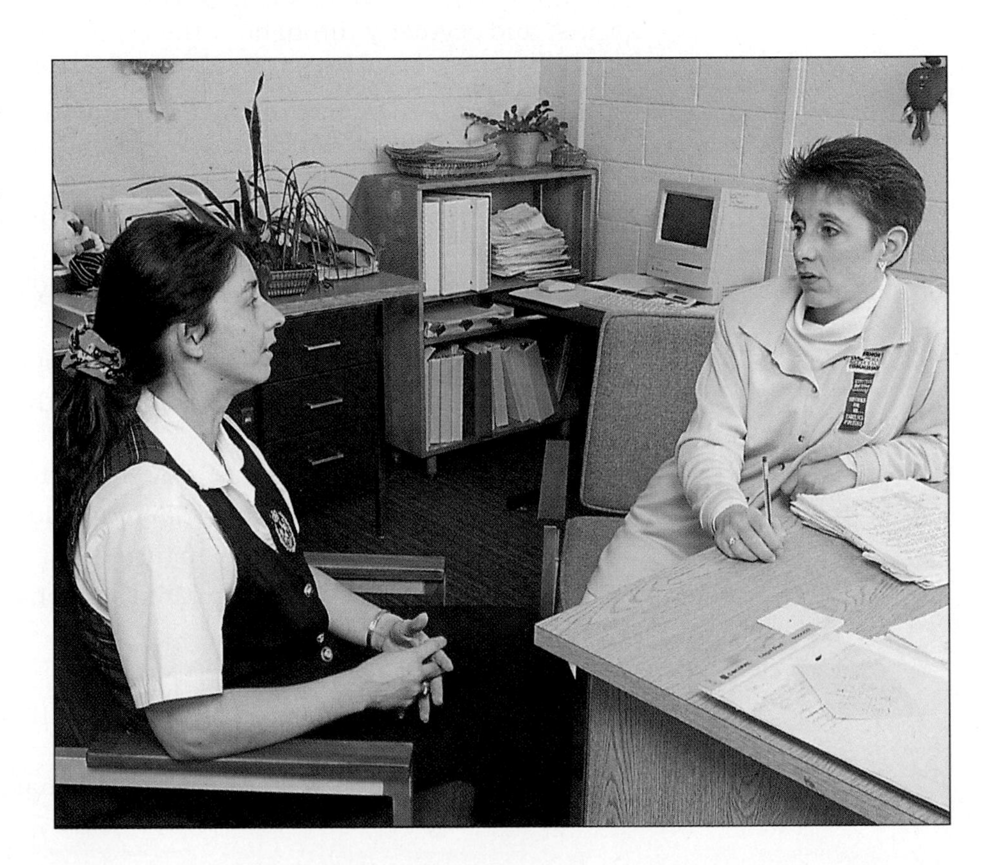

Collaborative development of programs depends on open communication among staff members, administrators, and parents.

formation about the program. Evaluation is a continuous component of the administrative process. There is a responsibility on the part of administration to identify areas of strengths and weaknesses within the center in order to determine appropriate solutions (Krechevsky, 1991).

Social science defines evaluation as being a process of research to gather information for decision making. It is a field that is continuously evolving. In the evaluation process, all aspects of the early childhood center are considered as a delivery system. In earlier decades, only a few of the most developed and well-funded programs conducted evaluations. Today, evaluations are required for most early childhood programs under state, local, and in some cases nationally recognized accreditation procedures.

The evaluation of an early childhood program involves both qualitative and quantitative reviews of the environment, curriculum, teachers, staff, and children's progress. Each of these areas contributes to the program's success.

Environmental Evaluations

Environmental evaluations can be conducted before the school year begins, and regularly throughout the semesters. Environments must be child-centered and as serviceable as possible.

- Divide the room into distinct areas of interest for centers (home, art block, quiet, construction, sand and water, music, and movement).
- Store materials in the area where they are used by the children.
- Provide an adequate amount and variety of materials in each area.
- Reserve space for displaying and storing children's work.
- Have each adult familiarize children with names and contents of each area.
- Change or add equipment throughout the year.
- Design the new preschool facility to include
  –Bathroom with child-level fixtures
  –Electrical outlets above children's reach or covered
  –Bulletin boards
  –Ample storage
- Ensure that centers are well stocked with appropriate materials.
- Store books in open-faced racks, and change the books periodically.

- Design room arrangements that accommodate children with special needs.

Evaluate the playground for the safety and developmental potential of an individual child. Offer equipment for large motor development and include areas (such as playhouses) for sociodramatic play. It is the administrator's responsibility to make certain all equipment is in good repair. A checklist can help the administrator in keeping an accurate record of materials and equipment conditions.

Teacher Evaluation

Teacher evaluation is a delicate art. It requires the administrator to be well informed about child development and to thoroughly understand the teacher's goals and objectives. The administrator's job is to determine if those goals and objectives are accomplished.

The best plans or tools are of little value if they are not implemented. Evaluation is, therefore, an essential part of every teacher's growth and a continual striving for improvement. Table 13.9 summarizes the administrative evaluation strategy.

Table 13.10 presents a sample appraisal log that can be used for staff development through teacher evaluation.

Evaluation of Children

Any evaluation of child performance is actually an evaluation of the program. If children are growing and developing physically, mentally, and emotionally, and at rates appropriate to their needs, the program can be considered a success. But if children are not developing, it is necessary for the administrator to investigate why the program is not meeting the needs of children.

"When a program is genuinely committed to assessment as a means of facilitating children's development and learning, numerous procedures can be used to assess each child's progress and to provide feedback on the effectiveness of the program for the child" (Almy, 1985, p. 227). Almy offers several types of evaluation for assessing student growth and development.

- Observations—portfolios including authentic assessment
- Informal or situational assessments of independent, collaborative, and dependent situations
- Checklists and teacher-developed appraisal systems
- The children's products
- Teacher records and accumulative data
- Standardized testing

TABLE 13.9 An Evaluation Policy for Administrators

1. Be thoroughly familiar with the evaluation policy of early childhood programs.
   a. Understand the evaluation instrument.
   b. Determine staff members to be evaluated.
   c. Carefully plan and explain the evaluation process to the staff.
      - Develop an atmosphere of trust, confidence, sharing, and mutual understanding.
      - Clarify mutual expectations.
2. Consider several factors in arriving at the final evaluation.
   a. Conduct classroom observations as the building blocks of the evaluation process.
      - Keep mental records of your observations.
      - Look for examples of specific teaching skills.
      - Prepare a record of observations and suggestions to discuss at a conference with the teacher.
   b. Carefully consider the teacher's competencies in job-related areas.
      - Are instructional competencies for individual children addressed?
      - Are teacher-child relations directed toward the growth of child competencies?
      - Are co-curricular activities provided to integrate ideas?
      - Are clerical duties of teachers clearly communicated?
      - Are staff duties effectively attained?
      - Are personal characteristics positive?
      - Is professional growth ongoing?
   c. Encourage teacher input as part of the evaluation process.
      - Allow teachers to submit a self-evaluation.
      - Be prepared to discuss information regarding the evaluation.
3. Conduct an effective evaluation conference as a vital element in the growth and development of good teaching skills.
   a. Before the conference, consider these key points.
      - What is the specific purpose of the conference?
      - How well does the person to be evaluated meet the job objectives (strengths and weaknesses as a teacher)?
      - Which performance areas need improvement?
      - Are assistance and resources available to help improve performance and progress toward reaching goals?
   b. Establish a positive and constructive environment during the conference.
4. Promote the evaluation process as pivotal in the development and growth of a strong educational environment within the school.
   a. The attitudes of the administrator and staff are important.
   b. Communication and understanding are essential for administrators.

The administrator should be familiar with the various types of pupil assessment for the district, campus, or system of child development centers of which the center is a part. Teachers should be encouraged to maintain accurate records of student progress and be able to interpret the findings. The success of young children in early childhood programs is an excellent demonstration of the continued need for such programs.

TABLE 13.10 Teacher Performance Data

Date	Observed	Comments
Classroom (Observations)		
• Organization of materials		
• Maintenance of materials		
• Required information displayed		
• Children's work displayed		
• Instructional centers		
• Atmosphere		
• Inviting environment		
Student Outcome (Observations)		
• Participation in class		
• Meets teacher objectives		
• Individual needs are noted		
• Appropriate materials are available		
• Cooperative opportunities are developed		
• Variation of activities		
Teaching Approaches (Observations)		
• Professional appearance		
• Voice		
• Appropriate groupings		
• Effective use of materials		
• Management of groups		
• Individual differences		
• Awareness of time		
• Advanced preparation		
• Rapport with parents		
• Participation in professional activities		
• Professional attitude		
• Use of agency resources		
• Participation in training		
Conference Notes		
Goals		
Concerns		
Teacher		
Evaluator		

Administrator's signature __________ Teacher's signature __________

Administrator's Self-Evaluation

In an effort to effectively stimulate the development of teachers, parents, and children, the administrator must constantly assess the administrative success of the program. It is not enough just to agree with the principles of good supervision; they must also be practiced. The most effective administrative evaluation includes an analysis of

TABLE 13.11 Administrator's Self-Evaluation Questions

1. Am I enthusiastic about the day?
2. Do I greet my staff and co-workers in an open manner that suggests I am glad to see them?
3. Am I flexible?
4. Do I accept suggestions and criticisms gracefully?
5. Do I maintain an attitude of self-assurance?
6. Am I patient even with those who depend on me?
7. Do I help others feel comfortable by being alert to their feelings?
8. Do I invite conversations?
9. Am I considerate of others in the requests made of them?
10. Am I practical in my expectations?
11. Am I mature in considering the problems of staff members?
12. Do I keep up with research in early childhood?
13. Do I maintain my role as a supervisor and remain alert to any changing responsibilities?
14. Do I organize for maximum efficiency?
15. Do I consider the inner world of the child in dealing with individuals?
16. Do I promote positive relationships among others and between myself and others?
17. Have I made a practice of taking an overview of situations rather than getting lost in details?
18. Do I encourage professional and personal growth for staff members?
19. Am I diplomatic in my dealings with others?
20. Am I dependable? Generous? Honest? Cooperative? Loyal? Respectful? Kind? Objective? Empathetic?

past performances. Table 13.11 presents a series of questions that may offer constructive insights for administrative self-evaluation.

SUMMARY

The duties of the administrator in early childhood are vast. These duties demand of the administrator competencies and skills in many areas. And the role of the administrator is expanding into other areas as early childhood education continues to grow.

The future of early childhood programs in the United States is uncertain, due in part to present economic constraints. Federal financial assistance is often on the edge of funding reductions.

The administrator may be called upon to enter the political arena in order to express the demand for quality early childhood programs. It is certain that the administrator will work closely with parents, teachers, and the community to ensure that early childhood programs do not encounter financial deprivation.

An important obligation of the early childhood administrator is continued professional growth through education and research. We anticipate that in addition to personal growth in these areas, greater emphasis will be placed on early childhood directors by university programs and administrative certification. Currently, a growing number of state programs require courses in the administration of early childhood education.

The role of the administrator is vital to the success of early childhood programs. It requires the very best of efforts by dedicated professionals.

TEST YOUR UNDERSTANDING

1. Discuss the leadership style most appropriate for administration of a child care program.
2. List five topics critical for a brochure describing an early childhood center.
3. Describe three strategies for involving parents in the center.
4. What is the significance of mentoring as it relates to individuals entering the early childhood profession?
5. What role does evaluation play in the continuing development of an early childhood center?
6. What would you assume to be the major tasks of an early childhood administrator?

LEARNING ACTIVITIES

1. Interview an early childhood administrator from the public and private sector (a public school principal and the director of a private or not-for-profit center). Discuss with each administrator their philosophy of early childhood, goals, assessment, and successes.
2. Tour an early childhood center and develop a marketing advertisement (such as a brochure) for the center.
3. Develop a series of questions you would ask a potential staff member applying for an early childhood system in your center.
4. Contact the area licensing agent for day care and nursery to determine the minimum standards for licensing child care in your area.

CHAPTER 14

Parent-Teacher Partnerships

CHAPTER OUTLINE

Developing Partnerships
- *Benefits*
- *Teacher Behaviors*

The Ecological Perspective

A Systems Framework

The Empathetic Element

Understanding Families

Communicating with Parents
- *Communication Styles*

Barriers to Collaboration

The Empowerment Paradigm

Parent-Teacher Conferences
- *Planning for Conferences*
- *Pitfalls*

Partnership Programs
- *Parents as Teachers*
- *Minnesota Early Childhood Family Education Program*
- *Kenan Trust Family Literacy Project*

KEY TERMS

Ecological perspective

Parents as Teachers

Minnesota Early Childhood Family Education Program

Kenan Trust Family Literacy Project

"I am so sorry," said the obviously distraught mother on the other end of the telephone line as the preschool teacher answered the phone. "I promise you my child will never behave badly in school again."

The teacher, confused for a moment, reassured the parent. "Nothing happened in school today that warrants an apology."

"Oh, but Reece told me he was really bad today." The teacher smiled to herself, remembering the children's rendition of the *Three Little Pigs*, and explained Reece's role as the big bad wolf in the impromptu performance. The mother chuckled and exclaimed, "Now I understand. He told me he was the baddest in the class today."

The teacher reassured the parent, explained the successful activity, and concluded, "Reece was the best bad wolf in school today."

A major challenge confronting the educational community is the development, nurturance, and maintenance of effective parent-teacher partnerships. For too long, many educators have failed to take advantage of building mutually beneficial relationships with parents. There is now a growing understanding that parents are the first and most important teachers of their children. Schools are very important to parents and families, but also need the support and resources of parents if maximum success is to be reached for individual children. The best type of relationship is clearly one in which parents are viewed as full-fledged partners with the teacher. This concept of true collaboration requires shared trust and equality in the relationship (Graves & Gargiulo, 1989).

Peterson (1987) identified several reasons why an effective parent-professional partnership is a critical component of successful early childhood education programs:

- Parents are the key teachers, socializing agents, and caregivers for their children.
- Parents can be effective intervention agents.
- Parents are in a particularly strategic position to note changes in the child's behavior or development.
- Parents' perspectives on the child's strengths and weaknesses can be extremely helpful to the professional in planning and implementing appropriate programs.

This type of involvement offers a framework for parents to build a positive perspective about their child as well as their own abilities as parents. Initiating partnerships during the child's early years offers many benefits for children, parents, and teachers.

DEVELOPING PARTNERSHIPS

The foundation for effective partnerships must include parents' and teachers' understanding of their roles in supporting children's development and learning. This also includes gaining an appreciation for their own growth as a parent or teacher (Swick, 1991). This process can enable schools and families to better realize how each can support the other in becoming full partners in the child's education and the community's development (Schaefer, 1982). Galinsky (1990) noted that the early years are not only a formative period for young children but also a challenging time for parents and teachers.

Parents welcome and need support as they face the many challenges of family life during their children's early years. Schaefer (1982) has stated that during the early stages of parenthood, the core behaviors required of parents for supporting healthy family life are formed: nurturing, teaching, and modeling.

Benefits

Efforts to support this time of parenting and family life have yielded several clear benefits (Galinsky, 1990; Gordon, 1977; Lightfoot, 1978; Swick, 1991):

- Parents can acquire information and support on critical parenting and child/family issues.
- Parents can engage in experiences in which they begin the development of their core parenting behaviors.
- Parents and children can engage in early partnership behaviors with significant helpers beyond the home.
- Families can alleviate or resolve at-risk situations that threaten them and can strengthen their ability to have meaningful relationships with each other and with their helpers in the community.

TEACHERS SPEAK OUT

We feel that parents are our school's most valuable resource. It is important that parents take an equal responsibility in observing the development of their child, and share those observations with the school. Together, we can best serve the needs of children.

While many schools historically have left these early involvements with parents to others in the community, a much more collaborative system involving teachers with parents and other helping professionals in the community is emerging as a way of enhancing children's school success (Cataldo, 1987; Comer, 1986; Epstein, 1984; Powell, 1988; Schaefer, 1982; Swick, 1984; Swick, 1991). A large part of the family's early learning style is formed before the child starts kindergarten (Swick, 1991). For some time, effective teachers have engaged in or supported these partnership efforts with families. An increase in partnerships has been partly the result of a recognition that parents, like teachers and other social systems, are growing, dynamic, and complex.

Teacher Behaviors

Initial experiences of children and parents in school environments should be nurturing and caring. Teachers should learn as much as possible about each child and family so that they can create positive strategies to build a foundation for school success. It is critical that the teacher be inviting and encouraging to parents about the child's classroom activities and school. Positive teacher attitudes and the involvement of parents are two key processes in ensuring a successful initiation to the child's school environment. Swick and Graves (1993, pp. 181–182) suggest five teacher behaviors in this process:

- Engage in shared learning experiences with parents where a success focus becomes the primary concern.
- Learn about parent and family cultural values and integrate these into the early relationships and activities with children and parents.
- Offer parents several different ways to get involved and provide supports that enable them to establish an involvement ethic.
- Engage parents right from the start in planning and managing children's early learning experiences with the school.
- Provide and pursue family-learning experiences (e.g., parent education, adult education, family reading) that focus on school readiness and success at the beginning of school entry.

During the past several decades, a perspective has emerged that gives early childhood educators new insights and strategies for relating to the needs of children and families during the child's early years. This view is called the ecological perspective.

THE ECOLOGICAL PERSPECTIVE

While the **ecological perspective** has a continuing historical foundation, its origins are in the work of the European gestalt psychologists (*gestalt* means "pattern" in German.) The gestalt perspective emphasizes the unity and integration of the whole person. For gestalt theorists, the human being cannot be reduced to the sum of its parts, as behaviorists believe.

The ecological perspective was popularized by Urie Bronfenbrenner's *The ecology of human development* (1979) as a means of understanding how people develop and learn. The ecological environment can be conceived as a set of nested structures, each inside another, like a set of Russian dolls. At the innermost level is the immediate setting containing the developing person. The developing person should be viewed as a growing, dynamic, and active individual who influences and is influenced by other people. The interaction between the developing person and the environment is viewed as a two-directional or reciprocal relationship.

In other words, a process of mutual accommodation occurs, to which both person and environment contribute. The environment that is relevant to human development is not limited to a single, immediate setting (home, school, or work). The ecological environment is broader and includes immediate settings and interactions between immediate settings (the relationship between home and school or home and workplace) and larger settings, including the culture (which also influences specific settings).

Bronfenbrenner (1979) argued that

> the understanding of human development demands more than the direct observation of behavior on the part of one or two persons in the same place; it requires examination of multiperson systems of interaction not limited to a single setting and must take into account aspects of the environment beyond the immediate situation containing the subject. (p. 21)

As Figure 14.1 illustrates, the ecological environment is composed of four structural levels (Bronfenbrenner, 1979, pp. 22–26):

- A microsystem is a pattern of activities, roles, and interpersonal relations experienced by the developing person in a given setting with particular physical and material characteristics.
- A mesosystem comprises the interrelations among two or more settings in which the developing person actively participates (such as, for a child, the relations among home, school, and neighborhood peer group; for an adult, among family, work, and social life).
- An exosystem refers to one or more settings that do not involve the developing person as an active participant, but in which events occur that affect, or are affected by, what happens in the setting containing the developing person.
- A macrosystem refers to consistencies, in the form and content of lower-order systems (micro-, meso-, and exo-) that exist, or could exist, at the level of the subculture or the culture as a whole, along with any belief systems or ideology underlying such consistencies.

FIGURE 14.1
Ecological Systems Theory

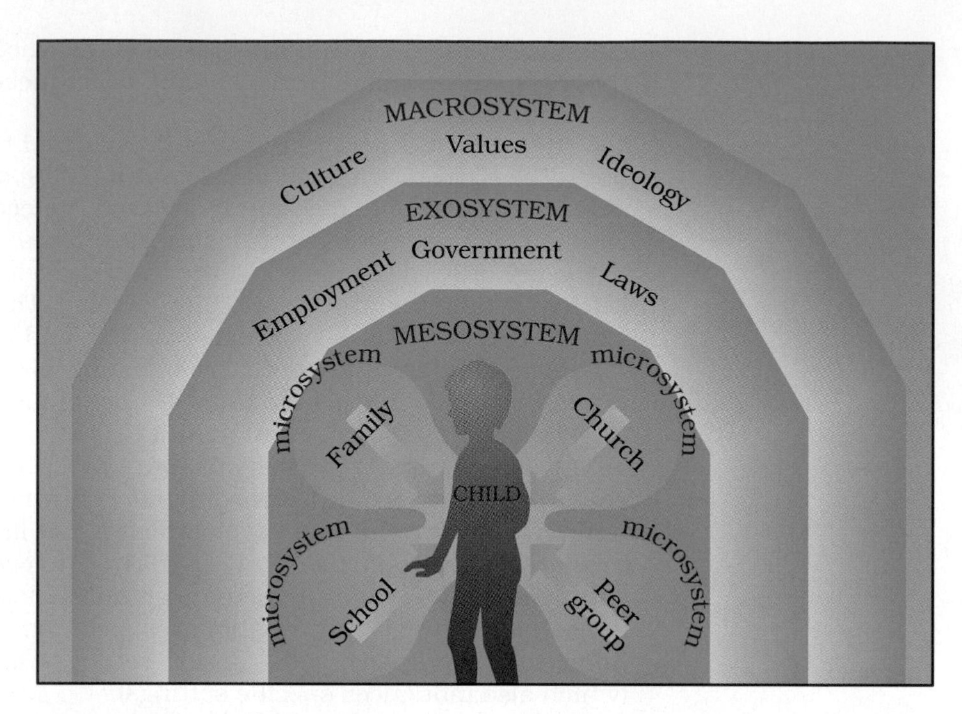

Source: A. Fogel and E. Melson, *Child development: Individual, family, and society* (St. Paul, MN: West, 1988, p. 50.)

A SYSTEMS FRAMEWORK

By viewing the family as a human learning system that is open to growth when mutually beneficial partnerships are formed, more positive results are possible for children, teachers, and parents. The concept of an ecology of human development and learning provides insights for teachers in better understanding families. This concept, which uses a systems framework for viewing human development, offers the following points as a foundation for gaining more understanding of families (Swick, 1987):

- All human systems are composed of elements that enable them to function.
- Human systems are connected to other systems in a transactional manner.
- The elements within a human system influence each other.
- Human systems strive to maintain their "integrity" through a needs-resources balancing process.

In the systems framework perspective, the development of individuals and families is seen as a dynamic process of person-environment relationships. In this sense the behavior of a child, a family, or a child and family is viewed as a part of a set of interrelated "systems" (physical, social, economic, spiritual, psychological, and ecological) that powerfully influence each other (Swick & Graves, 1993). For example, a child's passivity toward learning may be influenced by several person-environment factors such as malnutrition, abuse, poor physical health, poor dental health, family crises, or a combination of these and possibly others (Garbarino, 1982; Ford & Lerner, 1992).

THE EMPATHETIC ELEMENT

Swick and Graves (1993) have added an "empathetic" element to the ecological perspective. This provides the understanding dimension of how children and families function. It is based on the notion that human behavior is purposeful, and that this purpose is influenced by what happens within the person-family system as it relates to other social systems (Schwartzman, 1985). Therefore, human behavior can be understood and supported in achieving healthy and productive modes of living. By "understanding" (showing empathy) what is happening in families and assessing possible influences on the family's status, teachers can design strategies to promote well-being in the family. Through ecological-empathetic perspectives, early childhood educators can become sensitive to observable and subtle strengths as well as needs within the family system (Swick & Graves, 1993).

UNDERSTANDING FAMILIES

The term *understanding* represents a professional's ethical and humane position that all families have strengths, are important, and can make decisions that yield positive results. In this sense, to understand is to engage in meaningful and supportive dialogue with families. This is counter to the deficit model, in which families were viewed as having problems that needed intervention. It is an interactive focus that recognizes family needs, dynamics, and potential. Using this perspective calls for the teacher to view the partnership as an opportunity to engage in active involvements that are so lution oriented and build on family strengths (Swick & Graves, 1993).

The following perspectives should be sensitively explored by early childhood educators (Swick & Graves, 1993, pp. 56–57):

- Who are the families we serve? What do we know about these families that can empower us to be caring helpers?

Parents and teachers who have built partnerships understand how to ease the transition from home to the center.

- What do we know about ourselves as early childhood helping professionals? How do we think about the families we serve?
- What are the programs, services, and activities we offer families? Are they "enabling and empowering" in that they respond to family perceived needs?
- How do our program activities reflect family respect and family autonomy? Do we use parent input in the shaping of program activities?
- How is the uniqueness of each family's integrity accounted for in our programs? Are there opportunities for helpers and families to learn about each other's needs and strengths?
- What is the predominant view of our staff regarding families and our relationship with families? Is it one of positive nurturing partnerships or is it a cynical view?

TEACHERS SPEAK OUT

Teachers need to realize that they are not the child's parent. It is not up to a teacher to pass judgment or interfere with the child rearing practices of a family. Each family unit is different, and its individuality is acknowledged and respected.

As early childhood educators explore these questions and issues, we must realize the dramatic changes that have occurred in families during the last several decades. In the winter of 1990 a special issue of *Newsweek* magazine, titled "The Twenty-First Century Family," was published. The introductory article contained the following passage:

> The American family does not exist. Rather, we are creating many American families, of diverse styles and shapes. In unprecedented numbers, our families are unalike; we have fathers working while mothers keep house; fathers and mothers both working away from home; single parents; second marriages bringing children together from unrelated backgrounds; childless couples; unmarried couples, with and without children; gay and lesbian parents. We are living through a period of historic change in American family life. (*Newsweek*, 1990, p. 15)

Throughout this chapter, we use the term *parent*; however, we realize that many children have significant adults who may not be their biological parent, but accept primary caregiving responsibilities.

COMMUNICATING WITH PARENTS

The most important element in a successful parent-teacher partnership is effective communication. A true partnership between parents and teachers includes mutual respect and trust. To achieve this kind of relationship, each party must be willing to listen and respect the other's point of view. There is a real need for teachers to understand different communication styles. Included in this is a knowledge of how to communicate effectively verbally and nonverbally, to convey attentive caring, and to interpret messages from parents. Many teachers are fortunate to have frequent encounters with parents. It is important to remember, however, that the frequency of communication does not necessarily translate into a more effective relationship.

PARENTS SPEAK OUT

I've always enjoyed hearing anecdotes about my children's day at school. Just something they did or said. It makes me feel more a part of their school day. I also try to tell their teachers about things they do or say at home, especially if it involves school, teacher, or classmates.

A clear knowledge and understanding of expectations, obligations, and responsibilities by the parent and teacher is another essential element in the partnership. A parent handbook and a parent meeting at the very beginning of the year should thoroughly address this information and lay the foundation for an effective partnership. As with any relationship, time, respect, trust, and nurturance are required components. It is critical for the teacher to communicate clearly about the program philosophy as well as the philosophy regarding parent involvement. Parents need to know about daily schedules, fees, attendance policies, transportation policies, health and safety regulations, children's celebrations, recommendations for dress, parent meeting and parent conference schedules (Gestwicki, 1992).

Some handbooks describe general developmental characteristics of children and ways parents can assist in the child's natural growth and development processes. A handbook should also address teaching methods used, reporting procedures, materials needed, and facilities for parents in the school such as bulletin boards and lending libraries. Names, addresses, and telephone numbers of parent advisory committee members are also important to share with parents. The handbook should be clearly and concisely written in an easily understood style. Many teachers regularly reinforce much of this information in newsletters, meetings, and conferences throughout the year (Berger, 1987).

Home visits have proven to be a source of effective communication between teachers and families. Visiting in the home allows the teacher to view the home as a learning environment and gain information about the child and family. It also allows the teacher to model and demonstrate learning strategies with the parents. It is important to make certain the parents are comfortable with a visit (Powell, 1990). The close contact can contribute to the building of trust and respect between teacher and parents. Visits can be scheduled weekly, monthly, or less frequently depending on the nature and intent of the program.

Early childhood home visits are often used to build a partnership between the parents and the child's teacher. Establishing a clear purpose, organizing the planned activities, responding to parent needs, and involving the parents in the visits are vital steps in a successful home visit (Swick, 1991). Examples of activities may include sharing books, sharing stories, demonstrating learning experiences, and doing family activities together. These activities are usually short, simple tasks based on key learning skills. Table 14.1 gives several hints for involving parents in their child's education and development.

Communication Styles

Some styles of communication are perceived by the receiver as blaming, intimidating, and condescending. These styles should certainly be avoided. Styles that demonstrate empathy, understanding, and caring should be understood and used by teachers. Flake-Hobson and Swick (1979) have identified four basic communication styles.

TABLE 14.1
Hints for Involving Parents

- Involve parents in discussions about child development, discipline, or other pertinent topics.
- Involve parents in collaborative assessment activities.
- Involve parents in training programs or study groups.
- Involve parents in in support groups.
- Involve parents in teacher-parent conferences.
- Involve parents through notes and newsletters.
- Involve parents by providing lending libraries.
- Involve parents as helpers in the classroom.
- Build links with parents through technology.
- Involve parents in leadership and advocacy activities.

Source: K. J. Swick, *Teacher-parent partnerships to enhance school success in early childhood education* (Washington, DC: National Education Association, 1991).

These styles differ in the amount of risk involved and the amount of information that is shared and valued.

Style 1: Superficial. The superficial style is described as playful, sociable, and happy-go-lucky. It is very informal and remains on a surface level. Therefore, it is low on risk and low in giving and valuing information. The person who uses this style often speaks of another person's dress, hair, jewelry, or about the weather. There is little substance in the conversation.

Style 2: Command. The command style is much riskier, because it is often accusatory, intimidating, and manipulative. Since the nature of this style is blaming, the receiver often is defensive and obtains little information. An example of this style is the teacher who says, "You must let him do anything he wants!" or "Why do you let her watch so much television?"

Style 3: Intellectual. The intellectual style is often very impersonal and is used to convey objective information. It is a style that relies on big words and elaborate speech. This type is often received as condescending, because it uses a downward communication approach. The risk lies in the fact that it may not be understood. An example is the teacher who says, "It is imperative that we fully consider all possible alternatives before we commit to James's placement for next year."

Style 4: Caring. The caring style is high in risk because of its openness but also gives high information. This style requires the use of four sets of skills (Flake-Hobson & Swick, 1979):

- Listening
- Sharing self-information
- Establishing shared meaning through clarifying information received and sent
- Making a conscious commitment to care for the self and others that requires the individual to take risks in the relationship

An example of this style is the teacher who says, "I am concerned about Jimmy. He seems very tired in school. I wonder if he's getting enough sleep." This example expresses concern but in no way blames, accuses, or assumes that something happening at home is the source of a problem. It also implies that there may be something for the parent and the teacher to work on together for the mutual benefit of the child, parent, and teacher. Teachers who can develop this style will probably have many more positive interactions with parents. The next step in this interchange is careful and thoughtful listening by the teacher. Listening has been recognized as an effective tool of communication since the 1960s, when the work of Carl Rogers influenced psychological counseling. His "reflective listening" and the use of "I" messages have been used effectively in many teacher-parent conferences (Rogers, 1963).

The use of reflective listening is important, because a person cannot accurately respond to another unless the statement has been clearly heard and completely understood. This requires the teacher and parent to pay careful attention to verbal as well as nonverbal communication. A reflective response shows empathy while recognizing and validating the speaker's feelings. Here are some other qualities of reflective listening (Chinn, Winn, & Walters, 1978):

- It is empathetic.
- It uses labeling of specific feelings, not general ones.
- It begins by focusing on current feelings in the here and now.
- The listener's nonverbal messages-visible in facial expressions and gestures, audible in voice tone and volume-are congruent with his or her expressed verbal response.

Some general nonprioritized guidelines have been suggested for maximizing parent-professional partnerships (Sefton, Gargiulo, & Graves, 1991, p. 40):

- DO examine your attitude toward the child. Remember the child is an individual with unique needs, styles, and rates of growth, development, and learning.
- DON'T compare the child with other children. The child's progress should only be compared with previous growth and developmental levels.

- DO focus on the child's strengths and abilities, not weaknesses.
- DON'T be critical of parents. Be sensitive to the unique demands encountered daily by parents of the young child.
- DO remain open and accepting of the parents' feelings and behavior. DON'T make judgments about the family situation or the parents' manner of dealing with the child.
- DO respect the parents' right to choose their level of involvement and participation.
- DO demonstrate respect, concern, and a sincere desire to work cooperatively with the parents.
- DON'T threaten or manipulate parents into actions which may be uncomfortable for them.
- DO encourage parents to keep you informed of changes in the child's daily schedule or any situation that may affect the child, such as illness or the birth of a sibling.
- DO share information with parents. Keep parents informed of progress, activities, and special events. Use a variety of techniques: telephone calls, personal notes, bulletin boards, and newsletters.
- When communicating with parents, DO listen with the "third ear." DON'T hear only what the parent is saying. DO listen for the underlying feelings.
- DO remember that nonverbal communication often can convey feelings more accurately than words. Verbal behavior must be consistent with body language.
- DO be accountable. If you agree to assume responsibilities or gather information, be certain to follow through.
- DO communicate to parents in terms that are meaningful and understandable to them. DON'T use professional jargon.
- DO urge parents to discuss their concerns with you. Be available for the parents.
- DO solicit the parents' input. Seek suggestions from the parents about successful strategies for working with their child.
- DO express, in a nonthreatening manner, concerns you have with the child. DON'T focus on the child, focus on the behavior.

KIDS SPEAK UP

It's fun to have momma at school. She reads some stories and helps the teacher.

Boy, 5 years old

While the preceding list cannot ensure a successful partnership with all parents, it can assist in establishing a mutually respectful relationship.

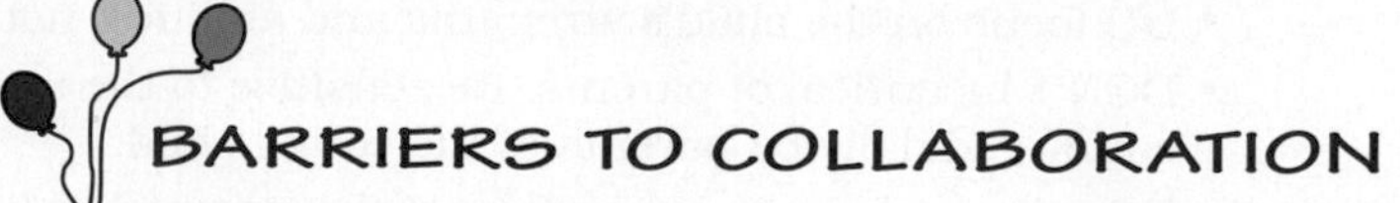

BARRIERS TO COLLABORATION

The question teachers posed years ago was, "Should we work with parents?" The question now has become, "How can we work with parents as partners?" Like all relationships between people barriers can exist between teachers and parents. While it is not instructive to place blame on one party or the other, it may be helpful to examine some of the reasons obstacles exist. Some who work with children view parents as a nuisance (Seligman & Seligman, 1980). Teachers have sometimes blamed parents for causing, or at least not preventing their child's problem (Seligman, 1979). Observers have noted that some professionals are opposed to parent involvement and are therefore reluctant to share responsibilities with parents (Gargiulo & Graves, 1991).

Some parents view their interactions with teachers as adversarial. Parents who have not had positive school experiences themselves may feel intimidated by the school. They may also feel fearful because the teacher is a professional who has earned a degree. This fearfulness and intimidation is sometimes unintentionally fostered by the professional. One of the most demeaning traits of professional people, according to Schultz (1987), is the tendency to deny parents' expertise and knowledge about their own child.

Barriers to collaboration can also be a product of the parents' behavior. Parents, like teachers, can also be demanding, uncooperative, defensive, and hostile. Kraft and Snell (1980) identified four types of parents frequently encountered by school personnel:

- The blame-oriented parent who regularly calls attention to shortcomings in the school.
- The invisible parent who takes no initiative and fails to respond to messages.
- The supercooperative parent who continually abuses the teacher's time.
- The pseudoexpert parent who knows more about education than the teacher.

Given this arena of mixed messages, misunderstanding, and intimidation, it is easy to understand how relationships between parents and professionals sometimes fail to develop (Gargiulo & Graves, 1991).

THE EMPOWERMENT PARADIGM

The term *empowerment* is being used by many people in a variety of contexts. In an ecological context, empowerment must be viewed as a process rather than an end state. Bronfenbrenner (1979), in his ecological perspective, stated that power emerges from the nature and structure of human relationships. "Critical to the person's integrity is not only the context of their experiences, but their perceptual orientation toward these events and processes" (Swick & Graves, 1993, p. 50). Often, a person's perceived reality is more important than what is literally happening. An empowering person is oriented toward events in a proactive and empathetic manner. The various ways people develop their perceptual focus has been the topic of many researchers and theorists (Hampden-Turner, 1981).

TEACHERS SPEAK OUT

Preschool teachers and parents can learn a great deal from each other.

Since individual interests, needs, affective development, and perceptual orientation evolve within the family ecology, the premises of family studies (particularly family systems research) are highly related with the empowerment paradigm. These premises include the following (Swick & Graves, 1993):

- Behavior takes place in a systems context.
- Individual development is intimately interrelated with the family's development.
- Family development is systematic.
- Events that influence any family member have some direct or indirect influence on the entire family system.

Within the family system, trust, attachment, self-esteem, social attitudes and behaviors, and many other processes and skills emerge in a nurturing, empowered family (Brubaker, 1993; Cataldo, 1987; Minuchin, 1984).

A sense of power or a sense of powerlessness is developed in the family ecology. Dunst, Trivette, and Deal (1988) have identified three enabling characteristics to assist in the empowerment process: ability to access and control needed resources, decision-making and problem-solving abilities, and instrumental behaviors for interacting effectively with others in the social exchange process. It is important to remember that the concept of empowerment is dynamic, interactive, and process-oriented.

Teachers who believe in the empowerment paradigm share the assumption that all families have strengths. Providing quality early childhood education programs, involving parents in partnerships, and supporting families can assist in empowering parents.

Teachers, administrators, and other school personnel are in a strategic position to promote positive interactions with families. If efforts are limited to either personal interactions or policy changes, much of the potential of the empowerment process can be lost. But if policies are changed to provide more and better parent involvement demonstrating mutual respect and meaningful involvement, benefits can be greater (Cochran & Dean, 1991).

PARENT-TEACHER CONFERENCES

Formal, scheduled conferences can produce anxiety on the part of the teacher and the parent. Casual conversations, newsletters, written notes sent by the child, telephone calls, and other means of informal communication are all very important in building and maintaining partnerships. The scheduled conference can provide an opportunity for free exchange of information and questions. It also gives both parties an opportunity to gain insight about the child's growth, development, and learning patterns.

The conference is sometimes associated with negativity because the general feeling among professionals and parents has been that a problem usually precipitates the need for a conference. This negativity can call up old feelings of parents when their family was called for a conference about them. It can also cause feelings of embarrassment, intimidation, and guilt. To avoid these feelings, teachers should clearly convey to parents that conferences are an important and routine part of the ongoing effort to share in the partnership of providing what is best for the child.

Here are a few of the many reasons teachers schedule parent-teacher conferences:

- To provide information related to the developmental level and abilities of the child.
- To discuss the progress the child is making toward meeting the objectives identified by the teacher.
- To show the parent samples of the child's work.
- To ask for information about the child that will enhance appropriate planning for the child.
- To reach consensus on future goals for the child.
- To provide time and privacy for an open exchange.

Planning for Conferences

Teachers should carefully select the times for conferences and strive to plan times that are mutually agreeable. Being flexible in planning to meet parents' needs demonstrates to the parents that the teacher

It is critical to keep communication lines open between parents and teachers.

has a serious commitment to involve parents in their child's care and education. Many teachers use a variety of communication methods when setting up conferences, including sending notes home, calling on the telephone, and making personal contacts.

To ensure a successful conference, make certain there is ample time and the setting is quiet and comfortable. Parents appreciate teachers who discuss specific tasks, behaviors, and abilities. Children's work samples, anecdotal notes, and notes from observations and interviews are all important documents to share with parents. Teachers who plan their objectives and jot down notes for the conference report success. Follow-up is also an important part of the conference. If an agreement is made to try a strategy, it is critical to follow through as planned.

Pitfalls

Gestwicki (1992, p. 221) describes the following pitfalls to avoid in planning successful conferences:

- Avoid using technical terminology.
- Avoid assuming the role of "expert."
- Avoid negative evaluations (i.e., "I'm having a problem with James," or "James is slow at learning").
- Avoid unprofessional conversation.
- Avoid giving advice.
- Avoid rushing into solutions.

PARTNERSHIP PROGRAMS

A variety of parent education and parent involvement programs exist throughout the country that build effective partnerships between parents and teachers. Family resource centers, parent education groups, mentoring projects, parent networking groups, and intergenerational teaming projects are some of the names used. The commitment to work as partners with parents and provide support systems to families is demonstrated in the three program examples we describe here. These programs focus on family strengths and use strategies that we discussed earlier in this chapter.

Parents as Teachers

One of the most widely recognized parent education programs in recent years is the **Parents as Teachers (PAT)** program, which evolved from the research of Burton L. White (1988). Parent education training begins in the third trimester of pregnancy and continues until the child's third birthday. Services include help (during pregnancy) for preparing the parent to be a parent, child development information, and developmental screenings for the child. The delivery of services takes place through home visits, group meetings, newsletters, parent centers, and referrals. The goals include educating parents about child development; helping parents gain confidence in their ability to parent; enhancing the cognitive, language, and social development of participating children; giving parents information about detecting problems; and helping parents develop positive connections with the program, school, and community.

KIDS SPEAK UP

My daddy is Santa Claus at school. He's not the *real* Santa Claus. He just helps. His stomach is real funny.

Girl, 4 years old

The content of the Parents as Teachers program was developed from White's (1988) seven phases of childhood development, discussed in his book *Educating the infant and toddler.* White also maintains a "Center for Parent Education" where resources, training, and services are provided. Here are some research findings of the Parents as Teachers program (Missouri Department of Education, 1985):

- Parents are more knowledgeable about child rearing practices and child development than parents not involved in the program.
- Risk factors in children were reduced by age 3 as compared to children of parents not involved in the program.
- Staff were effective in identifying developmental risks and in addressing them through interagency strategies.
- Parents are more positive toward school and community involvement than parents not involved in the program.
- Children are more advanced than other children in their language, problem solving, and social skills.

Minnesota Early Childhood Family Education Program

Minnesota Early Learning Design (MELD) was begun in 1973 and continues today. It is a classic parent education and family support program that can be found in over 80 locations in 19 states and 3 foreign countries. It has come to be known as MELD because of how successful the program "melds" the two primary components, information and support. The program strives to help parents establish networks involving not only other parents, but also various community resources. Parents are provided timely, age-specific, and unbiased child rearing information.

Parents teach and learn from each other as they meet together over a two-year period (through the child's second year). Elwood (1988) describes the overall organizational system of MELD as follows:

> Group leaders and volunteers who are trained and supervised by a site coordinator, a part-time professional who receives training over a 1-year period. Each MELD site maintains an ongoing but autonomous relationship with MELD's central office, which provides technical assistance and new program materials. Local agencies provide administrative and financial support to MELD groups. The MELD curriculum addresses issues of child health, child development, and family management. (p. 304)

Strengths of this program include goal setting, individualization of parent activities, and self-evaluation of local programs and agencies. Continuous evaluation has found (Elwood, 1988):

- Parents were consistent in attending and participating in group meetings.
- All of the mothers participating in the program received prenatal care.
- Almost half of the participants in the group meetings have been men.

- Of the mothers participating, 88 percent did not smoke during pregnancy.
- All of the children of the participating parents received well-baby checkups.
- Of the children of participating parents, 97 percent were free of serious accidents while in the program.
- Developmentally, children of participating families generally exceeded the criteria for their age as compared to other children.
- Of the children in the programs, 89 percent had updated immunizations.

This is certainly a very successful program, which has been adapted widely. It has achieved significant child, parent, and family strengthening tasks.

Kenan Trust Family Literacy Project

The **Kenan Trust Family Literacy Project** was initiated in the 1988–1989 school year with funding from the William R. Kenan, Jr., Charitable Trust. Its mission is to improve education for at-risk children and their parents through early intervention techniques designed to break the cycle of illiteracy. The four components of the program are parent literacy training, parenting and parent education, early childhood education, and human resources development. We briefly review each component below.

KIDS SPEAK UP

We wrote a story to our moms and dads about our trip to the circus . . . and drew a picture. The teacher made the letters for the story when we told her what to say. We colored it.

Boy, 5 years old

Parent Literacy Training. Individualized assistance on educational goals established by the parents is provided. These goals may vary from specific job training to general equivalency diploma (GED) courses.

Parenting and Parent Education. Parent Time (PT) and Parent and Children Time (PACT) make up the parenting and parent education component. During Parent Time, parents, teachers, and resource persons design programs of interest to discuss and study. These sessions usually occur in the early afternoon for periods of about 45 minutes. PT topics may include parent-child communication, discipline, job opportunities, community resources, and others.

PACT offers families an opportunity for joint activities that reinforce interaction among family members. During this time, the teacher models working with the children as parents observe. An additional part of the PACT is when activities planned by the children are carried out by the children with parents participating.

Early Childhood Education. The early childhood education part of the program involves the children engaged in learning activities guided by the High/Scope Curriculum. An active learning approach is supported by nurturing teachers who provide a range of activities and experiences.

Human Resources Development. The human resources development component includes parents studying various job-seeking skills. The program serves a variety of parent populations and is implemented in urban, rural, and suburban settings. Here are some findings of this project (Elwood, 1988):

- Parents and children made gains in academic performance, self-concept, social skills, and increasing control over their lives.
- Children made significant gains in self-concept, language, and problem-solving skills.
- Family literacy habits in the home improved substantially.
- Parent-child interactions became more nurturing and positive.
- Parents who participated regularly significantly improved their academic performance, their relationships with others, and their view of themselves.
- Parents who were fully committed to the program completed their adult education objectives with successful results.

Parents and teachers need to view their partnership as growth oriented experiences in which they strive to nurture each other toward becoming full partners in the child's learning and development. This requires an atmosphere of mutual trust, and a high regard for each other. This can best be accomplished if each partner focuses on strengths and maintains a positive, optimistic, outlook (Swick, 1993).

SUMMARY

In this chapter, we focus on opportunities for teachers to build effective partnerships with parents. We examine benefits to parents, teachers, and children. Parents are now viewed as active participants rather than mere recipients of services concerning their child's care and education. We also describe the rationale and foundation for effective relationships between parents and teachers. We examine Bronfenbrenner's (1979) ecological perspective as a framework for establishing and maintaining partnerships.

Also in this chapter, we thoroughly review the importance of communication. We explore styles of communication, considering bridges as well as barriers to effective communication. We examine guidelines for maximizing effective partnerships. We discuss conferences between parents and teachers, describing reasons for providing conferences as well as pitfalls to avoid. In a framework of empowerment, we discuss the critical components of trust, mutual respect, and meaningful involvement. We conclude the chapter by discussing several programs that have proved successful in implementing true partnerships between parents and teachers.

TEST YOUR UNDERSTANDING

1. Discuss reasons why effective parent-teacher partnerships are critical components of successful early childhood education programs.
2. Discuss how parents of young children nurture, teach, and serve as models for their children.
3. What kind of benefits can parents reap from building a partnership with teachers?
4. Using a view of the child as a system, discuss the reciprocal relationships found in the "mesosystem."
5. Discuss the benefits and risks of the "DO's" and "DON'Ts" addressed in the chapter.
6. How do the three partnership programs we described differ in the programs and services offered?

LEARNING ACTIVITIES

1. Interview an early childhood teacher about parent participation and involvement. Ask about the number of parents who participate in classroom activities, the types of communication used, the number of parent conferences, and other issues related to partnerships.
2. Attend a Parent-Teacher Association (PTA) or Parent-Teacher Organization (PTO) meeting and note who participates, who leads the meeting, and the types of issues addressed.
3. Write a brief paper explaining the importance of the five teacher behaviors discussed in the partnership process. Give examples.

4. Role play a parent-teacher interaction using several of the communication styles discussed in the chapter.
5. Role play a parent-teacher conference and have the students who are not assuming roles critique the role play.
6. In your community, find out how parents are involved in the school on a daily basis.

CHAPTER 15

Issues and Trends in Early Childhood Education

CHAPTER OUTLINE

Multicultural Education
- *Terminology*
- *Cultural Diversity in America*
- *From Melting Pot to Cultural Pluralism*
- *A Role for Schools*
- *Anti-Bias Curriculum*
- *Suggestions for Early Childhood Teachers*

Kindergarten Controversies
- *Kindergarten Entry Age*
- *Half-Day vs. Full-Day Kindergarten*
- *Kindergarten Curriculum*

Advocacy
- *Contributing to the Advocacy Role*
- *Building Advocacy Skills*

Quality Programs

Developmentally Appropriate Practice
- *SECA Position Statement*
- *NAEYC Position Statement*

Alternative Assessment

Readiness

Challenges for the Future

KEY TERMS

Multicultural

Multicultural education

Cultural pluralism

Anti-bias curriculum

Developmentally appropriate practice

Developmentally appropriate assessment

As the secretary answered the phone, a pleasant voice on the other end of the line began the conversation in a manner that had become quite common at the private kindergarten. The secretary responded to the caller's questions, realizing that a parent's initial telephone contact requesting information is very important.

The caller, apparently the father of a young child, asked general questions about the program for 5-year-olds. The secretary courteously answered his questions. As the father began to move from general questions about such things as tuition and supplies to more specific program questions, the secretary asked if he might like to speak to one of the teachers who was beginning a conference period.

The secretary passed the phone to the teacher and continued with her filing. She could hear the teacher's responses to the father. It was especially rewarding, she thought, to know that this parent had genuinely considered issues that were important to his child's needs. The teacher responded to questions related to enrollment size, the training of teachers and aides, multicultural awareness, language development, and academic approaches compared to developmentally appropriate settings. Clearly, this parent wanted the best for his child.

The teacher began to close the conversation. "Thank you for calling—we'll get some information in the mail to you." She paused to listen, then replied, "No. But I can make some predictions about what the program will be like when your child begins based on the trends of today's programs." The caller had apparently asked about the long-term characteristics of early childhood programs. "When will your child turn 5 years of age?" the teacher asked. There was a pause, and the secretary noticed the teacher was smiling. "I see," the teacher said, "and when is your wife's delivery date . . .?"

Public and private educational institutions are experiencing significant change. Schools of the next century will encounter many challenges. In comparison to the 1970s and 1980s, early childhood educators will confront an increasingly diverse student population, calls for greater accountability, heightened parent involvement, and intensified advocacy efforts on behalf of young children. Issues of affordability and quality of child care will also require attention. Even the role of kindergarten has generated controversy. These themes will affect the professional lives of many early childhood teachers. Early childhood professionals must be prepared to respond to change and the impact that it will have in their classrooms. The purpose of this chapter is to highlight selected topics considered important to the professional development of early childhood teachers.

MULTICULTURAL EDUCATION

As we briefly saw in Chapter 2, America's population is changing. Consequently, young children from many different lands will be attending early childhood programs and our public schools. An awareness and respect of this cultural diversity will become increasingly important for the early childhood professional.

Terminology

Many different labels have been used to describe the education of children from different cultural backgrounds. Sometimes, however, the terminology has contributed to inaccurate generalizations and incorrect information. Multicultural education, for example, has been a source of confusion and controversy (Tiedt & Tiedt, 1990). It is an ambiguous term that means different things to different people. In the following definitions, we attempt to clarify and describe the concepts. Several interpretations of the terms are presented. Our discussion is limited to the related themes of multicultural education and cultural pluralism.

Multicultural Education. In its simplest form, **multicultural** refers to more than one culture. The key to defining **multicultural education**, according to Tiedt and Tiedt (1990), can be found in the root word *culture*:

> Culture is a totality of values, beliefs, and behaviors common to a large group of people. A culture may include shared language and folklore, ideas and thinking patterns, communication styles—the "truths" accepted by members of the group." (p. 10)

These authors further state that every student grows up belonging to a particular culture. This cultural background influences the pupil's response to schooling and must be considered when planning learning activities.

> **TEACHERS SPEAK OUT**
>
> Today's day care teacher must keep in touch and in tune with the multicultural challenges in the day care classroom environment. Positive child guidance and self-esteem are no longer approached singularly. Ethnic differences must be learned, respected, and observed for families and care providers to work together successfully. The teacher needs to be aware of family needs to be able to make a difference in a child's life.

Sleeter and Grant (1988) believe that multicultural education is an umbrella concept that deals with issues of race, language, social class, and culture as well as handicap and gender. The term refers, therefore, to educational practices directed toward the social inequalities inherent in these topics.

Multicultural education can also be defined as providing equal educational opportunities to students whose language or cultural experiences suggest that they will encounter difficulties succeeding in traditional school programs (Ornstein & Levine, 1989).

Dean, Salend, and Taylor (1993) characterize multicultural education as a platform from which teachers "can promote goals of equal opportunity; racial, ethnic, and religious tolerance; and gender and sexual orientation awareness" (p. 40). Multicultural education also gives educators a chance to critically examine the content and values found in the traditional curriculum.

Finally, Gollnick and Chinn (1990) portray multicultural education as an educational strategy wherein the child's cultural background is valued and viewed positively. Teachers use the students' diversity in developing instructional strategies and supportive school environments.

Evident in the preceding definitions is a belief that early childhood educators need to embrace the cultural richness found in their classrooms. The cultural backgrounds of some students may be different from that of other youngsters, but different does not mean inferior or deficient. Cultural diversity is not synonymous with the terms *culturally deprived* or *culturally disadvantaged.* According to Sue (1981), all people inherit a cultural background; although it may differ from white, middle-class norms, this does not suggest that the pupil's background is deviant, defective, or impoverished. "Today, good preschool education values the cultural and linguistic diversity of children and their families" (Smith & Luckasson, 1992, p. 51). Teachers need to incorporate the reality of their children's lives in their instructional planning.

Cultural Pluralism. *Cultural pluralism* is the second term that requires clarification. Educators as well as professional groups describe this concept. Smith and her colleague (Smith & Luckasson, 1992) define **cultural pluralism** to mean "all cultural groups are valued components of the society, and the language and traditions of each group are maintained" (p. 42). Havighurst (1974, p. 587) offers an early, yet still valid description of cultural pluralism:

1. Mutual appreciation and understanding of the various cultures in the society;
2. Cooperation of the various groups in the civic and economic institutions of the society;
3. Peaceful coexistence of diverse lifestyles, folkways, manners, language patterns, religious beliefs, and family structures;

4. Autonomy for each subcultural group to work out its own social future, as long as it does not interfere with the same right for the other groups.

Our last description of cultural pluralism comes from the American Association of Colleges for Teacher Education (1972). This professional association realized, over twenty years ago, that

> to endorse cultural pluralism is to endorse the principle that there is no one model American . . . [and] is to understand and appreciate the differences that exist among the nation's citizens. It is to see these differences as a positive force. . . . Cultural pluralism is more than a temporary accommodation to placate racial and ethnic minorities. It is a concept that aims towards a heightened sense of being and of wholeness of the entire society based on the unique strengths of each of its parts. (p. 9)

These definitions stress that cultural pluralism allows for diversity while respecting differences and does not require the individual to abandon his or her cultural background (Sleeter & Grant, 1988).

Cultural Diversity in America

America's population is changing. The number of bilingual youngsters and children from culturally diverse backgrounds is rapidly increasing. Classrooms in the twenty-first century will be very

Schools in the United States are reflecting greater cultural diversity.

heterogeneous and evidence greater diversity than we find today. Changing demographics will present new challenges to schools and early childhood educators. Following are various reports and projections about our changing population:

- By the year 2000, approximately 33 percent of public school children will be from culturally diverse backgrounds (American Council on Education, 1988); Hispanics are predicted to be the largest group (U.S. Bureau of the Census, 1986).
- At least 50 percent of the student population in our 25 largest urban areas are from linguistically and culturally diverse groups (American Council on Education, 1988).
- Almost one-third of preschool children are members of minority groups (American Association of Colleges for Teacher Education, 1988).
- "Minority" students in New Mexico and Mississippi are actually the majority. It is projected that minority children in Texas and California will soon have the same status (Quality Education for Minorities Project, 1990).
- The number of language minority students is forecast to increase by 33 percent by the end of this century (Meyen, 1990).
- Youngsters from culturally and linguistically diverse populations will account for nearly 40 percent of all children in the U.S. by the year 2030 (Children's Defense Fund, 1989); by 2075, the proportion of children from these groups is expected to be more than 50 percent (Quality Education for Minorities Project, 1990).

What the preceding data fail to capture are the devastating consequences of the social and economic hardships frequently encountered by many multicultural families and their children. Approximately 22 percent of children under the age of 6 live in poverty (Graves, 1990a). Yet, more than 50 percent of all young African-American families with children and 40 percent of all Hispanic families reside in poverty (Children's Defense Fund, 1988). Researchers estimate that 24 percent of Native American families live in poverty; for those families on reservations, the rate of poverty is greater than 40 percent (Quality Education for Minorities Project, 1990).

Clearly, the ethnic makeup of our nation is changing. This increasing diversity will be reflected in our schools. The effectiveness of schools in meeting the needs of a multicultural population will largely depend on the teachers' ability to be responsive to cultural differences. Cultural awareness and sensitivity must become a priority for early childhood teachers.

From Melting Pot to Cultural Pluralism

Education in the United States has continually faced the issues of bilingualism and multiculturalism (Smith & Luckasson, 1992). In the early years of this century, one aim of schools was to assimilate immigrant children into American culture as quickly as possible. It was believed that public education could unify the population and inculcate the ideals of American society to diverse groups of people (Prince, Buckley, & Gargiulo, 1993). This "Americanizing" of our newest citizens required that they abandon their native languages, cultures, and beliefs. In their place, a new and unique American culture was to emerge. "Metaphorically, the United States was seen as a huge melting pot into which all diverse people were dumped to melt away the differences, thereby creating people who were very much alike" (Tiedt & Tiedt, 1990, p. 7).

The concept of a melting pot was derived from a play written by the English writer Israel Zangwill in 1908. Zangwill challenged the concept of "Americanization." He saw value in allowing the immigrants to preserve their cultural identity rather than insisting on conformity and becoming part of a homogenous culture. According to Smith and Luckasson (1992), "the melting pot model failed. Instead of creating a harmonious new culture, it lead to racism, segregation, poverty, and aggression toward individuals in each new immigrant group" (p. 42).

Beginning in the 1950s and 1960s came the slow realization that the melting pot had not blended its ingredients; in fact, as Ornstein and Levine (1989) note, ethnic identity was experiencing a rejuvenation. One outcome of this rebirth was the development of multicultural education in the late 1960s. This movement was aided by three commingling forces. Gay (1983) identifies these factors as the maturing civil rights movement, critical analyses of school textbooks and curricula, and a reexamination of cultural deficiency models (i.e., culturally disadvantaged or deprived).

Instead of the melting pot's stress on uniformity, the concept of cultural pluralism was emphasized (Ornstein & Levine, 1989). Racial and cultural diversity were recognized and prized. A new set of metaphors was introduced. The United States was likened to a tossed salad or patchwork quilt. In the viewpoint of Sleeter and Grant (1988):

> both metaphors depict an array of materials and objects of various sizes, shapes, and colors. Each is independent of the others, and each is unique, and they therefore form a collective total that is distinguished by its difference and diversity. (p. 140)

Today, a melting theory is inappropriate. Cultural diversity is perceived as a strength rather than a weakness. Citizens can be proud of their ethnic heritage instead of being ashamed of their differences (Tiedt & Tiedt, 1990).

A Role for Schools

Multicultural education plays a critical role in the education of our young children. Schools have the responsibility of fully meeting the needs of all children. Smith and Luckasson (1992) believe that unless schools consider the language and culture of all students, access to education is denied and an appropriate education is not being provided. Multicultural education must be an integral component of education at all levels. Schools, through multicultural education, can help develop positive attitudes and opinions about our multiethnic society and thereby enrich the lives of all students (Ornstein & Levine, 1989).

"The ultimate challenge of cultural pluralism lies in the ability of teachers and students to arrive at an understanding, an appreciation, and a respect for different languages, appearances, values, habits, and talents" (Poplin & Wright, 1983, p. 369). One vehicle for reaching this objective is through carefully constructed curricula and skillfully as well as sensitively presented instruction. A critical starting point is the early childhood educator. Effectiveness with multiethnic student populations requires teachers to understand and be comfortable with their own cultural backgrounds (Gollnick & Chinn, 1990). Of equal importance, young children need to understand their own cultural heritage. By understanding their background, pupils are then able to accept and appreciate the cultures of others (Tiedt & Tiedt, 1990). A goal of education, according to Gollnick and Chinn (1990), "is to help students value cultural differ-

Multicultural education plays a critical role in the education of our young children.

ences while realizing that individuals across cultures have many similarities" (p. 2).

Ideally, multicultural education should be fully integrated or infused within the school curriculum and not taught as a specialized course or fragmented units of study (Gay, 1975; Tiedt & Tiedt, 1990). Education that is multicultural is not something a teacher does once or twice a year; it is an ongoing process that permeates the entire curriculum. It can be found, for example, in the music, art, language arts, and literary experiences of young children.

Advocates of multicultural education urge that curriculum be revised to regularly present different perspectives and the contributions of diverse cultural groups (Sleeter & Grant, 1988). Curriculum materials, as well as classroom activities, need to be carefully evaluated to ensure that they sensitively portray accurate information about individual differences. Table 15.1 provides guidelines for early childhood teachers to use in evaluating instructional materials used in their classrooms. These twelve questions can assist the early childhood educator in developing appropriate multicultural curriculum.

Anti-Bias Curriculum

Children learn, at a very early age, about differences that are based on gender, ability, age, and language. Even very young children are capable of distinguishing differences between themselves and others. These observations have a powerful effect on the young child's emerging self-identity and beliefs and they influence their interactions with other children (Derman-Sparks, 1989).

Because racism, sexism, and stereotyping are so detrimental, Whaley and Swadner (1990) urge that multicultural education begin with infants and toddlers and continue throughout the school years. Multicultural awareness activities can be developed that are appropriate to the child's developmental level. One effective tool for combatting bias and prejudice in young children is the **anti-bias curriculum (ABC)** developed by Derman-Sparks (1989). This curriculum, published by the National Association for the Education of Young Children, extends the concept of multicultural education and encourages early childhood teachers to construct an anti-bias curriculum in their classrooms.

ABC is a value-based program that looks at differences as being positive and deserving of respect. Young children learn to be comfortable with diversity, to think critically, and to speak out and stand up for themselves and others when confronted with injustice and unfairness. The anti-bias curriculum includes a wide variety of activities and specific techniques that assist the child in developing confidence and a strong self-identity based on personal strengths rather than on the weaknesses of others. This curriculum model forms an integral part of daily school experiences. It attempts to de-

TABLE 15.1 Guidelines for Evaluating and Selecting Instructional Materials

1. Are the perspectives and contributions of people from diverse cultural and linguistic groups—both men and women, as well as people with disabilities—included in the curriculum?
2. Are there activities in the curriculum that will assist students in analyzing the various forms of the mass media for enthnocentrism, sexism, "handicapism," and stereotyping?
3. Are men and women, diverse cultural/racial groups, and people with varying abilities shown in both active and passive roles?
4. Are men and women, diverse cultural/racial groups, and people with disabilities shown in positions of power (i.e., the materials do not rely on the mainstream culture's character to achieve goals)?
5. Do the materials identify strengths possessed by so-called "underachieving" diverse populations? Do they diminish the attention given to deficits, to reinforce positive behaviors that are desired and valued?
6. Are members of diverse racial/cultural groups, men and women, and people with disabilities shown engaged in a broad range of social and professional activities?
7. Are members of a particular culture or group depicted as having a range of physical features (e.g., hair color, hair texture, variations in facial characteristics and body build)?
8. Do the materials represent historical events from the perspectives of the various groups involved or solely from the male, middle-class, and/or Western European perspective?
9. Are the materials free of ethnocentric or sexist language patterns that may make implications about persons or groups based solely on their culture, race, gender, or disability?
10. Will students from different ethnic and cultural backgrounds find the materials personally meaningful to their life experiences?
11. Are a wide variety of culturally different examples, situations, scenarios, and anecdotes used throughout the curriculum design to illustrate major intellectual concepts and principles?
12. Are culturally diverse content, examples, and experiences comparable in kind, significance, magnitude, and function to those selected from mainstream culture?

Source: From "Language differences" by C. Adger, W. Wolfram, and J. Detwyler, *Teaching Exceptional Children 26*, Fall 1993, p. 55. Copyright 1993 by The Council for Exceptional Children. Reprinted with permission.

velop an environment in which each youngster can achieve his or her fullest potential.

Derman-Sparks designed the ABC to go beyond what is usually found in multicultural curriculum. While incorporating the positive dimensions of multicultural curricula, the anti-bias model specifically avoids the pitfalls of a "tourist curriculum," which presents information and experiences that typically focus on external characteristics of different cultures such as food, clothing, entertainment, and national holidays. According to Derman-Sparks, a tourist approach to learning about differences is patronizing and emphasizes the "exotic" instead of examining the authentic, daily problems and experiences of different people. On the other hand, the anti-bias curriculum is more inclusive (Derman-Sparks, 1989, pp. 7–8):

a. It addresses more than cultural diversity by including gender and differences in physical ability;
b. It is based on children's developmental tasks as they construct identity and attitudes; and
c. It directly addresses the impact of stereotyping, bias, and discriminatory behavior in young children's development and interactions.

One final and important point needs to be made. The anti-bias approach to teaching young children is integrated into existing curriculum rather than being something that is added on to it. It necessitates that early childhood teachers demonstrate sensitivity and respect for individuality (Derman-Sparks, 1989).

Suggestions for Early Childhood Teachers

One objective of multicultural education is to develop an awareness, respect, and acceptance of all people who are part of our country. Teachers of young children play an important role in the efforts of schools to meet this goal. We offer the following suggestions to help early childhood educators incorporate cultural diversity in their daily classroom activities as well as effectively work with culturally diverse families.

- Instructional materials and assessment activities should reflect the cultural background of the children.
- Textbooks, visual displays, learning activities, and computer software should be free of bias and stereotype.
- Communications with non–English-speaking parents/caregivers should be in their native language; interpreters may be necessary for home visits or in-school contacts.

KIDS SPEAK UP

Nobody plays with Ninja turtles. I want to be a Mighty Morphin Power Ranger.

Boy, 4 years old

- Parents, grandparents, and community leaders of culturally diverse children should routinely be invited to visit the classroom, where they can demonstrate unique skills and share the customs, traditions, heritage, and folklore of their native lands.

- Early childhood teachers should learn as much as possible about their multicultural pupils and the child's cultural group; professional development activities might include foreign travel, workshop attendance, or developing resource files identifying community speakers, curricula materials, professional journals, media, and other sources of information for personal study.
- The holidays and festivals of different ethnic groups should be fully incorporated into classroom celebrations.
- Community volunteers can help teachers develop survival vocabulary—greetings and common words or phrases appropriate to the background of the children enrolled in their program.
- Staff development activities should be conducted using local experts and community leaders who can explain the role of the family, medical practices, communication patterns, child rearing strategies, academic expectations, and other issues from different cultural viewpoints.

It is an unmistakable fact that America's population is changing. These changes are amplified in the microcosm of our schools (Prince et al., 1993). As educators we are presented with the challenges, as well as the opportunities, this situation affords us. We must learn to live together—valuing diversity, respecting differences, sharing common beliefs, and trusting one another.

KINDERGARTEN CONTROVERSIES

While most people think of kindergarten as a happy and carefree experience for children, early childhood professionals are confronted with continuing controversy and debate about kindergartens. Some of the critical issues facing the early childhood educator focus on: At what age should a child begin kindergarten? Should kindergartens be an all-day or part-day experience? What is the purpose of a kindergarten program? We will briefly examine each of these three questions.

Kindergarten Entry Age

The age at which children enter kindergarten greatly varies; it can range from 5 to 8 years of age. Early childhood educators tend to favor enrolling older students who are more "mature" and exhibit greater readiness for the kindergarten experience. Younger kindergartners tend to have greater difficulties in comparison to their older classmates. Parents, on the other hand, are inclined to desire early entry age. Kindergartens typically enroll students whose fifth birth-

The role and function of kindergartens is subject to continuing controversy and debate.

day occurs before September 1 and, in some instances, as late as December 31 (see Table 2.3). Children whose parents seek early admission are sometimes asked to take a readiness test administered by the local school district. This assessment evaluates whether the youngster is likely to succeed in kindergarten. In addition to intellectual factors, social and behavioral characteristics are also considered when formulating an early admission decision. Some states have decided the question of early entry by requiring that students must be 5 years of age by September 1 of the year in which they wish to enroll. This issue, however, is not completely resolved, as noted by the findings of an annual survey of American education. Gallup (1986) discovered that 29 percent of the respondents were in favor of 4-year-olds (or younger) starting kindergarten, 41 percent believed youngsters should begin at age 5, and 18 percent considered age 6 the appropriate age to start school.

Half-Day vs. Full-Day Kindergarten

Which program is better—half-day or full-day kindergarten? Unfortunately, there is not an easy answer to this question. Each side of the issue has its proponents and advocates. Those who believe in half-day kindergartens stress that it represents a good way to move to an all-day first grade experience, and that 5-year-old children simply cannot handle more than just a few hours of school each day. Supporters of a full-day session dismiss this argument, maintaining that an all-day program is less rushed and provides for a more comprehensive curriculum. Many parents also believe that children in full-time kindergartens are more likely to be academically successful in the primary grades.

Frequently, proponents on both sides of the issue lose sight of the critical question, "What is best for the children?" Unfortunately, the research evidence does not provide a clear answer. One investigation that evaluated children in daily half-day kindergartens vs. pupils enrolled in alternate day full-day programs found no significant differences between the two models in the youngsters' academic achievement and social behavior (Gullo & Clements, 1984). Research also suggests that 5-year-old children are capable of handling all-day instruction, and that they benefit academically, emotionally, and socially from full-day programs (Gullo, Bersani, Clements, & Bayless, 1986; Lawton, 1988).

KIDS SPEAK UP

The sitter takes me to gymnastics after school.

Girl, 5 years old

While most states do not fully fund all-day kindergartens, there is a national movement toward all-day programming. In 1990, 42 percent of 5-year-old children who attended kindergarten were enrolled in all-day programs. In contrast, only about 12 percent attended all-day kindergartens in 1970 (National Center for Education Statistics, 1991). We predict that, in spite of tradition, as the benefits of providing an early education are recognized, an increasing number of kindergarten programs will become full time.

Kindergarten Curriculum

Our final area of debate and controversy surrounds the issue of kindergarten curriculum. What should kindergarten be like? Professionals and the public alike cannot seem to agree on the purpose of kindergartens. Kindergartens typically range from informal programs emphasizing socialization and preparation for the primary grades to those stressing academics and skill learning to such a high degree that they are almost identical to the first grade. Many years ago, Cohen and Rudolph (1977) observed this division:

> The kindergarten today is being beckoned into two opposite directions. One direction is that of supporting a "total learning" approach that does not focus on particular academic skills, but provides a foundation for them. The other approach is to provide formal skill learning. Often this results in borrowing from the early primary grades—in fact, of turning kindergarten into a watered down version of first grade. (p. 8)

One leading early childhood authority believes that in the past, kindergarten affected and modified the early grades; today, however, the primary grades seem to be strongly influencing public school kindergartens (Spodek, 1982).

Currently there are several conflicting points of view. Should kindergarten programs be formal or informal, child-directed or teacher-directed, and finally, concerned with child readiness or school readiness? There appears to be a national movement toward more skill-oriented, teacher-focused kindergartens. Many believe, however, that this trend is inconsistent with the learning and developmental characteristics of 5-year-olds. The Association for Childhood Education International (ACEI) in a position statement highly critical of a basic skills kindergarten program, stated (Moyer, Egertson, & Isenberg, 1987, p. 235):

> There is still a year of school called kindergarten, but today most kindergartens bear little resemblance to those of a generation ago . . . the curriculum of today's kindergarten focuses on specific skills to be learned, accompanied by great pressures on children to succeed . . . [leading to] this mismatch between the curriculum and the 5-year-old child.

Another professional association, the Southern Association on Children Under Six (now called the Southern Early Childhood Association) also expressed serious concerns about the movement toward skill-oriented kindergarten curriculum (Southern Association on Children Under Six, 1984). One popular weekly news magazine, *Newsweek*, even commented that at one time, "Kindergarten used to be a playground. Then it became a training ground" (Hymes, 1991, p. 272). These concerns focus on the developmental appropriateness of an academic curriculum for 5-year-olds. Furthermore, this movement, in which play is ignored as the primary means for learning, and subjects are taught as individual skills, is contradictory to the history of kindergartens (see Chapter 3) and is very distant from its original foundation in child development.

TEACHERS SPEAK OUT

Early Childhood Education, when practiced as a developmentally appropriate and interactive art, should be the model for all education.

Hymes (1991) cites an interesting example of the depth of this academically oriented approach. Florida, the first of seven states to require compulsory kindergarten for all 5-year-olds, established a Primary Education Program (PREP) that among other things, screens incoming kindergarten pupils. The purpose of PREP is to identify at-risk children and secure an appropriate instructional level for kindergartners. On the basis of their performance, youngsters can be assigned to one of three groups: developmental (at grade level), enrichment (above grade level), or preventative (a group for students performing below expectations).

Actions by the state of Georgia provide us with yet another example. In 1984, then-Governor Harris proposed compulsory kindergarten attendance for 5-year-olds. One segment of his plan called for the implementation of a kindergarten exit test to determine placement in either a first-grade classroom or enrollment in a transitional class. Hymes (1991) notes that in 1988 Georgia

> became the first state to require a standardized, multiple-choice, 90-minute test to determine which kindergartners could move on to first grade. Ninety-two percent of Georgia's 90,434 kindergartners passed. There was no report on what the testing did to the children or to the curriculum. (pp. 360–361)

Fortunately, this requirement was dropped after its initial year of operation, following many protests from parents as well as professionals.

We believe it is wrong for kindergarten teachers to label children as "delayed," "slow," or "immature" (as one of the authors was called). What they really mean is that kindergarten is not ready for the pupil, rather than the child not being ready for school. Thus, we should fix our programs, not the students. Stated another way, the curriculum should meet the needs of the student rather than asking the child to fit the demands of the curriculum.

ADVOCACY

A trend in the last decade related to the field of early childhood education is the importance of advocacy. Now more than ever, children are dependent on adults to provide a voice for their needs. The welfare of children in this country rests on our voting record, our lobbying efforts, and our participation in the political process. In partnership with parents and other professionals and citizen groups, early childhood educators must seize the power to create change. If this responsibility is not secured, children's needs will remain unheard and unmet.

PARENTS SPEAK OUT

The pre-tax exemption for child care proposal may be the most controversial issue to date. By the time I understand what it means, it may benefit my grandchildren and not my preschooler.

Early childhood advocacy essentially means standing up and speaking out for young children's needs. Experts have suggested that advocacy on behalf of children needs to become a part of our professional and ethical responsibilities (Goffin & Lombardi, 1988). A first step in becoming an advocate is to understand that children need a strong voice to address their needs. Another important element is to understand the processes of public policies and how they affect children's lives. Advocacy efforts attempt to improve the conditions and environments children are living in. For early childhood educators to become effective advocates, they must be well informed on issues in theory and practice, and they must be committed to sharing this knowledge with others.

Contributing to the Advocacy Role

Goffin and Lombardi (1988) have identified six ways for early childhood educators to contribute to the advocacy role:

1. *Sharing our knowledge.* Our beliefs and knowledge about children's needs, growth, development, and learning are solidly grounded in a knowledge base of research and effective practice. Therefore, we can and should assume responsibility for sharing this information with policymakers, parents, and other decision makers.

2. *Sharing our professional experiences.* Stories speak much louder than statistics in many cases. Early childhood educators experience first hand the impact of issues such as lack of accessibility of child care; lack of affordable child care; inappropriate curriculum; lack of adequate standards in child care; and conflicts between work and family. As a result, we have the responsibility to share the personal stories that give meaning to the statistics policymakers are presented.

I am sure that there are many ways of determining the best child care centers but we are a little old fashioned. We ask other parents who they recommend and why.

3. *Redefining the "bottom line" for children.* In the last twenty years, discussions about programs for young children have been included in discussions of job training, economic development, welfare, teenage pregnancy, and other social issues. Support and funding for children's programs is often now perceived as an investment in the future workforce. Experts have advised early childhood advocates to support children's issues that are connected to social concerns with broad political implications (Goffin, 1988).

4. *Standing up for our profession.* The field of early childhood education has a distinct professional knowledge base taken from research and theory. It is this knowledge base that guides our practice. We must take pride in this foundation and share information about research and theory that validates our profession.

5. *Activating parental power.* Our continuous interactions and partnerships with parents give us the opportunity to share common concerns and ideas for improving the quality of life for young children. Parents can be very effective advocates for children because of their commitment to their own children. By drawing on parent power, we can expand our base of advocates.

6. *Expanding the constituency for children.* Professionals in the field of early childhood education have natural connections with many other advocates who support quality programs, appropriate teaching practices, support services for families, and other issues. These people may be health care workers, human services personnel, professionals, volunteers, civic or religious groups, and others who are concerned with young children's needs and their welfare.

Building Advocacy Skills

Building skills in the area of advocacy requires keeping current on issues, being a change agent, and reaching agreement with other advocates. Three essential areas of expertise advocates need are content knowledge, advocacy strategies, and interpersonal skills. It is critically important for advocates to know the issues and be able to clearly articulate them verbally and in written form. Organizational skills and utilization of resources and support people are also very important. Lastly, having traits and skills like flexibility, reflective listening, shared decision making, and cooperative problem solving is advantageous for the advocate. Ideas for action are listed in Table 15.2.

QUALITY PROGRAMS

One of the most important components of quality in early childhood programs is the relationship between the teacher and child. Parents report that the type and quality of the attention their child receives significantly influences their decision in selecting one program over another (Galinsky, 1988). A study by Phillips, McCartney, and Scarr (1990) found that when children are talked to, asked questions, and encouraged to express themselves, their social development is enhanced. It was also found that these children were rated as more considerate, more intelligent, and task oriented. The teaching environment was found to be a strong predictor of the child's achievement.

TABLE 15.2 Actions Early Childhood Advocates Can Take

You can choose from many courses of action once you make a commitment to become an advocate for children, their families, and your profession. Here are a few of the choices:

- Share ideas for appropriate practice with other teachers and parents (instead of just observing disapprovingly).
- Explain to administrators why dittos are inappropriate learning tools for young children (rather than using them and feeling resentful that you have to practice your profession in ways inconsistent with its knowledge base).
- Explain to parents why children learn best through play (instead of bemoaning that parents are pushing their children or giving in and teaching with inappropriate methods and materials).
- Write a letter to the editor of a newspaper or magazine to respond to an article or letter (instead of just complaining about how other people don't understand the needs of children, their families, or their caregivers).
- Write to your state or federal legislators about a pending issue and share your experiences as a way to point out needs (rather than just assuming someone else will write).
- Meet someone new who is interested in early childhood education and ask her or him to join a professional group such as NAEYC, NBCDI, SACUS, or ACEI (instead of just wondering why the person isn't involved).
- Ask a friend to go with you to a legislator's town meeting (instead of staying home because you don't want to go alone).
- Volunteer to represent your professional group in a coalition to speak out on the educational needs of young children (instead of waiting to be asked or declining because you've never done it before).
- Agree to serve on a legislative telephone tree (rather than refusing because "my phone call won't matter anyway").
- Work and learn with others to develop a position statement on a critical issue (instead of saying "I don't really know much about this topic").
- Volunteer to speak at a school board meeting about NAEYC's position statement, *Developmentally Appropriate Practice in Early Childhood Programs Serving Children from Birth through Age 8* (Bredekamp, 1987), instead of resigning yourself to the fact that your school system doesn't understand much about early childhood education.
- Conduct a local or state survey of salaries in early childhood programs (instead of ignoring the issue because no one has the facts).
- Persuade colleagues that it is important to work toward accreditation from the National Academy of Early Childhood Programs (rather than assuming no one wants to improve the program).

Source: S. G. Goffin & J. Lombardi (1988), *Speaking out: Early childhood advocacy.* (Washington, DC: National Association for the Education of Young Children), p. 14. © S. G. Goffin & J. Lombardi.

In the National Child Care Staffing Study (Whitebrook, Howes, & Phillips, 1990), low program quality was associated with programs offering lower salaries, fewer benefits, and poorer working conditions. Children in such programs did less well on tests of social development and language development, key areas for later learning. Based on initial reports of program directors, the study found a 41 percent annual turnover rate among staff members. When data were analyzed based on results of follow-up calls, a 37 percent turnover rate was found by the researchers in just over six months (Whitebrook, et al., 1990).

Another component of quality in early childhood programs is resources. This includes group size, preparation and training of teachers, health and safety considerations, and adult-child ratios. In the Abt Associates National Day Care Study (1979), it was found that group size made a big difference in the program quality. In smaller groups, the adults spent more time interacting with the children; in large group settings, adults spent more time watching the children (Abt Associates, 1979). The National Child Care Staffing Study found that grouping fewer children per caregiver was associated with more developmentally appropriate activities. Teacher interactions were found to be more sensitive and less harsh (Whitebrook et al., 1990).

In the experience of the National Association for the Education of Young Children's accreditation system, more developmentally appropriate experiences occur when staff members have a combination of formal education and specific training in early childhood (Bredekamp, 1989). More research is needed to differentiate the types and amounts of quality of preparation and training, but the importance of specialized training in early childhood education is clear.

There has been a strong focus on the health and safety issues in programs for young children during the past few years. Researchers such as Susan Aronson have been studying health risks in programs. Aronson has found a relationship between frequent adult hand washing and programs in which children become ill less often (Aronson, 1987). Considering the costs of health care expenses and missed days of work by parents, the costs of children's illnesses and injury are a serious concern. Children's safety is another important factor. Safety can be enhanced when there are adequate adult-child ratios and small group sizes. A recent publication noted that nineteen states permit ratios of five or more infants to each adult (Adams, 1990). These ratios should be seriously questioned from the standpoint of quality of interactions as well as safety.

DEVELOPMENTALLY APPROPRIATE PRACTICE

In the 1980s the quality of our entire educational system came under close public scrutiny. While most of the attention focused on the secondary school and postsecondary education, the field of early childhood education has critically examined its practices in light of current knowledge and research in the area of children's growth, development, and learning. A trend in the last decade was to formalize instruction more in academic skills for young children. Despite the trend toward more formal instruction, there has been no comparable evidence of change in how children learn or what they need for optimal development. Elkind (1986) stated that the trend is based on misconceptions about early learning.

A growing body of research has emerged recently affirming that children learn most effectively through a concrete, play-oriented approach to early childhood education (Bredekamp, 1987). Several professional organizations have published position statements or other publications in support of the belief that young children learn through active, participatory, hands-on experiences with the teacher serving as a facilitator (Graves, 1990b).

SECA Position Statement

In 1984, the Southern Association on Children Under Six, now called the Southern Early Childhood Association (SECA), distributed their statement about the kindergarten experience. In the introduction, the authors stated "inappropriate teaching strategies such as workbooks, ditto sheets, and formal reading groups as well as academic skill-oriented curriculum content in kindergarten raise serious concerns" (Southern Association on Children Under Six, 1984). The paper includes a discussion of the importance of play and the importance of matching learning experiences to the children's stages and needs. It also contains guidelines for designing appropriate learning environments for kindergartners (see Appendix B for the complete

There is almost always social learning occurring in this type of play activity.

position statement). The statement speaks strongly about young children's development and learning:

1. Kindergarten children constantly strive to understand and make sense of their experiences.
2. Kindergarten children develop understandings through play and other natural learning strategies.
3. The social, emotional, intellectual, and physical needs of kindergarten children are interrelated.
4. While kindergarten children follow similar developmental sequences, they do so in unique ways and at different rates.
5. Kindergarten children need adults to help them make sense of their experiences.
6. The best learning environment for kindergarten children is one in which they can actively participate by manipulating objects and by expressing their ideas through many curricular areas.
7. Kindergarten children learn best when all of their development/learning needs and interests are nurtured through a broad and understanding curriculum.
8. The different learning styles, interests, and developmental needs of kindergarten children can best be facilitated through informal, flexible classroom arrangements that use interest centers and individualized activities and games.
9. Kindergarten children learn best when the curriculum is based on concrete experiences to which they can relate in meaningful ways.

NAEYC Position Statement

An outgrowth of a position statement by the National Association for the Education of Young Children (NAEYC) was the publication titled *Developmentally appropriate practice in early childhood programs serving children from birth through age 8* (Bredekamp, 1987). This publication represents the views of thousands of early childhood educators who are members of the largest professional organization in our country. According to this publication, the concept of developmental appropriateness has the following two dimensions:

- *Age appropriateness.* Research supports the notion that there are universal, predictable sequences of growth and change that occur in children during their first nine years of life. These changes take place in all areas of development—physical, social, emotional, and intellectual. Knowledge of typical growth and development prepare the learning environment and learning opportunities.

- *Individual appropriateness.* It is recognized that each child is a unique person with individual style, learning rates, personality, and background. Curriculum decisions and adult interactions should be considered when responding to individual differences. "Learning in young children is the result of interaction between the child's thoughts and experiences with materials, ideas, and people" (Bredekamp, 1987, p. 2). These experiences should be consistent with the child's developing abilities as they strive to challenge the child's interest and understanding.

Teachers of young children use this child development knowledge to identify the range of activities, materials, and appropriate behaviors for a specific group of individual children. The NAEYC publication describes how developmental appropriateness can be applied to four components of early childhood programs: curriculum; adult-child interactions; relations between home and program; and evaluation of children. See Appendix P for more information. Other organizations, like the National Association of State Boards of Education and the Early Childhood Education Consultants in State Departments of Education, have published similar papers supporting appropriate educational experiences for young children.

ALTERNATIVE ASSESSMENT

Legislation in sixteen states and more than half of the districts in another seven states mandate that schools conduct kindergarten entrance screening (Ellwein, Walsh, Eads, & Miller, 1991). Children are tested for the purpose of identifying their level of readiness and their likelihood of showing success in the kindergarten program. In many places, if children are deemed "unready," they are excluded from entering the program. In some areas children are not excluded, but parents are warned that they may experience "failure" and their children may be required to repeat a program or participate in an alternative program. One serious problem with this practice is that test results are not always accurate and are sometimes interpreted incorrectly. Several researchers have concluded that one popular admission test, the *Gesell School Readiness Test* (Gesell Institute for Human Development, 1980) can result in the misidentification of 50–60 percent of the children tested and placed in extra-year programs (Graue & Shepard, 1989; Shepard & Smith, 1985).

Over the past ten years parents, teachers, and educational experts have expressed concern over the use of standardized tests and the harmful effects on children and schools. A national trend is gaining momentum to abandon standardized testing in favor of alternative approaches that are developmentally appropriate. Several states—including North Carolina, Arizona, Texas, Missouri, and Mississippi—have recognized the inappropriateness of standardized testing for young children and have moved to stop some forms of testing (Southern Association on Children Under Six, 1990).

TEACHERS SPEAK OUT

A teacher must stand up for the rights and needs of young children.

Testing, and the emphasis on testing, seems to narrow academic programs. Many teachers feel pressured to teach the test and focus on "drill and kill," memorization, and an excess of teacher-directed activities. These activities may take the place of creative, problem-solving, discovery, and self-directed types of learning. Tests are often culturally biased and discriminate against poor and minority children. Many of the test items from the 200 million examinations given annually to children from preschool to grade 12 are drawn from middle-class culture. Scores are also often used by teachers for labeling or tracking children into a certain group. As most everyone agrees, testing is often stressful. The tension and anxiety that parents and teachers feel at testing time can be passed on to children.

Collecting information about children in order to make appropriate decisions in planning for their learning and development is an important task of the teacher. Curriculum decisions should be based on the most accurate and appropriate information available. An appropriate assessment procedure should be helpful to the child and the teacher. Criteria of developmentally appropriate assessment is as follows (Southern Association on Children Under Six, 1990):

- Assessment must be valid.
- Assessment should not include standardized tests, pencil and paper tasks, and multiple-choice items.
- Assessment must deal with the whole child.
- Assessment must involve repeated observations.
- Assessment be continuous over time.
- Assessment must use a variety of methods.
- Assessment information must be used to change the curriculum to meet the individual needs of the children in the program.

Some experts are recommending that information collected on each child be placed in an assessment portfolio. This portfolio becomes a record of the teacher's comments, his or her observations, and representative work from the child. The portfolio can include such items as academic and nonacademic work samples, notes from systematic observations of the child, checklists, anecdotal records from the teacher, and notes from interviews with parents or others (Southern Association on Children Under Six, 1991). Other entries that inform the teacher or parent about the progress of the child may be added.

READINESS

In 1988 the Southern Regional Education Board endorsed a school readiness goal. Since then, it has been adopted by each of the fifteen member states. In 1990, a similar focus of readiness was chosen by the National Governors Association as the first national education goal. The goal stated, "By the year 2000, all children will start school ready to learn" (National Governors Association, 1990). The initial reaction by many educators was not very positive. Professionals in the field of education wondered if this group realized that learning does not begin at the time a child enters school. Other thoughts concerned the many influences on education that are present in a child's life at the time of birth. Some questions that arose were, "Can we ensure adequate prenatal care, health care, child care, address all childrens' nutritional needs, and provide a strong economic base for all families?"

Other questions were raised about how this school readiness goal will be measured. Some people felt the goal suggested a national school admissions test for first grade. This thought may have helped generate more attention on the arguments against readiness tests that we discussed in this chapter. One of the main criticisms centers around the recognition that readiness is not just an educational issue. It is widely accepted that readiness is also a health issue, a social issue, and an economic issue. Therefore, the responsibility cannot simply reside at the elementary school where each child enters the public education system. These issues and this goal involve practically all aspects of our society. They are the combined responsibility of every institution and agency whose services or programs touch the lives of children and families (Southern Regional Education Board, 1992).

Table 15.3 lists specific objectives for meeting the readiness goal. These objectives relate to the provision of quality early childhood education programs, prenatal care and nutrition, health care, and parent involvement. Policymakers will use "proxies," defined as indicators that indirectly measure factors positively associated with readiness. The National Center for Education Statistics has been assembling the proxy data, which include national statistics on

TABLE 15.3
National Goals for Education Readiness

Readiness Goal 1: By the year 2000, all children in America will start school ready to learn.

Objectives:

- All disadvantaged and disabled children will have access to high-quality and developmentally appropriate preschool programs that help prepare children for school.
- Every parent in America will be a child's first teacher and devote time each day helping his or her preschool child learn; parents will have access to the training and support they need.
- Children will receive the nutrition and health care needed to arrive at school with healthy minds and bodies, and the number of low-birthweight babies will be significantly reduced through enhanced prenatal health systems.

Source: Southern Regional Education Board, *Readiness for school: The early childhood challenge* (Atlanta, GA: Author, 1992), p. 14.

- Low-birthweight babies
- Child nutrition
- Supply and demand of preschool services
- Prenatal care
- Percent of eligibles served by subsidized preschool programs
- Kinds of learning experiences provided in programs
- Child retention data in early grades

The National Center for Education Statistics is using the National Household Education Survey, a planned triennial telephone survey to a national sample of households, for the ongoing tracking of much of this information (Turnbull, 1990).

CHALLENGES FOR THE FUTURE

Many other issues will influence the field of early childhood education. The full implications of these issues have yet to emerge:

Year-round schools
National goals
National standards
Education reform
Multicultural education
Multi-age groupings
Outcome-based education

Authentic assessment
Collaboration
Violence
Homelessness
AIDS
Teen pregnancies
Health care

Affordability of care	Quality of care
Acceptability of care	Extended day programs

How will the profession respond to these issues through the 1990s and into the next century? What role will *you* play in responding to the challenges affecting the care and education of young children and services to their families?

SUMMARY

The field of early childhood education is experiencing significant changes and challenges. Early childhood teachers must be ready to deal with a wide range of issues that will affect their programs and the youngsters they serve. One example is the changing makeup of American society. As a nation we are becoming increasingly diverse: We are a country of many different people and cultures. Early childhood educators need to be sensitive to diversity and respect individuality. Multicultural education will play a crucial role as early childhood professionals attempt to meet the needs of all children regardless of their gender, ethnic background, language, and abilities. The anti-bias curriculum gives teachers the tools needed to confront bias, prejudice, and stereotyping.

Both kindergarten and pre-kindergarten teachers find themselves confronting several issues affecting their students. These issues focus on the critical questions of appropriate age of entry, curriculum, and length of school day. Unfortunately, there is no easy answer; therefore, it is crucial that the early childhood educator always have the best interests of the individual child in mind.

Teachers of young children in programs also face many issues and challenges. It is important for the early childhood educator of today to critically examine the role of advocate for young children and families. This role must become a part of the teacher's professional and ethical responsibility. Connected to this role is the teacher's role in ensuring quality in programs. Teachers and administrators must work collaboratively to improve working conditions, teacher-child ratios, teacher salaries, health and safety concerns, and other components of programming that influence quality.

Many professional organizations are speaking out in support of developmentally appropriate practices for children. An abundant body of research affirms that children learn most effectively through a concrete, play-oriented approach. Teachers must use the knowledge available to make decisions that guide curriculum and practice in programs.

Recent legislation and research on testing suggests that assessment practices used decades ago are no longer effective today. It is important for beginning as well as seasoned teachers to remain current on assessment practices. Another issue teachers should stay current on is school readiness. This issue, which has received much attention, is an important one for teachers of children from birth through age 8.

TEST YOUR UNDERSTANDING

1. What does the concept *multicultural education* mean to you?
2. The United States is no longer described as a melting pot; instead, it is characterized as a patchwork quilt. Why has this perspective changed?
3. How can early childhood teachers incorporate cultural diversity in their classrooms?
4. At what age do you think children should begin kindergarten?
5. Should kindergarten programs be full time or part time?
6. What is your opinion about what constitutes an appropriate kindergarten curriculum?
7. What is the early childhood educator's role in being an advocate for young children?
8. What are three ways a classroom teacher can demonstrate his/her role as an advocate?
9. What ways can classroom teachers have a positive impact on the quality of the education and care of children?
10. Discuss the definition of *developmentally appropriate practice* and ways teachers can ensure that their practices are appropriate for the children in their care.
11. What are the pros and cons of the alternative assessment issue?
12. What are the pros and cons of the readiness goal?

LEARNING ACTIVITIES

1. Interview three early childhood professionals about current issues in the field. Do you agree or disagree with their viewpoints on each topic? Why?
2. Talk to parents of children with a cultural and ethnic background different from your own. What are the parents' views about child rearing strategies, importance of early schooling, parent involvement in education, and any other issues affecting young children?
3. Observe an early childhood classroom that uses an anti-bias curriculum. Record at least five examples of the anti-bias curriculum being demonstrated. These may be behaviors, activities, language episodes, or other instances.
4. Choose one of the issues addressed in this chapter and write a one- or two-page paper discussing your reaction to the issue.

LET'S TALK ABOUT IT

If you were Austin's teacher, how would you have told his parents of your suspicions?

What would you do if a child asked you, "Why is Austin's daddy mad?"

What strategies can be utilized to help Lee experience success?

What might be some of Stephanie's frustrations?

Is it necessary for early childhood professionals to provide opportunities for all children to participate in special programs?

What do you do for those children whose parents do not want them to participate in special events?

Was Stephanie correct in going to the executive director about her situation?

Matt couldn't wait to share his experiences from a parent-teacher meeting that he observed. The infant specialist had invited Austin's parents to come in for a conference, because she suspected that Austin might have a developmental delay. "I was surprised by how matter-of-fact she was about this possibility," Matt reported. "It was cold. The father just looked at the ceiling, and the mother reached for her handkerchief. I have never seen two parents so crushed. Within a matter of five minutes, this teacher managed to change the lives of an entire family. She asked the parents if they had any questions while telling them she needed to leave shortly."

Lillian reflected on an incident she had observed while visiting the administrator's office for her session. Austin's father was at the center when everyone arrived the next morning. "Mr. Smith met the director at the door," Lillian said. "He was very angry about a teacher. The director could not get him to go into her office. The parents, teachers, and many of the children coming to school could hear what was said."

Mildred was very concerned about a young boy named Lee, whom she had observed in the after-school program. "The children seem to notice that Lee is different from them and often will not participate in any planned group activities," said Mildred, "Lee seems very unhappy because he cannot meet the expectations of the group leader." Mildred added, "I understand that it's very important to the parents that Lee have as much contact as possible with his typical peers."

Stephanie tells her group that she was volunteered by her cooperating teacher to serve on a committee preparing a seasonal parent program. "The group of children enrolled at Spring Hill is very diverse. I was concerned about how every child was going to meaningfully participate. I couldn't get help from my teacher, so I went to see the executive director who—I thought—knew about these things."

EPILOGUE

Graduation

In his senior year, Matt was elected president of the student chapter of the state early childhood association. Matt has secured a teaching job in a Head Start program in his home town. He hopes to pursue graduate studies in early childhood with an interest in young children with special needs.

Stephanie is a kindergarten teacher in an inner city school. Her entire class attended her wedding.

Mildred owns several child care franchises. She is a strong advocate for young children at the local and state level. She is undergoing training to be a validator for the National Association for the Education of Young Children.

Lillian's daughter graduated with a degree in early childhood education. Lillian, however, who never figured out when children learn how to read, was awarded a degree in accounting.

Appendixes

APPENDIX A

The National Association for the Education of Young Children Code of Ethical Conduct

PREAMBLE

NAEYC recognizes that many daily decisions required of those who work with young children are of a moral and ethical nature. The NAEYC Code of Ethical Conduct offers guidelines for responsible behavior and sets forth a common basis for resolving the principal ethical dilemmas encountered in early childhood education. The primary focus is on daily practice with children and their families in programs for children from birth to 8 years of age: preschools, child care centers, family day care homes, kindergartens, and primary classrooms. Many of the provisions also apply to specialists who do not work directly with children, including program administrators, parent educators, college professors, and child care licensing specialists.

Standards of ethical behavior in early childhood education are based on commitment to core values that are deeply rooted in the history of our field. We have committed ourselves to:

- Appreciating childhood as a unique and valuable stage of the human life cycle
- Basing our work with children on knowledge of child development
- Appreciating and supporting the close ties between the child and family
- Recognizing that children are best understood in the context of family, culture, and society
- Respecting the dignity, worth, and uniqueness of each individual (child, family member, and colleague)
- Helping children and adults achieve their full potential in the context of relationships that are based on trust, respect, and positive regard

The Code sets forth a conception of our professional responsibilities in four sections, each addressing an arena of professional relationships: 1) children, 2) families, 3) colleagues, and 4) community and society. Each section includes an introduction to the primary responsibilities of the early childhood practitioner in that arena, a set of ideals pointing in the direction of exemplary professional practice, and a set of principles defining practices that are required, prohibited, and permitted.

The ideals reflect the aspirations of practitioners. The principles are intended to guide conduct and assist practitioners in resolving ethical dilemmas encountered in the field. There is not necessarily a corresponding principle for each ideal. Both ideals and principles are intended to direct practitioners to those questions which, when responsibly answered, will provide the

---

This Code of Ethical Conduct and Statement of Commitment was prepared under the auspices of the Ethics Commission of the National Association for the Education of Young Children. The Commission members were Stephanie Feeney (Chairperson), Bettye Caldwell, Sally Cartwright, Carrie Cheek, Josué Cruz, Jr., Anne G. Dorsey, Dorothy M. Hill, Lilian G. Katz, Pamm Mattick, Shirley A. Norris, and Sue Spayth Riley. From Feeney, S., & Kipnis, K. (1989). A new code of ethics for early childhood educators. Code of ethical conduct and statement of commitment. *Young Children, 45* (1), 24–29.

basis for conscientious decision making. While the Code provides specific direction for addressing some ethical dilemmas, many others will require the practitioner to combine the guidance of the Code with sound professional judgment.

The ideals and principles in this Code present a shared conception of professional responsibility that affirms our commitment to the core values of our field. The Code publicly acknowledges the responsibilities that we in the field have assumed and in so doing supports ethical behavior in our work. Practitioners who face ethical dilemmas are urged to seek guidance in the applicable parts of this Code and in the spirit that informs the whole.

SECTION I: ETHICAL RESPONSIBILITIES TO CHILDREN

Childhood is a unique and valuable stage in the life cycle. Our paramount responsibility is to provide safe, healthy, nurturing, and responsive settings for children. We are committed to supporting children's development by cherishing individual differences, by helping them learn to live and work cooperatively, and by promoting their self-esteem.

Ideals

I-1.1—To be familiar with the knowledge base of early childhood education and to keep current through continuing education and in-service training.

I-1.2—To base program practices upon current knowledge in the field of child development and related disciplines and upon particular knowledge of each child.

I-1.3—To recognize and respect the uniqueness and the potential of each child.

I-1.4—To appreciate the special vulnerability of children.

I-1.5—To create and maintain safe and healthy settings that foster children's social, emotional, intellectual, and physical development and that respect their dignity and their contributions.

I-1.6—To support the right of children with special needs to participate, consistent with their ability, in regular early childhood programs.

Principles

P-1.1—Above all, we shall not harm children. We shall not participate in practices that are disrespectful, degrading, dangerous, exploitative, intimidating, psychologically damaging, or physically harmful to children. **This principle has precedence over all others in this Code.**

P-1.2—We shall not participate in practices that discriminate against children by denying benefits, giving special advantages, or excluding them from programs or activities on the basis of their race, religion, sex, national origin, or the status, behavior, or beliefs of their parents. (This principle does not apply to programs that have a lawful mandate to provide services to a particular population of children.)

P-1.3—We shall involve all of those with relevant knowledge (including staff and parents) in decisions concerning a child.

P-1.4—When, after appropriate efforts have been made with a child and the family, the child still does not appear to be benefitting from a program, we shall communicate our concern to the family in a positive way and offer them assistance in finding a more suitable setting.

P-1.5—We shall be familiar with the symptoms of child abuse and neglect and know community procedures for addressing them.

P-1.6—When we have evidence of child abuse or neglect, we shall report the evidence to the appropriate community agency and follow up to ensure that appropriate action has been taken. When possible, parents will be informed that the referral has been made.

P-1.7—When another person tells us of their suspicion that a child is being abused or neglected but we lack evidence, we shall assist that person in taking appropriate action to protect the child.

P-1.8—When a child protective agency fails to provide adequate protection for abused or neglected children, we acknowledge a collective ethical responsibility to work toward improvement of these services.

SECTION II: ETHICAL RESPONSIBILITIES TO FAMILIES

Families are of primary importance in children's development. (The term *family* may include others, besides parents, who are responsibly involved with the child.) Because the family and the early childhood educator have a common interest in the child's welfare, we acknowledge a primary responsibility to bring about collaboration between the home and school in ways that enhance the child's development.

Ideals

I-2.1—To develop relationships of mutual trust with the families we serve.

I-2.2—To acknowledge and build upon strengths and competencies as we support families in their task of nurturing children.

I-2.3—To respect the dignity of each family and its culture, customs, and beliefs.

I-2.4—To respect families' childrearing values and their right to make decisions for their children.

I-2.5—To interpret each child's progress to parents within the framework of a developmental perspective and to help families understand and appreciate the value of developmentally appropriate early childhood programs.

I-2.6—To help family members improve their understanding of their children and to enhance their skills as parents.

I-2.7—To participate in building support networks for families by providing them with opportunities to interact with program staff and families.

Principles

P-2.1—We shall not deny family members access to their child's classroom or program setting.

P-2.2—We shall inform families of program philosophy, policies, and personnel qualifications, and explain why we teach as we do.

P-2.3—We shall inform families of and, when appropriate, involve them in policy decisions.

P-2.4—We shall inform families of and, when appropriate, involve them in significant decisions affecting their child.

P-2.5—We shall inform the family of accidents involving their child, of risks such as exposures to contagious disease that may result in infection, and of events that might result in psychological damage.

P-2.6—We shall not permit or participate in research that could in any way hinder the eduction or development of the children in our programs. Families shall be fully informed of any proposed research projects involving their children and shall have the opportunity to give or withhold consent.

P-2.7—We shall not engage in or support exploitation of families. We shall not use our relationship with a family for private advantage or personal gain, or enter into relationships with family members that might impair our effectiveness in working with children.

P-2.8—We shall develop written policies for the protection of confidentiality and the disclosure of children's records. The policy documents shall be made available to all program personnel and families. Disclosure of children's records beyond family members, program personnel, and consultants having an obligation of confidentiality shall require familial consent (except in cases of abuse or neglect).

P-2.9—We shall maintain confidentiality and shall respect the family's right to privacy, refraining from disclosure of confidential information and intrusion into family life. However, when we are concerned about a child's welfare, it is permissible to reveal confidential information to agencies and individuals who may be able to act in the child's interest.

P-2.10—In cases where family members are in conflict we shall work openly, sharing our observations of the child, to help all parties involved make informed decisions. We shall refrain from becoming an advocate for one party.

P-2.11—We shall be familiar with and appropriately use community resources and professional services that support families. After a referral has been made, we shall follow up to ensure that services have been adequately provided.

SECTION III: ETHICAL RESPONSIBILITIES TO COLLEAGUES

In a caring, cooperative work place human dignity is respected, professional satisfaction is promoted, and positive relationships are modeled. Our primary responsibility in this arena is to establish and maintain settings and relationships that support productive work and meet professional needs.

A—Responsibilities to Co-Workers

Ideals

I-3A.1—To establish and maintain relationships of trust and cooperation with co-workers.
I-3A.2—To share resources and information with co-workers.
I-3A.3—To support co-workers in meeting their professional needs and in their professional development.
I-3A.4—To accord co-workers due recognition of professional achievement.

Principles

P-3A.1—When we have concern about the professional behavior of a co-worker, we shall first let that person know of our concern and attempt to resolve the matter collegially.
P-3A.2—We shall exercise care in expressing views regarding the personal attributes or professional conduct of co-workers. Statements should be based on firsthand knowledge and relevant to the interests of children and programs.

B—Responsibilities to Employers

Ideals

I-3B.1—To assist the program in providing the highest quality of service.
I-3B.2—To maintain loyalty to the program and uphold its reputation.

Principles

P-3B.1—When we do not agree with program policies, we shall first attempt to effect change through constructive action within the organization.
P-3B.2—We shall speak or act on behalf of an organization only when authorized. We shall take care to note when we are speaking for the organization and when we are expressing a personal judgment.

C—Responsibilities to Employees

Ideals

I-3C.1—To promote policies and working conditions that foster competence, well-being, and self-esteem in staff members.
I-3C.2—To create a climate of trust and candor that will enable staff to speak and act in the best interests of children, families, and the field of early childhood education.
I-3C.3—To strive to secure an adequate livelihood for those who work with or on behalf of young children.

Principles

P-3C.1—In decisions concerning children and programs, we shall appropriately utilize the training, experience, and expertise of staff members.
P-3C.2—We shall provide staff members with working conditions that permit them to carry out their responsibilities, timely and nonthreatening evaluation procedures, written grievance procedures, constructive feedback, and opportunities for continuing professional development and advancement.
P-3C.3—We shall develop and maintain comprehensive written personnel policies that define program standards and, when applicable, that specify the extent to which employees are accountable for their conduct outside the work place. These policies shall be given to new staff members and shall be available for review by all staff members.
P-3C.4—Employees who do not meet program standards shall be informed of areas of concern and, when possible, assisted in improving their performance.
P-3C.5—Employees who are dismissed shall be informed of the reasons for their termination. When a dismissal is for cause, justification must be based on evidence of inadequate or inappropriate behavior that is accurately documented, current, and available for the employee to review.
P-3C.6—In making evaluations and recommendations, judgments shall be based on fact and relevant to the interests of children and programs.

P-3C.7—Hiring and promotion shall be based solely on a person's record of accomplishment and ability to carry out the responsibilities of the position.

P-3C.8—In hiring, promotion, and provision of training, we shall not participate in any form of discrimination based on race, religion, sex, national origin, handicap, age, or sexual preference. We shall be familiar with laws and regulations that pertain to employment discrimination.

SECTION IV: ETHICAL RESPONSIBILITIES TO COMMUNITY AND SOCIETY

Early childhood programs operate within a context of an immediate community made up of families and other institutions concerned with children's welfare. Our responsibilities to the community are to provide programs that meet its needs and to cooperate with agencies and professions that share responsibility for children. Because the larger society has a measure of responsibility for the welfare and protection of children, and because of our specialized expertise in child development, we acknowledge an obligation to serve as a voice for children everywhere.

Ideals

I-4.1—To provide the community with high-quality, culturally sensitive programs and services.

I-4.2—To promote cooperation among agencies and professions concerned with the welfare of young children, their families, and their teachers.

I-4.3—To work, through education, research, and advocacy, toward an environmentally safe world in which all children are adequately fed, sheltered, and nurtured.

I-4.4—To work, through education, research, and advocacy, toward a society in which all young children have access to quality programs.

I-4.5—To promote knowledge and understanding of young children and their needs. To work toward greater social acknowledgment of children's rights and greater social acceptance of responsibility for their well-being.

I-4.6—To support policies and laws that promote the well-being of children and families. To oppose those that impair their well-being. To cooperate with other individuals and groups in these efforts.

I-4.7—To further the professional development of the field of early childhood education and to strengthen its commitment to realizing its core values as reflected in this Code.

Principles

P-4.1—We shall communicate openly and truthfully about the nature and extent of services that we provide.

P-4.2—We shall not accept or continue to work in positions for which we are personally unsuited or professionally unqualified. We shall not offer services that we do not have the competence, qualifications, or resources to provide.

P-4.3—We shall be objective and accurate in reporting the knowledge upon which we base our program practices.

P-4.4—We shall cooperate with other professionals who work with children and their families.

P-4.5—We shall not hire or recommend for employment any person who is unsuited for a position with respect to competence, qualifications, or character.

P-4.6—We shall report the unethical or incompetent behavior of a colleague to a supervisor when informal resolution is not effective.

P-4.7—We shall be familiar with laws and regulations that serve to protect the children in our programs.

P-4.8—We shall not participate in practices which are in violation of laws and regulations that protect the children in our programs.

P-4.9—When we have evidence that an early childhood program is violating laws or regulations protecting children, we shall report it to persons responsible for the program. If compliance is not accomplished within a reasonable time, we will report the violation to appropriate authorities who can be expected to remedy the situation.

P-4.10—When we have evidence that an agency or a professional charged with providing services to children, families, or teachers is failing to meet its obligations, we acknowledge a collective ethical responsibility to report the problem to appropriate authorities or to the public.

P-4.11—When a program violates or requires its employees to violate this Code, it is permissible, after fair assessment of the evidence, to disclose the identity of that program.

APPENDIX B

Developmentally Appropriate Assessment

The use of standardized tests has been increasing rapidly across the United States. An estimated 200 million examinations are given annually to children from preschool through grade 12. The South has been in the forefront of the testing explosion. Throughout the region, both school reform and accountability have been mistakenly equated with increases in test scores.

More recently, parents, teachers, and other experts have expressed concern over the use of tests and the harmful effects on children and their schools. A trend is developing in the southern states to abandon standardized testing in favor of developmentally appropriate means of assessment. Mississippi, North Carolina, Texas and Arizona have recognized the harmful effects and moved to stop some forms of testing for young children.

The Southern Association on Children Under Six recommends a ban of the routine, mass use of standardized intelligence, achievement, readiness and developmental screening tests for young children through the age of eight.

SACUS recognizes and endorses the important role of assessment in planning quality programs for young children. However, assessment practices must be developmentally appropriate and related to curriculum goals. The routine, mass use of standardized tests is inconsistent with these goals and often causes serious harm to both individual children and to educational programs.

Source: Southern Early Childhood Association, Little Rock, AR.

TESTING PRACTICES HARM YOUNG CHILDREN

Testing encourages *narrow academic programs.* Many teachers feel driven to teach to the test and therefore focus on drill, memorization, and force-fed bits of conventional information which may be on a test. School practices which require children to solve problems, respond to open-ended questions, be creative, and to take responsibility for their own learning are often overlooked as teachers teach to the test. Content which is not tested is frequently ignored, such as the arts and the sciences.

Tests are often culturally biased and discriminate against poor and minority children. Test scores sometimes reflect family income as well as achievement of ability. The test items are usually drawn from middle-class culture and therefore middle-class children are more likely to know the answers. This is unfair to children from a disadvantaged environment.

Test scores are often used by teachers and parents to label children as "average," "slowlearner," "gifted," or "special education." These labels tend to hide the beauty and uniqueness of individual children and to define human differences as problems. Labeling, often based on faulty data, can cause life long harm to children whose true potential is hidden by the label.

Tests are often the sole or primary basis for tracking children and for determining promotion to a grade, placement within class groups, or enrollment in a special program such as transitional first grade, or programs for the gifted. Children placed in a track, particularly in the "low group," are given watered down content that creates unequal opportunities to learn. This virtually guarantees that they will not do well on future tests and will be tracked for life. Since tests discriminate against poor and minority children, this causes re-segregation by grouping in schools. Retention is not educationally helpful and leads to school drop-out.

Testing for young children is often stressful. The tension and anxiety that teachers and parents feel about tests are often communicated to children. This may cause a fear of tests, dislike for school, and feelings of inadequacy on the part of children.

LIMITATIONS OF STANDARDIZED TESTING

Young children are *not good test-takers*. They are not physically adept at the skills required for test taking, which include managing a pencil, "bubbling-in," visual discrimination, sitting for long periods, following verbal directions, and are easily influenced by the test-giver.

The most important aspect of assessment is validity—that is, the extent to which an instrument measures what it claims to measure. The two most common types of early childhood instruments are intelligence tests and readiness tests. Because there is little agreement within the profession on a definition of intelligence and what constitutes school readiness there can be no confidence that tests measure either. Achievement tests are valid only if they test what children are expected to learn. For example, if a school has the goal of creative story telling but the test has no items on story telling, the test is not valid for this school.

Tests are generally of *low technical quality*. The Center for the Study of Evaluation reviewed some 800 published standardized tests for young children including over 3,900 sub-tests and found less than one percent to be minimally satisfactory.

MISUSES OF TEST DATA

Tests do not measure accountability. Achievement tests do not measure what children are learning and do not provide accurate information about the education of children. Therefore, test data should not be used as proof of the quality of the education which children receive.

The public and professionals alike share a common misconception that test scores are objective and scientific. This faulty assumption leads to an unjustified confidence in and reliance on test scores for decision making. This means that judgements about children are based on faulty data rather than data which reflect each child's personal course of development.

People outside the profession often misuse tests for their own purposes. Politicians frequently use test scores as part of their campaigns to show a vote for them will be a vote for better education. Test scores are frequently misused to justify budget requests, to judge teachers, and to determine merit pay. Schools frequently misuse tests to compare classrooms of children, screen out the "undesirable" and those children who supposedly cannot benefit from their program.

APPROPRIATE ASSESSMENT

Gathering information about children to make good judgement about their learning and development is a central part of the teacher's role. Teachers must make daily decisions about children which should be professional judgements based on accurate and appropriate information. A good assessment process must help children and never cause them harm.

CRITERIA OF GOOD ASSESSMENT

Assessment must be *valid*. It must provide information related to the goals and objectives of each program.

Assessment should *not include* standardized tests, which are group administered, pencil and paper, multiple choice, and claim to measure achievement.

Assessment must deal with the *whole child*. Programs must have goals and assessment processes which relate to children's physical, social, emotional, and mental development.

Assessment must involve *repeated observations*. Many observations help teachers find patterns of behavior and avoid quick decisions which may be based on unusual behavior by children.

Assessment must be *continuous* over time. Each child should be compared to his or her own individual course of development over time rather than to average behavior for a group.

Assessment must use a *variety of methods*. Gathering a wide variety of information from different sources enables informed and professional decisions.

Assessment information must be used to change the curriculum to meet the individual needs of the children in the program.

GOOD ASSESSMENT PRACTICES

Information collected should be placed in an *assessment portfolio*, which should be kept for each child. A portfolio is a record of the teacher's observations and comments as well as a wide selection of the representative work which has been selected by the child and teacher together. The portfolio should include, but not be limited to:

Work Samples

A collection of informal and formal work, academic and non-academic, that can include samples of writing (including drafts of work); processes and results of investigations, problem solving, and experiments, including photographs of products; art work; audiotapes and "running record" of the child's reading; interviews; and lists of books read.

Teacher Observations

These can be informal notes on the child's classroom, social and academic interactions, as well as more formal observation records of activities and progress. Parent and other sources of information can be included.

Checklists and Inventories

A checklist can indicate activities across a range of developmentally appropriate tasks, abilities and competencies in social, physical, intellectual, emotional and language areas. In general, observations should be based on regular activity, not only specially constructed or artificial activities such as tests.

Parent Conferences

Information should be gathered from the parent's perspective about developmental relationships within the family. This may include the parent's perspective of the social and emotional climate in the home.

Teacher Constructed Tests or Projects

Specific feedback on teacher-initiated or child-chosen learning tasks, to complement work samples and teacher observations with more structured or formal work.

Referral Decisions

When the opinion of another professional is required for eye examination, speech and hearing evaluation, or psychological screening, a record of the reasons for the referral as well as outcomes should be included.

CAUTIONS ON ASSESSMENT

Assessment information is not to be used as tests for grading, labeling, grouping, or retaining children.

Children have different styles, rates, and motivations for learning.

Expect diversity among children and treat these differences with respect and dignity.

All forms of assessment and evaluation can be misused and influenced by biases about race, gender, income level, and culture. Each individual must guard against personal bias influencing professional behavior.

OTHER ORGANIZATIONS CONCERNED WITH THE MISUSE OF TESTS

These national associations have expressed concern over the misuse and abuse of testing practices related to young children.

Association of Childhood Education International

National Association of Early Childhood Specialists in State Departments of Education

National Association of Early Childhood Teacher Educators

National Association of Elementary School Principals

National Association for the Education of Young Children

National Association of School Psychologists

National Association of State Boards of Education

National Education Association

National Association of Early Childhood Specialists

APPENDIX C

Anecdotal Record Sample

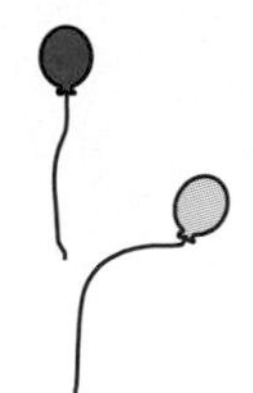

Name of child ______________ Date ______________________
Observer __________________ Time ______________________
Setting ____
Incident: ____
____
____
____
____
Comments: ____
Is this report cross-filed? Yes ________ No ________
Is supporting information available? Yes ________ No ________
What is it? ____
Where is it? ____

Source: C. Grace and E. F. Shores (1991). *The portfolio and its use: Developmentally appropriate assessment of young children.* Southern Early Childhood Association, Little Rock, AR. Used by permission.

APPENDIX D

Activity Chart Sample

Month ________________________________

Name ________________________________

	Sand & Water Play	Printing	Art	Music & Listening	Dramatic Play	Blocks	Math	Reading	Science	Language Arts	Social Studies
M											
T											
W											
T											
F											
M											
T											
W											
T											
F											
M											
T											
W											
T											
F											
M											
T											
W											
T											
F											
M											
T											
W											
T											
F											

Note: A check indicates the child completed the day's activity at the center.

Source: C. Grace and E. F. Shores (1991). *The portfolio and its use: Developmentally appropriate assessment of young children.* Southern Early Childhood Association, Little Rock, AR. Used by permission.

APPENDIX E

Systematic Record Sample

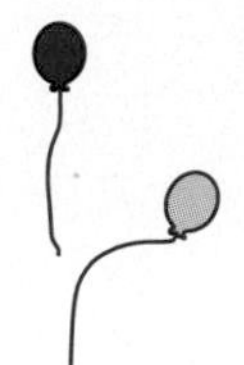

Directions: Each time a child comes to a center and completes an activity there, enter a tally mark in the appropriate space.
Child ______________________________
Observer ______________________________ Week of ______________________________

Learning Center	Day					Total
	Mon.	Tues.	Wed.	Thurs.	Fri.	
Science center						
Book center						
Puzzle center						
Art center						
Writing center						

Source: C. Grace and E. F. Shores (1991). *The portfolio and its use: Developmentally appropriate assessment of young children.* Southern Early Childhood Association, Little Rock, AR. Used by permission.

APPENDIX F

Kindergarten Checklist Sample

Student_____________________________ Age _____ Birthdate __________________
Teacher________________________ School ___________________ Academic Year ___

Checklist Marking Symbols

Satisfactory (S)	The skill or behavior has become a natural part of your child's actions.
Improvement Needed (I)	The skill or behavior has not become a natural part of your child's actions at this time.
Slash Mark (/)	The skill or behavior has not been taught in the curriculum at this time.

Skill or behavior	**Months**		
	1	**5**	**9**
Social/Emotional			
Responds to rights and feelings of others			
Remains involved until task is completed			
Demonstrates adequate attention span			
Works and plays independently			
Works and plays in group			
Takes care of self physically			
Takes care of own/others' materials			
Accepts authority easily			
Exhibits a cooperative attitude			
Exhibits eagerness to learn			
Verbal, Cognitive and Linguistic			
Asks questions for information and word meaning			
Shares ideas freely			
Acquires new vocabulary through experiences			
Knows meaning of morning, afternoon, night			
Knows meaning of spring, summer, fall, winter			
Knows days of week in sequence			
Verbalizes full name, phone number, home address, age, and birthday			

Source: C. Grace and E. F. Shores (1991). *The portfolio and its use: Developmentally appropriate assessment of young children.* Southern Early Childhood Association, Little Rock, AR. Used by permission.

continued

Kindergarten Checklist *(continued)*

Skill or behavior	**Months**		
	1	**5**	**9**
Uses "more," "less," "same," "different" correctly			
Recites songs and short fingerplays and poems			
Describes items and actions in pictures			
Distinguishes between living and non-living things			
Engages in imitative play and uses appropriate vocabulary (role plays real-life situations)			
Names at least seven basic colors			
Speaks clearly			
Listens to poems and stories with interest			
Exhibits curiosity about abstract words			
Understands left from right			
Can identify objects as to which is big, bigger, biggest, etc.			
Recognizes lower case letters (abcdefghijklmnopqrstuvwxyz)			
Recognizes upper case letters (ABCDEFGHIJKLMNOPQRSTUVWXYZ)			
Recognizes numerals to 20 (1 2 3 4 5 6 7 8 9 10 11 12 13 14 15 16 17 18 19 20)			
Recognizes likenesses and differences in letter sounds			
Enjoys looking at books			
Distinguishes rhyming words			
Distinguishes words beginning with same sound			
Knows left to right progression when looking at printed material			
Recognizes small number of printed words (labels, names, signs, etc.)			
Visual Perception			
Distinguishes differences among variety of shapes			
Identifies shapes in various sizes and positions			
Matches cut-out shapes of objects with actual objects			
Manipulates a variety of media to form objects			
Demonstrates understanding and usage of variety of spatial and positional terms			

continued

Kindergarten Checklist *(continued)*

Skill or behavior	**Months**		
	1	**5**	**9**
Demonstrates ability to complete puzzles with more than 10 pieces			
Manipulates a variety of media to form objects			
Constructs objects with blocks and other types of building materials			
Throws and catches a ball with some accuracy and performs most body movements with coordination			
Pre-number and Number Concepts			
Exhibits understanding of one-to-one correspondence			
Sorts objects according to function, size, and shape			
Identifies circle, square, triangle, rectangle, straight line			
Duplicates sequential order of objects or pictures			
Understands purpose of calendar			
Understands purpose of clock			
Tells time by the hour			
Understands "before" and "after"			
Understands purpose of thermometer			
Understands simple measurement techniques			
Joins sets of objects to sum of 10			
Separates sets out of 10			
Notes			

APPENDIX G

Sources: Standards/Guidelines for Playground Safety

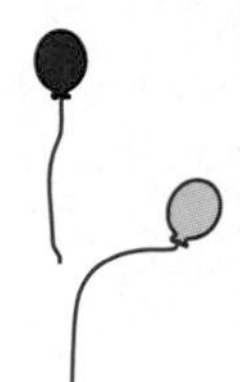

American Society for Testing and Materials. *Standard for Public Playground Equipment* and *Standard for Playground Surfacing*. 1916 Race Street, Philadelphia, PA 19103 (expected in 1992).

Canadian Institute of Child Health. (1984). *Draft for Children's Play Spaces and Equipment* (Draft 5, 1989). Canadian Institute of Child Health.

Deutsche Institut Fur Normung (D.I.N.). (1985). *Playground Equipment for Children: Concepts, Safety Requirements, Testing*. Berlin, West Germany: Deutsche Institut Fur Normung. Translation by British Standards Institution, Linford Wood, Milton Keynes, MK146LE. Tel: Milton Keynes (0908) 320033. Telex: 82577.

Kompan, Inc. (1984). *Playgrounds and Safety:* Comparisons between various playground equipment standards—American, Australian, British, German.

Seattle Department of Parks and Recreation. (1986). *Draft Design Guidelines for Play Areas*. Seattle, WA: 100 Dexter Avenue North, 98109.

U.S. Army Corps of Engineers. (1984). Planning and design of children's outdoor play environments—TM-803-11 (preliminary draft). Huntsville, AL: U.S. Corps of Engineers.

U.S. Consumer Product Safety Commission. (1981). *A Handbook for Public Playground Safety*, vol. I: General guidelines for new and existing playgrounds. Washington, DC: U.S. Consumer Product Safety Commission. Revised guidelines are scheduled for publication in late 1991.

______. (1981). *A Handbook for Public Playground Safety*, vol. II: Technical guidelines for equipment and surfacing. Washington, DC: U.S. Consumer Product Safety Commission.

Source: Reproduced by permission from *Play and Playscapes* by Joe L. Frost. Delmar Publishers, Inc., Albany, New York. Copyright 1992.

APPENDIX H

Infant-Toddler Playground Maintenance Checklist

Instructions: Check the playground thoroughly every week. Train all personnel to be alert constantly to playground hazards, and report and repair them promptly. Avoid the use of hazardous equipment until repaired.	**Date Checked**	**Repair Needed**	**Date Repaired**
1. Is there an 8–10-inch-deep ground cover (sand, or commercial material) under all swings, merry-go-rounds, slides, and climbing equipment? Is the resilient surface compacted or out of place? If concrete or asphalt is under equipment, is the manufactured impact attenuation product in place? Is pea gravel removed from the play area?			
2. Are there foreign objects or obstructions in the fall zones under and around fixed equipment?			
3. Are there obstructions to interfere with normal play activity?			
4. Are there climbing areas that would allow children to fall more than their reaching height when standing erect?			
5. Are concrete supports sticking above the ground? Are they secure?			
6. Are there sharp edges, broken parts, pinching actions, or loose bolts?			
7. Are there openings that could trap a child's head? Openings 3 to 9 inches wide should be avoided.			
8. Are there frayed cables, loose ropes, open S-hooks, or chains that could pinch or entangle?			
9. Are timbers rotting, splitting, termite infested, or excessively worn? Probe under ground for rotting and termites.			

Adapted from a checklist prepared for the Texas Department of Human Services by Joe L. Frost.

Infant-Toddler Playground Maintenance Checklist *(continued)*

	Date Checked	Repair Needed	Date Repaired
10. Are portable toys such as tricycles and wagons in good repair? Are small items that can choke children accessible to them?			
11. Are there protrusions that can catch clothing? Protrusions can include posts, bolts, and similar items.			
12. Are there crush points or shearing actions such as hinges and ends of seesaws and undercarriages of revolving equipment?			
13. Are swing seats excessively heavy? Do they have protruding parts such as animal noses or legs? Swing seats should be made of soft, pliable material.			
14. Is the fence at least 4 feet high and in good repair? Can gates be securely fastened? Is there a separate area for infants?			
15. Are there electrical hazards on the playground such as accessible air conditioners, switch boxes, or power lines?			
16. Are there collections of contaminated water on the playground?			
17. Are there toxic materials on the playground? Are bare metal decks and slides that can inflict burns exposed to the sun?			
18. Do the grass, trees, and shrubs need care? Are they poisonous?			
19. Do children wear inappropriate clothing, such as capes, on climbing and moving equipment?			
20. Does the adult-to-child supervision ratio equal ratios required for indoor activity?			

APPENDIX I

Maintenance Checklist

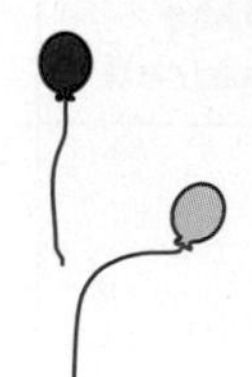

Date Detected	Date Repaired	
		• Hard surfaces under and around equipment in fall zones • Resilient surface material pitted or scattered • Insufficient space between equipment • Equipment not sized for age of children • Entrapment areas • Excessive or unprotected heights • Shearing and crushing mechanisms • Cracking, bending, warping, rusting, breaking or missing components • Pinching actions, open S hooks, deformed rings, links, etc. • Loose or uncapped bolts, nuts, etc. • Worn bearings or axles • Worn swing hangers (swivels) or chains • Metal slides in direct path of sun • Slide beds loose, metal edges accessible to fingers • Heavy swing seats or seats with protruding elements • Exposed or damaged concrete footings • Equipment improperly anchored • Sharp edges and points • Exposed or projecting elements, caps missing • Railings of insufficient height

Maintenance Checklist *(continued)*

Date Detected	Date Repaired	
		• Railings invite climbing (horizontal instead of vertical) • Exposed metal in tires or swing seats • Suspended elements (e.g., ropes, cables) in movement areas • Deteriorated (splintered, cracked, rotting) wood • Broken or missing railings, steps, swing seats, rungs, deck components, etc. • Slippery footing areas on decks, steps, walkways • Trash (broken glass, foreign objects, etc.) in area • Vandalism (fire damage, broken or missing parts) • Obstacles (rocks, roots, trash, badly placed equipment) in movement area • Poor drainage (standing water) • Accessible electrical apparatus (air conditioners, switch boxes) climbable poles, guy wires, ladders accessing electrical lines • Fence not installed or in need of repair, gates not securable (younger children), extra protection for pools • Signs illegible and in poor repair • Moving parts not lubricated • Toxic materials • Foreign material or equipment parts in fall zone

Source: Reproduced by permission from *Play and Playscapes* by Joe L. Frost. Delmar Publishers, Inc., Albany, New York. Copyright 1992.

APPENDIX J

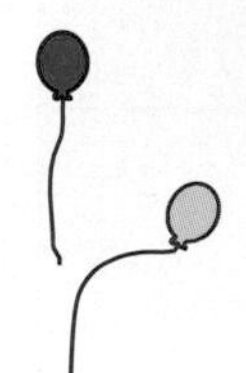

Developmentally Appropriate Equipment

BATTING TEE

Materials

- One 1-in. threaded diameter pipe 8 in. to 12 in. long
- One car radiator hose 12 in. to 18 in. long (inside diameter 1-½ in.)
- One block of wood 1 in. × 12 in. × 12 in.
- One pipe flange for 1-in. pipe to be mounted on the block
- Wood screws

Construction

1. Mount the flange on the block and screw the pipe into the flange.
2. Place the hose on the pipe.
3. For novelty, cut the base to resemble a "home plate" (Figure J.1).

FIGURE J.1 Batting Tee

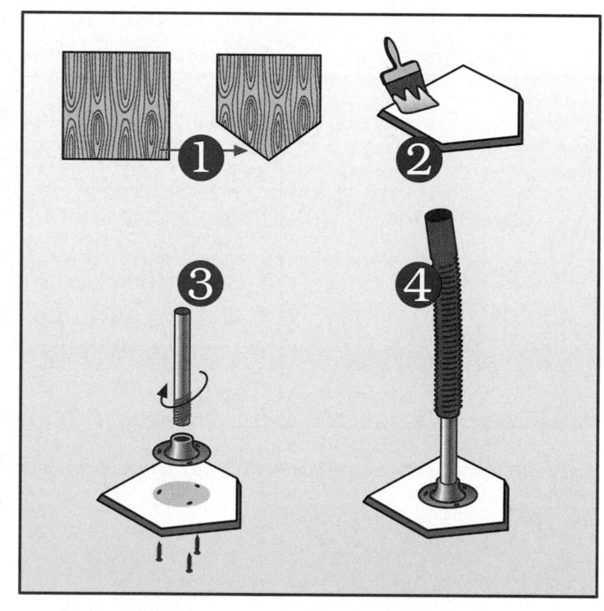

BIRDSEED TIMER

Materials

- Two 2-liter plastic soda bottles (leave the cap on one bottle)
- Three 27-in. wooden dowels
- Two 10-in. diameter circles (bases) cut from ½-in. plywood
- Glue
- Wood screws
- Birdseed (do not include sunflower seeds)
- Colorful plastic tape and duct tape

Construction

When completed, the timer will have the appearance of an hour glass.

1. Drill a 1/4-in. to 1/2-in. hole in the bottle cap (only one bottle will have a cap).
2. Place plastic tape at 3 to 4 equally spaced intervals around each bottle.
3. Fill one of the bottles ¾ full of birdseed and use duct tape to secure the two bottles together "top-to-top" (note: the bottles MUST be securely taped).
4. Place the two attached bottles so that one bottom rests on one of the bases. Place the other base on the opposite bottom.

5. Measure the distance between the two bases (it will be approximately 27 in.). The dowels must be cut to fit tightly between the two bases to hold the bottles in place.
6. Drill three ¼-in. holes in each base to hold the dowels according to the diagram. Fill the holes with glue, place the dowels in the holes and secure through the base with wood screws. (see Figure J.2).

FIGURE J.2 Birdseed Timer

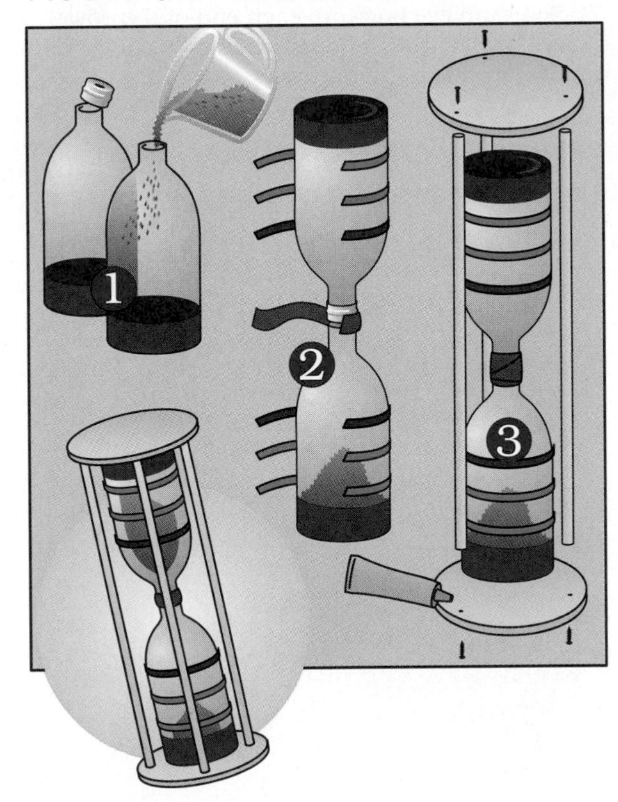

JUMPING MAT

Materials

- One non-skid rubber mat, 8 ft. to 10 ft. long
- Colorful latex enamel paint (variety of bright colors)
- One pair of cardboard foot patterns (cut to the size of a young child's feet)

Construction

1. Paint 2-in. wide colored lines, or 6-in. to 10-in. geometric shapes across the width of the mat at 8-in. to 12-in. intervals.
2. Draw and paint "feet" at one end of the mat to indicate the starting point and proper foot placement (see Figure J.3).

FIGURE J.3 Jumping Mat

JUMPING STANDARDS

Materials

- Two pieces of ¾-in. plywood (15 in. × 25 in.)
- Two bases (a 2-in. × 6-in. × 12-in. board with a 1-in. deep groove cut lengthwise in the middle)
- Colorful latex enamel paint (variety of colors)
- Glue
- Wood screws
- Dowel to be used as a crossbar

Construction

1. Cut the plywood according to the diagram with notches approximately 2 in. apart.
2. Secure the plywood frames into the 1-in. deep grooves of the bases with glue and wood screws.

3. Paint each section a different color (see Figure J.4).
4. Rest the crossbar in the notches.

FIGURE J.4 Jumping Standards

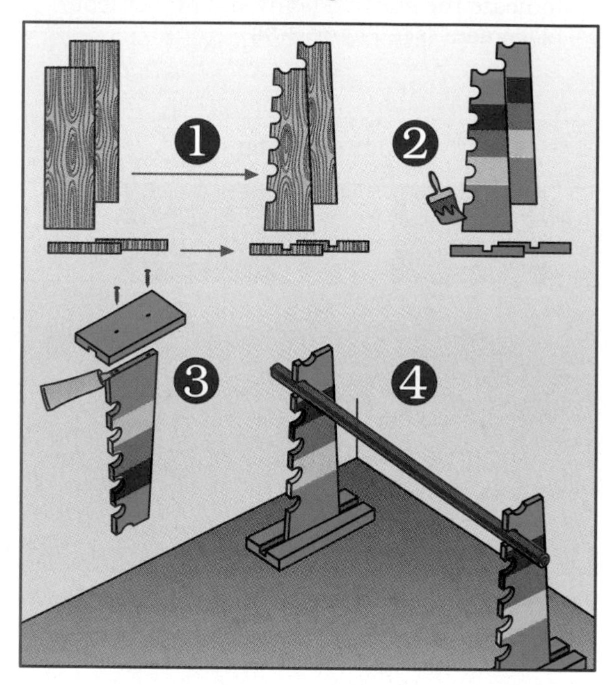

KICKING CHIMES

Materials

- One 1-in. metal pipe (total of 120-in. length)
- One 1-in. wooden dowel (5 ft. long)
- Cotton rope/cord
- Drill
- Metal pipe cutter
- Two eye bolts

Construction

1. Cut the 1-in. metal pipe into the following lengths: two 20 in., two 16 in., two 12 in., and one 24 in.
2. Drill holes large enough for the rope to go through into one end of each metal section, or place a cap with a threading hole on one end.
3. Drill holes 8 in. apart in the dowel; the holes need to be large enough for the rope.
4. Thread the ropes through the hole or cap in each pipe.
5. Thread the other end of the rope through one hole in the dowel.
6. Repeat this process with all pipes, allowing the chimes (pipes) to hang so that the chimes are even across the bottom (see Figure J.5).
7. Screw an eye bolt into each end of the dowel and use a rope to hang the chimes between two hooks or standards.

FIGURE J.5 Kicking Chimes

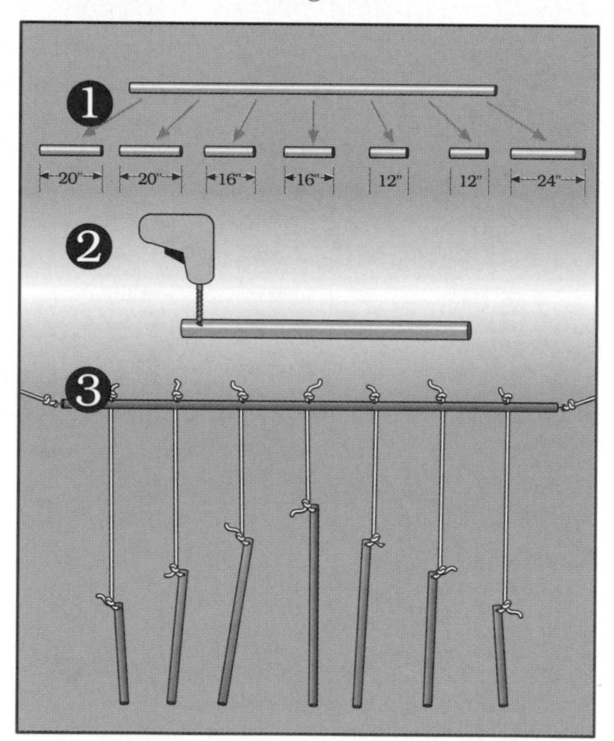

LARGE STATIONARY TARGETS

Materials

- One piece of muslin cloth or a bed sheet cut to 4 ft. × 6 ft.

- Colorful, latex enamel paint
- Cotton rope/cord

Construction

1. Paint a large, colorful cartoon or storybook character onto the cloth.
2. Sew a 2-in. hem in the top of the target and thread the cotton rope through the hem.
3. Hang the target between two wall hooks or standards.

NEAT FEET

Materials

- One nonskid rubber mat (size may range from 12 in. × 24 in. to 18 in. × 32 in.)
- One pair of cardboard foot patterns (cut to the size of a young child's feet)
- Colorful, latex enamel paint

Construction

1. Paint foot patterns for throwing or striking on the non-skid rubber mat as indicated in Figures J.6 and J.7.

FIGURE J.6 Neat Feet (throwing)

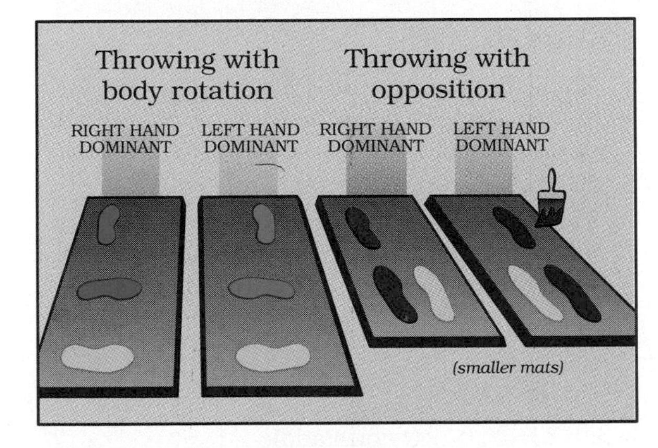

FIGURE J.7 Neat Feet (striking)

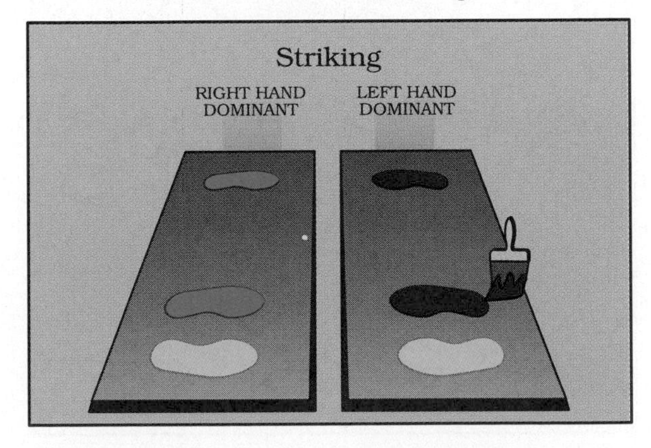

LUMMI STICKS

Materials

- One ¾-in. wooden dowel, or a cardboard cylinder from a slacks hanger (available from a commercial dry cleaner)
- Colorful contact paper or paint
- Plastic tape
- Newspaper
- Masking or duct tape

Construction

Lummi sticks can be made from wooden dowels or cardboard.

Wooden Dowels

Cut the 3⁄4-inch dowel into 10-in. to 12-in. lengths, sand the ends, and paint.

Cardboard

1. Take the cardboard cylinder from the slacks hanger and cut to a 10-in. to 12-in. length.
2. Cover with newspaper until the thickness is approximately ¾-in.
3. Roll tightly and secure with masking or duct tape at several points.
4. Cover with contact paper or plastic tape. Be sure the ends are covered securely.

2. Paint the feet on the "smoothest" side of the rubber mat. Mats should be made for right- and left-hand dominant children to use when throwing with opposition, throwing with body rotation and striking. Paint the "stepping foot" one color and the stationary foot a different color.

NYLON PADDLE

Materials

- One heavy wire clothes hanger
- Plastic or duct tape
- Nylon stocking (knee-high stockings work best)

Construction

1. Shape the hanger into a diamond or circular shape. Straighten the hook of the hanger and curl up the end to form a closed-loop handle.
2. Slip the stocking over the hanger.
3. Pull the stocking firmly, wrap the excess around the handle, tie and tape securely (see Figure J.8).

FIGURE J.8 Nylon Paddle

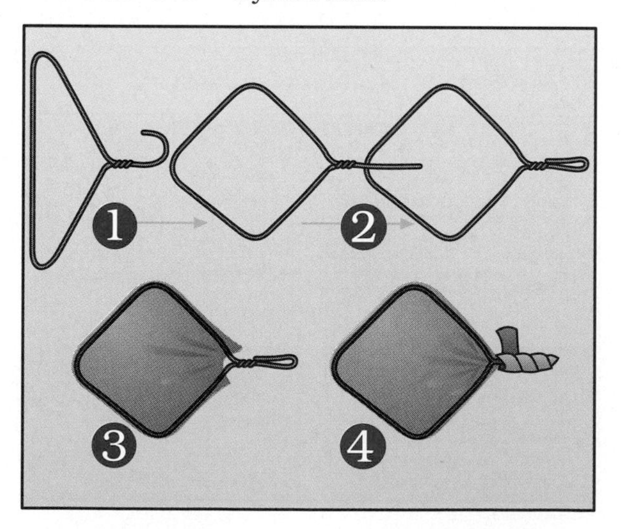

PENDULUM TARGET

Materials

- One fiberglass bicycle antenna
- One 2-ft. × 3-ft. piece of ¾-in. plywood to serve as a base
- A cloth or plexiglass target
- Hooks or velcro to attach the target to the antenna

Construction

1. Drill a ½-in. hole in the base.
2. Glue the antenna into the hole.
3. Attach the cloth or plexiglass target to the antenna. When hit, the target sways like a pendulum (see Figure J.9).

FIGURE J.9 Pendulum Target

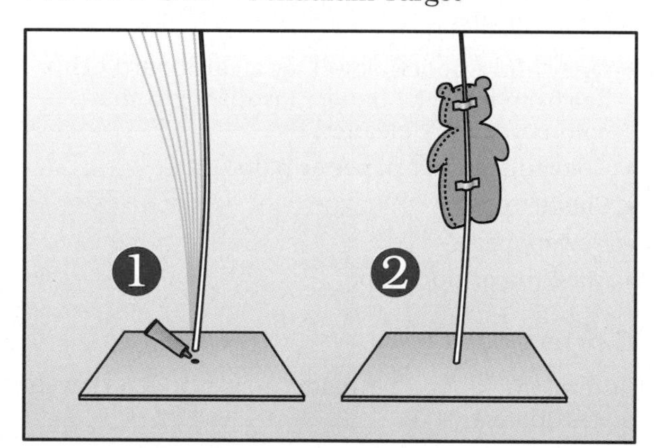

ROPE COIL

Materials

- One ½-in. to 1-in. diameter rope
- Duct or plastic tape

Construction

1. Cut the rope into 12-in. sections.

2. Form a circle with each section and securely tape the ends together (see Figure J.10).

FIGURE J.10 Rope Coil

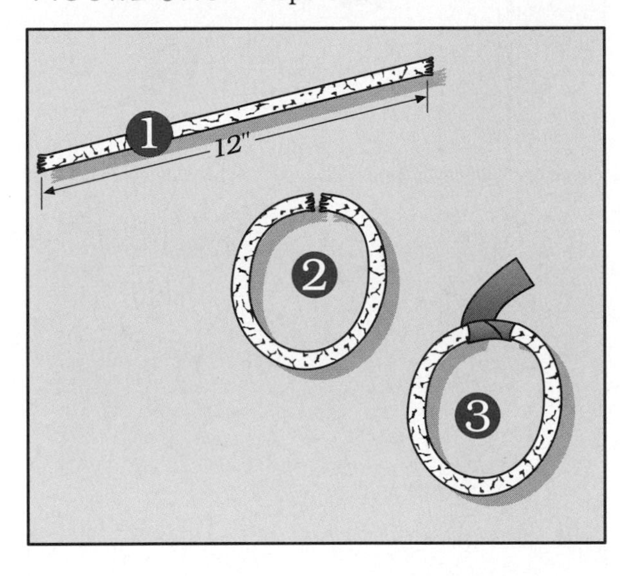

SCOOP

Materials

- One 1-gallon plastic bleach or milk container
- Plastic tape
- Scissors
- Utility knife

Construction

1. Hold the container by the handle with the top (cap end) closest to you.
2. Cut into a scoop shape as shown in the diagram.
3. Smooth the edges with scissors and cover with plastic tape to ensure safety and increase attractiveness (see Figure J.11).

FIGURE J.11 Scoop

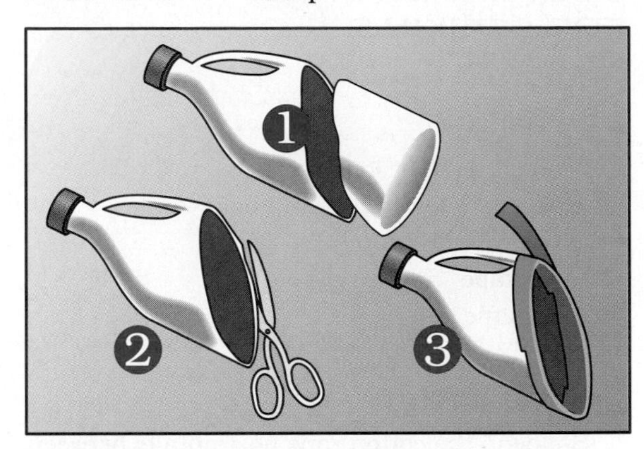

STARTER

Materials

- Two wooden blocks (1 in. × 4 in. × 10 in.)
- Two hinges
- Wood screws
- Two cabinet handles or knobs

Construction

1. Hinge the two wooden blocks together.
2. Attach the handles/knobs at desired locations (see Figure J.12).

FIGURE J.12 Starter

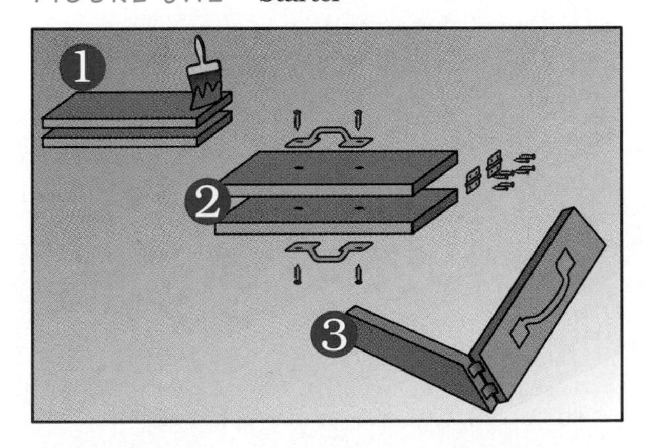

SUSPENDED BALL FOR STRIKING

Materials

- Nylon cord (10 ft. long)
- One metal shower curtain hook
- Cotton rope (10 ft. to 15 ft. long)
- Plastic tape
- One whiffle ball

Construction

1. Suspend the cotton rope horizontally between two standards or wall hooks.
2. Using the non-sticky side of the plastic tape, loosely secure the large end of the shower curtain hook to the cotton rope (this strategy allows the hook to slide on the rope as the ball is hit).
3. Tie an adjustable knot with the nylon rope; attach the single end of the rope to the whiffle ball (this allows for adjustment of ball height).
4. Attach the loop end of the hangman's knot to the small end of the shower curtain hook. (see Figure J.13).

FIGURE J.13 Suspended Ball for Striking

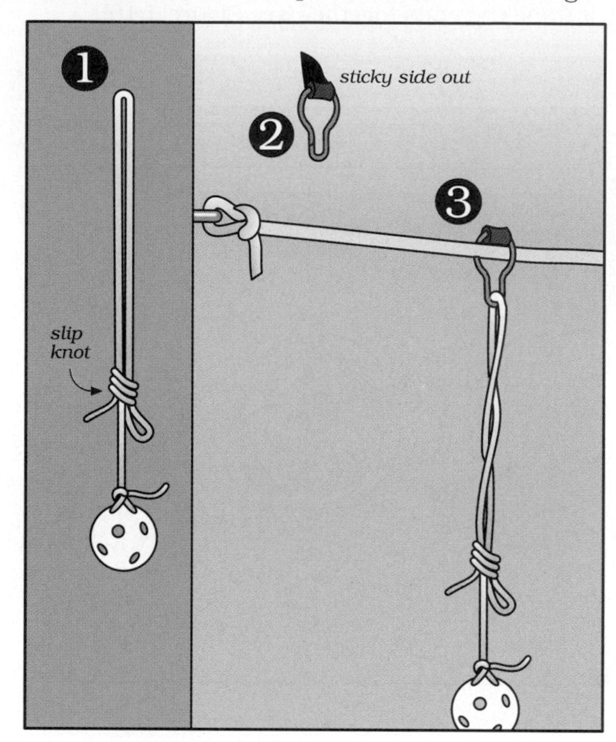

SUSPENDED BALL FOR CATCHING

Materials

- Nylon cord (10 ft. long)
- One metal shower curtain hook
- Cotton rope (10 ft. to 15 ft. long)
- Plastic tape
- One 6-in. to 10-in. foam ball
- Large metal washer

Construction

1. Refer to the procedures for the suspended ball for striking.
2. Use a sharp object such as a screwdriver to thread the single end of the rope with the adjustable knot through the foam ball.
3. Put the end of the rope through a large metal washer, then tie a knot. This procedure helps to keep the knot from pulling back through the ball (see Figure J.14).

YARN BALL

Materials

- One skein of yarn
- Kite cord
- Scissors
- One piece of cardboard (5 in. wide and 10 in. long)

Construction

1. Wrap the yarn around the cardboard 75 to 100 times, and cut the end from the remainder of the skein of yarn.

FIGURE J.14 Suspended Ball for Catching

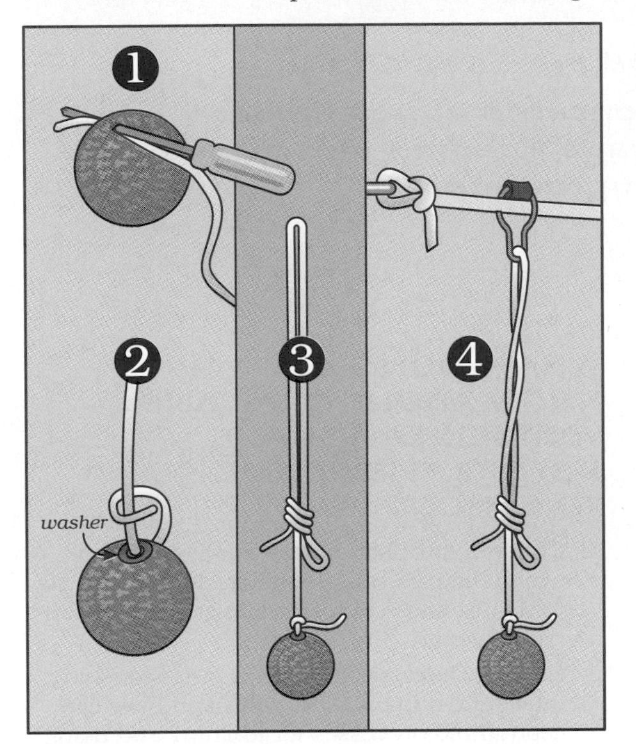

FIGURE J.15 Yarn Ball

2. Remove the wrapped yarn from the cardboard; use a piece of kite cord to tie it securely in the middle (we will refer to this as a looper).
3. Make three loopers. Tie the three loopers together securely (position the loopers together so that the middle of each looper is touching).
4. Trim the loops. Continue to trim the yarn until the ball is fluffy and approximately 4" in diameter. When completed, the ball should have a firm and full appearance. The key to a firm yarn ball is to tie each looper as tightly as possible with the kite cord (see Figure J.15).

APPENDIX K

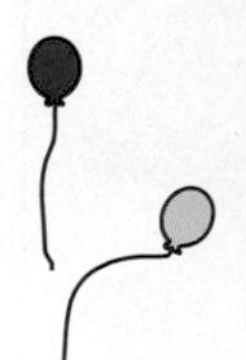

Literacy Development and Pre-First Grade

A Joint Statement of Concerns about Present Practices in Pre-First Grade Reading Instruction and Recommendations for Improvement

- Association for Childhood Education International
- Association for Supervision and Curriculum Development
- International Reading Association
- National Association for the Education of Young Children
- National Association of Elementary School Principals
- National Council of Teachers of English

OBJECTIVES FOR A PRE-FIRST GRADE READING PROGRAM

Literacy learning begins in infancy. Reading and writing experiences at school should permit children to build upon their already existing knowledge of oral and written language. Learning should take place in a supportive environment where children can build a positive attitude toward themselves and toward language and literacy. For optimal learning teachers should involve children actively in many meaningful, functional language experiences, including *speaking, listening, writing* and *reading.* Teachers of young children should be prepared in ways that acknowledge differences in language and cultural backgrounds and emphasize reading as an integral part of the language arts as well as of the total curriculum.

WHAT YOUNG CHILDREN KNOW ABOUT ORAL AND WRITTEN LANGUAGE BEFORE THEY COME TO SCHOOL

1. Children have had many experiences from which they are building their ideas about the functions and uses of oral language and written language.
2. Children have a command of language, have internalized many of its rules and have conceptualized processes for learning and using language.
3. Many children can differentiate between drawing and writing.
4. Many children are reading environmental print, such as road signs, grocery labels, and fast food signs.
5. Many children associate books with reading.
6. Children's knowledge about language and communication systems is influenced by their social and cultural backgrounds.
7. Many children expect that reading and writing will be sense-making activities.

Concerns

1. Many pre-first children are subjected to rigid, formal pre-reading programs with inappropriate expectations and experiences for their levels of development.

Source: "Literacy Development and Pre-First Grade," from *The Reading Teacher*, April 1986. Reprinted with permission of the International Reading Association.

2. Little attention is given to individual development or individual learning styles.
3. The pressures of accelerated programs do not allow children to be risk-takers as they experiment with language and internalize concepts about how language operates.
4. Too much attention is focused upon isolated skill development or abstract parts of the reading process, rather than upon the integration of oral language, writing and listening with reading.
5. Too little attention is placed upon reading for pleasure; therefore, children often do not associate reading with enjoyment.
6. Decisions related to reading programs are often based on political and economic considerations rather than on knowledge of how young children learn.
7. The pressure to achieve high scores on standardized tests that frequently are not appropriate for the kindergarten child has resulted in changes in the content of programs. Program content often does not attend to the child's social, emotional and intellectual development. Consequently, inappropriate activities that deny curiosity, critical thinking and creative expression occur all too frequently. Such activities foster negative attitudes toward communication skill activities.
8. As a result of declining enrollments and reduction in staff, individuals who have little or no knowledge of early childhood education are sometimes assigned to teach young children. Such teachers often select inappropriate methodologies.
9. Teachers of pre-first graders who are conducting individualized programs without depending upon commercial readers and workbooks need to articulate for parents and other members of the public what they are doing and why.

Recommendations

1. Build instruction on what the child already knows about oral language, reading and writing. Focus on meaningful experiences and meaningful language rather than merely on isolated skill development.
2. Respect the language the child brings to school, and use it as a base for language and literacy activities.
3. Ensure feelings of success for all children, helping them see themselves as people who can enjoy exploring oral and written language.
4. Provide reading experiences as an integrated part of the broader communication process, which includes speaking, listening and writing, as well as other communication systems such as art, math and music.
5. Encourage children's first attempts at writing without concern for the proper formation of letters or correct conventional spelling.
6. Encourage risk-taking in first attempts at reading and writing and accept what appear to be errors as part of children's natural patterns of growth and development.
7. Use materials for instruction that are familiar, such as well-known stories, because they provide the child with a sense of control and confidence.
8. Present a model for students to emulate. In the classroom, teachers should use language appropriately, listen and respond to children's talk, and engage in their own reading and writing.
9. Take time regularly to read to children from a wide variety of poetry, fiction and non-fiction.
10. Provide time regularly for children's independent reading and writing.
11. Foster children's affective and cognitive development by providing opportunities to communicate what they know, think and feel.
12. Use evaluative procedures that are developmentally and culturally appropriate for the children being assessed. The selection of evaluative measures should be based on the objectives of the instruction program and should consider each child's total development and its effect on reading performance.
13. Make parents aware of the reasons for a total language program at school and provide them with ideas for activities to carry out at home.
14. Alert parents to the limitations of formal assessments and standardized tests of pre-first graders' reading and writing skills.
15. Encourage children to be active participants in the learning process rather than passive recipients of knowledge, by using activities that allow for experimentation with talking, listening, writing and reading.

APPENDIX L

Appropriate and Inappropriate Practice for the Primary Grades

Component	Appropriate Practice	Inappropriate Practice
Integrated curriculum	The goals of the language and literacy program are for children to expand their ability to communicate orally and through reading and writing, and to enjoy these activities. Technical skills or subskills are taught as needed to accomplish the larger goals, not as the goal itself. Teachers provide generous amounts of time and a variety of interesting activities for children to develop language, writing, spelling, and reading ability, such as: looking through, reading, or being read high quality children's literature and nonfiction for pleasure and information; drawing, dictating, and writing about their activities or fantasies; planning and implementing projects that involve research at suitable levels of difficulty; creating teacher-made or child-written lists of steps to follow to accomplish a project; discussing what was read; preparing a weekly class newspaper; interviewing various people to obtain information for projects; making books of various kinds (riddle books, *what if* books,	The goal of the reading program is for each child to pass the standardized tests given throughout the year at or near grade level. Reading is taught as the acquisition of skills and subskills. Teachers teach reading only as a discrete subject. When teaching other subjects, they do not feel they are teaching reading. A sign of excellent teaching is considered to be silence in the classroom and so conversation is allowed infrequently during select times. Language, writing, and spelling instruction are focused on workbooks. Writing is taught as grammar and penmanship. The focus of the reading program is the basal reader, used only in reading groups, and accompanying workbooks and worksheets. The teacher's role is to prepare and implement the reading lesson in the teacher's guidebook for each group each day and to see that other children have enough seatwork to keep them busy throughout the reading group time. Phonics instruction stresses learning rules rather

Appropriate and Inappropriate Practice for the Primary Grades *(continued)*

Component	Appropriate Practice	Inappropriate Practice
Integrated curriculum	books about pets); listening to recordings or viewing high quality films of children's books; being read at least one high quality book or part of a book each day by adults or older children; using the school library and the library area of the classroom regularly. Some children read aloud daily to the teacher, another child, or a small group of children, while others do so weekly. Subskills such as learning letters, phonics, and word recognition are taught as needed to individual children and small groups through enjoyable games and activities. Teachers use the teacher's edition of the basal reader series as a guide to plan projects and hands-on activities relevant to what is read and to structure learning situations. Teachers accept children's invented spelling with minimal reliance on teacher-prescribed spelling lists. Teachers also teach literacy as the need arises when working on science, social studies, and other content areas.	than developing understanding of systematic relationships between letters and sounds. Children are required to complete worksheets or to complete the basal reader although they are capable of reading at a higher level. Everyone knows which children are in the slowest reading group. Children's writing efforts are rejected if correct spelling and standard English are not used.

Source: From *Developmentally Appropriate Practice in Early Childhood Programs Serving Children form Birth Through Age 8* (exp. ed.) (p.70) by S. Bredekamp, 1987, Washington, DC: National Association for the Education of Young Children. Copyright © 1987 by NAEYC. Reproduced by permission.

APPENDIX M

Materials for Math and Science

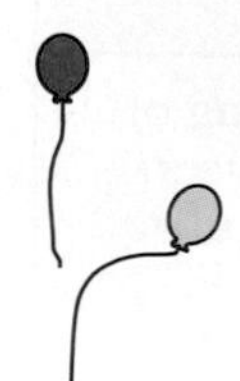

MATH

- Objects for classification, such as dollhouse furniture, different-colored beads, pebbles, and other raw materials
- Materials for making comparisons—that is, objects that are large and small, heavy and light, long and short, and have dark and light hues of the same color
- Materials for measuring, such as strings or yarn, measuring cups, scales, a trundle wheel, homemade rulers; many materials for counting, such as tongue depressors, counting chips (usually plastic and commonly referred to as poker chips), an abacus, cold drink cups, nuts, or other raw materials
- Materials for seeing part/whole relationship
- Materials for patterning, such as beads to string. Other patterning materials are commercially produced and include
  - –Cuisenaire rods—centimeter-square rods in lengths from 1 to 10 centimeters in various colors to differentiate their sizes
  - –Pattern blocks—wooden blocks in six colors and shapes that have uniform thickness
  - –Parquetry blocks and cards—wooden blocks of assorted colors and shapes with uniform thickness and pattern cards that children can follow
  - –Multibase blocks—wooden or plastic blocks that vary in color, shape, thickness, and size
  - –Geoboards—plastic or wooden boards with nails or pegs in an array, typically 5 in. by 5 in.
  - –Geoblocks—pieces of unfinished hardwood cut into a wide variety of shapes and sizes

SCIENCE

Bought or donated materials include

- Tripod magnifier stand
- Outdoor-indoor thermometer
- Magnets—horseshoe and bar
- Hand magnifier
- Rain gauge
- Aquarium
- Flashlight
- Tape recorder
- Prism
- Popcorn Popper
- Hot plate
- Balance scale

Consumable materials include

- Masking tape, transparent tape
- Batteries
- Paper towels
- Yarn
- Potting soil
- Sandpaper
- Fruits and vegetables
- Wax paper
- Paper bags
- Cotton balls
- String

From L. Ard and M. Pitts, *Room to grow: How to create quality early childhood environments*. Texas Association for the Education of Young Children. (Austin, TX: Texas Association for the Education of Young Children, 1990). pp. 80, 163.

- Paper cups
- Spices

Readily available materials include

- Plastic glasses, cups, bowls
- Measuring cups
- Tongs
- Sponges
- Spoons
- Dishpans
- Spatulas
- Plastic
- Spray bottles
- Ramp
- Lock and key

Items found in the natural environment include

- Feathers
- Leaves
- Twigs
- Rocks
- Soil samples
- Nonpoisonous plants
- Mosses
- Shells
- Bark
- Live insects
- Empty nests

APPENDIX N

Enriching Classroom Diversity with Books for Children

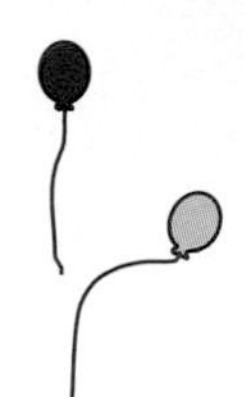

Think what a difference it would make in your classroom if you merely bought, often read and discussed, and sometimes did story-extension activities related to a number of these books! Buying and frequently using diversity books with your children can make the most homogeneous group more familiar with human diversity!

Children with Special Situations

Caines, J. (1973). *Abby*, New York: Harper & Row.

Clifton, L. (1983). *Everett Anderson's goodbye.* New York: Holt.

Remember books like Lionni's *Frederick* and Brown's *Arthur's eyes.*

Cooperation

Ancona, G. (1985). *Helping out.* New York: Clarion Books.

Burningham, J. (1973). *Mr. Gumpy's motor car.* New York: Crowell.

Galdone, P. (1973). *The little red hen.* Boston: Houghton Mifflin.

Iwamura, K. (1984), *Ton and Pan.* New York: Bradbury.

Lionni, L. (1973). *Swimmy*, New York: Knopf.

Mann, P. (1966). *The street of the flower boxes.* New York: Coward, McCann & Geoghegan.

Diverse Abilities: Children and Others with Disabilities

Aseltine, L. & Mueller, E. (1986). *I'm deaf and it's okay.* Niles, IL: Whitman.

Baker, P. (1986). *My first book of sign.* Washington, DC: Gallaudet University Press.

Bellet, J. (1984). *A-B-C-ing: An action alphabet.* New York: Crown.

Bourke, L. (1981). *Handmade ABC reading.* Reading, MA: Addison-Wesley.

Brown, T. (1991). *Someone special, just like you.* New York: Holt, Rinehart & Winston.

Cairo, S. (1985). *Our brother has Down's syndrome.* Willowdale, ON: Annick Press.

Children's Television Workshop. (1980). Sign language fun. New York: Random House.

dePaola, T. (1981). *Now one foot, now the other.* New York: Putnam.

Frank, D. (1974). *About handicaps: An open family book for parents and children together.* New York: Walker.

Greenfield, E. (1980). *Darlene*, New York: Methuen.

Head, B., & Seguin, J. (1975). *Who am I?* Pittsburgh: Family Communications.

Heide, F. (1979). *Sound of sunshine, sound of rain.* New York: Scholastic.

Jensen, V. A. (1983). *Catching.* New York: Putnam.

Larche, D. W. (1985). *Father Gander nursery rhymes.* Santa Barbara, CA: Advocacy Press.

Litchfield, A. (1976). *A button in her ear.* Niles, IL: Whitman.

Litchfield, A. (1977). *A cane in her hand.* Niles, IL: Whitman.

Peterson, J. (1977). *I have a sister, my sister is deaf.* New York: Harper & Row.

Powers, M. E. (1986). *Our teacher's in a wheelchair.* Niles, IL: Whitman.

Quinsey, M. B. (1986). *Why does that man have such a big nose?* Seattle: Parenting Press.

Rosenberg, M. (1983). *My friend Leslie.* New York: Lothrop, Lee & Shepard.

Sargent, S., & Wirt, D. A. (1983). *My favorite place.* New York: Abingdon.

Stein, S. B. (1974). *About handicaps.* New York: Walker.

Tickle Tune Typhoon. (1989). *Let's be friends* (video). Seattle: Tickle Tune Typhoon.

Wolf, B. (1974). *Don't feel sorry for Paul.* New York: Harper & Row.

Don't forget fairy tales and animal stories with antibias themes, such as "The Ugly Duckling," Lionni's *Cornelius*, Steig's *Amos and Boris*, and Waber's *You Look Ridiculous*.

Diverse Families, Special Relationships

Bauer, C. F. (1981). *My mom travels a lot.* New York: Frederick Warne.

Caines, J. (1977). *Daddy.* New York: Harper & Row.

Christiansen, C. B. (1989). *My mother's house, my father's house.* New York: Atheneum.

Dijs, C. (1991). *Are you my mommy? A pop-up book.* New York: Simon & Schuster.

Eisenberg, P. R. (1992). *You're my Nikki.* New York: Dial Books for Young Readers.

Flournoy, V. (1980). *The twins strike back.* New York: Dial.

Fox, M. (1985). *Wilfrid Gordon McDonald Partridge.* New York: Kane/Miller.

Greenberg, P. (1981). *I know I'm myself because.* New York: Human Sciences Press.

Greenfield, E. (1976). *First pink light.* New York: Scholastic.

Hest, A. (1984). *The crack-of-dawn walkers.* New York: Macmillan.

Hill, E. S. (1967). *Evan's corner.* New York: Rinehart and Winston.

Hines, A. G. (1986). *Daddy makes the best spaghetti.* New York: Clarion.

Johnson, A. (1990). *Do like Kyla.* New York: Orchard.

Keats, E. J. (1967). *Peter's chair.* New York: Harper & Row.

Perry, P., & Lynch, M. (1985). *Mommy and Daddy are divorced.* New York: Dial Books for Young Readers.

Polacco, P. (1988). *The keeping quilt.* New York: Simon & Schuster.

Rice, M., & Rice, C. (1987). *All about me.* Garden City, NY: Doubleday.

Rose, D. L. (1991). *Meredith's mother takes the train,* Morton Grove, IL: Albert Whitman.

Rosenberg, M. B. (1985). *Being a twin, having a twin.* New York: Lothrop, Lee & Shepard.

Rylant, C. (1982). *When I was young in the mountains.* New York: E. P. Dutton.

Schaffer, P. (1988). *How babies and families are made.* Berkeley, CA: Taber Sarah.

Scott, A. H. (1972). *On mother's lap.* New York: McGraw-Hill.

Simon, N. (1976). *All kinds of families.* Chicago: Albert Whitman.

Spier, P. (1980). *People.* New York: Doubleday.

Williams, B. (1975). *Kevin's grandma.* New York: Scholastic.

Williams, V. B. (1982). *A chair for my mother.* New York: Greenwillow.

Williams, V. B. (1990). *"More, more, more," said the baby*: 3 love stories. New York: Greenwillow.

Diverse Gender Behaviors

Behrens, J. (1985). *I can be a truck driver.* Chicago: Children's Press.

Caines, J. (1982). *Just us women.* New York: Harper & Row.

DeGrosbois, L., Lacelle, N., LaMothe, R., & Nantel, L. (1976). *Mommy works on dresses* (C. Bayard, Trans.). Toronto: Women's Press.

English, B. (1988). *Women at their work.* New York: Dial.

Kempler, S. (1981). *A man can be . . .* New York: Human Resources Press.

Lasker, J. (1972). *Mothers can do anything.* Niles, IL: Whitman.

Merriman, E. (1972). *Boys and girls, girls and boys.* New York: Holt, Rinehart & Winston.

Merriman, E. (1989). *Mommies at work.* New York: Simon & Schuster.

Omerod, J. (1981). *Sunshine.* New York: Lothrop, Lee & Shepard.

Portnoy, M. A. (1986). *Ima on the Bima.* Rockville, MD: Kar-Ben Copies.

Rockwell, A. (1981). *When we grow up.* New York: Dutton.

Wandro, M. (1981). *My daddy is a nurse.* Reading, MA: Addison Wesley.

Waxman, S. (1989). *What is a girl? What is a boy?* New York: Harper & Row.

Winthrop, E. (1985). *Tough Eddie.* New York: Dutton.

Zolotow, C. (1972). *William's doll.* New York: Harper & Row.

Environment

Altman, I., & Wohlwill, J. (Eds.). (1978). *Children and the environment.* New York: Plenum.

Bittinger, G. (1990). *Our world.* Everett, WA: Warren.

Cornell, J. B. (1979). *Sharing nature with young children.* Nevada City, CA: Ananda.

Earth Works Group. *Fifty simple things kids can do to recycle.* (1991). Berkeley, CA: Author.

Griffin, S. (1984). *Conservation seeds activities book.* Jefferson City, MO: Conservation Commission of the State of Missouri.

Holt, B. G. (1989). *Science with young children* (rev. ed.). Washington, DC: NAEYC.

Johnson, C. M. (1987). *Discovering nature with young people: An annotated bibliography and selection guide.* Westport, CT: Greenwood Press.

Link, M. (1981). *Outdoor education: A manual for teaching in nature's classroom.* Englewood Cliffs, NJ: Prentice-Hall.

McQueen, K., & Frassier, D. (1991). *Let's talk trash: The kids book about recycling.* Burlington, VT: Waterfront Books.

Nickelsburg, J. (1976). *Nature activities for early childhood.* Menlo Park, CA: Addison-Wesley.

Perry, G., & Rivkin, M. (1992). Teachers and science. *Young Children, 47*(4), 9–16.

Rivkin, M. (1992). Science is a way of life. *Young Children, 47*(4), 4–8.

Sisson, E. A. (1982). *Nature with children of all ages: Adventures for exploring, learning, and enjoying the world around us.* Englewood Cliffs, NJ: Prentice-Hall.

Skelsey, A., & Huckaby, G. (1973). *Growing up green.* New York: Workman.

Anti-animal stereotype

dePaola, T. (1981). *The hunter and his animals.* New York: Holiday House.

Nicki, P. (1988). *The story of a kind of wolf.* New York: North-South Books.

Low Income and Job Loss

Bethel, J. (1970). *Three cheers for Mother Jones.* New York: Holt, Rinehart & Winston.

Jordan, J. (1975). *New life: New room.* New York: Crowell.

Nolan, M. (1978). *My daddy don't go to work.* Minneapolis: Carolrhoda.

Quinlan, P. (1987). *My dad takes care of me.* Willowdale, ON: Annick Press.

Misuses of Power

Seuss, Dr. (1950). *Yertle the turtle and other stories.* New York: Random House.

Multicultural/Antibias (General)

All of us will shine (recording). Tickle Tune Typhoon. P. O. Box 15153, Seattle, WA 98115.

Anders, R. (1976). *A look at prejudice and understanding.* Minneapolis: Lerner.

Beim, J., & Beim, J. (1945). *Two is a team.* New York: Harcourt Brace Jovanovich.

Beim, J., & Beim, J. (1947). *The swimming hole.* New York: Morrow.

Clifton, L. (1976). *Everett Anderson's friend.* New York: Holt, Rinehart & Winston.

Cohen, B. (1983). *Molly's pilgrim.* New York: Lothrop, Lee & Shepard.

Corey, D. (1983). *You go away.* New York: Greenwillow.

Goldin, A. (1965). *Straight hair, curly hair.* New York: Harper & Row.

Hazen, B. S. (1985). *Why are people different? A book about prejudice.* New York: Golden Books.

Hug the earth (recording). (1985). Tickle Tune Typhoon, P. O. Box 15153, Seattle, WA 98115.

Jonas, A. (1982). *When you were a baby.* New York: Greenwillow.

Macmillan, D., & Freeman, D. (1987). *My best friend Martha Rodriguez.* New York: Julian Messner.

Martin, B., Jr. (1970). *I am freedom's child.* Oklahoma City: Bowmar.

Martin, B., Jr. (1983). *Brown bear, brown bear, what do you see?* New York: Holt, Rinehart & Winston.

Seuss, Dr. (1961). *The sneetches*. New York: Random House.

African American

Boone-Jones, M. (1968). *Martin Luther King, Jr.: A picture story*. Chicago: Children's Press.

Brenner, B. (1978). *Wagon Wheels*. New York: Harper & Row.

Church, V. (1971). *Colors around me*. Chicago: Afro-American Publishing.

Clifton, L. (1973). *The boy who didn't believe in spring*. New York: E. P. Dutton,

Clifton, L. (1980). *Don't you remember?* New York: Dalton.

Clifton, L. (1980). *My friend Jacob*. New York: Elsevier/Dutton.

Feelings, T., & Greenfield, E. (1981). *Daydreamers*. New York: Dial.

Greenfield, E. (1973). *Rosa Parks*. New York: Harper.

Greenfield, E. (1975). *Me and Nessie*. New York: Harper & Row.

Greenfield, E. (1978). *Honey, I love and other love poems*. New York: Crowell.

I'm gonna let it shine—a gathering of voices for freedom (recording), Round River Records, 301 Jacob St., Seekonk, MA 02771.

Keats, E. J. (1964). *Whistle for Willie*. New York: Viking Press.

McGovern, A. (1969) *Black is beautiful*. New York: Scholastic.

Meyer, L. D. (1988). *Harriet Tubman: They called me Moses*. Seattle: Parenting Press.

Schlank, C. H., & Metzker, B. (1989). *Martin Luther King, Jr.: A biography for young children*. Rochester AEYC, Box 356, Henrietta, NY 14467.

Showers, P. (1962). *Look at your eyes*. New York: Crowell.

Williams, V. B. (1986). *Cherries and cherry pits*. New York: Greenwillow.

Yarbrough, C. (1979). *Cornrows*. New York: Coward-McCann.

Simon, N. (1976). *Why am I different?* Niles, IL: Whitman.

Alaskan/Eskimo

Robinson, T. (1975). *An Eskimo birthday*. New York: Dodd, Mead.

Rogers, J. (1988). *Runaway mittens*. New York: Greenwillow.

Steiner, B. (1988). *Whale brother*. New York: Walker.

Chinese American

Fogel, J. (1979). *Wesley, Paul: Marathon runner*. New York: Lippincott.

Pinkwater, M. (1975). *Wingman*. New York: Dodd, Mead.

Hawaiian

Feeney, S. (1980). *A is for Aloha*. Honolulu: University of Hawaii Press.

Feeney, S. (1985). *Hawaii is a rainbow*. Honolulu: University of Hawaii Press.

Mower, N. (1984). *I visit my Tutu and Grandma*. Kailua, HI: Press Pacifica.

Hmong

Goldfarb. M. (1982). *Fighters, refugees, immigrants: A story of the Hmong*. Minneapolis: Carolrhoda.

Interracial

Adolf, A. (1973). *Black is brown is tan*. New York: Harper & Row.

Bunin, C., & Bunin S. (1976). *Is that your sister?* New York: Pantheon.

Mandelbaum, P. (1990). *You be me, I'll be you*. Brooklyn, NY: Kane/Miller.

Miller, M. (1991). *Whose shoe*. New York: Greenwillow.

Rosenberg, M. (1984). *Being adopted*. New York: Lothrop, Lee & Shepard.

Rosenberg, M. (1986). *Living in two worlds*. New York: Lothrop, Lee & Shepard.

Welber, R. (1972). *The train*. New York: Pantheon.

Japanese American

Bang, M. (1985). *The paper crane*. New York: Morrow.

Jewish American

Avni, F. (1986). *A child's look at . . . what it means to be Jewish* (recording). Alcazar, Box 429, Waterbury, VT 06676.

Avni, F. (1986). *Mostly matzah* (recording), Waterbury, VT: Alcazar.

Greene, J. D. (1986). *Nathan's Hanukkah bargain*. Kar-Ben Coples, Inc. 6800 Tildenwood Lane, Rockville, MD 20852.

Hirsh, M. (1984). *I love Hanukkah*. New York: Holiday House.

Korean American

Pack, M. (1978). *Aekyung's dream.* Chicago: Children's Press.

Latino

Atkinson, M. (1979). *Maria Teresa.* Carrboro, NC: Lollipop Power.

Martel, C. (1976). *Yagua days.* New York: Dial.

Long, Long Ago

Baylor, B. (1969). *Before you came this way.* New York: E. P. Dutton, (Native American)

Chang, K. (1977). *The iron moonhunter.* San Francisco: Children's Book Press. (Chinese American)

dePaola, T. (1983). *The legend of the bluebonnet.* New York: Putnam. (Native American)

Flournoy, V. (1985). *The patchwork quilt.* New York: Dial Books for Young Readers.

Hamilton, V. (1988). *In the beginning: Creation stories from around the world.* New York: Harcourt Brace Jovanovich.

Highwater, J. (1981). *Moonsong lullaby.* New York: Lothrop, Lee & Shepard. (Native American).

Levinson, R. (1986). *I go with my family to Grandma's.* New York: Dutton.

Monjo, F. N. (1970). *The drinking gourd.* New York: Harper & Row. (African American)

Native American

Bales, C. A. (1972). *Kevin Cloud: Chippewa boy in the city.* Chicago: Reilly & Lee.

Baylor, B. (1976). *Hawk, I'm your brother.* New York: Scribner's.

Blood, C., & Link, M. (1980). *The goat in the rug.* New York: Macmillan.

Cameron, A. (1988). *Spider woman.* Madeira Park, BC: Harbour.

Crowder, J. (1969). *Stephanie and the coyote.* Upper Strata, Box 278, Bernalillo, NM 87004.

Hayes, J. (1989). *Coyote and Native American folk tales* (recording). Santa Fe, NM: Trails West.

Hoyt-Goldsmith, D. (1990). *Totem pole.* New York: Holiday House.

Jeffers, S. (1991). *Brother eagle, sister sky.* New York: Dial Books.

Locke, K. (1983). *Lakota/Dakota flute music* (recording). Featherstone, P. O. Box 487, Brookings, SD 57006.

Locker, T. (1991). *The land of the gray wolf.* New York: Dial Books.

Martin, B., Jr., & Archambault, J. (1987). Knots on a counting rope. New York: Henry Holt.

New Mexico People and Energy Collective. (1981). *Red ribbons for Emma.* Berkeley, CA: New Seeds Press.

Shor, P. (1973). *When the corn is red.* New York: Abingdon.

Smith, M. M. (1984). *Grandmother's adobe dollhouse.* New Mexico Magazine, Bataan Memorial Building, Santa Fe, NM 87503.

Spanish

Ada, A. F. (1990). *Abecedario de los animales.* Madrid, Spain, Espasa Calpe.

Baden, R. (1990). *Y Domingo, siete [And Sunday makes seven].* Niles, IL: Albert Whitman.

Blue, R. (1971). *I am here/Yo estoy aqui.* New York: Franklin Watts.

Graw, J. S. (1989). *La ratita presumida [The little conceited rat].* Barcelona, Spain: Ediciones Hymsa.

Pomerantz, C. (1980). *The Tamarindo puppy and other poems.* New York: Greenwillow.

Rosario, I. (1987). *Idalia's project ABC: An urban alphabet book in English and Spanish.* New York: Holt, Rinehart & Winston.

Simon, N. (1974). *What do I do? Que hago?* Niles, IL: Whitman.

Suárez, M. (1989). *Los colores [Colors].* Mexico City: Editorial Grijalbo.

Vietnamese American

Constant, H. (1974). *First snow,* New York: Knopf.

Macmillan, D., & Freeman, D. (1987). *My best friend Duc Tran: Meeting a Vietnamese-American family.* New York: Julian Messner.

Shalant, P. (1988). *Look what we've brought you from Vietnam: Crafts, games, recipes, stories, and other cultural activities from new Americans.* New York: Julian Messner.

Can you think of stories that make the point that differences may be enriching? Lionni's *Fish Is Fish* comes to mind.

APPENDIX O

Definitions of Exceptional Children: Public Law 94—142

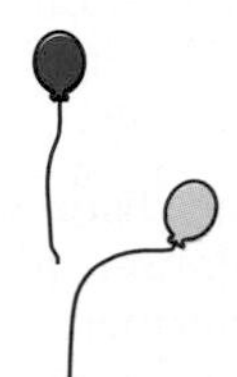

1. *Deaf.* A hearing impairment so severe that the child is impaired in processing linguistic information through hearing, with or without amplification, which adversely affects educational performance.

2. *Deaf-blind.* Concomitant hearing and visual impairments, the combination of which cause such severe communication and other developmental and educational problems that the child cannot be accommodated in special education programs solely for deaf or blind children.

3. *Hard of hearing.* A hearing impairment, whether permanent or fluctuating, that adversely affects a child's educational performance but is not included under the definition of *deaf* in this section.

4. *Mentally retarded.* Significantly subaverage general intellectual functioning existing concurrently with deficits in adaptive behavior and manifested during the developmental period, which adversely affect a child's educational performance.

5. *Multi-handicapped.* Concomitant impairments (such as mentally retarded-blind, mentally retarded-orthopedically impaired, etc.), the combination of which cause such severe educational problems that they cannot be accommodated in special education programs solely for one of the impairments. The term does not include deaf-blind children.

6. *Orthopedically impaired.* A severe orthopedic impairment, which adversely affects a child's educational performance. The term includes impairments caused by congenital anomaly (e.g., clubfoot, absence of some member, etc.), impairments caused by disease (e.g., poliomyelitis, bone tuberculosis, etc.) and impairments from other causes (e.g., cerebral palsy, amputations and fractures, or burns that cause contractures).

7. *Other health impaired.*

a. Having an autistic condition, which is manifested by severe communication and other developmental and educational problems; or

b. Having limited strength, vitality, or alertness, due to chronic or acute health problems such as a heart condition, tuberculosis, rheumatic fever, nephritis, asthma, sickle cell anemia, hemophilia, epilepsy, lead poisoning, leukemia, or diabetes, which adversely affect a child's educational performance.

8. *Seriously emotionally disturbed.*

a. A condition exhibiting one or more of the following characteristics over a long period of time and to a marked degree, which adversely affects educational performance:

- An inability to learn, which cannot be explained by intellectual, sensory, or health factors;
- An inability to build or maintain satisfactory interpersonal relationships with peers and teachers;
- Inappropriate types of behavior or feelings under normal circumstances;
- A general pervasive mood of unhappiness or depression; or
- A tendency to develop physical symptoms or fears associated with personal or school problems.

From the Federal Register, 1977, pp. 42478–42479.

b. The term includes children who are schizophrenic. The term does not include children who are socially maladjusted, unless it is determined that they are seriously emotionally disturbed.

9. *Specific learning disability.* A disorder in one or more of the basic psychological processes involved in understanding or in using language, spoken or written, that may manifest itself in an imperfect ability to listen, think, speak, read, write, spell, or to do mathematical calculations. The term includes such conditions as perceptual handicaps, brain injury, minimal brain dysfunction, dyslexia, and development aphasia. The term does not include children who have learning problems that are primarily the result of visual, hearing, or motor handicaps, or mental retardation, or emotional disturbance, or of environmental, cultural, or economic disadvantage.

10. *Speech impaired.* A communication disorder such as stuttering, impaired articulation, a language impairment, or a voice impairment, that adversely affects a child's educational performance.

11. *Visually handicapped.* A visual impairment that, even in correction, adversely affects a child's educational performance. The term includes both partially seeing and blind children.

APPENDIX P

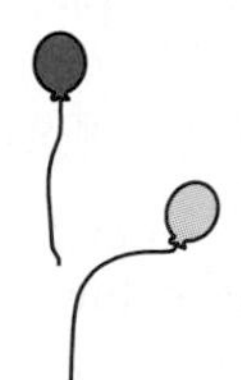

Developmentally Appropriate Practice in Early Childhood Programs Serving Children from Birth through Age 8

Introduction

The quality of our nation's educational system has come under intense public scrutiny in the 1980s. While much of the attention has been directed at secondary and postsecondary education, the field of early childhood education must also examine its practices in light of current knowledge of child development and learning.

The purpose of this paper is to describe developmentally appropriate practice in early childhood programs for administrators, teachers, parents, policy makers, and others who make decisions about the care and education of young children. An early childhood program is any part-day or full-day group program in a center, school, or other facility, that serves children from birth through age 8. Early childhood programs include child care centers, private and public preschools, kindergartens, and primary grade schools.

Rationale

In recent years, a trend toward increased emphasis on formal instruction in academic skills has emerged in early childhood programs. This trend toward formal academic instruction for younger children is based on misconceptions about early learning (Elkind, 1986). Despite the trend among some educators to formalize instruction, there has been no comparable evidence of change in what young children need for optimal development or how they learn. In fact, a growing body of research has emerged recently affirming that children learn most effectively through a concrete, play-oriented approach to early childhood education.

In addition to an increased emphasis on academics, early childhood programs have experienced other changes. The number of programs has increased in response to the growing demand for out-of-home care and education during the early years. Some characteristics of early childhood programs have also changed in the last few years. For example, children are now enrolled in programs at younger ages, many from infancy. The length of the program day for all ages of children has been extended in response to the need for extended hours of care for employed families. Similarly, program sponsorship has become more diverse. The public schools are playing a larger role in providing prekindergarten programs or before- and after-school child care. Corporate America is also becoming a more visible sponsor of child care programs.

Programs have changed in response to social, economic, and political forces; however, these changes have not always taken into account the basic developmental needs of young children, which have remained constant. The trend toward early academics, for example, is antithetical to what we know about how young children learn. Programs should be tailored to meet the needs of children, rather than expecting children to adjust to the demands of a specific program.

POSITION STATEMENT

The National Association for the Education of Young Children (NAEYC) believes that a high quality early childhood program provides a safe

---

and nurturing environment that promotes the physical, social, emotional, and cognitive development of young children while responding to the needs of families. Although the quality of an early childhood program may be affected by many factors, a major determinant of program quality is the extent to which knowledge of child development is applied in program practices—the degree to which the program is *developmentally appropriate.* NAEYC believes that high quality, developmentally appropriate programs should be available to all children and their families.

In this position paper, the concept of *developmental appropriateness* will first be defined. Then guidelines will be presented describing how developmental appropriateness can be applied to four components of early childhood programs: curriculum; adult-child interactions; relations between the home and program; and developmental evaluation of children. The statement concludes with a discussion of major policy implications and recommendations. These guidelines are designed to be used in conjunction with NAEYC's Criteria for High Quality Early Childhood Programs, the standards for accreditation by the National Academy of Early Childhood Programs (NAEYC, 1984).

Definition of Developmental Appropriateness

The concept of *developmental appropriateness* has two dimensions: age appropriateness and individual appropriateness.

1. *Age appropriateness.* Human development research indicates that there are universal, predictable sequences of growth and change that occur in children during the first 9 years of life. These predictable changes occur in all domains of development—physical, emotional, social, and cognitive. Knowledge of typical development of children within the age span served by the program provides a framework from which teachers prepare the learning environment and plan appropriate experiences.

2. *Individual appropriateness.* Each child is a unique person with an individual pattern and timing of growth, as well as individual personality, learning style, and family background. Both the curriculum and adults' interactions with children should be responsive to individual differences. Learning in young children is the result of interaction between the child's thoughts and experiences with materials, ideas, and people. These experiences should match the child's developing abilities, while also challenging the child's interest and understanding.

Teachers can use child development knowledge to identify the range of appropriate behaviors, activities, and materials for a specific age group. This knowledge is used in conjunction with understanding about individual children's growth patterns, strengths, interests, and experiences to design the most appropriate learning environment. Although the content of the curriculum is determined by many factors such as tradition, the subject matter of the disciplines, social or cultural values, and parental desires, for the content and teaching strategies to be developmentally appropriate they must be age appropriate and individually appropriate.

Children's play is a primary vehicle for and indicator of their mental growth. Play enables children to progress along the developmental sequence from the sensorimotor intelligence of infancy to preoperational thought in the preschool years to the concrete operational thinking exhibited by primary children (Fein, 1979; Fromberg, 1986; Piaget, 1952; Sponseller, 1982). In addition to its role in cognitive development, play also serves important functions in children's physical, emotional, and social development (Herron & Sutton-Smith, 1974). Therefore, child-initiated, child-directed, teacher-supported play is an essential component of developmentally appropriate practice (Fein & Rivkin, 1986).

GUIDELINES FOR DEVELOPMENTALLY APPROPRIATE PRACTICE

I. *Curriculum*

A developmentally appropriate curriculum for young children is planned to be appropriate for the age span of the children within the group and is implemented with attention to the different needs, interests, and developmental levels of those individual children.

A. *Developmentally appropriate curriculum provides for all areas of a child's development: physical, emotional, social, and cognitive through an integrated approach*

(Almy, 1975; Biber, 1984; Elkind, 1986; Forman & Kuschner, 1983; Kline, 1985; Skeen, Garner, & Cartwright, 1984; Spodek, 1985).

Realistic curriculum goals for children should address all of these areas in age-appropriate ways. Children's learning does not occur in narrowly defined subject areas; their development and learning are integrated. Any activity that stimulates one dimension of development and learning affects other dimensions as well.

B. *Appropriate curriculum planning is based on teachers' observations and recordings of each child's special interests and developmental progress* (Almy, 1975; Biber, 1984; Cohen, Stern, & Balaban, 1983; Goodwin & Goodwin, 1982).

Realistic curriculum goals and plans are based on regular assessment of individual needs, strengths, and interests. Curriculum is based on both age-appropriate and individually appropriate information. For example, individual children's family/cultural backgrounds—such as expressive styles, ways of interacting, play, and games—are used to broaden the curriculum for all children.

C. *Curriculum planning emphasizes learning as an interactive process. Teachers prepare the environment for children to learn through active exploration and interaction with adults, other children, and materials* (Biber, 1984; Fein, 1979; Forman & Kuschner, 1983; Fromberg, 1986; Goffin & Tull, 1985; Griffin, 1982; Kamii, 1985; Lay-Dopyera & Dopyera, 1986; Powell, 1986; Sponseller, 1982).

The process of interacting with materials and people results in learning. Finished products or "correct" solutions that conform to adult standards are not very accurate criteria for judging whether learning has occurred. Much of young children's learning takes place when they direct their own play activities. During play, children feel successful when they engage in a task they have defined for themselves, such as finding their way through an obstacle course with a friend or pouring water into and out of various containers. Such learning should not be inhibited by adult-established concepts of completion, achievement, and failure. Activities should be designed to concentrate on furthering emerging skills through creative activity and intense involvement.

D. *Learning activities and materials should be concrete, real, and relevant to the lives of young children* (Almy, 1975; Biber, 1984; Evans, 1984; Forman & Kuschner, 1983; Hawkins, 1970; Hirsch, 1984; Holt, 1979; Kamii, 1985; Kline, 1985; Piaget, 1972; Schickendanz, 1986; Seefeldt, 1986; Smith, 1985; Weber, 1984).

Children need years of play with real objects and events before they are able to understand the meaning of symbols such as letters and numbers. Learning takes place as young children touch, manipulate, and experiment with things and interact with people. Throughout early childhood, children's concepts and language gradually develop to enable them to understand more abstract or symbolic information. Pictures and stories should be used frequently to build upon children's real experiences.

Workbooks, worksheets, coloring books, and adult-made models of art products for children to copy are *not* appropriate for young children, especially those younger than 6. Children older than 5 show increasing abilities to learn through written exercises, oral presentations, and other adult-directed teaching strategies. However, the child's active participation in self-directed play with concrete, real-life experiences continues to be a key to motivated, meaningful learning in kindergarten and the primary grades.

Basic learning materials and activities for an appropriate curriculum include sand, water, clay, and accessories to use with them; hollow, table, and unit blocks; puzzles with varying numbers of pieces; many types of games; a variety of small manipulative toys; dramatic play props such as those for housekeeping and transportation; a variety of science investigation equipment and items to explore; a changing selection of appropriate and aesthetically pleasing books and recordings; supplies of paper, water-based paint and markers, and other materials for creative expression; large muscle equipment; field trips; classroom responsibilities, such as helping with routines; and positive interactions and problem-solving opportunities with other children and adults.

E. *Programs provide for a wider range of developmental interests and abilities than the chronological age range of the group would suggest. Adults are prepared to meet the needs of children who exhibit unusual interest and skills outside the normal developmental range* (Kitano, 1982; Languis, Sanders, & Tipps, 1980; Schickedanz, Schickedanz, & Forsyth, 1982; Souweine, Crimmins, & Mazel, 1981; Uphoff & Gilmore, 1985).

Activities and equipment should be provided for a chronological age range which in many cases is at least 12 months. However, the normal developmental age range in any group may be as much as 2 years. Some mainstreamed situations will demand a wider range of expectations. When the developmental age range of a group is more than 18 months, the need increases for a large variety of furnishings, equipment, and teaching strategies. The complexity of materials should also reflect the age span of the group. For example, a group that includes 3-, 4-, and 5-year-olds would need books of varying length and complexity; puzzles with varying numbers and sizes of pieces; games that require a range of skills and abilities to follow rules; and other diverse materials, teaching methods, and room arrangements.

F. *Teachers provide a variety of activities and materials; teachers increase the difficulty, complexity, and challenge of an activity as children are involved with it and as children develop understanding and skills* (Davidson, 1985; Ferreiro & Teberosky, 1982; Forman & Kaden, 1986; Gerber, 1982; Gilbert, 1981; Gonzalez-Mena & Eyer, 1980; Greenberg, 1976; Hill, 1979; Hirsch, 1984; Holt, 1979; Honig, 1980, 1981; Kamii, 1982, 1985; Kamii & DeVries, 1980; Lasky & Mukerji, 1980; McDonald, 1979; National Institute of Education, 1984; Schickedanz, 1986; Smith, 1982; Smith, 1983; Sparling, 1984; Stewart, 1982; Veach, 1977; Willert & Kamii, 1985; Willis & Ricciuti, 1975).

As children work with materials or activities, teachers listen, observe, and interpret children's behavior. Teachers can then facilitate children's involvement and learning by asking questions, making suggestions, or adding more complex materials or ideas to a situation. During a program year, as well as from one year to another, activities and environments for children should change in arrangement and inventory, and special events should also be planned. Examples of developmentally appropriate learning activities for various age groups follow.

1. *Infants and toddlers*

Infants and toddlers learn by experiencing the environment through their senses (seeing, hearing, tasting, smelling, and feeling), by physically moving around, and through social interaction. Nonmobile infants absorb and organize a great deal of information about the world around them, so adults talk and sing with them about what is happening and bring them objects to observe and manipulate. At times adults carry nonmobile infants around the environment to show them interesting events and people. Mobile infants and toddlers increasingly use toys, language, and other learning materials in their play.

Adults play a vital socialization role with infants and toddlers. Warm, positive relationships with adults help infants develop a sense of trust in the world and feelings of competence. These interactions are critical for the development of the children's healthy self-esteem. The trusted adult becomes the secure base from which the mobile infant or toddler explores the environment.

Important independence skills are being acquired during these years, including personal care such as toileting, feeding, and dressing. The most appropriate teaching technique for this age group is to give ample opportunities for the children to use self-initiated repetition to practice newly acquired skills and to experience feelings of autonomy and success. Infants will bat at, grasp, bang, or drop their toys. Patience is essential as a toddler struggles to put on a sweater. Imitation, hiding, and naming games are also important for learning at this age. Realistic toys will enable children to engage in increasingly complex types of play.

Two-year-olds are learning to produce language rapidly. They need simple books, pictures, puzzles, and music, and time and space for active play such as jumping, running, and dancing. Toddlers are acquiring social skills, but in groups there should be several of the same toy because egocentric toddlers are not yet able to understand the concept of sharing.

2. *Three-, 4-, and 5-year-olds*
Curriculum for 3-year-olds should emphasize language, activity, and movement, with major emphasis on large muscle activity. Appropriate activities include dramatic play, wheel toys and climbers, puzzles and blocks, and opportunities to talk and listen to simple stories.

Four-year-olds enjoy a greater variety of experiences and more small motor activities like scissors, art, manipulatives, and cooking. They are more able to concentrate and remember as well as recognize objects by shape, color, or size. Four-year-olds are developing basic math concepts and problem-solving skills.

Some 4-year-olds and most 5-year-olds combine ideas into more complex relations (for example, number concepts such as one-to-one correspondence) and have growing memory capacity and fine motor physical skills. Some 4-year-olds and most 5s display a growing interest in the functional aspects of written language, such as recognizing meaningful words and trying to write their own names. Activities designed solely to teach the alphabet, phonics, and penmanship are much less appropriate for this age group than providing a print-rich environment that stimulates the development of language and literacy skills in a meaningful context.

Curriculum for 4s and 5s can expand beyond the child's immediate experience of self, home, and family to include special events and trips. Five-year-olds are developing interest in community and the world outside their own. They also use motor skills well, even daringly, and show increasing ability to pay attention for longer times and in larger groups if the topic is meaningful.

3. *Six-, 7-, and 8-year-olds*
Six-year-olds are active and demonstrate considerable verbal ability; they are becoming interested in games and rules and develop concepts and problem-solving skills from these experiences. Most 6-year-olds and many 7- and 8-year-olds may be more mature mentally than physically. Therefore, hands-on activity and experimentation is more appropriate for this age group than fatiguing mechanical seatwork.

Seven-year-olds seem to need time to catch up and practice with many newly acquired physical and cognitive skills. They become increasingly able to reason, to listen to others, and to show social give-and-take.

Eight-year-olds combine great curiosity with increased social interest. Now they are able to learn about other, more distant peoples. During first, second, and third grade, children can learn from the symbolic experiences of reading books and listening to stories; however, their understanding of what they read is based on their ability to relate the written word to their own experience. Primary grade children also learn to communicate through written language, dictating or writing stories about their own experiences or fantasies. The same is true of the development of number concepts. Children's mathematical concepts develop from their own thinking during games and real-life experiences that involve quantification, such as cooking or carpentry.

G. *Adults provide opportunities for children to choose from among a variety of activities, materials, and equipment; and time to explore through active involvement. Adults facilitate children's engagement with materials and activities and extend the child's learning by asking questions or making suggestions that stimulate children's thinking* (Elkind, 1986; Forman & Kuschner, 1983; Goffin & Tull, 1985; Kamii & Lee-Katz, 1979; Lay-Dopyera & Dopyera, 1986; Sackoff & Hart, 1984; Skeen, Garner, & Cartwright, 1984; Sparling, 1984).

Children of all ages need uninterrupted periods of time to become involved, investigate, select, and persist at activities. The teacher's role in child-chosen activity is to prepare the environment with stimulating, challenging activity choices and then to facilitate children's engagement. In developmentally appropriate programs, adults:

1. provide a rich variety of activities and materials from which to choose.

   Such variety increases the likelihood of a child's prolonged or satisfied attention and increases independence and opportunity for making decisions.
2. offer children the choice to participate in a small group or in a solitary activity.
3. assist and guide children who are not yet able to use easily and enjoy child-choice activity periods.
4. provide opportunities for child-initiated, child-directed practice of skills as a self-chosen activity.

   Children need opportunities to repeat acquired skills to fully assimilate their learning. Repetition that is initiated and directed by the child, not adult-directed drill and practice, is most valuable for assimilation.

H. *Multicultural and nonsexist experiences, materials, and equipment should be provided for children of all ages* (Ramsey, 1979, 1982; Saracho & Spodek, 1983; Sprung, 1978).

Providing a wide variety of multicultural nonstereotyping materials and activities helps ensure the individual appropriateness of the curriculum and also

1. enhances each child's self-concept and esteem.
2. supports the integrity of the child's family,
3. enhances the child's learning processes in both the home and the early childhood program by strengthening ties.
4. extends experiences of children and their families to include knowledge of the ways of others, especially those whose share the community, and
5. enriches the lives of all participants with respectful acceptance and appreciation of differences and similarities among them.

   Multicultural experiences should not be limited to a celebration of holidays and should include foods, music, families, shelter, and other aspects common to all cultures.

I. *Adults provide a balance of rest and active movement for children throughout the program day* (Cratty, 1982; Curtis, 1986; Hendrick, 1986; Stewart, 1982; Willis & Ricciuti, 1975).

For infants and toddlers, naps and quiet activities such as listening to rhymes and music provide periodic rest from the intense physical exploration that is characteristic of this age group. Two-year-olds, and many 3's, will need morning and/or afternoon naps, and should also have periods of carefully planned transition to quieting-down or rousing, especially before and after eating and sleeping. Children at about 2½- to 3-years-old become able to maintain brief interest in occasional small-group, teacher-conducted activities, and may enjoy quiet stories, music, and fingerplays together between periods of intense activity. Most 4's and many 5's still need naps, especially if their waking days are very long as they are in some child care situations. Children at this age need planned alternations of active and quiet activities and are usually willing to participate in brief, interesting, small-group activities. Older children continue to need alternating periods of active and quiet activity throughout the day, beyond traditionally provided recess.

The pace of the program day will vary depending on the length of time children are present, but children should never be rushed and schedules should be flexible enough to take advantage of impromptu experiences. The balance between active and quiet activity should be maintained throughout the day by alternating activities.

J. *Outdoor experiences should be provided for children of all ages* (Cratty, 1982; Curtis, 1986; Frost & Klein, 1979).

Because their physical development is occurring so rapidly, young children through age 8 need daily outdoor experiences to practice large muscle skills, learn about outdoor environments, and experience freedom not always possible indoors. Outdoor time is an integral part of the curriculum and requires planning; it is not simply a time for children to release pent-up energy.

II. *Adult-Child Interaction*

The developmental appropriateness of an early childhood program is most apparent in the interactions between adults and children. Developmentally appropriate interactions are based on adults' knowledge and expectations of age-appropriate behavior in children balanced by adults' awareness of individual differences among children.

A. *Adults respond quickly and directly to children's needs, desires, and messages and adapt their responses to children's differing styles and abilities* (Bell & Ainsworth, 1972; Erikson, 1950; Genishi, 1986; Greenspan & Greenspan, 1985; Honig, 1980, 1981; Lozoff, Brillenham, Trause, Kennell, & Klaus, 1977; Shure & Spivak, 1978; Smith & Davis, 1976).

Appropriate responses vary with the age of the child. Adults should respond immediately to infants' cries of distress. The response should be warm and soothing as the adult identifies the child's needs. Adults should also respond appropriately to infants' vocalizations, manipulation of objects, and movement, as these are the ways infants communicate. Adults hold and touch infants frequently; talk and sing to infants in a soothing, friendly voice; smile and maintain eye contact with infants. For toddlers and 2-year-olds, adults remain close by, giving attention and physical comfort as needed. Adults repeat children's words, paraphrase, or use synonyms or actions to help assure toddlers that they are understood. As children get older, adult responses are characterized by less physical communication and more verbal responsiveness, although immediacy is still important. Positive responses such as smiles and interest, and concentrated attention on children's activity, are important. Adults move quietly and circulate among individuals in groups to communicate with children in a friendly and relaxed manner.

From infancy through the primary grades, adult communication with children is facilitated by sitting low or kneeling, and making eye contact. With all age groups, adults should also be aware of the powerful influence of modeling and other nonverbal communication; adults' actions should be compatible with their verbal messages and confirm that children understand their messages.

B. *Adults provide many varied opportunities for children to communicate* (Cazden, 1981; Genishi, 1986; Gordon, 1970, 1975; Greenspan & Greenspan, 1985; Lay-Dopyera & Dopyera, 1986; McAfee, 1985; Schachter & Strage, 1982; Schickendanz, 1986).

Children acquire communication skills through hearing and using language, and as adults listen and respond to what children say. Communication skills grow out of the desire to use language to express needs, insights, and excitement, and to solve problems. Children do not learn language, or any other concepts, by being quiet and listening to a lecture from an adult. Listening experiences—when there is something meaningful to listen to such as a story or poetry—can enrich language learning. Most language interaction with infants and toddlers is on an individual basis, although occasionally a group of two or three children may gather to hear an absorbing story. Throughout the preschool years, individual abilities to sit and pay attention will vary considerably, but time periods are short and groups should be small. During kindergarten and the primary grades, children can listen to directions or stories for longer periods of time (gradually expanding as children get older). Individual and small group interactions are still the most effective because children have the opportunity for two-way communication with adults and other children. Total group instructional techniques are *not* as effective in facilitating the development of communication skills and other learning in young children.

Equally important are opportunities for children to engage in two-way communication with others. Infants use crying and body movements to communicate. Adult responses to this communication, including the use of soothing language and descriptions of what is happening, build the foundation for children's ability to use language and their ability to feel good about themselves. Children rapidly expand their ability to understand language in their early years, and from about the age of 2, children can engage in increasingly interesting and lengthy conversations with adults and other children. These one-on-one exchanges are critical throughout the early years. Children's questions, and their responses to questions, particularly open-ended questions, provide valuable information about the individual's level of thinking.

C. *Adults facilitate a child's successful completion of tasks by providing support, focused attention, physical proximity, and verbal encouragement. Adults recognize that children learn from trial and error and that children's misconceptions reflect their developing thoughts* (Cohen, Stern, & Balaban, 1983; Elkind, 1986; Gottfried, 1983; Kamii, 1985; Piaget, 1950; Veach, 1977; Wallinga & Sweaney, 1985; Wellman, 1982; Zavitkovsky, Baker, Berlfein, & Almy, 1986).

Real successes are important incentives for people of all ages to continue learning and maintain motivation. Children learn from their own mistakes. Adults can examine the problem with the child and, if appropriate, encourage the child to try again or to find alternatives. Teachers plan many open-ended activities that have more than one right answer, and value the unique responses of individual children.

D. *Teachers are alert to signs of undue stress in children's behavior, and aware of appropriate stress-reducing activities and techniques* (Dreikurs, Grunwald, & Pepper, 1982; Elkind, 1986; Gazda, 1973; Honig, 1986; McCracken, 1986; Warren, 1977).

Formal, inappropriate instructional techniques are a source of stress for young children. When children exhibit stress-related behavior, teachers should examine the program to ensure that expectations are appropriate and not placing excessive demands on children.

When children experience stress from other sources, adults can find ways to reduce or eliminate the problem, or help children cope with it. Appropriate adult behaviors may include cuddling and soothing a crying infant; offering a toddler a favorite toy; providing books, water play, body movement, music, and quiet times for older children; and physically comforting and listening to the concerns of a child of any age who is in distress. Children's responses to stress are as individual as their learning styles. An understanding adult who is sensitive to individual children's reactions is the key to providing appropriate comfort.

E. *Adults facilitate the development of self-esteem by respecting, accepting and comforting children, regardless of the child's behavior* (Coppersmith, 1975; Gordon, 1970, 1975; Greenspan & Greenspan, 1985; Kobak, 1979; Kuczynski, 1983; Lickona, 1983; Moore, 1982; Mussen & Eisenberg-Bert, 1977; Riley, 1984; Rubin & Everett, 1982; Smith & Davis, 1976; Stone, 1978).

Understanding behavior that is not unusual for young children, such as messiness, interest in body parts and genital differences, crying and resistance, aggression, and later infraction of rules and truth, is the basis for appropriate guidance of young children. Developmentally appropriate guidance demonstrates respect for children. It helps them understand and grow, and is directed toward helping children develop self-control and the ability to make better decisions in the future.

Adult behaviors that are *never* acceptable toward children include: screaming in anger; neglect; inflicting physical or emotional pain; criticism of a child's person or family by ridiculing, blaming, teasing, insulting, name-calling, threatening, or using frightening or humiliating punishment. Adults should not laugh at children's behavior, nor discuss it among themselves in the presence of children.

F. *Adults facilitate the development of self-control in children* (Asher, Renshaw, & Hymel, 1982; Hoffman, 1975; Honig, 1985; Kopp, 1982; Lytton, 1979 Miller, 1984; Moore, 1982; Read, Gardner, & Mahler, 1986; Rogers & Ross, 1986; Schaffer, 1984; Stone, 1978; Wolfgang & Glickman, 1980; Yarrow, Scott, & Waxler, 1973; Yarrow & Waxler, 1976).

Children learn self-control when adults treat them with dignity and use discipline techniques such as

1. guiding children by setting clear, consistent, fair limits for classroom behavior; or in the case of older children, helping them to set their own limits;
2. valuing mistakes as learning opportunities;
3. redirecting children to more acceptable behavior or activity;
4. listening when children talk about their feelings and frustrations:
5. guiding children to resolve conflicts and modeling skills that help children to solve their own problems; and
6. patiently reminding children of rules and their rationale as needed.

G. *Adults are responsible for all children under their supervision at all times and plan for increasing independence as children acquire skills* (Stewart, 1982; Veach, 1977).

Adults must constantly and closely supervise and attend every child younger than the age of 3. They must be close enough to touch infants when awake, catch a climbing toddler before she hits the ground, be aware of every move of a 2-year-old, and be close enough to offer another toy when 2-year-olds have difficulty sharing. Adults must be responsible for 3- to 5-year-old children at all times, in an environment sufficiently open to permit it. Children older than 5 may be deemed, on individual bases, mature enough to leave the classroom or run independent errands within a building. This should happen only with the adult's permission and specific knowledge.

Children in all early childhood settings must be protected from unauthorized (by the guardian/family) adults and older children. Parents should be welcome visitors in the program, but provisions should be made for limited access to buildings, careful and close supervision of outdoor play areas, and policies which demand that visiting adults check with the administrative office before entering the children's areas. Constant adult vigilance is required with children birth through age 8 years. Young children should not be given the burden of protecting themselves from adults.

III. *Relations between the Home and Program*

To achieve individually appropriate programs for young children, early childhood teachers must work in partnership with families and communicate regularly with children's parents.

A. *Parents have both the right and the responsibility to share in decisions about their children's care and education. Parents should be encouraged to observe and participate. Teachers are responsible for establishing and maintaining frequent contacts with families* (Brazelton, 1984; Croft, 1979; Dittmann, 1984; Honig, 1982; Katz, 1980; Lightfoot, 1978; Moore, 1982; Weissbourd, 1981).

During early childhood, children are largely dependent on their families for identity, security, care, and a general sense of well-being. Communication between families and teachers helps build mutual understanding and guidance, and provides greater consistency for children. Joint planning between families and teachers facilitates major socialization processes, such as toilet learning, developing peer relationships, and entering school.

B. *Teachers share child development knowledge, insights, and resources as part of regular communication and conferences with family members* (Brazelton, 1984; Croft, 1979; Dittmann, 1984; Lightfoot, 1978).

Mutual sharing of information and insights about the individual child's needs and developmental strides help both the family and the program. Regular communication and understanding about child development form a basis for mutual problem solving about concerns regarding behavior and growth. Teachers seek information from parents about individual children. Teachers promote mutual respect by recognizing and acknowledging different points of view to help minimize confusion for children.

C. *Teachers, parents, agencies, programs, and consultants who may have educational responsibility for the child at different times should, with family participation, share developmental information about children as they pass from one level or program to another* (Lightfoot, 1978; Meisels, 1985; Read, Gardner, & Mahler, 1986; Ziegler, 1985).

Continuity of educational experience is critical to supporting development. Such continuity results from communication both horizontally, as children change programs within a given year, and vertically, as children move on to other settings.

IV. *Developmental Evaluation of Children*

Assessment of individual children's development and learning is essential for planning and implementing developmentally appropriate programs, but should be used with caution to prevent discrimination against individuals and to ensure accuracy. Accurate testing can only be achieved with reliable, valid instruments and such instruments developed for use with young children are extremely rare. In the absence of valid instruments, testing is not valuable. Therefore, assessment of young children should rely heavily on the results of observations of their development and descriptive data.

A. *Decisions that have a major impact on children such as enrollment, retention, or placement are not made on the basis of a single developmental assessment or screening device but consider other relevant information, particularly observations by teachers and parents. Developmental assessment of children's progress and achievements is used to adapt curriculum to match the developmental needs of children, to communicate with the child's family, and to evaluate* *the program's effectiveness* (Cohen, Stern, & Balaban, 1983; Goodwin & Goodwin, 1982; Meisels, 1985; Standards for Educational and Psychological Testing, 1985; Uphoff & Gilmore, 1985).

Scores on psychometric tests that measure narrowly defined academic skills should never be the sole criterion for recommending enrollment or retention in a program, or placement in special or remedial classes. Likewise, assessment of children should be used to evaluate the effectiveness of the curriculum, but the performance of children on standardized tests should not determine curriculum decisions.

B. *Developmental assessments and observations are used to identify children who have special needs and/or who are at risk and to plan appropriate curriculum for them* (Meisels, 1985).

This information is used to provide appropriate programming for these children and may be used in making professional referrals to families.

C. *Developmental expectations based on standardized measurements and norms should compare any child or group of children only to normative information that is not only age-matched, but also gender-, culture-, and socioeconomically appropriate* (Meisels, 1985; Standards for Educational and Psychological Testing, 1985; Uphoff & Gilmore, 1985).

The validity of comparative data analysis is questionable in the absence of such considerations.

D. *In public schools, there should be a developmentally appropriate placement for every child of legal entry age.*

No public school program should deny access to children of legal entry age on the basis of lack of maturational "readiness." For example, a kindergarten program that denies access to many 5-year-olds is not meeting the needs of its clients. Curriculum should be planned for the developmental levels of children and emphasize individual planning to address a wide range of developmental levels in a single classroom. It is the responsibility of the educational system to adjust to the developmental needs and levels of the children it serves; children should not be expected to adapt to an inappropriate system.

POLICIES ESSENTIAL FOR ACHIEVING DEVELOPMENTALLY APPROPRIATE EARLY CHILDHOOD PROGRAMS

The following policies are essential to implement NAEYC's Guidelines for Developmentally Appropriate Practice in Early Childhood Programs Serving Children From Birth Through Age 8. NAEYC strongly recommends that policy-making groups at the state and local levels consider the following when implementing early childhood programs.

A. *Early childhood teachers should have college-level specialized preparation in early childhood education/child development. Teachers in early childhood programs, regardless of credentialed status, should be encouraged and supported to obtain and maintain current knowledge of child development and its application to early childhood educational practice* (Almy, 1982; Feeney & Chun, 1985; NAEYC, 1982, 1985; Ruopp, Travers, Glantz, & Coelen, 1979).

Teachers must be knowledgeable about child development before they can implement a program based on child development principles. Implementing a developmentally appropriate program also requires preparation that is specifically designed for teaching young children through an individualized, concrete, experiential approach. Such preparation includes a foundation in theory and research of child development from birth through age 8, developmentally appropriate instructional methods, and field experiences.

B. *Early childhood teachers should have practical experience teaching the age group. Therefore, regardless of credentialed status, teachers who have not previously taught young children should have supervised experience with young children before they can be in charge of a group* (NAEYC, 1982, 1984).

C. *Implementation of developmentally appropriate early childhood programs requires limiting the size of the group and providing sufficient numbers of adults to provide individualized and age-appropriate care and education* (NAEYC, 1985; Ruopp, Travers, Glantz, & Coelen, 1979).

Even the most well-qualified teacher cannot individualize instruction and adequately supervise too large a group of young children. An acceptable adult-child ratio for 4- and 5-year-olds is 2 adults with no more than 20 children. Younger children require much smaller groups. Group size, and thus ratio of children to adults, should increase gradually through the primary grades.

REFERENCES

These references include both laboratory and clinical classroom research to document the broad-based literature that forms the foundation for sound practice in early childhood education.

Almy, M. (1975). *The early childhood educator at work.* New York: McGraw-Hill.

Almy, M. (1982). Day care and early childhood education. In E. Zigler & E. Gordon (Eds.), *Daycare: Scientific and social policy issues* (pp. 476–495). Boston: Auburn House.

Asher, S. R., Renshaw, P. D., & Humel, S. (1982). Peer relations and the development of social skills. In S. G. Moore & C. R. Cooper (Eds.), *The young child: Reviews of research* (Vol. 3, pp. 137–158). Washington, DC: NAEYC.

Bell, S., & Ainsworth, M. D. S. (1972). Infant crying and maternal responsiveness. *Child Development, 43,* 1171–1190.

Biber, B. (1984). *Early education and psychological development.* New Haven: Yale University Press.

Brazelton, T. B. (1984). Cementing family relationships through child care. In L. Dittman (Ed.), *The infants we care for* (rev. ed.) (pp. 9–20). Washington, DC: NAEYC.

Cazden, C. (Ed.), (1981). *Language in early childhood education* (rev. ed.), Washington, DC: NAEYC.

Cohen, D. H., Stern, V., & Balaban, N. (1983). *Observing and recording the behavior of young children* (3rd ed.). New York: Teachers College Press, Columbia University.

Coopersmith, S. (1975). Building self-esteem in the classroom. In S. Coopersmith (Ed.), *Developing motivation in young children.* San Francisco: Albion.

Cratty, B. (1982). Motor development in early childhood: Critical issues for researchers in the 1980s. In B. Spodek (Ed.), *Handbook of research in early childhood education.* New York: Free Press.

Croft, D. J. (1979). *Parents and teachers: A resource book for home, school, and community relations.* Belmont, CA: Wadsworth.

Curtis, S. (1986). New views on movement development and implications for curriculum in early childhood education. In C. Seefeldt (Ed.), *Early childhood curriculum: A review of current research.* New York: Teachers College Press, Columbia University.

Davidson, L. (1985). Preschool children's tonal knowledge: Antecedents of scale. In J. Boswell (Ed.), *The young child and music: Contemporary principles in child development and music education. Proceedings of the Music in Early Childhood Conference* (pp. 25–40). Reston, VA: Music Educators National Conference.

Dittmann, L. (1984). *The infants we care for.* Washington, DC: NAEYC.

Dreikurs, R., Grunwald, B., & Pepper, S., (1982). *Maintaining sanity in the classroom.* New York: Harper & Row.

Elkind, D. (1986, May). Formal education and early childhood education: An essential difference. *Phi Delta Kappan,* 631–636.

Erikson, E. (1950). *Childhood and society.* New York: Norton.

Evans, E. D. (1984). Children's aesthetics. In L. G. Katz (Ed.), *Current topics in early childhood education* (Vol. 5, pp. 73–104). Norwood, NJ: Ablex.

Feeney, S., & Chun, R. (1985). Research in review. Effective teachers of young children. *Young Children, 41*(1), 47–52.

Fein, G. (1979). Play and the acquisition of symbols. In L. Katz (Ed.), *Current topics in early childhood education* (Vol. 2). Norwood, NJ: Ablex.

Fein, G., & Rivkin, M. (Eds.). (1986). *The young child at play: Reviews of research* (Vol. 4). Washington, DC: NAEYC.

Ferreiro, E., & Teberosky, A. (1982). *Literacy before schooling.* Exeter, NH: Heinemann.

Forman, G., & Kaden, M. (1986). Research on science education in young children. In C. Seefeldt (Ed.), *Early childhood curriculum: A review of current research.* New York: Teachers College Press, Columbia University.

Forman, G., & Kuschner, D. (1983). *The child's construction of knowledge: Piaget for teaching children.* Washington, DC: NAEYC.

Fromberg, D. (1986). Play. In C. Seefeldt (Ed.), *Early childhood curriculum: A review of current research.* New York: Teachers College Press, Columbia University.

Frost, J. L., & Klein, B. L. (1979). *Children's play and playgrounds.* Austin, TX: Playgrounds international.

Gazda, G. M. (1973). *Human relations development: A manual for educators.* Boston: Allyn & Bacon.

Genishi, C. (1986). Acquiring language and communicative competence. In C. Seefeldt (Ed.), *Early childhood curriculum: A review of current research.* New York: Teachers College Press, Columbia University.

Gerber, M. (1982). What is appropriate curriculum for infants and toddlers? In B. Weissbourd & J. Musick (Eds.), *Infants: Their social environments.* Washington, DC: NAEYC.

Gilbert, J. P. (1981). Motoric music skill development in young children: A longitudinal investigation. *Psychology of Music, 9*(1), 21–24.

Goffin, S., & Tull, C. (1985). Problem solving: Encouraging active learning. *Young Children, 40*(3), 28–32.

Gonzales-Mena, J., & Eyer, D. W. (1980). *Infancy and caregiving.* Palo Alto, CA: Mayfield.

Goodwin, W., & Goodwin, L. (1982). Measuring young children. In B. Spodek (Ed.), *Handbook of research in early childhood education.* New York: Free Press.

Gordon, T. (1970). *Parent effectiveness training.* New York: Wyden.

Gordon, T. (1975). *Teacher effectiveness training.* New York: McKay.

Gottfried, A. (1983). Research in review. Intrinsic motivation in young children. *Young Children, 39*(1), 64–73.

Greenberg, M. (1976). Research in music in early childhood education: A survey with recommendations. *Council for Research in Music Education, 45,* 1–20.

Greenspan, S., & Greenspan, N. T. (1985). *First feelings: Milestones in the emotional development of your baby and child.* New York: Viking.

Griffin, E. F. (1982). *The island of childhood: Education in the special world of nursery school.* Teachers College Press, Columbia University.

Hawkins, D. (1970). Messing about in science. *ESS Reader,* Newton, MA: Education Development Center.

Hendrick, J. (1986). *Total learning: Curriculum for the young child* (2nd ed.). Columbus, OH: Merrill.

Herron, R., & Sutton-Smith, B. (1974). *Child's play.* New York: Wiley.

Hill, D. (1979). *Mud, sand, and water.* Washington, DC: NAEYC.

Hirsch, E. (Ed.). (1984). *The block book.* Washington, DC: NAEYC.

Hoffman, M. L. (1975). Moral internalization, parental power, and the nature of parent-child interaction. *Developmental Psychology, 11,* 228–239.

Holt, B. (1979). *Science with young children.* Washington, DC: NAEYC.

Honig, A. S. (1980). The young child and you—learning together. *Young Children, 35*(4), 2–10.

Honig, A. S. (1981). What are the needs of infants? *Young Children, 37*(1), 3–10.

Honig, A. S. (1982). Parent involvement in early childhood education. In B. Spodek (Ed.), *Handbook of research in early childhood education.* New York: Free Press.

Honig, A. S. (1985). Research in review. Compliance, control, and discipline (Parts 1 & 2). *Young Children, 40*(2) 50–58; *40*(3) 47–52.

Honig, A. S. (1986). Research in review. Stress and coping in children (Parts 1 & 2). *Young Children, 41*(4) 50–63; *41*(5) 47–59.

Kamii, C. (1982). *Number in preschool and kindergarten.* Washington, DC: NAEYC.

Kamii, C. (1985). Leading primary education toward excellence: Beyond worksheets and drill. *Young Children, 40*(6), 3–9.

Kamii, C., & DeVries, R. (1980). *Group games in early education.* Washington, DC: NAEYC.

Kamii, C., & Lee-Katz, L. (1979). Physics in early childhood education: A Piagetian approach. *Young Children, 34*(4), 4–9.

Katz, L. (1980). Mothering and teaching: Some significant distinctions. In L. Katz (Ed.), *Current topics in early childhood education* (Vol. 3, pp. 47–64). Norwood, NJ: Ablex.

Kitano, M. (1982). Young gifted children: Strategies for preschool teachers. *Young Children, 37*(4), 14–24.

Kline, L. W. (1985). *Learning to read, teaching to reach.* Newark, DE: LWK Enterprises.

Kobak, D. (1979). Teaching children to care. *Children Today, 8,* 6–7, 34–35.

Kohlberg, L., & Mayer, R. (1972). Development as the aim of education. *Harvard Educational Review, 42,* 449–496.

Kopp, C. B. (1982). Antecedents of self-regulation: A developmental perspective. *Developmental Psychology, 18*, 199–214.

Kuczynski, L. (1983). Reasoning, prohibitions, and motivations for compliance. *Developmental Psychology, 19*, 126–134.

Languis, M., Sanders, T., & Tipps, S. (1980). *Brain and learning: Directions in early childhood education.* Washington, DC: NAEYC.

Lasky, L., & Mukerji, R. (1980). *Art: Basic for young children.* Washington, DC: NAEYC.

Lay-Dopyera, M., & Dopyera, J. (1986). Strategies for teaching. In C. Seefeldt (Ed.), *Early childhood curriculum: A review of current research.* New York: Teachers College Press, Columbia, University.

Lightfoot, S. (1978). *Worlds apart: Relationships between families and schools.* New York: Basic.

Lickona, T. (1983). *Raising good children.* New York: Bantam.

Lozoff, B., Brillenham, G., Trause, M. A., Kennell, J. H., & Klaus, M. H. (1977, July). The mother-newborn relationship: Limits of adaptability. *Journal of Pediatrics, 91.*

Lytton, H. (1979). Disciplinary encounters between young boys and their mothers and fathers: Is there a contingency system? *Developmental Psychology, 15*, 256–268.

McAfee, O. (1985). Research report. Circle time: Getting past "Two Little Pumpkins." *Young Children, 40*(6), 24–29.

McCracken, J. B. (Ed.). (1986). *Reducing stress in young children's lives.* Washington, DC: NAEYC.

McDonald, D. T. (1979). *Music in our lives: The early years.* Washington, DC: NAEYC.

Meisels, S. (1985). *Developmental screening in early childhood.* Washington, DC: NAEYC.

Miller, C. S. (1984). Building self-control: Discipline for young children. *Young Children, 40*(1), 15–19.

Montessori, M. (1964). *The Montessori method.* Cambridge, MA: Robert Bentley.

Moore, S. (1982). Prosocial behavior in the early years: Parent and peer influences. In B. Spodek (Ed.), *Handbook of research in early childhood education.* New York: Free Press.

Mussen, P., & Eisenberg-Bert, N. (1977). *Roots of caring, sharing, and helping: The development of prosocial behavior in children.* San Francisco: Freeman.

NAEYC. (1982). *Early childhood teacher education guidelines for four- and five-year programs.* Washington, DC: NAEYC.

NAEYC. (1984). *Accreditation criteria and procedures of the National Academy of Early Childhood Programs.* Washington, DC: NAEYC.

NAEYC. (1985). *Guidelines for early childhood education programs in associate degree granting institutions.* Washington, DC: NAEYC.

National Institute of Education. (1984). *Becoming a nation of readers: The report of the Commission on Reading.* Washington, DC: U.S. Department of Education.

Piaget, J. (1950). *The psychology of intelligence.* London: Routledge & Kegan Paul.

Piaget, J. (1952). *The origins of intelligence in children.* (M. Cook, Trans.). New York: Norton. (Original work published 1936)

Piaget, J. (1972). *Science of education and the psychology of the child* (rev. ed.). New York: Viking. (Original work published 1965)

Powell, D. (1986). Effects of program approaches and teaching practices. *Young Children, 41*(6), 60–67.

Ramsey, P. G. (1979). Beyond "Ten Little Indians" and turkeys: Alternative approaches to Thanksgiving. *Young Children, 34*(6), 28–32, 49–52.

Ramsey, P. G. (1982). Multicultural education in early childhood. *Young Children, 37*(2), 13–24.

Read, K. H., Gardner, P., & Mahler, B. (1986). *Early childhood programs: A laboratory for human relationships* (8th ed.). New York: Holt, Rinehart & Winston.

Riley, S. S. (1984). *How to generate values in young children: Integrity, honesty, individuality, self-confidence.* Washington, DC: NAEYC.

Rogers, D. L., & Ross, D. D. (1986). Encouraging positive social interaction among young children. *Young Children, 41*(3), 12–17.

Rubin, K., & Everett, B. (1982). Social perspective-taking in young children. In S. G. Moore & C. R. Cooper (Eds.), *The young child: Reviews of research* (Vol. 3, pp. 97–114). Washington, DC: NAEYC.

Ruopp, R., Travers, J., Glantz, F., & Coelen C. (1979). *Children at the center. Final report of the National Day Care Study* (Vol. 1). Cambridge, MA: Abt Associates.

Sackoff, E., & Hart, R. (1984, Summer). Toys: Research and applications. *Children's Environments Quarterly*, 1–2.

Saracho, O., & Spodek, B. (Eds.). (1983). *Understanding the multicultural experience in early childhood education.* Washington, DC: NAEYC.

Schachter, F. F., & Strage, A. A. (1982). Adults' talk and children's language development. In S. G. Moore & C. R. Cooper (Eds.), *The young child: Reviews or research* (Vol. 3, pp. 79–96). Washington, DC: NAEYC.

Schaffer, H. R. (1984). *The child's entry into a social world.* Orlando, FL: Academic.

Schickedanz, J. (1986). *More than the ABCs: The early stages of reading and writing.* Washington, DC: NAEYC.

Schickedanz, J., Schickedanz, D. I., & Forsyth, P. D. (1982). *Toward understanding children.* Boston: Little, Brown.

Seefeldt, C. (1986). The visual arts in C. Seefeldt (Ed.), The early childhood curriculum: A review of current research. New York: Teachers College Press, Columbia University.

Shure, M. B., & Spivack, G. (1978). *Problem-solving techniques in childrearing.* San Francisco: Jossey-Bass.

Skeen, P., Garner, A. P., & Cartwright, S. (1984). *Woodworking for young children.* Washington, DC: NAEYC.

Smith, C. A., & Davis, D. E. (1976). Teaching children non-sense. *Young Children, 34*(3), 4–11.

Smith, F. (1982). *Understanding reading.* New York: Holt, Rinehart & Winston.

Smith, F. (1985). *Reading without nonsense* (2nd ed.). New York: Teachers College Press, Columbia University.

Smith, N. (1983). *Experience and art: Teaching children to paint.* New York: Teachers College Press, Columbia University.

Souweine, J., Crimmins, S., & Mazel, C. (1981). *Mainstreaming: Ideas for teaching young children.* Washington, DC: NAEYC.

Sparling, J. (1984). *Learning games for the first three years.* New York: Walker.

Spodek, B. (1985). *Teaching in the early years* (3rd ed.). Englewood Cliffs, NJ: Prentice-Hall.

Spodek, B. (Ed.), (1986). *Today's kindergarten: Exploring it's knowledge base, extending its curriculum.* New York: Teachers College Press, Columbia University.

Sponseller, D. (1982). Play and early education. In B. Spodek (Ed.), *Handbook of research in early childhood education.* New York: Free Press.

Sprung, B. (1978). *Perspectives on non-sexist early childhood education.* New York: Teachers College Press, Columbia University.

Sroufe, L. A. (1979). The coherence of individual development. *American Psychologist, 34,* 834–841.

Standards for educational and psychological testing. (1985). Washington, DC: American Psychological Association, American Educational Research Association, and National Council on Measurement in Education.

Stewart, I. S. (1982). The real world of teaching two-year-old children. *Young Children, 37*(5), 3–13.

Stone, J. G. (1978). *A guide to discipline* (rev. ed.). Washington, DC: NAEYC.

Uphoff, J. K., & Gilmore, J. (1985, September). Pupil age at school entrance—how many are ready for success? *Educational Leadership, 43,* 86–90.

Veach, D. M. (1977). Choice with responsibility. *Young Children, 32*(4), 22–25.

Wallinga, C. R., & Sweaney, A. L. (1985). A sense of real accomplishment: Young children as productive family members. *Young Children, 41*(1), 3–9.

Warren, R. M. (1977). *Caring: Supporting children's growth.* Washington, DC: NAEYC.

Weber, E. (1984). *Ideas influencing early childhood education: A theoretical analysis.* New York: Teachers College Press, Columbia University.

Weissbourd, B. (1981). Supporting parents as people. In B. Weissbourd & J. Musick (Eds.), *Infants; Their social environments.* Washington, DC: NAEYC.

Wellman, H. M. (1982). The foundations of knowledge: Concept development in the young child. In S. G. Moore & C. R. Cooper (Eds.), *The young child: Reviews of research* (Vol. 3, pp. 115–134). Washington, DC: NAEYC.

Willert, M., & Kamii, C. (1985). Reading in kindergarten: Direct versus indirect teaching. *Young Children, 40*(4), 3–9.

Willis, A., & Ricciuti, H. (1975). *A good beginning for babies: Guidelines for group care.* Washington, DC: NAEYC.

Wolfgang, C. H., & Glickman, C. D. (1980). *Solving discipline problems.* Boston: Allyn & Bacon.

Yarrow, M. R., Scott, P. M., & Waxler, C. Z. (1973). Learning concern for others. *Developmental Psychology, 8,* 240–260.

Yarrow, M. R., & Waxler, C. Z. (1976). Dimensions and correlates of prosocial behavior in young children. *Child Development, 47,* 118–125.

Zavitkovsky, D., Baker, K. R., Berlfein, J. R., & Almy, M. (1986). *Listen to the children.* Washington, DC: NAEYC.

Ziegler, P. (1985). Saying good-bye to preschool. *Young Children, 40*(3), 11–15.

APPENDIX Q

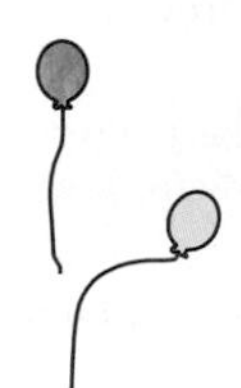

Developmentally Appropriate Educational Experiences in Kindergarten

The Southern Association on Children Under Six is a non-profit educational organization whose purpose is to work in behalf of young children and their families. One of its particular concerns is the development and dissemination of knowledge and understanding of young children.

The organization's eleven thousand members represent the wide range of people concerned with the education and development of young children. SACUS, through its history, has been supportive of its affiliate states to develop public school kindergarten programs and to strive for quality in those programs.

However, recent trends to incorporate developmentally inappropriate teaching strategies such as workbooks, ditto sheets, and formal reading groups as well as academic skill-oriented curriculum content in kindergarten, raise serious concerns. The Executive Board of the Southern Association on Children Under Six, therefore, has adopted the following position on developmentally appropriate educational experiences for kindergarten children.

BEGIN WITH THE NEEDS OF CHILDREN

A major mark of quality kindergarten programs is found in the relationship of learning activities to the children's developmental stages and needs. Quality programs use the child's natural learning abilities and interests to further his development. Thus, play is fundamental to the child's development and learning. In addition to these assumptions the following understandings regarding children's development should serve as guides to developing effective kindergarten programs.

- Kindergarten children constantly strive to understand and make sense of their experiences.
- Kindergarten children develop understanding through play and other natural learning strategies.
- The social, emotional, intellectual and physical needs of kindergarten children are interrelated.
- While kindergarten children follow similar developmental sequences, they do so in unique ways and at different rates.
- Kindergarten children need adults to help them make sense of their experiences.
- The best learning environment for kindergarten children is one in which they can actively participate by manipulating objects and by expressing their ideas through many curricular areas such as music, art, socio-drama, puppetry, and science projects.
- Kindergarten children learn best when all of their development/learning needs and interests are nurtured through a broad and understandable curriculum and guided by a caring teacher certified in Early Childhood Education.
- The different learning styles, interests, and developmental needs of kindergarten children can best be facilitated through informal, flexible classroom arrangements which utilize interest centers and individualized activities and games.
- Kindergarten children learn best when the curriculum is based on concrete experiences to which they can relate in meaningful ways.

Source: Southern Early Childhood Association, Little Rock, AR.

DESIGNING LEARNING ENVIRONMENTS TO MEET CHILDREN'S NEEDS

Kindergarten children are normally inquisitive, explorative and creative in their participation in the learning process. Their unique methods of learning should be supported. A rigid curriculum based on abstract, paper and pencil activities is not understood by them and interferes with their learning. The following guidelines are suggested for developing quality learning environments for kindergarten children.

- Select quality Early Childhood teachers who are knowledgeable in child growth and development, committed to children, and capable of designing programs that meet children's developmental needs.
- Design programs that have adult/child ratios which promote quality interaction in the classroom and allow for the development of close home school relationships.
- Design learning activities that involve children in using all of their senses.
- Create learning situations in which children can use both the real world and their fantasy world to experience the process of solving problems and creating new ideas.
- Capitalize on children's creativeness by providing dramatic play experiences, encouraging participation in artistic and musical expression and in scientific "hands-on" activities.
- Respond to the many facets of children's development by including social, physical, nutritional, intellectual, and emotional "content" in the kindergarten program.
- Provide many varied opportunities for kindergarten children to use language. Avoid narrowly defined reading programs which emphasize de-coding skills and expect the same level of readiness from all children. To meet the diverse needs and levels of children, use their experience as a basis for developing many language activities.
- Provide a participatory curriculum for fostering a sense of autonomy in kindergarten children. Encourage children's decision-making and design learning environments in which the child's needs, interests and discoveries are paramount.
- Utilize a variety of instructional approaches such as individualized learning and small group activities.
- Be intentionally personal in interactions with kindergarten children. Spend time listening to them and encourage them to express themselves both individually and in a variety of social situations.

A quality kindergarten includes many facets: the group planning of daily activities, individual discovery time; varied experiences with language stories and books, and other communicative arts; physical activity appropriate to the children's development; exploration activities by active manipulation of the natural scientific environment; opportunities for representing knowledge through social involvement in group living, role playing and other expressive means; program components that support children's health such as nutritious snacks and lunches, quiet time for reflecting on the day's activities; and many other indoor and outdoor learning situations.

ASSESSMENT: HELPING CHILDREN DEVELOP AND LEARN

Observations and informal assessments appropriate for kindergarten children are essential to understanding the many aspects of their development. Standardized paper and pencil tests are inappropriate for use with kindergarten children. Effective assessment attempts to insure that deficits are recognized, that remediation is designed, and that strengths are maximized. The following are appropriate guidelines for assessment procedures for kindergarten children.

- Assessment should be viewed as an ongoing process of analysis, a method of searching diligently for strengths and weaknesses so that individualized planning is provided for each child's development.
- Assessment techniques should be used in a caring manner that reflects children's sensitivity to unfamiliar situations.
- A variety of assessment techniques (appropriate developmental inventories, teacher observations, parent notations, and developmental profiles) should be used in continuous and

flexible ways to help teachers plan effective learning situations.

Assessment of children's development and learning must consider the "real world" in which the children live. It must recognize home life, cultural setting, and learning style orientation.

TOWARD QUALITY ENVIRONMENTS FOR KINDERGARTEN CHILDREN

It is crucial that schools provide children and families the best possible kindergarten experience. This experience must be based in knowledge that children develop and learn in a variety of ways. It must include responsive situations in classrooms in which children can actively engage in constructing, refining, and expanding knowledge through appropriate educational activities. All children, regardless of culture, handicaps, or other human differences, must have access to kindergarten programs that facilitate, not impede, their development. Teachers, parents, and other citizens must work together for programs that meet children's needs.

SELECTED REFERENCES

Urie Bronfenbrenner. *The ecology of human development.* Cambridge, Mass.: Harvard University Press, 1979.

David Elkind. *The hurried child: growing up too fast, too soon.* Reading, Mass.: Addison-Wesley Publishing, 1981.

Stephanie Feeney, Doris Christensen, & Eva Moravcik. *Who am I in the lives of children.* Columbus, Ohio: Charles E. Merrill, 1983.

Constance Kamii. Autonomy: the aim of education envisioned by Piaget, *Phi Delta Kappan*, February, 1984.

Marjorie Ramsey & Kathleen Bayles, *Kindergarten programs and practices.* St. Louis: C. V. Mosby, 1980.

Marguerita Rudolph & Dorothy Cohen. *Kindergarten and early schooling.* Englewood Cliffs, New Jersey: Prentice-Hall, 1984.

APPENDIX R

Organizations Concerned with Young Children

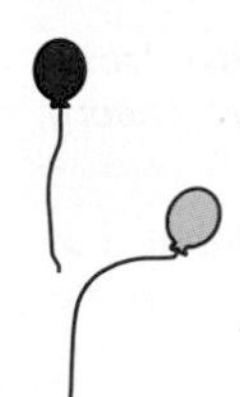

American Academy of Pediatrics
141 Northwest Point Boulevard
P. O. Box 927
Elk Grove Village, IL 60007

American Montessori Society (AMS)
150 Fifth Avenue, Suite 203
New York, NY 10010

Association for Childhood Education International (ACEI)
11501 Georgia Avenue, Suite 315
Wheaton, MD 20902

Children's Defense Fund
122 C Street NW
Washington, DC 20001

Child Welfare League of America, Inc.
440 First Street NW, Suite 310
Washington, DC 20001

Council for Early Childhood Professional Recognition
1341 G Street NW, Suite 400
Washington, DC 20005

Council for Exceptional Children (CEC)
1920 Association Drive
Reston, VA 22091

Educational Resources Information Center on Early Childhood Education (ERIC/ECE)
805 W. Pennsylvania Avenue
Urbana, IL 61801
Head Start Bureau
Department of Health and Human Services
330 C Street SW
Washington, DC 20013

High/Scope Educational Research Foundation
600 N. River Street
Ypsilanti, MI 48197

National Association for Family Day Care
815 15th Street NW, Suite 928
Washington, DC 20005

National Association for the Education of Young Children (NAEYC)
1509 Sixteenth Street NW
Washington, DC 20036

National Association of Child Care Resource and Referral Agencies
2116 Campus Drive SE
Rochester, MN 55904

National Black Child Development Institute
1463 Rhode Island Avenue NW
Washington, DC 20005

National Education Association (NEA)
1201 Sixteenth Street NW
Washington, DC 20036

Southern Early Childhood Association (SECA)
Box 5403
Brady Station
Little Rock, AR 72215

World Organization for Early Childhood Education
(Organisation Mondiale pour l'Education Prescolaire: QMEP)
1718 Connecticut Avenue NW
Washington, DC 20009

REFERENCES

Chapter 1

Almy, M. (1985). New challenges for teacher education: Facing political and economic realities. *Young Children, 40*(6), 10–11.

Association for Childhood Education International. (1983). *Preparation of early childhood teachers*. Wheaton, MD: Author.

Beck, C., & Gargiulo, R. (1983). Burnout in teachers of retarded and nonretarded children. *Journal of Educational Research, 76*(3), 169–173.

Benson, M., & Peters, D. (1988). The child development associate: Competence, training and professionalism. *Early Child Development and Care, 38*, 57–68.

Bredekamp, S. (1990). Setting and maintaining professional standards. In B. Spodek & O. Saracho (Eds.), *Early childhood teacher preparation* (pp. 138–152). New York: Teachers College Press.

Caldwell, B. (1987). Advocacy is everybody's business. *Child Care Information Exchange, 54*, 29–32.

Council for Early Childhood Professional Recognition. (1992). *Assessment system and competency standards for preschool caregivers*. Washington, DC: Author.

Derman-Sparks, L. (1989). *Anti-bias curriculum: Tools for empowering young children*. Washington, DC: National Association for the Education of Young Children.

Dresden, J., & Myers, B. (1989). Early childhood professionals: Toward self-definition. *Young Children, 44*(2), 62–66.

Early Childhood Teacher Certification. (1991). A position statement of the Association of Teacher Educators and the National Association for the Education of Young Children. *Young Children, 47*(1), 16–21.

Farson, R. (1978). *Birthrights*. New York: Macmillan.

Feeney, S., Christensen, D., & Moravcik, E. (1991). *Who am I in the lives of young children*? (4th ed.). New York: Macmillan.

Feeney, S., & Kipnis, K. (1985). Professional ethics in early childhood education. *Young Children, 40*(3), 54–56.

Feeney, S., & Kipnis, K. (1989). A new code of ethics for early childhood educators. Code of ethical conduct and statement of commitment. *Young Children, 45*(1), 24–29.

Feeney, S., & Sysko, L. (1986). Professional ethics in early childhood education: Survey results. *Young Children, 42*(1), 15–20.

Freudenberger, H. (1975). The staff burnout syndrome in alternative institutions. *Psychotherapy: Theory, Research and Practice, 12*, 73–83.

Freudenberger, H. (1977). Burnout: Occupational hazard of the child care worker. *Child Care Quarterly, 6*, 90–99.

Gargiulo, R. (1985). *Working with parents of exceptional children*. Boston: Houghton Mifflin.

Goffin, S. (1988). Putting our advocacy efforts into a new context. *Young Children, 43*(3), 52–56.

Graves, S. (1987). Ethical behavior in early childhood education. *Scope, 46*(1), 4–5.

Graves, S. (1990). Early childhood education. In T.E.C. Smith, *Introduction to education* (2nd ed., pp. 182–219). St. Paul, MN: West.

Hess, R., & Croft, D. (1981). *Teachers of young children* (3rd ed.) Boston: Houghton Mifflin.

Hildebrand, V. (1990). *Guiding young children* (4th ed.). New York: Macmillan.

Howsam, R., Corrigan, D., Denemark, G., & Nash, R. (1976). *Education as a profession*. Washington, DC: American Association of Colleges for Teacher Education.

Katz, L. (1972). Development stages of preschool teachers. *Elementary School Journal, 73*(1), 50–54.

Katz, L. (1988). Where is early childhood education as a profession? In B. Spodek, O. Saracho, & D. Peters (Eds.), *Professionalism and the early childhood practitioner* (pp. 75–83). New York: Teachers College Press.

Katz, L., & Goffin, S. (1990). Issues in the preparation of teachers of young children. In B. Spodek & O. Saracho (Eds.), *Early childhood teacher preparation* (pp. 192–208). New York: Teachers College Press.

Katz, L., & Ward, E. (1978). *Ethical behavior in early childhood education*. Washington, DC: National Association for the Education of Young Children.

Kerckhoff, R., & McPhee, J. (1984). Receptivity to child-rights legislation. *Young Children, 39*(2), 58–61.

Lawton, J. (1988). *Introduction to child care and early childhood education*. Glenview, IL: Scott, Foresman and Co.

Lindberg, L., & Swedlow, R. (1985). *Young children*. Boston: Allyn & Bacon.

Lombardi, J. (1986). Training for public policy and advocacy. *Young Children, 41*(4), 65–69.

Maxim, G. (1985). *The very young* (2nd ed.). Belmont, CA: Wadsworth.

Mattingly, M. (1977). Sources of stress and burnout in professional child care work. *Child Care Quarterly, 6*, 127–137.

McCarthy, J. (1988). *Early childhood teacher certification requirements.* Washington, DC: National Association for the Education of Young Children.

Morrison, G. (1991). *Early childhood education today* (5th ed.). New York: Macmillan.

Morrison, G. (1993). *Contemporary curriculum K–8.* Boston: Allyn & Bacon.

National Association for the Education of Young Children. (1982). *Early childhood teacher education guidelines for four- and five-year programs.* Washington, DC: Author.

National Association for the Education of Young Children. (1985). *Guidelines for early childhood education programs in associate degree granting institutions.* Washington, DC: Author.

National Center for Education Statistics. (1991). *Digest of education statistics: 1991.* Washington, DC: U.S. Government Printing Office.

Ott, D., Zeichner, K., & Price, G. (1990). Research horizons and the quest for a knowledge base in early childhood teacher education. In B. Spodek & O. Saracho (Eds.), *Early childhood teacher preparation* (pp. 188–137). New York: Teachers College Press.

Partin, R., & Gargiulo, R. (1980). Burned out teachers have no class! Prescriptions for teacher educators. *College Student Journal, 14*(4), 365–368.

Perry, G. (1990). Alternate modes of teacher preparation. In C. Seefeldt (Ed.), *Continuing issues in early childhood education* (pp. 173–200). Columbus, OH: Merrill.

Powell, D., & Dunn, L. (1990). Non-baccalaureate teacher education in early childhood education. In B. Spodek & O. Saracho (Eds.), *Early childhood teacher preparation* (pp. 45–66). New York: Teachers College Press.

Saracho, O. (1984). Perception of the teaching process in early childhood education through role analysis. *Journal of the Association for the Study of Perception, International, 19*(1), 26–29.

Seaver, J., Cartwright, C., Ward, C., & Heasley, C. (1979). *Careers with young children: Making your decision.* Washington, DC: National Association for the Education of Young Children.

Seefeldt, C., & Barbour, N. (1990). *Early childhood education* (2nd ed.). Columbus, OH: Merrill.

Spodek, B., & Saracho, O. (1988). Professionalism in early childhood education. In B. Spodek, O. Saracho, & D. Peters (Eds.), *Professionalism and the early childhood practitioner* (pp. 59–74). New York: Teachers College Press.

Spodek, B., & Saracho, O. (1990). Preparing early childhood teachers. In B. Spodek & O. Saracho (Eds.), *Early childhood teacher preparation* (pp. 23–44). New York: Teachers College Press.

Spodek, B., Saracho, O., & Davis, M. (1991). *Foundations of early childhood education* (2nd ed.). Englewood Cliffs, NJ: Prentice Hall.

Spodek, B., Saracho, O., & Peters, D. (1988). Professionalism, semi-professionalism, and craftsmanship. In B. Spodek, O. Saracho, & D. Peters (Eds.), *Professionalism and the early childhood practitioner* (pp. 3–9). New York: Teachers College Press.

United Nations. (1959). *Declaration of the rights of the child* (Resolution No. 1386). New York: Author.

U.S. Department of Labor. (1992). *Occupational projections and training data* (Bulletin 2401). Washington, DC: U.S. Government Printing Office.

Wilkens, A., & Blank, H. (1986). Child care: Strategies to move the issue forward. *Young Children, 42*(1), 68–72.

Wittmer, J., & Myrick, R. (1974). *Facilitative teaching: Theory and practice.* Santa Monica, CA: Goodyear.

Chapter 2

Abt Associates. (1979). *Children at the center. Final report of the National Day Care Study.* Cambridge, MA: Author.

Beatty, J. (1990). A post-cold war budget. *The Atlantic Monthly, 265*(2), 74–82.

Berrueta-Clement, J., Schweinhart, L., Barnett, W., Epstein, A., & Weikart, D. (1984). Changed lives: The effects of the Perry Preschool Program on youths through age 19. *Monographs of the High/Scope Education Research Foundation, 8.*

Brown, B. (1985). Head Start: How research changed public policy. *Young Children, 40*(5), 9–13.

Children's Defense Fund. (1991). *The state of America's children 1991.* Washington, DC: Author.

Cohen, D. (1990, May 23). "Silver Ribbon Panel" calls for upgrading 25-year-old Head Start. *Education Week*, p. 17.

Elam, S., Rose, L., & Gallup, A. (1991). The 23rd annual Gallup/PDK Poll of the public's attitudes toward the public schools. *Phi Delta Kappan, 73*(1), 41–56.

Elam, S., Rose, L., & Gallup, A. (1992). The 24th annual Gallup/PDK Poll of the public's attitudes toward the public schools. *Phi Delta Kappan, 74*(1), 41–53.

Federal Register. (1990, June 18). *55*(117), p. 24838.

Gallup, A. (1986). The 18th annual Gallup Poll of the public's attitudes toward the public schools. *Phi Delta Kappan, 68*(1), 43–59.

Graves, S. (1990a). Early childhood education. In T.E.C. Smith, *Introduction to education* (2nd ed., pp. 189–219). St. Paul, MN: West.

Graves, S. (1990b). *Social and economic issues affecting children and families.* SACUS Public Policy Institute Report (No. 3). Little Rock, AR: Southern Association on Children under Six.

Gullo, D. (1992). *Developmentally appropriate teaching in early childhood.* Washington, DC: National Education Association.

Hess, R., & Croft, D. (1981). *Teachers of young children* (3rd ed.). Boston: Houghton Mifflin.

Heward, W., & Orlansky, M. (1988). *Exceptional children* (3rd ed.). Columbus, OH: Merrill.

Hymes, J. (1991). *Early childhood education: Twenty years in review.* Washington, DC: National Association for the Education of Young Children.

Joffe, C. (1977). *Friendly intruders: Child care professions and family life.* Berkeley, CA: University of California Press.

Lawton, J. (1988). *Introduction to child care and early childhood education.* Glenview, IL: Scott Foresman.

Lazar, I., Hubbel, V., Murray, H., Rosche, M., & Royce, J. (1977). *The persistence of preschool effects: A long-term follow-up of fourteen infant and preschool experiments.* Washington, DC: U.S. Department of Health, Education and Welfare, Administration on Children, Youth and Families.

National Association for the Education of Young Children. (1984). *Accreditation criteria and procedures of the National Academy of Early Childhood Programs.* Washington, DC: Author.

National Center for Education Statistics. (1991). *Digest of education statistics: 1991.* Washington, DC: U.S. Government Printing Office.

Poplin, M., & Wright, P. (1983). The concept of cultural pluralism: Issues in special education. *Learning Disability Quarterly, 6*, 367–371.

Quality Education for Minorities Pr*tion that works: An action plan f* *norities.* Cambridge, MA: Mas ...usetts Institute of Technology.

Read, K. (1960). *The nurs... school: A human relationship laboratory* (3r... ed.). Philadelphia: W.B. Saunders.

Read, K. (1971). *The nursery school: A human relationship laboratory* (5th ed.). Philadelphia: W.B. Saunders.

Robinson, H. (1983). *Exploring teaching in early childhood education* (2nd ed.). Boston: Allyn and Bacon.

Schweinhart, L., Berrueta-Clement, J., Epstein, A., & Weikart, D. (1985). The promise of early childhood education. *Phi Delta Kappan, 66*(8), 548–553.

Schweinhart, L., & Weikart, D. (1985). Evidence that good early childhood programs work. *Phi Delta Kappan, 66*(8), 545–551.

Schweinhart, L., & Weikart, D. (1986). What do we know so far? *Young Children, 41*(2), 49–55.

Spodek, B., Saracho, O., & Davis, M. (1991). *Foundations of early childhood education* (2nd ed.). Englewood Cliffs, NJ: Prentice Hall.

U.S. Bureau of the Census. (1976). *Status: A monthly chart book of social and economic trends.* Washington, DC: U.S. Government Printing Office.

U.S. Bureau of the Census. (1989). *Changes in American family life* (Current Population Reports, Series P–23, No. 163). Washington, DC: U.S. Government Printing Office.

U.S. Bureau of the Census. (1992a). *School enrollment—Social and economic characteristics of students: October 1990* (Current Population Reports, Series P–20, No. 460). Washington, DC: U.S. Government Printing Office.

U.S. Bureau of the Census. (1992b). *Who's minding the kids? Child care arrangements: Fall 1988* (Current Population Reports, P 70–30). Washington, DC: U.S. Government Printing Office.

U.S. Bureau of the Census. (1992c). *Statistical abstract of the United States 1992* (112th ed.). Washington, DC: U.S. Government Printing Office.

Willer, B., Hofferth, S., Kisker, E., Divine-Hawkins, P., Farquhar, E., & Glantz, F. (1991). *The demand and supply of child care in 1990.* Washington, DC: National Association for the Education of Young Children.

Willer B., & Johnson, L. (1989). *The crisis is real: Demographics on the problems of recruiting and retaining early childhood staff.* Washington, DC: National Association for the Education of Young Children.

ʼapter 3

Abt Associates. (1977). *Education as experimentation: A planned variation approach.* Cambridge, MA: Author.

Aires, P. (1962). *Centuries of childhood.* New York: Vantage Books.

Bereiter, C., & Englemann, S. (1966). *Teaching disadvantaged children in the preschool.* Englewood Cliffs, NJ: Prentice Hall.

de Mause, L. (Ed.). (1974). *This history of childhood.* New York: Psychohistory Press.

Dewey, J. (1916). *Democracy and education.* New York: Macmillan.

Gargiulo, R. (1990). Child abuse and neglect: An overview. In R. Goldman & R. Gargiulo (Eds.), *Children at risk* (pp. 1–36). Austin, TX: Pro-Ed.

Gargiulo, R., & Cerna, M. (1992). Special education in Czechoslovakia: Characteristics and issues. *International Journal of Special Education, 7*(1), 60–70.

Gargiulo, R., & Graves, S. (1993). Early childhood special education: Lessons from Eastern Europe. *Day Care and Early Education, 21*(1), 36–37.

Gilkeson, E., & Bowman, G. (1976). *The focus is on children.* New York: Bank Street Publications.

Ginsburg, H., & Opper, S. (1969). *Piaget's theory of intellectual development.* Englewood Cliffs, NJ: Prentice Hall.

Goffin, S. (1990). Government's responsibility in early childhood care and education: Renewing the debate. In C. Seefeldt (Ed.), *Continuing issues in early childhood education* (pp. 9–26). Columbus, OH: Merrill.

Graves, S. (1990). Early childhood education. In T. E. C. Smith, *Introduction to education* (2nd ed., pp. 182–219). St. Paul, MN: West.

Graves, S., & Gargiulo, R. (1994). Early childhood education in three Eastern European countries. *Childhood Education, 70*(4), 205–209.

Hess, R., & Croft, D. (1981). *Teachers of young children* (3rd ed.). Boston: Houghton Mifflin.

Hewes, D. (1990). Historical foundations of early childhood teacher training: The evaluation of kindergarten teacher preparation. In B. Spodek & O. Saracho (Eds.), *Early childhood teacher preparation* (pp. 1–22). New York: Teachers College Press.

Hohmann, N., Banet, B., & Weikart, D. (1979). *Young children in action: A manual for preschool educators.* Ypsilanti, MI: High/Scope Press.

Katz, L. (1988). Engaging children's minds: The implications of research for early childhood education. In C. Warger (Ed.), *A resource guide to public school early childhood programs* (pp. 32–62). Alexandria, VA: Association for Supervision and Curriculum Development.

Klein, J. (1973). Making or breaking it: The teacher's role in model (curriculum) implementation. *Young Children, 28*, 359–366.

Lawton, J. (1988). *Introduction to child care and early childhood education.* Glenview, IL: Scott Foresman.

Maxim, G. (1985). *The very young* (2nd ed.). Belmont, CA: Wadsworth.

Montessori, M. (1965). *Dr. Montessori's own handbook.* New York: Schocken Books.

Morrison, G. (1991). *Early childhood education today* (5th ed.). New York: Macmillan.

Mounts, N., & Roopnarine, J. (1987). Application of behavioristic principles to early childhood education. In J. Roopnarine & J. Johnson (Eds.), *Approaches to early childhood education* (pp. 127–142). Columbus, OH: Merrill.

Osborn, D. (1980). *Early childhood education in historical perspective.* Athens, GA: Education Associates.

Peabody, E. (May 1882). Origin and growth of the kindergarten. *Education*, 523.

Piaget, J., & Inhelder, B. (1969). *The psychology of the child.* New York: Basic Books.

Seefeldt, C. (1990). *Continuing issues in early childhood education.* Columbus, OH: Merrill.

Segal, J. (1978). *A child's journey.* New York: McGraw-Hill.

Spodek, B. (1991). Early childhood curriculum and cultural definitions of knowledge. In B. Spodek & O. Saracho (Eds.), *Issues in early childhood curriculum* (pp. 1–20). New York: Teachers College Press.

Spodek, B., Saracho, O., & Davis, M. (1991). *Foundations of early childhood education* (2nd ed.). Englewood Cliffs, NJ: Prentice Hall.

Steiner, G. (1976). *The children's cause.* Washington, DC: Brookings Institution.

Weikart, D. (1971). *Early childhood special education for intellectually subnormal and/or culturally different children.* Ypsilanti, MI: High/Scope Education Research Foundation.

Weikart, D., & Schweinhart, L. (1987). The High/Scope cognitively oriented curriculum in early education. In J. Roopnarine & J. Johnson (Eds.), *Approaches to early childhood education* (pp. 253–268). Columbus, OH: Merrill.

Zimiles, H. (1987). The Bank Street approach. In J. Roopnarine & J. Johnson (Eds.), *Approaches to early childhood education* (pp. 163–178). Columbus, OH: Merrill.

Chapter 4

Beaty, J. (1990). *Observing the development of the young child.* Columbus, OH: Merrill.

Brown, M. H. (Ed.). (1988). *Quality environments: Developmentally appropriate experiences for young children.* Champaign, IL: Stipes.

Cook R. E., Tessier, A., & Armbruster, V. B. (1991). *Adapting early childhood curricula for children with special needs.* Columbus, OH: Merrill.

Grace, C. & Shores, E. (1991). *The portfolio and its use: Developmentally appropriate assessment of young children.* Little Rock, AR: Southern Association on Children Under Six.

Hills, T. (1992). Reaching potentials through appropriate assessment. In Bredekamp, S. & Rosegrant, T. (Eds.), *Reaching potentials: Appropriate curriculum and assessment for young children* (Vol. 1, pp. 43–63). Washington, DC: National Association for the Education of Young Children.

Meisels, S. J. & Steele, D. M. (1991). *The early childhood portfolio collection process.* Ann Arbor, MI: Center for Human Growth and Development, University of Michigan.

National Association for the Education of Young Children & the National Association of Early Childhood Specialists in State Departments of Education. (1991) Guidelines for appropriate curriculum content and assessment in programs serving children ages 3 through 8. *Young Children, 46*(3), 21–38.

Northwest Regional Educational Laboratory. (1991). *Alternative program evaluation ideas for early childhood programs.* Portland, OR: Author.

Southern Association on Children Under Six. (1990). *Developmentally appropriate assessment.* Little Rock, AR: Author.

Chapter 5

Barnes, K. (1971). Preschool play norms: A replication. *Developmental Psychology, 5*, 99–103.

Buhler, C. (1935). *From birth to maturity.* London: Routledge and Kegan Paul.

Dimidjian, V. J. (1991). *Play's place in public education for young children.* Washington, DC: National Education Association.

Dodge, M. K., & Frost, J. L. (1986). Children's dramatic play: Influence of thematic and nonthematic settings. *Childhood Education, 62*, 166–170.

Eddowes, E. A. (1991). The benefits of solitary play. *Dimensions, 20*, 31–34.

Ellis, M. J. (1973). *Why people play.* Englewood Cliffs, NJ: Prentice Hall.

Frost, J. L. (1992). *Play and playscapes.* Albany, NY: Delmar.

Gilmore, J. B. (1971). Play: A special behavior. In R. E. Herron & B. Sutton-Smith (Eds.), *Child's play* (pp. 343–355). New York: Wiley.

Guddemi, M., & Jambor, T. (1993). *Playscapes at KinderCare: An action training guide.* Montgomery, AL: KinderCare.

Johnson, J. E., Christie, J. F., & Yawkey, T. D. (1987). *Play and early childhood development.* Glenview, IL: Scott Foresman.

McGrew, W. C. (1972). An ethological study of children's behavior. New York: Academic Press.

Neumann, E. A. (1971). *The elements of play.* New York: MSS Information Corp.

Parten, M. B. (1932). Social participation among preschool children. *Journal of Abnormal and Social Psychology, 27*, 243–269.

Peck, J., & Goldman, R. (March 1978). The behavior of kindergarten children under selected conditions of the physical and social environment. Paper presented at the American Educational Research Association. Toronto, Canada.

Peters, D. L., Neisworth, J. T., & Yawkey, T. D. (1985). *Early childhood education: From theory to practice.* Monterey, CA: Brooks/Cole.

Phyfe-Perkins, E. (1980). Children's behavior in preschool settings—A review of research concerning the influence of the physical environment. In L. G. Katz (Ed.), *Current topics in early childhood education* (Vol. 3, pp. 99–125). Norwood, NJ: Ablex.

Piaget, J. (1962). *Play, dreams, and imitation in childhood.* New York: Norton.

Piaget, J. (1977). *The development of thought: Equilibration of cognitive structures.* New York: Viking.

Pellegrini, A. (1988). Elementary school children's rough-and-tumble play and social competence. *Developmental Psychology, 24*, 802–806.

Rubin, K. H., Fein, G. G., & Vandenberg, B. (1983). Play. In Heatherington, M. E. (Ed.), *Carmichael's manual of child psychology: Social development* (pp. 693–774). New York: Wiley.

Rubin, K. H., Maioni, T. L., & Hornung, M. (1976). Free play behaviors in middle and lower class preschoolers: Parten and Piaget revisited. *Child Development, 47*, 414-419.

Schwartzman, H. B. (1978). *Transformations: The anthropology of play.* New York: Plenum.

Smilansky, S. (1968). *The effects of sociodramatic play on disadvantaged preschool children.* New York: Wiley.

Smith, P. K., & Connolly, K. J. (1980). *The ecology of preschool behavior.* Cambridge, England: Cambridge University Press.

Spodek, B., & Saracho, O. N. (1988). The challenge of educational play. In D. Bergen (Ed.), *Play as a medium for learning and development: A handbook of theory and practice* (pp. 9–22). Portsmouth, NH: Heinemann.

Spodek, B., Saracho, O. N., & Davis, M.D. (1991). *Foundations of early childhood education: Teaching three-, four-, and five-year-old children.* Englewood Cliffs, NJ: Prentice Hall.

Swick, K. J., Brown, M. H., & Graves, S. B. (1984). Developmentally appropriate educational experiences for kindergarten. *Dimensions, 12*, 25.

Van Hoorn, J., Nourot, P., Scales, B., & Alward, K. (1993). *Play at the center of the curriculum.* New York: Merrill.

Vygotsky, L. S. (1967). Play and its role in the mental development of the child. *Soviet Psychology, 12*, 62–76.

White, R. F. (1959). Motivation reconsidered: The concept of competence. *Psychological Review, 66*, 297–333.

Wood, D., McMahon, L., & Cranstoun, Y. (1980). *Working with under fives.* Ypsilanti, MI: High/Scope Press.

Chapter 6

Amabile, T. M., & Hennessey, B.A. (1988). The motivation for creativity in children. In A. K. Boggiano & T. Pittman (Eds.), *Achievement motivation: A social developmental perspective.* NY: Cambridge University Press.

Baer, J. (1993). *Creative and divergent thinking.* Hillsdale, NJ: Erlbaum.

Baron, J. B., & Sternberg, R. J. (1987). *Teaching thinking skills.* NY: W. H. Freeman.

Bloom, B. S. (1964). *Stability and change in human characteristics.* NY: Wiley.

Bloom, B. S., Englehart, M. D., Furst, E. J., Hill, W. H., & Krathwohl, D. R. (1956). *Taxonomy of educational objectives.* NY: Mckay.

Bredekamp, S. (1987). *Developmentally appropriate practices in early childhood programs serving children from birth through age 8.* Washington, DC: National Association for the Education of Young Children.

Bredekamp, S., & Rosegrant, T. (1992). *Reaching potentials: Appropriate curriculum and assessment for young children.* Washington, DC: National Association for the Education of Young Children.

Bredekamp, S. (1993). Reflections on Reggio Emilia. *Young Children, 49*(1), 13–17.

Cherry C., Godwin, D., & Staples, J. (1989). *Is the left brain always right? A guide to whole child development.* Belmont, CA: David S. Lake.

Chukowsky, K. (1968). *From two to five.* Berkeley, CA: University of California Press.

Clark, B. (1986). *Optimizing learning integrative education model in the classroom.* Columbus, OH: Merrill.

Clark, B. (1988). *Growing up gifted: Developing the potential of children at home and at school.* Columbus, OH: Merrill.

Clemens, S. G. (1991). Art in the classroom: Making every day special. *Young Children, 46*(2), 4–11.

Csikszentmihalyi, M. (1988). Society, culture and persons: A systems view of creativity. In R. Sternberg (Ed.), *The nature of creativity.* New York, NY: Cambridge University Press.

Draper, T. W., Larsen, J. M., Haupt, J. H., Robinson, C. C., & Hart, C. (1993, March). *Family emotional climate as a mediating variable between parent education and social competence in an advantaged subculture.* Paper presented at the biennial meeting of the Society for Research in Child Development, New Orleans, LA.

Edwards, C. P., & Springate, K. (1993). Inviting children into project work. *Dimensions of Early Childhood, 22*(1), 9–12.

Eisner, E. W. (1992). The misunderstood role of the arts in human development. *Phi Delta Kappan, 73*(8), 591–595.

Elkind, D. (1994). *Sympathetic understanding of the child: Birth through sixteen.* Boston, MA: Allyn and Bacon.

Fein, G. C. (1986). Pretend play. In D. Gorlitz & J. F. Wohwill (Eds.), *Curiosity imagination, and play.* Hillsdale, NJ: Erlbaum.

Galin, D. (1976). Educating both halves of the brain. *Childhood Education, 53*(1), 17–20.

Gandini, L. (1993). Fundamentals of Reggio Emilia approach to early childhood education. *Young Children, 49*(1), 4–8.

Gardner, H. (1989). *To open minds.* NY: Harper Collins.

Gardner, H. (1993). *Multiple intelligence.* New York: Harper Collins.

Getzel, J., & Csikszentmihalyi, M. (1976). *The creative vision.* New York: Wiley.

Getzel, J., & Jackson, D. (1962). *Creativity and intelligence.* New York: Wiley and Sons.

Grady, M. P., & Luecke, E. A. (1978). *Education and the brain.* Bloomington, IN: Phi Delta Kappa Educational Foundation.

Guilford, J. P. (1967). *The structure of intellect.* New York: MacGraw Hill.

Hanna, J. L. (1992). Connections: Arts, academics, and productive citizens. *Phi Delta Kappan, 73*(8), 601–607.

Heller, W. (1990, May/June). Of one mind: Second thoughts about the brain's dual nature. *The Sciences*, 38–44.

Hellige, J. B. (1990). Hemispheric asymmetry. *Annual Review of Psychology, 41.* Palo Alto, CA: Annual Review.

Helson, R. M. (1993, August). *Issues of change and stability in creative lives.* Paper presented at the meeting of the American Psychological Association, Toronto.

Hendricks, J. (1994). *Total learning developmental curriculum for the young child.* NY: Macmillan.

Jalongo, M. R. (1990). The child's right to the expressive arts: Nurturing the imagination as well as the intellect. *Childhood Education, 66*(4), 195–201.

Katz, L. (1990). Impressions of Reggio Emilia preschools. *Young Children, 45*(6), 11–12.

Lowenfeld, V. (1954). *Your child and his art: A guide for parents.* NY: Macmillan.

Lowenfeld, V., & Brittain, W. L. (1987). *Creative and mental growth.* NY: Macmillan.

MacKinnon, D. W. (1962). The nature and nurture of creative talent. *American Psychologist, 17*, 484–495.

Maxim, G. W. (1989). *The very young: Guiding children from infancy through the early years.* Columbus, OH: Merrill.

Mayesky, M. (1990). *Creative activities for young children.* NY: Delmar.

Moran, J. D., Milgram, R., Sawyers, J. K., & Fu, V. R. (1983). Original thinking in preschool children. *Child Development, 54*, 921–926.

Moyer, J. (1990). Whose creation is it anyway? *Childhood Education, 66*(3), 130–131.

New, R. (1990). Excellent early education: A city in Italy has it. *Young Children, 45*(6), 4–10.

New, R. (1993). Cultural variations on developmentally appropriate practices: Challenges to theory and practice. In C. Edwards, L. Gandini, & G. Forman (Eds.), *The hundred languages of children: The Reggio Emilia Approach to Early Childhood Education* (pp. 215–232). Norwood, NJ: Ablex.

Ornstein, R. E. (1977). *The psychology of consciousness.* New York: Harcourt Brace Jovanovich.

Ornstein, R. (1978). The split and whole brain. *Human Nature, 1*(5), 76–83.

Parnes, S. J. (1967). *Creative behavior guidebook.* New York: Charles Scribner's Sons.

Perkins, D. (1984, September). Creativity by design. *Educational Leadership, 42*, 18–25.

Restak, R. M. (1988). *The mind.* New York: Bantam Books.

Runco, M. A. (1991). *Divergent thinking.* Norwood, NJ: Ablex.

Santrock, J. W., & Yussen, S. (1992). *Child Development.* Dubuque, IA: Wm. C. Brown.

Schiamberg, L. C. (1989). *Child and Adolescent Development.* NY: Macmillan.

Seigler, R. S. (1991). *Children's thinking.* Englewood Cliffs, NJ: Prentice Hall.

Sisk, D. (1987). *Creative teaching of the gifted.* New York: McGraw Hill.

Tegano, D. W., Moran, J. D., & Sawyers, J. K. (1991). *Creativity in early childhood classrooms.* Washington, DC: National Education Association.

Torrance, E. P., (1962). *Guiding creative talent.* Englewood Cliffs, NJ: Prentice Hall.

Torrance, E. P., (1963). Adventuring in creativity. *Childhood Education, 40*(2), 79–87.

Torrance, E. P. (1969). *Creativity.* Sioux Falls, SD: Adapt Press.

Wakefield, J. F. (1991). *Creative thinking: Problem solving skills and the arts orientation.* Norwood, NJ: Ablex.

Wallach, M. A., & Kogan, N. (1965). *Modes of thinking in young children.* New York: Holt, Rinehart, and Winston.

Warner, L. (1990). Basic musical concepts for preschoolers. *Dimensions, 16*(4), 13–14.

Weikart, D. (1990). *Quality preschool programs: A long term social investment.* New York: Ford Foundation.

Williams, C. K., & Kamii, C. (1987). How do children learn by handling objects? *Young Children, 42*(1), 23–26.

Winner, E. (1989). Development in the visual arts. In W. Damon (Ed.), *Child Development Today and Tomorrow.* San Francisco, CA: Jossey Bass.

Wolfe, A. D. (1990). Art postcards: Another aspect of your aesthetics program? *Young Children, 45*(2), 39–43.

Chapter 7

Almy, M. (1985). *The early childhood educator at work.* NY: McGraw-Hill.

Anselmo, S., & Zinck, R. A. (1987). Computers for young children? Perhaps. *Young Children, 42*(3), 22–27.

Ard, L. & Pitts, M. (1990). *Room to grow: How to create quality early childhood environments.* Austin, TX: Texas Association for the Education of Young Children.

Apelman, M. (1984). Appendix I: Stages of block building. In E. S. Hirsch, *The block book.* Washington, DC: National Association for the Education of Young Children.

Bereiter, C., & Englemann, S. (1966). *Teaching the culturally disadvantaged child in the preschool.* Englewood Cliffs, NJ: Prentice Hall.

Bredekamp, S., & Rosegrant, T. (1992). *Reaching potentials: Appropriate curriculum and assessment for young children (vol. 1).* Washington, DC: National Association for the Education of Young Children.

Burns, S., Goin, L. Donlon, J. T. (1990). A computer in my room. *Young Children, 45*(2), 62–67.

Burton, L. (1991). *Joy in learning: Making it happen in early childhood classes.* Washington, DC: National Education Association.

Cartwright, S. (1990). Learning with large blocks. *Young Children, 45*(3), 38–41.

Christie, J., & Wardle, F. (1992). How much time is needed to play? *Young Children, 47*(3), 28–33.

Crosser, S. (1992). Managing the early childhood classroom. *Young Children, 47*(2), 23–29.

Cryan, J. R., & Surbeck, E. (1979). *Early childhood education: Foundations for lifelong learning.* Bloomington, IN: Phi Delta Kappa Educational Foundation.

Cummings, C. (1989). *Translating guidelines into practice.* Saginaw: Mid-Michigan Association for the Education of Young Children.

Danielson, K. E. (1990). Creating interest in words with literature. *Childhood Education, 66*(4), 220–225.

Day, D. (1983). *Early childhood education: A human ecological approach.* Glenview, IL: Scott, Foresman.

Day, B. D. (1988). *Early childhood education: Creative learning activities.* New York: Macmillan.

Day, B. D. (1992). Early childhood education: A developmental perspective. *Kappa Delta Pi Record, 28*(3), 66–69.

Decker, C. A., & Decker, J. R. (1988). *Planning and administering early childhood programs.* Columbus, OH: Merrill.

DeVries, R., & Kohlberg, L. (1990). *Constructive early education: Overview and comparison with other programs.* Washington, DC: National Association for the Education of Young Children.

Dodge, D. T., Goldhammer, M., & Colker, L. J. (1988). The creative curriculum. Washington, DC: Creative Associates International.

Elkind, D. (1994). *A sympathetic understanding of the child: Birth to sixteen.* Boston, MA: Allyn and Bacon.

Erikson, E. (1963). *Childhood and society.* New York: Norton.

Ferreiro, E., & Teberosky, A. (1982). *Literacy before schooling.* Portsmouth, NH: Heinemann.

Foster, J. R., & Rogers, L. R. (1970). Housing early childhood education in Texas. *Innovative Resources, 5*, 5–12.

Gehrke, N. (1979). Rituals of the hidden curriculum. In K. Yamamoto (Ed.), *Children in time and space.* New York: Teachers College Press.

Haugland, S., & Shade, D. (1990). *Developmental evaluation of software for young children.* New York: Delmar.

Headley, N. E. (1966). *Education in the kindergarten* (4th ed.). New York: American Book.

Hirsch, E. S. (1984). *The block book.* Washington, DC: National Association for the Education of Young Children.

Hitz, R. (1987). Creative problem solving through music activities. *Young Children, 42*(2), 12–17.

Hohmann, C., Banet, B., & Weikart, D. (1979). *Young children in action.* Ypsilanti, MI: High/Scope Press.

Hyson, M. C., & Eyman, A. (1986). Approaches to computer literacy in early childhood teacher education. *Young Children, 41*(6), 54–59.

Irlen, H. (1991). *Reading by the colors.* NY: Avery Publishing.

Jefferson, R. E. (1968). Indoor facilities. In S. Sunderland & N. Gray (Eds.), *Housing for early childhood education* (pp. 32–40). Washington, DC: Association for Childhood Educators International.

Johnson, H. M. (1933). *The art of block building.* New York: Bank Street College Education.

Kennedy, D. (1991). The young child's experience of space and child care center design: A practical meditation. *Children's Environments Quarterly, 8* (1), 37–48.

Kostelnik, M. J. (1992). Myths associated with developmentally appropriate programs. *Young Children, 47*(4), 17–23.

Kostelnik, M. J., Soderman, A. K., & Whiren, A. P. (1993). *Developmentally appropriate programs in early childhood education.* New York: Macmillan.

Kritchevsky, S., Prescott, E., & Walling, L. (1977). *Planning environments for young children: Physical space* (2nd ed.). Washington, DC: National Association for the Education of Young Children.

Leeper, S. H., Witherspoon, R. L., & Day, B. (1984). *Good schools for young children.* NY: Macmillan.

Lewis, B. (1979) Time and space in schools. In K. Yamamoto (Ed.), *Children in time and space* (pp. 16–24). New York: Teachers College Press.

Loughlin, C. E. (1977). Understanding the learning environment. *Elementary School Journal, 78*(2), 1–5.

Loughlin, C. E., & Martin, M. D. (1987). *Supporting literacy: Developing effective learning environments.* New York: Teachers College Press.

Malecki, C. L. (1990). Teaching whole science: In a departmentalized elementary setting. *Childhood Education, 66*(4), 232–236.

Meltz, B. F. (1990). A little privacy: Children need space to call their own. *Tallahassee Democrat, 4*, 1.

Myers, B. K., & Mauer, K. (1987). Teaching with less talking: Learning in the kindergarten. *Young Children, 42*(5), 20–27.

Myhre, S. (1993). Enhancing your dramatic play area through the use of prop boxes. *Young Children, 48*(5), 6–11.

Nunnelley, J. C. (1990). Beyond turkeys, Santas, snowmen, and hearts: How to plan innovative curriculum themes. *Young Children, 46*(1), 24–29.

Osborn, D. K. (1991). *Early childhood education in historical perspective* (3rd ed.). Athens, GA: Daze Press.

Pattillo, J., & Vaughn, E. (1992). *Learning centers for child-centered classrooms.* Washington, DC: National Education Association.

Piaget, J. (1952). *The origins of intelligence of children* (M. Cook, Trans.). New York: International University Press.

Readdick, C. A. (1993). Solitary pursuits: Supporting children's privacy needs in early childhood settings. *Young Children,* 49(1), 60–64.

Sampson, F. K. (1970). *Contrast rendition and school lighting.* New York: Educational Facilities Laboratory.

Seefeldt, C., & Barbour, N. (1990). *Early childhood education: An introduction.* Columbus, OH: Merrill.

Shapiro, S. (1975). Preschool ecology: A study of three environmental variables. *Reading Improvement, 12,* 236–241.

Snider, S. L. (1994). *Integrating developmentally appropriate curriculum and learning style preferences: Effects on standardized test performance of second grade students.* Unpublished master's thesis, Texas Woman's University, Denton, TX.

Stein, C. (1975). School lighting re-evaluated. *American School and University, 48,* 70–78.

Swick, K. (1989). Appropriate use of computers with young children. *Educational Technology,* 7–13.

Taylor, A. P., & Vlustos, G. (1983). *School zone: Learning environments for children.* NY: Van Nostrand Reinhold Company.

Teale, W., & Sulzby, E. (Eds.). (1986). *Emergent literacy: Writing and reading.* Norwood, NJ: Ablex.

Vygotsky, L. S. (1978). Mind in society: The development of *psychological processes.* Cambridge, MA: Harvard University Press.

Waldrop, C. S., & Scarborough, A. M. (1990). Crayons and markers. *Dimensions, 16*(4), 15–18.

Willis, C., & Lindberg, L. (1967). *Kindergarten for today's children.* Chicago: Follett.

Zeegers, S. (1991). *Privacy in day care setting.* Unpublished manuscript.

Zimring, C. M. (1981). Stress and the designed environment. *Journal of Social Issues, 37*(1), 145–171.

Chapter 8

American Alliance for Health, Physical Education, Recreation, and Dance (in press). *Developmentally appropriate practice in movement programs for young children.* Reston, VA: Author.

American Alliance for Health, Physical Education, Recreation, and Dance (1986). *Movement programs for young children: A position paper.* Reston, VA: Author.

Esbensen, S. (1990). Play environments for young children: Design perspectives. In S. Wortham & J. Frost (Eds.), *Playgrounds for young children: national survey and perspectives* (pp. 49–68). Reston, VA: American Alliance for Health, Physical Education, Recreation, and Dance.

Frost, J. (1992). *Play and playscapes.* Albany, NY: Delmar.

Gabbard, C. (1992). *Lifelong motor development.* Dubuque, IA: William C. Brown.

Gabbard, C., LeBlanc, E., & Lowy, S. (1987). *Physical education for children: Building the foundation.* Englewood Cliffs, NJ: Prentice-Hall.

Gallahue, D. (1993). *Developmental physical education for today's children* (2nd ed.). Dubuque, IA: Brown & Benchmark.

Haywood, K. (1986). *Lifespan motor development.* Champaign, IL: Human Kinetics.

Jaffe, M., & Kosakov, C. (1982). The motor development of fat babies. *Clinical Pediatrics, 27,* 619–621.

Jambor, T., & Palmer, D. (1991). *Playground safety manual.* Birmingham, AL: The Alabama Chapter of American Academy of Pediatrics.

Kuntzleman, C., & Reiff, G. (1992). The decline of American children's fitness levels. *Research Quarterly for Exercise and Sport, 63,* 107–111.

Lowrey, G. (1986). *Growth and development of children* (7th ed.). Chicago: Year Book Medical.

Martin, P. C., & Vincent, E. L. (1960). *Human development.* New York: Ronald.

McGinnis, M. (1987). Introduction. National youth fitness study II. *Journal of Physical Education, Recreation and Dance, 58,* 50.

Payne, G. V., & Isaacs, L. D. (1991). *Human motor development* (2nd ed.). Mountain View, CA: Mayfield.

Ross, J., & Pate, R. (1987). The national children and youth fitness survey: A summary of findings. *Journal of Physical Education, Recreation and Dance, 58,* 51–56.

Siedentop, D., Herkowitz, J., & Rink, J. (1984). *Elementary physical education methods.* Englewood Cliffs, NJ: Prentice-Hall.

Sommerfield, D., & Dunn, C. (1988). Project OLE: Outdoor learning environments for children. In L. Bruya (Ed.), *Play spaces for children: A new beginning* (pp. 166–176). Reston, VA: American Alliance for Health, Physical Education, Recreation, and Dance.

Thompson, D., Bruya, L., & Crawford, M. (1990). Maintaining play environments: Training, checklists and documentation. In S. Wortham & J. Frost (Eds.), *Playgrounds for young children: National survey and perspectives* (pp. 103–146). Reston, VA: American Alliance for Health, Physical Education, Recreation, and Dance.

Warrell, E. (1988). A system to establish playground safety in the school. In L. Bruya (Ed.), *Play spaces for children: A new beginning* (pp. 139–164). Reston, VA: American Alliance for Health, Physical Education, Recreation, and Dance.

Wortham, S., & Frost, J. (1990). Introduction. In S. Wortham & J. Frost (Eds.), *Playgrounds for young children: National survey and perspectives* (pp. 1–4). Reston, VA: American Alliance for Health, Physical Education, Recreation, and Dance.

Chapter 9

Anderson, G. S. (1984). *A whole language approach to reading.* Lanham, MD: University Press of America.

Bird, L. (1987). What is whole language? In "Dialogue," D. Jacobs (Ed.), *Teachers networking: The whole language newsletter, 1*(1).

Boehnlein, M. (1987). Reading intervention for high-risk first graders. *Educational Leadership, 44*, 32–37.

Bredekamp, S. (Ed.). (1987). *Developmentally appropriate practice* (Expanded edition). Washington, DC: National Association for the Education of Young Children.

Brown, M. H., Cromer, P. S., & Weinberg, S. (1986). Shared book experiences in kindergarten: Helping children come to literacy. *Early Childhood Research Quarterly, 1*, 397–405.

Calkins, L. M. (1986). *The art of teaching writing.* Exeter, NH: Heinnemann Educational Books.

Chomsky, C. (1971). Write first, read later. *Childhood Education, 47*, 296–299.

Chomsky, N. (1968). *Language and mind.* New York: Harcourt, Brace, and World.

Clark, E. V. (1973). What's in a word? On the child's acquisition of semantics in his first language. In T. E. Moore (Ed.), *Cognitive development and the acquisition of language.* New York, NY: Academic Press.

Clark, E. V. (1979). Building a vocabulary: Words for objects, actions, and relations. In P. Fletcher & M. Garman (Eds.), *Language acquisition: Studies in first language development.* Cambridge, MA: Cambridge University Press.

Clark, M. M. (1976). *Young fluent readers.* London: Heinemann Educational Books.

Clay, M. M. (1966). *Emergent reading behavior.* Doctoral dissertation, University of Aukland.

Cohen, D. (1968). The effect of literature on vocabulary and reading achievement. *Elementary English, 45*, 209–213, 217.

Commission on Reading. (1984). *Becoming a nation of readers.* Washington, DC: National Institute of Education, 119.

Cullinan, B. E., Jagger, A., & Strickland, D. (1974). Language expansion for black children in the primary grades: A research report. *Young Children, 29*, 98–112.

Cushenberry, D. C. (1989). *Building elementary reading skills through whole language and literature.* Springfield, IL: Charles C. Thomas.

Dewey, J. (1938). *Experience in education.* New York: Collier.

Dewey, J. (1943). *The child and the curriculum and the school and society.* Chicago: University of Chicago Press.

Donaldson, M. C., & Balfour, G. (1968). Less is more: A study of language comprehension in children. *British Journal of Psychology, 59*, 461–472.

Duckworth, E. (1987) *The having of wonderful ideas.* New York: Teachers College Press.

Durkin, D. (1966). *Children who read early.* New York, NY: Teachers College Press.

Eldridge, J. L., & Butterfield, D. (1986). Alternatives to traditional reading instruction. *The Reading Teacher, 40*, 32–37.

Ferreiro, E., & Teberosky, A. (1982). *Literacy before schooling.* Exeter, NH: Heinemann Educational Books.

Fountas, I. C., & Hannigan, I. L. (1989). Making sense of whole language: The pursuit of informed teacher. *Childhood Education, 65*(3), 133–137.

Golinkoff, R. M. (1983). The preverbal messages: Insights into the transition period. In R. M. Golinkoff (Ed.), *The transition from prelinguistic to linguistic communication.* Hillside, NJ: Erlbaum.

Goodman, K. (1986). *What's whole in whole language?* Portsmouth, NH: Heinemann.

Goodman, K. (1988). Look what they've done to Judy Blume: The basalization of children's literature. *The New Advocate, 1*, 29–41.

Goodman, K. S., & Goodman, Y. M. (1981). *A whole-language comprehension-centered view of reading development.* Occasional paper No. 1, Tucson, AZ: Program in Language and Literacy.

Goodman, K., Smith, E. B., Meredith, R., & Goodman, Y. (1987). *Language and thinking in school.* New York: Richard C. Owen.

Goodman, Y. (1980). The roots of literacy. In M. Douglas (Ed.), *Claremont Reading Conference forty-fourth yearbook*. Claremont, CA: Claremont Reading Conference.

Goodman, Y. & Altwerger, B. (1981). Print awareness in preschool children: A study of the development of literacy in preschool children (Occasional Paper 4). Tucson, AZ: Arizona Center for Research and Development Program in Language and Literacy.

Goodman, Y. (1984). The development of initial literacy. In H. Goelman, A. Oberg, & F. Smith (Eds.), *Awakening to literacy*. Exeter, NH: Heinemann Educational Books.

Goodman, Y. (1985). Kidwatching: Observing children in the classroom. In A. Jagger & M. Smith-Burke (Eds.), *Observing the Language Learner* (pp. 9–17). Newark, DE: International Reading Association.

Goodman, Y. (1989). Roots of the whole language movement. *The Elementary School Journal, 90*(2).

Goodman, Y., Watson, D., & Burke C. (1987). *Reading miscue inventory*. New York: Richard C. Owens.

Graves, D. (1983). *Writing: Teachers and children at work*. Portsmouth, NH: Heinemann.

Griffiths, P. (1979). Speech acts and early sentences. In P. Fletcher & M. Garman (Eds.), *Language acquisition: Studies in first language development*. Cambridge: Cambridge University Press.

Halliday, M. (1975). *Learning how to mean*. New York, NY: Elsevier.

Hansen, J. S. (1969). The impact of the home literacy environment on reading attitude. *Elementary English, 46*, 17–24.

Harste, J. C., Woodward, V. A., & Burke, C. L. (1984). *Language stories and literacy lessons*. Portsmouth, NH: Heinemann.

Heath, S. B. (1980). The functions and uses of literacy. *Journal of Communication, 30*, 123–133.

Hiebert, E. H., & Colt, J. (1989). Patterns of literature-based reading instruction. *The Reading Teacher, 43*(1), 22–28.

Holdaway, D. (1979). *Foundations of literacy*. Sydney: Ashton Scholastic.

Holdaway, D. (1982). Shared book experience: Teaching reading using favorite books. *Theory into Practice, 21*, 293–300.

Holdaway, D. (1986). The structure of natural learning as a basis for literacy instruction. In M. Sampson (Ed.), *The pursuit of literacy: Early reading and writing*. Dubuque, IA: Kendall/Hunt.

Hoskisson, K. (1979). Learning to read naturally. *Language Arts, 53*, 489–496.

International Reading Association. (1985). *Literacy development and pre-first grade*. Newark, DE: IRA.

Larrick, N. (1987). Illiteracy starts too soon. *Phi Delta Kappan, 69*, 184–189.

Leichter, H. P. (1984). Families as environments for literacy. In H. Goelman, A. Oberg, & F. Smith (Eds.), *Awakening to literacy*. Exeter, NH: Heinemann Educational Books.

Lenneberg, E. (1967). *Biological foundations of language*. New York, NY: Wiley.

Manning, M. M., Manning, G. L., Long, R., & Wolfson, B. (1987). *Reading and writing in the primary grades*. Washington, DC: National Education Association.

McGee, L., & Richgels, D. (1990). *Literacy's beginnings: Supporting young readers and writers*. Needham Heights, MA: Allyn and Bacon.

McNeil, D. (1970). *The acquisition of language: The study of developmental psycholinguistics*. New York: Harper & Row.

Morrow, L. M. (1983). Home and school correlates of early interest in literature. *Journal of Educational Research, 76*, 221–230.

Morrow, L. M. (1985). Retelling stories: A strategy for improving children's comprehension, concept of story structure and oral language complexity. *Elementary School Journal, 85*, 647–661.

Morrow, L. M. (1989). *Literacy development in the early years: Helping children read and write*. Englewood Cliffs, NJ: Prentice-Hall, Inc.

Nelson, K. (1973). Structure and strategy in learning to talk. *Monograph for the Society for Research in Child Development, 38*(1–2).

Newman, J. M. (1985). Introduction. In J. Newman (Ed.), *Whole language*. Portsmouth, NH: Heinemann.

Owens, R. E. (1992). *Language development: An introduction* (3rd Ed.). New York: Merrill.

Piaget, J., & Inhelder, B. (1969). *The psychology of the child*. New York, NY: Basic Books.

Pickering, C. T. (1989). Whole language: A new signal for expanding literacy. *Reading Improvement, 26*(2).

Pinnell, G., & Haussler, M. (1988). *Impact of language research on curriculum*. Newark, DE: International Reading Association.

Read, C. (1975). *Children's categorization of speech sounds in English* (National Research Report 17). Urbana, IL: National Council of Teachers of English.

Rye, J. (1982). *Cloze procedure and the teaching of reading*. Exeter, NH: Heinemann Educational Books.

Salinger, T. (1988). *Language arts and literacy for young children*. Columbus, OH: Merrill.

Searfoss, L. W., & Readence, J. E. (1985). *Helping children learn to read*. Englewood Cliffs, NJ: Prentice-Hall.

Smith, F. (1973). *Psycholinguistics and reading*. New York: Holt, Rinehart & Winston.

Smith, F. (1983). A metaphor for literacy: Creating words or shunting information? In F. Smith (Ed.), *Essays into literacy*. Exeter, NH: Heinemann Educational Books.

Smith, F. (1984). The creative achievement of literacy. In H. Hoelman, A. Oberg, & F. Smith (Eds.), *Awakening to Literacy* (pp. 143–153). Portsmouth, NH: Heinemann.

Smith, T. E. C., Aldridge, J. T., & Graves, S. B. (in press). *Teaching reading*. St. Paul, MN: West.

Southside Teachers Support Group (Eds.). (1985). *What is the whole language approach? A pamphlet for parents*. (Available from Edmonton Public Schools, Edmonton, Alberta, Canada.)

Taylor, D. (1983). *Family literacy*. Exeter, NH: Heinemann Educational Books.

Teale, W. (1978). Positive environments for learning to read: What studies of early readers tell us. *Language Arts, 55*, 922–923.

Teale, W. (1982). Toward a theory of how children learn to read and write naturally. *Language Arts, 59*, 555–570.

Teale, W. (1984). Reading to young children: Its significance to literacy development. In H. Goelman, A. Oberg, & F. Smith (Eds.), *Awakening to literacy*. Exeter, NH: Heinemann Educational Books.

Thorndike, E. L. (1973). *Reading comprehension education in fifteen countries: An empirical study*. New York: Wiley.

Tunnell, M. D., & Jacobs, J. S. (1989). Using "real" books: Research findings on literature-based reading instruction. *The Reading Teacher, 42*(7), 470–477.

Vygotsky, L. S. (1978). *Mind in society*. M. Cole, V. John-Steiner, S. Scribner, & E. Souberman (Eds.), Cambridge, MA: Harvard University Press.

Vygotsky, L. S. (1981). The genesis of higher mental functions. In J. J. Wertsch (Ed.), *The concept of activity*. White Plains, NY: M. E. Sharpe.

Watson, D. (1989). Defining and describing whole language. *The Elementary School Journal, 90*, 129–141.

Weaver, C. (1988). *Reading process and practice: From socio-psycholinguistics to whole language*. Portsmouth, NH: Heinemann.

Wiseman, D. E., & Robeck, C. P. (1983). The written language behavior of two socio-economic groups of preschool children, *Reading Psychology, 4*, 349–363.

Chapter 10

Ard, L., & Pitts, M. (Eds.) (1990). *Room to grow: How to create quality early childhood environments*. Austin, TX: Texas Association for the Education of Young Children.

Bredderman, T. (1982). Activity science: The evidence shows it matters. *Science and Children, 20*(1), 39–41.

Brewer, J. (1992). *Introduction to early childhood education*. Needham Heights, MA: Allyn and Bacon.

Copeland, R. (1970). *How children learn mathematics: Teaching implications of Piaget's research*. London: Collier-Macmillan Limited.

Curriculum and evaluation standards for school mathematics. (1989). Reston, VA: The National Council of Teachers of Mathematics.

Dewey, J. (1910). *How we think*. New York: D. C. Heath.

Hohmann, M., Banet, B., & Weikart, D. (1979). *Young children in action*. Ypsilanti, MI: High/Scope Press.

Holt, B. (1977). *Science with young children*. Washington, DC: National Association for the Education of Young Children.

Iatridis, M. (1986). *Teaching science to children: A resourcebook*. New York: Garland.

Kamii, C., & DeVries, R. (1978). *Physical knowledge in preschool education*. Englewood Cliffs, NJ: Prentice-Hall.

Kamii, C. (1982). *Number in preschool and kindergarten*. Washington, DC: National Association for the Education of Young Children.

Klein, A. (1991). About ants: Discovery learning in the primary grades. *Young Children, 46*(5), 23–27.

Krough, S. (1990). *The integrated early childhood curriculum*. New York: McGraw-Hill Publishing Company.

Maxim, G. (1989). *The very young*. Columbus, Ohio: Merrill Publishing Company.

Piaget, J. (1950). *The psychology of intelligence*. New York: Harcourt, Brace.

Piaget, J. (1954). *The constructions of reality in the child*. New York: Basic.

Piaget, J. (1965). *The child's conception of number*. New York: W. W. Norton.

Piaget, J., & Inhelder, B. (1963). *The child's conception of space*. London: Routledge and Kegan Paul.

Schinkendanz, J., York, M., Steward, I., & White, D. (1990). Strategies for teaching young children. Englewood Cliffs, NJ: Prentice-Hall.

Scott, L., & Gardner, J. (1978). *Mathematical experiences for young children*. New York: McGraw Hill.

Seefeldt, C., & Barbour, N. (1990). *Early childhood education*. Columbus, OH: Merrill Publishing Company.

Shymansky, J., Kyle, W., & Alport, J. (1982). How effective were hands-on science programs of yesterday? *Science and Children, 20*(1), 14-15.

Chapter 11

Anderson, L. F. (1990). A rationale for global education. In R. S. Brandt (Ed.), *Global education: From thought to action*, Alexandria, VA: Association for Supervision and Development.

Archer, S. L. (1989). The status of identity: Reflections on the need for intervention. *Journal of Adolescence, 12*, 345–359.

Archer, S. L. (1991). Identify development, gender differences. In R. M. Lerner, A. C. Petersen, & J. Brooks-Gunn (Eds.), *Encyclopedia of Adolescence* (Vol. 1). New York: Garland.

Atwood, V. A. (1986). Elementary social studies: Cornerstone or crumbling mortar. In *Elementary school social studies: Research as a guide to practice*. Washington, DC: National Council for the Social Studies.

Block, M. N. (1986). Social Education of Young Children. In C. Cornbleth (Ed.), *An invitation to research in social education*. Washington, DC: National Council for the Social Studies.

Bricker, D. C. (1989). *Classroom life as civic education*. New York: Teachers College Press, Columbia University.

Burns, S. M., & Brainerd, C. J. (1979). Effects of constructive and dramatic play on perspective-taking in very young children. *Developmental Psychology, 15*, 512–521.

Cawelti, G. (1993). *Challenges and achievements of American education*. Alexandria, VA: Association for Supervision and Curriculum Development.

Clark, L., DeWolf, S., & Clark, C. (1992). Teaching teachers to avoid having culturally assaultive classrooms. *Young Children, 47*(5) 4–9.

Clemens, H. M., Fielder, W. R., & Tabachnick, B. R. (1966). *Social study: Inquiry in elementary classrooms*. New York: Bobbs-Merrill.

Damon, W. (1988). *The moral child*. New York: Free Press.

Derman-Sparks, L. (1993). Revisiting multicultural education: What children need to live in a diverse society. *Dimensions of Early Childhood, 21*(2). 6–9.

Derman-Sparks, L., & Ramsey, P. G. (1992). Multicultural education reaffirmed. *Young Children, 47*(2), 10–11.

Dewey, J. (1944). *Democracy and education*. New York: Free Press.

Eccles, J. S. (1993, March). *Parents as gender role socializers during middle childhood and adolescence*. Paper presented at the biennial meeting of the society for Research in Child Development, New Orleans, LA.

Eccles, J. S., & Midgley, C. (1990). Changes in academic motivation and self-perception during early adolescence. In R. Montemayer, G. R. Adams, & T. P. Gullotta (Eds.) *From childhood to adolescence: A transitional period?* Newbury Park, CA: Sage.

Eccles, J. S., MacIver, D., & Lange, L. (1986, March). *Classroom practices and motivation to study math*. Paper presented at the annual meeting of the American Educational Research Association, San Francisco, CA.

Elkind, D. (1993). *Image of the young child*. Washington, DC: National Association for the Education of Young Children.

Erikson, E. H. (1950). *Childhood and society*. New York: Norton.

Erikson, E. H. (1968). *Identity: Youth and crisis*. New York: Norton.

Froebel, F. W. (1887). *Education of man*. Translated by M. W. Hailman. New York: Appelton.

Gardner, H. (1983). *Frames of mind*. New York: Basic.

Gilligan, C. (1990). Teaching Shakespeare's sister. In C. Gilligan, N. Lyons, & T. Hammer (Eds.), *Making connections: The relational words of adolescent girls*. Cambridge, MA: Harvard University Press.

Gough, P. B. (1993). Dealing with diversity. *Phi Delta Kappan, 75*(1), 3.

Grief, E. B. (1979, March) *Sex differences in parent-child conversations: Who interrupts who?* Paper presented at the Biennial Meeting of the Society for Research in Child Development, San Francisco, CA.

Hanson, C. (1993). Imagine, if you will, the following. New York: U.N. Demographic Data Division, United Nations Children's Fund.

Havighurst, R. J. (1953). *Human development and education*. New York: Aldine.

Hendrick, J. (1990). Total learning. Toronto, Ontario, Canada: Macmillan.

Jones, E., & Derman-Sparks, L. (1992). Meeting the challenge of diversity. *Young Children, 47*(2), 16.

Katz, L., & Chard, S. C. (1992). *Engaging children's minds: The project approach*. Norwood, NJ: Ablex.

Kohlberg, L. (1978). Moral stages and moralization: The cognitive development approach. In T. Fickona (Ed.). *Moral Development and Behavior*. New York: Holt, Reinhart, & Winston.

Kohn, A. (1992). Choices for children. *Phi Delta Kappan, 75*(1), 8–20.

Lally, J. R., Mangione, P. L., Honig, A. S., & Wittmer, D. S. (1988). More pride, less delinquency: Findings from the ten year follow-up study of the Syracuse university family development research program. *Zero to 3, 8*(4), 13–18.

Lazar, I., & Darlington, R. (1982). Lasting effects of early education: A report from the consortium for longitudinal studies. *Monographs of the Society for Research in Child Development, 47*(3, serial no. 195).

Lewis, M. (1987). Early sex-role behavior and school age adjustment. In J. M. Reinisch, L. A. Rosenblum, & S. A. Sanders (Eds.), *Masculinity-femininity: Basic perspectives.* New York: Oxford University Press.

Maccoby, E. E. (1989, August). *Gender and relationships: A developmental account.* Paper presented at the meeting of the American Psychological Association, New Orleans, LA.

Marcia, C. (1990). Identity and self development. In R. M. Lerner, A. C. Peterson, & J. Brooks-Gunn (Eds.), *Encyclopedia of Adolescence* (vol. 1). New York: Garland.

Maslow, A. H. (1954). *Motivation and personality.* New York: Harper Collins.

Maslow, A. H. (1971). *The farther reaches of human nature.* New York: Viking Penguin.

Matthews, W. S., Beebe, S., & Bopp, W. (1980). Spatial perspective-taking and pretend play. *Perceptual and Motor Skills, 51,* 49–50.

McAvoy-Baptiste, L., Baptiste, H. P., & Hughes, K. (1993). Muticultural education: A valuable necessity for everyone. *Texas Association for the Education of Young Children, 18*(4), 15.

McCracken, J. B. (1990). Helping children love themselves and others: A professional handbook for family day care. Washington, DC: Children's Foundation.

Montessori, M. (1912). *The Montessori method.* New York: Stokes.

Morrissett. I. (1983). *Social studies in the 1980s: A report of project SPAN.* Alexandria, VA: Association for Supervision and Curriculum Development.

Ornstein, A. C., & Levine, D. O. (1990). Multicultural education: Trends and issues. In Z. W. Chevalier (Ed.), *Issues and advocacy in early childhood education.* Boston: Allyn & Bacon.

Osborn, D. K. (1975). *Early childhood education in historical perspective.* Athens, GA: Early Childhood Education Learning.

Parker, W. C. (1991). Reviewing the social studies curriculum. Alexandria, VA: Association for Supervision and Curriculum Development.

Phillips, C. (1992). Forward. In B. Neugebauer (Ed.), *Alike and Different.* Washington, DC: National Association for the Education of Young Children.

Piaget, J. (1932). *The moral judgment of the child.* New York: Harcourt Brace Jovanovich.

Piaget, J. (1970). Piaget's theory. In P. H. Mussen (Ed.), *Manual of Child Psychology* (vol. D.). New York: Wiley.

Rogers, C. R. (1961). *On becoming a person.* Boston: Houghton Mifflin.

Rosen, C. E. (1974). The effects of sociodramatic play on problem-solving behavior among culturally disadvantaged preschool children. *Child Development, 45*(10), 22–45.

Saltz, E., Dixon D., & Johnson, R. (1977). Training disadvantaged preschoolers on various fantasy activities: Effects on cognitive functioning and impulse control. *Child Development, 48,* 367–380.

Santrock, J. W., & Yussen, S. R. (1992). *Child development.* Dubuque, IA: Wm. C. Brown.

Seefeldt, C. (1989). *Social studies for the preschool-primary child.* Columbus, OH: Merrill.

Seefeldt, C. (1993). Social studies learning for freedom. *Young Children, 8*(3), 4–9.

Serbin, L. A. (1980, Fall). Play activities and the development of visual-spatial skills. *Equal Play,* 6–9.

Serbin, L. A., O'Leary, K. D., Kent, R. N., & Tonick, E. J. (1973). A comparison of teacher response to a preacademic and problem behavior of boys and girls. *Child Development, 22,* 796–804.

Sluder, L. C. (1987). *An investigation into the relationship of sex differences in reading readiness and the achievement of conservation skills of entering first grade students.* Paper presented to the International Association of the Jean Piaget Society, Eighteenth Annual Session, Philadelphia, PA.

Smith, P. K., Daglish, M., & Herzmark, M. G. (1981). A comparison of the effects of fantasy play tutoring and skills tutoring in nursery classes. *International Journal of Behavioral Development, 4,* 421–441.

Smith, P. K., & Sydall, S. (1978). Play and nonplay tutoring in preschool children: Is it play or tutoring which matters? *British Journal of Educational Psychology, 48,* 315–325.

Snyder, A. (1972). *Dauntless women in childhood education.* Washington, DC: Association for Childhood Education International.

Spodek, B., Saracho, O. N., & Davis, M. D. (1987). *Foundations of early childhood education.* Englewood Cliffs, NJ: Prentice-Hall.

Tavris, C., & Wade, C. (1984). *The longest war: Sex differences in perspective.* New York: Harcourt Brace & Jovanovich.

Turiel, E. (1966). An experimental test of sequentiality of developmental stages in the child's moral judgments. *Journal of Personality and Social Psychology, 3,* 611–618.

Walker, L. J. (1991). Family interaction and the development of moral reasoning. *Child Development, 62,* 264–283.

Walker, L. J. (1993, March). Is the family a sphere of moral growth for children? Paper presented at the biennial meeting of the Society for Research in Child Development, New Orleans, LA.

Walker, L. J., & Taylor, J. H. (1991). Stage transitions in moral reasoning: A longitudinal study of developmental processes. *Developmental Psychology, 27,* 330–337.

Wall, J. A. (1993, March). *Susceptibility to antisocial peer pressure in Mexican-American adolescents and its relation to acculturation.* Paper presented at meeting of the Society for Research in Child Development, New Orleans, LA.

Weikart, D. P. (1989). *Quality preschool programs: A long social investment.* New York: Ford Foundation.

Weikart, D. P. (1993). *Long-term positive effects in the Perry Preschool Head Start program.* Unpublished data, High Scope Foundation, Ypsilanti, MI.

Chapter 12

Allen, K. (1992). *The exceptional child: Mainstreaming in early childhood education* (2nd ed.). Albany, NY: Delmar.

Bailey, D., & Wolery, M. (1992). *Teaching infants and preschoolers with disabilities* (2nd ed.). New York: Merrill.

Blacher, J. (1984). Sequential stages of parental adjustments to the birth of a child with disabilities. *Mental Retardation, 22,* 55–68.

Brain, G. (1979). The early planners. In E. Zigler & J. Valentine (Eds.), *Project Head Start: A legacy of the war on poverty* (pp. 72–77). New York: Free Press.

Bronfenbrenner, U. (1979). *The ecology of human development: Experiments by nature and design.* Cambridge, MA: Harvard University Press.

Casto, G., & Mastropieri, M. (1986). The efficacy of early intervention programs: A meta-analysis. *Exceptional Children, 52,* 417–424.

Clarke, A., & Clarke, A. (1976). *Early experience: Myth and evidence.* New York: Free Press.

Cook, R., Tessier, A., & Klein, M. (1992). *Adapting early childhood curricula for children with special needs* (3rd ed.). New York: Merrill.

Cross, A. (1977). Diagnosis. In L. Cross and K. Goin (Eds.), *Identifying handicapped children: A guide to casefinding, screening, diagnosis, assessment and evaluation* (pp. 25–34). New York: Walker.

Deal, A., Dunst, C., & Trivette, C. (1989). A flexible and functional approach to developing Individualized Family Service Plans. *Infants and Young Children, 1,* 32–43.

Dumars, K., Duran-Flores, D., Foster, C., & Stills, S. (1987). Screening for developmental disabilities. In H. Wallace, R. Biehl, L. Taft, & A. Oglesby (Eds.), *Handicapped children and youth* (pp. 111–125). New York: Human Sciences Press.

Dunst, C. (1986). Overview of the efficacy of early intervention programs: Methodological and conceptual considerations. In L. Bickman & D. Weatherford (Eds.), *Evaluating early intervention programs for severely handicapped children and their families* (pp. 79–147). Austin, TX: Pro-Ed.

Dunst, C., & Snyder, S. (1986). A critique of the Utah State University early intervention meta-analysis research. *Exceptional Children, 53,* 269–276.

Dunst, C., Trivette, C., & Deal, A. (1988). *Enabling and empowering families: Principles and guidelines for practice.* Cambridge, MA: Brookline Books.

Fallen, N., & Umansky, W. (1985). *Young children with special needs* (2nd ed.). Columbus, OH: Merrill.

Federal Register. (1977, August 23). Washington, DC: U.S. Government Printing Office, *42*(163).

Fewell, R. (1991). Trends in the assessment of infants and toddlers with disabilities. *Exceptional Children, 58,* 166–173.

Filler, J. (1983). Service models for handicapped infants. In S. Garwood & R. Fewell (Eds.), *Educating handicapped infants* (pp. 369–386). Rockville, MD: Aspen.

Garber, H., & Heber, R. (1977). The Milwaukee Project: Indications of the effectiveness of early intervention in preventing mental retardation. In P. Mittler (Ed.), *Research to practice in mental retardation: Care and intervention* (Vol. 1, pp. 119–127). Baltimore: University Park Press.

Gargiulo, R. (1985). *Working with parents of exceptional children.* Boston: Houghton Mifflin.

Gargiulo, R. & Graves, S. (1991). Parental feelings. The forgotten component when working with parents of handicapped preschool children. *Childhood Education, 67,* 176–178.

Graves, S., & Gargiulo, R. (1989). Parents and early childhood professionals as program partners: Meeting the needs of the preschool exceptional child. *Dimensions, 17,* 23–24.

Hallahan, D., & Kauffman, J. (1991). *Exceptional children* (5th ed.). Englewood Cliffs, NJ: Prentice Hall.

Hanson, M., & Lynch, E. (1989). *Early intervention.* Austin, TX: Pro-Ed.

Hardman, M., Drew, C., Egan, M., & Wolf, B. (1993). *Human exceptionality: Society, school and family* (4th ed.). Needham Heights, MA: Allyn & Bacon.

Heber, R., & Garber, H. (1975). The Milwaukee Project: A study of the use of family intervention to prevent cultural-familial mental retardation. In B. Friedlander, G. Sterritt, & G. Kirk (Eds.), *Exceptional infant: Assessment and intervention* (pp. 399–433). New York: Brunner/Mazel.

Heward, W., & Orlansky, M. (1988). *Exceptional children* (3rd ed.). Columbus, OH: Merrill.

Kaufman, M., Gottlieb, J., Agard, J., & Kukic, M. (1975). Mainstreaming: Toward an explication of the construct. In E. Meyen, G. Vergason, & R. Whelan (Eds.), *Alternatives for teaching exceptional children* (pp. 35–54). Denver: Love Publishing.

Koppelman, J. (1986). Reagan signs bills expanding services to handicapped preschoolers. *Report to Preschool Programs, 18*, 3–4.

Kroth, R. (1978). Parents: Powerful and necessary allies. *Teaching Exceptional Children, 10*, 88–90.

Lazar, I. (1981). Early intervention is effective. *Educational Leadership, 38*, 303–305.

Lazar, I., & Darlington, R. (1979). *Summary report: Lasting effects after preschool.* (DHEW Publication No. OHDS 80–30179). Washington, DC: U.S. Government Printing Office.

Lazar, I., & Darlington, R. (Eds.). (1982). Lasting effects of early education: A report from the Consortium for Longitudinal Studies. *Monographs of the Society for Research in Child Development, 47* (2&3 Serial No. 195).

Lerner, J., Mardell-Czudnowski, C., & Goldenberg, D. (1987). *Special education for the early years* (2nd ed.). Englewood Cliffs, NJ: Prentice Hall.

Meyen, E. (1990). *Exceptional children* (2nd ed.). Denver: Love Publishing.

Michaelis, C. (1980). *Home and school partnership in exceptional education.* Rockville, MD: Aspen.

Morrison, G. (1978). *Parent involvement in the home, school, and community.* Columbus, OH: Merrill.

Odom, S., & Speltz, M. (1983). Program variations in preschools for handicapped and nonhandicapped children: Mainstreamed vs. integrated special education. *Analysis and Intervention in Developmental Disabilities, 3*, 89–104.

Pavia, L. (1992). Introducing the early childhood teacher to IEP. *Day Care and Early Education, 19*, 38–40.

Peterson, N. (1987). *Early intervention for handicapped and at-risk children.* Denver: Love Publishing.

Polloway, E., Patton, J., Payne, J., & Payne, R. (1989). *Strategies for teaching learners with special needs* (4th ed.). Columbus: OH: Merrill.

Ramey, C., & Campbell, F. (1977). Prevention of developmental retardation in high risk children. In P. Mittler (Ed.), *Research to practice in mental retardation: Care and intervention* (Vol. 1, pp. 157–164). Baltimore: University Park Press.

Ramey, C., & Campbell, F. (1984). Preventive education for high risk children: Cognitive consequences of the Carolina Abecedarian Project. *American Journal of Mental Deficiency, 88*, 515–523.

Ramey, C., & Smith, B. (1977). Assessing the intellectual consequences of early intervention with high-risk infants. *American Journal of Mental Deficiency, 81*, 318–324.

Sailor, W., Anderson, J., Halvorsen, A., Doering, K., Filler, J., & Goetz, L. (1989). *The comprehensive local school.* Baltimore: Paul H. Brookes.

Sailor, W., Gerry, M., & Wilson, W. (1991). Policy implications of emergent full inclusion models for the education of students with severe disabilities. In M. Wang, H. Walberg, & M. Reynolds (Eds.), *Handbook of special education* (Vol. 4, pp. 175–193.) New York: Pergamon Press.

Salvia, J., & Ysseldyke, J. (1978). *Assessment in special and remedial education.* Boston: Houghton Mifflin.

Schulz, J. (1987). *Parents and professionals in special education.* Boston: Allyn & Bacon.

Sefton, K., Gargiulo, R., & Graves, S. (1991). Working with families of children with special needs. *Day Care and Early Education, 18*, 40.

Seligman, M., & Seligman, P. (1980). The professional's dilemma: Learning to work with parents. *Exceptional Parent, 10*, 11–13.

Smith, S. (1990). Individualized education program (IEP) in special education—From intent to acquiescence. *Exceptional Children, 57*, 6–13.

Smith, B., & Strain, P. (1984). *The argument for early intervention.* Reston, VA: ERIC Information Service Digest, ERIC Clearinghouse on Handicapped and Gifted Children (ERIC Document Reproduction Service No. ED 262 502).

Strain, P., & Smith, B. (1986). A counter-interpretation of early intervention effects: A response to Casto and Mastropieri. *Exceptional Children, 53*, 260–265.

Striefel, S., Killoran, J., & Quintero, M. (1991). *Functional integration for success: Preschool intervention.* Austin, TX: Pro-Ed.

Swick, K. (1987). *Perspectives on understanding and working with families.* Champaign, IL: Stipes.

Tjossem, T. (1976). Early intervention: Issues and approaches. In T. Tjossem (Ed.), *Intervention strategies for high-risk and handicapped children* (pp. 3–33). Baltimore: University Park Press.

Trohanis, P. (1989). An introduction to PL 99–457 and the national policy agenda for serving young children with special needs and their families. In J. Gallagher, P. Trohanis, & R. Clifford (Eds.), *Policy implementation and PL 99–457: Planning for young children with special needs* (pp. 1–17). Baltimore: Paul H. Brookes.

Turnbull, A., & Turnbull, H. (1982). Parent involvement in the education of handicapped children: A critique. *Mental Retardation, 20*, 115–122.

Turnbull, A., & Turnbull, H. (1990). *Families, professionals, and exceptionality: A special partnership* (2nd ed.). Columbus, OH: Merrill.

U.S. Department of Education. (1991). *Thirteenth Annual Report to Congress on the Implementation of the Individuals with Disabilities Act.* Washington, DC: U.S. Government Printing Office.

U.S. Department of Education. (1992). *Fourteenth Annual Report to Congress on the Implementation of the Individuals with Disabilities Act.* Washington, DC: U.S. Government Printing Office.

Webster, E. (1977). *Counseling with parents of handicapped children.* New York: Grune & Stratton.

White, K., Bush, D., & Casto, G. (1986). Let the past be prologue: Learning from previous reviews of early intervention efficacy research. *Journal of Special Education, 19*, 417–428.

Widerstrom, A., Mowder, B., & Sandall, S. (1991). *At-risk and handicapped newborns and infants.* Englewood Cliffs, NJ: Prentice Hall.

Will, M. (1986). Educating students with learning problems: A shared responsibility. *Exceptional Children, 54*, 411–416.

Wolfensberger, W. (1972). *Normalization: The principle of normalization in human services.* Toronto: National Institute on Mental Retardation.

Zigler, E., & Valentine, J. (Eds.). (1979). *Project Head Start: A legacy of the war on poverty.* New York: Free Press.

Chapter 13

Almy, M. (1985). *The early childhood educator at work.* New York: McGraw-Hill.

Bloom, P. J. (1988). *A great place to work.* Washington, DC: National Association for the Education of Young Children.

Bloom, P. J. (1993). But I'm worth more than that. *Young Children, 48*(3), 65–68.

Boyer, M., Gerst, C., & Eastwood, S. (1990). *Between a rock and a hard place: Raising rates raise wages.* Minneapolis, MN: Child Care Worker Alliance.

Bredekamp, S. (1992). The early childhood profession coming together. *Young Children, 47*(6), 36–39.

Bredekamp, S., & Rosegrant, T. (1992). *Reaching potentials: Appropriate curriculum and assessment for young children.* Washington, DC: National Association for the Education of Young Children.

Bundy, B. F. (1991). Fostering communications between parents and preschools. *Young Children, 46*(2), 12–22.

Carmichael, V., Clark, M. W., & Leonard, B. (1977) *Administration of schools for young children.* New York: Teachers College Press, Columbia University.

Caruso, J. J., & Faucett, M. T. (1986). *Supervision of early childhood education: A developmental perspective.* New York: Teachers College Press, Columbia University.

Cherry, C., Harkness, B., & Kuzma, K. (1987). *Nursery school & day care center management guide*, 2nd Ed. Belmont, CA: David S. Lake.

Children's Defense Fund. (1994). *State of America's children.* Washington, DC: Author.

Click, P. M., & Click, D. W. (1990). *Administration of schools for young children.* Albany, NY: Delmar.

Curtis, L. (1978). Twenty ideas to help parents enjoy your program. *Day Care and Early Education, 6*, 43.

Daresh, J. C., & Playko, M. (1990, September). Mentor programs: Focus on the beginning principal. NASSP Bulletin, 73-77.

Decker, C. A., & Decker, J. R. (1988). *Planning and administering early childhood programs.* Columbus, OH: Merrill.

DiGeronimo, J. M. (1993). A buddy system for rookie teachers. *Phi Delta Kappan, 75*(4), 348.

Galvez-Hjornevick, C. (1986, January). Mentoring among teachers: A review of the literature. *Journal of Teacher Education*, 6–11.

Hewes, D., & Hartmen, B. (1972). *Early childhood education: A workbook for administrators.* Belmont, CA: David S. Lake.

Hildebrand, V. (1990). *Management of child development centers.* New York: Macmillan.

Joffe, C. (1986). *Friendly intruders: Childcare professionals and family life.* Berkeley, CA: University of California Press.

Kaplan-Sanoff, M., & Yablans-Magid, R. (1981). *Exploring early childhood reading and practice.* New York: Macmillan.

Krechevsky, M. (1991). Project spectrum: An innovative assessment alternative. *Educational Leadership, 47*(4), 17–23.

Playko, M. (1990, May) What it means to be mentored. *National Association Secondary School Principals Bulletin*, 29–32.

Schweinhart, L. J., & Weikart, D. P. (1986). Consequences of three preschool curriculum models through age 15. *Early Childhood Research Quarterly, 1*(1), 15–45.

Weikart, D. (1979). Reopening the case for public preschool education. *The High Scope Report*, (4).

Chapter 14

Berger, E. H. (1987). *Parents as partners in education: The school and home working together.* Columbus, OH: Merrill.

Bronfenbrenner, U. (1979). *The ecology of human development: Experiments by nature and design.* Cambridge: Harvard University Press.

Brubaker, T. (Ed.), (1993). *Family relations: Challenges for the future.* Newbury Park, CA: Sage.

Cataldo, C. (1987). *Parent education for early childhood.* New York: Teachers College Press.

Chinn, P. C., Winn, J., & Walters, R. H. (1978). *Two-way talking with parents of special children: A process of positive communication.* St. Louis: C. V. Mosby.

Cochran, M., & Dean, C. (1991). Home-school relations and the empowerment process. *Elementary School Journal, 91*(3), 261–269.

Comer, J. (1986). Parental participation in the schools. *Phi Delta Kappan, 67*, 442–446.

Dunst, C., Trivette, C., & Deal, A. (1988). *Enabling and empowering families: Principles and guidelines for practice.* Cambridge, MA: Brookline.

Elwood, A. (1988). Prove to me that MELD makes a difference. In H. Weiss & F. Jacobs (Eds.), *Evaluating family programs.* New York: Aldine de Gruyter.

Epstein, J. (1984). *Single parents and the schools: The effect of marital status on parent and teacher evaluations.* Baltimore, MD: Center for Social Organization of Schools, The Johns Hopkins University.

Flake-Hobson, C., & Swick, K. J. (1979). Communication strategies for parents and teachers or how to say what you mean. *Dimensions, 7*(4), 112–115.

Fogel, A., & Melson, E. (1988). *Child development: Individual, family, and society.* St. Paul, MN: West.

Ford, D., & Lerner, R. (1992). *Developmental systems theory: An integrative approach.* Newbury Park, CA: Sage.

Galinsky, E. (1990). Parents and Teachers/Caregivers: Sources of tension, sources of support. *Young Children, 43*(3), 4–12.

Garbarino, J. (1982). *Children and families in the social environment.* New York: Aldine de Gruyter.

Gargiulo, R. M., & Graves, S. B. (1991). Parental feelings: The forgotten component when working with parents of handicapped preschool children. *Childhood Education, 67*(3), 176–178.

Gestwicki, C. (1992). *Home, school and community relations.* Albany, NY: Delmar.

Gordon, I. (1977). *Research report of parent oriented home-based early childhood education programs.* Gainesville, FL: Institute for Human Development, University of Florida.

Graves, S. B., & Gargiulo, R. M. (1989). Parents and early childhood professionals as program partners: Meeting the needs of the preschool exceptional child. *Dimensions, 18*,(1), 23–24.

Hampden-Turner, C. (1981). *Maps of the mind.* New York: Macmillan.

Kraft, S., & Snell, M. (1980). Parent-teacher conflict: Coping with parental stress. *The Pointer, 24*, 29–37.

Lightfoot, S. (1978). *Worlds apart: Relationships between families and school.* New York: Basic Books.

Minuchin, S. (1984). *Family kaleidoscope.* Cambridge, MA: Harvard University Press.

Missouri Department of Education (1985). *An evaluation summary: New parents as teachers program.* Columbia, MO: Missouri Department of Education.

Peterson, N. (1987). *Early intervention for handicapped and at-risk children.* Denver: Love.

Powell, D. (1988). *Parent education as early childhood intervention.* Norwood, NJ: Ablex.

Powell, D. (1990). Home visiting in the early years: Policy and program design decisions. *Young Children, 45*(6), 65–73.

Rogers, C. (1963). *On becoming a person.* Boston, Houghton Mifflin.

Schaefer, E. (1982). Parent-professional interaction: Research, parental, professional, and policy perspectives. In R. Haskins, & D. Adams, (Eds.), *Parent education and public policy.* Norwood, NJ: Ablex.

Schultz, J. (1987). *Parents and professionals in special education.* Boston: Allyn & Bacon.

Schwartzman, J. (1985). *Families and other systems.* New York: Guilford.

Sefton, K., Gargiulo, R. M., & Graves, S. B. (1991). Working with families of children with special needs. *Day Care and Early Education, 16*,(3), 40.

Seligman, M. (1979). *Strategies for helping parents of exceptional children.* New York: Free Press.

Seligman, M., & Seligman, P. (1980). The professional's dilemma: Learning to work with parents. *Exceptional parent, 10*, 11–13.

Swick, K. J. (1984). *Inviting parents into the young child's world.* Champaign, IL: Stipes.

Swick, K. J. (1987). *Perspectives on understanding and working with families.* Champaign, IL: Stipes.

Swick, K. J. (1991). *Teacher-parent partnerships to enhance school success in early childhood education.* Washington, DC: National Education Association.

Swick, K. J. (1993). *Strengthening parents and families during the early childhood years.* Champaign, IL: Stipes.

Swick, K. J., & Graves, S. B. (1993). *Empowering at-risk families during the early childhood years.* Washington, DC: National Education Association.

The twenty-first century family. (1990, winter). *Newsweek Special Edition.*

White, B. (1988). *Educating the infant and toddler.* Lexington, MA: D. C. Heath (Lexington Books).

Chapter 15

Abt Associates. (1979). *Children at the center. Final report of the National Day Care Study.* Cambridge, MA: Author.

Adams, G. (1990). *Who knows how safe? The status of state efforts to ensure quality child care.* Washington, DC: Children's Defense Fund.

American Association of Colleges for Teacher Education. (1972). *No one model American: A statement of multicultural education.* Washington, DC: Author.

American Association of Colleges for Teacher Education. (1988). *Teacher education pipeline: Schools, colleges and departments of education enrollments by race and ethnicity.* Washington, DC: Author.

American Council on Education. (1988). *One-third of a nation. A report by the Commission on Minority Participation in Education and American Life.* Washington, DC: Author.

Aronson, S. (1987). Maintaining health in child care settings. In B. M. Caldwell (Ed.), *Group care for young children: A supplement to parental care.* Proceedings of the 12th Johnson & Johnson Pediatric Round Table. Lexington, MA: Lexington Books.

Bredekamp, S. (1987). *Developmentally appropriate practice in early childhood programs serving children from birth through age 8* (expanded ed.). Washington, DC: National Association for the Education of Young Children.

Bredekamp, S. (1989). *Regulating child care quality: Evidence from NAEYC's accreditation system.* Washington, DC: National Association for the Education of Young Children.

Children's Defense Fund. (1988). *Vanishing dreams: The growing economic plight of America's young families.* Washington, DC: Author.

Children's Defense Fund. (1989). *A vision for America's future.* Washington, DC: Author.

Cohen, D., & Rudolph, M. (1977). *Kindergarten and early schooling.* Englewood Cliffs, NJ: Prentice-Hall.

Dean, A., Salend, S., & Taylor, L. (1993). Multicultural education. *Teaching Exceptional Children, 26*(1), 40–43.

Derman-Sparks, L. (1989). *Anti-bias curriculum: Tools for empowering young children.* Washington, DC: National Association for the Education of Young Children.

Elkind, D. (1986). Formal education and early childhood education: An essential difference. *Phi Delta Kappan, 67*(9), 631–636.

Ellwein, M. C., Walsh, D. J., Eads, G. M., & Miller, A. (1991). Using readiness tests to route kindergarten students: The snarled intersection of psychometrics, policy, and practice. *Educational Evaluation and Policy Analysis, 13*(2), 159–175.

Galinsky, E. (1988). The impact of child care problems on the job and at home. Paper presented at the Wingspread Conference on Child Care Action Campaign, Racine, WI.

Gallup, A. (1986). The 18th annual Gallup Poll of the public's attitudes toward the public schools. *Phi Delta Kappan, 68*(1), 43–59.

Gay, G. (1975). Organizing and designing culturally pluralistic curriculum. *Educational Leadership, 33,* 176–183.

Gay, G. (1983). Multiethnic education: Historical developments and future prospects. *Phi Delta Kappan, 64,* 560–563.

Gesell Institute for Human Development. (1980). *Gesell School Readiness Test.* Rosemont, NJ: Programs for Education.

Goffin, S. (1988). Putting our advocacy efforts into a new context. *Young Children, 43*(3), 52–56.

Goffin, S., & Lombardi, J. (1988). *Speaking out: Early childhood advocacy.* Washington, DC: National Association for the Education of Young Children.

Gollnick, D., & Chinn, P. (1990). *Multicultural education in a pluralistic society* (3rd ed.). New York: Macmillan.

Graue, M. E., & Shepard, L. A. (1989). Predictive validity of the Gesell School Readiness Tests. *Early Childhood Research Quarterly, 4,* 303–315.

Graves, S. (1990a). *Social and economic issues affecting children and families* (report no. 3). Little Rock, AR: Southern Association on Children Under Six.

Graves, S. (1990b). Early childhood education. In T.E.C. Smith, *Introduction to education* (2nd ed., pp. 189–219). St. Paul, MN: West.

Gullo, D., Bersani, C., Clements, D., & Bayless, K. (1986). A comparative study of all-day, alternate-day, and half-day kindergarten schedules: Effects on achievement and classroom social behaviors. *Journal of Research in Childhood Education, 1*, 87–94.

Gullo, D., & Clements, D. (1984). The effects of kindergarten schedules on achievement, classroom behavior, and attendance. *Journal of Educational Research, 78*, 51–56.

Havighurst, R. (1974). The American Indian: From assimilation to cultural pluralism. *Educational Leadership, 31*, 585–589.

Heward, W., & Orlansky, M. (1988). *Exceptional children* (3rd ed.). Columbus, OH: Merrill.

Hymes, J. (1991). *Early childhood education: Twenty years in review.* Washington, DC: National Association for the Education of Young Children.

Lawton, J. (1988). *Introduction to child care and early childhood education.* Glenview, IL: Scott Foresman.

Meyen, E. (1990). *Exceptional children* (2nd ed.). Denver: Love.

Moyer, J., Egerston, H., & Isenberg, J. (1987). The child-centered kindergarten. *Childhood Education, 63*(4), 235–242.

National Center for Education Statistics. (1991). *Digest of education statistics: 1991.* Washington, DC: U.S. Government Printing Office.

National Governors' Association. (1990). *National education goals.* A statement adopted by the members of the National Governors' Association in Charlottesville, VA, on February 25, 1990.

Ornstein, A., & Levine, D. (1989). *Foundations of education* (4th ed.). Boston: Houghton Mifflin.

Phillips, D., McCartney, K., & Scarr, S. (1990). Child-care quality and children's social development. *Developmental Psychology, 23*(4), 537–543.

Poplin, M., & Wright, P. (1983). The concept of cultural pluralism: Issues in special education. *Learning Disability Quarterly 6*, 367–371.

Prince, J., Buckley, M., & Gargiulo, R. (1993). The laboratory school: Has its time come again? *Education, 113*(3), 473–479.

Quality Education for Minorities Project. (1990). *Education that works: An action plan for the education of minorities.* Cambridge, MA: Massachusetts Institute of Technology.

Shepard, L. A., & Smith, M. L. (1985). *The Boulder Valley kindergarten study: Retention practices and retention effects.* Boulder, CO: Boulder Valley Public Schools.

Sleeter, C., & Grant, C. (1988). *Making choices for multicultural education.* Columbus, OH: Merrill.

Smith, D., & Luckasson, R. (1992). *Introduction to special education.* Boston: Allyn & Bacon.

Southern Association on Children Under Six. (1984). *Position statement on developmentally appropriate educational experiences for kindergarten.* Little Rock, AR: Author.

Southern Association on Children Under Six. (1990). *Developmentally appropriate assessment: A position paper.* Little Rock, AR: Author.

Southern Association on Children Under Six. (1991). *The portfolio and its use: Developmentally appropriate assessment of young children.* Little Rock, AR: Author.

Southern Regional Education Board. (1992). *Readiness for school: The early childhood challenge.* Atlanta, GA: Author.

Spodek, B. (1982). The kindergarten: A retrospective and contemporary look. In L. Katz (Ed.), *Current topics in early childhood education* (vol. 4, pp. 173–191). Norwood, NJ: Ablex.

Sue, D. (1981). *Counseling the culturally different: Theory and practice.* New York: Wiley.

Swick, K., Brown, M., & Graves, S. B. (1984). Developmentally appropriate educational experiences for kindergarten. *Dimensions, 12*(4), 25.

Tiedt, P., & Tiedt, I. (1990). *Multicultural teaching: A handbook of activities, information, and resources.* (3rd ed.). Boston: Allyn & Bacon.

Turnbull, B. J. (1990). *Readiness for school: Issues brief.* Washington, DC: Policy Studies Associates and Office of Educational Research and Improvement.

U.S. Bureau of the Census. (1986). *Projections of the Hispanic population: 1983 to 2080* (Serial P–25). Washington, DC: U.S. Government Printing Office.

Whaley, K., & Swadner, E. (1990). Multicultural education in infant and toddler settings. *Childhood Education, 66*, 238–240.

Whitebrook, M., Howes, C., & Phillips, D. (1990). *Who cares? Child care teachers and the quality of care in America.* A final report of the National Child Care Staffing Study. Oakland, CA: Child Care Employee Project.

GLOSSARY

Accommodation. According to Piaget, an alteration of existing cognitive structures to allow for new information; involves a change in understanding.

Accreditation. Recognition by an external agency that a program meets established standards and expectations. Accreditation is voluntary and often suggests that specific standards have been met. The National Association for the Education of Young Children is one organization that offers accreditation standards.

Adaptation. In Piaget's cognitive theory, the process of adjusting to new situations via the interplay of assimilation and accommodation.

Advocacy. Strategies for influencing the political process on behalf of children, their families, and the profession. An important function of early childhood professionals.

Anecdotal records. Factual, nonjudgmental observations of observed activity.

Anti-bias curriculum. An inclusive, value-based curriculum model that extends the principles of multicultural education. An integral component of daily school experiences.

Assessment. The use of a comprehensive evaluation system to determine the quality of a program or the progress of a child.

Assimilation. In Piaget's terms, the inclusion of new information and experiences into already present cognitive schemes or structures.

Associative play. Play in which several children play together, but in a loosely organized fashion.

At-risk. Describing a child with exposure to certain adverse conditions and circumstances known to have a high probability of resulting in learning and development difficulties.

Attribute. The identifiable features of an object, situation, person, or event.

Auditory discrimination. The ability to distinguish differences between sounds that are closely similar. Sounds from the environment, animals, and humans are the foundations for auditory discrimination.

Autocratic management. Dictatorial approach to issues. Primary decision and policy maker. A style of management that uses little or no collaboration with others.

Autonomy vs. shame and doubt. Second stage of Erikson's stages of development, typically occurring between 1 and 3 years of age.

Behaviorist theory. A theory that bases its understanding of children on the belief that behavior can be shaped by rewards and punishment.

Bias. A tendency to accept or reject certain people or things.

Burnout. A debilitating response to ongoing stress. Typically results in emotional and physical exhaustion.

Center-based services. Group-oriented service delivery model for young children with special needs. Intervention and educational services provided in settings other than the child's home.

Cephalocaudal. A term that literally means "head to tail." It is used to explain how physical growth and development of motor skills progress longitudinally from the head to the feet.

Chapter I. A federal educational program aimed at improving the academic achievement of disadvantaged and educationally at-risk students. Originally known as Title I.

Checklists. Lists of specific traits or behaviors arranged in a logical order. Checklists are helpful for teachers to use in noting the presence or absence of certain traits or behaviors.

Child care center. A place providing care for children; settings may vary. Adults attend to the physical, social, emotional, and intellectual needs of the children. Fees are usually charged for services.

Child Development Associate (CDA). A national credential awarded to child care workers signifying competency in working with young children. Individuals must complete a rigorous assessment process.

Classification. Process for organizing objects, language, or activities into categories.

Class inclusion. The ability to consider more than one attribute of a group. For example, children may or may not consider both color and texture when sorting, comparing, or classifying a group of objects.

Cognitive developmental theory. The theory described by and elaborated on by Jean Piaget. This theory refers to the thinking and reasoning abilities of the child.

Comparing. Observing or manipulating two or more objects to determine similarities and differences.

Conservation. An awareness that occurs as individuals are able to understand that objects or materials maintain the same quantity although the form or arrangement of the materials may change.

Constructivist. A theory, based on the research and writings of Jean Piaget, that all individuals build their knowledge through experience with people and objects, and that construction occurs from within each person.

Conventional reasoning. The second stage in Kohlberg's theory of moral development, involving interpersonal norms and social system morality.

Convergent thinking. A thinking process that produces one correct answer. Standardized testing, worksheets, coloring sheets, and the replication of a common model are examples of single-answer activities that promote convergent thinking.

Cooperative play. Play in which each child accepts a designated role and each is dependent on the others for achieving the goals of the play.

Creative impulses. Self-initiated systems that satisfy needs and interests that occur before a child knows the correct or acceptable answer to a situation.

Creativity. The ability to approach something in a novel or unusual manner. The approach is new to the individual generating the idea and often appreciated by others.

Cultural pluralism. The belief that diverse ethnic, racial, and cultural groups are valued and appreciated; differences are respected and seen as contributing to the overall strength of society.

Curriculum domains. Areas of curricular emphasis for children 3 to 5 years of age. Key elements include cognitive development, motor development, language development, social/emotional development, self-help skills, and play skills.

Democratic management. Authoritative style of management that encourages the involvement of others in the decision-making process.

Department of Human Resources and Services. State agency charged with the responsibility of managing and maintaining supplemental programs including child care licensing, aid to families with dependent children, child abuse, and food subsidies.

Developmental delay. A concept defined by individual states when referring to young children with special needs. A delay is usually determined on the basis of various developmental assessments.

Developmental scales. A screening instrument used by teachers to help identify skills and strengths that children possess.

Developmentally appropriate assessment. Using a variety of procedures and data that are appropriate for making decisions related to planning, implementing, and evaluating children's progress, growth, and development.

Developmentally appropriate practice. As defined by the National Association for the Education of Young Children, the definition of this term has two dimensions: age appropriateness and individual appropriateness. *Age appropriate* refers to the universal, predictable sequences of growth and change that occur in all children during their first nine years. *Individual appropriate* refers to the recognition that each person is unique with individual styles, rates of learning, personalities, and backgrounds.

Disability. An inability to do something; a reduced capacity to perform in a specific way.

Discovery learning. Strategies that encourage children to discover information by formulating questions, forming a methodology for discovery, developing a hypothesis, implementing procedures, and summarizing their findings. The discovery method is guided by the teacher, who provides the stimulus for inquiry and allows children to learn through active involvement.

DISTAR. A highly structured behavioral approach to teaching young children that focuses on the development of specific skills and abilities.

Divergent thinking. A thinking process that produces many possible answers to the same question, a characteristic of creativity. Activities that are considered to be open ended, such as work with clay and paints, stimulate divergent thinking and education of children.

Early childhood. Generally regarded as the time period between birth and 8 years of age.

Early childhood education. A field of study concerned with the learning and development of children from birth through age 8. Also refers to the many programs and services providing early educational experiences—infancy through the primary grades.

Ecological perspective. The basic tenets of this perspective are that individuals or family units are influenced by the events and experiences that occur in their lives (their ecology), and that these events and experiences can be understood and influenced to promote healthy modes of development and learning.

Emergent literacy. The natural process of how language develops. The concept assumes that the child has acquired some knowledge in language, reading, and writing before beginning school. The process occurs through interactions with print and materials and through interactions in social contexts.

Empowering. Applying strategies whereby individuals gain a sense of control over their future as a result of their own efforts and activities.

Empty spaces. Paths, dividers, or undesignated areas. Undesignated areas can be used for activities that occur throughout the year.

Enabling. Providing the means and opportunities for persons to do something to meet their goals or needs.

Environmental ownership. The ability to relate or to feel possession of and comfort in one's classroom, school, or space.

Equilibration. According to Piaget's theorizing, the cognitive process by which a person attempts to balance new information with already existing data.

Even Start. An early childhood program initiated by federal legislation. The focus of this parent-child education effort is on young children and their caregivers from impoverished backgrounds.

Exceptional children. Children who differ from society's view of normalcy.

Foundational movement. The third rung of the motor development ladder, which provides the building blocks needed for participation in a lifetime of activity. It includes three movement categories: movement awareness, fundamental motor skills, and fitness.

Fundamental motor skills. The building blocks for future sport skill development. It includes three categories: stability, locomotor, and manipulative skills.

Gifts. A Froebelian term referring to manipulative objects, such as balls and wooden blocks, used as tools for learning in Froebel's curriculum.

Graphing. Organizing mathematical or scientific information into a visual media in order to record or share the information with others.

Handicap. The consequences or impact encountered by or imposed on a child with a disability as he or she attempts to function and interact in the environment.

Head Start. A federally funded program aimed at young children in poverty; designed to increase the chances of success in school and opportunity for achievement.

Home-based services. A type of service delivery model for young children with special needs. Intervention provided in the youngster's home by the primary caregiver. Professionals make regular visits to work directly with the child and to provide instruction to the caregiver.

Home Start. A derivation of the Head Start program; designed to provide comprehensive services to young children and their parents in the home through the utilization of home visitors.

Inclusion. The belief that all children with disabilities should be educated in regular education classrooms in their neighborhood schools. Placements should be age and grade appropriate.

Individualized educational program (IEP). Required by federal legislation. A customized educational plan, constructed by a team, for each child with special needs.

Individualized family service plan (IFSP). A written document mandated by federal law. Designed as a guide for services for infants, toddlers, and their families. Developed by a team of professionals and the parent(s).

Initiative vs. guilt. Third stage of Erikson's psychosocial development, observed during the preschool years.

Inquiry method. A method that begins with inquiry, initiated by the student or teacher, and requires the active involvement of children in solving the problem. Children question, manipulate, and register their discoveries.

In-service. Ongoing training for staff members actively involved in the care and education of children. In-service may be specified by either licensing or accreditation agencies.

Interviews. One of the most effective and easy means of gathering information about a child.

Kenan Trust Family Literacy Project. A parent-oriented program initiated in the 1988–1989 school year designed to break the cycle of illiteracy and undereducation by combining efforts to improve the literacy and parenting skills of undereducated adults.

Key experiences. Components of the Cognitively Oriented Curriculum. Used by teachers to help structure the curriculum while promoting intellectual development.

Kindergarten. An early childhood program designed primarily for 4- and 5-year-old children. Usually sponsored by the public schools, although large numbers of youngsters attend private and church-affiliated programs. Originally a German term meaning "children's garden."

Kinesthetic. Learning through touch or manipulation.

Laissez-faire management. A style of management in which little or no leadership is provided. Employees are self-directed.

Lanham Act. Legislation enacted during the Second World War; this act established day care centers so mothers could work in defense-related industries.

Learning center. Areas designed to provide children with specific opportunities to explore and learn.

Learning through movement. One aspect of the goal of educational movement programs. It focuses on using movement as a means of developing the cognitive and affective domains.

Learning to move. A focus on movement awareness, skills acquisition, and fitness enhancement. Learning to move is one aspect of the goal of educational movement programs.

Least restrictive environment (LRE). A concept requiring that children with special needs be educated, to the maximum extent appropriate, with their typical classmates. Setting is individually determined for each pupil with exceptionalities.

Left cerebral hemisphere. The cerebrum is composed of two halves, called *hemispheres*, that are connected by a band of fibers called the *corpus callosum*. The left cerebral hemisphere refers to the logical brain, which controls such functions as hearing, speech, and verbal information processing.

Licensing. Recognition by a specific agency that a program meets and maintains specific standards under the supervision of the issuing agency.

Logico-mathematical knowledge. Also referred to as *logical mathematical knowledge*; one of three ways Piaget identifies the knowledge all individuals possess. This knowledge is formed by the individual and involves arranging, organizing, and assigning value to the world.

Mainstreaming. The process of integrating children with special needs into classes and schools with their typical peers.

Manipulatives. Materials that contribute to the child's development of skills through handling and movement.

Maturation. The qualitative changes occurring with age that cause an individual to progress to a higher level of functioning. Maturation is a fixed order of progression that is primarily innate and genetically determined.

Mentoring. The interaction of experienced staff members with new employees to provide transitional support and encouragement.

Minnesota Early Childhood Family Education Program. A program begun in 1973 to help parents establish support networks involving not only other parents, but also various other community resources. Another goal is to provide parents with accurate, age-specific, and unbiased child rearing information.

Motor development. The study of changes in performance of motor skills throughout the lifespan and the factors that influence these changes.

Multicultural. Referring to more than one culture. Also used to describe programs that incorporate an appreciation and respect for differences among children and their heritage.

Multicultural education. A term with many interpretations. Typically refers to educational strategies that value, promote, and accept cultural, racial, linguistic, and ethnic diversity.

Multisensory approach. Techniques used to convey information through the five senses combined with physical movement. Children compare, contrast, and categorize information in a natural inquiry method.

National Academy of Early Childhood Programs. National accreditation program for early childhood programs under the direction of the National Association for the Education of Young Children.

Nativist theory. A language development theory presented by Noam Chomsky based on the idea that language is creative and develops innately.

Neonate. A newborn child.

Normalization. Philosophical concept that every person with a disability has the right to a normal life-style. Each citizen should be integrated, in all aspects of their daily living experiences, to the maximum extent possible.

Occupations. A Froebelian concept describing arts and crafts type activities used to develop eye-hand coordination and fine motor skills.

Olfactory discrimination. The ability to discern similarities and differences using the senses of taste and smell.

Onlooker play. Play in which the child who is playing individually is simultaneously observing those playing in the same area.

Operations. The concept that numbers can be changed by taking groups of objects apart or putting them together. Addition, subtraction, multiplication, and division are forms of operations.

Ordering. Seriating; placing objects or pictures in sequence according to ranked order such as weight, length, height, value, or age.

Parallel play. Play in which several children are playing in close proximity to each other but are playing independently.

Parent cooperative preschool. Educational program for young children organized and supported by parents. Parents play a role in the daily operations of the program.

Parents as Teachers. A program that emerged from the research and development work of Burton L. White. This parent education program targets women in the third trimester of their pregnancy and provides services until the child's third birthday. Services include preparation for parenthood, child development information, and developmental screenings.

Perceptual motor development. A phase of development that incorporates new experiences, past experiences, and purposeful movement in a motor response.

Physical growth. The quantitative, structural changes that occur with age.

Physical knowledge. One of three categories of knowledge according to Piagetian theory. Refers to the descriptive properties of an object, place, or thing that are learned by sensory or external experiences.

Play spaces. Areas specifically identified with materials that are designated to serve a particular purpose.

Postconventional reasoning. The third stage in Kohlberg's theory of moral development associated with community rights versus individual rights and universal ethical principles.

Preconventional reasoning. The first stage in Kohlberg's theory of moral development, which involves (1) punishment and obedience, and (2) orientation and individualism.

Pre-exercise theory. A theory of play based on philosopher Karl Groos' belief that play serves to strengthen instincts needed for the future. This theory is sometimes called *practice theory*.

Prejudice. Preconceived ideas and opinions typically formed without the benefit of adequate knowledge or facts; an intolerance of others.

Prekindergarten. A program for young children in preparation for kindergarten, which focuses on social and cognitive activities.

Prepared environment. An important component in a Montessori classroom; a planned and orderly setting containing specially developed tasks and materials designed to promote children's learning.

Preschool. Early school experiences for children between the ages of 2 and 5 years. Usually a half-day program with emphasis on social-emotional development; a learning environment within a play setting.

Primary grades. School program serving youngsters in the first, second, and third grades; children ages 6 through 8. Curriculum is typically academically oriented.

Problem solving. Going through the following steps of investigation: determining that a problem exists, gathering data about the problem, formulating hypotheses, testing the hypotheses, gathering additional data if necessary, and drawing conclusions.

Profession. An occupation that results from years of study coupled with specialized training and skills.

Professional. An individual engaged in a profession; a person who uses his or her skills and abilities for the betterment of others.

Progressives. Advocates of the philosophy of Progressive Education, a movement away from Froebel's principles and practices regarding kindergarten to one focused on children's interest and principles of child development.

Progressivism. A school of thought founded by John Dewey. Emphasis placed on interest of children rather than activities chosen by the teacher.

Project approach. The use of themes or topics to unify learning experiences.

Project Follow-Through. A federal program that attempts to continue the gains developed through Head Start. Funding is available for children in kindergarten through the third grade. Children receive educational, health, and social service benefits.

Proximodistal. A term that explains how physical growth and motor control progress from the midline of the body around the spinal column outward to the extremities.

Rating scales. Tools that indicate the degree to which a person exhibits a certain trait or behavior.

Recapitulation theory. The notion that children reenact the developmental stages of the human race in their play: animal, savage, tribal member, etc. This theory was extended by G. Stanley Hall.

Recreation theory. This theory, proposed by the German poet Moritz Lazarus, states that the purpose of play is to restore energy expended in work.

Regular education initiative (REI). An approach for educating children with special needs; special and regular educators work cooperatively in providing services to pupils with exceptionalities in the regular classroom.

Right cerebral hemisphere. The cerebrum is composed of two halves, called *hemispheres*, that are connected by a band of fibers called the *corpus callosum*. The right section of the brain interprets the world through patterns, images, and emotions.

Room arrangement. The placement of centers, equipment, and materials within the learning environment in a manner that reinforces learning.

Schema. According to Piaget, a cognitive organizational pattern or framework that provides a foundation for the development of cognitive structures used in thinking.

Self-concept. The ability of a person to think of themselves. A self-opinion that develops as one interacts with others. Positive or negative self-concepts are influenced by the individual's interpretation of how others perceive them.

Self-expressive activities. Open-ended activities that allow many opportunities for expression without conforming to specific criteria or expectations. Self-expressive activities are divergent in nature.

Sensitive periods. Stages of development early in life during which, according to Montessori, a child is especially capable of learning particular skills or behaviors.

Seriation. The concept through which children sequence objects in accordance to a ranked order. Aspects of seriation include rankings such as weight, length, height, value, or age.

Socialization. A process of learning about an individual's role and the role of others in their community. Skills of socialization are influenced by the expectations of a group or a larger society.

Socio-conventional knowledge. Understandings that are acquired through cultural and social experiences.

Solitary play. Play in which children engage without regard for what other children around them are doing.

Spatial relations. Awareness of space in relation to one's body, understanding the relationship of objects, and recognizing the shapes of objects.

Surplus energy theory. According to this theory, each living thing generates a certain amount of energy to meet survival needs. This theory can be traced back to Friedrich Schiller, a German poet, and Herbert Spencer, a British philosopher.

Systematic observation. Regular, deliberate, and thoughtful listening, watching, and recording of a child's behavior.

Tactile discrimination. Information acquired by a person's ability to distinguish similarities and differences through the sense of touch.

Temporal. Relating to time.

Theory Z management. Management style that encourages collaboration of all members of an organization. Such managers use both autocratic and democratic management styles as the situation warrants.

Trust vs. mistrust. First stage of Erikson's psychosocial stage. Observed during the first year of life. Positive outcome is that a sense of well-being and mutual trust exists. Negative outcome is a feeling of distrust of the world.

Unoccupied play. According to Parten, this term refers to times when children are not playing.

Values. Personal concepts; things an individual believes in and cherishes.

Visual discrimination. The skills related to a child's ability to distinguish color, shape, and pattern for the purposes of categorizing, classifying, sequencing, and organizing information.

Vygotskian theory. A theory of language development introduced by Vygotsky. He believed that children learn through maturation and the stimulation of social interactions. His view was that development occurs as innate, biological maturation interacts with social experiences.

Work samples. Examples of a child's work that have been saved as records of the child's progress.

Works Progress Administration (WPA). Established during the Great Depression; federal dollars used to fund nursery schools in an effort to provide employment for educators and other school personnel.

Zone of proximal development. According to Vygotsky, this term refers to the distance between the child's actual development level as determined by independent problem solving and the level of potential development as determined through problem solving under adult guidance or in collaboration with more capable peers.

NAME INDEX

SUBJECT INDEX

M

PHOTO CREDITS

PART ONE

8: ©1989 Arthur Tilley, FPG International. **11:** ©1985 Janice Rubin, Black Star. **18:** Elizabeth Crews. **20:** Paul Conklin/PhotoEdit. **31:** Michael Newman/PhotoEdit. **34:** Bill Horsman, Stock Boston. **42:** Joseph Nettis, Stock Boston. **59:** Tony Freeman/PhotoEdit. **61:** Elizabeth Crews. **63:** Michael Newman/PhotoEdit. **77:** ©1993 Steve Winter, Black Star. **80:** Scott Robinson, Tony Stone Images. **83:** Culver Pictures. **84:** Culver Pictures. **87:** Culver Pictures. **91:** Culver Pictures. **98:** Elizabeth Crews. **106:** Culver Pictures. **114:** Elizabeth Crews.

PART TWO

122: David Young-Wolff/PhotoEdit. **126:** ©1991 Arthur Tilley, FPG International. **134:** David Young-Wolff/PhotoEdit. **135:** Mary Kate Denny/PhotoEdit. **139:** Frank Siteman, Stock Boston. **144:** Martin Rogers, Tony Stone Images. **151:** Elizabeth Crews. **152:** Jeff Greenberg/PhotoEdit. **154:** Elizabeth Crews. **161:** Mary Kate Denny/PhotoEdit. **164:** Richard Hutchings/PhotoEdit. **168:** Andy Sacks, Tony Stone Images. **172:** Elizabeth Crews. **180:** Tony Freeman/PhotoEdit. **194:** Elizabeth Crews.

PART THREE

198: Myrleen Ferguson/PhotoEdit. **202:** ©1992 Bill Losh, FPG International. **205:** Elizabeth Crews. **219:** Elena Rooraid/PhotoEdit. **223:** Vic Bider/PhotoEdit. **224:** ©1992 G&J, Black Star. **228:** David Young-Wolff/PhotoEdit. **238:** Telegraph Colour Library, FPG International. **249:** Myrleen Ferguson/PhotoEdit. **265:** ©1992 Cindy Karp, Black Star. **282:** The Image Bank. **288:** Tony Freeman/PhotoEdit. **290:** Tony Freeman/PhotoEdit. **293:** ©1992 Rick Freidman, Black Star. **297:** Elizabeth Crews. **322:** The Image Bank. **327:** Bob Daemmrich, Stock Boston. **330:** Tony Freeman/PhotoEdit. **334:** ©1990 Bob Krist, Black Star. **343:** Minnesota Zoo. **345:** David Young-Wolff/PhotoEdit. **352:** The Image Bank. **355:** Stephen McBrady/PhotoEdit. **362:** Michael Newman/PhotoEdit. **368:** Elizabeth Crews. **378:** Frank Siteman, Stock Boston.

PART FOUR

386: Myrleen Ferguson/PhotoEdit. **390:** Don Smetzer, Tony Stone Images. **395:** Elizabeth Crews. **399:** Bob Daemmrich/Stock, Boston. **402:** Elizabeth Crews. **407:** Elizabeth Crews. **411:** Michael Newman/PhotoEdit. **417:** Bob Daemmrich, Stock Boston. **431:** Laura Dwight/PhotoEdit. **436:** Tony Garcia, Tony Stone Images. **445:** Billy E. Barnes/PhotoEdit. **450:** David Young-Wolff/PhotoEdit. **456:** Dennis MacDonald/PhotoEdit. **459:** Jim Pickerell, Stock Boston. **466:** Dan Bosler, Tony Stone Images. **474:** Robert Brenner/PhotoEdit. **483:** Elizabeth Crews. **490:** The Image Bank. **495:** Elizabeth Crews. **498:** Elizabeth Crews. **503:** Elizabeth Crews. **511:** Lawrence Migdale, Stock Boston.

TEXT CREDITS

Text Credits

Chapter 1, page 28: Feeney, S., and K. Kipnis (1989). A new code of ethics for early childhood educators. Code of ethical conduct and statement of commitment. *Young Children, 45*(1), 24–29. Used with permission.

Chapter 1, pages 33–34: Hess, Robert D., and Doreen J. Croft. *Teachers of Young Children.* Third Edition. Copyright © 1981 by Houghton Mifflin Company. Used with permission.

Chapter 3, page 102: Reprinted with the permission of Macmillan College Publishing Company from *Early Childhood Education Today,* 5th edition, by George S. Morrison. Copyright © 1991 by Macmillan College Publishing Company, Inc.

Chapter 3, pages 113, 116: Reprinted with the permission of Macmillan College Publishing Company from *Approaches to Early Childhood Education* by Jaipaul L. Roopnarine and James E. Johnson. Copyright © 1987 by Macmillan College Publishing Company, Inc.

Chapter 12, pages 433–434: Sefton, K., R. Gargiulo, and S. Graves. Working with families of children with special needs. *Day Care and Early Education, 18*(3), 40.

Chapter 14, page 470 and pages 473–474: Swick, K., and S. Graves (1993). *Empowering At-Risk Families During the Early Childhood Years,* pp. 181–182 and pp. 56–57. Copyright © 1993. Reprinted by permission of the NEA Professional Library. Washington D.C.: National Education Association.

Chapter 14, pages 478–479: Sefton, K., R. Gargiulo, and S. Graves. Working with families of children with special needs. *Day Care and Early Education, 18*(3), 40.